American Government

Readings and Cases

TWELFTH EDITION

Peter Woll
Brandeis University

HarperCollins*CollegePublishers*

This book is dedicated to
my mother,
RUTH C. WOLL,
and to the memory of my father,
JOHN W. WOLL

Acquisitions Editor: Leo A. W. Wiegman
Project and Art Coordination, Text and Cover Design: York Production Services
Manufacturing Manager: Hilda Koparanian
Electronic Page Makeup: R.R. Donnelley and Sons Company, Inc.
Printer and Binder: R.R. Donnelley and Sons Company, Inc.
Cover Printer: Color-Imetry Corp.

American Government: Readings and Cases, 12/e.

Library of Congress Cataloging-in-Publication Data

American government : readings and cases / [edited by] Peter Woll.—
    12th ed.
        p. cm.
    Includes bibliographical references (p.).
    ISBN 0-673-52438-8
    1. United States—Politics and government. I. Woll, Peter, 1933-.
JK21.A445   1995
320.473—dc20
                                                                95-16988
                                                                    CIP

        97 98 9 8 7 6 5 4

Contents

power. Each branch of government is given the necessary means and motives to resist encroachments from coordinate branches.

Interpreting the Constitution

CHAPTER 2

Federalism   **51**

Constitutional Background: National versus State Power

The Supremacy of National Law

A Perspective on Federalism: Present and Future

CHAPTER 3
Civil Liberties and Civil Rights   103

The Nationalization of the Bill of Rights

Freedom of Speech and Press

Freedom of Expression: The Skokie Case

Dissenting from the Supreme Court's decision that denied review in the Skokie case (selection 14), Justice Blackmun argued that the high court should answer the compelling First Amendment questions that were raised.

Equal Protection of the Laws: School Desegregation

State laws that establish separate public educational facilities based on race violate the equal protection of the laws clause of the Fourteenth Amendment. Separate facilities are inherently unequal even though they may be equal physically.

Because of varied local school problems relating to desegregation, the federal district courts are delegated the authority to implement the 1954 *Brown* decision. These courts are to proceed "with all deliberate speed," while balancing the community and personal interests involved.

The Judicial Sources of Major Political Controversies over Civil Liberties and Rights

Religious Freedom and the Issue of School Prayer

The First Amendment's establishment clause requires a "wall of separation" between Church and State. It prohibits even nondenominational state-sponsored prayers in public schools.

The Right to Abortion

The constitutional right to privacy grants women the absolute right to have abortions during the first trimester of their pregnancies. Thereafter states have the authority to regulate abortions to preserve the health and life of the mother, and to protect potential life.

Some Thoughts on Autonomy and Equality in Relation to *Roe v. Wade*

A Supreme Court justice argues that the Court might have avoided the legal and political controversy that followed *Roe* v. *Wade* had it used gender equality considerations rather the "right" to privacy as the basis of its decision.

Affirmative Action

Equal Protection, Voting Rights, and Racial Gerrymandering

Part Two
Political Parties, Electoral Behavior, and Interest Groups   183

CHAPTER 4   185
Political Parties and the Electorate

Constitutional Background

Political Parties in Divided Government

Divided We Govern

Critics of divided government have proposed more disciplined political parties to unify the president and the congress, thereby helping to overcome the effects of the separation of powers. However, the divided government that the separation of powers helps to create works as well as the unified government that party discipline would establish.

Functions and Types of Elections

A Theory of Critical Elections

Critical elections begin a long-term realignment from the previously dominant party to a new majority party.

Party Decline and Electoral Decay

Politics By Other Means

Political parties and elections play a central role in the democratic process. Party decline and electoral decay have intensified institutional conflict and politics by other means.

Voting Behavior: Rational or Irrational?

Democratic Practice and Democratic Theory

Although democratic theory assumes that all voters are rational and interested in participating in elections, in fact many citizens are irrational in making political choices and often are apathetic.

Political Campaigns and the Electorate

The Responsible Electorate

Voters are not fools, and contrary to the views of many political candidates and their advisers, a wise electorate more often than not knows and votes its interests.

CHAPTER 5
Interest Groups   231

The Nature and Functions of Interest Groups

30 David B. Truman   **233**

The Governmental Process
There is no "national interest" apart from the interests of pressure groups. Pressure groups provide the necessary linkage between people and government, and by pursuing their own interests these groups define the national interest.

31 Theodore J. Lowi   **239**

The End of Liberalism: The Indictment
The group theory of politics is inadequate because of its failure to recognize a national interest and the need for legitimate governmental bodies to develop standards of law that will be above the selfish interests of pressure groups.

32 V. O. Key, Jr.   **243**

Pressure Groups
Interest groups interact with government primarily through the voices of their leadership, which often do not reflect the involvement of the membership of the groups.

Pressure Group Politics

33 Walter Isaacson   **248**

Running with the PACs
Political action committees win friends and influence elections by supplying the most important grist for the electoral mill—money.

Money, PACs, and Elections

34 Larry J. Sabato   **258**

The Misplaced Obsession with PACs
PAC-bashing is overdone. PACs have not changed the political landscape, but reflect in new ways the underlying forces that have always characterized the political process.

Part Three

NATIONAL GOVERNMENT INSTITUTIONS   267

CHAPTER 6
The Presidency   269

Presidential Character and Style

The President and the Media

Presidential Power in Foreign and Domestic Affairs

Presidential Leadership and Political Parties

The Presidency in Divided Government

CHAPTER 7
The Bureaucracy   333

Constitutional Background

The Political Roots and Consequences of Bureaucracy

The Courts and Administrative Agencies

CHAPTER 8

Congress   357

Constitutional Background: Representation of Popular, Group, and National Interests

Federalist 53, 56, 57, 58, 62, and 63
The functions of the House and Senate are fundamentally different. The House, popularly elected for a two-year term, stands close to the people and represents popular interests on matters of local concern. Senators, indirectly elected for staggered six-year terms, are more detached, deliberative, and conservative. A primary responsibility of the Senate is to act as a conservative check on the House.

Congress and the Washington Political Establishment

The Rise of the Washington Establishment
Congress, always with an eye to the reelection of its members, has created a vast federal bureaucracy to implement programs that ostensibly benefit constituents. Members of Congress, who gain credit for establishing the programs in the first place, step in once again to receive credit for handling constituent complaints against the bureaucracy.

Committee Chairman as Part of the Washington Establishment

Congress and the Quest for Power
The pursuit of personal power within Congress supports decentralization and the dispersion of power on Capitol Hill, which is particularly reflected in committee domination of the legislative process. However, presidential assaults on Congress occasionally cause members to subordinate their desire for personal aggrandizement to strengthen Congress as an institution.

Congress and the Media

Media Power and Congressional Power
Television has transformed congressional politics in many ways. Members of Congress often spend as much time with the media as they do on their legislative work. Media exposure is essential not only to reelection but to a successful Capitol Hill career.

Congress and the Electoral Connection

Congress and Campaign Finance Reform

Interpreting the Constitution

The Contemporary Debate over Constitutional Interpretation

The Tempting of America
A provocative jurist argues that the original intent of the Constitution rather than political or social considerations should guide judges. In the political arena the Supreme Court should not substitute its judgment for that of Congress or state legislatures.

For "Loose" Construction
A Supreme Court justice proclaims that the Court should flexibly interpret the Constitution to make decisions that are in tune with changing popular aspirations.

Preface for the Twelfth Edition

American Government provides key classic and contemporary readings and cases that introduce students to the underpinnings and current practices of American government. It also complements regular textbooks by illustrating and amplifying important issues and concepts, and at the same time, due to the organization and design of the book, it is suitable for use as a core textbook. Included are extensive notes that prepare for, connect, and comment on the selections and point out their significance within the broader context of American government.

General Subjects

The text covers all of the topics traditionally taught in introductory American Government courses. The Constitution and its underpinnings begin the book with readings to help students understand constitutional theory, practice, and politics. Readings in the first two chapters on the Constitution and federalism, respectively, explain how the Constitution was framed, the nature of the separation of powers, and the unique aspects of American federalism. The first section of the book concludes with a chapter on civil liberties and civil rights that includes the basic cases introductory students should know.

Readings on political parties, electoral behavior, and interest groups comprise the next section of the text. From James Madison's skeptical view of factions in *Federalist 10*, through V. O. Key, Jr.'s theory of critical elections and David Truman's group theory, students develop a framework within which they can evaluate the critical and changing role parties, elections, and interest groups play in the governmental process.

In-depth chapters on the presidency, bureaucracy, Congress, and the judiciary come next and complete the book. As in all parts of the book, the selections in these chapters balance classical and contemporary readings to give students a comprehensive overview of American government in theory and action.

The New Edition

The new edition contains up-to-date and relevant material designed to stimulate student interest and discussion and at the same time to show how our government works. As in previous editions, a balance is maintained among classic selections, important historical and current constitutional law cases, and contemporary readings that pinpoint and analyze evolving political trends.

The twelfth edition continues to give students a view of their rich political heritage through classic readings from *The Federalist*. Particularly emphasized in Chapter 1 on Constitutional government are *Federalist Papers 47, 48,* and *51* (on the separation of powers and checks and balances); *10* (on parties and interest groups); *39* (on federalism); *70* (on the presidency); and *78* (on judicial review). Also kept is Laurence Tribe and Michael Dorf's succinct selection—"How Not to Read the Constitution"—which helps students understand the frugality of constitutional language and the complexities of defining "original intent."

Chapter 2 on federalism retains the classic selections by James Madison, Alexis de Tocqueville, and Morton Grodzins. A new selection by Alice M. Rivlin focuses on contemporary trends in federalism, and calls for a reexamination of patterns of government to reflect the need for a greater sharing of power between the federal government and the states.

Following the precedent of previous editions, the book presents throughout major Supreme Court cases, including *Marbury v. Madison* (1803), *McCullough v. Maryland* (1819), and the key cases that have set the tone of contemporary constitutional law. The Supreme Court and the judiciary continue to be uniquely powerful in our political system.

Chapter 3 on civil liberties and civil rights retains the historic case *Gideon v. Wainwright* (1963) that nationalized the right to counsel; the Skokie case that confronts students with compelling issues of freedom of expression; and *Brown v. Board of Education* [1954] and its implementing decision that teach students the constitutional basis of school desegregation and provide insights into political realities of Supreme Court decision making. The chapter concludes with cases that have sparked contemporary political controversies over civil liberties and civil rights. *Engel v. Vitale* [1962]) covers school prayer, an issue that continues to rear its head in the political campaigns of 1990s. The right to abortion and affirmative action, covered respectively in *Roe v. Wade* [1973] and *Regents of the University of California v. Bakke* [1978], also continue to be politically controversial.

In a new Chapter 3 selection Supreme Court Justice Ruth Bader Ginsberg focuses on *Roe v. Wade* and presents the provocative thesis that a different Supreme Court approach to defining the right to abortion might have avoided or at least substantially reduced the continuing political controversy over the decision. Also new to this edition is *Shaw v. Reno* [1993], which demonstrates how the Supreme Court is grappling with the meaning of equal protection in relation to voting rights and racial gerrymandering.

In all other areas the revised edition is strengthened with updated, pertinent selections. Particularly stressed are the themes of divided government, party decline and electoral decay, and the administrative presidency. New readings also cover the important role the judiciary plays in reviewing administrative and congressional action.

Added to Chapter 4 on political parties and the electorate is David R. Mayhew's provocative selection entitled "Divided We Govern." For much of the twentieth century, political scientists have criticized divided government and argued for disciplined parties. But Mayhew argues that the eighteenth-century divided government model that discourages political parties works as well as the unified government that party discipline would establish. The revisionist approach to the eighteenth-century separation of powers and checks and balances system supporting the Madisonian model of government is becoming increasingly popular among political scientists and is reflected in other new selections in the twelfth edition.

Also new to Chapter 4 is Benjamin Ginsberg and Martin Shefter's innovative reading on party decline and electoral decay entitled "Politics By Other Means." The authors argue that the decline of political parties and elections has given rise to politics by other means, intensifying institutional conflict and the use of litigation and the criminal justice system to bring about political closure that divided government and pluralistic politics fails to produce.

Chapter 5 on interest groups retains the great classics by David B. Truman, Theodore J. Lowi, and V. O. Key, Jr. that present the group theory of politics, criticize it, and explain some of the intricacies of group political action. New to the twelfth edition is Larry J. Sabato's selection entitled, "The Misplaced Obsession with PACs." PAC-bashing is overdone, suggests Sabato, for PACs have not changed the political landscape but reflect in new ways the underlying forces that have always characterized the political process.

As the book turns to national governmental institutions, the presidency is first in line. Three important new selections complement the wide array of classic readings from Alexander Hamilton to Clinton Rossiter, Richard E. Neustadt, James David Barber and Aaron Wildavsky that define this chapter. Sidney M. Milkis, in "The Presidency and Political Parties," shows that an institutionalized "administrative presidency" more than partisan politics defines presidential leadership. Charles O. Jones, in "The Presidency in a Separated System," stresses the limits on presidential power in our divided governmental system. Finally, presidential scholar Thomas Cronin continues the theme of presidential limits in his reading, "How Much Is His Fault?" The Clinton presidency, argues Cronin, is but one example of how popular expectations about presidential power outrun political realities.

Turning to Chapter 7 on the bureaucracy, R. Shep Melnick contributes an important new reading, "Administrative Law and Bureaucratic Reality," which shows students the complex and often conflicting role that courts play in the administrative process. The new selection nicely complements my own discussion of constitutional democracy and bureaucratic power at the opening of the chapter, and James Q. Wilson's classic, "The Rise of the Bureaucratic State."

A list of star authors continues to make Chapter 8 on the congress compelling and particularly interesting to students. Richard F. Fenno, Jr., Morris P. Fiorina, David Mayhew, and Lawrence C. Dodd give a multidimensional and interesting view of Congress. Fresh selections in the twelfth edition, by Norman J. Ornstein, on "The New Republican Congress"; Richard Morin and David S. Broder of *The Washington Post* on "Why Americans Hate Congress"; and Frank J. Sorauf on "The Special Politics of Campaign Finance," make the chapter even more timely, informative, and exciting than in previous editions.

Finally, in Chapter 8 on the judiciary, Supreme Court Justice Stephen R. Breyer contributes a new selection entitled, "On The Uses of Legislative History in Interpreting Statutes." He enlightens students on the intricacies of judicial decision-making and at the same time shows how the congressional process, and the limits of statutory language, support a broad judicial approach to ensure fairness to individuals and to preserve the integrity of the legislative process.

Chapter 9 on the judiciary retains timeless classic selections including, Alexander Hamilton's depiction of the role of the judiciary in *Federalist 78*; Chief

Justice John Marshall's historic *Marbury* v. *Madison* opinion; John P. Roche, on judicial self-restraint; and Robert H. Bork and William J. Brennan, Jr., who argue eloquently for their contrasting positions on the proper role of the Supreme Court in constitutional interpretation.

As in previous editions, an extensive Instructor's Manual accompanies the textbook. In addition to being a comprehensive guide to the selections, the manual contains background material, and discussion and multiple-choice questions. At the instructor's discretion any part of the manual may be reproduced for students as an instructional aid.

Acknowledgments

Unfortunately space does not permit me to thank the numerous individuals who over the years have generously given their time, energy, and ideas to help me make this work a major American government source book. My colleagues Sid Milkis and Shep Melnick continue to give me valuable suggestions as new editions unfold. Stephen Rockwell aided me in research for the new edition and made many invaluable suggestions. I would also like to thank my HarperCollins editor, Leo A. W. Wiegman, whose ideas and professional skills helped immeasurably in the preparation of the new edition. Finally, I would like to give special thanks to Phyllis Gibson, who not only faultlessly word-processed the manuscript changes, but also drew on her own professional background in publishing to smooth the manuscript's path to completion.

Peter Woll

Part One

❖❖❖

The Setting of the American System

❖❖❖

CONSTITUTIONAL GOVERNMENT

The Founding Fathers were consummate politicians, but also brilliant political philosophers in their own right. They did not hesitate to draw upon the rich Western tradition of political philosophy as they searched for an ideal model of government. Above all, they wanted a government responsive to the people but also one of balanced and limited powers.

Constitutional Democracy:
The Rule of Law

The Western political heritage has emphasized the importance of democracy and the rule of law. Aristotle's *Politics* stressed the viability of democracy, provided there are sufficient checks upon unlimited popular rule.

The American constitutional tradition reflects the beliefs of many political philosophers. One of the most dominating figures is John Locke. It is not suggested that Locke was read by most of the colonists, but only that his ideas invariably found their way into many writings of eighteenth-century America, most importantly the Declaration of Independence. In a letter to Henry Lee in 1825, Thomas Jefferson wrote:

"When forced . . . to resort to arms for redress, an appeal to the tribunal of the world was deemed proper for our justification. This was the object of the Declaration of Independence. Not to find out new principles, or new arguments, never before thought of, not merely to say things which had never been said before; but to place before mankind the common sense of the subject, in terms so plain and firm as to command their assent, and to justify ourselves in the independent stand we are compelled to take. Neither aiming at originality of principle or sentiment, nor yet copied from any particular and previous writing, it was intended to be an expression of the American mind, and to give to that expression the proper tone and spirit called for by the occasion. All its authority rests then on the harmonizing sentiments of the day, whether expressed in conversation, in letters, printed essays, or in the elementary books of public right [such] as Aristotle, Cicero, Locke, Sidney, etc. . . ."

In May 1790, Jefferson wrote: "Locke's little book on government is perfect as far as it goes." Although Jefferson's admiration of Locke was perhaps greater than that of many other colonists, his views did reflect a mood of eighteenth-century America. Locke's *Second Treatise, of Civil Government* attempted to trace the reasons why people enter into political societies in the first place. The eighteenth century, no less than the twentieth, was an era characterized by attempts to be "scientific" in political formulations. Locke's *Second Treatise,* first published in 1690, reflected the scientific emphasis that was to prevail so widely beginning in the eighteenth century. To Locke, natural law was objectively valid, and therefore once ascertained, governments based upon it would have a superior claim to legitimacy. Locke is notable for his discussions of natural law, from which he derived the "best" form of government. In reading Locke, one should observe how much importance he placed upon property rights and the right of the people to dissolve government once it no longer meets their legitimate expectations.

1

John Locke

SECOND TREATISE, OF CIVIL GOVERNMENT

❖❖❖❖❖❖❖

Of the State of Nature

To understand political power aright, and derive it from its original, we must consider what estate all men are naturally in, and that is, a state of perfect freedom to order their actions, and dispose of their possessions and persons as they think fit, within the bounds of the laws of Nature, without asking leave or depending upon the will of any other man.

A state also of equality, wherein all the power and jurisdiction is reciprocal, no one having more than another, there being nothing more evident than that creatures of the same species and rank, promiscuously born to all the same advantages of Nature, and the use of the same faculties, should also be equal one amongst another, without subordination or subjection, unless the lord and master of them all should, by any manifest declaration of his will, set one above another, and confer on him, by an evident and clear appointment, an undoubted right to dominion and sovereignty. . . .

But though this be a state of liberty, yet it is not a state of license; though man in that state have an uncontrollable liberty to dispose of his person or possessions, yet he had not liberty to destroy himself, or so much as any creature in his possession, but where some nobler use than its bare preservation calls for it. The state of Nature has a law of Nature to govern it, which obliges every one, and reason, which is that law, teaches all mankind who will but consult it, that being all equal and independent, no one ought to harm another in his life, health, liberty or possessions. . . . And, being furnished with like faculties, sharing all in one community of Nature, there cannot be supposed any such subordination among us that may authorize us to destroy one another, as if we were made for one another's uses, as the inferior ranks of creatures are for ours. Every one as he is bound to preserve himself, and not to quit his station wilfully, so by the like reason, when his own preservation comes not in competition, ought he as much as he can to preserve the rest of mankind, and not unless it be to do justice on an offender, take away or impair the life, or what tends to the preservation of life, the liberty, health, limb, or goods of another.

And that all men may be restrained from invading others' rights, and from doing hurt to one another, and the law of Nature be observed, which willeth the peace and preservation of all mankind, the execution of the law of Nature is in that state put into every man's hands, whereby every one has a right to punish the transgressors of that law to such a degree as may hinder its violation. For the law of Nature would, as all other laws that concern men in this world, be in vain if there were nobody that in the state of Nature had a power to execute that law, and thereby preserve the innocent and restrain offenders; and if any one in the state of Nature may punish another for any evil he has done, every one may do so. For in that state of perfect equality, where naturally there is no superiority or jurisdiction of one over another, what any may do in prosecution of that law, every one must needs have a right to do.

And thus, in the state of Nature, one man comes by a power over another, but yet no absolute or arbitrary power to use a criminal, when he has got him in his hands, according to the passionate heats or boundless extravagancy of his own will, but only to retribute him so far as calm reason and conscience dictate, what is proportionate to his transgression, which is so much as may serve for reparation and restraint. . . .

Every offence that can be committed in the state of Nature may, in the state of Nature, be also punished equally, and as far forth, as it may, in a commonwealth. For—though it would be beside my present purpose to enter here into the particulars of the law of Nature, or its measures of punishment, yet it is certain there is such a law, and that too as intelligible and plain to a rational creature and a studier of that law as the positive laws of commonwealths, nay, possibly plainer; as much as reason is easier to be understood than the fancies and intricate contrivances of men, following contrary and hidden interests put into words. . . .

Of the Ends of Political Society and Government

If man in the state of Nature be so free as has been said, if he be absolute lord of his own person and possessions, equal to the greatest and subject to nobody, why will he part with his freedom, this empire, and subject himself to the dominion and control of any other power? To which it is obvious to answer, that though in the state of Nature he hath such a right, yet the enjoyment of it is very uncertain and constantly exposed to the invasion of others; for all being kings as much as he, every man his equal, and the greater part no strict observers of equity and justice, the enjoyment of the property he has in this state is very unsafe, very insecure. This makes him willing to quit this condition which, however free, is full of fears and continual dangers; and it is not without reason that he seeks out and is willing to join in society with others who are already united, or have a mind to unite for the mutual preservation of their lives, liberties, and estates, which I call by the general name—property.

The great and chief end, therefore, of men uniting into commonwealths, and putting themselves under government, is the preservation of their property; to which in the state of Nature there are many things wanting.

Firstly, there wants an established, settled, known law, received and allowed by common consent to be the standard of right and wrong, and the common measure to decide all controversies between them. For though the law of Nature be plain and intelligible to all rational creatures, yet men, being biased by their interest, as well as ignorant for want of study of it, are not apt to allow of it as a law binding to them in the application of it to their particular cases.

Secondly, in the state of Nature there wants a known and indifferent judge, with authority to determine all differences according to the established law. For every one in that state being both judge and executioner of the law of Nature, men being partial to themselves, passion and revenge is very apt to carry them too far, and with too much heat in their own cases, as well as negligence and unconcernedness, make them too remiss in other men's.

Thirdly, in the state of Nature there often wants power to back and support the sentence when right, and to give it due execution. They who by any injustice offended will seldom fail where they are able by force to make good their injustice. Such resistance many times makes the punishment dangerous, and frequently destructive to those who attempt it.

Thus mankind, notwithstanding all the privileges of the state of Nature, being but in an ill condition while they remain in it are quickly driven into society. Hence it comes to pass, that we seldom find any number of men live any time together in this state. The inconveniences that they are therein exposed to by the irregular and uncertain exercise of the power every man has of punishing the transgressions of others, make them take sanctuary under the established laws of government, and therein seek the preservation of their property. It is this makes them so willingly give up every one his single power of punishing to be exercised by such alone as shall be appointed to it amongst them, and by such rules as the community, or those authorised by them to that purpose, shall agree on. And in this we have the original right and rise of both the legislative and executive power as well as of the governments and societies themselves.

For in the state of Nature to omit the liberty he has of innocent delights, a man has two powers. The first is to do whatsoever he thinks fit for the preservation of himself and others within the permission of the law of Nature; by which law, common to them all, he and all the rest of mankind are one community, make up one society distinct from all other creatures, and were it not for the corruption and viciousness of degenerate men, there would be no need for any other, no necessity that men should separate from this great and natural community, and associate into lesser combinations. The other power a man has in the state of Nature is the power to punish the crimes committed against that law. Both these he gives up when he joins in a private, if I may so call it, or particular political society, and incorporates into any commonwealth separate from the rest of mankind.

The first power—viz., of doing whatsoever he thought fit for the preservation of himself and the rest of mankind, he gives up to be regulated by laws made by the society, so far forth as the preservation of himself and the rest of that society shall require; which laws of the society in many things confine the liberty he had by the law of Nature.

Secondly, the power of punishing he wholly gives up, and engages his natural force, which he might before employ in the execution of the law of Nature, by his own single authority, as he thought fit, to assist the executive power of the society as the law thereof shall require. For being now in a new state, wherein he is to enjoy many conveniences from the labor, assistance, and society of others in the same community, as well as protection from its whole strength, he is to part also with as much of his natural liberty, in providing for himself, as the good, prosperity, and safety of the society shall require, which is not only necessary but just, since the other members of the society do the like.

But though men when they enter into society give up the equality, liberty, and executive power they had in the state of Nature into the hands of the society, to be so far disposed of by the legislative as the good of the society shall require, yet it being only with an intention in every one the better to preserve himself, his liberty and property (for no rational creature can be supposed to change his condition with an intention to be worse), the power of the society or legislative constituted by them can never be supposed to extend farther than the common against those three defects above mentioned that made the state of Nature so unsafe and uneasy. And so, whoever has the legislative or supreme power of any commonwealth, is bound to govern by established standing laws, promulgated and known to the people, and not by extemporary decrees, by indifferent and upright judges, who are to decide controversies by those laws; and to employ the force of the community at home only in the execution of such laws, or abroad to prevent or redress foreign injuries and secure the community from inroads and invasion. And all this to be directed to no other end but the peace, safety, and public good of the people. . . .

Of the Extent of
the Legislative Power

The great end of men's entering into society being the enjoyment of their properties in peace and safety, and the great instrument and means of that being the laws established in that society, the first and fundamental positive law of all commonwealths is the establishing of the legislative power, as the first and fundamental natural law, which is to govern even the legislative itself, is the preservation of the society and (as far as will consist with the public good) of every person in it. This legislative is not only the supreme power of the commonwealth, but sacred and unalterable in the hands where the community have once placed it. Nor can any edict of anybody else, in what form soever conceived, or by what power soever backed, have the force and obligation of a law which has not its sanction from that legislative which the public has chosen and appointed it; for without this the law could not have that which is absolutely necessary to its being a law, the consent of the society, over whom nobody can have a power to make laws but by their own consent and by authority received from them. . . .

These are the bounds which the trust that is put in them by the society and the law of God and Nature have set to the legislative power of every commonwealth, in all forms of government. First: They are to govern by promulgated established laws, not to be varied in particular cases, but to have one rule for rich and poor, for the favorite at Court and the countryman at plough. Secondly: These laws also ought to be designed for no other end ultimately but the good of the people. Thirdly: They must not raise taxes on the property of the people without the consent of the people given by themselves or their deputies. And this properly concerns only such governments where the legislative is always in being, or at least where the people have not reserved any part of the legislative to deputies, to be from time to time chosen by themselves. Fourthly: Legislative neither must nor can transfer the power of making laws to anybody else, or place it anywhere but where the people have. . . .

Of the Dissolution
of Government

The constitution of the legislative [authority] is the first and fundamental act of society, whereby provision is made for the continuation of their union under the direction of persons and bonds of laws, made by persons authorised thereunto, by the consent and appointment of the people, without which no one man, or number of men, amongst them can have authority of making laws that shall be binding to the rest. When any one, or more, shall take upon them to make laws whom the people have not appointed so to do, they make laws without authority, which the people are not therefore bound to obey; by which means they come again to be out of subjection, and may constitute to themselves a new legislative, as they think best, being in full liberty to resist the force of those who, without authority, would impose anything upon them. . . .

Whosoever uses force without right—as every one does in society who does it without law—puts himself into a state of war with those against whom he so uses it, and in that state all former ties are cancelled, all other rights cease, and every one has a right to defend himself, and to resist the aggressor. . . .

Here it is like the common question will be made: Who shall be judge whether the prince or legislative act contrary to their trust? This, perhaps, ill-affected and factious men may spread amongst the people, when the prince only makes use of his due prerogative. To this I reply, The people shall be judge; for who shall be judge whether his trustee or deputy acts well and according to the trust reposed in him, but he who deputes him and must, by having deputed him, have still a power to discard him when he fails in his trust? If this be reasonable in particular cases of private men, why should it be otherwise in that of the greatest moment, where the welfare of millions is concerned and also where the evil, if not prevented, is greater, and the redress very difficult, dear, and dangerous? . . .

To conclude. The power that every individual gave the society when he entered into it can never revert to the individuals again, as long as the society lasts, but will always remain in the community; because without this there can be no community— no commonwealth, which is contrary to the original agreement; so also when the society hath placed the legislative in any assembly of men, to continue in them and their successors, with direction and authority for providing such successors, the legislative can never revert to the people whilst that government lasts; because, having provided a legislative with power to continue for ever, they have given up their political power to the legislative, and cannot resume it. But if they have set limits to the duration of their legislative, and made this supreme power in any person or assembly only temporary; or else when, by the miscarriages of those in authority, it is forfeited; upon the forfeiture of their rulers, or at the determination of the time set, it reverts to the society, and the people have a right to act as supreme, and continue the legislative in themselves or place it in a new form, or new hands, as they think good.

❖❖ The influence of John Locke goes far beyond his impact on the thinking of the founding fathers of the United States, such as Thomas Jefferson. Some scholars (among them, Louis Hartz, *The Liberal Tradition in America*) have interpreted the American political tradition in terms of the pervasive attachment to the ideas and values set forth in the writings of Locke. There is little question that American political life has been uniquely characterized by widespread adherence to the fundamental principles about the relations among people, society, and government expressed in Locke's writings.

It is not just that we have representative government, with institutions similar in structure and function to those of the constitutional democracy described in Locke's *Second Treatise,* but that through the years we have probably maintained, more than any other society, a widespread agreement about the fundamental human values cherished by Locke. His emphasis upon the sanctity of private property has been paramount in the American political tradition from the very beginning. Moreover, Locke's views on the nature of man are shared by most Americans. All our governmental institutions, processes, and traditions rest upon principles such as the primacy of the individual, man's inborn ability to exercise reason in order to discern truth and higher principles of order and justice, and a political and social equality among people in which no person shall count for more than another in determining the actions of government and their application. We may not have always practiced these ideals, but we have been *theoretically* committed to them.

FRAMING THE CONSTITUTION: ELITIST OR DEMOCRATIC PROCESS?

A remarkable fact about the United States government is that it has operated for two hundred years on the basis of a written Constitution. Does this suggest unusual sagacity on the part of the Founding Fathers, or exceptional luck? What was involved in framing the Constitution?

In the following selection John P. Roche suggests that the framing of the Constitution was essentially a democratic process involving the reconciliation of a variety of state, political, and economic interests. Roche writes that "the Philadelphia Convention was not a College of Cardinals or a council of Platonic guardians working in a manipulative, predemocratic framework; it was a *nationalist* reform caucus that had to operate with great delicacy and skill in a political cosmos full of enemies to achieve one definitive goal—popular approbation." Roche recognizes that the framers, collectively, were an elite, but he is careful to point out that they were a political elite dedicated for the most part to establishing an effective and at the same time controlled national government that would be able to overcome the weaknesses of the Articles of Confederation. The framers were not, says Roche, a cohesive elite dedicated to a particular set of political or economic assumptions beyond the simple need to create a national government that would be capable of reconciling disparate state interests. The Constitution was "a vivid demonstration of effective democratic political action, and of the forging of a national elite which literally persuaded its countrymen to hoist themselves by their own bootstraps."

2

John P. Roche

THE FOUNDING FATHERS: A REFORM CAUCUS IN ACTION

❖❖❖❖❖❖❖

Over the last century and a half, the work of the Constitutional Convention and the motives of the Founding Fathers have been analyzed under a number of different ideological auspices. To one generation of historians, the hand of God was moving in the assembly; under a later dispensation, a dialectic (at various levels of philosophical sophistication) replaced the Deity: "relationships of production" moved into the niche previously reserved for Love of Country. Thus in counterpart to the *zeitgeist*, the framers have undergone miraculous metamorphoses: at one time acclaimed as liberals and bold social engineers, today they appear in the guise of sound Burkean conservatives, men who in our time would subscribe to *Fortune*, look to Walter Lippmann for political theory, and chuckle patronizingly at the antics of Barry Goldwater. The implicit assumption is that if James Madison were among us, he would be President of the Ford Foundation, while Alexander Hamilton would chair the Committee for Economic Development.

The "Fathers" have thus been admitted to our best circles; the revolutionary ferocity which confiscated all Tory property in reach and populated New Brunswick with outlaws has been converted by the "Miltown School" of American historians into a benign dedication to "consensus" and "prescriptive rights." The Daughters of the American Revolution have, through the ministrations of Professors Boorstin, Hartz, and Rossiter, at last found ancestors worthy of their descendants. It is not my purpose here to argue that the "Fathers" were, in fact, radical revolutionaries; that proposition has been brilliantly demonstrated by Robert R. Palmer in his *Age of the Democratic Revolution*. My concern is with the future position that not only were they revolutionaries, but also they were democrats. Indeed, in my view, there is one fundamental truth about the Founding Fathers that *every* generation of zeitgeisters has done its best to obscure: they were first and foremost superb democratic politicians. I suspect that in a contemporary setting, James Madison would be Speaker of

"The Founding Fathers," by John P. Roche, *APSR*, December 1961. Copyright © 1961 by the American Political Science Association. Reprinted by permission of the American Political Science Association.

the House of Representatives and Hamilton would be the *eminence grise* dominating (*pace* Theodore Sorensen or Sherman Adams) the Executive Office of the President. They were, with their colleagues, *political men*—not metaphysicians, disembodied conservatives or Agents of History—and as recent research into the nature of American politics in the 1780s confirms, they were committed (perhaps willy-nilly) to working within the democratic framework, within a universe of public approval. Charles Beard *and* the filiopietists to the contrary notwithstanding, the Philadelphia Convention was not a College of Cardinals or a council of Platonic guardians working within a manipulative, predemocratic framework; it was a *nationalist* reform caucus which had to operate with great delicacy and skill in a political cosmos full of enemies to achieve the one definitive goal—popular approbation.

Perhaps the time has come, to borrow Walton Hamilton's fine phrase, to raise the framers from immortality to mortality, to give them credit for their magnificent demonstration of the art of democratic politics. The point must be reemphasized: they *made* history and did it within the limits of consensus. There was nothing inevitable about the future in 1787; the *zeitgeist*, that fine Hegelian technique of begging causal questions, could only be discerned in retrospect. What they did was to hammer out a pragmatic compromise which would both bolster the "national interest" and be acceptable to the people. What inspiration they got came from their collective experience as professional politicians in a democratic society. As John Dickinson put it to his fellow delegates on August 13, "Experience must be our guide. Reason may mislead us."

In this context, let us examine the problems they confronted and the solutions they evolved. The Convention has been described picturesquely as a counter-revolutionary junta and the Constitution as a coup d'état, but this has been accomplished by withdrawing the whole history of the movement for constitutional reform from its true context. No doubt the goals of the constitutional elite were "subversive" to the existing political order, but it is overlooked that their subversion could only have succeeded if the people of the United States endorsed it by regularized procedures. Indubitably they were "plotting" to establish a much stronger central government than existed under the Articles, but only in the sense in which one could argue equally well that John F. Kennedy was, from 1956 to 1960, "plotting" to become President. In short, on the fundamental *procedural* level, the Constitutionalists had to work according to the prevailing rules of the game. Whether they liked it or not is a topic for spiritualists—and is irrelevant: one may be quite certain that had Washington agreed to play the de Gaulle (as the Cincinnati once urged), Hamilton would willingly have held his horse, but such fertile speculation in no way alters the actual context in which events took place.

I

When the Constitutionalists went forth to subvert the Confederation, they utilized the mechanisms of political legitimacy. And the roadblocks which confronted them were formidable. At the same time, they were endowed with certain potent political assets. The history of the United States from 1786 to 1790 was largely one of a masterful employment of political expertise by the Constitutionalists as against bumbling, erratic behavior by the opponents of reform. Effectively, the Constitutionalists had to induce the states, by democratic techniques of coercion, to emasculate themselves. To be specific, if New York had refused to join the new Union, the project was doomed; yet before New York was safely in, the reluctant state legislature had *suasponte* to take the following steps: (1) agree to send delegates to the Philadelphia Convention; (2) provide maintenance for these delegates (these were distinct stages: New Hampshire was early in naming delegates, but did not provide for their maintenance until July); (3) set up the special ad hoc convention to decide on ratification; and (4) concede to the decision of the ad hoc convention that New York should participate. New York admittedly was a tricky state, with a strong interest in a status quo which permitted her to exploit New Jersey and Connecticut, but the same legal hurdles existed in every state. And at the risk of becoming boring, it must be reiterated that the *only* weapon in the Constitutionalist arsenal was an effective mobilization of public opinion.

The group which undertook this struggle was an interesting amalgam of a few dedicated nationalists with the self-interested spokesmen of various parochial bailiwicks. The Georgians, for example, wanted a strong central authority to provide military protection for their huge, underpopulated state against the Creek Confederacy; Jerseymen and Connecticuters wanted to escape from economic bondage to New York; the Virginians hoped to establish a system which would give that great state its rightful place in the councils of the republic. The dominant figures in the politics of these states therefore cooperated in the call for the Convention. In other states, the thrust towards national reform was taken up by opposition groups who added the "national interest" to their weapons system; in Pennsylvania, for instance, the group fighting to revise the Constitution of 1776 came out four-square behind the Constitutionalists, and in New York, Hamilton and the Schuyler *ambiance* took the same tack against George Clinton. There was, of course, a large element of personality in the affair: there is reason to suspect that Patrick Henry's opposition to the Convention and the Constitution was founded on his conviction that Jefferson was behind both, and a close study of local politics elsewhere would surely reveal that others supported the Constitution for the simple (and politically quite sufficient) reason that the "wrong" people were against it.

To say this is not to suggest that the Constitution rested on a foundation of impure or base motives. It is rather to argue that in politics there are no immaculate conceptions, and that in the drive for a stronger general government, motives of all sorts played a part. Few men in the history of mankind have espoused a view of the "common good" or "public interest" that militated against their private status; even Plato with all his reverence for disembodied reason managed to put philosophers on top of the pile. Thus it is not surprising that a number of diversified private interests joined to push the nationalist public interest; what would have been surprising was the absence of such a pragmatic united front. And the fact remains that, however motivated, these men did demonstrate a willingness to compromise their parochial interest in behalf of an ideal which took shape before their eyes and under their ministrations.

As Stanley Elkins and Eric McKitrick have suggested in a perceptive essay [76 *Political Science Quarterly* 181 (1961)], what distinguished the leaders of the Constitutionalist caucus from their enemies was a "Continental" approach to political, economic and military issues. To the extent that they shared an institutional base of operations, it was the Continental Congress (thirty-nine of the delegates to the Federal Convention had served in Congress), and this was hardly a locale which inspired respect for the state governments. Robert de Jouvenal observed French politics half a century ago and noted that a revolutionary Deputy had more in common with a nonrevolutionary Deputy than he had with a revolutionary non-Deputy; similarly one can surmise that membership in the Congress under the Articles of Confederation worked to establish a Continental frame of reference, that a Congressman from Pennsylvania and one from South Carolina would share a universe of discourse which provided them with a conceptual common denominator vis-à-vis their respective state legislatures. This was particularly true with respect to external affairs: the average state legislator was probably about as concerned with foreign policy then as he is today, but Congressmen were constantly forced to take the broad view of American prestige, were compelled to listen to the reports of Secretary John Jay and to the dispatches and pleas from their frustrated envoys in Britain, France, and Spain. From considerations such as these, a "Continental" ideology developed which seems to have demanded a revision of our domestic institutions primarily on the ground that only by invigorating our general government could we assume our rightful place in the international arena. Indeed, an argument with great force—particularly since Washington was its incarnation—urged that our very survival in the Hobbesian jungle of world politics depended upon a reordering and strengthening of our national sovereignty.

The great achievement of the Constitutionalists was their ultimate success in convincing the elected representatives of a majority of the white male population that change was imperative. A small group of political leaders with a Continental vision and essentially a consciousness of the United States' *international* impotence, provided the matrix of the movement. To their standard other leaders rallied with their own parallel ambitions. Their great assets were (1) the presence in their caucus of the one authentic American "father figure," George Washington, whose prestige was enormous; (2) the energy and talent of their leadership (in which one must include the towering intellectuals of the time, John Adams and Thomas Jefferson, despite their absence abroad), and their communications "network," which was far superior to anything on the opposition site; (3) the preemptive skill which made "their" issue The Issue and kept the locally oriented opposition permanently on the defensive; and (4) the subjective consideration that these men were spokesmen of a new and compelling credo: *American* nationalism, that ill-defined but nonetheless potent sense of collective purpose that emerged from the American Revolution.

Despite great institutional handicaps, the Constitutionalists managed in the mid-1780s to mount an offensive which gained momentum as years went by. Their greatest problem was lethargy, and paradoxically, the number of barriers in their path may have proved an advantage in the long run. Beginning with the initial battle to get the Constitutional Convention called the delegates appointed, they could never relax, never let up the pressure. In practical terms, this meant that the local "organizations" created by the Constitutionalists were perpetually in movement building up their cadres for the next fight. (The word *organization* has to be used with great caution: a political organization in the United States—as in contemporary England—generally consisted of a magnate and his following, or a coalition of magnates. This did not necessarily mean that it was "undemocratic" or "aristocratic," in the Aristotelian sense of the word: while a few magnates such as the Livingstons could draft their followings, most exercised their leadership without coercion on the basis of popular endorsement. The absence of organized opposition did not imply the impossibility of competition any more than low public participation in elections necessarily indicated an undemocratic suffrage.)

The Constitutionalists got the jump on the "opposition" (a collective noun: oppositions would be more correct) at the outset with demand for a Convention. Their opponents were caught in an old political trap: they were not being asked to approve any specific program of reform, but only to endorse a meeting to discuss and recommend needed reforms. If they took a hard line at the first stage, they were put in the position of glorifying the status quo and of denying the need for *any* changes. Moreover, the Constitutionalists could go to the people with a persuasive argument for "fair play"—"How can you condemn reform before you know precisely what is involved?" Since the state legislatures obviously would have the final say on any proposals that might emerge from the Convention, the Constitutionalists were merely reasonable men asking for a chance. Besides, since they did not make any concrete proposals at that stage, they were in a position to capitalize on every sort of generalized discontent with the Confederation.

Perhaps because of their poor intelligence system, perhaps because of overconfidence generated by the failure of all previous efforts to alter the Articles, the opposition awoke too late to the dangers that confronted them in 1787. Not only did the Constitutionalists manage to get every state but Rhode Island (where politics was enlivened by a party system reminiscent of the "Blues" and the "Greens" in the Byzantine Empire) to appoint delegates to Philadelphia, but when the results were in, it appeared that they dominated the delegations. Given the apathy of the opposition, this was a natural phenomenon: in an ideologically nonpolarized political atmosphere those who get appointed to a special committee are likely to be the men who supported the movement for its creation. Even George Clinton, who seems to have been the first opposition leader to awake to the possibility of trouble, could not prevent the New York legislature from appointing Alexander Hamilton—though he did have the foresight to send two of his henchmen to dominate the delegation. Incidentally, much has been made of the fact that the delegates to Philadelphia were not elected by the people; some have adduced this fact as evidence of the "undemocratic" character of the gathering. But put in the context of the time, this argument is wholly specious: the central government under the Articles was considered a creature of the component states and in all the states but Rhode Island, Connecticut, and New Hampshire, members of the national Congress were chosen by the state legislatures. This was not a consequence of elitism or fear of the mob; it was a logical extension of states' rights doctrine to guarantee that the national institution did not end-run the state legislatures and make direct contact with the people.

II

With delegations safely named, the focus shifted to Philadelphia. While waiting for a quorum to assemble, James Madison got busy and drafted the so-called Randolph or Virginia Plan with the aid of the Virginia delegation. This was a political master-stroke. Its consequence was that once business got underway, the framework of the discussion was established on Madison's terms. There was no interminable argument over agenda; instead the delegates took the Virginia Resolutions—"just for purposes of discussion"—as their point of departure. And along with Madison's proposals, many of which were buried in the course of the summer, went his major premise: a new start on a Constitution rather than piecemeal amendment. This was not necessarily revolutionary—but Madison's proposal that this "lump sum" amendment go into effect after approval by nine states (the Articles required unanimous state approval for any amendment) was thoroughly subversive.

Standard treatments of the Convention divide the delegates into "nationalists" and "states' righters" with various improvised shadings ("moderate nationalists," etc.), but these are *a posteriori* categories which obfuscate more than they clarify. What is striking to one who analyzes the Convention as a case study in democratic politics is the lack of clear-cut ideological divisions in the Convention. Indeed, I submit that the evidence—Madison's *Notes*, the correspondence of the delegates, and debates on ratification—indicates that this was a remarkably homogeneous body on the ideological level. Yates and Lansing, Clinton's two chaperones for Hamilton, left in disgust on July 10. (Is there anything more tedious than sitting through endless disputes on matters one deems fundamentally misconceived? It takes an iron will to spend a hot summer as an ideological *agent provocateur*.) Luther Martin, Maryland's bibulous narcissist, left on September 4 in a huff when he discovered that others did not share his self-esteem; others went home for personal reasons. But the hard core of delegates accepted a grinding regimen throughout the attrition of a Philadelphia summer precisely because they shared the Constitutionalist goal.

Basic differences of opinion emerged, of course, but these were not ideological; they were *structural*. If the so-called "states' rights" group had not accepted the fundamental purposes of the Convention, they could simply have pulled out and by doing so have aborted the whole enterprise. Instead of bolting, they returned day after day to argue and to compromise. An interesting symbol of this basic homogeneity was the initial agreement on secrecy: these professional politicians did not want to become prisoners of publicity; they wanted to retain that freedom of maneuver which is only possible when men are not forced to take public stands in the preliminary stages of negotiation. There was no legal means of binding the tongues of the delegates: at any stage in the game a delegate with basic principled objections to the emerging project could have taken the stump (as Luther Martin did after his exit) and denounced the Convention to the skies. Yet Madison did not even inform Thomas Jefferson in Paris of the course of the deliberations and available correspondence indicates that the delegates generally observed the injunction. Secrecy is certainly uncharacteristic of any assembly marked by strong ideological polarization. This was noted at the time: the *New*

York Daily Advertiser, August 14, 1787, commented that the "profound secrecy hitherto observed by the Convention [we consider] a happy omen, as it demonstrates that the spirit of party on any great and essential point cannot have arisen to any height."

Commentators on the Constitution who have read *The Federalist* in lieu of reading the actual debates have credited the Fathers with the invention of a sublime concept called "Federalism." Unfortunately *The Federalist* is probative evidence for only one proposition: that Hamilton and Madison were inspired propagandists with a genius for retrospective symmetry. Federalism, as the theory is generally defined, was an improvisation which was later promoted into a political theory. Experts on "federalism" should take to heart the advice of David Hume, who warned in his *Of the Rise and Progress of the Arts and Sciences* that "there is no subject in which we must proceed with more caution than in [history], lest we assign causes which never existed and reduced what is merely contingent to stable and universal principles." In any event, the final balance in the Constitution between the states and the nation must have come as a great disappointment to Madison, while Hamilton's unitary views are too well known to need elucidation.

It is indeed astonishing how those who have glibly designated James Madison the "father" of Federalism have overlooked the solid body of fact which indicates that he shared Hamilton's quest for a unitary central government. To be specific, they have avoided examining the clear import of the Madison-Virginia Plan, and have disregarded Madison's dogged inch-by-inch retreat from the bastions of centralization. The Virginia Plan envisioned a unitary national government effectively freed from and dominant over the states. The lower house of the national legislature was to be elected directly by the people of the states with membership proportional to population. The upper house was to be selected by the lower and two chambers would elect the executive and choose the judges. The national government would be thus cut completely loose from the states.

The structure of the general government was freed from state control in a truly radical fashion, but the scope of the authority of the national sovereign as Madison initially formulated it was breathtaking—it was a formulation worthy of the Sage of Malmesbury himself. The national legislature was to be empowered to disallow the acts of state legislatures, and the central government was vested, in addition to the powers of the nation under the Articles of Confederation, with plenary authority wherever "the separate States are incompetent or in which the harmony of the United States may be interrupted by the exercise of individual legislation." Finally, just to lock the door against state intrusion, the national Congress was to be given the power to use military force on recalcitrant states. This was Madison's "model" of an ideal national government, though it later received little publicity in *The Federalist*.

The interesting thing was the reaction of the Convention to this militant program for a strong autonomous central government. Some delegates were startled, some obviously leery of so comprehensive a project of reform, but nobody set off any fireworks and nobody walked out. Moreover, in the two weeks that followed, the Virginia Plan received substantial endorsement *en principe;* the initial temper of the gathering can be deduced from the approval "without debate or dissent," on May 31, of the Sixth Resolution which granted Congress the authority to disallow state legislation "contravening *in its opinion* the Articles of Union." Indeed, an amendment was included to bar states from contravening national treaties.

The Virginia Plan may therefore be considered, in ideological terms, as the delegates' Utopia, but as the discussions continued and became more specific, many of those present began to have second thoughts. After all, they were not residents of Utopia or guardians in Plato's Republic who could simply impose a philosophical ideal on subordinate strata of the population. They were practical politicians in a democratic society, and no matter what their private dreams might be, they had to take home an acceptable package and defend it—and their own political futures—against predictable attack. On June 14 the breaking point between dream and reality took place. Apparently realizing that under the Virginia Plan, Massachusetts, Virginia, and Pennsylvania could virtually dominate the national government—and probably appreciating that to sell this program to "the folks back home" would be impossible—the delegates from the small states dug in their heels and demanded time for a consideration of alternatives. One gets a graphic sense of the inner politics from John Dickinson's reproach to Madison: "You see the consequences of pushing things too far. Some of the members from the small States wish for two branches in the General Legislature and are friends to a good National Government; but we would sooner submit to a foreign power than . . . be deprived of an equality of suffrage in both branches of the Legislature, and thereby be thrown under the domination of the large States."

The bare outline of the *Journal* entry for Tuesday, June 14, is suggestive to anyone with extensive experience in deliberative bodies. "It was moved by Mr. Patterson [sic, Paterson's name was one of those consistently misspelled by Madison and everybody else] seconded by Mr. Randolph that the further consideration of the report from the Committee of the whole House [endorsing the Virginia Plan] be postponed till tomorrow and before the question for postponement was taken. It was moved by Mr. Randolph seconded by Mr. Patterson that the House adjourn." The House adjourned by obvious prearrangement of the two principals: since the preceding Saturday when Brearley and Paterson of New Jersey had announced their fundamental discontent with the representational features of the Virginia Plan, the informal pressure had certainly been building up to slow down the steamroller. Doubtless there were extended arguments at the Indian Queen between Madison and Paterson, the latter insisting that events were moving rapidly towards a probably disastrous conclusion, towards a political suicide pact. Now the process of accommodation was put into action smoothly—and wisely, given the character and strength of the doubters. Madison had the votes, but this was one of those situations where the enforcement of mechanical majoritarianism could easily have destroyed the objectives of the majority: the Constitutionalists were in quest of a qualitative as well as a quantitative consensus. This was hardly from deference to local Quaker custom; it was a political imperative if they were to attain ratification.

III

According to the standard script, at this point the "states' rights" group intervened in force behind the New Jersey Plan, which has been characteristically portrayed as a reversion to the status quo under the Articles of Confederation with but minor modifications. A careful examination of the evidence indicates that only in a marginal sense is this an accurate description. It is true that the New Jersey Plan put the states back into the institutional picture, but one could argue that to do so was a recognition of political reality rather than an affirmation of states' rights. A serious case can be made that the advocates of the New Jersey Plan, far from being ideological addicts of states' rights, intended to substitute for the Virginia Plan a system which would both retain strong national power and have a chance of adoption in the states. The leading spokesman for the project asserted quite clearly that his views were based more on counsels of expediency than on principle; said Paterson on June 16: "I came here not to speak my own sentiments, but the sentiments of those who sent me. Our object is not such a Government. as may be best in itself, but such a one as our Constituents have authorized us to prepare, and as they will approve." This is Madison's version; in Yates's transcription, there is a crucial sentence following the remarks above: "I believe that a little practical virtue is to be preferred to the finest theoretical principles, which cannot be carried into effect." In his preliminary speech on June 9, Paterson had stated "to the public mind we must accommodate ourselves," and in his notes for this and his later effort as well, the emphasis is the same. The *structure* of government under the Articles should be retained:

> 2. Because it accords with the Sentiments of the People.
>   [Proof:]   1.   Coms. [Commissions from state legislatures defining the juris
>   diction of the delegates]
>   2.   News-papers—Political Barometer. Jersey never would have
>   sent Delegates under the first [Virginia] Plan—
>
> Not here to sport Opinions of my own. Wt. [What] can be done. A little practical Virtue preferable to Theory.

This was a defense of political acumen, not of states' rights. In fact, Paterson's notes of his speech can easily be construed as an argument for attaining the substantive objectives of the Virginia Plan by a sound political route, i.e., pouring the new wine in the old bottles. With a shrewd eye, Paterson queried:

> Will the Operation, and Force of the [central] Govt. depend upon the mode of Representn.—No—it will depend upon the Quantum of Power lodged in the leg. ex. and judy. Departments—Give [the existing] Congress the same Powers that you intend to give the two Branches, [under the Virginia Plan] and I apprehend they will act with as much Propriety and more Energy. . . .

In other words, the advocates of the New Jersey Plan concentrated their fire on what they held to be the *political liabilities* of the Virginia Plan—which were matters of institutional structure—rather than on the proposed scope of national authority. Indeed, the Supremacy Clause of the Constitution first saw the light of day in Paterson's Sixth Resolution; the New Jersey Plan contemplated the use of military force to secure compliance with national law; and finally Paterson made clear his view that under either the Virginia or the New Jersey systems, the general government would ". . . act on individuals and not on states." From the states' rights viewpoint, this was heresy: the fundament of that doctrine was the proposition that any central government had as its constituents the states, not the people, and could only reach the people through the agency of the state government.

Paterson then reopened the agenda of the Convention, but he did so within a distinctly nationalist framework. Paterson's position was one of favoring a strong central government in principle, but opposing one which in fact *put the big states in the saddle*. (The Virginia Plan, for all its abstract merits, did very well by Virginia.) As evidence for this speculation, there is a curious and intriguing proposal among Paterson's preliminary drafts of the New Jersey Plan:

> Whereas it is necessary in Order to form the People of the U.S. of America in to a Nation, that the States should be consolidated, by which means all the Citizens thereof will become equally intitled to and will equally participate in the same Privileges and Rights ... it is therefore resolved, that all the Lands contained within the Limits of each state individually, and of the U.S. generally be considered as constituting one Body or Mass, and be divided into thirteen or more integral parts.
>
> Resolved, That such Divisions or integral Parts shall be styled Districts.

This makes it sound as though Paterson was prepared to accept a strong unified central government along the lines of the Virginia Plan if the existing states were eliminated. He may have gotten the idea from his New Jersey colleague Judge David Brearley, who on June 9 had commented that the only remedy to the dilemma over representation was "that a map of the U.S. be spread out, that all the existing boundaries be erased, and that a new partition of the whole be made into 13 equal parts." According to Yates, Brearley added at this point, "then a government on the present [Virginia Plan] system will be just."

This proposition was never pushed—it was patently unrealistic—but one can appreciate its purpose: it would have separated the men from the boys in the large-state delegations. How attached would the Virginians have been to their reform principles if Virginia were to disappear as a component geographical unit (the largest) for representational purposes? Up to this point, the Virginians had been in the happy position of supporting high ideals with that inner confidence born of knowledge that the "public interest" they endorsed would nourish their private interest. Worse, they had shown little willingness to compromise. Now the delegates from the small states announced that they were unprepared to be offered up as sacrificial victims to a "national interest" which reflected Virginia's parochial ambition. Caustic Charles Pinckney was not far off when he remarked sardonically that "the whole [conflict] comes to this": "Give N. Jersey an equal vote, and she will dismiss her scruples, and concur in the Natl. system." What he rather unfairly did not add was that the Jersey delegates were not free agents who could adhere to their private convictions; they had to take back, sponsor and risk their reputations on the reforms approved by the Convention—and in New Jersey, not in Virginia.

Paterson spoke on Saturday, and one can surmise that over the weekend there was a good deal of consultation, argument, and caucusing among the delegates. One member at least prepared a full length address: on Monday Alexander Hamilton, previously mute, rose and delivered a six-hour oration. It was a remarkably apolitical speech; the gist of his position was that *both* the Virginia and New Jersey Plans were inadequately centralist, and he detailed a reform program which was reminiscent of the Protectorate under the Cromwellian *Instrument of Government* of 1653. It has been suggested that Hamilton did this in the best political tradition to emphasize the moderate character of the Virginia Plan, to give the cautious delegates something *really* to worry about; but this interpretation seems somehow too clever. Particularly since the sentiments Hamilton expressed happened to be completely consistent with those he privately—and sometimes publicity—expressed throughout his life. He wanted, to take a striking phrase from a letter to George Washington, a "strong well mounted government"; in essence, the Hamilton Plan contemplated an elected life monarch, virtually free of public control, on the Hobbesian ground that only in this fashion could strength and stability be achieved. The other alternatives, he argued, would put policy-making at the mercy of the passions of the mob; only if the sovereign was beyond the reach of selfish influence would it be possible to have government in the interests of the whole community.

From all accounts, this was a masterful and compelling speech, but (aside from furnishing John Lansing and Luther Martin with ammunition for later use against the Constitution) it made little impact. Hamilton was simply transmitting on a different wavelength from the rest of the delegates; the latter adjourned after his great effort, admired his rhetoric, and then returned to business. It was rather as if they had taken a day off to attend the opera. Hamilton, never a particularly patient man or much of a negotiator, stayed for another ten days and then left, in considerable disgust, for New York. Although he came back to Philadelphia sporadically and attended the last two weeks of the Convention, Hamilton played no part in the laborious task of hammering out the Constitution. His day came later when he led the New York Constitutionalists into the savage imbroglio over ratification—an arena in which his unmatched talent for dirty political infighting may well have won the day. For instance, in the New York Ratifying Convention, Lansing threw back into Hamilton's teeth the sentiments the latter had expressed in his June 18 oration in the Convention. However, having since retreated to the fine defensive positions immortalized in the *The Federalist*, the Colonel flatly denied that he had ever been an enemy of the states, or had believed that conflict between states and nation was inexorable! As Madison's authoritative *Notes* did not appear until 1840, and there had been no press coverage, there was no way to verify his assertions, so in the words of the reporter, "a warm personal altercation between [Lansing and Hamilton] engrossed the remainder of the day [June 28, 1788]."

IV

On Tuesday morning, June 19, the vacation was over. James Madison led off with a long, carefully reasoned speech analyzing the New Jersey Plan which, while intellectually vigorous in its criticisms, was quite conciliatory in mood. "The great difficulty," he observed, "lies in the affair of Representation; and if this could be adjusted, all others would be surmountable." (As events were to demonstrate, this diagnosis was correct.) When he finished, a vote was taken on whether to continue with the Virginia Plan as the nucleus for a new constitution: seven states voted "Yes"; New York, New Jersey, and Delaware voted "No"; and Maryland, whose position often depended on which delegates happened to be on the floor, divided. Paterson, it seems, lost decisively; yet in a fundamental sense he and his allies had achieved their purpose: from that day onward, it could never be forgotten that the state governments loomed ominously in the background and that no verbal incantations could exorcise their power. Moreover, nobody bolted the Convention: Paterson and his colleagues took their defeat in stride and set to work to modify the Virginia Plan, particularly with respect to its provisions on representation in the national legislature. Indeed, they won an immediate rhetorical bonus; when Oliver Ellsworth of Connecticut rose to move that the word "national" be expunged from the Third Virginia Resolution ("Resolved that a *national* Government ought to be established consisting of a *supreme* Legislative, Executive and Judiciary"), Randolph agreed and the motion passed unanimously. The process of compromise had begun.

For the next two weeks, the delegates circled around the problem of legislative representation. The Connecticut delegation appears to have evolved a possible compromise quite early in the debates, but the Virginians and particularly Madison (unaware that he would later be acclaimed as the prophet of "federalism") fought obdurately against providing for equal representation of states in the second chamber. There was a good deal of acrimony and at one point Benjamin Franklin—of all people—proposed the institution of a daily prayer; practical politicians in the gathering, however, were meditating more on the merits of a good committee than on the utility of Divine intervention. On July 2, the ice began to break when through a number of fortuitous events—and one that seems deliberate—the majority against equality of representation was converted into a dead tie. The Convention had reached the stage where it was "ripe" for a solution (presumably all the therapeutic speeches had been made), and the South Carolinians proposed a committee. Madison and James Wilson wanted none of it, but with only Pennsylvania dissenting, the body voted to establish a working party on the problem of representation.

The members of this committee, one from each state, were elected by the delegates—and a very interesting committee it was. Despite the fact that the Virginia Plan had held majority support up to that date, neither Madison nor Randolph was selected (Mason was the Virginian) and Baldwin of Georgia, whose shift in position had resulted in the tie, was chosen. From the composition, it was clear that this was not to be a "fighting" committee: the emphasis in membership was on what might be described as "second-level political entrepreneurs." On the basis of the discussions up to that time, only Luther Martin of Maryland could be described as a "bitter-ender." Admittedly, some divination enters into this sort of analysis, but one does get a sense of the mood of the delegates from these choices—including the interesting selection of Benjamin Franklin, despite his age and intellectual wobbliness, over the brilliant and incisive Wilson or the sharp, polemical Gouverneur Morris, to represent Pennsylvania. His passion for conciliation was more valuable at this juncture than Wilson's logical genius, or Morris's acerbic wit.

There is a common rumor that the framers divided their time between philosophical discussions of government and reading the classics in political theory. Perhaps this is as good a time as any to note that their concerns were highly practical, that they spent little time canvassing abstractions. A number of them had some acquaintance with the history of political theory (probably gained from reading John Adam's monumental compilation *A Defense of the Constitutions of Government*, the first volume of which appeared in 1786), and it was a poor rhetorician indeed who could not cite Locke, Montesquieu, or Harrington *in sup-*

port of a desired goal. Yet up to this point in the deliberations, no one had expounded a defense of states' rights or the "separation of powers" on anything resembling a theoretical basis. It should be reiterated that the Madison model had no room either for the states or for the "separation of powers": effectively *all* governmental power was vested in the national legislature. The merits of Montesquieu did not turn up until *The Federalist;* and although a perverse argument could be made that Madison's ideal was truly in the tradition of John Locke's *Second Treatise of Government,* the Locke whom the American rebels treated as an honorary president was a pluralistic defender of vested rights, not of parliamentary supremacy.

It would be tedious to continue a blow-by-blow analysis of the work of the delegates; the critical fight was over representation of the states and once the Connecticut Compromise was adopted on July 17, the Convention was over the hump. Madison, James Wilson, and Gouverneur Morris of New York (who was there representing Pennsylvania!) fought the compromise all the way in a last-ditch effort to get a unitary state with parliamentary supremacy. But their allies deserted them and they demonstrated after their defeat the essential opportunist character of their objections—using "opportunist" here in a nonpejorative sense, to indicate a willingness to swallow their objections and get on with the business. Moreover, once the compromise had carried (by five states to four, with one state divided), its advocates threw themselves vigorously into the job of strengthening the general government's substantive powers—as might have been predicted, indeed, from Paterson's early statements. It nourishes an increased respect for Madison's devotion to the art of politics, to realize that this dogged fighter could sit down six months later and prepare essays for *The Federalist* in contradiction to his basic convictions about the true course the Convention should have taken.

V

Two tricky issues will serve to illustrate the later process of accommodation. The first was the institutional position of the Executive. Madison argued for an executive chosen by the national legislature and on May 29 this had been adopted with a provision that after his seven-year term was concluded, the chief magistrate should not be eligible for reelection. In late July this was reopened and for a week the matter was argued from several different points of view. A good deal of desultory speech-making ensued, but the gist of the problem was the opposition from two sources to election by the legislature. One group felt that the states should have a hand in the process; another small but influential circle urged direct election by the people. There were a number of proposals: election by the people, election by state governors, by electors chosen by state legislatures, by the national legislature (James Wilson, perhaps ironically, proposed at one point that an Electoral College be chosen by lot from the national legislature!), and there was some resemblance to three-dimensional chess in the dispute because of the presence of two other variables, length of tenure and reeligibility. Finally, after opening, reopening, and re-reopening the debate, the thorny problem was consigned to a committee for absolution.

The Brearley Committee on Postponed Matters was a superb aggregation of talent and its compromise on the Executive was a masterpiece of political improvisation. (The Electoral College, its creation, however, had little in its favor as an *institution*—as the delegates well appreciated.) The point of departure for all discussion about the presidency in the Convention was that in immediate terms, the problem was nonexistent; in other words, everybody present knew that under any system devised, George Washington would be President. Thus they were dealing in the future tense and to a body of working politicians the merits of the Brearley proposal were obvious: everybody got a piece of cake. (Or to put it more academically, each viewpoint could leave the Convention and argue to its constituents that it had *really* won the day.) First, the state legislatures had the right to determine the mode of selection of the electors; second, the small states received a bonus in the Electoral College in the form of a guaranteed minimum of three votes while the big states got acceptance of the principle of proportional power; third, if the state legislatures agreed (as six did in the first presidential election), the people could be involved directly in the choice of electors; and finally, if no candidate received a majority in the College, the right of decision passed to the national legislature with each state exercising equal strength. (In the Brearley recommendation, the election went to the Senate, but a motion from the floor substituted the House; this was accepted on the ground that the Senate already had enough authority over the executive in its treaty and appointment powers.)

This compromise was almost too good to be true, and the farmers snapped it up with little debate or controversy. No one seemed to think well of the College as an *institution;* indeed, what evidence there is suggests that there was an assumption that once Washington had finished his tenure as President, the electors would cease to produce majorities and the Chief Executive would usually be chosen in the House. George Mason observed casually that the selection would be made in the House nineteen times in twenty and no one seriously disputed this point. The vital aspect of the Electoral College was that it got the Convention over the hurdle and protected everybody's interests. The future was left to cope with the problem of what to do with this Rube Goldberg mechanism.

In short, the framers did not in their wisdom endow the United States with a college of Cardinals—the Electoral College was neither an exercise in applied Platonism nor an experiment in indirect government based on elitist distrust of the masses. It was merely a jerry-rigged improvisation which has subsequently been endowed with a high theoretical content. When an elector from Oklahoma in 1960 refused to cast his vote for Nixon (naming Byrd and Goldwater instead) on the ground that the Founding Fathers intended him to exercise his great independent wisdom, he was indulging in historical fantasy. If one were to indulge in counter-fantasy, he would be tempted to suggest that the Fathers would be startled to find the College still in operation—and perhaps even dismayed at their descendants' lack of judgment or inventiveness.

The second issue on which some substantial practical bargaining took place was slavery. The morality of slavery was, by design, not at issue; but in its other concrete aspects, slavery colored the arguments over taxation, commerce, and representation. The "Three-Fifths Compromise," that three-fifths of the slaves would be counted both for representation and for purposes of direct taxation (which was drawn from the past—it was a formula of Madison's utilized by Congress in 1783 to establish the basis of state contributions to the Confederation treasury), had allayed some Northern fears about Southern overrepresentation (no one then foresaw the trivial role that direct taxation would play in later federal financial policy), but doubts still remained. The Southerners, on the other hand, were afraid that Congressional control over commerce would lead to the exclusion of slaves or to their excessive taxation as imports. Moreover, the Southerners were disturbed over "navigation acts," i.e., tariffs, or special legislation providing, for example, that exports be carried only in American ships; as a section depending upon exports, they wanted protection from the potential voracity of their commercial brethren of the Eastern states. To achieve this end, Mason and others urged that the Constitution include a proviso that navigation and commercial laws should require a two-thirds vote in Congress.

These problems came to a head in late August and, as usual, were handed to a committee in the hope that, in Gouverneur Morris's words, "these things may form a bargain among the Northern and Southern States." The Committee reported its measures of reconciliation on August 25, and on August 29 the package was wrapped up and delivered. What occurred can best be described in George Mason's dour version (he anticipated Calhoun in his conviction that permitting navigation acts to pass by majority vote would put the South in economic bondage to the North—it was mainly on this ground that he refused to sign the Constitution):

> The Constitution as agreed to till a fortnight before the Convention rose was such a one as he would have set his hand and heart to. . . . [Until that time] The 3 New England States were constantly with us in all questions . . . so that it was these three States with the 5 Southern ones against Pennsylvania, Jersey and Delaware. With respect to the importation of slaves, [decision-making] was left to Congress. This disturbed the two Southern-most States who knew the Congress would immediately suppress the importation of slaves. Those two States therefore struck up a bargain with the three New England States. If they would join to admit slaves for some years, the two Southern-most States would join in changing the clause which required the 2/3 of the Legislature in any vote [on navigation acts]. It was done.

On the floor of the Convention there was a virtual love-feast on this happy occasion. Charles Pinckney of South Carolina attempted to overturn the committee's decision, when the compromise was reported to the Convention, by insisting that the South needed protection from the imperialism of the Northern states. But his Southern colleagues were not prepared to rock the boat and General C. C. Pinckney arose to spread oil on the suddenly ruffled waters; he admitted that:

> It was in the true interest of the S[outhern] States to have no regulation of commerce; but considering the loss brought on the commerce of the Eastern States by the Revolution, their liberal conduct towards the views of South Carolina [on the regulation of the slave trade] and the interests the weak Southn. States had in being united with the strong Eastern states, he thought it proper that no fetters should be imposed on the power of making commercial regulations; *and that his constituents, though prejudiced against the Eastern States, would be reconciled to this liberality.* He had himself prejudices against the Eastern States before he came here,

but would acknowledge that he had found them as liberal and candid as any men whatever. (Italics added.)

Pierce Butler took the same tack, essentially arguing that he was not too happy about the possible consequences, but that a deal was a deal. Many Southern leaders were later—in the wake of the "Tariff of Abominations"—to rue this day of reconciliation; Calhoun's *Disquisition on Government* was little more than an extension of the argument in the Convention against permitting a Congressional majority to enact navigation acts.

VI

Drawing on their vast collective political experience, utilizing every weapon in the politician's arsenal, looking constantly over their shoulders at their constituents, the delegates put together a Constitution. It was a makeshift affair; some sticky issues (for example, the qualification of voters) they ducked entirely; others they mastered with that ancient instrument of political sagacity, studied ambiguity (for example, citizenship); and some they just overlooked. In this last category, I suspect, fell the matter of the power of the federal courts to determine the constitutionality of acts of Congress. When the judicial article was formulated (Article III of the Constitution), deliberations were still in the stage where the legislature was endowed with broad power under the Randolph formulation, authority which by its own terms was scarcely amenable to judicial review. In essence, courts could hardly determine when "the separate States are incompetent or . . . the harmony of the United States may be interrupted"; the national legislature, as critics pointed out, was free to define its own jurisdiction. Later the definition of legislative authority was changed into the form we know, a series of stipulated powers, *but the delegates never seriously reexamined the jurisdiction of the judiciary under this new limited formulation.* All arguments on the intention of the framers in this matter are thus deductive and *a posteriori,* though some obviously make more sense than others.

The framers were busy and distinguished men, anxious to get back to their families, their positions, and their constituents, not members of the French Academy devoting a lifetime to a dictionary. They were trying to do an important job, and do it in such a fashion that their handiwork would be acceptable to very diverse constituencies. No one was rhapsodic about the final document, but it was a beginning, a move in the right direction, and one they had reason to believe the people would endorse. In addition, since they had modified the impossible amendment provisions of the Articles (the requirement of unanimity which could always be frustrated by "Rogues Island") to one demanding approval by only three-quarters of the states, they seemed confident that gaps in the fabric which experience would reveal could be rewoven without undue difficulty.

So with a neat phrase introduced by Benjamin Franklin (but devised by Gouverneur Morris) which made their decision sound unanimous, and an inspired benediction by the Old Doctor urging doubters to doubt their own infallibility, the Constitution was accepted and signed. Curiously, Edmund Randolph, who had played so vital a role throughout, refused to sign, as did his fellow Virginian George Mason and Elbridge Gerry of Massachusetts. Randolph's behavior was eccentric, to say the least—his excuses for refusing his signature have a factitious ring even at this late date; the best explanation seems to be that he was afraid that the Constitution would prove to be a liability in Virginia politics, where Patrick Henry was burning up the countryside with impassioned denunciations. Presumably, Randolph wanted to check the temper of the populace before he risked his reputation, and perhaps his job, in a fight with both Henry and Richard Henry Lee. Events lend some justification to this speculation: after much temporizing and use of the conditional subjunctive tense, Randolph endorsed ratification in Virginia and ended up getting the best of both worlds.

Madison, despite his reservations about the Constitution, was the campaign manager in ratification. His first task was to get the Congress in New York to light its own funeral pyre by approving the "amendments" to the Articles and sending them on to the state legislatures. Above all, momentum had to be maintained. The anti-Constitutionalists, now thoroughly alarmed and no novices in politics, realized that their best tactic was attrition rather than direct opposition. Thus they settled on a position expressing qualified approval but calling for a second Convention to remedy various defects (the one with the most demagogic appeal was the lack of a Bill of Rights). Madison knew that to accede to this demand would be equivalent to losing the battle, nor would he agree to conditional approval (despite wavering even by Hamilton). This was an all-or-nothing proposition: national salvation or national impotence with no intermediate positions possible. Unable to get Congressional approval, he settled for second best: a unanimous resolution of Congress transmitting the Constitution to the states for whatever action they saw fit to take. The opponents then moved from New York and the Congress, where they had attempted to attach amendments and conditions, to the states for the final battle.

At first the campaign for ratification went beautifully: within eight months after the delegates set their names to the document, eight states had ratified. Only in Massachusetts had the result been close (187–168). Theoretically, a ratification by one more state convention would set the new government in motion, but in fact until Virginia and New York acceded to the new Union, the latter was a fiction. New Hampshire was the next to ratify; Rhode Island was involved in its characteristic political convulsions (the legislature there sent the Constitution out to the towns for decision by popular vote and it got lost among a series of local issues); North Carolina's convention did not meet until July and then postponed a final decision. This is hardly the place for an extensive analysis of the conventions of New York and Virginia. Suffice it to say that the Constitutionalists clearly out-maneuvered their opponents, forced them into impossible political positions, and won both states narrowly. The Virginia Convention could serve as a classic study in effective floor management: Patrick Henry had to be contained, and a reading of the debates discloses a standard two-stage technique. Henry would give a four- or five-hour speech denouncing some section of the Constitution on every conceivable ground (the federal district, he averred at one point, would become a haven for convicts escaping from state authority!); when Henry subsided, "Mr. Lee of Westmoreland" would rise and literally poleax him with sardonic invective (when Henry complained about the militia power, "Lighthorse Harry" really punched below the belt: observing that while the former Governor had been sitting in Richmond during the Revolution, *he* had been out in the trenches with the troops and thus felt better qualified to discuss military affairs). Then the gentlemanly Constitutionalists (Madison, Pendleton, and Marshall) would pick up the matters at issue and examine them in the light of reason.

Indeed, modern Americans who tend to think of James Madison as a rather desiccated character should spend some time with this transcript. Probably Madison put on his most spectacular demonstration of nimble rhetoric in what might be called "The Battle of the Absent Authorities." Patrick Henry in the course of one of his harangues alleged that Jefferson was known to be opposed to Virginia's approving the Constitution. This was clever: Henry hated Jefferson, but was prepared to use any weapon that came to hand. Madison's riposte was superb: First, he said that with all due respect to the great reputation of Jefferson, he was not in the country and therefore could not formulate an adequate judgment; second, no one should utilize the reputation of an outsider—the Virginia Convention was there to think for itself; third, if there were to be recourse to outsiders, the opinions of George Washington should certainly be taken into consideration; and finally, he knew from privileged personal communications from Jefferson that in fact the latter *strongly favored* the Constitution. To devise an assault route into this rhetorical fortress was literally impossible.

VII

The fight was over; all that remained now was to establish the new frame of government in the spirit of its framers. And who were better qualified for this task than the framers themselves? Thus victory for the Constitution meant simultaneous victory for the Constitutionalists; the anti-Constitutionalists either capitulated or vanished into limbo—soon Patrick Henry would be offered a seat on the Supreme Court and Luther Martin would be known as the Federalist "bull-dog." And irony of ironies, Alexander Hamilton and James Madison would shortly accumulate a reputation as the formulators of what is often alleged to be our political theory, the concept of "federalism." Also, on the other side of the ledger, the arguments would soon appear over what the framers "really meant"; while these disputes have assumed the proportions of a big scholarly business in the last century, they began almost before the ink on the Constitution was dry. One of the best early ones featured Hamilton versus Madison on the scope of presidential power, and other framers characteristically assumed positions in this and other disputes on the basis of their political convictions.

Probably our greatest difficulty is that we know so much more about what the framers *should have meant* than they themselves did. We are intimately acquainted with the problems that their Constitution should have been designed to master; in short, we have read the mystery story backwards. If we are to get the right "feel" for their time and their circumstances, we must in Maitland's phrase, "think ourselves back into a twilight." Obviously, no one can pretend completely to escape from the solipsistic web of his own environment, but if the effort is made, it is possible to appreciate the past roughly on its own terms. The first step in this process is to abandon the academic premise that because we can ask a question, there must be an answer.

Thus we can ask what the farmers meant when they gave Congress the power to regulate interstate and foreign commerce, and we emerge, reluctantly perhaps, with the reply that they may not have known what they meant, that there may not have been any semantic consensus. The Convention was not a seminar in analytic philosophy or linguistic analysis. Commerce was *commerce*—and if different interpretations of the word arose, later generations could worry about the problem of definition. The delegates were in a hurry to get a new government established; when definitional arguments arose, they characteristically took refuge in ambiguity. If different men voted for the same proposition for varying reasons, that was politics (and still is); if later generations were unsettled by this lack of precision, that would be their problem.

There was a good deal of definitional pluralism with respect to the problems the delegates did discuss, but when we move to the question of extrapolated intentions, we enter the realm of spiritualism. When men in our time, for instance, launch into elaborate talmudic exegesis to demonstrate that federal aid to parochial schools is (or is not) in accord with the intentions of the men who established the Republic and endorsed the Bill of Rights, they are engaging in historical Extra-Sensory Perception. (If one were to join this E.S.P. contingent for a minute, he might suggest that the hard-boiled politicians who wrote the Constitution and Bill of Rights would chuckle scornfully at such an invocation of authority: obviously a politician would chart his course on the intentions of the living, not of the dead, and count the number of Catholics in his constituency.)

The Constitution, then, was not an apotheosis of "constitutionalism," a triumph of architectonic genius; it was a patch-work sewn together under the pressure of both time and events by a group of extremely talented democratic politicians. They refused to attempt the establishment of a strong, centralized sovereignty on the principle of legislative supremacy for the excellent reason that the people would not accept it. They risked their political fortunes by opposing the established doctrines of state sovereignty because they were convinced that the existing system was leading to national impotence and probably foreign domination. For two years, they worked to get a convention established. For over three months, in what must have seemed to the faithful participants an endless process of give-and-take, they reasoned, cajoled, threatened, and bargained amongst themselves. The result was a Constitution which the people, in fact, by democratic processes, did accept, and a new and far better national government was established.

Beginning with the inspired propaganda of Hamilton, Madison, and Jay, the ideological build-up got under way. *The Federalist* had little impact on the ratification of the Constitution, except perhaps in New York, but this volume had enormous influence on the image of the Constitution in the minds of future generations, particularly on historians and political scientists who have an innate fondness for theoretical symmetry. Yet, while the shades of Locke and Montesquieu *may* have been hovering in the background, and the delegates *may* have been unconscious instruments of a transcendent *telos*, the careful observer of the day-to-day work of the Convention finds no overarching principles. The "separation of powers" to him seems to be a by-product of suspicion, and "federalism" he views as a *pis aller*, as the farthest point the delegates felt they could go in the destruction of state power without themselves inviting repudiation.

To conclude, the Constitution was neither a victory for abstract theory nor a great practical success. Well over half a million men had to die on the battlefields of the Civil War before certain constitutional principles could be defined—a baleful consideration which is somehow overlooked in our customary tributes to the far-sighted genius of the framers and to the supposed American talent for "constitutionalism." The Constitution was, however, a vivid demonstration of effective democratic political action, and of the forging of a national elite which literally persuaded its countrymen to hoist themselves by their own boot straps. American pro-consuls would be wise not to translate the Constitution into Japanese, or Swahili, or treat it as a work of semi-Divine origin; but when students of comparative politics examine the process of nation-building in countries newly freed from colonial rule, they may find the American experience instructive as a classic example of the potentialities of a democratic elite.

❖❖John Roche's article on the framing of the Constitution was written as an attack upon a variety of views that suggested the Constitution was not so much a practical political document as an expression of elitist views based upon political philosophy and economic interests. One such elitist view was that of Charles A. Beard, who published his famous *An Economic Interpretation of the Constitution* in 1913. He suggested that the Constitution was nothing more than the work of an economic elite that was seeking to preserve its property. This elite, according to Beard, consisted of landholders, creditors, merchants, public bondholders, and wealthy lawyers. Beard demonstrated that many of the delegates to the convention fell into one of these categories.

According to Beard's thesis, as the delegates met, the primary concern of most of them was to limit the power of popular majorities and thus protect their own property interests. To Beard, the antimajoritarian attributes that he felt existed in the Constitution were a reflection of the less numerous creditor class attempting to protect itself against incursions by the majority. Specific provisions as well were put into the Constitution with a view towards protecting property, such as the clause prohibiting states from impairing contracts, coining money, or emitting bills of credit. Control over money was placed in the hands of the national government, and in Article VI of the Constitution it was provided that the new government was to guarantee all debts that had been incurred by the national government under the Articles of Confederation.

Ironically, Beard, like Roche, was attempting to dispel the prevailing notions of his time that the Constitution had been formulated by philosopher kings whose wisdom could not be challenged. But while Roche postulates a loosely knit practical political elite, Beard suggests the existence of a cohesive and even conspiratorial economic elite. The limitation on majority rule was an essential component of this economic conspiracy.

The Constitution does contain many provisions that limit majority rule. Beard claimed that the Constitution from initial adoption to final ratification was never supported by the majority of the people. The holding of a constitutional convention in the first place was never submitted to a popular vote, nor was the Constitution that was finally agreed upon ratified by a popular referendum. The selection of delegates to state ratifying conventions was not executed through universal suffrage, but on the basis of the suffrage qualifications that applied in the states and that were within the discretion of state legislatures. The limited suffrage in the states severely restricted popular participation in ratification of the Constitution.

Beard's thesis was startling at the time it was published in 1913. As it came under close examination, it was revealed that the evidence simply did not support Beard's hypothesis. Key leaders of the convention, including Madison, were not substantial property owners. Several important opponents to ratification of the Constitution were the very members of the economic elite that Beard said conspired to thrust the Constitution upon an unknowing public.

Before Beard presented his narrow thesis in 1913, he had published in 1912 *The Supreme Court and the Constitution.* The major theme of the book was that the Supreme Court was intended to have the authority to review acts of Congress under the terms of the original Constitution. At the same time, the book presents Beard's elitist view of the framing of the Constitution in a somewhat broader context than it was presented in *An Economic Interpretation of the Constitution* published a year later. But the earlier work clearly contains the economic theme, as in the passage where Beard states that the framers of the Constitution were "anxious above everything else to safeguard the rights of private property against any levelling tendencies on the part of the propertyless masses." The following selection contains Beard's overview of the framing and adoption of the Constitution and highlights his economic theme and his belief in the antimajoritarian attributes of the Constitution.

8

Charles A. Beard

FRAMING THE CONSTITUTION

As Blackstone[1] shows by happy illustration the reason and spirit of a law are to be understood only by an inquiry into the circumstances of its enactment. The under-

---

Chapter X from *The Economic Basis of Politics and Related Writings by Charles A. Beard*, compiled and annotated by William Beard, Vintage Books, Inc., © 1957 by William Beard and Miriam B. Vagts. Reprinted with permission of William Beard and the Estate of Miriam B. Vagts.

[1]*Compiler's Note*: Blackstone, Sir William (1723–1780). Distinguished commentator on the laws of England, judge, and teacher.

lying purposes of the Constitution [of the United States], therefore, are to be revealed only by a study of the conditions and events which led to its formation and adoption.

At the outset it must be remembered that there were two great parties at the time of the adoption of the Constitution—one laying emphasis on strength and efficiency in government and the other on its popular aspects. Quite naturally the men who led in stirring up the revolt against Great Britain and in keeping the fighting temper of the Revolutionists at the proper heat were the boldest and most radical thinkers—men like Samuel Adams, Thomas Paine, Patrick Henry, and Thomas Jefferson. They were not, generally speaking, men of large property interests or of much practical business experience. In a time of disorder, they could consistently lay more stress upon personal liberty than upon social control; and they pushed to the extreme limits those doctrines of individual rights which had been evolved in England during the struggles of the small landed proprietors and commercial classes against royal prerogative, and which corresponded to the economic conditions prevailing in America at the close of the eighteenth century. They associated strong government with monarchy, and came to believe that the best political system was one which governed least. A majority of the radicals viewed all government, especially if highly centralized, as a species of evil, tolerable only because necessary and always to be kept down to an irreducible minimum by a jealous vigilance.

Jefferson put the doctrine in concrete form when he declared that he preferred newspapers without government to government without newspapers. The Declaration of Independence, the first state Constitutions, and the Articles of Confederation bore the impress of this philosophy. In their anxiety to defend the individual against all federal interference and to preserve to the states a large sphere of local autonomy, these Revolutionists had set up a system too weak to accomplish the accepted objects of government; namely, national defense, the protection of property, and the advancement of commerce. They were not unaware of the character of their handiwork, but they believed with Jefferson that "man was a rational animal endowed by nature with rights and with an innate sense of justice and that he could be restrained from wrong and protected in right by moderate powers confided to persons of his own choice." Occasional riots and disorders, they held, were preferable to too much government.

The new American political system based on these doctrines had scarcely gone into effect before it began to incur opposition from many sources. The close of the Revolutionary struggle removed the prime cause for radical agitation and brought a new group of thinkers into prominence. When independence had been gained, the practical work to be done was the maintenance of social order, the payment of the public debt, the provision of a sound financial system, and the establishment of conditions favorable to the development of the economic resources of the new country. The men who were principally concerned in this work of peaceful enterprise were not the philosophers, but men of business and property and the holders of public securities. For the most part they had had no quarrel with the system of class rule and the strong centralization of government which existed in England. It was on the question of policy, not of governmental structure, that they had broken with the British authorities. By no means all of them, in fact, had even resisted the policy of the mother country, for within the ranks of the conservatives were large numbers of Loyalists who had remained in America, and, as was to have been expected, cherished a bitter feeling against the Revolutionists, especially the radical section which had been boldest in denouncing the English system root and branch. In other words, after the heat and excitement of the War of Independence were over and the new government, state and national, was tested by the ordinary experiences of traders, financiers, and manufacturers, it was found inadequate, and these groups accordingly grew more and more determined to reconstruct the political system in such a fashion as to make it subserve their permanent interests.

Under the state constitutions and the Articles of Confederation established during the Revolution, every powerful economic class in the nation suffered either immediate losses or from impediments placed in the way of the development of their enterprises. The holders of the securities of the Confederate government did not receive the interest on their loans. Those who owned Western lands or looked with longing eyes upon the rich opportunities for speculation there chaffed at the weakness of the government and its delays in establishing order on the frontiers. Traders and commercial men found their plans for commerce on a national scale impeded by local interference with interstate commerce. The currency of the states and the nation was hopelessly muddled. Creditors everywhere were angry about the depreciated paper money which the agrarians had made and were attempting to force upon those from whom they had borrowed specie. In short, it was a war between business and populism. Under the Articles of Confederation populism had a free hand, for majorities in the state legislatures were omnipotent. Anyone who reads the economic history of the time will see why the solid conservative interests of the country were weary of talk about the "rights of the people" and bent upon establishing firm guarantees for the rights of property.

The Congress of the Confederation was not long in discovering the true character of the futile authority which the Articles had conferred upon it. The necessity for new sources of revenue became apparent even while the struggle for independence was yet undecided, and, in 1781, Congress carried a resolution to the effect that it should be authorized to lay a duty of five percent on certain goods. This moderate proposition was defeated because Rhode Island rejected it on the grounds that "she regarded it the most precious jewel of sovereignty that no state shall be called upon to open its purse but by the authority of the state and by her own officers." Two years later Congress prepared another amendment to the Articles providing for certain import duties, the receipts from which, collected by state officers, were to be applied to the payment of the public debt; but three years after the introduction of the measure, four states, including New York, still held out against its ratification, and the project was allowed to drop. At last, in 1786, Congress in a resolution declared that the requisitions for the last eight years had been so irregular in their operation, so uncertain in their collection, and so evidently unproductive, that a reliance on them in the future would be no less dishonorable to the understandings of those who entertained it than it would be dangerous to the welfare and peace of the Union. Congress, thereupon, solemnly added that it had become its duty "to declare most explicitly that the crisis had arrived when the people of the

United States, by whose will and for whose benefit the federal government was instituted, must decide whether they will support their rank as a nation by maintaining the public faith at home and abroad, or whether for the want of a timely exertion in establishing a general review and thereby giving strength to the Confederacy, they will hazard not only the existence of the Union but those great and invaluable privileges for which they have so arduously and so honorably contended."

In fact, the Articles of Confederation had hardly gone into effect before the leading citizens also began to feel that the powers of Congress were wholly inadequate. In 1780, even before their adoption, Alexander Hamilton proposed a general convention to frame a new constitution, and from that time forward he labored with remarkable zeal and wisdom to extend and popularize the idea of a strong national government. Two years later, the Assembly of the State of New York recommended a convention to revise the Articles and increase the power of Congress. In 1783, Washington, in a circular letter to the governors, urged that it was indispensable to the happiness of the individual states that there should be lodged somewhere a supreme power to regulate and govern the general concerns of the confederation. Shortly afterward (1785), Governor Bowdoin, of Massachusetts, suggested to his state legislature the advisability of calling a national assembly to settle upon and define the powers of Congress; and the legislature resolved that the government under the Articles of Confederation was inadequate and should be reformed; but the resolution was never laid before Congress.

In January, 1786, Virginia invited all the other states to send delegates to a convention at Annapolis to consider the question of duties on imports and commerce in general. When this convention assembled in 1786, delegates from only five states were present, and they were disheartened at the limitations on their powers and the lack of interest the other states had shown in the project. With characteristic foresight, however, Alexander Hamilton seized the occasion to secure the adoption of a recommendation advising the states to choose representatives for another convention to meet in Philadelphia the following year "to consider the Articles of Confederation and to propose such changes therein as might render them adequate to the exigencies of the union." This recommendation was cautiously worded, for Hamilton did not want to raise any unnecessary alarm. He doubtless believed that a complete revolution in the old system was desirable, but he knew that, in the existing state of popular temper, it was not expedient to announce his complete program. Accordingly no general reconstruction of the political system was suggested; the Articles of Confederation were merely to be "revised"; and the amendments were to be approved by the state legislatures as provided by that instrument.

The proposal of the Annapolis convention was transmitted to the state legislatures and laid before Congress. Congress thereupon resolved in February, 1787, that a convention should be held for the sole and express purpose of revising the Articles of Confederation and reporting to itself and the legislatures of the several states such alterations and provisions as would when agreed to by Congress and confirmed by the states render the federal constitution adequate to the exigencies of government and the preservation of the union.

In pursuance of this call, delegates to the new convention were chosen by the legislatures of the states or by the governors in conformity to authority conferred by the legislative assemblies.[2] The delegates were given instructions of a general nature by their respective states, none of which, apparently, contemplated any very far-reaching changes. In fact, almost all of them expressly limited their representatives to a mere revision of the Articles of Confederation. For example, Connecticut authorized her delegates to represent and confer for the purpose mentioned in the resolution of Congress and to discuss such measures "agreeable to the general principles of Republican government" as they should think proper to render the Union adequate. Delaware, however, went so far as to provide that none of the proposed alterations should extend to the fifth part of the Articles of Confederation guaranteeing that each state should be entitled to one vote.

It was a truly remarkable assembly of men that gathered in Philadelphia on May 14, 1787, to undertake the work of reconstructing the American system of government. It is not merely patriotic pride that compels one to assert that never in the history of assemblies has there been a convention of men richer in political experience and in practical knowledge, or endowed with a profounder insight into the springs of human action and the intimate essence of government. It is indeed an astounding fact that at one time so many men skilled in statecraft could be found on the very frontiers of civilization among a population numbering about four million whites. It is no less a cause for admiration that their instrument of government should have survived the trials and crises of a century that saw the wreck of more than a score of paper constitutions.

All the members had had a practical training in politics. Washington, as commander-in-chief of the Revolutionary forces, had learned well the lessons and problems of war, and mastered successfully the no less difficult problems of administration. The two Morrises had distinguished themselves in grappling with financial questions as trying and perplexing as any which statesmen had ever been compelled to face. Seven of the delegates had gained political wisdom as governors of their native states; and no less than twenty-eight had served in Congress either during the Revolution or under the Articles of Confederation. These were men trained in the law, versed in finance, skilled in administration, and learned in the political philosophy of their own and all earlier times. Moreover, they were men destined to continue public service under the government which they had met to construct—Presidents, Vice-Presidents, heads of departments, Justices of the Supreme Court were in that imposing body. . . .

As Woodrow Wilson had concisely put it, the framers of the Constitution represented "a strong and intelligent class possessed of unity and informed by a conscious solidarity of interests."[3] . . .

---

[2]Rhode Island alone was unrepresented. In all, sixty-two delegates were appointed by the states; fifty-five of these attended sometime during the sessions; but only thirty-nine signed the finished document.

[3]Woodrow Wilson, *Division and Reunion* (New York: Longmans, Green, & Co., 1893), p. 12.

The makers of the federal Constitution represented the solid, conservative, commercial and financial interests of the country—not the interests which denounced and proscribed judges in Rhode Island, New Jersey, and North Carolina, and stoned their houses in New York. The conservative interests, made desperate by the imbecilities of the Confederation and harried by state legislatures, roused themselves from the lethargy, drew together in a mighty effort to establish a government that would be strong enough to pay the national debt, regulate interstate and foreign commerce, provide for national defense, prevent fluctuations in the currency created by paper emissions, and control the propensities of legislative majorities to attack private rights. . . . The radicals, however, like Patrick Henry, Jefferson, and Samuel Adams, were conspicuous by their absence from the convention.[4] . . .

[The makers of the Constitution were convened] to frame a government which would meet the practical issues that had arisen under the Articles of Confederation. The objections they entertained to direct popular government, and they were undoubtedly many, were based upon their experience with popular assemblies during the immediately preceding years. With many of the plain lessons of history before them, they naturally feared that the rights and privileges of the minority would be insecure if the principle of majority rule was definitely adopted and provisions made for its exercise. Furthermore, it will be remembered that up to that time the right of all men, as men, to share in the government had never been recognized in practice. Everywhere in Europe the government was in the hands of a ruling monarch or at best a ruling class; everywhere the mass of the people had been regarded principally as an arms-bearing and tax-paying multitude, uneducated, and with little hope or capacity for advancement. Two years were to elapse after the meeting of the grave assembly at Philadelphia before the transformation of the Estates General into the National Convention in France opened the floodgates of revolutionary ideas on human rights before whose rising tide old landmarks of government are still being submerged. It is small wonder, therefore, that, under the circumstances, many of the members of that august body held popular government in slight esteem and took the people into consideration only as far as it was imperative "to inspire them with the necessary confidence," as Mr. Gerry frankly put it.[5]

Indeed, every page of the laconic record of the proceedings of the convention preserved to posterity by Mr. Madison shows conclusively that the members of that assembly were not seeking to realize any fine notions about democracy and equality, but were striving with all the resources of political wisdom at their command to set up a system of government that would be stable and efficient, safeguarded on one hand against the possibilities of despotism and on the other against the onslaught of majorities. In the mind of Mr. Gerry, the evils they had experienced flowed "from the excess of democracy," and he confessed that while he was still republican, he

---

[4]*Compiler's Note:* The contents of this paragraph have been taken from positions on pp. 75–76 and 88 of the original text of *The Supreme Court and the Constitution* and placed here to emphasize the economic theme.

[5]Jonathan Elliot, *The Debates in the Several State Conventions on the Adoption of the Federal Constitution* (Washington, D.C.: The Editor, 1827–1830), vol. v, p. 160.

"had been taught by experience the danger of the levelling spirit."[6] Mr. Randolph in offering to the consideration of the convention his plan of government, observed "that the general object was to provide a cure for the evils under which the United States labored; that, in tracing these evils to their origin, every man had found it in the turbulence and follies of democracy; that some check therefore was to be sought for against this tendency of our governments; and that a good Senate seemed most likely to answer the purpose."[7] Mr. Hamilton, in advocating a life term for Senators, urged that "all communities divide themselves into the few and the many. The first are rich and well born and the other the mass of the people who seldom judge or determine right."

Gouverneur Morris wanted to check the "precipitancy, changeableness, and excess" of the representatives of the people by the ability and virtue of men "of great and established property—aristocracy; men who from pride will support consistency and permanency. . . . Such an aristocratic body will keep down the turbulence of democracy." While these extreme doctrines were somewhat counter-balanced by the democratic principles of Mr. Wilson who urged that "the government ought to possess, not only first, the force, but second the mind or sense of the people at large," Madison doubtless summed up in a brief sentence the general opinion of the convention when he said that to secure private rights against majority factions, and at the same time to preserve the spirit and form of popular government, was the great object to which their inquiries had been directed.[8]

They were anxious above everything else to safeguard the rights of private property against any leveling tendencies on the part of the propertyless masses. Gouverneur Morris, in speaking on the problem of apportioning representatives, correctly stated the sound historical fact when he declared: "Life and liberty were generally said to be of more value than property. An accurate view of the matter would, nevertheless, prove that property was the main object of society. . . . If property, then, was the main object of government, certainly it ought to be one measure of the influence due to those who were to be affected by the government".[9] Mr. King also agreed that "property was the primary object of society".[10] and Mr. Madison warned the convention that in framing a system which they wished to last for ages they must not lose sight of the changes which the ages would produce in the forms and distribution of property. In advocating a long term in order to give independence and firmness to the Senate, he described these impending changes: "An increase of population will of necessity increase the proportion of those who will labor under all the hardships of life and secretly sigh for a more equal distribution of its blessings. These may in time outnumber those who are placed above the feelings of indigence. According to the equal laws of suffrage, the power will slide into the hands of the former. No agrarian attempts have yet been made in this country, but

---

[6]*Ibid.*, vol. v, p. 136.
[7]*Ibid.*, vol. v, p. 138.
[8]*The Federalist,* No. 10.
[9]Elliot's *Debates, op. cit.,* vol. v, p. 279.
[10]*Ibid.*, p. 280·

symptoms of a levelling spirit, as we have understood have sufficiently appeared, in a certain quarter, to give notice of the future danger".[11] And again, in support of the argument for a property qualification on voters, Madison urged: "In future times, a great majority of the people will not only be without landed, but any other sort of property. These will either combine, under the influence of their common situation,—in which case the rights of property and the public liberty will not be secure in their hands,—or, what is more probable, they will become the tools of opulence and ambition; in which case there will be equal danger on another side".[12] Various projects for setting up class rule by the establishment of property qualifications for voters and officers were advanced in the convention, but they were defeated. . . .

> The absence of such property qualifications is certainly not due to any belief in Jefferson's free-and-equal doctrine. It is due rather to the fact that the members of the convention could not agree on the nature and amount of the qualifications. Naturally a landed qualification was suggested, but for obvious reasons it was rejected. Although it was satisfactory to the landed gentry of the South, it did not suit the financial, commercial, and manufacturing gentry of the North. If it was high, the latter would be excluded; if it was low it would let in the populistic farmers who had already made so much trouble in the state legislatures with paper-money schemes and other devices for "relieving agriculture." One of the chief reasons for calling the convention and framing the Constitution was to promote commerce and industry and to protect personal property against the "depredations" of Jefferson's noble freeholders. On the other hand a personal-property qualification, high enough to please merchant princes like Robert Morris and Nathaniel Gorham would shut out the Southern planters. Again, an alternative of land or personal property, high enough to afford safeguards to large interests, would doubtless bring about the rejection of the whole Constitution by the troublemaking farmers who had to pass upon the question of ratification.[13] . . .

Nevertheless, by the system of checks and balances placed in the government, the convention safeguarded the interests of property against attacks by majorities. The House of Representatives, Mr. Hamilton pointed out, "was so formed as to render it particularly the guardian of the poorer orders of citizens,"[14] while the Senate was to preserve the rights of property and the interests of the minority against the demands of the majority.[15] In the tenth number of *The Federalist*, Mr. Madison argued in a philosophic vein in support of the proposition that it was necessary to base the political system on the actual conditions of "natural inequality." Uniformity of interests throughout the state, he contended, was impossible on account of the diversity in the faculties of men, from which the rights of property originated;

---

[11]*Ibid.*, p. 243.

[12]*Ibid.*, p. 387.

[13]*Compiler's Note:* This single paragraph from "Whom Does Congress Represent?" *Harper's Magazine,* Jan. 1930, pp. 144–152, has been inserted here because of its value in amplifying the passages from *The Supreme Court and the Constitution.* Reprinting from this article by Beard has been done with the permission of *Harper's Magazine.*

[14]Elliot's *Debates, op. cit.,* vol. v, p. 244.

[15]*Ibid.,* vol. v, p. 203.

the protection of these faculties was the first object of government; from the protection of different and unequal faculties of acquiring property the possession of different degrees and kinds of property immediately resulted; from the influence of these on the sentiments and views of the respective proprietors ensued a division of society into different interests and parties; the unequal distribution of wealth inevitably led to a clash of interests in which the majority was liable to carry out its policies at the expense of the minority; hence, he added, in concluding this splendid piece of logic, "the majority, having such coexistent passion or interest, must be rendered by their number and local situation unable to concert and carry into effect schemes of oppression"; and in his opinion it was the great merit of the newly framed Constitution that it secured the rights of the minority against "the superior force of an interested and overbearing majority."

This very system of checks and balances, which is undeniably the essential element of the Constitution, is built upon the doctrine that the popular branch of the government cannot be allowed full sway, and least of all in the enactment of laws touching the rights of property. The exclusion of the direct popular vote in the election of the President; the creation, again by indirect election, of a Senate which the framers hoped would represent the wealth and conservative interests of the country;[16] and the establishment of an independent judiciary appointed by the President with the concurrence of the Senate—all these devices bear witness to the fact that the underlying purpose of the Constitution was not the establishment of popular government by means of parliamentary majorities.

Page after page of *The Federalist* is directed to that portion of the electorate which was disgusted with the "mutability of the public councils." Writing on the presidential veto Hamilton says: "The propensity of the legislative department to intrude upon the rights, and absorb the powers, of other departments has already been suggested and repeated. . . . It may perhaps be said that the power of preventing bad laws included the power of preventing good ones; and may be used to the one purpose as well as the other. But this objection will have little weight with those who can properly estimate the mischiefs of that inconstancy and mutability in the laws which form the greater blemish in the character and genius of our governments. They will consider every institution calculated to restrain the excess of law-making and to keep things in the same state in which they happen to be at any given period, as more likely to do good than harm; because it is favorable to greater stability in the system of legislation. The injury which may be possibly done be defeating a few good laws will be amply compensated by the advantage of preventing a number of bad ones."

When the framers of the Constitution had completed the remarkable instrument which was to establish a national government capable of discharging effectively certain great functions and checking the propensities of popular legislatures to attack the rights of private property, a formidable task remained before them— the task of securing the adoption of the new frame of government by states torn with popular dissensions. They knew very well that the state legislatures which had

---

[16]*Compiler's Note:* Popular election of senators was achieved in 1913 through the Seventeenth Amendment to the constitution.

been so negligent in paying their quotas [of money] under the Articles [of Confederation] and which had been so jealous of their rights, would probably stick at ratifying such a national instrument of government. Accordingly they cast aside that clause in the Articles requiring amendments to be ratified by the legislatures of all the states; and advised that the new Constitution should be ratified by conventions in the several states composed of delegates chosen by the voters.[17] They furthermore declared—and this is a fundamental matter—that when the conventions of nine states had ratified the Constitution the new government should to into effect so far as those states were concerned. The chief reason for restoring to ratifications by conventions is laid down by Hamilton in the twenty-second number of *The Federalist:* "It has not a little contributed to the infirmities of the existing federal system that it never had a ratification by the people. Resting on no better foundation than the consent of the several legislatures, it has been exposed to frequent and intricate questions concerning the validity of its powers; and has in some instances given birth to the enormous doctrine of a right of legislative repeal. Owing its ratification to the law of a state, it has been contended that the same authority might repeal the law by which it was ratified. However gross a heresy it may be to maintain that a party to a compact has a right to revoke that compact, the doctrine itself has respectable advocates. The possibility of a question of this nature proves the necessity of laying the foundations of our national government deeper than in the mere sanction of delegated authority. The fabric of American empire ought to rest on the solid basis of the consent of the people. The streams of national power ought to flow immediately from that pure original foundation of all legitimate authority."

Of course, the convention did not resort to the revolutionary policy of transmitting the Constitution directly to the conventions of the several states. It merely laid the finished instrument before the Confederate Congress with the suggestion that it should be submitted to "a convention of delegates chosen in each state by the people thereof, under the recommendation of its legislature, for their assent and ratification; and each convention assenting thereto and ratifying the same should give notice thereof to the United States in Congress assembled." The convention went on to suggest that when nine states had ratified the Constitution, the Confederate Congress should extinguish itself by making provision for the elections necessary to put the new government into effect. . . .

After the new Constitution was published and transmitted to the states, there began a long and bitter fight over ratification. A veritable flood of pamphlet literature descended upon the country, and a collection of these pamphlets by Hamilton, Madison, and Jay, brought together under the title of *The Federalist*—though clearly a piece of campaign literature—has remained a permanent part of the contemporary sources on the Constitution and has been regarded by many lawyers as a commentary second in value only to the decisions of the Supreme Court. Within a year the champions of the new government found themselves victorious, for on June 21, 1788, the ninth state, New Hampshire, ratified the Constitution, and accordingly

---

[17]*Compiler's Note:* The original text, p. 75, comments: "It was largely because the framers of the Constitution knew the temper and class bias of the state legislatures that they arranged that the new Constitution should be ratified by conventions."

the new government might go into effect as between the agreeing states. Within a few weeks, the nationalist party in Virginia and New York succeeded in winning these two states, and in spite of the fact that North Carolina and Rhode Island had not yet ratified the Constitution, Congress determined to put the instrument into effect in accordance with the recommendations of the convention. Elections for the new government were held; the date March 4, 1789, was fixed for the formal establishment of the new system; Congress secured a quorum on April 6; and on April 30 Washington was inaugurated at the Federal Hall in Wall Street, New York.

❖❖ Charles A. Beard suggests that there is a dichotomy between the values of the Constitution and those of the Declaration of Independence, between Jefferson and his followers on the one hand, and Madison and Hamilton on the other. He suggest that Jefferson and the Revolutionists supported political equality and individual freedom and opposed a strong central government. The spirit of the Revolution, argues Beard, spawned the Articles of Confederation, which purposely created a weak and ineffective government. The Revolutionists, in general, were not men of property and thus did not believe that a strong central government was necessary to protect their interests. By contrast, the framers of the Constitution reflected the spirit of Alexander Hamilton, who ironically was not a man of substantial property himself, but who advocated an energetic and dominant national government. Hamilton, like many of the framers, was a strong proponent of governmental protection of property interests.

LIMITATION OF GOVERNMENTAL POWER
AND OF MAJORITY RULE

The most accurate and helpful way to characterize our political system is to call it a constitutional democracy. The term implies a system in which the government is regulated by laws that control and limit the exercise of political power. In a constitutional democracy people participate in government on a limited basis. A distinction should be made between an unlimited democratic government and a constitutional democracy. In the former, the people govern through the operation of a principle such as majority rule without legal restraint; in the latter, majority rule is curtailed and checked through various legal devises. A constitutional system is one in which the formal authority of government is restrained. The checks upon government in a constitutional society customarily include a division or fragmentation of authority that prevents government from controlling all sectors of human life.

Hamilton noted in *Federalist 1*, "It seems to have been reserved to the people of this country, to decide by their conduct and example, the important question, whether societies of men are really capable or not, of establishing good government from reflection and choice, or whether they are forever destined to depend, for their political constitutions, on accident and force." The framers of our Constitution attempted to structure the government in such a way that it would meet the needs and aspirations of the people and at the same time check the arbitrary exercise of political power. The doctrine of the separation of powers was designed to prevent any one group from gaining control of the national governmental apparatus. The selections reprinted here from *The Federalist,* which was written between October 1787 and August 1788, outline the theory and mechanism of the separation of powers.

4

James Madison

FEDERALIST 47

❖❖❖❖❖❖❖

I proceed to examine the particular structure of this government, and the distribution of this mass of power among its constituent parts.

One of the principal objections inculcated by the more respectable adversaries to the constitution, is its supposed violation of the political maxim, that the legislative, executive, and judiciary departments, ought to be separate and distinct. In the structure of the federal government, no regard, it is said, seems to have been paid to this essential precaution in favor of liberty. The several departments of power are distributed and blended in such a manner, as at once to destroy all symmetry and beauty of form; and to expose some of the essential parts of the edifice to the danger of being crushed by the disproportionate weight of other parts.

No political truth is certainly of great intrinsic value, or is stamped with the authority of more enlightened patrons of liberty, than that on which the objection is founded. The accumulation of all powers, legislative, executive, and judiciary, in the same hands, whether of one, a few, or many, and whether hereditary, self-appointed, or elective, may justly be pronounced the very definition of tyranny. Were the federal constitution, therefore, really chargeable with this accumulation of power, or with a mixture of powers, having a dangerous tendency to such an accumulation, no further arguments would be necessary to inspire a universal reprobation of the system. I persuade myself, however, that it will be made apparent to every one, that the charge cannot be supported, and that the maxim on which it relies has been totally misconceived and misapplied.

The oracle who is always consulted and cited on this subject, is the celebrated Montesquieu. If he be not the author of this invaluable precept in the science of politics, he has the merit of at least displaying and recommending it most effectually to the attention of mankind. . . .

From . . . facts, by which Montesquieu was guided, it may clearly be inferred, that in saying, "there can be no liberty, where the legislative and executive powers are united in the same person, or body of magistrates"; or "if the power of judging, be not separated from the legislative and executive powers," he did not mean that these departments ought to have no *partial agency* in, or no *control* over, the acts of each other. His meaning . ?. can amount to no more than this, that where the *whole* power of one department is exercised by the same hands which possess the *whole* power of another department, the fundamental principles of a free constitution are subverted. . . .

If we look into the constitutions of the several states, we find, that notwithstanding the emphatical, and, in some instances, the unqualified terms in which this axiom has been laid down, there is not a single instance in which the several departments of power have been kept absolutely separate and distinct. . . .

The constitution of Massachusetts has observed a sufficient, though less pointed caution, in expressing this fundamental article of liberty. It declares, "that the legislative department shall never exercise the executive and judicial powers, or either of them: the executive shall never exercise the legislative and judicial powers, or either of them: the judicial shall never exercise the legislative and executive powers, or either of them." This declaration corresponds precisely with the doctrine of Montesquieu. . . . It goes no farther than to prohibit any one of the entire departments from exercising the powers of another department. In the very constitution to which it is prefixed, a partial mixture of powers has been admitted. . . .

FEDERALIST 48

❖❖❖❖❖❖❖

. . . I shall undertake in the next place to show, that unless these departments be so far connected and blended, as to give to each a constitutional control over the others, the degree of separation which the maxim requires, as essential to a free government, can never in practice be duly maintained.

It is agreed on all sides, that the powers properly belonging to one of the departments ought not to be directly and completely administered by either of the other departments. It is equally evident, that neither of them ought to possess, directly or indirectly, an overruling influence over the others in the administration of their respective powers. It will not be denied, that power is of an encroaching nature, and that it ought to be effectually restrained from passing the limits assigned to it. After discriminating, therefore, in theory, the several classes of power, as they may in their nature be legislative, executive, or judiciary; the next, and most difficult task, is to provide some practical security for each, against the invasion of the others. What this security ought to be, is the great problem to be solved.

Will it be sufficient to mark, with precision, the boundaries of these departments, in the constitution of the government, and to trust to these parchment barriers against the encroaching spirit of power? This is the security which appears to have been principally relied on by the compilers of most American constitutions. But experience assures us, that the efficacy of the provision has been greatly overrated; and that some more adequate defense is indispensably necessary for the more feeble, against the more powerful members of the government. The legislative department is everywhere extending the sphere of its activity, and drawing all power into its impetuous vortex. . . .

In a government where numerous and extensive prerogatives are placed in the hands of an hereditary monarch, the executive department is very justly regarded as the source of danger, and watched with all the jealousy which a zeal for liberty ought to inspire. In a democracy, where a multitude of people exercise in person the legislative functions, and are continually exposed, by their incapacity for regular deliberation and concerted measures, to the ambitious intrigues of their executive magistrates, tyranny may well be apprehended on some favorable emergency, to start up in the same quarter. But in a representative republic, where the executive magistracy is carefully limited, both in the extent and the duration of its power; and where the legislative is exercised by an assembly, which is inspired by a supposed influence over the people, with an intrepid confidence in its own strength; which is sufficiently numerous to feel all the passions which actuate a multitude; yet not so numerous as to be incapable of pursuing the objects of its passions, by means which reason prescribes; it is against the enterprising ambition of this department, that the people ought to indulge all their jealousy and exhaust all their precautions.

The legislative department derives a superiority in our governments from other circumstances. Its constitutional powers being at once more extensive, and less susceptible of precise limits, it can, with the greater facility, mask, under complicated and indirect measures, the encroachment which it makes on the coordinate departments. It is not infrequently a question of real nicety in legislative bodies, whether the operation of a particular measure will, or will not extend beyond the legislative sphere. On the other side, the executive power being restrained within a narrower compass, and being more simple in its nature; and the judiciary being described by landmarks, still less uncertain, projects of usurpation by either of these departments would immediately betray and defeat themselves. Nor is this all: as the legislative department alone has access to the pockets of the people, and has in some constitutions full discretion, and in all a prevailing influence over the pecuniary rewards of those who fill the other departments; a dependence is thus created in the latter, which gives still greater facility to encroachment of the former. . . .

FEDERALIST 51

To what expedient then shall we finally resort, for maintaining in practice the necessary partition of power among the several departments, as laid down in the constitution? The only answer that can be given is, that as all these exterior provisions are found to be inadequate, the defect must be supplied, by so contriving the interior structure of the government, as that its several constituent parts may, by their mutual relations, be the means of keeping each other in their proper places. . . .

In order to lay a due foundation for that separate and distinct exercise of the different powers of government, which, to a certain extent, is admitted on all hands to be essential to the preservation of liberty, it is evident that each department should have a will of its own; and consequently should be so constituted, that the members of each should have as little agency as possible in the appointment of the members of the others. . . .

It is equally evident, that the members of each department should be as little dependent as possible on those of the others, for the emoluments annexed to their offices. Were the executive magistrate, or the judges, not independent of the legislature in this particular, their independence in every other, would be merely nominal.

But the great security against a gradual concentration of the several powers in the same department, consists in giving to those who administer each department, the necessary constitutional means, and personal motives, to resist encroachments of the others. The provision for defense must in this, as in all other cases, be made commensurate to the danger of attack. Ambition must be made to counteract ambition. The interest of the man must be connected with the constitutional rights of the place. It may be a reflection on human nature, that such devices should be necessary to control the abuses of government. But what is government itself, but the greatest of all reflections on human nature? If men were angels, no government would be necessary. If angels were to govern men, neither external nor internal controls on government would be necessary. In framing a government, which is to be administered by men over men, the great difficulty lies in this: you must first enable the government to control the governed; and in the next place, oblige it to control itself. A dependence on the people is, no doubt, the primary control on the government; but experience has taught mankind the necessity of auxiliary precautions.

This policy of supplying by opposite and rival interests, the defect of better motives, might be traced through the whole system of human affairs, private as well as public. We see it particularly displayed in all the subordinate distributions of power; where the constant aim is, to divide and arrange the several offices in such a manner, as that each may be a check on the other; that the private interest of every individual, may be a sentinel over the public rights. These inventions of prudence cannot be less requisite to the distribution of the supreme powers of the state.

But it is not possible to give each department an equal power of self-defense. In republican government, the legislative authority necessarily predominates. The remedy for this inconvenience is, to divide the legislature into different branches; and to render them by different modes of election, and different principles of action, as little connected with each other, as the nature of their common functions, and their common dependence on the society will admit. It may even be necessary to guard against dangerous encroachments, by still further precautions. As the weight of the legislative authority requires that it should be thus divided, the weakness of the executive may require, on the other hand, that it should be fortified. An absolute negative on the legislature, appears, at first view, to be the natural defense with which the executive magistrate should be armed. But perhaps it would be neither altogether safe, nor alone sufficient. On ordinary occasions, it might not be exerted with the requisite firmness; and on extraordinary occasions, it might be perfidiously abused. May not this defect of an absolute negative be supplied by some qualified connection between this weaker department, and the weaker branch of the stronger department, by which the latter may be led to support the constitutional rights of the former, without being too much detached from the rights of its own department?

INTERPRETING THE CONSTITUTION

The preceding selections have offered contrasting views on the framing, nature, and purpose of the Constitution. As background, John Locke's political philosophy expressed in his *Second Treatise, Of Civil Government* (1690) supported the political beliefs of many eighteenth-century Americans in government as a social contract between rulers and ruled to protect the natural rights of citizens to life, liberty, and, very importantly, property.

To John Roche, the Constitution was a practical political document reflecting compromises among state delegations with contrasting political and economic interests, and being advocates of strong national power and proponents of states' rights. Charles Beard saw the Constitution as a reflection of the interests of property owners and creditors who feared that the rule of the debtor majority would inflate currency, cancel debts, and deprive creditors of their rightful property. James Madison's selections from *The Federalist* suggest a mistrust of government, a wary view of both political leaders and the people, and an emphasis upon the need for governmental checks and balances to prevent the arbitrary exercise of political power. Madison also distrusted what he termed "faction," by which he meant political parties or special-interest groups, which he considered intrinsically to be opposed to the national interest (see *Federalist 10,* Chapter 4).

The separation of powers among the executive, legislative, and judicial branches is an outstanding characteristic of our constitutional system. A uniquely American separation of powers incorporated an *independent* executive, pitting the president against Congress and requiring their cooperation to make the government work. The separation of powers was a constitutional filter through which political demands had to flow before they could be translated into public policies.

James Madison clearly saw the separation-of-powers system, incorporating checks and balances among the branches of government, as a process that would help to prevent arbitrary and excessive governmental actions. The three branches of the government, but particularly the president and Congress, would have independent political bases, motivations, and powers that would both enable and encourage them to compete with each other.

While Madison saw the separation of powers as an important limit upon arbitrary government, Alexander Hamilton represented a different point of view. He viewed the independent presidency, a central component of the separation of powers, as an office that could make the national government energetic and effective. "Energy in the executive is the definition of good government," wrote Hamilton in *The Federalist,* No. 70, and the constitutional separation of powers would provide that energy rather than simply making the president of a co-equal branch subject to congressional whims or Supreme Court constraints.

History has, at different times, borne out the views of both Madison and Hamilton regarding the effect of the separation of powers. During times of relative political tranquility the president and Congress have often been stalemated in a deadlock of democracy. But Hamilton's imperial presidency has taken charge in times of crisis, such as during the Civil War, Franklin D. Roosevelt's New Deal in the 1930s, and the Second World War in the 1940s.

The Constitution is a frugal, bare-bones document that has, almost miraculously and with very few amendments, remained in place for over 200 years. It was not, however, a perfect governmental plan, for the nation had to fight a bloody Civil War to establish the principle of *e pluribus unum* once and for all.

While reverence for the Constitution is an important strand in our political history, it has not prevented sharp political controversy over how the Constitution should be interpreted. The framers themselves did not see eye to eye on many constitutional provisions, interpreting them in different ways. To buttress their positions political opponents have often cited the Constitution, claiming that it supports their side. For example, during George Washington's presidency Thomas Jefferson argued that the Constitution should be strictly interpreted to limit Congress to its explicit Article I powers, which did not allow establishment of a national bank. Secretary of the Treasury Alexander Hamilton took the "loose" constructionist approach in support of the bank. Hamilton argued that while Article I of the Constitution did not explicitly give Congress the authority to create a national bank, Congress could imply such authority under its enumerated power to regulate commerce among the states. Both men were using the same Constitution to support their contrasting political positions.

The historic debate over whether or not the Constitution should be read "strictly" or "loosely" has metamorphosed into another and related debate over the importance of "original intent" in constitutional interpretation. Judge Robert Bork, for example, argues in selection 64 in Chapter 9 that the Supreme Court has often erred in not following the original intent of the framers. The authors of the following selection, however, claim that the framers of the Constitution knew they had forged a flexible document that future generations would be able to adapt to their values and needs.

Laurence H. Tribe and Michael C. Dorf

How Not to Read the
Constitution

❖❖❖❖❖❖❖❖

From its very creation, the Constitution was perceived as a document that sought to strike a delicate balance between, on the one hand, governmental power to accomplish the great ends of civil society and, on the other, individual liberty. As James Madison put it in *The Federalist Papers*, "[i]f men were angels, no government would be necessary. If angels were to govern men, neither external nor internal controls on government would be necessary. In framing a government which is to be administered by men over men, the great difficulty lies in this: you must first enable the government to control the governed; and in the next place oblige it to control itself. A dependence on the people is, no doubt, the primary control on the government; but experience has taught mankind the necessity of auxiliary precautions." Although Madison initially opposed the inclusion of a Bill of Rights in the Constitution, as his correspondence with Thomas Jefferson shows, he became convinced that judicially enforceable rights are among the necessary "auxiliary precautions" against tyranny.

In the Constitution of the United States, men like Madison bequeathed to subsequent generations a framework for balancing liberty against power. However, it is only a framework; it is not a blueprint. Its Eighth Amendment prohibits the infliction of "cruel and unusual punishment," but gives no examples of permissible or impermissible punishments. Article IV requires that "[t]he United States shall guarantee to every State in this Union a Republican Form of Government," but attempts no definition of republican government. The Fourteenth Amendment proscribes state abridgments of the "privileges or immunities of citizens of the United States," but contains no catalogue of privileges or immunities.

How then ought we to go about the task of finding concrete commandments in the Constitution's majestically vague admonitions? If there is genuine controversy over how the Constitution should be read, certainly it cannot be because the disputants have access to different bodies of information. After all, they all have exactly the same text in front of them, and that text has exactly one history, however complex, however multifaceted. But of course different people believe different things about how that history bears on the enterprise of constitutional interpretation. . . .

Perhaps the disputants agree on what *counts* as "the Constitution," but simply approach the same body of textual and historical materials with different visions, different premises, and different convictions. But *that* assumption raises an obvious question: How are those visions, premises, and convictions relevant to how this brief text ought to be read? Is reading the text just a *pretext* for expressing the reader's vision in the august, almost holy terms of constitutional law? Is the Constitution simply a mirror in which one sees what one wants to see? . . .

Reading the Constitution or Writing One?

The belief that we must look beyond the specific views of the Framers to apply the Constitution to contemporary problems is not necessarily a "liberal" position. Indeed, not even the most "conservative" justices today believe in a jurisprudence of original intent that looks only to the Framers' unenacted views about particular institutions or practices. Consider the following statement made by a Supreme Court justice in 1976:

> The framers of the Constitution wisely spoke in general language and left to succeeding generations the task of applying that language to the unceasingly changing environment in which they would live. . . . Where the framers . . . used general language, they [gave] latitude to those who would later interpret the instrument to make that language applicable to cases that the framers might not have foreseen.

The author was not Justice William Brennan or Justice Thurgood Marshall, but then-Justice William Rehnquist. Or consider the statement by Justice White, joined by Justice Rehnquist in a 1986 opinion for the Court: "As [our] prior cases clearly show, . . . this Court does not subscribe to the simplistic view that constitutional interpretation can possibly be limited to the 'plain meaning' of the Constitution's text or to the subjective intention of the Framers. The Constitution," wrote Justice White, "is not a deed setting forth the precise metes and bounds of its subject matter; rather, it is a document announcing fundamental principles in value-laden terms that leave ample scope for the exercise of normative judgment by those charged with interpreting and applying it."

So the "conservatives" on the Court, no less than the "liberals," talk as though *reading* the Constitution requires much more than passively discovering a fixed meaning planted there generations ago. Those who wrote the document, and those who voted to ratify it, were undoubtedly projecting their wishes into an indefinite future. If writing is wish-*projection*, is reading merely an exercise in wish-*fulfillment*—not fulfillment of the wishes of the *authors*, who couldn't have begun to foresee the way things would unfold, but fulfillment of the wishes of *readers*, who perhaps use the language of the Constitution simply as a mirror to dress up their own political or moral preferences in the hallowed language of our most fundamental document? Justice Joseph Story feared that that might happen when he wrote in 1845: "How easily men satisfy themselves that the Constitution is exactly what they wish it to be."

To the extent that this is so, it is indefensible. The authority of the Constitution, its claim to obedience and the force that we permit it to exercise in our law and over our lives, would lose all legitimacy if it really were only a mirror for the readers' ideas and ideals. Just as the original intent of the Framers—even if it could be captured in the laboratory, bottled, and carefully inspected under a microscope—will not yield a satisfactory determinate interpretation of the Constitution, so too at the other end of the spectrum we must also reject as completely unsatisfactory the idea of an empty, or an infinitely malleable, Constitution. We must find principles of interpretation that can anchor the Constitution in some more secure, determinate, and external reality. But that is no small task.

One basic problem is that the text itself leaves so much room for the imagination. Simply consider the preamble, which speaks of furthering such concepts as "Justice" and the "Blessings of Liberty." It is not hard, in terms of concepts that fluid and that plastic, to make a linguistically plausible argument in support of more than a few surely incorrect conclusions. Perhaps a rule could be imposed that it is improper to refer to the preamble in constitutional argument on the theory that it is only an introduction, a preface, and not part of the Constitution *as enacted*. But even if one were to invent such a rule, which has no apparent grounding in the Constitution itself, it is hardly news that the remainder of the document is filled with lively language about "liberty," "due process of law," "unreasonable searches and seizures," and so forth—words that, although not *infinitely* malleable, are capable of supporting meanings at opposite ends of virtually any legal, political, or ideological spectrum.

It is therefore not surprising that readers on both the right and left of the American political center have invoked the Constitution as authority for strikingly divergent conclusions about the legitimacy of existing institutions and practices, and that neither wing has found it difficult to cite chapter and verse in support of its "reading" of our fundamental law. As is true of other areas of law, the materials of constitutional law require construction, leave room for argument over meaning, and tempt the reader to import his or her vision of the just society into the meaning of the materials being considered. . . .

When all of the Constitution's supposed unities are exposed to scrutiny, criticisms of its inconsistency with various readers' sweeping visions of what it ought to be become considerably less impressive. Not all need be reducible to a single theme. Inconsistency—even inconsistency with democracy—is hardly earth-shattering. Listen to Walt Whitman: "Do I contradict myself? Very well then, I contradict myself." "I am large, I contain multitudes," the Constitution replies.

Chapter 2

❖❖❖

FEDERALISM

The United States government utilizes a "federal" form to secure certain political and economic objectives. This chapter identifies both the traditional and modern goals of American federalism from the writings of important theorists who have examined general and specific problems in national-state relationships. The validity of federalism is also analyzed.

Constitutional Background: National Versus State Power

No subject attracted greater attention or was more carefully analyzed at the time of the framing of the Constitution than federalism. *The Federalist* devoted a great deal of space to proving the advantages of a federal form of government relative to a confederacy, since the Constitution was going to take some of the power traditionally within the jurisdiction of state governments and give it to a newly constituted national government.

The victory of the nationalists at the Constitutional Convention of 1787, which resulted in sovereign states giving up a significant portion of their authority to a new national government, is remarkable by any standard of measurement. Today, when the creation of the Union is largely taken for granted, it is difficult to appreciate the environment of the Revolutionary period, a time when the states wanted at all costs to protect their newly won freedom from an oppressive British government. The constitution of 1787 was accepted as a matter of necessity as much as desire.

It was against the background of Articles of Confederation that Hamilton wrote in *The Federalist* about the advantages of the new "federal" system that would be created by the Constitution. The Articles of Confederation had been submitted to the states in 1777 and were finally ratified by all of the states in 1781, Maryland being the only holdout after 1779. The "League of Friendship" that had been created among the states by the Articles had proved inadequate to meeting even the minimum needs of union. The government of the Articles of Confederation had many weaknesses, for it was essentially a league of sovereign states, joined together more in accordance with principles of international agreement than in accordance with the rules of nation states. Most of the provisions of the Articles of Confederation concerned the foreign relations of the new government, and matters of national defense and security. For this purpose a minimum number of powers were granted to the national government, which, however, had no executive or judicial authority and was therefore incapable of independent enforcement. National actions were dependent upon the states for enforcement, and under Article Two "each state retains its sovereignty, freedom and independence, and every power, jurisdiction and right, which is not by this confederation expressly delegated to the United States, in Congress assembled." The paucity of authority delegated to the central government under the Articles left the sovereignty of the states intact. And the national government was totally dependent upon the states as agents of enforcement of what little authority it could exercise. The government of the Articles of Confederation then, without an executive or judicial branch, and without such crucial authority as the power to tax and regulate commerce, required a drastic overhaul if it was to become a national government in fact as well as in name.

In the following selections from *The Federalist,* Alexander Hamilton argues the advantages of the new federal Constitution, and at the same time attempts to alleviate the fears of his opponents that the new government would intrude upon and possibly eventually destroy the sovereignty of the states. The national government, he wrote, must be able to act directly upon the citizens of the states to regulate the common concerns of the nation. He found the system of the Articles of Confederation too weak, allowing state evasion of national power. Augmenting the authority of the national government would not destroy state sovereignty, because of the inherent strength of the individual states (which at the time Hamilton wrote were singly and collectively far more powerful than any proposed national government). Moreover, there would be no incentives for ambitious politicians to look to the states to realize their goals, for the scope of national power was sufficient to occupy temptations for political aggrandizement.

6

Alexander Hamilton

FEDERALIST 16

❖❖❖❖❖❖❖

The . . . death of the confederacy . . . is what we now seem to be on the point of experiencing, if the federal system be not speedily renovated in a more substantial form. It is not probable, considering the genius of this country, that the complying states would often be inclined to support the authority of the union, by engaging in a war against the non-complying states. They would always be more ready to pursue the milder course of putting themselves upon an equal footing with the delinquent members, by an imitation of their example. And the guilt of all would thus become the security of all. Our past experience has exhibited the operation of this spirit in its full light. There would, in fact, be an insuperable difficulty in ascertaining when force would with propriety be employed. In the article of pecuniary contribution, which would be the most usual source of delinquency, it would often be impossible to decide whether it had proceeded from disinclination, or inability. The pretense of the latter would always be at hand. And the case must be very flagrant in which its fallacy could be detected with sufficient certainty to justify the harsh expedient of compulsion. It is easy to see that this problem alone, as often as it should occur, would open a wide field to the majority that happened to prevail in the national council, for the exercise of factious views, of partiality, and of oppression.

It seems to require no pains to prove that the states ought not to prefer a national constitution, which could only be kept in motion by the instrumentality of a large army, continually on foot to execute the ordinary requisitions or decrees of the government. And yet this is the plain alternative involved by those who wish to deny it the power of extending its operations to individuals. Such a scheme, if practicable at all, would instantly degenerate into a military despotism; but it will be found in every light impracticable. The resources of the union would not be equal to the maintenance of any army considerable enough to confine the larger states within the limits of their duty; nor would the means ever be furnished of forming such an army in the first instance. Whoever considers the populousness and strength of several of these states singly at the present juncture, and looks forward to what they will become, even at the distance of half a century, will at once dismiss as idle and visionary any scheme which aims at regulating their movements by laws, to operate upon them in their collective capacities, and to be executed by a coercion applicable to them in the same capacities. A project of this kind is little less romantic than the monster-taming spirit attributed to the fabulous heroes and demigods of antiquity. . . .

The result of these observations to an intelligent mind must clearly be this, that if it be possible at any rate to construct a federal government capable of regulating the common concerns, and preserving the general tranquillity, it must be founded, as to the objects committed to its case, upon the reverse of the principle contended for by the opponents of the proposed constitution [i.e., a confederacy]. It must carry its agency to the persons of the citizens. It must stand in need of no intermediate legislations; but must itself be empowered to employ the arm of the ordinary magistrate to execute its own resolutions. The majesty of the national authority must be manifested through the medium of the courts of justice. The government of the union, like that of each state, must be able to address itself immediately to the hopes and fears of individuals; and to attract to its support, those passions which have the strongest influence upon the human heart. It must, in short, possess all the means, and have a right to resort to all the methods, of executing the powers with which it is entrusted, that are possessed and exercised by the governments of the particular states.

To this reasoning it may perhaps be objected, that if any state should be disaffected to the authority of the union, it could at any time obstruct the execution of its laws, and bring the matter to the same issue of force, with the necessity of which the opposite scheme is reproached.

The plausibility of this objection will vanish the moment we advert to the essential difference between a mere NONCOMPLIANCE and a DIRECT and ACTIVE RESISTANCE. If the interposition of the state legislatures be necessary to give effect to a measure of the union [as in a confederacy], they have only NOT TO ACT, OR TO ACT EVASIVELY, and the measure is defeated. This neglect of duty may be disguised under affected but unsubstantial provisions so as not to appear, and of course not to excite any alarm in the people for the safety of the constitution. The state leaders may even make a merit of their surreptitious invasions of it, on the ground of some temporary convenience, exemption, or advantage.

But if the execution of the laws of the national government should not require the intervention of the state legislatures; if they were to pass into immediate operation upon the citizens themselves, the particular governments could not interrupt their progress without an open and violent exertion of an unconstitutional power. No omission, nor evasions, would answer the end. They would be obliged to act, and in such a manner, as would leave no doubt that they had encroached on the national rights. An experiment of this nature would always be hazardous in the face of a constitution in any degree competent to its own defense, and of the people enlightened enough to distinguish between a legal exercise and an illegal usurpation of authority. The success of it would require not merely a factious majority in the legislature, but the concurrence of the courts of justice, and of the body of the people. . . .

Federalist 17

An objection, of a nature different from that which has been stated and answered in my last address, may, perhaps, be urged against the principle of legislation for the individual citizens of America. It may be said, that it would tend to render the government of the union too powerful, and to enable it to absorb those residuary authorities, which it might be judged proper to leave with the states for local purposes. Allowing the utmost latitude to the love of power, which any reasonable man can require, I confess I am at a loss to discover what temptation the persons entrusted with the administration of the general government could ever feel to divest the states of the authorities of that description. The regulation of the mere domestic police of a state, appears to me to hold out slender allurements to ambition. Commerce, finance, negotiation, and war, seem to comprehend all the objects which have charms for minds governed by that passion; and all the powers necessary to those objects, ought, in the first instance, to be lodged in the national depository. The administration of private justice between the citizens of the same state; the supervision of agriculture, and of other concerns of a similar nature; all those things, in short, which are proper to be provided for by local legislation, can never be desirable cares of a general jurisdiction. It is therefore improbable, that there should exist a disposition in the federal councils, to usurp the powers with which they are connected; because the attempt to exercise them would be as troublesome as it would be nugatory; and the possession of them, for that reason, would contribute nothing to the dignity, to the importance, or to the splendor, of the national government.

But let it be admitted, for argument's sake, that mere wantonness, and lust of domination, would be sufficient to beget that disposition; still, it may be safely affirmed, that the sense of the constituent body of the national representatives, or in other words, of the people of the several states, would control the indulgence of so extravagant an appetite. It will always be far more easy for the state governments to encroach upon the national authorities, than for the national government to encroach upon the state authorities. The proof of this proposition turns upon the greater degree of influence which the state governments, if they administer their affairs with uprightness and prudence, will generally possess over the people; a circumstance which at the same time teaches us, that there is an inherent and intrinsic weakness in all federal constitutions; and that too much pain cannot be taken in their organization, to give them all the force which is compatible with the principles of liberty.

The superiority of influence in favor of the particular governments, would result partly from the diffusive construction of the national government; but chiefly from the nature of the objects to which the attention of the state administrations would be directed.

It is a known fact in human nature, that its affections are commonly weak in proportion to the distance of diffusiveness of the object. Upon the same principle that a man is more attached to his family than to his neighborhood, to his neighborhood than to the community at large, the people of each state would be apt to feel a strong bias towards their local governments, than towards the government of the union, unless the force of that principle should be destroyed by a much better administration of the latter.

This strong propensity of the human heart, would find powerful auxiliaries in the objects of state regulation.

The variety of more minute interests, which will necessarily fall under the superintendence of the local administrations, and which will form so many rivulets of influence, running through every part of the society, cannot be particularized, without involving a detail too tedious and uninteresting to compensate for the instruction it might afford.

There is one transcendent advantage belonging to the province of the state governments, which alone suffices to place the matter in a clear and satisfactory light—I mean the ordinary administration of criminal and civil justice. This, of all others, is the most powerful, most universal and most attractive source of popular obedience and attachment. It is this, which, being the immediate and visible guardian of life and property; having its benefits and its terrors in constant activity before the public eye; regulating all those personal interests, and familiar concerns, to which the sensibility of individuals is more immediately awake; contributes, more than any other circumstance, to impress upon the minds of the people affection, esteem, and reverence towards the government. This great cement of society, which will diffuse itself almost wholly through the channels of the particular governments, independent of all other causes of influence, would insure them so decided an empire over their respective citizens, as to render them at all times a complete counterpoise, and not infrequently dangerous rivals to the power of the union.

❖❖ In *Federalist 39,* James Madison stated that the new Constitution was both federal and national. He attempted to answer arguments that the Constitution destroyed the confederacy of sovereign states and replaced it with a national government. In answering this argument Madison used the term *federal* as it was used by the objectors to the Constitution he was attempting to answer. They essentially used *federal* and *confederacy* interchangeably, each term referring to a system requiring agreement among the states before certain actions could be taken. Because agreement was required among the states for ratification, for example, Madison referred to the establishment of the Constitution as a *federal* and not a national act. Madison suggested that the character of the House of Representatives, which derives its powers from the people, was national rather than federal. Conversely, the Senate, representing the states equally, was federal, not national. With regard to the powers of the national government, Madison claimed that in operation they are national because they allow the national government to act directly upon the people, but in extent they are federal because they are limited, the states having agreed to delegate only a certain number of powers to the national government. A truly national government would not be limited in the scope of its powers.

7

James Madison

FEDERALIST 39

❖❖❖❖❖❖❖

The last paper having concluded the observations which were meant to introduce a candid survey of the plan of government reported by the convention, we now proceed to the execution of that part of our undertaking.

The first question that offers itself is whether the general form and aspect of the government be strictly republican. It is evident that no other form would be reconcilable with the genius of the people of America; with the fundamental principles of the Revolution; or with that honorable determination which animates every votary of freedom to rest all our political experiments on the capacity of mankind for self-government. If the plan of the convention, therefore, be found to depart from the republican character, its advocates must abandon it as no longer defensible.

What, then, are the distinctive characters of the republican form? Were an answer to this question to be sought, not by recurring to principles but in the application of the term by political writers to the constitutions of different States, no satisfactory one would ever be found. Holland, in which no particle of the supreme authority is derived from the people, has passed almost universally under the denomination of a republic. The same title has been bestowed on Venice, where absolute power over the great body of the people is exercised in the most absolute manner by a small body of hereditary nobles. Poland, which is a mixture of aristocracy and of monarchy in their worst forms, has been dignified with the same appellation. The government of England, which has one republican branch only, combined with an hereditary aristocracy and monarchy, has with equal impropriety been frequently placed on the list of republics. These examples, which are nearly as dissimilar to each other as to a genuine republic, show the extreme inaccuracy with which the term has been used in political disquisitions.

If we resort for a criterion to the different principles on which different forms of government are established, we may define a republic to be, or at least may bestow the name on, a government which derives all its powers directly or indirectly from the great body of the people, and is administered by persons holding their offices during pleasure for a limited period, or during good behavior. It is *essential* to such a government that it be derived from the great body of the society, not from an inconsiderable proportion or a favored class of it; otherwise a handful of tyrannical nobles, exercising their oppressions by a delegation of their powers, might aspire to the rank of republicans and claim for their government the honorable title of republic. It is *sufficient* for such a government that the persons administering it be appointed, either directly or indirectly, by the people; and that they hold their appointments by either of the tenures just specified; otherwise every government in the United States, as well as every other popular government that has been or can be well organized or well executed, would be degraded from the republican character. According to the constitution of every State in the Union, some or other of the officers of government are appointed indirectly only by the people. According to most of them, the chief magistrate himself is so appointed. And according to one, this mode of appointment is extended to one of the co-ordinate branches of the legislature. According to all the constitutions, also, the tenure of the highest offices is extended to a definite period, and in many instances, both within the legislative and executive departments, to a period of years. According to the provisions of most of the constitutions, again, as well as according to the most respectable and received opinions on the subject, the members of the judiciary department are to retain their offices by the firm tenure of good behavior.

On comparing the Constitution planned by the convention with the standard here fixed, we perceived at once that it is, in the most rigid sense, conformable to it. The House of Representatives, like that of one branch at least of all the State legislatures, is elected immediately by the great body of the people. The Senate, like the present Congress and the Senate of Maryland, derives its appointment indirectly from the people. The President is indirectly derived from the choice of the people, according to the example in most of the States. Even the judges, with all other officers of the Union, will, as in the several States, be the choice, though a remote choice, of the people themselves. The duration of the appointments is equally conformable to the republican standard and to the model of State constitutions. The House of Representatives is periodically elective, as in all the States; and for the period of two years, as in the State of South Carolina. The Senate is elective for the period of six years, which is but one year more than the period of the Senate of Maryland, and but two more than that of the Senators of New York and Virginia. The President is to continue in office for the period of four years; as in New York and Delaware the chief magistrate is elected for three years, and in South Carolina for two years. In the other States the election is annual. In several of the States, however, no explicit provision is made for the impeachment of the chief magistrate. And in Delaware and Virginia he is not impeachable till out of office. The President of the United States is impeachable at any time during his continuance in office. The tenure by which the judges are to hold their places is, as it unquestionably ought to be, that of good behavior. The tenure of the ministerial offices generally will be a subject of legal regulation, conformable to the reason of the case and the example of the State constitutions.

Could any further proof be required of the republican complexion of this system, the most decisive one might be found in its absolute prohibition of titles of nobility, both under the federal and the State governments; and in its express guaranty of the republican form to each of the latter.

"But it was not sufficient," say the adversaries of the proposed Constitution, "for the convention to adhere to the republican form. They ought with equal care to have preserved the *federal* form, which regards the Union as a *Confederacy* of sovereign states; instead of which they have framed a *national* government, which regards the Union as a *consolidation* of the States." And it is asked by what authority this bold and radical innovation was undertaken. The handle which has been made of this objection requires that it should be examined with some precision.

Without inquiring into the accuracy of the distinction on which the objection is founded, it will be necessary to a just estimate of its force, first, to ascertain the real character of the government in question; secondly, to inquire how far the convention were authorized to propose such a government; and thirdly, how far the duty they owed to their country could supply any defect of regular authority.

First.—In order to ascertain the real character of the government, it may be considered in relation to the foundation on which it is to be established; to the sources from which its ordinary powers are to be drawn; to the operation of those powers; to the extent of them; and to the authority by which future changes in the government are to be introduced.

On examining the first relation, it appears, on one hand, that the Constitution is to be founded on the assent and ratification of the people of America, given by deputies elected for the special purpose; but, on the other, that this assent and ratification is to be given by the people, not as individuals composing one entire nation, but as composing the distinct and independent States to which they respectively belong. It is to be the assent and ratification of the several States, derived from the supreme authority in each State—the authority of the people themselves. The act, therefore, establishing the Constitution will not be a *national* but a *federal* act.

That it will be a federal and not a national act, as these terms are understood by the objectors—the act of the people, as forming so many independent States, not as forming one aggregate nation—is obvious from this single consideration: that it is to result neither from the decision of a *majority* of the people of the Union, nor from that of a *majority* of the States. It must result from the *unanimous* assent of the several States that are parties to it, differing not otherwise from their ordinary assent than in its being expressed, not by the legislative authority, but by that of the people themselves. Were the people regarded in this transaction as forming one nation, the will of the majority of the whole people of the United States would bind the minority, in the same manner as the majority in each State must bind the minority; and the will of the majority must be determined either by a comparison of the individual votes, or by considering the will of the majority of the States as evidence of the will of a majority of the people of the United States. Neither of these rules has been adopted. Each State, in ratifying the Constitution, is considered as a sovereign body independent of all others, and only to be bound by its own voluntary act. In this relation, then, the new Constitution will, if established, be a *federal* and not a *national* constitution.

The next relation is to the sources from which the ordinary powers of government are to be derived. The House of Representatives will derive its powers from the people of America; and the people will be represented in the same proportion and on the same principle as they are in the legislature of a particular State. So far the government is *national*, not *federal*. The Senate, on the other hand, will derive its powers from the States as political and coequal societies; and these will be represented on the principle of equality in the Senate, as they now are in the existing

Congress. So far the government is *federal*, not *national*. The executive power will be derived from a very compound source. The immediate election of the President is to be made by the States in their political characters. The votes allotted to them are in a compound ratio, which considers them partly as distinct and coequal societies, partly as unequal members of the same society. The eventual election, again, is to be made by that branch of the legislature which consists of the national representatives; but in this particular act they are to be thrown into the form of individual delegations from so many distinct and coequal bodies politic. From this aspect of the government it appears to be of a mixed character, presenting at least as many *federal* as *national* features.

The difference between a federal and national government, as it relates to the *operation of the government*, is by the adversaries of the plan of the convention supposed to consist in this, that in the former the powers operate on the political bodies composing the confederacy in their political capacities; in the latter, on the individual citizens composing the nation in their individual capacities. On trying the Constitution by this criterion, it falls under the *national* not the *federal* character; though perhaps not so completely as has been understood. In several cases, and particularly in the trial of controversies to which States may be parties, they must be viewed and proceeded against in their collective and political capacities only. But the operation of the government on the people in their individual capacities, in its ordinary and most essential proceedings, will, in the sense of its opponents, on the whole, designate it, in this relation, a *national* government.

But if the government be national with regard to the *operation* of its powers, it changes its aspect again when we contemplate it in relation to the extent of its powers. The idea of a national government involves in it not only an authority over the individual citizens, but an indefinite supremacy over all persons and things, so far as they are objects of lawful government. Among a people consolidated into one nation, this supremacy is completely vested in the national legislature. Among communities united for particular purposes, it is vested partly in the general and partly in the municipal legislatures. In the former case, all local authorities are subordinate to the supreme; and may be controlled, directed, and abolished by it at pleasure. In the latter, the local or municipal authorities form distinct and independent portions of the supremacy, no more subject, within their respective spheres, to the general authority than the general authority is subject to them, within its own sphere. In this relation, then, the proposed government cannot be deemed a *national* one; since its jurisdiction extends to certain enumerated objects only, and leaves to the several States a residuary and inviolable sovereignty over all other objects. It is true that in controversies relating to the boundary between the two jurisdictions, the tribunal which is ultimately to decide is to be established under the general government. But this does not change the principle of the case. The decision is to be impartially made, according to the rules of the Constitution; and all the usual and most effectual precautions are taken to secure this impartiality. Some such tribunal is clearly essential to prevent an appeal to the sword and a dissolution of the compact; and that it ought to be established under the general rather than under the local governments, or, to speak more properly, that it could be safely established under the first alone, is a position not likely to be combated.

If we try the Constitution by its last relation to the authority by which amendments are to be made, we find it neither wholly *national* nor wholly *federal*. Were it wholly national, the supreme and ultimate authority would reside in the *majority* of the people of the Union; and this authority would be competent at all times, like that of a majority of every national society to alter or abolish its established government. Were it wholly federal, on the other hand, the concurrence of each State in the Union would be essential to every alteration that would be binding on all. The mode provided by the plan of the convention is not founded on either of these principles. In requiring more than a majority, and particularly in computing the proportion by *States*, not by *citizens*, it departs from the national and advances towards the *federal* character; in rendering the concurrence of less than the whole number of States sufficient, it loses again the *federal* and partakes of the *national* character.

The proposed Constitution, therefore, even when tested by the rules laid down by its antagonists, is, in strictness, neither a national nor a federal Constitution, but a composition of both. In its foundation it is federal, not national; in the sources from which the ordinary powers of the government are drawn, it is partly federal and partly national; in the operation of these powers, it is national, not federal; in the extent of them, again, it is federal, not national; and, finally in the authoritative mode of introducing amendments, it is neither wholly federal nor wholly national.

PUBLIUS

❖❖ In *The Federalist,* Alexander Hamilton and James Madison were careful to point out the advantages of the federal form of government that would be established by the Constitution, both over the government that had existed under the Articles of Confederation and in general terms. Because many state political leaders were highly suspicious of the national government that would be created by the new Constitution, much of the efforts of Hamilton and Madison were directed toward allaying their fears. Above all, they both stated, the energy of the national government would never be sufficient to coerce the states into giving up any portion of their sovereignty. Moreover, Hamilton stated in *Federalist 17* that there would be no incentive for national politicians to take away the reserved powers of the states. The sphere of national power, although limited, was considered entirely adequate to absorb even the most ambitious politicians. And James Madison, in *Federalist 39,* was careful to point out that the jurisdiction of the national government extended only to certain enumerated objects, implying that the residual sovereignty of the states was in fact greater than the sovereignty of the national government.

Alexis de Tocqueville, an aristocratic French observer of the American political and social scene in the early 1830s, acknowledged his debt to the writers of *The Federalist* in helping him to understand American government. Many of the sanguine views of Hamilton and Madison about the prospects for the new Constitution were echoed in Tocqueville's analysis of American institutions forty years later.

Tocqueville had set out for the United States in 1831, with his friend Gustave de Beaumont, ostensibly to examine the American prison system with a view toward prison reform in France. Tocqueville was a French judicial officer, who after the July Revolution of 1830 became disenchanted with the new government of Louis Philippe, and, in a broader context, with the continual turmoil that he saw in French political institutions. While the investigation of prisons served as a ready excuse for a leave of absence from governmental duties, Tocqueville and Beaumont's real interest was in studying American society and government. It was their feeling that democracy was probably the wave of the future and that whatever lessons could be learned from the American experiment would undoubtedly be a useful guide to the future of European society.

Tocqueville was in the United States for only nine months, from May 1831 until February 1832, but during this time he traveled over most of the country east of the Mississippi, staying long enough in various places to gain wide knowledge of local customs and institutions. Most of Tocqueville's observations about the United States were objectively optimistic about the future of democracy, yet his most hopeful expectations were not always realized. In particular, after leaving the United States, he became concerned with the possibility of what he called "tyranny of the majority," which he wrote would be an inevitable consequence of egalitarian tendencies in democratic societies such as the United States. The framers of the Constitution, too, were worried about unbridled majority rule in government, and felt that governmental tyranny by the majority would be curtailed by such institutional devices as the separation of powers, checks and balances, and federalism, the latter being a division of authority between the national government and the states. While the framers of the Constitution felt that the possibility of the tyranny of the majority was primarily a governmental problem, Tocqueville saw it as a societal dilemma, produced by the egalitarian ethic. Therefore, to Tocqueville, constitutional devices by themselves would not be sufficient to control the inevitable tendency toward majority despotism in an egalitarian society.

The following selection is taken from Tocqueville's discussion of the characteristics of federalism as he saw it in operation in 1831. In his discussion Tocqueville uses the terms *confederation* and *federalism* interchangeably. To him, the American federal system was one type of confederation. This is important to note because Hamilton, in his discussion of federalism in *The Federalist*, spoke of federalism in the new Constitution as replacing the "confederacy," by which he meant the government that existed under the Articles of Confederation. Most American writers on politics distinguish federalism and confederacy in the same way that Hamilton did, essentially by identifying federalism with the system of the Constitution, and a confederacy with the system of the Articles of Confederation. Under this more common definition of federalism, a federal system is one in which the national government has authority that is separate and distinct from that of the constituent states, an authority that operates directly upon the citizens of the states rather than upon the states as entities. Dual sovereignty is a characteristic of American federalism, whereas under the Articles of Confederation the national government had no authority distinct from the states, and it could not operate without their consent.

The breadth of Tocqueville's analytical method is revealed in his discussion of American federalism. He examines the broad social and political forces operating in society, refers to historical and comparative experience, and analyzes constitutional forms and institutional characteristics. His approach is both empirical and analytical. Tocqueville recognizes that while the theory of federalism may be clear, it is very difficult to apply it without some further clarification. This has certainly been true of the American federal system. As Tocqueville noted: "The sovereignty of the union is so involved in that of the states that it is impossible to distinguish its boundaries at the first glance. The whole structure of the government is artificial and conventional, and it would be ill adapted to a people which has not been long accustomed to conduct its own affairs, or to one in which the science of politics has not descended to the humblest classes of society. I have never been more struck by the good sense and the practical judgment of the Americans than in the manner in which they elude the numberless difficulties resulting from their federal constitution." Tocqueville implied that after all is said and done, federalism as well as other constitutional forms worked because of the good sense and pragmatism of the American people, which overcame constitutional ambiguity. This is why federalism worked in the United States, but, according to Tocqueville, failed in other countries that attempted to imitate the United States Constitution.

In reading the following selection, students should look for Tocqueville's views on (1) the outstanding characteristics of American federalism, (2) the major advantages of federalism, and (3) significant disadvantages of the federal form of government. What evidence does Tocqueville use to buttress his arguments for the advantages and disadvantages of federalism? What changes have occurred since 1831 that might lead to a different perspective on federalism today?

8

Alexis de Tocqueville

DEMOCRACY IN AMERICA: THE FEDERAL CONSTITUTION

❖❖❖❖❖❖❖

Characteristics of the Federal Constitution of the United States of America as Compared with All Other Federal Constitutions

The United States of America does not afford the first or the only instance of a confederation, several of which have existed in modern Europe, without referring to those of antiquity. Switzerland, the Germanic Empire, and the Republic of the

Low Countries either have been or still are confederations. In studying the constitutions of these different countries one is surprised to see that the powers with which they invested the federal government are nearly the same as those awarded by the American Constitution to the government of the United States. They confer upon the central power the same rights of making peace and war, of raising money and troops, and of providing for the general exigencies and the common interests of the nation. Nevertheless, the federal government of these different states has always been as remarkable for its weakness and inefficiency as that of the American Union is for its vigor and capacity. Again, the first American Confederation perished through the excessive weakness of its government; and yet this weak government had as large rights and privileges as those of the Federal government of the present day, and in some respects even larger. But the present Constitution of the United States contains certain novel principles which exercise a most important influence, although they do not at once strike the observer.

This Constitution, which may at first sight be confused with the federal constitutions that have preceded it, rests in truth upon a wholly novel theory, which may be considered as a great discovery in modern political science. In all the confederations that preceded the American Constitution of 1789, the states allied for a common object agreed to obey the injunctions of a federal government; but they reserved to themselves the right of ordaining and enforcing the execution of the laws of the union. The American states which combined in 1789 agreed that the Federal government should not only dictate the laws, but execute its own enactments. In both cases the right is the same, but the exercise of the right is different; and this difference produced the most momentous consequences.

In all the confederations that preceded the American Union the federal government, in order to provide for its wants, had to apply to the separate governments; and if what it prescribed was disagreeable to any one of them, means were found to evade its claims. If it was powerful, it then had recourse to arms; if it was weak, it connived at the resistance which the law of the union, its sovereign, met with, and did nothing, under the plea of inability. Under these circumstances one of two results invariably followed: either the strongest of the allied states assumed the privileges of the federal authority and ruled all the others in its name[1]; or the federal government was abandoned by its natural supporters, anarchy arose between the confederates, and the union lost all power of action.[2]

In America the subjects of the Union are not states, but private citizens: the national government levies a tax, not upon the state of Massachusetts, but upon each inhabitant of Massachusetts. The old confederate governments presided over communities, but that of the Union presides over individuals. Its force is not bor-

---

[1]This was the case in Greece when Philip undertook to execute the decrees of the Amphictyons; in the Low Countries, where the province of Holland always gave the law; and in our own time in the Germanic Confederation, in which Austria and Prussia make themselves the agents of the Diet and rule the whole confederation in its name.

[2]Such has always been the situation of the Swiss Confederation, which would have perished ages ago but for the mutual jealousies of its neighbors.

rowed, but self-derived; and it is served by its own civil and military officers, its own army, and its own courts of justice. It cannot be doubted that the national spirit, the passions of the multitude, and the provincial prejudices of each state still tend singularly to diminish the extent of the Federal authority thus constituted and to facilitate resistance to its mandates; but the comparative weakness of a restricted sovereignty is an evil inherent in the federal system. In America each state has fewer opportunities and temptations to resist; nor can such a design be put in execution (if indeed it be entertained) without an open violation of the laws of the Union, a direct interruption of the ordinary course of justice, and a bold declaration of revolt; in a word, without taking the decisive step that men always hesitate to adopt.

In all former confederations the privileges of the union furnished more elements of discord than of power, since they multiplied the claims of the nation without augmenting the means of enforcing them; and hence the real weakness of federal governments has almost always been in the exact ratio of their nominal power. Such is not the case in the American Union, in which, as in ordinary governments, the Federal power has the means of enforcing all it is empowered to demand. . . .

Advantages of the Federal System in General, and Its Special Utility in America

. . . In small states, the watchfulness of society penetrates everywhere, and a desire for improvement pervades the smallest details; the ambition of the people being necessarily checked by its weakness, all the efforts and resources of the citizens are turned to the internal well-being of the community and are not likely to be wasted upon an empty pursuit of glory. The powers of every individual being generally limited, his desires are proportionally small. Mediocrity of fortune makes the various conditions of life nearly equal, and the manners of the inhabitants are orderly and simple. Thus, all things considered, and allowance being made for the various degrees of morality and enlightenment, we shall generally find more persons in easy circumstances, more contentment and tranquillity, in small nations than in large ones.

When tyranny is established in the bosom of a small state, it is more galling than elsewhere, because, acting in a narrower circle, everything in that circle is affected by it. It supplies the place of those great designs which it cannot entertain, by a violent or exasperating interference in a multitude of minute details; and it leaves the political world, to which it properly belongs, to meddle with the arrangements of private life. Tastes as well as actions are to be regulated; and the families of the citizens, as well as the state, are to be governed. This invasion of rights occurs but seldom, however, freedom being in truth the natural state of small communities. The temptations that the government offers to ambition are too weak and the resources of private individuals are too slender for the sovereign power easily to fall into the grasp of a single man; and should such an event occur, the subjects of the state can easily unite and overthrow the tyrant and the tyranny at once by a common effort.

Small nations have therefore always been the cradle of political liberty; and the fact that many of them have lost their liberty by becoming larger shows that their freedom was more a consequence of their small size than of the character of the people.

The history of the world affords no instance of a great nation retaining the form of republican government for a long series of years;[3] and this had led to the conclusion that such a thing is impracticable. For my own part, I think it imprudent for men who are every day deceived in relation to the actual and the present, and often taken by surprise in the circumstances with which they are most familiar, to attempt to limit what is possible and to judge the future. But it may be said with confidence, that a great republic will always be exposed to more perils than a small one.

All the passions that are most fatal to republican institutions increase with an increasing territory, while the virtues that favor them do not augment in the same proportion. The ambition of private citizens increases with the power of the state; the strength of parties with the importance of the ends they have in view; but the love of country, which ought to check these destructive agencies, is not stronger in a large than in a small republic. It might, indeed, be easily proved that it is less powerful and less developed. Great wealth and extreme poverty, capital cities of large size, a lax morality, selfishness, and antagonism of interests are the dangers which almost invariably arise form the magnitude of states. Several of these evils scarcely injure a monarchy, and some of them even contribute to its strength and duration. In monarchical states the government has its peculiar strength; it may use, but it does not depend on, the community; and the more numerous the people, the stronger is the prince. But the only security that a republican government possesses against these evils lies in the support of the majority. This support is not, however, proportionably greater in a large republic than in a small one; and thus, while the means of attack perpetually increase, in both number and influence, the power of resistance remains the same; or it may rather be said to diminish, since the inclinations and interests of the people are more diversified by the increase of the population, and the difficulty of forming a compact majority is constantly augmented. It has been observed, moreover, that the intensity of human passions is heightened not only by the importance of the end which they propose to attain, but by the multitude of individuals who are animated by them at the same time. Everyone has had occasion to remark that his emotions in the midst of a sympathizing crowd are far greater than those which he would have felt in solitude. In great republics, political passions become irresistible, not only because they aim at gigantic objects, but because they are felt and shared by millions of men at the same time.

It may therefore be asserted as a general proposition that nothing is more opposed to the well-being and the freedom of men than vast empires. Nevertheless, it

---

[3]I do not speak of a confederation of small republics, but of a great consolidated republic.

is important to acknowledge the peculiar advantages of great states. For the very reason that the desire for power is more intense in these communities than among ordinary men, the love of glory is also more developed in the hearts of certain citizens, who regard the applause of a great people as a reward worthy of their exertions and an elevating encouragement to man. If we would learn why great nations contribute more powerfully to the increase of knowledge and the advance of civilization than small states, we shall discover an adequate cause in the more rapid and energetic circulation of ideas and in those great cities which are the intellectual centers where all the rays of human genius are reflected and combined. To this it may be added that most important discoveries demand a use of national power which the government of a small state is unable to make: in great nations the government has more enlarged ideas, and is more completely disengaged from the routine of precedent and the selfishness of local feeling; its designs are conceived with more talent and executed with more boldness.

In time of peace the well-being of small nations is undoubtedly more general and complete; but they are apt to suffer more acutely from the calamities of war than those great empires whose distant frontiers may long avert the presence of the danger from the mass of the people, who are therefore more frequently afflicted than ruined by the contest.

But in this matter, as in many others, the decisive argument is the necessity of the case. If none but small nations existed, I do not doubt that mankind would be more happy and more free; but the existence of great nations is unavoidable.

Political strength thus becomes a condition of national prosperity. It profits a state but little to be affluent and free if it is perpetually exposed to be pillaged or subjugated; its manufactures and commerce are of small advantage if another nation has the empire of the seas and gives the law in all the markets of the globe. Small nations are often miserable, not because they are small, but because they are weak; and great empires prosper less because they are great than because they are strong. Physical strength is therefore one of the first conditions of the happiness and even of the existence of nations. Hence it occurs that, unless very peculiar circumstances intervene, small nations are always united to large empires in the end, either by force or by their own consent. I do not know a more deplorable condition than that of a people unable to defend itself or to provide for its own wants.

The federal system was created with the intention of combining the different advantages which result from the magnitude and the littleness of nations; and a glance at the United States of America discovers the advantages which they have derived from its adoption.

In great centralized nations the legislator is obliged to give a character of uniformity to the laws, which does not always suit the diversity of customs and of districts; as he takes no cognizance of special cases, he can only proceed upon general principles; and the population are obliged to conform to the requirements of the laws, since legislation cannot adapt itself to the exigencies and the customs of the population, which is a great cause of trouble and misery. This disadvantage does not exist in confederations; Congress regulates the principal measures of the national government, and all the details of the administration are reserved to the provincial legislatures. One can hardly imagine how much this division of sovereignty contributes to the well-being of each of the states that compose the Union. In these small communities, which are never agitated by the desire of aggrandizement or the care of self-defense, all public authority and private energy are turned towards internal improvements. The central government of each state, which is in immediate relationship with the citizens, is daily apprised of the wants that arise in society; and new projects are proposed every year, which are discussed at town meetings or by the legislature, and which are transmitted by the press to stimulate the zeal and to excite the interest of the citizens. This spirit of improvement is constantly alive in the American republics, without compromising their tranquillity; the ambition of power yields to the less refined and less dangerous desire for well-being. It is generally believed in America that the existence and the permanence of the republican form of government in the New World depend upon the existence and the duration of the federal system; and it is not unusual to attribute a large share of the misfortunes that have befallen the new states of South America to the injudicious erection of great republics instead of a divided and confederate sovereignty.

It is incontestably true that the tastes and the habits of republican government in the United States were first created in the townships and the provincial assemblies. In a small state, like that of Connecticut, for instance, where cutting a canal or laying down a road is a great political question, where the state has no army to pay and no wars to carry on, and where much wealth or much honor cannot be given to the rulers, no form of government can be more natural or more appropriate than a republic. But it is this same republican spirit, it is these manners and customs of a free people, which have been created and nurtured in the different states, that must be afterwards applied to the country at large. The public spirit of the Union is, so to speak, nothing more than an aggregate or summary of the patriotic zeal of the separate provinces. Every citizen of the United States transfers, so to speak, his attachment to his little republic into the common store of American patriotism. In defending the Union he defends the increasing prosperity of his own state or county, the right of conducting its affairs, and the hope of causing measures of improvement to be adopted in it which may be favorable to his own interests; and these are motives that are wont to stir men more than the general interests of the country and the glory of the nation.

On the other hand, if the temper and the manners of the inhabitants especially fitted them to promote the welfare of a great republic, the federal system renders their task less difficult. The confederation of all the American states presents none of the ordinary inconveniences resulting from large associations of men. The Union is a great republic in extent, but the paucity of objects for which its government acts assimilates it to a small state. Its acts are important, but they are rare. As the sovereignty of the Union is limited and incomplete, its exercise is not dangerous to liberty; for it does not excite those insatiable desires for fame and power which have proved so fatal to great republics. As there is no common center to the country, great capital cities, colossal wealth, abject poverty, and sudden revolutions are alike unknown; and political passion, instead of spreading over the land like a fire on the prairies, spends it strength against the interests and the individual passions of every state.

Nevertheless, tangible objects and ideas circulate throughout the Union as freely as in a country inhibited by one people. Nothing checks the spirit of enterprise. The government invites the aid of all who have talents or knowledge to serve it. Inside of the frontiers of the Union profound peace prevails, as within the heart of some great empire; abroad it ranks with the most powerful nations of the earth: two thousand miles of coast are open to the commerce of the world; and as it holds the keys of a new world, its flag is respected in the most remote seas. The Union is happy and free as a small people, and glorious and strong as a great nation.

Why the Federal System is Not Practicable for All Nations, and How the Anglo-Americans Were Enabled to Adopt It

. . . I have shown the advantages that the Americans derive from their federal system; it remains for me to point out the circumstances that enabled them to adopt it, as its benefits cannot be enjoyed by all nations. The accidental defects of the federal system which originate in the laws may be corrected by the skill of the legislature, but there are evils inherent in the system which cannot be remedied by any effort. The people must therefore find in themselves the strength necessary to bear the natural imperfections of their government.

The most prominent evil of all federal systems is the complicated nature of the means they employ. Two sovereignties are necessarily in presence of each other. The legislator may simplify and equalize as far as possible the action of these two sovereignties, by limiting each of them to a sphere of authority accurately defined; but he cannot combine them into one or prevent them from coming into collision at certain points. The federal system, therefore, rests upon a theory which is complicated at the best, and which demands the daily exercise of a considerable share of discretion on the part of those it governs. . . .

In examining the Constitution of the United States, which is the most perfect federal constitution that ever existed, one is startled at the variety of information and the amount of discernment that it presupposes in the people whom it is meant to govern. The government of the Union depends almost entirely upon legal fictions; the Union is an ideal nation, which exists, so to speak, only in the mind, and whose limits and extent can only be discerned by the understanding.

After the general theory is comprehended, many difficulties remain to be solved in its application; for the sovereignty of the Union is so involved in that of the states that it is impossible to distinguish its boundaries at the first glance. The whole structure of the government is artificial and conventional, and it would be ill adapted to a people which has not been long accustomed to conduct its own affairs, or to one in which the science of politics has not descended to the humblest classes of society. I have never been more struck by the good sense and the practical judgment of the Americans than in the manner in which they elude the numberless difficulties resulting from their Federal Constitution. I scarcely ever met with a plain American citizen who could not distinguish with surprising facility the obligations created by the laws of Congress from those created by the laws of his own state, and who, after having discriminated between the matters which come under the cognizance of the Union and those which the local legislature is competent to regulate, could not point out the exact limit of the separate jurisdictions of the Federal courts and the tribunals of the state.

The Constitution of the United States resembles those fine creations of human industry which ensure wealth and renown to their inventors, but which are profitless in other hands. . . .

The second and most fatal of all defects, and that which I believe to be inherent in the federal system, is the relative weakness of the government of the Union. The principle upon which all confederations rest is that of a divided sovereignty. Legislators may render this partition less perceptible, they may even conceal it for a time from the public eye, but they cannot prevent it from existing; and a divided sovereignty must always be weaker than an entire one. The remarks made on the Constitution of the United States have shown with what skill the Americans, while restraining the power of the Union within the narrow limits of a federal government, have given it the semblance, and to a certain extent the force, of a national government. By this means the legislators of the Union have diminished the natural danger of confederations, but have not entirely obviated it.

The American government, it is said, does not address itself to the states, but transmits its injunctions directly to the citizens and compels them individually to comply with its demands. But if the Federal law were to clash with the interests and the prejudices of a state, it might be feared that all the citizens of that state would conceive themselves to be interested in the cause of a single individual who refused to obey. If all the citizens of the state were aggrieved at the same time and in the same manner by the authority of the Union, the Federal government would vainly attempt to subdue them individually; they would instinctively unite in a common defense and would find an organization already prepared for them in the sovereignty that their state is allowed to enjoy. Fiction would give way to reality, and an organized portion of the nation might then contest the central authority.

The same observation holds good with regard to the Federal jurisdiction. If the courts of the Union violated an important law of a state in a private case, the real though not the apparent contest would be between the aggrieved state represented by a citizen and the Union represented by its courts of justice.

He would have but a partial knowledge of the world who should imagine that it is possible by the aid of legal fictions to prevent men from finding out and employing those means of gratifying their passions which have been left open to them. The American legislators, though they have rendered a collision between the two sovereignties less probable, have not destroyed the causes of such a misfortune. It may even be affirmed that, in case of such a collision, they have not been able to ensure the victory of the Federal element. The Union is possessed of money and troops, but the states have kept the affections and the prejudices of the people. The sovereignty of the Union is an abstract being, which is connected with but few external objects; the sovereignty of the states is perceptible by the senses, easily understood, and constantly active. The former is of recent creation, the latter is coeval with the people itself. The sovereignty of the Union is factitious, that of the states is natural and self-existent, without effort, like the authority of a parent. The sovereignty of the nation affects a few of the chief interests of society; it represents an immense but remote country, a vague and ill-defined sentiment. The authority of the states controls every individual citizen at every hour and in all circumstances; it protects his property, his freedom, and his life; it affects at every moment his well-being or his misery. When we recollect the traditions, the customs, the prejudices of local and familiar attachment with which it is connected, we cannot doubt the superiority of a power that rests on the instinct of patriotism, so natural to the human heart.

Since legislators cannot prevent such dangerous collisions as occur between the two sovereignties which coexist in the Federal system, their first object must be, not only to dissuade the confederate states from warfare, but to encourage such dispositions as lead to peace. Hence it is that the Federal compact cannot be lasting unless there exists in the communities which are leagued together a certain number of inducements to union which render their common dependence agreeable and the task of the government light. The Federal system cannot succeed without the presence of favorable circumstances added to the influence of good laws. All the nations that have ever formed a confederation have been held together by some common interests, which served as the intellectual ties of association. . . .

The circumstance which makes it easy to maintain a Federal government in America is not only that the states have similar interests, a common origin, and a common language, but they have also arrived at the same stage of civilization, which almost always renders a union feasible. I do not know of any European nation, however small, that does not present less uniformity in its different provinces than the American people, which occupy a territory as extensive as one half of Europe. The distance from Maine to Georgia is about one thousand miles; but the difference between the civilization of Maine and that of Georgia is slighter than the difference between the habits of Normandy and those of Brittany. Maine and Georgia, which are place at the opposite extremities of a great empire, have therefore more real inducements to form a confederation than Normandy and Brittany, which are separated only by a brook.

The geographical position of the country increased the facilities that the American legislators derived from the usages and customs of the inhabitants; and it is to this circumstance that the adoption and the maintenance of the Federal system are mainly attributable.

The most important occurrence in the life of a nation is the breaking out of a war. . . . A long war almost always reduces nations to the wretched alternative of being abandoned to ruin by defeat or to despotism by success. War therefore renders the weakness of a government most apparent and most alarming; and I have shown that the inherent defect of federal governments is that of being weak.

The federal system not only has no centralized administration, and nothing that resembles one, but the central government itself is imperfectly organized, which is always a great cause of weakness when the nation is opposed to other countries which are themselves governed by a single authority. In the Federal Constitution of the United States, where the central government has more real force than in any other confederation, this evil is extremely evident. . . .

How does it happen, then, that the American Union, with all the relative perfection of its laws, is not dissolved by the occurrence of a great war? It is because it has no great wars to fear. Placed in the center of an immense continent, which offers a boundless field for human industry, the Union is almost as much insulated from the world as if all its frontiers were girt by the ocean. . . .

The great advantage of the United States does not, then, consist in a Federal Constitution which allows it to carry on great wars, but in a geographical position which renders such wars extremely improbable.

No one can be more inclined than I am to appreciate the advantages of the federal system, which I hold to be one of the combinations most favorable to the prosperity and freedom of men. I envy the lot of those nations which have been able to adopt it; but I cannot believe that any confederate people could maintain a long or an equal contest with a nation of similar strength in which the government is centralized. A people which, in the presence of the great military monarchies of Europe, should divide its sovereignty into fractional parts would, in my opinion, by that very act abdicate its power, and perhaps its existence and its name. But such is the admirable position of the New World that man has no other enemy than himself, and that, in order to be happy and to be free, he has only to determine that he will be so.

THE SUPREMACY OF NATIONAL LAW

Tracing the historical development of nation-state relationships, one finds that there has been constant strife over the determination of the boundaries of national power in relation to the reserved powers of the states. The Civil War did not settle once and for all the difficult question of national versus state power. The Supreme Court has played an important role in the development of the federal system, and some of its most historic opinions have upheld national power at the expense of the states. In the early period of the Court, Chief Justice John Marshall in *McCulloch* v. *Maryland,* 4 Wheaton 316 (1819), stated two doctrines that have had a profound effect upon the federal system: (1) the doctrine of implied powers, and (2) the doctrine of the supremacy of national law. The former enables Congress to expand its power into numerous areas affecting states directly. By utilizing the commerce clause, for example, Congress may now regulate what is essentially *intrastate* commerce, for the Court has held that this is implied in the original clause giving Congress the power to regulate commerce among the several states. The immediate issues in *McCulloch* v. *Maryland* were, first, whether or not Congress had the power to incorporate, or charter, a national bank; second, if Congress did have such a power, although nowhere stated in the Constitution, did the existence of such a bank prevent state action that would interfere in its operation?

9

McCULLOCH v. MARYLAND
4 WHEATON 316 (1819)

Mr. Chief Justice Marshall delivered the opinion of the Court, saying in part:

In the case now to be determined, the defendant, a sovereign state, denies the obligation of a law enacted by the legislature of the Union; and the plaintiff, on his part, contests the validity of an act which has been passed by the legislature of that state. The Constitution of our country, in its most interesting and vital parts, is to be considered; the conflicting powers of the government of the Union and of its members, as marked in that Constitution, are to be discussed; and an opinion given, which may essentially influence the great operations of the government. . . .

If any one proposition could command the universal assent of mankind, we might expect it would be this: that the government of the Union, though limited in its powers, is supreme within its sphere of action. This would seem to result necessarily from its nature. It is the government of all; its powers are delegated by all; it represents all, and acts for all. Though any one state may be willing to control its operations, no state is willing to allow others to control them. The nation, on those subjects on which it can act, must necessarily bind its component parts. But this question is not left to mere reason: the people have, in express terms, decided it, by saying, "this Constitution, and the laws of the United States, which shall be made in pursuance thereof," "shall be the supreme law of the land," and by requiring that the members of the state legislatures, and the officers of the executive and judicial departments of the states, shall take the oath of fidelity to it. . . .

A constitution, to contain an accurate detail of all the subdivisions of which its great powers will admit, and of all the means by which they may be carried into execution, would partake of the prolixity of a legal code, and could scarcely be embraced by the human mind. It would probably never be understood by the public. Its nature, therefore, requires that only its great outlines should be marked, its important objects designated, and the minor ingredients which compose those objects be deduced from the nature of the objects themselves. That this idea was entertained by the framers of the American Constitution, is not only to be inferred from the nature of the instrument, but from the language. . . .

Although, among the enumerated powers of government, we do not find the word "bank," or "incorporation," we find the great powers to lay and collect taxes; to borrow money; to regulate commerce; to declare and conduct a war; and to raise and support armies and navies. The sword and the purse, all the external relations, and no inconsiderable portion of the industry of the nation, are entrusted to its government. It can never be pretended that these vast powers draw after them others of inferior importance, merely because they are inferior. Such an idea can never be advanced. But it may, with great reason, be contended, that a government, entrusted with such ample powers, on the due execution of which the happiness and prosperity of the nation so vitally depends, must also be entrusted with ample means for their execution. The power being given, it is the interest of the nation to facilitate its execution. It can never be their interest, and cannot be presumed to have been their intention, to clog and embarrass its execution by withholding the most appropriate means. Throughout this vast republic, from the St. Croix to the Gulf of Mexico, from the Atlantic to the Pacific, revenue is to be collected and expended, armies are to be marched and supported. The exigencies of the nation may require, that the treasure raised in the North should be transported to the South, that raised in the East conveyed to the West, or that this order should be reversed. Is that construction of the Constitution to be preferred which would render these operations difficult, hazardous, and expensive? Can we adopt that construction (unless the words imperiously require it) which would impute to the framers of that instrument, when granting these powers for the public good, the intention of impeding their exercise by withholding a choice of means? If, indeed, such be the mandate of the Constitution, we have only to obey; but that instrument does not profess to enumerate the means by which the powers it confers may be executed; nor does it prohibit the creation of a corporation, if the existence of such a being be essential to the beneficial exercise of those powers. It is, then, the subject of fair inquiry, how far such means may be employed. . . .

We admit, as all must admit, that the powers of the government are limited, and that its limits are not to be transcended. But we think the sound construction of the Constitution must allow to the national legislature that discretion, with respect to the means by which the powers it confers are to be carried into execution, which will enable that body to perform the high duties assigned to it, in the manner most beneficial to the people. Let the end be legitimate, let it be within the scope of the Constitution, and all means which are appropriate, which are plainly adapted to that end, which are not prohibited, but consist with the letter and spirit of the Constitution, are constitutional. . . .

It being the opinion of the court that the act incorporating the bank is constitutional; and that the power of establishing a branch in the state of Maryland might be properly exercised by the bank itself, we proceed to inquire:

Whether the state of Maryland may, without violating the Constitution, tax that branch? . . .

That the power of taxation is one of vital importance; that it is retained by the states; that it is not abridged by the grant of a similar power to the government of the Union; that it is to be concurrently exercised by the two governments: are truths which have never been denied. But, such is the paramount character of the Constitution, that its capacity to withdraw any subject from the action of even this power, is admitted. The states are expressly forbidden to lay any duties on imports or exports, except what may be absolutely necessary for executing their inspection laws. If the obligation of this prohibition must be conceded—if it may restrain a state from the exercise of its taxing power of imports and exports; the same paramount character would seem to restrain, as it certainly may restrain, a state from such other exercise of this power, as is in its nature incompatible with, and repugnant to, the constitutional laws of the Union. A law, absolutely repugnant to another, as entirely repeals that other as if express terms of repeal were used.

On this ground the counsel for the bank place its claim to be exempted from the power of a state to tax its operations. There is no express provision for the case, but the claim has been sustained on a principle which so entirely pervades the Constitution, is so intermixed with the materials which compose it, so interwoven with its web, so blended with its texture, as to be incapable of being separated from it, without rending it into shreds.

This great principle is, that the Constitution and the laws made in pursuance thereof are supreme; that they control the Constitution and laws of the respective states, and cannot be controlled by them. From this, which may be almost termed an axiom, other propositions are deduced as corollaries, on the truth or error of which, and on their application to this case, the cause has been supposed to depend. These are, 1. That a power to create implies a power to preserve. 2. That a power to destroy, if wielded by a different hand, is hostile to, and incompatible with, these powers to create and preserve. 3. That where this repugnancy exists, that authority which is supreme must control, not yield to that over which it is supreme. . . .

If we apply the principle for which the state of Maryland contends, to the Constitution generally, we shall find it capable of changing totally the character of that instrument. We shall find it capable of arresting all the measures of the government, and of prostrating it at the foot of the states. The American people have declared their Constitution, and the laws made in pursuance thereof, to be supreme; but this principle would transfer the supremacy, in fact, to the states. . . .

The court has bestowed on this subject its most deliberate consideration. The result is a conviction that the states have no power, by taxation or otherwise, to retard, impede, burden, or in any manner control, the operations of the constitutional laws enacted by Congress to carry into execution the powers vested in the general government. That is, we think, the unavoidable consequence of that supremacy which the Constitution has declared. . . .

❖❖ Constitutional doctrine regarding the power of the national government to regulate commerce among the states to promote general prosperity has been clarified in a series of Supreme Court cases. At issue is the interpretation of the power to "regulate commerce with foreign nations, and among the several States," granted to Congress in Article 1. Some of these cases have emphasized the role of the national government as umpire, enforcing certain rules of the game within which the free enterprise system functions; others have emphasized the positive role of the government in regulating the economy.

A key case supporting the supremacy of the national government in commercial regulation was *Gibbons* v. *Ogden,* 9 Wheaton 1 (1824). The New York legislature, in 1798, granted Robert R. Livingston the exclusive privilege to navigate by steam the rivers and other waters of the state, provided he could build a boat that would travel at four miles an hour against the current of the Hudson River. A two-year time limitation was imposed, and the conditions were not met; however, New York renewed its grant for two years in 1803 and again in 1807. In 1807 Robert Fulton, who now held the exclusive license with Livingston, completed and put into operation a steamboat that met the legislative conditions. The New York legislature now provided that a five-year extension of their monopoly would be given to Livingston and Fulton for each new steamboat they placed into operation on New York waters. The monopoly could not exceed thirty years, but during that period anyone wishing to navigate New York waters by steam had first to obtain a license from Livingston and Fulton, who were given the power to confiscate unlicensed boats. New Jersey and Connecticut passed retaliatory laws, the former authorizing confiscation of any New York ship for each ship confiscated by Livingston and Fulton, the latter prohibiting boats licensed in New York from entering Connecticut waters. Ohio also passed retaliatory legislation. Open commercial warfare seemed a possibility among the states of the union.

In 1793 Congress passed an act providing for the licensing of vessels engaged in the coasting trade, and Gibbons obtained under this statute a license to operate boats between New York and New Jersey. Ogden was engaged in a similar operation under an exclusive license issued by Livingston and Fulton, and thus sought to enjoin Gibbons from further operation. The New York court upheld the exclusive grants given to Livingston and Fulton, and Gibbons appealed to the Supreme Court. Chief Justice Marshall made it quite clear that (1) states cannot interfere with a power granted to Congress by passing conflicting state legislation, and (2) the commerce power includes anything affecting "commerce among the states" and thus may include *intrastate* as well as interstate commerce. In this way the foundation was laid for broad national control over commercial activity.

❖❖ Over its history the Supreme Court has interpreted the commerce clause both to expand and contract the authority of the national government. After Chief Justice John Marshall's era ended in 1836, the Court gradually adopted a more restrictive view of the national commerce power, protecting state sovereignty over many areas of commercial regulation that Marshall clearly would have allowed Congress to regulate. The Supreme Court did not fully return to the broad commerce clause interpretation of the *Gibbons* case until 1937, when it reluctantly capitulated to Franklin D. Roosevelt's New Deal and the centralized government it represented. The restoration of the Marshall Court's definition of the commerce power removed constitutional restraints upon Congress.

Since 1937 the Supreme Court has essentially upheld congressional interpretations of its own authority under the commerce clause. While the commerce power is generally used to support economic regulation, Congress turned to the commerce clause for the legal authority to enact the Civil Rights Act of 1964. The public accommodations section of the bill, Title II, proscribed discrimination in public establishments, including inns, hotels, motels, restaurants, motion-picture houses, and theaters. The law declared that the "operations of an establishment affects commerce . . . if . . . it serves or offers to serve interstate travelers or a substantial portion of the food which it serves or gasoline or other products which it sells, has moved in commerce . . . [or if] it customarily presents films, performances, athletic teams, exhibitions, or other sources of entertainment which move in commerce." In *Heart of Atlanta Motel, Inc.* v. *United States,* 379 US 241 (1964), the Supreme Court upheld the law under the commerce clause. The motel-plaintiff contended that it was in no way involved in interstate commerce, arguing that while some of its guests might be occasionally engaged in commerce, "persons and people are not part of trade or commerce . . . people conduct commerce and engage in trade, but people are not part of commerce and trade." But the Court accepted the government's argument that racial discrimination in public accommodations impedes interstate travel by those discriminated against, causing disruption of interstate commerce which Congress has the authority to prevent.

The Supreme Court did briefly resurrect the commerce clause as a limit on congressional power over the states in *National League of Cities* v. *Usery,* 426 US 833 (1976). A sharply divided Court held that Congress could not regulate governmental activities that were an integral part of state sovereignty. The decision overturned provisions of the Fair Labor Standards Act that governed state employees. The Court's majority opinion argued that states had traditionally controlled their employees, a responsibility within state sovereignty because the states through their own democratic processes should have the autonomy to decide for themselves how they would manage their public sector.

It was not long, however, before the Court reversed the *National League of Cities* decision, holding in *Garcia* v. *San Antonio Metropolitan Transit Authority,* 83L Ed. 2d 10 16 (1985), that Congress could apply minimum-wage requirements to the states and their localities. Again the vote was closely divided, 5–4, and this time the majority opinion struck a distinct note of judicial self-restraint, concluding: "We doubt that courts ultimately can identify principled constitutional limitations on the scope of Congress' commerce clause powers over the states merely by relying on *a priori* definitions of state sovereignty." The Court found nothing in the Fair Labor Standards Act that violated state sovereignty, implying that it was up to Congress and not the courts to determine the extent of its power under the commerce clause. Sharp dissents were registered in the case, possibly indicating that in the future the issue once again may be joined and a more conservative Supreme Court majority uphold some commerce clause restraints against national regulation of state governments. The *Garcia* decision is directly in line with Court precedents since 1937 that have supported virtually unlimited congressional authority under the commerce clause.

A Perspective on Federalism: Present and Future

In the following selection, the role of the states in the political system is discussed from the perspective that the nature of intergovernmental relations reflects underlying political conditions and realities. As James Madison pointed out in *Federalist 39,* The original constitutional scheme of federalism represented a delicate balance between national and state ("federal") interests. But, under the original constitutional design, the national government was not to intervene directly in the affairs of state governments; and the problems of subsidiary local governments within states were not considered to be separate from the problems of the states themselves, and therefore, they were a proper matter for resolution by the individual state governments.

Morton Grodzins points out that strict separation of national and state functions has never really existed, and that even before the Constitution of 1787 a national statute passed by the Continental Congress gave grants-in-aid of land to the states for public schools. Tocqueville also comments on the difficulties of formally separating, in theory, the responsibilities of national, state, and local governments. The history of the federal system has seen the ebb and flow of national dominance over the states; centralization and decentralization have been the cyclical themes of federalism and intergovernmental relations. The thrust of the New Deal was toward centralization through the use of federal grant-in-aid programs, a philosophy that dominated the government until the emergence of the "New Federalism" of the Nixon administration, which supported decentralization of power from the national to the state governments. The move toward decentralization was broadly supported by the Republican party. Revenue sharing was inaugurated by President Nixon to transfer national funds to the states, without stipulation of how the money was to be spent. The revenue-sharing procedure was in direct contrast to the grant-in-aid programs, which allowed for state receipt of federal money upon the condition of state adherence to national standards. President Reagan's New Federalism proposed the merging of grant-in-aid programs into block grants to the states leading eventually to a reduced federal role in financing state and local governments. The continuing conflict between the themes and realities of centralization and decentralization are examined in the following selection.

10

Morton Grodzins

THE FEDERAL SYSTEM

❖❖❖❖❖❖❖❖

Federalism is a device for dividing decisions and functions of government. As the constitutional fathers well understood, the federal structure is a means, not an end. The pages that follow are therefore not concerned with an exposition of American federalism as a formal, legal set of relationships. The focus, rather, is on the purpose of federalism, that is to say, on the distribution of power between central and peripheral units of government.

    From Morton Grodzins, ed., *Goals for Americans: The Report of the President's Commission on National Goals* (New York: The American Assembly), pp. 265–282. Reprinted by permission.

I. The Sharing of Functions

The American form of government is often, but erroneously, symbolized by a three-layer cake. A far more accurate image is the rainbow or marble cake, characterized by an inseparable mingling of differently colored ingredients, the colors appearing in vertical and diagonal strands and unexpected whirls. As colors are mixed in the marble cake, so functions are mixed in the American federal system. Consider the health officer, styled "sanitarian," of a rural county in a border state. He embodies the whole idea of the marble cake of government.

The sanitarian is appointed by the state under merit standards established by the federal government. His base salary comes jointly from state and federal funds, the county provides him with an office and office amenities and pays a portion of his expenses, and the largest city in the county also contributes to his salary and office by virtue of his appointment as a city plumbing inspector. It is impossible from moment to moment to tell under which governmental hat the sanitarian operates. His work of inspecting the purity of food is carried out under federal standards; but he is enforcing state laws when inspecting commodities that have not been in interstate commerce; and somewhat perversely he also acts under state authority when inspecting milk coming into the county from producing areas across the state border. He is a federal officer when impounding impure drugs shipped from a neighboring state; a federal-state officer when distributing typhoid immunization serum; a state officer when enforcing standards of industrial hygiene; a state-local officer when inspecting the city's water supply; and (to complete the circle), a local officer when insisting that the city butchers adopt more hygienic methods of handling their garbage. But he cannot and does not think of himself as acting in these separate capacities. All business in the county that concerns public health and sanitation he considers his business. Paid largely from federal funds, he does not find it strange to attend meetings of the city council to give expert advice on matters ranging from rotten apples to rabies control. He is even deputized as a member of both the city and county police forces.

The sanitarian is an extreme case, but he accurately represents an important aspect of the whole range of governmental activities in the United States. Functions are not neatly parceled out among the many governments. They are shared functions. It is difficult to find any governmental activity which does not involve all three of the so-called "levels" of the federal system. In the most local of local functions—law enforcement or education, for example—the federal and state governments play important roles. In what, a priori, may be considered the purest central government activities—the conduct of foreign affairs, for example—the state and local governments have considerable responsibilities, directly and indirectly.

The federal grant programs are only the most obvious example of shared functions. They also most clearly exhibit how sharing serves to disperse governmental powers. The grants utilize the greater wealth-gathering abilities of the central government and establish nationwide standards, yet they are "in aid" of functions carried out under state law, with considerable state and local discretion. The national supervision of such programs is largely a process of mutual accommodation. Leading state and local officials, acting through their professional organizations, are in considerable part responsible for the very standards that national officers try to persuade all state and local officers to accept.

Even in the absence of joint financing, federal-state-local collaboration is the characteristic mode of action. Federal expertise is available to aid in the building of a local jail (which may later be used to house federal prisoners), to improve a local water purification system, to step up building inspections, to provide standards for state and local personnel in protecting housewives against dishonest butchers' scales, to prevent gas explosions, or to produce a land use plan. States and localities, on the other hand, take important formal responsibilities in the development of national programs for atomic energy, civil defense, the regulation of commerce, and the protection of purity in foods and drugs; local political weight is always a factor in the operation of even a post office or a military establishment. From abattoirs and accounting through zoning and zoo administration, any governmental activity is almost certain to involve the influence, if not the formal administration, of all three planes of the federal system.

II. Attempts to Unwind the Federal System

[From 1947 to 1960] there [were] four major attempts to reform or reorganize the federal system: the first (1947– 149) and second (1953–55) Hoover Commissions on Executive Organization; the Kestnbaum Commission on Intergovernmental Relations (1953–55); and the Joint Federal-State Action Committee (1957–59). All four of these groups . . . aimed to minimize federal activities. None of them . . . recognized the sharing of functions as the characteristic way American governments do things. Even when making recommendations for joint action, these official commissions [took] the view (as expressed in the Kestnbaum report) that "the main tradition of American federalism [is] the tradition of separateness." All four . . . in varying degrees, worked to separate functions and tax sources.

The history of the Joint Federal-State Action Committee is especially instructive. The committee was established at the suggestion of President Eisenhower, who charged it, first of all, "to designate functions which the States are ready and willing to assume and finance that are now performed or financed wholly or in part by the Federal Government." He also gave the committee the task of recommending "Federal and State revenue adjustments required to enable the States to assume such functions".[1]

The President's third suggestion was that the committee "identify functions and responsibilities likely to require state or federal attention in the future and . . . recommend the level of state effort, or federal effort, or both, that will be needed to assure effective action." The committee initially devoted little attention to this problem. Upon discovering the difficulty of making separatist recommendations, i.e., for turning over federal functions and taxes to the states, it developed a series of proposals looking to greater effectiveness in intergovernmental collaboration. The committee was succeeded by a legislatively based, 26-member Advisory Commission on Intergovernmental Relations, established September 29, 1959.

The committee subsequently established seemed most favorably situated to accomplish the task of functional separation. It was composed of distinguished and able men, including among its personnel three leading members of the President's Cabinet, the director of the Bureau of the Budget, and ten state governors. It had the full support of the President at every point, and it worked hard and conscientiously. Excellent staff studies were supplied by the Bureau of the Budget, the White House, the Treasury Department, and, from the state side, the Council of State Governments. It had available to it a large mass of research data, including the sixteen recently completed volumes of the Kestnbaum Commission. There existed no disagreements on party lines within the committee and, of course, no constitutional impediments to its mission. The President, his Cabinet members, and all the governors (with one possible exception) on the committee completely agreed on the desirability of decentralization-via-separation-of-functions-and-taxes. They were unanimous in wanting to justify the committee's name and to produce action, not just another report.

The committee worked for more than two years. It found exactly two programs to recommend for transfer from federal to state hands. One was the federal grant program for vocational education (including practical-nurse training and aid to fishery trades); the other was federal grants for municipal waste treatment plants. The programs together cost the federal government less than $80 million in 1957, slightly more than two percent of the total federal grants for that year. To allow the states to pay for these programs, the committee recommended that they be allowed a credit against the federal tax on local telephone calls. Calculations showed that this offset device, plus an equalizing factor, would give every state at least 40 percent more from the tax than it received from the federal government in vocational education and sewage disposal grants. Some states were "equalized" to receive twice as much.

The recommendations were modest enough, and the generous financing feature seemed calculated to gain state support. The President recommended to Congress that all points of the program be legislated. None of them was, none has been since, and none is likely to be.

III. A Point of History

The American federal system has never been a system of separated governmental activities. There has never been a time when it was possible to put neat labels on discrete "federal," "state," and "local" functions. Even before the Constitution, a statute of 1785, reinforced by the Northwest Ordinance of 1787, gave grants-in-land to the states for public schools. Thus the national government was a prime force in making possible what is now taken to be the most local function of all, primary and secondary education. More important, the nation, before it was fully organized, established by this action a first principle of American federalism: the national government would use its superior resources to initiate and support national programs, principally administered by the states and localities.

The essential unity of state and federal financial system was again recognized in the earliest constitutional days with the assumption by the federal government of the Revolutionary War debts of the states. Other points of federal-state collaboration during the Federalist period concerned the militia, law enforcement, court practices, the administration of elections, public health measures, pilot laws, and many other matters.

The nineteenth century is widely believed to have been the preeminent period of duality in the American system. Lord Bryce at the end of the century described (in *The American Commonwealth*) the federal and state governments as "distinct and separate in their action." The system, he said, was "like a great factory wherein two sets of machinery are at work, their revolving wheels apparently intermixed, their bands crossing one another, yet each set doing its own work without touching or hampering the other." Great works may contain gross errors. Bryce was wrong. The nineteenth century, like the early days of the republic, was a period principally characterized by intergovernmental collaboration.

Decisions of the Supreme Court are often cited as evidence of nineteenth-century duality. In the early part of the century the Court, heavily weighted with Federalists, was intent upon enlarging the sphere of national authority; in the later years (and to the 1930s) its actions were in the direction of paring down national powers and indeed all governmental authority. Decisions referred to "areas of exclusive competence" exercised by the federal government and the states; to their powers being "separated and distinct"; and to neither being able "to intrude within the jurisdiction of the other."

Judicial rhetoric is not always consistent with judicial action, and the Court did not always adhere to separatist doctrine. Indeed, its rhetoric sometimes indicated a positive view of cooperation. In any case, the Court was rarely, if ever, directly confronted with the issue of cooperation versus separation as such. Rather it was concerned with defining permissible areas of action for the central government and the states; or with saying with respect to a point at issue whether any government could take action. The Marshall Court contributed to intergovernmental cooperation by the very act of permitting federal operations where they had not existed before. Furthermore, even Marshall was willing to allow interstate commerce to be affected by the states in their use of the police power. Later courts also upheld state laws that had an impact on interstate commerce, just as they approved the expansion of the national commerce power, as in statutes providing for the control of telegraphic communication or prohibiting the interstate transportation of lotteries, impure foods and drugs, and prostitutes. Similar room for cooperation was found outside the commerce field, notably in the Court's refusal to interfere with federal grants-in-land or cash to the states. Although research to clinch the point has not been completed, it is probably true that the Supreme Court from 1800 to 1936 allowed far more federal-state collaboration than it blocked.

Political behavior and administrative action of the nineteenth century provide positive evidence that, throughout the entire era of so-called dual federalism, the many governments in the American federal system continued the close administrative and fiscal collaboration of the earlier period. Governmental activities were not extensive. But relative to what governments did, intergovernmental cooperation during the last century was comparable with that existing today.

Occasional presidential vetoes (from Madison to Buchanan) of cash and land grants are evidence of constitutional and ideological apprehensions about the extensive expansion of federal activities which produced widespread intergovernmental collaboration. In perspective, however, the vetoes are a more important evidence of the continuous search, not least by state officials, for ways and means to involve the central government in a wide variety of joint programs. The search was successful.

Grants-in-land and grants-in-services from the national government were of first importance in virtually all the principal functions undertaken by the states and their local subsidies. Land grants were made to the states for, among other purposes, elementary schools, colleges, and special educational institutions; roads, canals, rivers, harbors, and railroads; reclamation of desert and swamp lands; and veterans' welfare. In fact whatever was at the focus of state attention became the recipient of national grants. (Then, as today, national grants established state emphasis as well as followed it.) If Connecticut wished to establish a program for the care and education of deaf and dumb, federal money in the form of a land grant was found to aid that program. If higher education relating to agriculture became a pressing need, Congress could dip into the public domain and make appropriate grants to states. If the need for swamp drainage and flood control appeared, the federal government could supply both grants-in-land and, from the Army's Corps of Engineers, the services of the only trained engineers then available.

Aid also went in the other direction. The federal government, theoretically in exclusive control of the Indian population, relied continuously (and not always wisely) on the experience and resources of state and local governments. State militias were an all-important ingredient in the nation's armed forces. State governments became unofficial but real partners in federal programs for homesteading, reclamation, tree culture, law enforcement, inland waterways, the nation's internal communications system (including highway and railroad routes), and veterans' aid of various sorts. Administrative contacts were voluminous, and the whole process of interaction was lubricated, then as today, by constituent-conscious members of Congress.

The essential continuity of the collaborative system is best demonstrated by the history of the grants. The land grant tended to become a cash grant based on the calculated disposable value of the land, and the cash grant tended to become an annual grant based upon the national government's superior tax powers. In 1887, only three years before the frontier was officially closed, thus signalizing the end of the disposable public domain, Congress enacted the first continuing cash grants.

A long, extensive, and continuous experience is therefore the foundation of the present system of shared functions characteristic of the American federal system, what we have called the marble cake of government. It is a misjudgment of our history and our present situation to believe that a neat separation of governmental functions could take place without drastic alterations in our society and system of government.

IV. Dynamics of Sharing: The Politics of the Federal System

Many causes contribute to dispersed power in the federal system. One is the simple historical fact that the states existed before the nation. A second is in the form of creed, the traditional opinion of Americans that expresses distrust of centralized power and places great value in the strength and vitality of local units of government. Another is pride in locality and state, nurtured by the nation's size and by variations of regional and state history. Still a fourth cause of decentralization is the sheer wealth of the nation. It allows all groups, including state and local governments, to partake of the central government's largesse, supplies room for experimentation and even waste, and makes unnecessary the tight organization of political power that must follow when the support of one program necessarily means the deprivation of another.

In one important respect, the Constitution no longer operates to impede centralized government. The Supreme Court since 1937 has given Congress a relatively free hand. The federal government can build substantive programs in many areas on the taxation and commerce powers. Limitations of such central programs based on the argument, "it's unconstitutional," are no longer possible as long as Congress (in the Court's view) acts reasonably in the interest of the whole nation. The Court is unlikely to reverse this permissive view in the foreseeable future.

Nevertheless, some constitutional restraints on centralization continue to operate. The strong constitutional position of the states—for example, the assignment of two Senators to each state, the role given the states in administering even national elections, and the relatively few limitations on their lawmaking powers—establishes the geographical units as natural centers of administrative and political strength. Many clauses of the Constitution are not subject to the same latitude of interpretation as the commerce and tax clauses. The simple, clearly stated, unambiguous phrases—for example, the President "shall hold his office during the term of four years"—are subject to change only through the formal amendment process. Similar provisions exist with respect to the terms of Senators and Congressmen and the amendment process. All of them have the effect of retarding or restraining centralizing action of the federal government. The fixed terms of the President and members of Congress, for example, greatly impede the development of nationwide, disciplined political parties that almost certainly would have to precede continuous large-scale expansion of federal functions.

The constitutional restraints on the expansion of national authority are less important and less direct today than they were in 1879 or 1936. But to say that they are less important is not to say that they are unimportant.

The nation's politics reflect these decentralizing causes and add some of their own. The political parties of the United States are unique. They seldom perform the function that parties traditionally perform in other countries, the function of gathering together diverse strands of power and welding them into one. Except during the period of nominating and electing a President and for the essential but nonsubstantive business of organizing the houses of Congress, the American parties rarely coalesce power at all. Characteristically they do the reverse, serving as a canopy under which special and local interests are represented with little regard for anything that can be called a party program. National leaders are elected on a party ticket, but in Congress they must seek cross-party support if their leadership is to be effective. It is a rare President during rare periods who can produce legislation without facing the defection of substantial numbers of his own party. (Wilson could do this in the first session of the Sixty-Third Congress; but Franklin D. Roosevelt could not, even during the famous hundred days of 1933.) Presidents whose parties form the majority of the Congressional houses must still count heavily on support from the other party.

The parties provide the pivot on which the entire governmental system swings. Party operations, first of all, produce in legislation the basic division of functions between the federal government, on the one hand, and state and local governments, on the other. The Supreme Court's permissiveness with respect to the expansion of national powers has not in fact produced any considerable extension of exclusive federal functions. The body of federal law in all fields has remained, in the words of Henry M. Hart, Jr., and Herbert Wechsler, "interstitial in its nature," limited in objective and resting upon the principal body of legal relationships defined by state law. It is difficult to find any area of federal legislation that is not significantly affected by state law.

In areas of new or enlarged federal activity, legislation characteristically provides important roles for state and local governments. This is as true of Democratic as of Republican administrations and true even of functions for which arguments of efficiency would produce exclusive federal responsibility. Thus the unemployment compensation program of the New Deal and the airport program of President Truman's administration both provided important responsibilities for state governments. In both cases attempts to eliminate state participation were defeated by a cross-party coalition of pro-state votes and influence. A large fraction of the Senate is usually made up of ex-governors, and the membership of both houses is composed of men who know that their reelection depends less upon national leaders or national party organization than upon support from their home constituencies. State and local officials are key members of these constituencies, often central figures in selecting candidates and in turning out the vote. Under such circumstances, national legislation taking state and local views heavily into account is inevitable.

Second, the undisciplined parties affect the character of the federal system as a result of Senatorial and Congressional interference in federal administrative programs on behalf of local interests. Many aspects of the legislative involvement in administrative affairs are formalized. The Legislative Reorganization Act of 1946, to take only one example, provided that each of the standing committees "shall exercise continuous watchfulness" over administration of laws within its jurisdiction. But the formal system of controls, extensive as it is, does not compare in importance with the informal and extralegal network of relationships in producing continuous legislative involvement in administrative affairs.

Senators and Congressmen spend a major fraction of their time representing problems of their constituents before administrative agencies. An even larger fraction of Congressional staff time is devoted to the same task. The total magnitude of such "case work" operations is great. In one five-month period of 1943 the Office of Price Administration received a weekly average of 842 letters from members of Congress. If phone calls and personal contacts are added, each member of Congress on the average presented the OPA with a problem involving one of his constituents twice a day in each five-day work week. Data for less vulnerable agencies during less intensive periods are also impressive. In 1958, to take only one example, the Department of Agriculture estimated (and underestimated) that it received an average of 159 Congressional letters per working day. Special Congressional liaison staffs have been created to service this mass of business, though all higher officials meet it in one form or another. The Air Force in 1958 had, under the command of a major general, 137 people (55 officers and 82 civilians) working it its liaison office.

The widespread, consistent, and in many ways unpredictable character of legislative interference in administrative affairs has many consequences for the tone and character of American administrative behavior. From the perspective of this paper, the important consequence is the comprehensive, day-to-day, even hour-by-hour, impact of local views on national programs. No point of substance or procedure is immune from Congressional scrutiny. A substantial portion of the entire weight of this impact is on behalf of the state and local governments. It is a weight that can alter procedures for screening immigration applications, divert the course of a national highway, change the tone of an international negotiation, and amend a social security law to accommodate local practices or fulfill local desires.

The party system compels administrators to take a political role. This is a third way in which the parties function to decentralize the American system. The administrator must play politics for the same reason that the politician is able to play in administration: the parties are without program and without discipline.

In response to the unprotected position in which the party situation places him, the administrator is forced to seek support where he can find it. One ever-present task is to nurse the Congress of the United States, that crucial constituency which ultimately controls his agency's budget and program. From the administrator's view, a sympathetic consideration of Congressional request (if not downright submission to them) is the surest way to build the political support without which the administrative job could not continue. Even the completely task-oriented administrator must be sensitive to the need for Congressional support and to the relationship between case work requests, on one side, and budgetary and legislative support, on the other. "You do a good job handling the personal problems and requests of a Congressman," a White House officer said, "and you have an easier time convincing him to back your program." Thus there is an important link between the nursing of Congressional requests, requests that largely concern local matters, and the most comprehensive national programs. The administrator must accommodate to the former as a price of gaining support for the latter.

One result of administrative politics is that the administrative agency may become the captive of the nationwide interest group it serves or presumably regulates. In such cases no government may come out with effective authority: the winners are the interest groups themselves. But in a very large number of cases, states and localities also win influence. The politics of administration is a process of making peace with legislators who for the most part consider themselves the guardians of local interests. The political role of administrators therefore contributes to the power of states and localities in national programs.

Finally, the way the party system operates gives American politics their overall distinctive tone. The lack of party discipline produces an openness in the system that allows individuals, groups, and institutions (including state and local governments) to attempt to influence national policy at every step of the legislative-administrative process. This is the "multiple-crack" attribute of the American government. "Crack" has two meanings. It means not only many fissures or access points; it also means, less statically, opportunities for wallops or smacks at government.

If the parties were more disciplined, the result would not be a cessation of the process by which individuals and groups impinge themselves upon the central government. But the present state of the parties clearly allows for a far greater operation of the multiple crack than would be possible under the conditions of centralized party control. American interest groups exploit literally uncountable access points in the legislative-administrative process. If legislative lobbying, from committee stages to the conference committee, does not produce results, a Cabinet secretary is called. His immediate associates are petitioned. Bureau chiefs and their aides are hit. Field officers are put under pressure. Campaigns are instituted by which friends of the agency apply a secondary influence on behalf of the interested party. A conference with the President may be urged.

To these multiple points for bringing influence must be added the multiple voices of the influencers. Consider, for example, those in a small town who wish to have a federal action taken. The easy merging of public and private interest at the local level means that the influence attempt is made in the name of the whole community, thus removing it from political partisanship. The Rotary Club as well as the City Council, the Chamber of Commerce and the mayor, eminent citizens and political bosses—all are readily enlisted. If a conference in a Senator's office will expedite matters, someone on the local scene can be found to make such a conference possible and effective. If technical information is needed, technicians will supply it. State or national professional organizations of local officials, individual Congressmen and Senators, and not infrequently whole state delegations will make the local cause their own. Federal field officers, who service localities, often assume local views. So may elected and appointed state officers. Friendships are exploited, and political mortgages called due. Under these circumstances, national policies are molded by local action.

In summary, then, the party system functions to devolve power. The American parties, unlike any other, are highly responsive when directives move from the bottom to the top, highly unresponsive from top to bottom. Congressmen and Senators can rarely ignore concerted demands from their home constituencies; but no party leader can expect the same kind of response from those below, whether he be a President asking for Congressional support or a Congressman seeking aid from local or state leaders.

Any tightening of the party apparatus would have the effect of strengthening the central government. The four characteristics of the system, discussed above, would become less important. If control from the top were strictly applied, these hallmarks of American decentralization might entirely disappear. To be specific, if disciplined and program-oriented parties were achieved: (1) It would make far less likely legislation that takes heavily into account the desires and prejudices of the highly decentralized power groups and institutions of the country, including the state and local governments. (2) It would to a large extent prevent legislators, individually and collectively, from intruding themselves on behalf of non-national interests in national administrative programs. (3) It would put an end to the administrator's search for his own political support, a search that often results in fostering state, local, and other non-national powers. (4) It would dampen the process by which individuals and groups, including state and local political leaders, take advantage of multiple cracks to steer national legislation and administration in ways congenial to them and the institutions they represent.

Alterations of this sort could only accompany basic changes in the organization and style of politics which, in turn, presuppose fundamental changes at the parties' social base. The sharing of functions is, in fact, the sharing of power. To end this sharing process would mean the destruction of whatever measure of decentralization exists in the United States today.

V. Goals for the System of Sharing

The Goal of Understanding

Our structure of government is complex, and the politics operating that structure are mildly chaotic. Circumstances are ever-changing. Old institutions mask intricate procedures. The nation's history can be read with alternative glosses, and what is nearest at hand may be furthest from comprehension. Simply to understand the federal system is therefore a difficult task. Yet without understanding there is little possibility of producing desired changes in the system. Social structures and processes are relatively impervious to purposeful change. They also exhibit intricate interrelationships so that change induced at point "A" often produces unanticipated results at point "Z." Changes introduced into an imperfectly understood system are as likely to produce reverse consequences as the desired ones.

This is counsel of neither futility nor conservatism for those who seek to make our government a better servant of the people. It is only to say that the first goal for those setting goals with respect to the federal system is that of understanding it.

Two Kinds of Decentralization

The recent major efforts to reform the federal system have in large part been aimed at separating functions and tax sources, at dividing them between the federal government and the states. All of these attempts have failed. We can now add that their success would be undesirable.

It is easy to specify the conditions under which an ordered separation of functions could take place. What is principally needed is a majority political party, under firm leadership, in control of both Presidency and Congress, and, ideally but not necessarily, also in control of a number of states. The political discontinuities, or the absence of party links, (1) between the governors and their state legislatures, (2) between the President and the governors, and (3) between the President and Congress clearly account for both the picayune recommendations of the Federal-State Action Committee and for the failure of even those recommendations in Congress. If the President had been in control of Congress (that is, consistently able to direct a majority of House and Senate votes), this alone would have made possible some genuine separation and devolution of functions. The failure to decentralize by order is a measure of the decentralization of power in the political parties.

Stated positively, party centralization must precede governmental decentralization by order. But this is a slender reed on which to hang decentralization. It implies the power to centralize. A majority party powerful enough to bring about ordered decentralization is far more likely to choose in favor of ordered centralization. And a society that produced centralized national parties would, by that very fact, be a society prepared to accept centralized government.

Decentralization by order must be contrasted with the different kind of decentralization that exists in the United States. It may be called the decentralization of mild chaos. It exists because of the existence of dispersed power centers. This form of decentralization is less visible and less neat. It rests on no discretion of central authorities. It produces at times specific acts that many citizens may consider undesirable or evil. But power sometimes wielded even for evil ends may be desirable power. To those who find value in the dispersion of power, decentralization by mild chaos is infinitely more desirable than decentralization by order. The preservation of mild chaos is an important goal for the American federal system.

Oiling the Squeak Points

In a governmental system of genuinely shared responsibilities, disagreements inevitably occur. Opinions clash over proximate ends, particular ways of doing things become the subject of public debate, innovations are contested. These are not basic defects in the system. Rather, they are the system's energy-reflecting life blood. There can be no permanent "solutions" short of changing the system itself by elevating one partner to absolute supremacy. What can be done is to attempt to produce conditions in which conflict will not fester but be turned to constructive solutions of particular problems.

A long list of specific points of difficulty in the federal system can be easily identified. No adequate congressional or administrative mechanism exists to review the patchwork of grants in terms of national needs. There is no procedure by which to judge, for example, whether the national government is justified in spending so much more for highways than for education. The working force in some states is inadequate for the effective performance of some nationwide programs, while honest and not-so-honest graft frustrates efficiency in others. Some federal aid programs distort state budgets, and some are so closely supervised as to impede state action in meeting local needs. Grants are given for programs too narrowly defined, and overall programs at the state level consequently suffer. Administrative, accounting, and auditing difficulties are the consequence of the multiplicity of grant programs. City officials complain that the states are intrusive fifth wheels in housing, urban redevelopment, and airport building programs.

Some differences are so basic that only a demonstration of strength on one side or another can solve them. School desegregation illustrates such an issue. It also illustrates the correct solution (although not the most desirable method of reaching it): in policy conflicts of fundamental importance, touching the nature of democracy itself, the view of the whole nation must prevail. Such basic ends, however, are rarely at issue, and sides are rarely taken with such passion that loggerheads are reached. Modes of settlement can usually be found to lubricate the squeak points of the system.

A pressing and permanent state problem, general in its impact, is the difficulty of raising sufficient revenue without putting local industries at a competitive disadvantage or without an expansion of sales taxes that press hardest on the least wealthy. A possible way of meeting this problem is to establish a state-levied income tax that could be used as an offset for federal taxes. The maximum level of the tax which could be offset would be fixed by federal law. When levied by a state, the state collection would be deducted from federal taxes. But if a state did not levy the tax, the federal government would. An additional fraction of the total tax imposed by the states would be collected directly by the federal government and used as an equalization fund, that is, distributed among the less wealthy states. Such a tax would almost certainly be imposed by all states since not to levy it would give neither political advantage to its public leaders nor financial advantage to its citizens. The net effect would be an increase in the total personal and corporate income tax.

The offset has great promise for strengthening state governments. It would help produce a more economic distribution of industry. It would have obvious financial advantages for the vast majority of states. Since a large fraction of all state income is used to aid political subdivisions, the local governments would also profit, though not equally as long as cities are underrepresented in state legislatures. On the other hand, such a scheme will appear disadvantageous to some low-tax states which profit from the in-migration of industry (though it would by no means end all state-by-state tax differentials). It will probably excite the opposition of those concerned over governmental centralization, and they will not be assuaged by methods that suggest themselves for making both state and central governments bear the psychological impact of the tax. Although the offset would probably produce an across-the-board tax increase, wealthier persons, who are affected more by an income tax than by other levies, can be expected to join forces with those whose fear is centralization. (This is a common alliance and, in the nature of things, the philosophical issue rather than financial advantage is kept foremost.)

Those opposing such a tax would gain additional ammunition from the certain knowledge that federal participation in the scheme would lead to some federal standards governing the use of the funds. Yet the political strength of the states would keep these from becoming onerous. Indeed, inauguration of the tax offset as a means of providing funds to the states might be an occasion for dropping some of the specifications for existing federal grants. One federal standard, however, might be possible because of the greater representation of urban areas in the constituency of Congress and the President than in the constituency of state legislatures: Congress might make a state's participation in the offset scheme dependent upon a periodic reapportionment of state legislatures.

The income tax offset is only one of many ideas that can be generated to meet serious problems of closely meshed governments. The fate of all such schemes ultimately rests, as it should, with the politics of a free people. But much can be done if the primary technical effort of those concerned with improving the federal system were directed not at separating its interrelated parts but at making them work together more effectively. Temporary commissions are relatively inefficient in this effort, though they may be useful for making general assessments and for generating new ideas. The professional organizations of government workers do part of the job of continuously scrutinizing programs and ways and means of improving them. A permanent staff, established in the President's office and working closely with state and local officials, could also perform a useful and perhaps important role.

The Strength of the Parts

Whatever governmental "strength" or "vitality" may be, it does not consist of independent decision-making in legislation and administration. Federal-state interpenetration here is extensive. Indeed, a judgment of the relative domestic strength of the two planes must take heavily into account the influence of one on the other's decisions. In such an analysis the strength of the states (and localities) does not weigh lightly. The nature of the nation's politics makes federal functions more vulnerable to state influence than state offices are to federal influence. Many states, as the Kestnbaum Commission noted, live with "self-imposed constitutional limitations" that make it difficult for them to "perform all of the services that their citizens require." If this has the result of adding to federal responsibilities, the states' importance in shaping and administering federal programs eliminates much of the sting.

The geography of state boundaries, as well as many aspects of state internal organization, are the products of history and cannot be justified on any grounds of rational efficiency. Who, today, would create major governmental subdivisions the size of Maryland, Delaware, New Jersey, or Rhode Island? Who would write into Oklahoma's fundamental law an absolute state debt limit of $500,000? Who would design (to cite only the most extreme cases) Georgia's and Florida's gross underrepresentation of urban areas in both houses of the legislature?

A complete catalogue of state political and administrative horrors would fill a sizeable volume. Yet exhortations to erase them have roughly the same effect as similar exhortations to erase sin. Some of the worst inanities—for example, the boundaries of the states, themselves—are fixed in the national constitution and defy alteration for all foreseeable time. Others, such as urban underrepresentation in state legislatures, serve the overrepresented groups, including some urban ones, and the effective political organization of the deprived groups must precede reform.

Despite deficiencies of politics and organizations that are unchangeable or slowly changing, it is an error to look at the states as static anachronisms. Some of them—New York, Minnesota, and California, to take three examples spanning the country—have administrative organizations that compare favorably in many ways with the national establishment. Many more in recent years have moved rapidly towards integrated administrative departments, statewide budgeting, and central leadership. The others have models-in-existence to follow, and active professional organizations (led by the Council of State Governments) promoting their development. Slow as this change may be, the states move in the direction of greater internal effectiveness.

The pace toward more effective performance at the state level is likely to increase. Urban leaders, who generally feel themselves disadvantaged in state affairs, and suburban and rural spokesmen, who are most concerned about national centralization, have a common interest in this task. The urban dwellers want greater equality in state affairs, including a more equitable share of state financial aid; nonurban dwellers are concerned that city dissatisfactions should not be met by exclusive federal, or federal-local, programs. Antagonistic, rather than amiable, cooperation may be the consequence. But it is a cooperation that can be turned to politically effective measures for a desirable upgrading of state institutions.

If one looks closely, there is scant evidence for the fear of the federal octopus, the fear that expansion of central programs and influence threatens to reduce the states and localities to compliant administrative arms of the central government. In fact, state and local governments are touching a larger proportion of the people in more ways than ever before; and they are spending a higher fraction of the total national product than ever before. Federal programs have increased, rather than diminished, the importance of the governors; stimulated professionalism in state agencies; increased citizen interest and participation in government; and, generally, enlarged and made more effective the scope of state action.[2] It may no longer be true in any significant sense that the states and localities are "closer" than the federal government to the people. It is true that the smaller governments remain active and powerful members of the federal system.

Central Leadership: The Need for Balance

The chaos of party processes makes difficult the task of presidential leadership. It deprives the President of ready-made Congressional majorities. It may produce, as in the chairmen of legislative committees, power-holders relatively hidden from public scrutiny and relatively protected from presidential direction. It allows the growth of administrative agencies which sometimes escape control by central officials. These are prices paid for a wide dispersion of political power. The cost is tolerable because the total results of dispersed power are themselves desirable and because, where clear national supremacy is essential, in foreign policy and military affairs, it is easiest to secure.

Moreover, in the balance of strength between the central and peripheral governments, the central government has on its side the whole secular drift towards the concentration of power. It has on its side technical developments that make

---

[2]See the valuable report, *The Impact of Federal Grants-in-Aid on the Structure and Functions of State and Local Governments,* submitted to the Commission on Intergovernmental Relations by the Governmental Affairs Institute (Washington, 1955).

central decisions easy and sometimes mandatory. It has on its side potent purse powers, the result of superior tax-gathering resources. It has potentially on its side the national leadership capacities of the presidential office. The last factor is the controlling one, and national strength in the federal system has shifted with the leadership desires and capacities of the Chief Executive. As these have varied, so there has been an almost rhythmic pattern: periods of central strength put to use alternating with periods of central strength dormant.

Following a high point of federal influence during the early and middle years of the New Deal, the postwar years have been, in the weighing of central-peripheral strength, a period of light federal activity. Excepting the Supreme Court's action in favor of school desegregation, national influence by design or default has not been strong in domestic affairs. The danger now is that the central government is doing too little rather than too much. National deficiencies in education and health require the renewed attention of the national government. Steepening population and urbanization trend lines have produced metropolitan area problems that can be effectively attacked only with the aid of federal resources. New definitions of old programs in housing and urban redevelopment, and new programs to deal with air pollution, water supply, and mass transportation are necessary. The federal government's essential role in the federal system is that of organizing, and helping to finance, such nationwide programs.

The American federal system exhibits many evidences of the dispersion of power not only because of formal federalism but more importantly because our politics reflect and reinforce the nation's diversities-within-unity. Those who value the virtues of decentralization, which writ large are virtues of freedom, need not scruple at recognizing the defects of those virtues. The defects are principally the danger that parochial and private interests may not coincide with, or give way to, the nation's interest. The necessary cure for these defects is effective national leadership.

The centrifugal force of domestic politics needs to be balanced by the centripetal force of strong presidential leadership. Simultaneous strength at center and periphery exhibits the American system at its best, if also at its noisiest. The interests of both find effective spokesmen. States and localities (and private interest groups) do not lose their influence opportunities, but national policy becomes more than the simple consequence of successful, momentary concentrations of non-national pressures: it is guided by national leaders.

❖❖ The author of the following selection, as Director of the Office of Management and Budget and before that of the Congressional Budget Office, had wide experience in both the Executive branch and on Capitol Hill. From both vantage points she has had to deal with the Federal budget and the complex issues it presents. In the following selection she argues that the dominant role of the Federal Government in relation to the states must be reconsidered in light of new economic and political trends.

11

Alice M. Rivlin

THE CASE FOR RETHINKING FEDERALISM

❖❖❖❖❖❖❖

The argument about which functions should be exercised by the federal government and which by the states has been going on for more than two hundred years. There are no "right" answers. The prevailing view shifts with changing perceptions of the needs of the country and the relative competence and responsiveness of the states and the federal government.

Until the 1930s, the federal government had limited powers and spent relatively little money except in time of war. Government services were not as extensive as they are now, and most were performed by states and their localities. In this period of "dual federalism," the powers of the federal government and the states were viewed as separate and distinct, not overlapping. Then, over the half century between 1930 and 1980, Americans laid increasing responsibilities on the central government. All levels of government grew, but the power, functions, and budget of the federal government grew most rapidly.

Americans turned to Washington for two distinct sets of reasons. First, the collapse of the economy in the Great Depression convinced many people of the need for national institutions to strengthen the economy and deal with problems that states could not be expected to handle on their own. The federal government created social security, set up the unemployment insurance system, developed river basins to control flooding and produce power, supported agricultural prices, strengthened banking and credit systems, and began regulating many economic activities.

Second, activist and reformers turned to Washington, especially in the 1960s, out of frustration with the way states and localities were performing their traditional functions. Compared with the federal government, states had limited capacities and resources. Their staffs were unsophisticated and unprofessional. Their legislatures, dominated by rural members, were unresponsive to city dwellers and minorities. Many state governments were overtly racist. Hence the federal government enacted a range of programs designed to influence the level and nature of state spending in areas that had traditionally been states' responsibilities, such as education, job training, health services, waste treatment, and housing. Many federal grants bypassed states entirely and went directly to local governments, especially big cities.

The surge of federal activities had many positive results, but it also diffused accountability and directed the energies of reformers toward Washington. Citizens concerned about improving state and local services began joining national organizations to lobby for federal money, rather than working at the state or local level. States and localities, even universities, established Washington offices, hired consultants, and acquired expertise in federal grantsmanship.

The proliferation of federal programs, projects, offices, and agencies in so many parts of the country made the federal government increasingly unmanageable. It resembled a giant conglomerate that has acquired too many different kinds of businesses and cannot coordinate its own activities or manage them all effectively from central headquarters.

Then the reaction set in. The flood of federal funds for state and local government crested in the late 1970s and ebbed in the 1980s. Tax cuts and defense spending increases created a huge federal budget deficit that precluded new federal domestic activities. States and cities had to rely more on their own resources. Moreover, the perception of superior federal competence, which had propelled Washington into many traditionally state areas, faded. Reforms gave states stronger governors, more representative legislatures, and more professional and sophisticated civil servants. Meanwhile, the federal government lost some of its former luster. The savings and loan debacle and scandals in defense procurement and housing programs undermined the presumption that the federal government managed more effectively than the states. The intertwining of state and local responsibilities and the diffusion of accountability remained, however.

In the 1990s the United States faces an urgent need to revitalize its economy and to get its political system off dead center and functioning responsively again. There are at least four reasons to think that reraising the fundamental questions of federalism—which level of government should do what and where the revenues should come from—would help in meeting these challenges.

The Impact of Global Interdependence

The first reason is that dramatic changes in the world are radically altering the tasks facing national governments. Rapid advances in the technology of transportation, communications, and weaponry have shrunk distances and intertwined the United States with the rest of the world, intimately and irreversibly. Goods, services, money, and people are flowing easily across oceans and borders. So are economic, political, and environmental problems.

Global interdependence requires international cooperation to solve common problems and some delegation of sovereignty to supranational authorities. The Gulf war and growing nuclear capacity in developing nations leave no doubt that stronger international controls are needed on sophisticated weapons. The rapidly thinning ozone layer dramatizes the stake that all nations have in controlling harmful atmospheric emissions.

Despite its political appeal, isolationism is no longer a viable option. If the United States is to protect its own citizens and help shape a more habitable world, it must take an active part in international partnerships focused on everything from chemical weapons to acid rain to narcotics traffic. These partnerships are already demanding increasing attention from both the executive and legislative branches of the federal government.

Global interdependence creates a paradox for the U.S. government. On the one hand, since both the president and Congress will be spending greater time and energy on international affairs, domestic policy will get less attention in Washington. At the same time, global interdependence makes domestic policy more important than ever. The United States needs rising productivity, a skilled labor force, and modern physical capital, both public and private, if it is to generate the improved standard of living necessary not only to foster domestic well-being, but also to play an effective role in international partnerships. The added complexity of Washington's international role strengthens the case for sorting out domestic responsibilities more clearly. Washington cannot do everything and should not try. The states should take responsibility for a larger and more clearly defined segment of the domestic agenda.

Top-down and Bottom-up Reform

A second and more important reason for rethinking the division of responsibilities is that some of the policies needed to revitalize the American economy require bottom-up community effort that cannot be imposed from the top down. They require experimentation and adaptation to local and regional conditions, and that can come only from the state and local level, not from Washington.

Improving education will take bottom-up reform. Presidential speeches and photo opportunities, national testing and assessment, federally funded experimental schools, even new grants spent in accordance with federal guidelines, can make only marginal contributions to fixing the schools. Education in America will not improve significantly until states and communities decide they want better schools. Making education more effective will take parents who care, committed teachers, community support, and accountable school officials. An "education president" can help focus media attention on schooling, but he risks diluting state and local responsibility by implying that Washington can actually produce change.

The popular federal Head Start program demonstrates that preschool education helps children from poor families cope better in school. The negative legacy of Head Start, however, is that states and communities have come to believe that the responsibility for preschool education lies with Washington, not with them. Change would come more rapidly if concerned citizens, parents, and educators worked to improve their own preschools instead of lobbying Washington to allocate more funds for Head Start.

Street crime, drug use, and teenage pregnancy are all examples of problems that the federal government can deplore but cannot fix. A resurgence of community concern and effort is needed. Social services, housing, community development, and most infrastructure also must be carefully adapted to the needs of particular places. Federal grants can help defray the costs, but at the price of confusing the issue of who is responsible and who needs to take action.

On the other hand, there are important public functions that Washington performs well and state and local governments cannot address effectively. First, there are inherently central responsibilities, like national defense and foreign affairs, for which the federal government must represent and defend the interests of the country as a whole. Second, there are activities whose benefits clearly spill over state lines—such as air traffic control, basic scientific research, and prevention of river pollution or acid rain. Individual states have little incentive to undertake these programs because so much of the benefit would go to people in other states. Third, there are programs whose work-ability depends on having a uniform national system, such as social security.

Social security is perhaps the federal government's greatest domestic success. It is well administered and immensely popular. People are less resentful of social security taxes than other taxes, because they know what the money goes for and they expect benefits themselves. Because it involves tracking people over a lifetime, social security could not easily be handled by the states; too many people would move in and out of state systems and end up with conflicting and overlapping coverage.

The federal government is also best adapted to solving the double problem of controlling rapidly rising health costs and providing health insurance to the whole population. The U.S. health care system is the most expensive in the world, now consuming more than one-eighth of everything the nation produces, but it does not provide commensurate benefits. Millions of people are left out or inadequately insured. State-by-state efforts to expand insurance coverage and control medical costs are not likely to be successful. Sentiment is growing for some kind of national health insurance system that would provide universal coverage for basic health services and would control costs by setting reimbursement rates for doctors, hospitals, and other medical providers.

Another important role that the federal government is uniquely positioned to play at the moment is increasing national saving. Americans are saving by contributing to social security. The social security system is currently running significant annual surpluses because taxes collected exceed benefits paid out. These reserves will be needed to pay benefits to the large baby boom generation when its members retire. They ought to be used to help finance the productive investment needed to generate higher incomes in the future. At present, however, the social security surpluses are simply being lent to the rest of the government to offset part of the huge federal budget deficit. For the savings of working Americans to be used productively, the federal deficit must be eliminated.

The Need for More Tax Revenue

The third reason for focusing on the assignment of tasks to federal and state governments is that all levels of government are in serious financial difficulties. Even if some services are cut back and others are run more efficiently, more revenues are needed to eliminate deficits at the federal, state, and local levels, to accomplish the productivity agenda, and to reform health care financing. If taxes must go up, it is important to consider which level of government will make best use of the revenues.

The federal fiscal crisis. The federal budget deficit is the biggest single impediment to revitalizing the American economy. It diverts a large portion of America's inadequate supply of saving into financing the ongoing expenses of the government rather than productivity-enhancing investment. It puts upward pressure on interest rates and requires that a substantial share of federal tax revenues be devoted to debt service. It has paralyzed the federal government's ability to address new problems, at home and abroad, and weakened its ability to combat recession.

Despite more than a decade of efforts to reduce it, the federal deficit is definitely not withering away. To be sure, the recession and the savings and loan bailout combined to increase the deficit in 1991 and 1992 to levels that are not likely to continue. Even without these temporary upward pressures, however, the Congressional Budget Office (CBO) projects that the federal deficit will still be above $200 billion in 1996. Moreover, the CBO expects the deficit to rise significantly by the beginning of the next century if policies are not changed. Why would CBO expect the deficit to rise if tax and spending laws do not change? A big part of the answer is that the costs of medicare and medicaid are projected to keep going up faster than revenues if nothing is done to control medical care prices.

The unfortunate fact is that if the federal government retains its present portfolio of responsibilities (even with declining defense spending), it cannot balance the budget, much less get to surplus, *without raising taxes*. Even bigger tax hikes will be required if the federal government is to take on new responsibilities. The only option for eliminating the deficit without a significant federal revenue increase would be to count on the states for the productivity agenda and also to devolve big chunks of current federal responsibilities to the states. This would move the financing crisis from the federal to the state level.

The state fiscal crisis. Increasing the responsibilities of state and local governments is a dubious proposition because they too are in fiscal trouble. At first glance, their fiscal distress seems more temporary than that of the federal government. State and local governments generally suffer serious fiscal stress in recessions. Their revenues fall off as sales, income, and property values stop growing or decline while claims on their services continue to increase. Because, unlike the federal government, states and localities cannot normally borrow to cover operating expenses, they are forced to raise taxes and cut services as soon as their reserves are exhausted.

Even after the economy returns to moderate growth, however, there are reasons for pessimism about the prospects for state and local finance in the 1990s. The fiscal health of state and local governments declined in the second half of the 1980s. Pressures for spending outran revenues. The fiscal stress, especially in cities, reflected the growth in crime, drug addiction, AIDS, homelessness, and poverty, all of which continued to increase through the long recovery from the recession of the early 1980s. Moreover, a major villain of the federal budget drama appears again at the state and local level. Rising medical care costs, especially for medicaid, have put enormous pressure on state and local budgets that seems unlikely to abate.

Thus all levels of government will probably face continuing fiscal stress in the 1990s. Policies to revitalize the economy—increased public investment, a federal surplus, health financing reform—cannot be undertaken without more revenue at some level of government. The public seems angry and dissatisfied with government, however, and unwilling either to increase its support or to accept a lower level of services.

Dissatisfaction with Government

The fourth reason for questioning the jobs assigned to various levels of government in the 1990s is the American public's dissatisfaction with politics and politicians. Many Americans have "tuned out" political debate and stopped participating in elections. Polls reveal declining confidence in political leaders, rising skepticism that public officials care about the views of ordinary people, disgust at political campaigns, and cynicism about the democratic process.

There are many possible reasons for the disparagement of government: the need to blame someone for the stresses of a faltering economy, the influence of big money on political campaigns, the negativism of political advertising, and the insensitivity of politicians to the damage done to their collective image by even minor peccadillos such as getting parking tickets fixed. Some blame the ideological polarization of the major parties—the capture of the Republicans by ultraconservatives and the Democrats by extreme liberals—for leaving the pragmatic, middle-of-the-road majority without leadership. Others point to the widening gulf between elites, who see public policy as a matter of technical control, and a general public that correctly perceives the elites' contempt for citizens' opinions.

The blurring of state and federal roles contributes to cynicism about politics. For example, much of the rhetoric in the 1988 presidential campaign concerned issues over which presidents have little control—crime, drugs, education, child care, and industrial development. Voters care about these issues, but they also know that Washington is too remote from them to make a difference. Candidates for federal office undermine their credibility by implying these problems have national solutions and by refusing to address serious federal issues, such as the budget deficit.

Voters also appear more willing to pay taxes if they know that revenues will be used for identifiable services important to them. Polls show voters opposed to paying more taxes for undisclosed purposes but willing to pay for improved schools or increased environmental protection. In recent years the federal government's general revenues (other than social security and medicare payroll taxes) have declined as a percentage of GNP, while state and local revenues have increased substantially.

Perhaps taxpayers are clearer about their need for state and local services and are more willing to pay for them than for the more remote services of the federal government. Despite substantial increases in payroll taxes for social security and medicare in recent decades, polls show these taxes are less unpopular than the federal income tax, presumably because taxpayers know what the payroll taxes buy and value the benefits. Hence the most feasible way to increase revenue may be to earmark new taxes for a particular federal benefit such as health insurance or for improved services at the state and local level.

Proposals for the Future

This focus on federalism suggests several quite drastic proposals aimed at reenergizing the American economy and restoring confidence in the political system. Their basic theme is that the federal and state governments should divide the jobs to be done and get moving.

- *The productivity agenda.* The states should take charge of the primary public investment needed to increase productivity and raise incomes, especially to improve education and skill training and modernize infrastructure.
- *Devolution.* The federal government should eliminate most of its programs in education, housing, highways, social services, economic development, and job training.
- *Common shared taxes.* With federal blessing, or even the assistance of the federal government, states should strengthen their revenue systems by cooperating in collecting common taxes to be shared among them on a formula basis.
- *Health care financing.* The federal government should adopt a plan that will ensure basic health insurance coverage for everyone and control the increase in health costs.
- *Federal budget surplus.* The federal government should run a surplus in its whole budget (counting social security), thus reducing federal debt service costs and adding to the pool of saving available to finance private investment.

These proposals fit together. State responsibility for the productivity agenda would sharpen the distinction between federal and state tasks, making it easier for citizens to understand what each level of government does and to blame the right set of officials for poor performance. Devolution would take whole areas of public spending out of the federal budget, making it easier to move that budget toward surplus. More important, making clear that the devolved functions belong to the states, not the federal government, would transfer pressure for increased spending in these areas from Washington to state capitals and help keep federal deficits from recurring.

The resulting fiscal pressure on states and localities would be alleviated in two ways. First, federal responsibility for health care financing, coupled with strong cost controls, would relieve states and localities of the escalating burden of medicaid and reduce the cost of other public medical care. Second, the adoption of one or more common shared taxes would improve the states' collective revenue-raising capacity.

One example of a common shared tax would be a uniform state sales tax (or value-added tax) collected at the same rate on the same items and shared on the basis of population. A uniform corporation income tax, collected along with the federal income tax and shared on a formula basis, would make tax compliance simpler for multistate corporations. A common state energy tax could reduce pollution and promote conservation as well as raising revenue.

The idea of states sharing common taxes is a radical departure from the American tradition that each state must go it alone in levying taxes. In other federal systems, tax sharing is more usual. In Germany, for example, the central government collects most of the taxes and shares the proceeds with the *Länder* (states). German taxpayers, individual and corporate, fill out only one income tax return, for both federal and state taxes. German firms pay a value-added tax whose proceeds are shared between the federal government and the states, with disproportionate shares going to the least affluent states to help equalize services.

As the American economy becomes more national and international, the case for more coordination of state taxation increases. People, companies, sales, and services move with greater ease across borders. One consequence is that states and localities have to worry about keeping their tax rates from getting out of line with those of other jurisdictions. Another is that more and more companies, and even individuals, owe taxes in multiple jurisdictions. The resulting complexity is costly for both taxpayers and tax collectors.

Like federal grants, common shared taxes could be designed to improve the relative position of the least affluent states. Unlike federal grants, however, they would not cause confusion about which level of government has responsibility for particular programs or impose federal rules and guidelines on state and local authorities.

To revive the American dream, citizens must find new energy and commitment to revitalize the myriad institutions that influence American life—families, businesses, schools, unions, churches, clubs, and government at all levels. They must be willing to experiment, restructure, and try new approaches to old and new problems. In the words of David Osborne and Ted Gaebler, they must even "reinvent government" by breaking out of old hierarchical patterns and empowering those closest to the problems to participate in finding solutions.

A first step is to reexamine that peculiarly American institution, federalism. The current confusion of responsibilities between federal and state government is undermining confidence in government and impeding the implementation of policies needed to restore a healthy economy. Sorting out the roles more clearly could break the logjam, help both levels function more effectively, and improve both domestic and foreign policy.

Chapter 3

❖❖❖

CIVIL LIBERTIES AND CIVIL RIGHTS

Civil liberties and civil rights cover a very broad area. Among the most funda-mental civil liberties are those governing the extent to which individuals can speak, write, and read what they choose. The democratic process requires the free exchange of ideas. Constitutional government requires the protection of minority rights and, above all, the right to dissent.

The Nationalization of the Bill of Rights

It is clear from the debate over the inclusion of the Bill of Rights in the Consti-tution of 1787 that its provisions were certainly never intended to be prohibi-tions upon state action. The Bill of Rights was added to the Constitution to sat-isfy state governments that the same rights which they generally accorded to their own citizens under state constitutions would apply with respect to the national government, and act as a check upon abridgments by the national government of civil liberties and civil rights. Proponents of a separate bill of rights wanted specific provisions to limit the powers of the national govern-ment, which, *in its own sphere,* could act directly upon citizens of the state.

Article X, which is not so much a part of the Bill of Rights as an expression of the balance of authority that exists between the national government and the states in the Constitution, provides that "the powers not delegated to the United States by the Constitution, nor prohibited by it to the states are reserved to the states respectively or to the people." Under the federal system each member of the community is both (1) a citizen of the United States and (2) a citizen of the particular state in which he or she resides. The rights and obliga-tions of each citizenship class are determined by the legal divisions of authority set up in the Constitution. Apart from specific limits upon state power to abridge civil liberties and civil rights, as for example the prohibitions of Section 10 against state passage of any bills of attainder or ex post facto laws, there is nothing in the main body of the Constitution or the Bill of Rights that controls state action. Originally it was up to the states to determine the protections they would give to their own citizens against state actions. The applicability of the Bill of Rights to national action only was affirmed in *Barron* v. *Baltimore*, 7 Peters 243 (1833).

The adoption of the Fourteenth Amendment in 1868 potentially limited the discretion that the states had possessed to determine the civil liberties and rights of citizens within their sphere of authority. The Fourteenth Amendment provided that:

> 1. All persons born or naturalized in the United States, and subject to the jurisdiction thereof, are citizens of the United States and of the state wherein they reside. No state shall make or enforce any law which shall abridge the privileges or immunities of citizens of the United States; nor shall any state deprive any person of life, liberty, or property, without due process of law; nor deny to any person within its jurisdiction the equal protection of the laws. . . .
>
> 5. The Congress shall have power to enforce, by appropriate legislation, the provisions of this article.

Although the Fourteenth Amendment appeared to be a tough restriction upon state action, its provisions were equivocal and required clarification by the Supreme Court before they could take effect. The history of the Fourteenth Amendment suggested that it was designed to protect the legal and political rights of blacks against state encroachment, and was not to have a broader application. In the *Slaughterhouse Cases,* 16 Wallace 36 (1873), the Supreme Court held that the privileges and immunities clause of the Fourteenth Amendment did nothing to alter the authority of the states to determine the rights and obligations of citizens subject to state action. Under this doctrine the Bill of Rights could not be made applicable to the states.

It was not until *Gitlow* v. *New York*, 268 U.S. 652 (1925), that the Court finally announced that the substantive areas of freedom of speech and of press of the First Amendment are part of the "liberty" protected by the Fourteenth Amendment due process clause; however, in Gitlow's case the Court found that the procedures that had been used in New York to restrict his freedom of speech did not violate due process. In *Near* v. *Minnesota*, 283 U.S. 697 (1931), the Court for the first time overturned a state statute as a violation of the Fourteenth Amendment due process clause because it permitted prior censorship of the press. *Gitlow* and *Near* were limited because they incorporated only the freedom of speech and press provisions of the First Amendment under the due process clause of the Fourteenth Amendment. The cases marked the beginning of a slow and tedious process of "incorporation" of most of the provisions of the Bill of Rights as part of the due process clause of the Fourteenth Amendment. The process of incorporation did not begin in earnest until the Warren Court, and then not until the 1960s. By the late 1970s all of the Bill of Rights was incorporated as protections against state action, with the exceptions of the rights to grand jury indictment, trial by jury in *civil* cases, the right to bear arms, protection against excessive bail and fines, and protection against involuntary quartering of troops in private homes.[1]

The following case presents an example of incorporation of the right to counsel under the due process clause of the Fourteenth Amendment. In cases prior to *Gideon* v. *Wainwright*, decided in 1963, the Court had upheld an ad hoc right to counsel in individual cases. That is, it had held that the facts of a particular case warranted granting the right to counsel as part of due process under the Fourteenth Amendment for that particular case only. By such ad hoc determinations, the Court was able to exercise self-restraint in relation to federal-state relations, by not requiring a general right to counsel in all state criminal cases. *Powell* v. *Alabama*, 287 U.S. 45 (1932), was an example of such an ad hoc inclusion of the right to counsel in a specific case, where, in a one-day trial, seven black men had been convicted of raping two white girls, and sentenced to death. The Court held that under the circumstances of the case the denial of counsel by the Alabama courts to the defendants violated the due process clause of the Fourteenth Amendment. In *Powell*, however, the Court did not incorporate the right to counsel in all criminal cases under this due process clause. It only provided that "in a capital case, where the defendant is unable to employ counsel, and is incapable adequately of making his own defense because of ignorance, feeblemindedness, illiteracy, or the like, it is the duty of the court, whether requested or not, to assign counsel for him as a necessary requisite of due process of law. . . ." The *Powell* case was widely interpreted as nationalizing (incorporating) the right to counsel in all *capital* cases. The Court reaffirmed its refusal to incorporate the right to counsel in all criminal cases in *Betts* v. *Brady*, 316 U.S. 455 (1942). There the Court held that the Sixth Amendment applies only to trials in federal courts and that the right to counsel is not a fundamental right, essential to a fair trial, and therefore is not required in all cases under the due process clause of the Fourteenth Amendment. The Court emphasized that whether or not the right to counsel would be required depended upon the circumstances of the case in which it was requested.

In *Gideon* v. *Wainwright* the Court finally nationalized the right to counsel in all criminal cases under the due process clause of the Fourteenth Amendment. The case represented, in 1963, an important step in the progression toward nationalization of most of the Bill of Rights. While Justice Roberts, writing for the majority of the Court in the *Betts* case in 1942, found that the right to counsel was not fundamental to a fair trial, Justice Black, who had dissented in the Betts case, writing for the majority in *Gideon* v. *Wainwright* in 1962, held that the right to counsel was fundamental and essential to a fair trial and therefore was protected by the due process clause of the Fourteenth Amendment. In *Gideon*, Justice Black noted:

---

[1]For an excellent discussion of the incorporation of most of the Bill of Rights under the due process clause of the Fourteenth Amendment, see Henry J. Abraham, *Freedom and the Court*, 3d ed. (New York: Oxford University Press, 1977), chap. 3.

We accept the *Brady* assumption, based as it was on our prior cases, that a provision of the Bill of Rights which is "fundamental and essential to a fair trial" is made obligatory upon the states by the Fourteenth Amendment. We think the Court in *Betts* was wrong, however, in concluding that the Sixth Amendment's guarantee of counsel is not one of the fundamental rights.

The history of Supreme Court interpretation of the Fourteenth Amendment due process clause reveals the Court acting both politically and ideologically. In the period from 1868 to 1925 the Court was careful to exercise judicial self-restraint in interpreting the Fourteenth Amendment, in part because of the conservative views of most of the justices that the Court should not impose national standards of civil liberties and civil rights upon the states. The Court did not believe in self-restraint in all areas, as is demonstrated by its use of the due process clause of the Fourteenth Amendment to impose its own views on the proper relationship between the states and business. The Court read the Fourteenth Amendment due process clause in such a way as to protect the property interests of business against state regulation. Many such laws were found to be taking the liberty or property of business without due process. Beginning with *Gitlow* v. *New York* in 1925, the Court for the first time added substance to the due process clause of the Fourteenth Amendment in the area of civil liberties by including First Amendment freedoms of speech and press as part of the "liberty" of the due process clause.

While the Supreme Court is sensitive to the political environment in which it functions, the ways in which it has interpreted the due process clause of the Fourteenth Amendment suggest that ideological convictions are more important than pressure from political majorities. During the era of economic substantive due process under the Fourteenth Amendment, which ended in 1937, the Court was really taking an elitist position that did not agree with the political majorities in many states that were behind the regulatory laws that the Court struck down. Nor can it be said that when the Court began to add substance in civil liberties and civil rights to the due process clause and extend procedural protection that it was supported by political majorities. In fact, the Warren Court's extension of the Fourteenth Amendment due process clause, particularly in the area of criminal rights, caused a political outcry among the states and their citizens who felt that law enforcement efforts would be unduly impeded. When the Court, in *Griswold* v. *Connecticut* in 1965, went beyond the explicit provisions of the Bill of Rights to find a right of privacy to strike down Connecticut's birth control statute that prevented the use of contraceptives in the state, even Justice Black, a strong supporter of incorporating the Bill of Rights under the due process clause, took objection. He found in the *Griswold* decision a return to substantive due process in a form that was unacceptable, because it was adding substance to the clause that was not explicitly provided for in the intent of the Fourteenth Amendment, which he had held in *Adamson* v. *California* in 1946 to be total inclusion of the Bill of Rights. The *Griswold* decision was not unpopular politically, but when the Court in *Roe* v. *Wade* in 1973 used the right of privacy to strike down a Texas abortion statute, and in effect declare all state laws that absolutely prohibited abortion to be unconstitutional, a nationwide antiabortion movement was organized to overturn the decision by mobilizing political support behind a constitutional amendment. The Supreme Court has certainly not, in the area of interpretation of the Fourteenth Amendment, acted solely out of political motives.[2]

The following case presents an example of the way in which the Supreme Court gradually incorporated the Bill of Rights under the Fourteenth Amendment. Behind the decision to nationalize the right to counsel in *Gideon* v. *Wainwright* a fascinating series of events had occurred.[3] By the time the *Gideon* case was called up the Court was purposely looking for an appropriate case from which it could incorporate the right to counsel under the due process clause of the Fourteenth Amendment. The Court felt that Gideon's case presented the kind of circumstances that would be publicly accepted as requiring the right to counsel to ensure fairness. In granting certiorari to Gideon's *in forma pauperis* petition ("in the manner of the pauper," a permission to sue without incurring liability for costs) the Court had in effect already made up its mind about the decision. By the appointment of attorney Abe Fortas, later to become a member of the Court (although eventually forced to resign because of conflict-of-interest charges), one of the most distinguished lawyers in the country, the Court guaranteed an eloquent and persuasive brief for the petitioner, Earl Gideon. The Court felt that the right to counsel was a right whose time had come by 1963.

12

GIDEON V. WAINWRIGHT
372 U.S. 335 (1963)

❖❖❖❖❖❖❖

. . . Mr. Justice Black delivered the opinion of the Court, saying in part:

Petitioner was charged in a Florida state court with having broken and entered a poolroom with intent to commit a misdemeanor. This offense is a felony under Florida law. Appearing in court without funds and without a lawyer, petitioner asked the court to appoint counsel for him, whereupon the following colloquy took place:

---

[2]The forces affecting Supreme Court decision making are discussed in the selections by William J. Brennan, Jr., and John P. Roche in Chapter 9.

[3]The story of the case is brilliantly told by Anthony Lewis, in *Gideon's Trumpet* (New York: Random House, 1964).

In this selection some footnotes are omitted: all are renumbered.

The COURT: Mr. Gideon, I am sorry, but I cannot appoint Counsel to represent you in this case. Under the laws of the State of Florida, the only time the Court can appoint Counsel to represent a Defendant is when that person is charged with a capital offense. I am sorry, but I will have to deny your request to appoint Counsel to defend you in this case.

The DEFENDANT: The United States Supreme Court says I am entitled to be represented by Counsel.

Put to trial before a jury, Gideon conducted his defense about as well as could be expected from a layman. He made an opening statement to the jury, cross-examined the State's witnesses, presented witnesses in his own defense, declined to testify himself, and made a short argument "emphasizing his innocence to the charge contained in the Information filed in this case." The jury returned a verdict of guilty, and petitioner was sentenced to serve five years in the state prison. Later, petitioner filed in the Florida Supreme Court this habeas corpus petition attacking his conviction and sentence on the ground that the trial court's refusal to appoint counsel for him denied him rights "guaranteed by the Constitution and the Bill of Rights by the United States Government."[1] Treating the petition for habeas corpus as properly before it, the State Supreme Court, "upon consideration thereof" but without an opinion, denied all relief. Since 1942, when *Betts v. Brady*, 316 U.S. 455 . . . was decided by a divided Court, the problem of a defendant's federal constitutional right to counsel in a state court has been a continuing source of controversy and litigation in both state and federal courts. To give this problem another review here, we granted certiorari. 370 U.S. 908. . . . Since Gideon was proceeding *in forma pauperis*, we appointed counsel to represent him and requested both sides to discuss in their briefs and oral arguments the following: "Should this Court's holding in *Betts v. Brady* . . . be reconsidered?"

I

The facts upon which Betts claimed that he had been unconstitutionally denied the right to have counsel appointed to assist him are strikingly like the facts upon which Gideon here bases his federal constitutional claim. Betts was indicted for robbery in a Maryland state court. On arraignment, he told the trial judge of his lack of funds to hire a lawyer and asked the court to appoint one for him. Betts was advised that it was not the practice in that county to appoint counsel for indigent defendants except in murder and rape cases. He then pleaded not guilty, had witnesses summoned, cross-examined the State's witnesses, examined his own, and chose not to testify himself. He was found guilty by the judge, sitting without a jury, and sentenced to eight years in prison. Like Gideon, Betts sought release by habeas corpus, alleging that he had been denied the right to assistance of counsel in violation of the Fourteenth Amendment. Betts was denied any relief, and on review this

---

[1]Later in the petition for habeas corpus, signed and apparently prepared by the petitioner himself, he stated, "I, Clarence Earl Gideon, claim that I was denied the rights of the 4th, 5th and 14th amendments of the Bill of Rights."

Court affirmed. It was held that a refusal to appoint counsel for an indigent defendant charged with a felony did not necessarily violate the Due Process Clause of the Fourteenth Amendment, which for reasons given the Court deemed to be the only applicable federal constitutional provision. The Court said:

> Asserted denial [of due process] is to be tested by an appraisal of the totality of facts in a given case. That which may, in one setting, constitute a denial of fundamental fairness, shocking to the universal sense of justice, may, in other circumstances, and in the light of other considerations, fall short of such denial. 316 U.S., at 462. . . .

Treating due process as "a concept less rigid and more fluid than those envisaged in other specific and particular provisions of the Bill of Rights," the Court held that refusal to appoint counsel under the particular facts and circumstances in the Betts case was not so "offensive to the common and fundamental ideas of fairness" as to amount to a denial of due process. Since the facts and circumstances of the two cases are so nearly indistinguishable, we think the *Betts* v. *Brady* holding if left standing would require us to reject Gideon's claim that the Constitution guarantees him the assistance of counsel. Upon full reconsideration we conclude that *Betts* v. *Brady* should be overruled.

II

The Sixth Amendment provides, "In all criminal prosecutions, the accused shall enjoy the right . . . to have the Assistance of Counsel for his defence." We have construed this to mean that in federal courts counsel must be provided for defendants unable to employ counsel unless the right is competently and intelligently waived. Betts argued that this right is extended to indigent defendants in state courts by the Fourteenth Amendment. In response the Court stated that, while the Sixth Amendment laid down "no rule for the conduct of the states, the question recurs whether the constraint laid by the amendment upon the national courts expresses a rule so fundamental and essential to a fair trial, and so, to due process of law, that it is made obligatory upon the states by the Fourteenth Amendment." 316 U.S., at 465. . . . In order to decide whether the Sixth Amendment's guarantee of counsel is of this fundamental nature, the Court in Betts set out and considered "[r]elevant data on the subject . . . afforded by constitutional and statutory provisions subsisting in the colonies and the states prior to the inclusion of the Bill of Rights in the national Constitution, and in the constitutional, legislative, and judicial history of the states to the present date." 316 U.S., at 465. . . . On the basis of this historical data the Court concluded that "appointment of counsel is not a fundamental right, essential to a fair trial." 316 U.S., at 471. . . . It was for this reason the Betts Court refused to accept the contention that the Sixth Amendment's guarantee of counsel for indigent federal defendants was extended to or, in the words of that Court, "made obligatory upon the states by the Fourteenth Amendment." Plainly, had the Court concluded that appointment of counsel for an indigent criminal defendant was "a fundamental right, essential to a fair trial," it would have held that the Fourteenth Amendment requires appointment of counsel in a state court, just as the Sixth Amendment requires in a federal court.

We think the Court in Betts had ample precedent for acknowledging that those guarantees of the Bill of Rights which are fundamental safeguards of liberty immune from federal abridgment are equally protected against state invasion by the Due Process Clause of the Fourteenth Amendment. This same principle was recognized, explained, and applied in *Powell* v. *Alabama*, 287 U.S. 45 (1932), a case upholding the right of counsel, where the Court held that despite sweeping language to the contrary in *Hurtado* v. *California*, 110 U.S. 516 (1884), the Fourteenth Amendment "embraced" those "fundamental principles of liberty and justice which lie at the base of all our civil and political institutions," even though they had been "specifically dealt with in another part of the Federal Constitution." 287 U.S., at 67. . . . In many cases other than Powell and Betts, this Court has looked to the fundamental nature of original Bill of Rights guarantees to decide whether the Fourteenth Amendment makes them obligatory on the States. Explicitly recognized to be of this "fundamental nature" and therefore made immune from state invasion by the Fourteenth, or some part of it, are the First Amendment's freedoms of speech, press, religion, assembly, association, and petition for redress of grievances. For the same reason, though not always in precisely the same terminology, the Court has made obligatory on the States the Fifth Amendment's command that private property shall not be taken for public use without just compensation, the Fourth Amendment's prohibition of unreasonable searches and seizures, and the Eighth's ban on cruel and unusual punishment. On the other hand, this Court in *Palko* v. *Connecticut*, 301 U.S. 319 . . . (1937), refused to hold that the Fourteenth Amendment made the double jeopardy provision of the Fifth Amendment obligatory on the States. In so refusing, however, the Court, speaking through Mr. Justice Cardozo, was careful to emphasize that "immunities that are valid as against the federal government by force of the specific pledges of particular amendments have been found to be implicit in the concept of ordered liberty, and thus, through the Fourteenth Amendment, become valid as against the states" and that guarantees "in their origin . . . effective against the federal government alone" had by prior cases "been taken over from the earlier articles of the Federal Bill of Rights and brought within the Fourteenth Amendment by a process of absorption." 302 U.S., at 324–325, 326. . . .

We accept *Betts* v. *Brady's* assumption, based as it was on our prior cases, that a provision of the Bill of Rights which is "fundamental and essential to a fair trial" is made obligatory upon the States by the Fourteenth Amendment. We think the Court in Betts was wrong, however, in concluding that the Sixth Amendment's guarantee of counsel is not one of these fundamental rights. Ten years before *Betts* v. *Brady*, this Court, after full consideration of all the historical data examined in Betts, had unequivocally declared that "the right to the aid of counsel is of this fundamental character." *Powell* v. *Alabama*, 287 U.S. 45 . . . (1932). While the Court at the close of its Powell opinion did by its language, as this Court frequently does, limit its holding to the particular facts and circumstances of that case, its conclusions about the fundamental nature of the right to counsel are unmistakable. Several years later, in 1936, the Court reemphasized what it had said about the fundamental nature of the right to counsel in this language:

We concluded that certain fundamental rights, safeguarded by the first eight amendments against federal action, were also safeguarded against state action by the due process of law clause of the Fourteenth Amendment, and among them the fundamental right of the accused to the aid of counsel in a criminal prosecution. *Grosjean v. American Press Co.*, 297 U.S. 233 . . . (1936).

And again in 1938 this Court said:

[The assistance of counsel] is one of the safeguards of the Sixth Amendment deemed necessary to insure fundamental human rights of life and liberty. . . . The Sixth Amendment stands as a constant admonition that if the constitutional safeguards it provides be lost, justice will not 'still be done.' *Johnson v. Zerbst*, 304 U.S. 458 . . . (1938). To the same effect, see *Avery v. Alabama*, 308 U.S. 444 . . . (1940), and *Smith v. O'Grady*, 312 U.S. 329 . . . (1941).

In light of these and many other prior decisions of this Court, it is not surprising that the Betts Court, when faced with the contention that "one charged with crime, who is unable to obtain counsel, must be furnished counsel by the state," conceded that "[e]xpressions in the opinions of this court lend color to the argument . . ." 316 U.S., at 462–463. . . . The fact is that in deciding as it did—that "appointment of counsel is not a fundamental right, essential to a fair trial"—the Court in *Betts* v. *Brady* made an abrupt break with its own well-considered precedents. In returning to these old precedents, sounder we believe than the new, we but restore constitutional principles established to achieve a fair system of justice. Not only these precedents but also reason and reflection require us to recognize that in our adversary system of criminal justice, any person haled into court, who is too poor to hire a lawyer, cannot be assured a fair trial unless counsel is provided for him. This seems to us to be an obvious truth. Governments, both state and federal, quite properly spend vast sums of money to establish machinery to try defendants accused of crime. Lawyers to prosecute are everywhere deemed essential to protect the public's interest in an orderly society. Similarly, there are few defendants charged with crime, few indeed, who fail to hire the best lawyers they can get to prepare and present their defenses. That government hires lawyers to prosecute and defendants who have the money hire lawyers to defend are the strongest indications of the widespread belief that lawyers in criminal courts are necessities, not luxuries. The right of one charged with crime to counsel may not be deemed fundamental and essential to fair trials in some countries, but it is in ours. From the very beginning, our state and national constitutions and laws have laid great emphasis on procedural and substantive safeguards designed to assure fair trials before impartial tribunals in which every defendant stands equal before the law. This noble ideal cannot be realized if the poor man charged with crime has to face his accusers without a lawyer to assist him. A defendant's need for a lawyer is nowhere better stated than in the moving words of Mr. Justice Sutherland in *Powell* v. *Alabama*:

The right to be heard would be, in many cases, of little avail if it did not comprehend the right to be heard by counsel. Even the intelligent and educated layman has small and sometimes no skill in the science of law. If charged with crime, he is incapable, generally, of determining for himself whether the indictment is good or bad. He is unfamiliar with the rules of evidence. Left without the aid of counsel he may be put on trial without a proper charge, and convicted upon incompetent evidence, or evidence irrelevant to the issue or other wise inadmissible. He lacks both the skill and knowledge adequately to prepare his defense, even though he have a perfect one. He requires the guiding hand of counsel at every step in the proceedings against him. Without it, though he be not guilty, he faces the danger of conviction because he does not know how to establish his innocence. 287 U.S., at 68–69. . . .

The Court in *Betts* v. *Brady* departed from the second wisdom upon which the Court's holding in *Powell* v. *Alabama* rested. Florida, supported by two other States, has asked that *Betts* v. *Brady* be left intact. Twenty-two States, as friends of the Court, argue that Betts was "an anachronism when handed down" and that it should now be overruled. We agree.

The judgment is reversed and the cause is remanded to the Supreme Court of Florida for further action not inconsistent with this opinion.

Reversed.

Chief Justice Warren, and Justices Brennan, Stewart, White, and Goldberg join in the opinion of the Court.

Mr. Justice Douglas joins the opinion, giving a brief historical resume of the relation between the Bill of Rights and the Fourteenth Amendment. Mr. Justice Clark concurs in the result. Mr. Justice Harlan concurs in the result.

❖❖ FREEDOM OF SPEECH AND PRESS

There are many reasons why we should support freedom of speech and press. One of these is the impossibility of proving the existence of an Absolute Truth. No person or group can be infallible. The "best" decisions are those that are made on the basis of the most widespread information available pertaining to the subject at hand. Freedom of information is an integral part of the democratic process. In this selection from John Stuart Mill's famous essay *On Liberty,* published in 1859, the justifications for permitting liberty of speech and press are discussed.

13

John Stuart Mill

LIBERTY OF THOUGHT
AND DISCUSSION

❖❖❖❖❖❖❖

The time, it is to be hoped, is gone by when any defense would be necessary of the "liberty of the press" as one of the securities against corrupt or tyrannical government. No argument, we may suppose, can now be needed, against permitting a legislature or an executive, not identified in interest with the people, to prescribe opinions to them, and determine what doctrines or what arguments they shall be allowed to hear. This aspect of the question, besides, has been so often and so triumphantly enforced by preceding writers, that it needs not be specially insisted on in this place. Though the law of England, on the subject of the press, is as servile to this day as it was in the time of the Tudors, there is little danger of its being actually put in force against political discussion, except during some temporary panic, when fear of insurrection drives ministers and judges from their propriety; and, speaking generally, it is not, in constitutional countries, to be apprehended, that the government, whether completely responsible to the people or not, will often attempt to control the expression of opinion, except when in doing so it makes itself the organ of the general intolerance of the public. Let us suppose, therefore, that the government is entirely at one with the people, and never thinks of exerting any power of coercion unless in agreement with what it conceives to be their voice. But I deny the right of the people to exercise such coercion, either by themselves or by their government. The power itself is illegitimate. The best government has no more title to it than the worst. It is as noxious, or more noxious, when exerted in accordance with public opinion, than when in opposition to it. If all mankind minus one, were of one opinion, and only one person were of the contrary opinion, mankind would be no more justified in silencing that one person, than he, if he had the power, would be justified in silencing mankind. Were an opinion a personal possession of no value except to the owner; if to be obstructed in the enjoyment of it were simply a private injury, it would make some difference whether the injury was inflicted only on a few persons or on many. But the peculiar evil of silencing the expression of an opinion is, that it is robbing the human race; posterity as well as the existing generation; those who dissent from the opinion, still more than those who hold it. If the opinion is right, they are deprived of the opportunity of exchanging error for truth: if wrong, they lose, what is almost as great a benefit, the clearer perception and livelier impression of truth, produced by its collision with error.

It is necessary to consider separately these two hypotheses, each of which has a distinct branch of the argument corresponding to it. We can never be sure that the opinion we are endeavoring to stifle is a false opinion; and if we were sure, stifling it would be an evil still.

First: the opinion which it is attempted to suppress by authority may possibly be true. Those who desire to suppress it, of course deny its truth; but they are not infallible. They have no authority to decide the question for all mankind, and exclude every other person from the means of judging. To refuse a hearing to an opinion, because they are sure that it is false, is to assume that *their* certainty is the same thing as *absolute* certainty. All silencing of discussion is an assumption of infallibility. Its condemnation may be allowed to rest on this common argument, not the worse for being common.

Unfortunately for the good sense of mankind, the fact of their fallibility is far from carrying the weight in their practical judgment, which is always allowed to it in theory; for while every one well knows himself to be fallible, few think it necessary to take any precautions against their own fallibility, or admit the supposition that any opinion, of which they feel very certain, may be one of the examples of the error to which they acknowledge themselves to be liable. Absolute princes, or others who are accustomed to unlimited deference, usually feel this complete confidence in their own opinions on nearly all subjects. People more happily situated, who sometimes hear their opinions disputed, and are not wholly unused to be set right when they are wrong, place the same unbounded reliance only on such of their opinions as are shared by all who surround them, or to whom they habitually defer: for in proportion to a man's want of confidence in his own solitary judgment, does he usually repose, with implicit trust, on the infallibility of "the world" in general. And the world, to each individual, means the part of it with which he comes in contact; his party, his sect, his church, his class of society: the man may be called, by comparison, almost liberal and largeminded to whom it means anything so comprehensive as his own country or his own age. Nor is his faith in this collective authority at all shaken by his being aware that other ages, countries, sects, churches, classes, and parties have thought, and even now think, the exact reverse. He devolves upon his own world the responsibility of being in the right against the dissentient worlds of other people; and it never troubles him that mere accident has decided which of these numerous worlds is the object of his reliance, and that the same causes which make him a Churchman in London, would have made him a Buddhist or a Confucian in Peking. Yet it is as evident in itself, as any amount of argument can make it, that ages are not more infallible than individuals; every age having held many opinions which subsequent ages have deemed not only false but absurd; and it is as certain that many opinions, now general, will be rejected by future ages, as it is that many, once general, are rejected by the present.

The objection likely to be made to this argument, would probably take some such form as the following. There is no greater assumption of infallibility in forbidding the propagation of error, than in any other thing which is done by public authority on its own judgment and responsibility. Judgment is given to men that they may use it. Because it may be used erroneously, are men to be told that they ought not to use it at all? To prohibit what they think pernicious, is not claiming exemption from error, but fulfilling the duty incumbent on them, although fallible, of acting on their conscientious conviction. If we were never to act on our opinions, because those opinions may be wrong, we should leave all our interests uncared for, and all our duties unperformed. An objection which applies to all conduct, can be no valid objection to any conduct in particular. It is the duty of governments, and of individuals, to form the truest opinions they can; to form them carefully, and never impose them upon others unless they are quite sure of being right. But when they are sure (such reasoners may say), it is not conscientiousness but cowardice to shrink from acting on their opinions, and allow doctrines which they honestly think dangerous to the welfare of mankind, either in this life or in another, to be scattered abroad without restraint, because other people, in less enlightened times, have persecuted opinions now believed to be true. Let us take care, it may be said, not to make the same mistake: but governments and nations have made mistakes in other things, which are not denied to be fit subjects for the exercise of authority: they have laid on bad taxes, made unjust wars. Ought we therefore to lay on no taxes, and, under whatever provocation, make no wars? Men, and governments, must act to the best of their ability. There is no such thing as absolute certainty, but there is assurance sufficient for the purposes of human life. We may, and must, assume our opinion to be true for the guidance of our own conduct: and it is assuming no more when we forbid bad men to pervert society by the propagation of opinions which we regard as false and pernicious.

I answer, that it is assuming very much more. There is the greatest difference between presuming an opinion to be true, because, with every opportunity for contesting it, it had not been refuted, and assuming its truth for the purpose of not permitting its refutation. Complete liberty of contradicting and disproving our opinion, is the very condition which justifies us in assuming its truth for purposes of action; and on no other terms can a being with human faculties have any rational assurance of begin right.

When we consider either the history of opinion, or the ordinary conduct of human life, to what is it to be ascribed that the one and the other are no worse than they are? Not certainly to the inherent force of the human understanding; for, on any matter not self-evident, there are ninety-nine persons totally incapable of judging of it, for one who is capable; and the capacity of the hundredth person is only comparative; for the majority of the eminent men of every past generation held many opinions now known to be erroneous, and did or approved numerous things which no one will now justify. Why is it, then, that there is on the whole a preponderance among mankind of rational opinions and rational conduct? If there really is this preponderance—which there must be, unless human affairs are, and have always been, in an almost desperate state—it is owing to a quality of the human mind, the source of everything respectable in man either as an intellectual or as a moral being, namely, that his errors are corrigible. He is capable of rectifying his mistakes, by discussion and experience. Not by experience alone. There must be discussion, to show how experience is to be interpreted. Wrong opinions and practices gradually yield to fact and argument: but facts and arguments, to produce any effect on the mind, must be brought before it. Very few facts are able to tell their own story, without comments to bring out their meaning. The whole strength and value, then, of human judgment, depending on the one property, that it can be set right when it is wrong, reliance can be placed on it only when the means of setting it right are kept constantly at hand. In the case of any person whose judgment is really deserving of confidence, how has it become so? Because he has kept his mind open to criticism of his opinions and conduct. Because it has been his practice to listen to all that could be said against him; to profit by as much of it as was just, and expound to himself, and upon occasion to others, the fallacy of what was fallacious. Because he has felt, that the only way in which a human being can make some approach to knowing the whole of a subject, is by hearing what can be said about it by persons of every variety of opinion, and studying all modes in which it can be looked at by every character of mind. No wise man ever acquired his wisdom in any mode but this; nor is it in the nature of human intellect to become wise in any other manner. The steady habit of correcting and completing his own opinion by collating it with those of others, so far from causing doubt and hesitation in carrying it into practice, is the only stable foundation for a just reliance on it: for, being cognizant of all that can, at least obviously, be said against him, and having taken up his position against all gainsayers—knowing that he has sought for objections and difficulties, instead of avoiding them, and has shut out no light which can be thrown upon the subject from any quarter—he has a right to think his judgment better than that of any person, or any multitude, who have not gone through a similar process.

It is not too much to require that what the wisest of mankind, those who are best entitled to trust their own judgment, find necessary to warrant their relying on it, should be submitted to by that miscellaneous collection of a few wise and many foolish individuals, called the public. The most intolerant of churches, the Roman Catholic Church, even at the canonization of a saint, admits, and listens patiently to, a "devil's advocate." The holiest of men, it appears, cannot be admitted to posthumous honors, until all that the devil could say against him is known and weighed. If even the Newtonian philosophy were not permitted to be questioned, mankind could not feel as complete assurance of its truth as they now do. The beliefs which we have most warrant for, have no safeguard to rest on, but a standing invitation to the whole world to prove them unfounded. . . .

We have now recognized the necessity to the mental well-being of mankind (on which all their other well-being depends) of freedom of opinion, and freedom of the expression of opinion, on four distinct grounds; which we will now briefly recapitulate.

First, if any opinion is compelled to silence, that opinion may, for aught we can certainly know, be true. To deny this is to assume our own infallibility.

Secondly, though the silenced opinion be an error, it may, and very commonly does, contain a portion of truth; and since the general or prevailing opinion on any subject is rarely or never the whole truth, it is only by the collision of adverse opinions that the remainder of the truth has any chance of begin supplied.

Thirdly, even if the received opinion be not only true, but the whole truth; unless it is suffered to be, and actually is, vigorously and earnestly contested, it will, by most of those who receive it, be held in the manner of a prejudice, with little comprehension of feeling of its rational grounds. And not only this, but fourthly, the meaning of the doctrine itself will be in danger of being lost, or enfeebled, and deprived of its vital effect on the character and conduct: the dogma becoming a mere formal profession, inefficacious for good, but cumbering the ground, and preventing the growth of any real and heartfelt conviction from reason or personal experience.

Before quitting the subject of freedom of opinion, it is fit to take some notice of those who say, that the free expression of all opinions should be permitted, on condition that the manner be temperate, and do not pass the bounds of fair discussion. Much might be said on the impossibility of fixing where these supposed bounds are to be placed; for if the test be offence to those whose opinion is attacked, I think experience testifies that this offence is given whenever the attack is telling and powerful, and that every opponent who pushes them hard, and whom they find it difficult to answer, appears to them, if he shows any strong feeling on the subject, an intemperate opponent. But this, though an important consideration in a practical point of view, merges in a more fundamental objection. Undoubtedly the manner of asserting an opinion, even though it be a true one, may be very objectionable, and may justly incur severe censure. But the principal offences of the kind are such as it is mostly impossible, unless by accidental self-betrayal, to bring home to conviction. The gravest of them is, to argue sophistically, to suppress facts or arguments, to misstate the elements of the case, or misrepresent the opposite opinion. But all this, even to the most aggravated degree, is so continually done in perfect good faith, by persons who are not considered, and in many other respects may not deserve to be considered, ignorant or incompetent, that it is rarely possible on adequate grounds conscientiously to stamp the misrepresentation as morally culpable; and still less could law presume to interfere with this kind of controversial misconduct. With regard to what is commonly meant by intemperate discussion, namely, invective, sarcasm, personality, and the like, the denunciation of these weapons would deserve more sympathy if it were ever proposed to interdict them equally to both sides; but it is only desired to restrain the employment of them against the prevailing opinion: against the unprevailing they may not only be used without general disapproval, but will be likely to obtain for him who uses them the praise of honest zeal and righteous indignation. Yet whatever mischief arises from their use, is greatest when they are employed against the comparatively defenceless; and whatever unfair advantage can be derived by any opinion from this mode of asserting it, accrues almost exclusively to received opinions. The worst offence of this kind which can be committed by a polemic, is to stigmatize those who hold the contrary opinion as bad and immoral men. To calumny of this sort, those who hold any unpopular opinion are peculiarly exposed, because they are in general few and uninfluential, and nobody but themselves feels much interest in seeing justice done them; but this weapon is, from the nature of the case, denied to those who attack a prevailing opinion: they can neither use it with safety to themselves, nor, if they could, would it do anything but recoil on their own cause. In general, opinions contrary to those commonly received can only obtain a hearing by studied moderation of language, and the most cautious avoidance of unnecessary offence, from which they hardly ever deviate even in a slight degree without losing ground: while unmeasured vituperation employed on the side of the prevailing opinion, really does deter people from professing contrary opinions, and from listening to those who profess them. For the interest, therefore, of truth and justice, it is far more important to restrain this employment of vituperative language than the other; and, for example, if it were necessary to choose, there would be much more need to discourage offensive attacks on infidelity, than on religion. It is, however, obvious that law and authority have no business with restraining either, while opinion ought, in every instance, to determine its verdict by the circumstances of the individual case; condemning every one, on whichever side of the argument he places himself, in whose mode of advocacy either want of candor, or malignity, bigotry, or intolerance of feeling manifest themselves; but not inferring these vices from the side which a person takes, though it be the contrary side of the question to our own: and giving merited honor to every one, whatever opinion he may hold, who had calmness to see and honesty to state what his opponents and their opinions really are, exaggerating nothing to their discredit, keeping nothing back which tells, or can be supposed to tell, in their favor. This is the real morality of public discussion; and if often violated, I am happy to think that there are many controversialists who to a great extent observe it, and a still greater number who conscientiously strive towards it.

❖❖ Mill does not justify absolute liberty of speech and press but implies that there are boundaries—although difficult to determine—to public debate. Democratic governments have always been faced with this dilemma: At what point can freedom of speech and press be curtailed? The Supreme Court has had difficulty in making decisions in areas involving censorship and loyalty and security. Freedom of speech and press cannot be used to destroy the very government that protects civil liberties.

Justice Holmes, in *Schenck* v. *United States,* 249 U.S. 47 (1919), stated his famous "clear and present danger" test, which subsequently was applied at both the national and state levels, for deciding whether or not Congress could abridge freedom of speech under the First Amendment:

> The most stringent protection of free speech would not protect a man in falsely shouting fire in a theatre and causing a panic. It does not protect a man from an injunction against uttering words that may have all the effects of force. . . . The question in every case is whether the words used are used in such circumstances and are of such a nature as to create a clear and present danger that they will bring about the substantive evils that Congress has a right to prevent. It is a question of proximity and degree. When a nation is at war many things that might be said in time of peace are such a hindrance to its efforts that their utterance will not be endured so long as men fight and that no Court could regard them as protected by any constitutional right.

❖❖ FREEDOM OF EXPRESSION: THE SKOKIE CASE

The Skokie case is one of the most famous free speech cases in the twentieth century. It was even a television miniseries starring Danny Kaye. The case involved an incident in Skokie, Illinois, during the years 1977–1978, when the American Nazi party attempted to assemble and march in the village of 70,000 persons, a majority of whom were Jewish and a substantial number survivors of the German Nazi concentration camps in World War II. The situation was rife for violence as the town's residents announced their plans to stop the demonstration at all costs.

Skokie ordinances required permits for parades and public assemblies, and prohibited political party members who wore uniforms from publicly demonstrating. Also proscribed was the dissemination of material intended to incite religious or racial hatred. The Nazis did not meet the requirements because they intended to wear uniforms with swastika arm bands while carrying placards defending free speech for white persons.

After being denied an assembly permit, the National Socialist (Nazi) party, with the help of the American Civil Liberties Union, brought an action in the federal district court to declare the village ordinances unconstitutional, alleging that they violated the First and Fourteenth Amendments' freedom of speech and right to assemble clauses. The court declared the ordinances unconstitutional on a number of grounds, including the fact that they could be interpreted not only to limit speech that would incite civil disorder but also to suppress unpopular but legitimate views. Moreover, one of the ordinances "does not merely punish speech after it is spoken, but requires a person to obtain permission before he may speak at all. It is, in other words, a prior restraint on the content of speech [which] bears a heavy presumption of unconstitutionality."[1]

The district court found that the presumption of unconstitutionality of the Skokie ordinances could not be overcome, for "the distinction of protected and unprotected speech in this area is very hard to draw and the evidence in this case shows clearly that plaintiffs' opinions are so unpopular in Skokie that it is highly doubtful that village officials would issue a permit under any circumstances. Second, defendants' admission that there is no clear and present danger that the kind of speech prohibited by this ordinance would cause violence and disorders in the village severely undercuts the village's need for a prior restraint. Finally, the permit system lacks adequate procedural safeguards."[2]

The Village of Skokie appealed the district court's decision to the federal court of appeals, which rendered the following opinion that was implicitly upheld by a majority of the United States Supreme Court when it denied certiorari (appeal). Four Supreme Court justices, however, dissented from the denial of certiorari in the Skokie case in a brief opinion given at the end of the following selection.

14
COLLIN V. SMITH
578 F.2D 1197 (1978)

❖❖❖❖❖❖❖

Circuit Court Judge Pell delivered the following opinion:

Plaintiff-appellee, the National Socialist Party of America (NSPA) is a political group described by its leader, plaintiff-appellee Frank Collin, as a Nazi party. Among NSPA's more controversial and generally unacceptable beliefs are that black persons are biologically inferior to white persons, and should be expatriated to

---

[1]*Collin* v. *Smith*, 447 F.Supp. 676, 699 (1978).
[2]Ibid.

Africa as soon as possible; that American Jews have "inordinate . . . political and financial power" in the world and are "in the forefront of the international Communist revolution." NSPA members affect a uniform reminiscent of those worn by members of the German Nazi Party during the Third Reich,[1] and display a swastika thereon and on a red, white, and black flag they frequently carry.

The Village of Skokie, Illinois, a defendant-appellant, is a suburb north of Chicago. It has a large Jewish population,[2] including as many as several thousand survivors of the Nazi holocaust in Europe before and during World War II. Other defendants-appellants are Village officials.

When Collin and NSPA announced plans to march in front of the Village Hall in Skokie on May 1, 1977, Village officials responded by obtaining in state court a preliminary injunction against the demonstration. After state courts refused to stay the injunction pending appeal, the United States Supreme Court ordered a stay, *National Socialist Party of America* v. *Village of Skokie*. The injunction was subsequently reversed first in part, *Village of Skokie* v. *National Socialist Party of America*, and then in its entirety. On May 2, 1977, the Village enacted three ordinances to prohibit demonstrations such as the one Collin and NSPA had threatened.[3] This lawsuit seeks declaratory and injunctive relief against enforcement of the ordinances.

Village Ordinance No. 77-5-N-994 (hereinafter designated, for convenience of reference, as 994) is a comprehensive permit system for all parades or public assemblies of more than 50 person.[4] It requires permit applicants to obtain $300,000 in public liability insurance and $50,000 in property damage insurance. Id., §§ 27-54, 27-56(j). One of the prerequisites for a permit is a finding by the appropriate official (s) that the assembly

> will not portray criminality, depravity or lack of virtue in, or incite violence, hatred, abuse or hostility toward a person or group of persons by reason of reference to religious, racial, ethnic, national or regional affiliation.

Id., § 27-56(c). Another is a finding that the permit activity will not be conducted "for an unlawful purpose," id., § 27-56(i). None of this ordinance applies to activities of the Village itself or of a governmental agency, id., § 27-51, and any provision of the ordinance may be waived by unanimous consent of the Board of Trustees of the Village, id., § 27-64. To parade or assemble without a permit is a crime, punishable by fines from $5 to $500. Id., § 27-65.

---

[1]In Collin's words: "We wear brown shirts with a dark brown tie, a swastika pin on the tie, a leather shoulder strap, a black belt with buckle, dark brown trousers, black engineer boots, and either a steel helmet or a cloth cap, depending on the situation, plus a swastika arm band on the left arm and an American flag patch on the right arm."

[2]In 1974, 40,500 of the Village's 70,000 population were Jewish.

[3]The district court herein found as a matter of legislature intent that the ordinances in question were designed to cover Nazi marches. The appellants do not attack the finding.

[4]Section 27-52 of the ordinances requires application for a permit at least 30 days before the proposed parade. Like some other provisions of 994, it is not challenged here. We are informed that appellees by registered letter of April 11, 1978, have applied for a permit to demonstrate on June 25, 1978.

Village Ordinance No. 77-5-N-995 (995) prohibits

[t]he dissemination of any materials within the Village of Skokie which promotes and incites hatred against persons by reason of their race, national origin, or religion, and is intended to do so

Id., § 28-43.1. "Dissemination of materials" includes

publication or display or distribution of posters, signs, handbills, or writings and public display of marking and clothing of symbolic significance.

Id., § 28-43.2. Violation is a crime punishable by fine of up to $500, or imprisonment of up to six months. Id., § 28.43.4. Village Ordinance No. 77-5-N-996 (996) prohibits public demonstrations by members of political parties while wearing "military-style" uniforms, § 28.42.1, and violation is punishable as in 995.

Collin and NSPA applied for a permit to march on July 4, 1977, which was denied on the ground the application disclosed an intention to violate 996. The Village apparently applies 994 § 27-56(i) so that an intention to violate 995 or 996 establishes an "unlawful purpose" for the march or assembly. The permit application stated that the march would last about a half hour, and would involve 30 to 50 demonstrators wearing uniforms including swastikas and carrying a party banner with a swastika and placards with statements thereon such as "White Free Speech," "Free Speech for the White Man," and "Free Speech for White America." A single file sidewalk march that would not disrupt traffic was proposed, without speeches or the distribution of handbills or literature.[5] Counsel for the Village advises us that the Village does not maintain that Collin and NSPA will behave other than as described in the permit application(s).

The district court, after considering memoranda, exhibits, depositions, and live testimony, issued a comprehensive and thorough opinion granting relief to Collin and NSPA. The insurance requirements of 994 were invalidated as insuperable obstacles to free speech in Skokie, and §§ 27-56(c) and (i) (the latter when used to deny permits on the basis of anticipated violations of 955 or 996) were adjudged impermissible prior restraints. Ordinance 995 was determined to be fatally vague and overbroad, and 996 was invalidated as overbroad and patently unjustified.

On its appeal, the Village concedes the invalidity of the insurance requirements as applied to these plaintiffs and of the uniform prohibition of 996.

I

The conflict underlying this litigation has commanded substantial public attention, and engendered considerable and understandable emotion. We would hopefully surprise no one by confessing personal views that NSPA's beliefs and goals are repugnant to the core values held generally by residents of this country, and, indeed, to much of what we cherish in civilization. As judges sworn to defend the Constitution, however, we cannot decide this or any case on that basis. Ideological tyranny,

---

[5]A renewed permit application for June 25, 1978, was sent to the Village on April 11, 1978, and contains similar recitations.

no matter how worthy its motivation, is forbidden as much to appointed judges as to elected legislators.

The record in this case contains the testimony of a survivor of the Nazi holocaust in Europe. Shortly before oral argument in this case, a lengthy and highly publicized citizenship revocation trial of an alleged Nazi war criminal was held in a federal court in Chicago, and in the week immediately after argument here, a four-part "docudrama" on the holocaust was nationally televised and widely observed. We cannot then be unmindful of the horrors associated with the Nazi regime of the Third Reich, with which to some real and apparently intentional degree appellees associate themselves.[6] Nor does the record allow us to ignore the certainty that appellees know full well that, in light of their views and the historical associations they would bring with them to Skokie, many people would find their demonstration extremely mentally and emotionally disturbing, or the suspicion that such a result may be relished by appellees.

But our task here is to decide whether the First Amendment protects the activity in which appellees wish to engage, not to render moral judgment on their views or tactics. No authorities need be cited to establish the proposition, which the Village does not dispute, that First Amendment rights are truly precious and fundamental to our national life. Nor is this truth without relevance to the saddening historical images this case inevitably arouses. It is, after all, in part the fact that our constitutional system protects minorities unpopular at a particular time or place from governmental harassment and intimidation, that distinguishes life in this country from life under the Third Reich.

Before undertaking specific analysis of the clash between the Village ordinances and appellees' desires to demonstrate in Skokie, it will be helpful to establish some general principles of pertinence to the decision required of us. Putting to one side for the moment the question of whether the content of appellees' views and symbols makes a constitutional difference here, we find we are unable to deny that the activities in which the appellees wish to engage are within the ambit of the First Amendment.

[1–3]

These activities involve the "cognate rights" of free speech and free assembly. . . .

[4, 5]

No doubt, the Nazi demonstration could be subjected to reasonable regulation of its time, place, and manner. . . . [But] because the ordinances turn on the content of the demonstration, they are necessarily not time, place, or manner regulations. *Mosley, supra; Konigsberg v. State Bar of California.*

Legislating against the content of First Amendment activity, however, launches the government on a slippery and precarious path. . . .

---

[6]Collin testified, however, that NSPA did not advocate genocide as a solution to the "Jewish problem," but was content to expose to the American people what his group conceived that problem to be.

II

We first consider ordinance 995, prohibiting the dissemination of materials which would promote hatred towards persons on the basis of their heritage. The Village would apparently apply this provision to NSPA's display of swastikas, their uniforms, and, perhaps, to the content of their placards.[7]

[8]

The ordinance cannot be sustained on the basis of some of the more obvious exceptions to the rule against content control. While some would no doubt be willing to label appellees' views and symbols obscene, the constitutional rule that obscenity is unprotected applies only to material with erotic content. . . . Furthermore, although the Village introduced evidence in the district court tending to prove that some individuals, at least, might have difficulty restraining their reactions to the Nazi demonstration, the Village tells us that it does not rely on a fear of responsive violence to justify the ordinance, and does not even suggest that there will be any physical violence if the march is held.[8] . . .

Four basic arguments are advanced by the Village to justify the content restrictions of 995. First, it is said that the content criminalized by 995 is "totally lacking in social content," and that it consists of "false statements of fact" in which there is "no constitutional value" (*Gertz v. Robert Welch, Inc.*). We disagree that, if applied to the proposed demonstration, the ordinance can be said to be limited to "statements of fact," false or otherwise. No handbills are to be distributed; no speeches are planned. To the degree that the symbols in question can be said to assert anything specific, it must be the Nazi ideology, which cannot be treated as a mere false "fact."

[9]

. . .

The Village's second argument, and the one on which principal reliance is placed, centers on *Beauharnais v. Illinois*. There a conviction was upheld under a statute prohibiting, in language substantially (and perhaps not unintentionally) similar[9] to that used in the ordinance here, the dissemination of materials promoting racial or religious hatred. The closely-divided Court stated that the criminal punishment of libel of an *individual* raised no constitutional problems. . . .

---

[7]Collin, at least, in his verified complaint, alleged that Village officials advised him that this and the other ordinances would be applied to his and NSPA's proposed demonstration, and the Village has never suggested that this ordinance might not be applied thereto.

[8]The Village understandably offers no guarantee that there will not be violence, but commendably advises us that if a final order in this case requires it to permit the march, it will make every effort to protect the demonstrators (and the Village) from responsive violence.

[9]The actual language in *Beauharnais, see id.* at 251, 72 S.Ct. 725, invoked specifically the depiction of criminality, depravity, unchastity, or lack of virtue in target groups, and is thus most like the language of 994 § 27-56(c), discussed *infra*.

In our opinion *Beauharnais* does not support ordinance 995. . . . [T]he rationale of that decision turns quite plainly on the strong tendency of the prohibited utterances to cause violence and disorder.

It may be questioned, . . . whether the *tendency to induce violence* approach sanctioned implicitly in *Beauharnais* would pass constitutional muster today. Assuming that it would, however, it does not support ordinance 995, because the Village, as we have indicated, does not assert appellees' possible violence, an audience's possible responsive violence, or possible violence against third parties by those incited by appellees, as justifications for 995. . . .

[10]

The Village's third argument is that it has a policy of fair housing, which the dissemination of racially defamatory material could undercut. We reject this argument without extended discussion. That the effective exercise of First Amendment rights may undercut a given government's policy on some issue is, indeed, one of the purposes of those rights. No distinction is constitutionally admissible that turns on the intrinsic justice of the particular policy in issue.

The Village's fourth argument is that the Nazi march, involving as it does the display of uniforms and swastikas, will create a substantive evil that is has a right to prohibit: the infliction of psychic trauma on resident holocaust survivors and other Jewish residents.[10] The Village points out that Illinois recognizes the "new tort" of intentional infliction of severe emotional distress. . . . Assuming that specific individuals could proceed in tort under this theory to recover damages probably occasioned by the proposed march, and that a First Amendment defense would not bar the action,[11] it is nonetheless quite a different matter to criminalize protected First Amendment conduct in anticipation of such results.

. . .

[13]

It is said that the proposed march is not speech, or even "speech plus," but rather an invasion, intensely menacing no matter how peacefully conducted. The Village's expert psychiatric witness, in fact, testified that the effect of the march would be much the same regardless of whether uniforms and swastikas were displayed, due to the intrusion of self-proclaimed Nazis into what he characterized as predominately Jewish "turf." There is room under the First Amendment for the government to

---

[10]Ironically the witnessing of the television show "Holocaust" might seem to have the same trauma producing possibilities. The extent to which the residents of Skokie may have willingly exposed themselves to the painful reminders of this production might have been pertinent to the psychic trauma issue if the airing had occurred prior to the district court evidentiary hearing.

[11]These questions, of course, are not before us, and we intimate no view thereon, one way or the other.

protect targeted listeners from offensive speech, but only when the speaker intrudes on the privacy of the home, or a captive audience cannot practically avoid exposure. . . .

This case does not involve intrusion into people's homes. There *need be* no captive audience, as Village residents may, if they wish, simply avoid the Village Hall for thirty minutes on a Sunday afternoon, which no doubt would be their normal course of conduct on a day when the Village Hall was not open in the regular course of business. Absent such intrusion or captivity, there is no justifiable substantial privacy interest to save 995 from constitutional infirmity, when it attempts, by fiat, to declare the entire Village, at all times, a privacy zone that may be sanitized from the offensiveness of Nazi ideology and symbols.

[14]

We conclude that 995 may not be applied to criminalize the conduct of the proposed demonstration. . . . [T]he ordinance could conceivably be applied to criminalize dissemination of *The Merchant of Venice* or a vigorous discussion of the merits of reverse racial discrimination in Skokie. . . .

III

[15]

Our decision that 995 cannot constitutionally be applied to the proposed march necessarily means that a permit for the march may not be denied on the basis of anticipated violations thereof. . . .

The preparation and issuance of this opinion has not been an easy task, or one which we have relished. Recognizing the implication that often seems to follow over-protestation, we nevertheless feel compelled once again to express our repugnance at the doctrines which the appellees desire to profess publicly. Indeed, it is a source of extreme regret that after several thousand years of attempting to strengthen the often thin coating of civilization with which humankind has attempted to hide brutal animal-like instincts, there would still be those who would resort to hatred and vilification of fellow human beings because of their racial background or their religious beliefs, or for that matter, because of any reason at all.

Retaining meaning in civil rights, particularly those many of the founding fathers believed sufficiently important as to delay the approval of the Constitution until they could be included in the Bill of Rights, seldom seems to be accomplished by the easy cases, however, and it was not so here.

Although we would have thought it unnecessary to say so, it apparently deserves emphasis in the light of the dissent's reference to this court apologizing as to the result, that our *regret* at the use appellees plan to make of their rights is not in any sense an *apology* for upholding the First Amendment. The result we have reached is dictated by the fundamental proposition that if these civil rights are to remain vital for all, they must protect not only those society deems acceptable, but also those whose ideas it quite justifiably reject and despises.

The judgment of the district court is AFFIRMED.

15
SMITH V. COLLIN
439 U.S. 916 (1978)

❖❖❖❖❖❖❖

Certiorari denied.

Mr. Justice Blackmun, with whom Mr. Justice White joins, dissenting [from denial of certiorari]:

It is a matter of regret for me that the Court denies certiorari [review] in this case, for this is litigation that rests upon critical, disturbing, and emotional facts, and the issues cut down to the very heart of the First Amendment.

The village of Skokie, Ill., a suburb of Chicago, in 1974 had a population of approximately 70,000 persons. A majority were Jewish; of the Jewish population a substantial number were survivors of World War II persecution. In March 1977, respondents Collin and the National Socialist Party of America, which Collin described as a "Nazi organization," publicly announced plans to hold an assembly in front of the Skokie Village Hall. On May 2, the village enacted three ordinances. The first established a permit system for parades and public assemblies and required applicants to post public liability and property damage insurance. The second prohibited the dissemination of material that incited racial or religious hatred with intent so to incite. The third prohibited public demonstrations by members of political parties while wearing military-style uniforms.

On June 22, respondent Collin applied for a permit under the first ordinance. His application stated that a public assembly would take place on July 4, would consist of persons demonstrating in front of the Village Hall, would last about a half hour, and would not disrupt traffic. It also stated that the participants would wear uniforms with swastikas and would carry placards proclaiming free speech for white persons, but would not distribute handbills or literature. The permit was denied.

Skokie's Village Hall stood on a street that was zoned commercial. There were residential areas, however, adjoining to the North, South, and West. The front of the Village Hall was visible from dwellings in those areas.

Upon the rejection of the permit application, respondents filed a complaint in the United States District Court for the Northern District of Illinois against the president of the village of Skokie, its manager, its corporation counsel, and the village itself. Respondents asked that the ordinances be declared void and their enforcement enjoined. The District Court, after receiving evidence, ruled that the ordinances were unconstitutional on their face, and granted the requested declaratory and injunctive relief. It filed a comprehensive opinion. The United States Court of Appeals for the Seventh Circuit, with one judge dissenting in part, affirmed:

A permit then was issued to respondents for a demonstration on the afternoon of June 25, 1978, in front of the Village Hall. Respondents, however, shifted their assembly from Skokie to Chicago where activities took place on June 24 and July 9.

Other aspects of the controversy already have reached this Court. In April 1977, the Circuit Court of Cook County, Ill., entered an injunction against respondents prohibiting them, within the village, from parading in the National Socialist uniform, displaying the swastika, or displaying materials that incite or promote hatred against persons of the Jewish or any other faith. The Illinois Appellate Court denied an application for stay pending appeal. The Supreme Court of Illinois, in turn, denied a stay and also denied leave for an expedited appeal. Relief was sought here. This Court, *per curiam* but by a divided vote, reversed the denial of a stay and remanded the case for further proceedings. *National Socialist Party v. Skokie*.

On remand, the Illinois Appellate Court reviewed and modified the injunction the Circuit Court had entered and this time upheld only that portion thereof that prevented the display of swastikas "in the course of a demonstration, march, or parade." *Village of Skokie v. National Socialist Party*. The Supreme Court of Illinois denied an application for stay pending expedited review. Mr. Justice Stevens, as Circuit Justice, denied a stay of the injunction as so modified. The Illinois Supreme Court ultimately reversed the remaining injunctive feature, "albeit reluctantly," and with one justice dissenting.

Thereafter, the village and its codefendants in the present federal litigation filed an application to stay the Seventh Circuit's mandate or, in the alternative, to stay enforcement of the injunction entered by the District Court. This Court, with two Justices dissenting, denied the application.

These facts and this chronology demonstrate, I believe, the pervading sensitivity of the litigation. On the one hand, we have precious First Amendment rights vigorously asserted and an obvious concern that, if those asserted rights are not recognized, the precedent of a "hard" case might offer a justification for repression in the future. On the other hand, we are presented with evidence of a potentially explosive and dangerous situation, enflamed by unforgettable recollections of traumatic experiences in the second world conflict. Finally, Judge Sprecher of the Seventh Circuit observed that "each court dealing with these precise problems (the Illinois Supreme Court, the District Court and this Court) feels the need to apologize for its result."

Furthermore, in *Beauharnais v. Illinois* (1952), this Court faced up to an Illinois statute that made it a crime to exhibit in any public place a publication that portrayed "depravity, criminality, unchastity, or lack of virtue of a class of citizens, of any race, color, creed or religion," thereby exposing such citizens "to contempt, derision, or obloquy." The Court, by a divided vote, held that, as construed and applied, the statute did not violate the liberty of speech guaranteed as against the States by the Due Process Clause of the Fourteenth Amendment.

I stated in dissent when the application for stay in the present litigation was denied that I feel the Seventh Circuit's decision is in some tension with *Beauharnais*. That case has not been overruled or formally limited in any way.

I therefore would grant certiorari in order to resolve any possible conflict that may exist between the ruling of the Seventh Circuit here and *Beauharnais*. I also feel that the present case affords the Court an opportunity to consider whether, in the context of the facts that this record appears to present, there is no limit whatsoever to the exercise of free speech. There indeed may be no such limit, but when citizens assert, not casually but with deep conviction, that the proposed demonstration is scheduled at a place and in a manner that is taunting and overwhelmingly offensive to the citizens of that place, that assertion, uncomfortable though it may be for judges, deserves to be examined. It just might fall into the same category as one's "right" to cry "fire" in a crowded theater, for "the character of every act depends upon the circumstances in which it is done." *Schenck* v. *United States*.

❖❖ EQUAL PROTECTION OF THE LAWS: SCHOOL DESEGREGATION

By now most students are thoroughly familiar with the evolution of the "separate but equal" doctrine first enunciated by the Supreme Court in *Plessy* v. *Ferguson,* 163 U.S. 537 (1896). Students should note that what is involved in cases in this area is legal interpretation of the provision in the Fourteenth Amendment that no state may deny "to any person within its jurisdiction the equal protection of the laws." The *Plessy* case stated that separate but equal accommodations, required by state law to be established on railroads in Louisiana, did not violate the equal protection of the laws clause of the Fourteenth Amendment. The Court went on to say that the object of the Fourteenth Amendment:

> . . . was undoubtedly to enforce the absolute equality of the two races before the law, but in the nature of things it could not have been intended to abolish distinction based upon color, or to enforce social, as distinguished from political, equality, or a commingling of the two races upon terms unsatisfactory to either. Laws permitting, and even requiring, their separation in places where they are liable to be brought into contact do not necessarily imply the inferiority of either race to the other, and have been generally, if not universally, recognized as within the competency of the state legislatures in the exercise of their police power. The most common instance of this is connected with the establishment of separate schools for white and colored children, which has been held to be a valid exercise of the legislative power even by courts of States where the political rights of the colored race have been longest and most earnestly enforced.

Both the police power and education are within the reserved powers of the states; they are reserved, however, only insofar as they do not conflict with provisions of the Constitution. The Supreme Court, in *Brown* v. *Board of Education,* 347 U.S. 483 (1954), finally crystallized its interpretation of the equal protection of the laws clause in a way that resulted in a significant decrease in state power in an area traditionally reserved to states, namely, education. In addition, a general principle was established which extended far beyond the field of education.

16
BROWN V. BOARD OF EDUCATION OF TOPEKA 347 U.S. 483 (1954)

❖❖❖❖❖❖❖

Mr. Chief Justice Warren delivered the opinion of the Court, saying in part:

These cases come to us from the states of Kansas, South Carolina, Virginia, and Delaware. They are premised on different facts and different local conditions, but a common legal question justifies their consideration together in this consolidated opinion.

In each of the cases, minors of the Negro race, through their legal representatives, seek the aid of the courts in obtaining admission to the public schools of their community on a nonsegregated basis. In each instance, they had been denied admission to schools attended by white children under laws requiring or permitting segregation according to race. This segregation was alleged to deprive the plaintiffs of the equal protection of the laws under the Fourteenth Amendment. In each of the cases other than the Delaware case, a three-judge federal district court denied relief to the plaintiffs on the so-called "separate but equal" doctrine announced by this Court in *Plessy v. Ferguson.*...

The plaintiffs contend that segregated public schools are not "equal" and cannot be made "equal," and that hence they are deprived of the equal protection of the laws. Because of the obvious importance of the question presented, the Court took jurisdiction....

In the first cases in this Court construing the Fourteenth Amendment, decided shortly after its adoption, the Court interpreted it as proscribing all state-imposed discriminations against the Negro race. The doctrine of "separate but equal" did not make its appearance in this Court until 1896 in the case of *Plessy v. Ferguson, supra,* involving not education but transportation. American courts have since labored with the doctrine for over half a century. In this Court, there have been six cases involving the "separate but equal" doctrine in the field of public education.... In more recent cases, all on the graduate school level, inequality was found in that specific benefits enjoyed by white students were denied to Negro students of the same educational qualifications.... In none of these cases was it necessary to reexamine the doctrine to grant relief to the Negro plaintiff. And in *Sweatt v. Painter* [339 U.S.

629 (1950)], the Court expressly reserved decision on the question whether *Plessy v. Ferguson* should be held inapplicable to public education.

In the instant cases, that question is directly presented. Here, unlike *Sweatt v. Painter*, there are findings below that the Negro and white schools involved have been equalized, or are being equalized, with respect to buildings, curricula, qualifications and salaries of teachers, and other "tangible" factors. Our decision, therefore, cannot turn on merely a comparison of these tangible factors in the Negro and white schools involved in each of the cases. We must look instead to the effect of segregation itself on public education.

In approaching this problem, we cannot turn the clock back to 1868 when the Amendment was adopted, or even to 1896 when *Plessy v. Ferguson* was written. We must consider public education in the light of its full development and its present place in American life throughout the Nation. Only in this way can it be determined if segregation in public schools deprives these plaintiffs of the equal protection of the laws.

Today, education is perhaps the most important function of state and local governments. Compulsory school attendance laws and the great expenditures for education both demonstrate our recognition of the importance of education to our democratic society. It is required in the performance of our most basic public responsibilities, even service in the armed forces. It is the very foundation of good citizenship. Today it is a principal instrument in awakening the child to cultural values, in preparing him for later professional training, and in helping him to adjust normally to his environment. In these days, it is doubtful that any child may reasonably be expected to succeed in life if he is denied the opportunity of an education. Such an opportunity, where the state has undertaken to provide it, is a right which must be made available to all on equal terms.

We come then to the question presented: Does segregation of children in public schools solely on the basis of race, even though the physical facilities and other "tangible" factors may be equal, deprive the children of the minority group of equal educational opportunities? We believe that it does.

In *Sweatt v. Painter, supra,* in finding that a segregated law school for Negroes could not provide them equal educational opportunities, this Court relied in large part on "those qualities which are incapable of objective measurement but which make for greatness in a law school." In *MacLaurin v. Oklahoma State Regents, supras* [339 U.S. 637 (1950)], the Court, in requiring that a Negro admitted to a white graduate school be treated like all other students, again resorted to intangible considerations: "his ability to study, to engage in discussions and exchange views with other students, and, in general, to learn his profession." Such considerations apply with added force to children in grade and high schools. To separate them from others of similar age and qualifications solely because of their race generates a feeling of inferiority as to their status in the community that may affect their hearts and minds in a way unlikely ever to be undone. The effect of this separation of their educational opportunities was well stated by a finding in the Kansas case by a court which nevertheless felt compelled to rule against the Negro plaintiffs:

> Segregation of white and colored children in public schools has a detrimental effect upon the colored children. The impact is greater when it has the sanction of the law; for the policy of separating the races is usually interpreted as denoting the inferiority of the Negro group. A sense of inferiority affects the motivation of a child to learn. Segregation with the sanction of law, therefore, has a tendency to retard the educational and mental development of Negro children and to deprive them of some of the benefits they would receive in a racially integrated school system.

Whatever may have been the extent of psychological knowledge at the time of *Plessy* v. *Ferguson*, this finding is amply supported by modern authority. Any language in *Plessy* v. *Ferguson* contrary to this finding is rejected.

We conclude that in the field of public education the doctrine of "separate but equal" has no place. Separate educational facilities are inherently unequal. Therefore, we hold that the plaintiffs and others similarly situated for whom the actions have been brought are by reason of the segregation complained of, deprived of the equal protection of the laws guaranteed by the Fourteenth Amendment. This disposition makes unnecessary any discussion whether such segregation also violates the Due Process Clause of the Fourteenth Amendment.

Because these are class actions, because of the wide applicability of this decision, and because of the great variety of local conditions, the formulation of decrees in these cases presents problems of considerable complexity. On reargument, the consideration of appropriate relief was necessarily subordinate to the primary question—the constitutionality of segregation in public education. We have now announced that such segregation is a denial of the equal protection of the laws. In order that we may have the full assistance of the parties in formulating decrees, the cases will be restored to the docket, and the parties are requested to present further argument on Questions 4 and 5 previously propounded by the Court for the re-argument this Term [which deal with the implementation of desegregation]. The Attorney General of the United States is again invited to participate. The Attorneys General of the states requiring or permitting segregation in public education will also be permitted to appear as *amici curiae* upon request to do so by September 15, 1954, and submission of briefs by October 1, 1954. It is so ordered.

❖❖ On the same day the decision was announced in the *Brown* case (1954), the Court held that segregation in the District of Columbia was unconstitutional on the basis of the due process clause of the Fifth Amendment. (See *Bolling* v. *Sharpe, 347* U.S. 497 [1954].) This situation reversed the normal one in that a protection explicitly afforded citizens of states was not expressly applicable against the national government, and could be made so only through interpreting it into the concept of due process of law.

After hearing the views of all interested parties in the *Brown* case the Court, on May 31, 1955, announced its decision concerning the implementation of desegregation in public schools.

17

BROWN V. BOARD OF
EDUCATION OF TOPEKA
349 U.S. 294 (1955)

❖❖❖❖❖❖❖❖

Mr. Chief Justice Warren delivered the opinion of the Court, saying in part:

These cases were decided on May 17, 1954. The opinions of that date, declaring the fundamental principle that racial discrimination in public education is unconstitutional, are incorporated herein by reference. All provisions of federal, state, or local law requiring or permitting such discrimination must yield to this principle. There remains for consideration the manner in which relief is to be accorded.

Because these cases arose under different local conditions and their disposition will involve a variety of local problems, we requested further argument on the question of relief. . . . The parties, the United States, and the states of Florida, North Carolina, Arkansas, Oklahoma, Maryland, and Texas filed briefs and participated in the oral argument.

These presentations were informative and helpful to the Court in its consideration of the complexities arising from the transition to a system of public education freed of racial discrimination. The presentations also demonstrated that substantial steps to eliminate racial discrimination in public schools have already been taken, not only in some of the communities in which these cases arose, but in some of the states appearing as *amici curiae*, and in other states as well. Substantial progress has been made in the District of Columbia and in the communities in Kansas and Delaware involved in this litigation. The defendants in the cases coming to us from South Carolina and Virginia are awaiting the decision of this Court concerning relief.

Full implementation of these constitutional principles may require solution of varied local school problems. School authorities have the primary responsibility for elucidating, assessing, and solving these problems; courts will have to consider whether the action of school authorities constitutes good faith implementation of the governing constitutional principles. Because of their proximity to local conditions and the possible need for further hearings, the courts which originally heard these cases can best perform this judicial appraisal. Accordingly, we believe it appropriate to remand the cases to those courts.

In fashioning and effectuating the decrees, the courts will be guided by equitable principles. Traditionally, equity has been characterized by a practical flexibility in shaping its remedies and by a facility for adjusting and reconciling public and private needs. These cases call for the exercise of these traditional attributes of equity power. At stake is the personal interest of the plaintiffs in admission to public schools as soon as practicable on a nondiscriminatory basis. To effectuate this interest may call for elimination of a variety of obstacles in making the transition to school systems operated in accordance with the constitutional principles set forth in our May 17, 1954, decision. Courts of equity may properly take into account the public interest in the elimination of such obstacles in a systematic and effective manner. But it should go without saying that the vitality of these constitutional principles cannot be allowed to yield simply because of disagreement with them.

While giving weight to these public and private considerations, the courts will require that the defendants make a prompt and reasonable start toward full compliance with our May 17, 1954, ruling. Once such a start has been made, the courts may find that additional time is necessary to carry out the ruling in an effective manner. The burden rests upon the defendants to establish such time as is necessary in the public interest and is consistent with good faith compliance at the earliest practicable date. To that end, the courts may consider problems related to administration, arising from the physical condition of the school plant, the school transportation system, personnel, revision of school districts and attendance areas into compact units to achieve a system of determining admission to the public schools on a nonracial basis, and revision of local laws and regulations which may be necessary in solving the foregoing problems. They will also consider the adequacy of any plans the defendants may propose to meet these problems and to effectuate a transition to a racially nondiscriminatory school system. During this period of transition, the courts will retain jurisdiction of these cases.

The judgments below, except that in the Delaware case, are accordingly reversed and the cases are remanded to the District Courts to take such proceedings and enter such orders and decrees consistent with this opinion as are necessary and proper to admit to public schools on a racially nondiscriminatory basis with all deliberate speed the parties to these cases. The judgment in the Delaware case—ordering the immediate admission of the plaintiffs to schools previously attended only by white children—is affirmed on the basis of the principles stated in our May 17, 1954, opinion, but the case is remanded to the Supreme Court of Delaware for such further proceedings as that Court may deem necessary in the light of this opinion.

It is so ordered.

❖❖ After the second decision of the Supreme Court in *Brown* v. *Board of Education* in 1955, it soon became clear that many southern states would proceed with deliberate speed not to implement the desegregation of public schools but to obstruct the intent of the Supreme Court. The Southern Manifesto, signed by 101 congressmen from 11 southern states in 1956, clearly indicated the line that would be taken by many southern members of Congress to justify defiance of the Supreme Court. The gist of the manifesto was simply that the Supreme Court did not have the constitutional authority to interfere in an area such as education, which falls within the reserved powers of the states.

After the two *Brown* decisions in 1954 and 1955, the implementation of desegregation in the South was very slow. Ten years later, less than 10 percent of the black pupils in the lower educational levels in the southern states that had had legally segregated education before were enrolled in integrated schools. It was not until 1970 that substantial progress was made in the South. Between 1968 and 1970 the percentage of black students in all-black schools in 11 southern states decreased from 68.0 percent to 18.4 percent. One device used to circumvent the Supreme Court's decisions was to establish de facto dual school systems, similar to those that exist in most northern cities, whereby students are assigned to schools on the basis of the neighborhoods in which they live. Such systems are not de jure segregation because they are not based upon a law requiring segregation per se, but simply upon school board regulations assigning pupils on the basis of where they live. De facto school systems can be as segregated as were the de jure systems previously existing in the South, but the question is to what extent can courts interfere to break up de facto segregation patterns since they are not based upon legal stipulations?

In *Swann* v. *Charlotte-Mecklenburg County Board of Education,* 402 U.S. 1 (1971), the Supreme Court held that in southern states with a history of legal segregated education the district courts have broad power to assure "unitary" school systems by requiring (1) reassignment of teachers, so that each school faculty will reflect a racial balance similar to that which exists in the community as a whole; (2) reassignment of pupils to reflect a racial ratio similar to that which exists within the total community; (3) the use of noncontiguous school zones and the grouping of schools for the purpose of attendance to bring about racial balance; and (4) the use of busing of elementary and secondary school students within the school system to achieve racial balance.

This case and companion cases were referred to at the time as school "busing" cases, and caused tremendous controversy within the South because communities felt they were not being treated on an equal basis with their northern counterparts, where de facto segregation is for the most part not subject to judicial intervention. The Nixon administration, which favored neighborhood schools, was firmly opposed to the transportation of students beyond normal geographic school zones to achieve racial balance. Democratic Senator Ribicoff of Connecticut attempted to attach an amendment to an administration-sponsored bill providing $1.5 billion to aid school districts in the South in the desegregation of facilities that would have required nationwide integration of pupils from intercity schools with children from the suburbs. The amendment was defeated on April 21, 1971, by a vote of 51 to 35, with most Republicans voting against it and 13 of 34 northern Democrats opposed. Busing remains a highly controversial political issue.

Swann v. *Charlotte-Mecklenburg County Board* (1971) held that the courts could order busing of schoolchildren within the limits of the city school district if necessary to achieve desegregated educational facilities. In the case of Charlotte-Mecklenburg, the limits of the city school district included the surrounding county. However, only 18 of the country's 100 largest city school districts contained both the inner city and the surrounding county. In cities such as San Francisco, Denver, Pasadena, and Boston, court-ordered busing plans pertained only to the central city school district. In 1974 the Supreme

Court reviewed a busing plan for Detroit ordered by a federal district court and sustained by the court of appeals that would have required the busing of students among 54 separate school districts in the Detroit metropolitan area to achieve racially balanced schools. The decision of the lower federal court in the Detroit case set a new precedent that required busing among legally separate school districts. Proponents of the Detroit busing plan argued that the central city of Detroit was 70 percent black and that the only way integration could be achieved would be to link the school district of Detroit with the surrounding white suburban school districts. In *Milliken* v. *Bradley,* 418 U.S. 717 (1974), the Supreme Court held that the court-ordered Detroit busing plan could not be sustained under the equal protection clause of the Fourteenth Amendment, which was the constitutional provision relied upon in the lower court's decision to require busing. The Supreme Court found that there was no evidence of disparate treatment of white and black students among the 53 outlying school districts that surround Detroit. The only evidence of discrimination was within the city limits of Detroit itself. Therefore, since the outlying districts did not violate the equal protection clause they could not be ordered to integrate their systems with that of Detroit. Since discrimination was limited to Detroit, the court order to remedy the situation must be limited to Detroit also. The effect of the decision is to leave standing court orders for busing within school districts, but to prevent the forced merger of inner city schools with legally separate suburban school districts.

THE JUDICIAL SOURCES OF MAJOR POLITICAL CONTROVERSIES OVER CIVIL LIBERTIES AND RIGHTS

Chief Justice John Marshall in the early nineteenth century laid the groundwork for Supreme Court involvement in politics when he declared that "it is emphatically the province and duty of the Judicial Department to say what the law is." Ironically, in the same case he invented the doctrine of "political questions," proclaiming that the courts should not become involved in those matters more appropriately decided by legislative bodies. Marshall muted that note of judicial self-restraint, however, by his implicit recognition that the courts and not legislatures ultimately would decide what matters fell within their jurisdiction.

Chief Justice Marshall's proclamation of judicial power in *Marbury* v. *Madison* also incorporated the doctrine of judicial review. The authority to declare what the law is included the power to review acts of Congress and judge their constitutionality. The *Marbury* case, however, did not involve a major confrontation with Congress. The Court merely held that Congress could not grant it the mandamus power in original jurisdiction, which had been done in the judiciary Act of 1789. Essentially the Court was interpreting the scope of its own powers, not those of Congress.

Inevitably, however, the power of judicial review pushed the Supreme Court and lower federal courts as well into political controversies as they ruled not only on congressional laws but far more importantly on the actions of state legislatures and courts. As of early 1985 the Supreme Court had held only 135 provisions of federal laws to be unconstitutional in whole or in part out of a total of approximately 91,000 public and private bills that had been passed. By contrast, the Court had overturned on constitutional grounds 970 state laws and provisions of state constitutions, 800 of these rulings coming after 1870.[1] By far the greatest political controversies have been over Supreme Court rulings affecting the states, as the nation for most of its history struggled over the question of how far national power should intrude upon state sovereignty.

Controversies surrounding Supreme Court decisions on civil liberties and civil rights have almost entirely involved Supreme Court rulings on the permissible scope of state power. In the early nineteenth century Chief Justice John Marshall's decisions in the historic cases of *McCulloch* v. *Maryland* (1819) and *Gibbons* v. *Ogden* (1823) raised the ire of states' rights advocates who widely proclaimed that the Court's actions would bring about the dissolution of the Union. The Supreme Court had unequivocally upheld national supremacy and wide congressional powers over the states.

Almost a century and a half after the *McCulloch* decision, the Supreme Court was again embroiled in a political controversy, not concerning the extent of congressional power over the states, an issue that had finally been settled in favor of the national government during the New Deal, but over how far national civil liberties and rights standards should be applied to the states. Under the chief justiceship of former California governor Earl Warren, an activist and interventionist Supreme Court in the 1960s completed the process of applying most of the provisions of the Bill of Rights to the states under the due process clause of the Fourteenth Amendment. Before the Warren era the Court had been very reluctant to extend parts of the Bill of Rights to the states, weighing heavily against such action considerations of federalism that supported state sovereignty. It nationalized only what in the view of a majority of the justices were fundamental freedoms and rights without which the democratic process and individual liberty could not survive.

RELIGIOUS FREEDOM AND THE ISSUE OF SCHOOL PRAYER

As early as 1940 the Supreme Court nationalized the *free exercise* clause of the First Amendment, but it was not until 1947 that a majority of justices agreed that the *establishment* clause of the First Amendment was also a fundamental liberty protected by the due process clause of the Fourteenth Amendment[2].

---

[1]Henry J. Abraham, *The Judiciary: The Supreme Court in the Governmental Process*, 6th ed. (Boston: Allyn & Bacon, 1983), p. 164.

[2]The two cases nationalizing the First Amendment free exercise and establishment clauses were, respectively, *Cantwell* v. *Connecticut*, 310 U.S. 296 (1940) and *Everson* v. *Board of Education*, 330 U.S. 1 (1947).

The First Amendment provision embodying the establishment and free exercise clauses states: "Congress shall make no law respecting an establishment of religion, or prohibiting the free exercise thereof." While little controversy surrounded the Supreme Court's nationalization of these provisions, its 1962 decision in Engel v. Vitale, given in the following selection, holding that religious freedom required a ban on prayers in public schools, caused a political backlash that continued into the 1980s, one that seemed to grow in intensity as the years passed. As the Moral Majority and the Christian Right became politically active in the 1980s, one of their major goals was the restoration of prayers in public schools. They supported state efforts to pass legislation that would get around the school prayer decision by requiring moments of silence rather than prayers to open school days. However, the Supreme Court held in 1985 that an Alabama moment-of-silence statute authorizing public school teachers to hold a one-minute period of silence for "meditation or voluntary prayer" each school day violated the establishment clause of the First Amendment.[3] Of particular concern to the Court were statements by the sponsors of the legislation that they intended the law to restore prayer to public schools. Even conservative justices, such as Sandra Day O'Connor, who supported completely voluntary moments of silence in public schools during which prayers might be given, agreed that the Alabama statute had no secular effect and was an impermissible official encouragement of prayers. The following case originated the school prayer controversy.

18
ENGEL V. VITALE
370 U.S. 421 (1962)

❖❖❖❖❖❖❖

Mr. Justice Black delivered the opinion of the Court, saying in part:

The respondent Board of Education of Union Free School District No. 9, New Hyde Park, New York, acting in its official capacity under state law, directed the School District's principal to cause the following prayer to be said aloud by each class in the presence of a teacher at the beginning of each school day:

> Almighty God, we acknowledge our dependence upon Thee, and we beg Thy blessings upon us, our parents, our teachers and our country.

This daily procedure was adopted on the recommendation of the State Board of Regents, a governmental agency created by the state Constitution to which the New

---

[3]*Wallace v. Jaffree*, 86 L Ed. 2d 29 (1985).

York Legislature has granted broad supervisory, executive, and legislative powers over the state's public school system. These state officials composed the prayer which they recommended and published as a part of their "Statement on Moral and Spiritual Training in the Schools," saying: "We believe that this Statement will be subscribed to by all men and women of good will, and we call upon all of them to aid in giving life to our program."

Shortly after the practice of reciting the Regents' prayer was adopted by the School District, the parents of ten pupils brought this action in a New York State Court insisting that use of this official prayer in the public schools was contrary to the beliefs, religions, or religious practices of both themselves and their children. Among other things, these parents challenged the constitutionality of both the state law authorizing the School District to direct the use of prayer in public schools and the School District's regulation ordering the recitation of this particular prayer on the ground that these actions of official governmental agencies violate that part of the First Amendment of the federal Constitution which commands that "Congress shall make no law respecting an establishment of religion"—a command which was "made applicable to the state of New York by the Fourteenth Amendment of the said Constitution." The New York Court of Appeals, over the dissents of Judges Dye and Fuld, sustained an order of the lower state courts which had upheld the power of New York to use the Regents' prayer as a part of the daily procedures of its public schools so long as the schools did not compel any pupil to join in the prayer over his or her parents' objection. We granted certiorari to review this important decision involving rights protected by the First and Fourteenth Amendments.

We think that by using its public school system to encourage recitation of the Regents' prayer, the state of New York has adopted a practice wholly inconsistent with the Establishment Clause. There can, of course, be no doubt that New York's program of daily classroom invocation of God's blessings as prescribed in the Regents' prayer is a religious activity. It is a solemn avowal of divine faith and supplication for the blessings of the Almighty. The nature of such a prayer has always been religious, none of the respondents has denied this and the trial court expressly so found. . . .

The petitioners contend among other things that the state laws requiring or permitting use of the Regents' prayer must be struck down as a violation of the Establishment Clause because the prayer was composed by governmental officials as a part of a governmental program to further religious beliefs. For this reason, petitioners argue, the state's use of the Regents' prayer in its public school system breaches the constitutional wall of separation between church and state. We agree with that contention since we think that the constitutional prohibition against laws respecting an establishment of religion must at least mean that in this country it is no part of the business of government to compose official prayers for any group of the American people to recite as a part of a religious program carried on by government.

It is a matter of history that this very practice of establishing governmentally composed prayers for religious services was one of the reasons which caused many of our early colonists to leave England and seek religious freedom in America. The Book of Common Prayer, which was created under governmental direction and which was approved by Acts of Parliament in 1548 and 1549, set out in minute detail the accepted form and content of prayer and other religious ceremonies to be used in the established, tax-supported Church of England. The controversies over the Book and what should be its content repeatedly threatened to disrupt the peace of that country as the accepted forms of prayer in the established church changed with the views of the particular ruler that happened to be in control at the time. Powerful groups representing some of the varying religious views of the people struggled among themselves to impress their particular views upon the government and obtain amendments of the Book more suitable to their respective notions of how religious services should be conducted in order that the official religious establishment would advance their particular religious beliefs. Other groups, lacking the necessary political power to influence the government on the matter, decided to leave England and its established church and seek freedom in America from England's governmentally ordained and supported religion.

It is an unfortunate fact of history that when some of the very groups which had most strenuously opposed the established Church of England found themselves sufficiently in control of colonial governments in this country to write their own prayers into law, they passed laws making their own religion the official religion of their respective colonies. Indeed, as late as the time of the Revolutionary War, there were established churches in at least eight of the thirteen former colonies and established religions in at least four of the other five. But the successful Revolution against English political domination was shortly followed by intense opposition to the practice of establishing religion by law. . . .

By the time of the adoption of the Constitution, our history shows that there was a widespread awareness among many Americans of the dangers of a union of church and state. . . . The First Amendment was added to the Constitution to stand as a guarantee that neither the power nor the prestige of the federal government would be used to control, support or influence the kinds of prayer the American people can say—that the people's religions must not be subjected to the pressures of government for change each time a new political administration is elected to office. Under that amendment's prohibition against governmental establishment of religion, as reinforced by the provisions of the Fourteenth Amendment, government in this country, be it state or federal, is without power to prescribe by law any particular form of prayer which is to be used as an official prayer in carrying on any program of governmentally sponsored religious activity.

There can be no doubt that New York's state prayer program officially establishes the religious beliefs embodied in the Regents' prayer. The respondents' argument to the contrary, which is largely based upon the contention that the Regents' prayer is "nondenominational" and the fact that the program, as modified and approved by state courts, does not require all pupils to recite the prayer but permits those who wish to do so to remain silent or be excused from the room, ignores the essential nature of the program's constitutional defects. Neither the fact that the prayer may be denominationally neutral, nor the fact that its observance on the part of the students is voluntary can serve to free it from the limitations of the Establishment Clause, as it might from the Free Exercise Clause, of the First Amendment, both of which are operative against the states by virtue of the Fourteenth Amendment. Although these two clauses may in certain instances overlap, they forbid two quite different kinds of governmental encroachment upon religious freedom. The Establishment Clause, unlike the Free Exercise Clause, does not depend upon any showing of direct governmental compulsion and is violated by the enactment of laws which establish an official religion whether those laws operate directly to coerce nonobserving individuals or not. This is not to say, of course, that laws officially prescribing a particular form of religious worship do not involve coercion of such individuals. When the power, prestige and financial support of government is placed behind a particular religious belief, the indirect coercive pressure upon religious minorities to conform to the prevailing officially approved religion is plain. But the purposes underlying the Establishment Clause go much further than that. Its first and most immediate purpose rested on the belief that a union of government and religion tends to destroy government and to degrade religion. The history of governmentally established religion, both in England and in this country, showed that whenever government had allied itself with one particular form of religion, the inevitable result has been that it had incurred the hatred, disrespect and even contempt of those who held contrary beliefs. That same history showed that many people had lost their respect for any religion that had relied upon the support of government to spread its faith. The Establishment Clause thus stands as an expression of principle on the part of the Founders of our Constitution that religion is too personal, too sacred, too holy, to permit its "unhallowed perversion" by a civil magistrate. Another purpose of the Establishment Clause rested upon an awareness of the historical fact that governmentally established religions and religious persecutions go hand in hand. The founders knew that only a few years after the Book of Common Prayer became the only accepted form of religious services in the established Church of England, an Act of Uniformity was passed to compel all Englishmen to attend those services and to make it a criminal offense to conduct or attend religious gatherings of any other kind—a law which was consistently flouted by dissenting religious groups in England and which contributed to widespread persecutions of people like John Bunyan who persisted in holding "unlawful [religious] meetings . . . to the great disturbance and distraction of the good subjects of this kingdom. . . ." And they knew that similar persecutions had received the sanction of law in several of the colonies in this country soon after the establishment of official religions in those colonies. It was in large part to get completely away from this sort of systematic religious persecution that the Founders brought into being our Nation, our Constitution, and our Bill of Rights with its prohibition against any governmental establishment of religion. The New York laws officially prescribing the Regents' prayer are inconsistent with both the purposes of the Establishment Clause and with the Establishment Clause itself.

It has been argued that to apply the Constitution in such a way as to prohibit state laws respecting an establishment of religious services in public schools is to indicate a hostility toward religion or toward prayer. Nothing, of course, could be more wrong. The history of man is inseparable from the history of religion. And perhaps it is not too much to say that since the beginning of that history many people have devoutly believed that "More things are wrought by prayer than this world dreams of." It was doubtless largely due to men who believed this that there grew up a sentiment that caused men to leave the crosscurrents of officially established state religions and religious persecution in Europe and come to this country filled with the hope that they could find a place in which they could pray when they pleased to the God of their faith in the language they chose. And there were men of this same faith in the power of prayer who led the fight for adoption of our Constitution and also for our Bill of Rights with the very guarantees of religious freedom that forbid the sort of governmental activity which New York has attempted here. These men knew that the First Amendment, which tried to put an end to governmental control of religion and of prayer, was not written to destroy either. They knew rather that it was written to quiet well-justified fears which nearly all of them felt arising out of an awareness that governments of the past had shackled men's tongues to make them speak only the religious thoughts that government wanted them to speak and to pray only to the God that government wanted them to pray to. It is neither sacrilegious nor antireligious to say that each separate government in this country should stay out of the business of writing or sanctioning official prayers and leave that purely religious function to the people themselves and to those the people choose to look to for religious guidance.

It is true that New York's establishment of its Regents' prayer as an officially approved religious doctrine of that state does not amount to a total establishment of one particular religious sect to the exclusion of all others—that, indeed, the governmental endorsement of that prayer seems relatively insignificant when compared to the governmental encroachments upon religion which were commonplace 200 years ago. To those who may subscribe to the view that because the Regents' official prayer is so brief and general there can be no danger to religious freedom in its governmental establishment, however, it may be appropriate to say in the words of James Madison, the author of the First Amendment:

> [I]t is proper to take alarm at the first experiment on our liberties. . . . Who does not see that the same authority which can establish Christianity, in exclusion of all other Religions, may establish with the same ease any particular sect of Christians, in exclusion of all other Sects? That the same authority which can force a citizen to contribute three pence only of his property for the support of any one establishment, may force him to conform to any other establishment in all cases whatsoever?

The judgment of the Court of Appeals of New York is reversed and the cause remanded for further proceedings not inconsistent with this opinion.

Reversed and remanded.

Mr. Justice Frankfurter took no part in the decision of this case.

Mr. Justice White took no part in the consideration or decision of this case.

Mr. Justice Douglas concurred in a separate opinion.

Mr. Justice Stewart, dissenting:

A local school board in New York has provided that those pupils who wish to do so may join in a brief prayer at the beginning of each school day, acknowledging their dependence upon God and asking His blessing upon them and upon their parents, their teachers, and their country. The court today decides that in permitting this brief nondenominational prayer the school board has violated the Constitution of the United States. I think this decision is wrong.

The Court does not hold, nor could it, that New York has interfered with the free exercise of anybody's religion. For the state courts have made clear that those who object to reciting the prayer must be entirely free of any compulsion to do so, including any "embarrassments and pressure." Cf. *West Virginia State Board of Education* v. *Barnette*, 319 U.S. 624. But the Court says that in permitting school children to say this simple prayer, the New York authorities have established "an official religion."

With all respect, I think the Court has misapplied a great constitutional principle. I cannot see how an "official religion" is established by letting those who want to say a prayer say it. On the contrary, I think that to deny the wish of these school children to join in reciting this prayer is to deny them the opportunity of sharing in the spiritual heritage of our nation.

The Court's historical review of the quarrels over the Book of Common Prayer in England throws no light for me on the issue before us in this case. England had then and has now an established church. Equally unenlightening, I think, is the history of the early establishment and later rejection of an official church in our own states. For we deal here not with the establishment of a state church, which would, of course, be constitutionally impermissible, but with whether school children who want to begin their day by joining in prayer must be prohibited from doing so. Moreover, I think that the Court's task, in this as in all areas of constitutional adjudication, is not responsibly aided by the uncritical invocation of metaphors like the "wall of separation," a phrase nowhere to be found in the Constitution. What is relevant to the issue here is not the history of an established church in sixteenth-century England or in eighteenth-century America, but the history of the religious traditions of our people, reflected in countless practices of the institutions and officials of our government.

At the opening of each day's session of this Court we stand, while one of our officials invokes the protection of God. Since the days of John Marshall our Crier has said, "God save the United States and this Honorable Court." Both the Senate and the House of Representatives open their daily sessions with prayer. Each of our Presidents, from George Washington to John F. Kennedy, has upon assuming his office asked the protection and help of God.

The Court today says that the state and federal governments are without constitutional power to prescribe any particular form of words to be recited by any group of the American people on any subject touching religion. The third stanza of "The Star-Spangled Banner," made our national anthem by Act of Congress in 1931, contains these verses:

Blest with victory and peace, may the heav'n rescued land
Praise the Pow'r that hath made and preserved us a nation!

> Then conquer we must, when our cause it is just,
> And this be our motto, "In God is our Trust."

In 1954 Congress added a phrase to the Pledge of Allegiance to the Flag so that it now contains the words "one Nation *under* God indivisible, with liberty and justice for all." In 1952 Congress enacted legislation calling upon the President each year to proclaim a National Day of Prayer. Since 1865 the words "IN GOD WE TRUST" have been impressed on our coins.

Countless similar examples could be listed, but there is no need to belabor the obvious. It was all summed up by this Court just ten years ago in a single sentence: "We are a religious people whose institutions presuppose a Supreme Being." *Zoarch v. Clauson*, 343 U.S. 306, 313.

I do not believe that this Court, or the Congress, or the President has by the actions and practices I have mentioned established an "official religion" in violation of the Constitution. And I do not believe the state of New York has done so in this case. What each has done has been to recognize and to follow the deeply entrenched and highly cherished spiritual traditions of our nation—traditions which come down to us from those who almost two hundred years ago avowed their "firm reliance on the Protection of Divine Providence" when they proclaimed the freedom and independence of this brave new world.

I dissent.

THE RIGHT TO ABORTION

Ironically, while the "liberal" Warren Court stirred political controversy with its school prayer and many other decisions extending civil liberties and rights to the states, it was the "conservative" Supreme Court under the chief justiceship of Warren Burger, who was appointed by Republican President Richard M. Nixon in 1969, that raised an even greater political storm by holding in the following case that the Fourteenth Amendment incorporates a right to privacy that grants women the absolute right to abortion during the first trimester of pregnancy. When the decision was handed down in 1973, a majority of states strictly regulated abortions, which could be performed if at all only to protect the life of the mother. The moral codes of many religions, particularly the Catholic church, forbid abortions under any circumstances.

Supporters of the abortion decision argued that while the issue was indeed a moral one for most people, women had a constitutionally protected right to decide whether or not they would have an abortion. Opponents not only emphatically opposed abortion on moral grounds, but also attacked the Court for acting as a supralegislature by imposing its own values upon democratically elected state legislative bodies that were regulating abortion in response to the demands of popular majorities.

The Supreme Court's abortion decision did seem to resurrect "substantive due process," a doctrine under which the Court had in the past judged the fairness of state legislation in terms not of explicitly stated constitutional standards but on the basis of its own values. The Bill of Rights does not contain a general right of privacy, although it may be fairly implied, as Justice Douglas wrote for a majority of the Court in *Griswold* v. *Connecticut*, 381 U.S. 479 (1965), from First Amendment freedoms of association, Fourth Amendment protections against unreasonable searches and seizures, and the Fifth Amendment shield against self-incrimination.

Whether emanating indirectly from the Bill of Rights or considered to be part of the liberty protected by the Fourteenth Amendment, the right of privacy that the Supreme Court applied in its abortion decision is highly subjective and gives the justices great leeway to impose their own concepts of privacy rights upon legislative bodies. But judicial decisions, especially those of the Supreme Court, always express the values of those making them. The justices did go beyond a strict construction of the Bill of Rights in upholding a woman's right to abortion. However, they had previously interpreted the Fourteenth Amendment due process clause just as subjectively in each case in the step-by-step process of nationalization of most of the provisions of the Bill Rights.

The Anglo-American system of law and jurisprudence has always supported the concept of a higher law that ultimately the courts must interpret and apply. In Great Britain, however, Parliament became supreme after the Glorious Revolution of 1688, preventing judicial review of parliamentary laws. Our Supreme Court, on the other hand, continues to be the final judge of what the law is, and inevitably its decisions will involve the Court in major political controversies, as has been the case in the following opinion.

19
ROE V. WADE
410 U.S. 113 (1973)

❖❖❖❖❖❖❖❖

Mr. Justice Blackmun delivered the opinion of the Court:

V

The principal thrust of appellant's attack on the Texas statutes is that they improperly invade a right, said to be possessed by the pregnant woman, to choose to terminate her pregnancy. Appellant would discover this right in the concept of personal "liberty" embodied in the Fourteenth Amendment's Due Process Clause; or in personal, marital, familial, and sexual privacy said to be protected by the Bill of Rights or its penumbras, see *Griswold* v. *Connecticut* [1965] . . . *Eisenstadt* v. *Baird* [1972]

... (White, J., concurring in result); or among those rights reserved to the people by the Ninth Amendment, *Griswold* v. *Connecticut*, ... (Goldberg, J., concurring). Before addressing this claim, we feel it desirable briefly to survey, in several aspects, the history of abortion, for such insight as that history may afford us, and then to examine the state purposes and interests behind the criminal abortion laws.

VI

It perhaps is not generally appreciated that the restrictive criminal abortion laws in effect in a majority of States today are of relatively recent vintage. Those laws, generally proscribing abortion or its attempt at any time during pregnancy except when necessary to preserve the pregnant woman's life, are not of ancient or even of common-law origin. Instead, they derive from statutory changes effected, for the most part, in the latter half of the 19th century. . . .

VII

Three reasons have been advanced to explain historically the enactment of criminal abortion laws in the 19th century and to justify their continued existence.

It has been argued occasionally that these laws were the product of a Victorian social concern to discourage illicit sexual conduct. Texas, however, does not advance this justification in the present case, and it appears that no court or commentator has taken the argument seriously. The appellants and amici contend, moreover, that this is not a proper state purpose at all and suggest that, if it were, the Texas statutes are overbroad in protecting it since the law fails to distinguish between married and unwed mothers.

A second reason is concerned with abortion as a medical procedure. When most criminal abortion laws were first enacted, the procedure was a hazardous one for the woman. This was particularly true prior to the development of antisepsis. Antiseptic techniques, of course, were based on discoveries by Lister, Pasteur, and others first announced in 1867, but were not generally accepted and employed until about the turn of the century. Abortion mortality was high. Even after 1900, and perhaps until as late as the development of antibiotics in the 1940's, standard modern techniques such as dilation and curettage were not nearly so safe as they are today. Thus, it has been argued that a State's real concern in enacting a criminal abortion law was to protect the pregnant woman, that is, to restrain her from submitting to a procedure that placed her life in serious jeopardy.

Modern medical techniques have altered this situation. Appellants and various amici refer to medical data indicating that abortion in early pregnancy, this is, prior to the end of the first trimester, although not without its risk, is now relatively safe. Mortality rates for women undergoing early abortions, where the procedure is legal, appear to be as low as or lower than the rates for normal childbirth. Consequently, any interest of the State in protecting the woman from an inherently hazardous procedure, except when it would be equally dangerous for her to forgo it, has largely disappeared. Of course, important state interests in the area of health and medical standards do remain.

The State has a legitimate interest in seeing to it that abortion, like any other medical procedure, is performed under circumstances that insure maximum safety for the patient. This interest obviously extends at least to the performing physician and his staff, to the facilities involved, to the availability of aftercare, and to adequate provision for any complication or emergency that might arise. The prevalence of high mortality rates at illegal "abortion mills" strengthens, rather than weakens, the State's interest in regulating the conditions under which abortions are performed. Moreover, the risk to the woman increases as her pregnancy continues. Thus, the State retains a definite interest in protecting the woman's own health and safety when an abortion is proposed at a late stage of pregnancy.

The third reason is the State's interest—some phrase it in terms of duty—in protecting prenatal life. Some of the argument for this justification rests on the theory that a new human life is present from the moment of conception. The State's interest and general obligation to protect life then extends, it is argued, to prenatal life. Only when the life of the pregnant mother herself is at stake, balanced against the life she carries within her, should the interest of the embryo or fetus not prevail. Logically, of course, a legitimate state interest in this area need not stand or fall on acceptance of the belief that life begins at conception or at some other point prior to live birth. In assessing the State's interest, recognition may be given to the less rigid claim that as long as at least *potential* life is involved, the State may assert interests beyond the protection of the pregnant woman alone.

Parties challenging state abortion laws have sharply disputed in some courts the contention that a purpose of these laws, when enacted, was to protect prenatal life. . . .

It is with these interests, and the weight to be attached to them, that this case is concerned.

VIII

The Constitution does not explicitly mention any right of privacy. In a line of decisions, however, going back perhaps as far as *Union Pacific R. Co. v. Botsford* [1891] . . . , the Court has recognized that a right of personal privacy, or a guarantee of certain areas or zones of privacy, does exist under the Constitution. In varying contexts, the Court or individual Justices have, indeed, found at least the roots of that right in the First Amendment, *Stanley* v. *Georgia* [1969] . . . ; in the Fourth and Fifth Amendments, *Terry* v. *Ohio* [1968] . . . , *Katz* v. *United States* [1967] . . . ; in the penumbras of the Bill of Rights, *Griswold* v. *Connecticut* [1965] . . . ; in the Ninth Amendments, id., at 486, . . . (Goldberg, J., concurring); or in the concept of liberty guaranteed by the first section of the Fourteenth Amendment, see *Meyer* v. *Nebraska* [1923]. . . . These decisions make it clear that only personal rights that can be deemed "fundamental" or "implicit in the concept of ordered liberty," *Palko* v. *Connecticut* [1937] . . . , are included in this guarantee of personal privacy. They also make it clear that the right has some extension to activities relating to marriage, *Loving* v. *Virginia* [1967] . . . ; procreation, *Skinner* v. *Oklahoma* [1942] . . . ; contraception, *Eisenstadt* v. *Baird* [1972]. . . .

This right of privacy, whether it be founded in the Fourteenth Amendment's concept of personal liberty and restrictions upon state action, as we feel it is, or, as the District Court determined, in the Ninth Amendment's reservation of rights to the people, is broad enough to encompass a woman's decision whether or not to terminate her pregnancy. The detriment that the State would impose upon the pregnant woman by denying this choice altogether is apparent. Specific and direct harm medically diagnosable even in early pregnancy may be involved. Maternity, or additional offspring, may force upon the woman a distressful life and future. Psychological harm may be imminent. Mental and physical health may be taxed by child care. There is also the distress, for all concerned, associated with the unwanted child, and there is the problem of bringing a child into a family already unable, psychologically and otherwise, to care for it. In other cases, as in this one, the additional difficulties and continuing stigma of unwed motherhood may be involved. All these are factors the woman and her responsible physician necessarily will consider in consultation.

On the basis of elements such as these, appellant and some amici argue that the woman's right is absolute and that she is entitled to terminate her pregnancy at whatever time, in whatever way, and for whatever reason she alone chooses. With this we do not agree. Appellant's arguments that Texas either has no valid interest at all in regulating the abortion decision, or no interest strong enough to support any limitation upon the woman's sole determination, is unpersuasive. The Court's decisions recognizing a right of privacy also acknowledge that some state regulation in areas protected by that right is appropriate. As noted above, a State may properly assert important interests in safeguarding health, in maintaining medical standards, and in protecting potential life. At some point in pregnancy, these respective interests become sufficiently compelling to sustain regulation of the factors that govern the abortion decision. The privacy right involved, therefore, cannot be said to be absolute. In fact, it is not clear to us that the claim asserted by some amici that one has an unlimited right to do with one's body as one pleases bears a close relationship to the right of privacy previously articulated in the Court's decisions. The Court has refused to recognize an unlimited right of this kind in the past. *Jacobson v. Massachusetts* [1905] . . . (vaccination); *Buck v. Bell* [1927] . . . (sterilization).

We, therefore, conclude that the right of personal privacy includes the abortion decision, but that this right is not unqualified and must be considered against important state interests in regulation.

Where certain "fundamental rights" are involved, the Court has held that regulation limiting these rights may be justified only by a "compelling state interest," . . . and that legislative enactments must be narrowly drawn to express only the legitimate state interests at stake. . . .

IX

The District Court held that the appellee failed to meet his burden of demonstrating that the Texas statute's infringement upon Roe's rights was necessary to support a compelling state interest. . . . Appellee argues that the State's determination to recognize and protect prenatal life from and after conception constitutes a compelling state interest. As noted above, we do not agree fully with either formulation.

A. The appellee and certain amici argue that the fetus is a "person" within the language and meaning of the Fourteenth Amendment. In support of this, they outline at length and in detail the well-known facts of fetal development. If this suggestion of personhood is established, the appellant's case, of course, collapses, for the fetus' right to life is then guaranteed specifically by the Amendment. The appellant conceded as much on reargument. On the other hand, the appellee conceded on reargument that no case could be cited that holds that a fetus is a person within the meaning of the Fourteenth Amendment.

The Constitution does not define "person" in so many words. Section 1 of the Fourteenth Amendment contains three references to "person." The first, in defining "citizens," speaks of "persons born or naturalized in the United States." The word also appears both in the Due Process Clause and in the Equal Protection Clause. "Person" is used in other places in the Constitution. . . . But in nearly all these instances, the use of the word is such that it has application only postnatally. None indicates, with any assurance, that it has any possible prenatal application.

All this, together with our observation, supra, that throughout the major portion of the 19th century prevailing legal abortion practices were far freer than they are today, persuades us that the word "person," as used in the Fourteenth Amendment, does not include the unborn. . . .

B. The pregnant woman cannot be isolated in her privacy. She carries an embryo and, later, a fetus, if one accepts the medical definitions of the developing young in the human uterus. . . . The situation therefore is inherently different from marital intimacy, or bedroom possession of obscene material, or marriage, or procreation, or education, with which *Eisenstadt, Griswold, Stanley, Loving, Skinner, Pierce,* and *Meyer* were respectively concerned. As we have intimated above, it is reasonable and appropriate for a State to decide that at some point in time another interest, that of health of the mother or that of potential human life, becomes significantly involved. The woman's privacy is no longer sole and any right of privacy she possesses must be measured accordingly.

Texas urges that, apart from the Fourteenth Amendment, life begins at conception and is present throughout pregnancy, and that, therefore, the State has a compelling interest in protecting that life from and after conception. We need not resolve the difficult question of when life begins. When those trained in the respective disciplines of medicine, philosophy, and theology are unable to arrive at any consensus, the judiciary, at this point in the development of man's knowledge, is not in a position to speculate as to the answer.

It should be sufficient to note briefly the wide divergence of thinking on this most sensitive and difficult question. . . .

X

In view of all this, we do not agree that, by adopting one theory of life, Texas may override the rights of the pregnant woman that are at stake. We repeat, however, that the State does have an important and legitimate interest in preserving and protecting the health of the pregnant woman, whether she be a resident of the State or a nonresident who seeks medical consultation and treatment there, and that it has still *another* important and legitimate interest in protecting the potentiality of human life. These interests are separate and distinct. Each grows in substantiality as the woman approaches term and, at a point during pregnancy, each becomes "compelling."

With respect to the State's important and legitimate interest in the health of the mother, the "compelling" point, in the light of present medical knowledge, is at approximately the end of the first trimester. This is so because of the now-established medical fact, referred to above . . . that until the end of the first trimester mortality in abortion may be less than mortality in normal childbirth. It follows that, from and after this point, a State may regulate the abortion procedure to the extent that the regulation reasonable relates to the preservation and protection of maternal health. Examples of permissible state regulation in this area are requirements as to the qualifications of the person who is to perform the abortion; as to the licensure of that person; as to the facility in which the procedure is to be performed, that is, whether it must be a hospital or may be a clinic or some other place of less-than-hospital status; as to the licensing of the facility; and the like.

This means, on the other hand, that, for the period of pregnancy prior to this "compelling" point, the attending physician, in consultation with his patient, is free to determine, without regulation by the State, that, in his medical judgment, the patient's pregnancy should be terminated. If that decision is reached, the judgment may be effectuated by an abortion free of interference by the State.

With respect to the State's important and legitimate interest in potential life, the "compelling" point is at viability. This is so because the fetus then presumably has the capability of meaningful life outside the mother's womb. State regulation protective of fetal life after viability thus has both logical and biological justifications. If the State is interested in protecting fetal life after viability, it may go so far as to proscribe abortion during that period, except when it is necessary to preserve the life or health of the mother.

Measured against these standards, Art. 1196 of the Texas Penal Code, in restricting legal abortions to those "procured or attempted by medical advice for the purpose of saving the life of the mother," sweeps too broadly. The statute makes no distinction between abortions performed early in pregnancy and those performed later, and it limits to a single reason, "saving" the mother's life, the legal justification for the procedure. The statute, therefore, cannot survive the constitutional attack made upon it here. . . .

XI

To summarize and to repeat:

1. A state criminal abortion statute of the current Texas type, that excepts from criminality only a *lifesaving* procedure on behalf of the mother, without regard to pregnancy stage and without recognition of the other interests involved, is violative of the Due Process Clause of the Fourteenth Amendment.

(a) For the stage prior to approximately the end of the first trimester, the abortion decision and its effectuation must be left to the medical judgment of the pregnant woman's attending physician.

(b) For the stage subsequent to approximately the end of the first trimester, the State, in promoting its interest in the health of the mother, may, if it chooses, regulate the abortion procedure in ways that are reasonably related to maternal health.

(c) For the stage subsequent to viability, the State in promoting its interest in the potentiality of human life may, if it chooses, regulate, and even proscribe, abortion except where it is necessary, in appropriate medical judgment, for the preservation of the life or health of the mother.

2. The State may define the term "physician," as it has been employed in the preceding numbered paragraphs of this Part XI of this opinion, to mean only a physician currently licensed by the State, and may proscribe any abortion by a person who is not a physician as so defined.

In *Doe* v. *Bolton* [1973] . . . procedural requirements contained in one of the modern abortion statutes are considered. That opinion and this one, of course, are to be read together. . . .

Mr. Chief Justice Burger concurred.

Mr. Justice Douglas concurred.

Mr. Justice Stewart, concurring:

In 1963, this Court, in *Ferguson* v. *Skrupa*, . . . purported to sound the death knell for the doctrine of substantive due process, a doctrine under which many state laws had in the past been held to violate the Fourteenth Amendment. As Mr. Justice Black's opinion for the Court in *Skrupa* put it: "We have returned to the original constitutional proposition that courts do not substitute their social and economic beliefs for the judgment of legislative bodies, who are elected to pass laws.". . .

Barely two years later, in *Griswold* v. *Connecticut*, . . . the Court held a Connecticut birth control law unconstitutional. In view of what had been so recently said in *Skrupa*, the Court's opinion in *Griswold* understandably did its best to avoid reliance on the Due Process Clause of the Fourteenth Amendment as the ground for decision. Yet, the Connecticut law did not violate any provision of the Bill of Rights, nor any other specific provision of the Constitution. So it was clear to me then, and it is equally clear to me now, that the *Griswold* decision can be rationally understood only as a holding that the Connecticut statute substantively invaded the "liberty" that is protected by the Due Process Clause of the Fourteenth Amendment. As so understood, *Griswold* stands as one in a long line of pre-*Skrupa* cases decided under the doctrine of substantive due process, and I now accept it as such.

"In a Constitution for a free people, there can be no doubt that the meaning of 'liberty' must be broad indeed." . . . The Constitution nowhere mentions a specific right of personal choice in matters of marriage and family life, but the "liberty" protected by the Due Process Clause of the Fourteenth Amendment covers more than those freedoms explicitly named in the Bill of Rights. . . .

Several decisions of this Court make clear that freedom of personal choice in matters of marriage and family life is one of the liberties protected by the Due Process Clause of the Fourteenth Amendment. *Loving* v. *Virginia*, . . . *Griswold* v. *Connecticut.* . . . In *Eisenstadt* v. *Baird*, . . . we recognized "the right of the *individual*, married or single, to be free from unwarranted governmental intrusion into matters so fundamentally affecting a person as the decision whether to bear or beget a child." That right necessarily includes the right of a woman to decide whether or not to terminate her pregnancy. "Certainly the interests of a woman in giving of her physical and emotional self during pregnancy and the interest that will be affected throughout her life by the birth and raising of a child are of a far greater degree of significance and personal intimacy than the right to send a child to private school protected in *Pierce* v. *Society of Sisters* [1925]. . . , or the right to teach a foreign language protected in *Meyer* v. *Nebraska.* . . . "

Mr. Justice Rehnquist, dissenting:

. . . I have difficulty in concluding, as the Court does, that the right of "privacy" is involved in this case. Texas, by the statute here challenged, bars the performance of a medical abortion by a licensed physician on a plaintiff such as Roe. A transaction resulting in an operation such as this is not "private" in the ordinary usage of that word. . . .

If the Court means by the term "privacy" no more than that the claim of a person to be free from unwanted state regulation of consensual transactions may be a form of "liberty" protected by the Fourteenth Amendment, there is no doubt that similar claims have been upheld in our earlier decisions on the basis of the liberty. I agree with the statement of Mr. Justice Stewart in his concurring opinion that the "liberty," against deprivation of which without due process the Fourteenth Amendment protects, embraces more than the rights found in the Bill of Rights. But that liberty is not guaranteed absolutely against deprivation, only against deprivation without due process of law. The test traditionally applied in the area of social and economic legislation is whether or not a law such as that challenged has a rational relation to a valid state objective. . . . But the Court's sweeping invalidation of any restrictions on abortion during the first trimester is impossible to justify under that standard, and the conscious weighing of competing factors that the Court's opinion apparently substitutes for the established test is far more appropriate to a legislative judgment than to a judicial one.

The Court eschews the history of the Fourteenth Amendment in its reliance on the "compelling state interest" test. . . . But the Court adds a new wrinkle to this test by transposing it from the legal considerations associated with the Equal Protection Clause of the Fourteenth Amendment to this case arising under the Due Process Clause of the Fourteenth Amendment. Unless I misapprehend the consequences of this transplanting of the "compelling state interest test," the Court's opinion will accomplish the seemingly impossible feat of leaving this area of the law more confused than it found it.

While the Court's opinion quotes from the dissent of Mr. Justice Holmes in *Lochner* v. *New York*, the result it reaches is more closely attuned to the majority

opinion of Mr. Justice Peckham in that case. As in *Lochner* and similar cases applying substantive due process standards to economic and social welfare legislation, the
adoption of the compelling state interest standard will inevitably require this Court
to examine the legislative policies and pass on the wisdom of these policies in the
very process of deciding whether a particular state interest put forward may or may
not be "compelling." The decision here to break pregnancy into three distinct
terms and to outline the permissible restrictions the State may impose in each one,
for example, partakes more of judicial legislation than it does of a determination of
the intent of the drafters of the Fourteenth Amendment.

The fact that a majority of the States reflecting, after all the majority sentiment in those States, have had restrictions on abortions for at least a century is a
strong indication, it seems to me, that the asserted right to an abortion is not "so
rooted in the traditions and conscience of our people as to be ranked as fundamental," *Snyder* v. *Massachusetts* [1934]. . . . Even today, when society's views on
abortion are changing, the very existence of the debate is evidence that the
"right" to an abortion is not so universally accepted as the appellant would have
us believe.

To reach its result, the Court necessarily has had to find within the scope of the
Fourteenth Amendment a right that was apparently completely unknown to the
drafters of the Amendment. As early as 1821, the first state law dealing directly
with abortion was enacted by the Connecticut Legislature. . . . By the time of the
adoption of the Fourteenth Amendment in 1868, there were at least 36 laws enacted by state or territorial legislatures limiting abortion. While many States have
amended or updated their laws, 21 of the laws on the books in 1868 remain in effect
today. . . .

. . . The only conclusion possible from this history is that the drafters did not
intend to have the Fourteenth Amendment withdraw from the States the power to
legislate with respect to this matter. . . .

Mr. Justice White, joined by Mr. Justice Rehnquist, dissented.

❖❖ The Court's decision in *Roe* v. *Wade* (1973) almost immediately mobilized
pro-life forces who pressured Congress for a constitutional amendment to
overturn the *Roe* decision. Elected officials were caught in a political vise on
the issue, which they considered a no-win situation. Pro-lifers constituted a
powerful political movement but not a majority of the American people who,
after the *Roe* decision, favored the pro-choice position although not necessarily the practice of abortion.

For their part, politicians more often than not ducked the abortion issue by
making vague statements such as, "I am personally against abortion but I must
uphold and respect the Supreme Court's decision on the matter." Before the
Roe decision, many states were well on their way toward liberalizing their
abortion statutes in an environment that was relatively free of political rancor.

Ironically, the *Roe* decision galvanized political opposition to abortion and forced politicians, however reluctantly, to deal with the issue. As state statutes regulating abortion were struck down one after the other, the pro-life movement gathered more steam than converts.

While pressing for a constitutional amendment, the pro-lifers knew that their best hope was to convince the Supreme Court to overturn *Roe* v. *Wade*. Litigation had produced the decision, and litigation could overturn it if the Court's composition changed to a more conservative, pro-life viewpoint.

Ronald Reagan's election to the presidency in 1980 gave the pro-lifers renewed hopes for change. Reagan took a strong pro-life position, putting the issue at the top of his social agenda. During his eight years as president he was able to make three conservative appointments to the Supreme Court—Sandra Day O'Connor, Antonin Scalia, and Anthony M. Kennedy. Reagan and the pro-lifers had reason to hope that these new justices might tip the Court's scale in favor of overruling *Roe* v. *Wade*.

The suspense on both sides of the abortion issue was almost unbearable as the Court in 1989 reviewed a circuit court decision that had struck down a Missouri abortion law on the ground that it violated the principles of *Roe* v. *Wade*. The law prohibited the use of public facilities or employees to perform abortions, and prohibited the use of public funds for abortion counseling. The following decision, while not overruling *Roe* v. *Wade*, marked the beginning of a change in the Court's attitude on the abortion issue. A *plurality* of justices, led by Chief Justice William H. Rehnquist, began a process of dismantling *Roe*, but did not take the final step, urged by Justice Scalia, of overturning it. Justice Blackmun, who had written the *Roe* opinion, dissented along with Justices Brennan and Marshall. Blackmun wrote, "The simple truth is that *Roe* would not survive the plurality's analysis, and that the plurality provides no substitute for *Roe*'s protective umbrella. I fear for the future. I fear for the liberty and equality of the millions of women who have lived and come of age in the sixteen years since *Roe* was decided. I fear for the integrity of, and public esteem for, this Court." He concluded, "For today, at least, the law of abortion stands undisturbed. For today, the women of this nation still retain the liberty to control their destinies. But the signs are evident and very ominous and a chill wind blows."

While it seems unlikely that the Supreme Court will overrule *Roe* v. *Wade* in its entirety, the Rehnquist Court has allowed states to regulate abortion to a greater degree than *Roe* v. *Wade* would have permitted. Chief Justice Rehnquist, Justice Antonin Scalia, and other Justices have rejected much of Justice Blackmun's reasoning in *Roe* v. *Wade*'s majority opinion.

Conservatives have broadly attacked Roe's affirmation of the constitutional right to privacy, first "discovered" in *Griswold* v. *Connecticut* (1965), to support the right to abortion. In the following selection Supreme Court Justice Ruth Bader Ginsburg argues that had the court used gender equality considerations to strike down the statute in Roe it might well have avoided the legal and political controversy over the case that continues to rage.

20

Ruth Bader Ginsburg

SOME THOUGHTS ON AUTONOMY AND EQUALITY IN RELATION TO ROE V. WADE[1]

The 1973 United States Supreme Court decision in *Roe* v. *Wade* sparked a legal and political controversy that continues to this day. Judge Ginsburg suggests that the *Roe* opinion would have been more acceptable if it had not gone beyond a ruling on the extreme statute involved in the case. She agrees with commentary maintaining that the Court should have adverted specifically to sex equality considerations. Such an approach might have muted the criticism of the *Roe* decision. The breadth and detail of the *Roe* opinion ironically may have stimulated, rather than discourage, antiabortion measures, particularly with respect to public funding of abortion.

These remarks contrast two related areas of constitutional adjudication: gender-based classification and reproductive autonomy. In both areas, the Burger Court, in contrast to the Warren Court, has been uncommonly active. The two areas are intimately related in this practical sense: the law's response to questions subsumed under these headings bears pervasively on the situation of women in society. Inevitably, the shape of the law on gender-based classification and reproductive autonomy indicates and influences the opportunity women will have to participate as men's full partners in the nation's social, political, and economic life.

Doctrine in the two areas, however, has evolved in discrete compartments. The High Court has analyzed classification by gender under an equal protection/sex discrimination rubric; it has treated reproductive autonomy under a substantive due process/personal autonomy headline not expressly linked to discrimination against women. The Court's gender classification decisions overturning state and federal legislation, in the main, have not provoked large controversy; the Court's initial 1973 abortion decision, *Roe* v. *Wade*, on the other hand, became and remains a storm center. *Roe* v. *Wade* sparked public opposition and academic criticism, in part, I believe, because the Court ventured too far in the change it ordered and presented an incomplete justification for its action. I will attempt to explain these twin perspectives on *Roe* later in this Essay.

"Some Thoughts on Autonomy and Equality in Relation to *Roe v. Wade*," by Ruth Bader Ginsburg, *North Carolina Law Review*, Volume 63, 1985. Reprinted by permission of the North Carolina Law Review.

[1]*North Carolina Law Review,* volume 63, 1984, pp. 375–386.

Preliminarily, I will relate why an invitation to speak at Chapel Hill on any topic relating to constitutional law led me to think about gender-based classification coupled with *Roe* and its aftermath. In 1971, just before the Supreme Court's turning-point gender-classification decision in *Reed* v. *Reed,* and over a year before *Roe* v. *Wade,* I visited a neighboring institution to participate in a conference on women and the law. I spoke then of the utility of litigation attacking official line-drawing by sex. My comments focused on the chance in the 1970s that courts, through constitutional adjudication, would aid in evening out the rights, responsibilities, and opportunities of women and men. I did not mention the abortion cases then on the dockets of several lower courts—I was not at that time or any other time thereafter personally engaged in reproductive-autonomy litigation. Nonetheless, the most heated questions I received concerned abortion.

The questions were pressed by black men. The suggestion, not thinly veiled, was that legislative reform and litigation regarding abortion might have less to do with individual autonomy or discrimination against women than with restricting population growth among oppressed minorities. The strong word "genocide" was uttered more than once. It is a notable irony that, as constitutional law in this domain has unfolded, women who are not poor have achieved access to abortion with relative ease; for poor women, however, a group in which minorities are disproportionately represented, access to abortion is not markedly different from what it was in pre-*Roe* days.

I will summarize first the Supreme Court's performance in cases challenging explicit gender-based classification—a development that has encountered no significant backlash—and then turn to the far more turbulent reproductive autonomy area.

The Warren Court uncabined the equal protection guarantee in diverse settings, but line drawing by sex was a quarter in which no change occurred in the 1950s and 1960s. From the 1960s until 1971, the record remained unbroken: the Supreme Court rejected virtually every effort to overturn sex-based classification by law. Without offense to the Constitution, for example, women could be kept off juries and could be barred from occupations ranging from lawyer to bartender.

In the 1970s overt sex-based classification fell prey to the Burger Court's intervention. Men could not be preferred to women for estate administration purposes, the Court declared in the pivotal *Reed* v. *Reed* decision. Married women in the military could not be denied fringe benefits—family housing and health care allowances—accorded married men in military service, the High Court held in *Frontiero* v. *Richardson.* Social security benefits, welfare assistance, and workers' compensation secured by a male's employment must be secured, to the same extent, by a female's employment, the Supreme Court ruled in a progression of cases: *Weinberger* v. *Wiesenfeld, Califano* v. *Goldfarb, Califano* v. *Westcott,* and *Wengler* v. *Druggists Mutual Insurance Co.* Girls are entitled to the same parental support as boys, the Supreme Court stated in *Stanton* v. *Stanton.* Evidencing its neutrality, the Court declared in *Craig* v. *Boren* that boys must be permitted to buy 3.2 percent beer at the same age as girls and, in *Orr* v. *Orr,* that alimony could not be retained as a one-way street: a state could compel able men to make payments to women in need only if it also held women of means accountable for payments to men unable to fend for themselves. Louisiana's rule, derived from

Napoleon's Civil Code, designating husband head and master of the household, was held in *Kirchberg* v. *Feenstra* to be offensive to the evolving sex equality principle.

However sensible—and noncontroversial—these results, the decisions had a spectacular aspect. The race cases that trooped before the Warren Court could be viewed as moving the federal judiciary onto the course set by the Reconstruction Congress a century earlier in the post-Civil War amendments. No similar foundation, set deliberately by actors in the political arena, can account for the Burger Court sex discrimination decisions. Perhaps for that reason, the Court has proceeded cautiously. It has taken no giant step. In its most recent decision, *Mississippi University for Women* v. *Hogan*, the High Court recognized the right of men to a nursing school education at an institution maintained by the state for women only. But it earlier had declined to condemn a state property tax advantage reserved for widows, a state statutory rape law penalizing males but not females, and draft registration limited to males. It has formally reserved judgment on the question whether, absent ratification of an equal rights amendment, sex, like race, should rank as a suspect classification.

The Court's gender-based classification precedent impelled acknowledgment of a middle-tier equal protection standard of review, a level of judicial scrutiny demanding more than minimal rationality but less than a near-perfect fit between legislative ends and means. This movement away from the empty-cupboard interpretation of the equal protection principle in relation to sex equality claims largely trailed and mirrored changing patterns in society—most conspicuously, the emergence of the two-career family. The Court's decisions provoked no outraged opposition in legislative chambers. On the contrary, in a key area in which the Court rejected claims of impermissible sex-based classification, Congress indicated a different view, one more sensitive to discrimination against women.

That area, significantly in view of the Court's approach to reproductive choice, was pregnancy. In 1974 the Court decided an issue pressed by pregnant school teachers forced to terminate their employment, or take unpaid maternity leave, months before the anticipated birth date. Policies singling out pregnant women for disadvantageous treatment discriminated invidiously on the basis of sex, the teachers argued. The Court bypassed that argument; instead, the Court rested its decision holding mandatory maternity leaves unconstitutional on due process/conclusive presumption reasoning. Some weeks later, the Court held that a state-operated disability income protection plan could exclude normal pregnancy without offense to the equal protection principle. In a statutory setting as well, under Title VII, the Court later ruled, as it earlier had held in a constitutional context, that women unable to work due to pregnancy or childbirth could be excluded from disability coverage. The classifications in these disability cases, according to the Court, were not gender-based on their face, and were not shown to have any sex-discriminatory effect. All "nonpregnant persons," women along with men, the Court pointed out, were treated alike.

With respect to Title VII, Congress prospectively overruled the Court in 1978. It amended the statute to state explicitly that classification on the basis of sex includes classification on the basis of pregnancy. That congressional definition is not controlling in constitutional adjudication, but it might stimulate the Court one day to revise its position that regulation governing "pregnant persons" is not sex-based.

Roe v. Wade, in contrast to decisions involving explicit male/female classification, has occasioned searing criticism of the Court, over a decade of demonstrations, a stream of vituperative mail addressed to Justice Blackmun (the author of the opinion), annual proposals for overruling *Roe* by constitutional amendment, and a variety of measures in Congress and state legislatures to contain or curtail the decision. In 1973, when *Roe* issued, abortion law was in a state of change across the nation. There was a distinct trend in the states, noted by the Court, "toward liberalization of abortion statutes." Several states had adopted the American Law Institute's Model Penal Code approach setting out grounds on which abortion could be justified at any stage of pregnancy; most significantly, the Code included as a permissible ground preservation of the woman's physical or mental health. Four states—New York, Washington, Alaska, and Hawaii—permitted physicians to perform first-trimester abortions with virtually no restrictions. This movement in legislative arenas bore some resemblance to the law revision activity that eventually swept through the states establishing no-fault divorce as the national pattern.

The Texas law at issue in *Roe* made it a crime to "procure an abortion" except "by medical advice for the purpose of saving the life of the mother." It was the most extreme prohibition extant. The Court had in close view two pathmarking opinions on reproductive autonomy: first, a 1965 precedent, *Griswold* v. *Connecticut,* holding inconsistent with personal privacy, somehow sheltered by due process, a state ban on the use of contraceptives even by married couples; second, a 1972 decision, *Eisenstadt* v. *Baird,* extending *Griswold* to strike down a state prohibition on sales of contraceptives except to married persons by prescription. The Court had already decided *Reed* v. *Reed,* recognizing the arbitrariness in the 1970s of a once traditional gender-based classification, but it did not further pursue that avenue in *Roe.*

The decision in *Roe* appeared to be a stunning victory for the plaintiffs. The Court declared that a woman, guided by the medical judgment of her physician, had a "fundamental" right to abort a pregnancy, a right the Court anchored to a concept of personal autonomy derived from the due process guarantee. The Court then proceeded to define with precision the state regulation of abortion henceforth permissible. The rulings in *Roe,* and in a companion case decided the same day, *Doe* v. *Bolton,* were stunning in this sense: they called into question the criminal abortion statutes of every state, even those with the least restrictive provisions.

Roe announced a trimester approach Professor Archibald Cox has described as "read[ing] like a set of hospital rules and regulations." During the first trimester, "the abortion decision and its effectuation must be left to the medical judgment of the pregnant woman's attending physician"; in the next, roughly three-month stage, the state may, if it chooses, require other measures protective of the woman's health. During the final months, "the stage subsequent to viability," the state also may concern itself with an emerging interest, the "potentiality of human life"; at that stage, the state "may, if it chooses, regulate, and even proscribe, abortion except where it is necessary, in appropriate medical judgment, for the preservation of the life or health of the mother."

Justice O'Connor, ten years after *Roe*, described the trimester approach as "on a collision course with itself." Advances in medical technology would continue to move *forward* the point at which regulation could be justified as protective of a woman's health, and to move *backward* the point of viability, when the state could proscribe abortions unnecessary to preserve the patient's life or health. The approach, she thought, impelled legislatures to remain *au courant* with changing medical practices and called upon courts to examine legislative judgments, not as jurists applying "neutral principles," but as "science review boards."

I earlier observed that, in my judgment, *Roe* ventured too far in the change it ordered. The sweep and detail of the opinion stimulated the mobilization of a right-to-life movement and an attendant reaction in Congress and state legislatures. In place of the trend "toward liberalization of abortion statutes" noted in *Roe*, legislatures adopted measures aimed at minimizing the impact of the 1973 rulings, including notification and consent requirements, prescriptions for the protection of fetal life, and bans on public expenditures for poor women's abortions.

Professor Paul Freund explained where he thought the Court went astray in *Roe*, and I agree with his statement. The Court properly invalidated the Texas proscription, he indicated, because "[a] law that absolutely made criminal all kinds and forms of abortion could not stand up; it is not a reasonable accommodation of interests." If *Roe* had left off at that point and not adopted what Professor Freund called a "medical approach," physicians might have been less pleased with the decision, but the legislative trend might have continued in the direction in which it was headed in the early 1970s. "[S]ome of the bitter debate on the issue might have been averted," Professor Freund believed; "[t]he animus against the Court might at least have been diverted to the legislative halls." Overall, he thought that the *Roe* distinctions turning on trimesters and viability of the fetus illustrated a troublesome tendency of the modern Supreme Court under Chief Justices Burger and Warren "to specify by a kind of legislative code the one alternative pattern that will satisfy the Constitution."

I commented at the outset that I believe the Court presented an incomplete justification for its action. Academic criticism of *Roe*, charging the Court with reading its own values into the due process clause, might have been less pointed had the Court placed the woman alone, rather than the woman tied to her physician, at the center of its attention. Professor Karst's commentary is indicative of the perspective not developed in the High Court's opinion; he solidly linked abortion prohibitions with discrimination against women. The issue in *Roe*, he wrote, deeply touched and concerned "women's position in society in relation to men."

It is not a sufficient answer to charge it all to women's anatomy—a natural, not man-made, phenomenon. Society, not anatomy, "places a greater stigma on unmarried women who become pregnant than on the men who father their children." Society expects, but nature does not command, that "women take the major responsibility . . . for child care" and that they will stay with their children, bearing nurture and support burdens alone, when fathers deny paternity or otherwise refuse to provide care or financial support for unwanted offspring.

I do not pretend that, if the Court had added a distinct sex discrimination theme to its medically oriented opinion, the storm *Roe* generated would have been less furious. I appreciate the intense divisions of opinion on the moral question and recognize that abortion today cannot fairly be described as nothing more than birth control delayed. The conflict, however, is not simply one between a fetus' interests and a woman's interests, narrowly conceived, nor is the overriding issue state versus private control of a woman's body for a span of nine months. Also in the balance is a woman's autonomous charge of her full life's course—as Professor Karst put it, her ability to stand in relation to man, society, and the state as an independent, self-sustaining, equal citizen.

On several occasions since *Roe* the Court has confronted legislative responses to the decision. With the notable exception of the public funding cases, the Court typically has applied *Roe* to overturn or limit efforts to impede access to abortion. I will not survey in the brief compass of this Essay the Court's series of opinions addressing: regulation of the abortion decisionmaking process; specifications regarding personnel, facilities, and medical procedures; and parental notification and consent requirements in the case of minors. Instead, I will simply highlight the Court's statement last year reaffirming *Roe*'s "basic principle that a woman has a fundamental right to make the highly personal choice whether or not to terminate her pregnancy." In *City of Akron* v. *Akron Center for Reproductive Health, Inc.*, the Court acknowledged arguments it continues to hear that *Roe* "erred in interpreting the Constitution." Nonetheless, the Court declared it would adhere to *Roe* because "*stare decisis*, while perhaps never entirely persuasive on a constitutional question, is a doctrine that demands respect in a society governed by the rule of law."

I turn, finally, to the plight of the woman who lacks resources to finance privately implementation of her personal choice to terminate her pregnancy. The hostile reaction to *Roe* has trained largely on her.

Some observers speculated that the seven-two judgment in *Roe* was motivated at least in part by pragmatic considerations—population control concerns, the specter of coat hanger abortions, and concerns about unwanted children born to impoverished women. I recalled earlier the view that the demand for open access to abortions had as its real purpose suppressing minorities. In a set of 1977 decisions, however, the Court upheld state denial of medical expense reimbursement or hospital facilities for abortions sought by indigent women. Moreover, in a 1980 decision, *Harris* v. *McRae*, the Court found no constitutional infirmity in the Hyde Amendment, which excluded even medically necessary abortions from Medicaid coverage. After these decisions, the Court was accused of sensitivity only to the Justices' own social milieu—"of creating a middle-class right to abortion."

The argument for constitutionally mandated public assistance to effectuate the poor woman's choice ran along these lines. Accepting that our Constitution's Bill of Rights places restraints, not affirmative obligations, on government, counsel for the impoverished women stressed that childbirth was publicly subsidized. As long as the government paid for childbirth, the argument proceeded, public funding could not be denied for abortion, often a safer and always a far less expensive course, short and long run. By paying for childbirth but not abortion, the complainants maintained, government increased spending and intruded upon or steered a choice *Roe* had ranked as a woman's "fundamental" right.

The Court responded that, like other individual rights secured by the Constitution, the right to abortion is indeed a negative right. Government could not intervene by blocking a woman's utilization of her own resources to effectuate her decision. It could not "'impose its will by force of law.'" But *Roe* did not demand government neutrality, the Court reasoned; it left room for substantive government control to this extent: Action "deemed in the public interest"—in this instance, protection of the potential life of the fetus—could be promoted by encouraging childbirth in preference to abortion.

Financial need alone, under the Court's jurisprudence, does not identify a class of persons whose complaints of disadvantageous treatment attract close scrutiny. Generally, constitutional claims to government benefits on behalf of the poor have prevailed only when tied to another bark—a right to travel interstate, discrimination because of out-of-wedlock birth, or gender-based discrimination. If the Court had acknowledged a woman's equality aspect, not simply a patient-physician autonomy constitutional dimension to the abortion issue, a majority perhaps might have seen the public assistance cases as instances in which, borrowing a phrase from Justice Stevens, the sovereign had violated its "duty to govern impartially."

I have tried to discuss some features of constitutional adjudication concerning sex equality, in relation to the autonomy and equal-regard values involved in cases on abortion. I have done so tentatively and with trepidation. *Roe* v. *Wade* is a decision I approached gingerly in prior comment; until now I have limited my remarks to a brief description of what others have said. While I claim no original contribution, I have endeavored here to state my own reflections and concerns.

Roe, I believe, would have been more acceptable as a judicial decision if it had not gone beyond a ruling on the extreme statute before the Court. The political process was moving in the early 1970s, not swiftly enough for advocates of quick, complete change, but majoritarian institutions were listening and acting. Heavy-handed judicial intervention was difficult to justify and appears to have provoked, not resolved, conflict.

The public funding of abortion decisions appear incongruous following so soon after the intrepid 1973 rulings. The Court did not adequately explain why the "fundamental" choice principle and trimester approach embraced in *Roe* did not bar the sovereign, at least at the previability stage of pregnancy, from taking sides.

Overall, the Court's *Roe* position is weakened, I believe, by the opinion's concentration on a medically approved autonomy idea, to the exclusion of a constitutionally based sex-equality perspective. I understand the view that for political reasons the reproductive autonomy controversy should be isolated from the general debate on equal rights, responsibilities, and opportunities for women and men. I expect, however, that organized and determined opposing efforts to inform and persuade the public on the abortion issue will continue through the 1980s. In that process there will be opportunities for elaborating in public forums the equal-regard conception of women's claims to reproductive choice uncoerced and unsteered by government.

AFFIRMATIVE ACTION

The Supreme Court has unequivocally ruled that racial discrimination by law is unconstitutional. When the law treats *racial* groups differently, it is almost invariably the case that the Court will declare the law to be a violation of the equal protection clause of the Fourteenth Amendment or, where federal action is involved, the standards of equal protection required under the due process clause of the Fifth Amendment.[1]

Before the era of the Warren court, which began in 1953 and led immediately to the *Brown* decision, the Supreme Court applied a "rational-relation" or "conceivable-basis" test to determine if legislative classifications that treated separate groups of people differently constituted a violation of equal protection standards. Generally, under these tests the Court upheld the legislative classifications if it found there was a rational relationship between the classifications and legislative goals. Such classifications were also upheld if the Court found a conceivable basis upon which to support the reasoning of the legislature in creating classifications. These equal protection standards are referred to as the "old equal protection."

The Warren court inaugurated the "new equal protection" standards to apply to legislative classifications based on race or other "suspect" group classifications. For example, gender classifications have come to be regarded by the Burger court as at least partly suspect.[2] The new equal protection standards required the demonstration of a "compelling" governmental interest to uphold the legislative classifications under review. The new equal protection standards also required the demonstration of a compelling governmental interest to sustain legislative classifications that burdened fundamental rights. For example, in *Shapiro* v. *Thompson,* 394 U.S. 618 (1969), the Warren court reviewed challenges to state and District of Columbia laws denying welfare assistance to persons who had not resided within their jurisdictions for at least one year immediately prior to applying for assistance. The Court found that the laws burdened the fundamental right to travel, and therefore could be sustained only upon the demonstration of a compelling governmental interest. The Court found no such compelling interest present and held the laws to be unconstitutional. The application of the new equal protection standard is called *strict judicial scrutiny.* When the Court employs this strict judicial scrutiny, the invariable effect is to declare unconstitutional the classification in the law under review.

In the *Bakke* case, presented below, the opinions of Justices Powell and Brennan discuss the circumstances under which strict judicial scrutiny is required by the equal protection clause of the Fourteenth Amendment. This case arose out of a complex set of circumstances. Title VI of the Civil Rights Act of 1964 provided that no person was to be "subjected to discrimination under

---

[1]An important exception to the rigid application of equal protection standards to racial classification was the holding of the Supreme Court in *Korematsu* v. *United States,* 323 U.S. 214 (1944), which upheld a racial classification that treated Japanese-Americans differently than other citizens. The Court found that the federal government could exclude Japanese-Americans from military zones on the West Coast on the ground of national security, a holding that in effect supported the establishment of relocation centers for Japanese-American citizens during World War II.

[2]See, for example, *Frontiero* v. *Richardson,* 411 U.S. 677 (1973).

any program or activity receiving federal financial assistance." The Department of Health, Education and Welfare found this section to require affirmative action programs by private institutions receiving federal aid, to achieve a racial balance among employees and, in institutions of higher learning, within their student bodies as well. Throughout the country, pressure from civil rights groups, women, and other minorities prompted the adoption of affirmative action plans that contained racial classifications providing for the favored treatment of racial minorities in school admissions and private employment.

The *Bakke* case was initiated by Allan Bakke, a 36-year-old white engineer who decided that he wanted to become a doctor. In 1973 and 1974 he applied, unsuccessfully, for admission to the University of California Medical School at Davis. The school informed Bakke that there were too many qualified applicants and that it could admit only one out of 26 in 1973, and one out of 37 in 1974. However, 16 of the 100 openings in the Davis medical school were set aside for minority applicants. Bakke's objective qualifications, such as his Medical College Admission Test scores and his undergraduate grades, were better than those of some of the minority applicants who were accepted during the years when he was rejected. The minority applicants competed among themselves for the 16 places reserved for them, making it possible to admit minority students with different qualifications than were required of nonminority applicants. Bakke claimed that the admissions procedures violated the equal protection clause and Title VI of the Civil Rights Act of 1964.

The trial court in the *Bakke* case held that the admissions program established racial quotas in violation of the equal protection clause and Title VI. However, the court refused to order the admission of Bakke to the medical school because of his failure to prove that he would have been admitted in the absence of the special program for minorities. The California Supreme Court sustained the trial court's finding that the program violated the equal protection clause and the Civil Rights Act but overruled the trial court's denial of an order that Bakke be admitted. The United States Supreme Court granted certiorari to the California Supreme Court to review the case.

The California Supreme Court, by a five-four vote, ruled that Bakke should be admitted to the Davis Medical School. The majority on the issue of admittance agreed that the racial quota system at the school was not an acceptable means to decide who should be admitted. The majority justices favoring admission and a ban on quotas were Powell, Burger, Stevens, Rehnquist, and Stewart. Brennan, White, Marshall, and Blackmun dissented on these issues, arguing that "Davis's special admissions program cannot be said to violate the Constitution simply because it has set aside a predetermined number of places for qualified minority applicants. . . ."

Justice Louis F. Powell, who was in the majority favoring admission and a ban on quotas, joined with the four justices who dissented from the Court's decision and opinion on those issues to form another majority that held that an applicant's race can be considered in deciding who should be admitted to a university program.

21

REGENTS OF THE UNIVERSITY OF CALIFORNIA
v. BAKKE
438 U.S. 265 (1978)

❖❖❖❖❖❖❖

Mr. Justice Powell announced the judgment of the Court and wrote an opinion:

For the reasons stated in the following opinion, I believe that so much of the judgment of the California court as holds petitioner's special admissions program unlawful and directs that respondent be admitted to the Medical School must be affirmed. For the reasons expressed in a separate opinion, my Brothers The Chief Justice, Mr. Justice Stewart, Mr. Justice Rehnquist, and Mr. Justice Stevens concur in this judgment.

I also conclude for the reasons stated in the following opinion that the portion of the court's judgment enjoining petitioner from according any consideration to race in its admissions process must be reversed. For reasons expressed in separate opinions, my Brothers Mr. Justice Brennan, Mr. Justice White, Mr. Justice Marshall, and Mr. Justice Blackmun concur in this judgment.

Affirmed in part and reversed in part.

II

B

The language of § 601 [of the Civil Rights Act of 1964], like that of the Equal Protection Clause, is majestic in its sweep:

> No person in the United States shall, on the ground of race, color, or national origin, be excluded from participation in, be denied the benefits of, or be subjected to discrimination under any program or activity receiving Federal financial assistance.

The concept of "discrimination," like the phrase "equal protection of the laws," is susceptible of varying interpretations, for as Mr. Justice Holmes declared, "[a] word is not a crystal, transparent and unchanged, it is the skin of a living thought and may vary greatly in color and content according to the circumstances and the time in which it is used." . . . We must, therefore, seek whatever aid is available in determining the precise meaning of the statute before us. . . . Examination of the voluminous legislative history of Title VI reveals a congressional intent to halt federal funding of entities that violate a prohibition of racial discrimination similar to that of the Constitution. Although isolated statements of various legislators, taken out of context, can be marshaled in support of the proposition that § 601 enacted a purely color-blind scheme, without regard to the reach of the Equal Protection Clause, these comments must be read against the background of both the problem that Congress was addressing and the broader view of the statute that emerges from a full examination of the legislative debates.

The problem confronting Congress was discrimination against Negro citizens at the hands of recipients of federal moneys. Indeed, the color blindness pronouncements [of Congress] generally occur in the midst of extended remarks dealing with the evils of segregation in federally funded programs. Over and over again, proponents of the bill detailed the plight of Negroes seeking equal treatment in such programs. There simply was no reason for Congress to consider the validity of hypothetical preferences that might be accorded minority citizens; the legislators were dealing with the real and pressing problem of how to guarantee those citizens equal treatment.

In addressing that problem, supporters of Title VI repeatedly declared that the bill enacted constitutional principles. . . .

In the Senate, Senator Humphrey declared that the purpose of Title VI was "to insure that Federal funds are spent in accordance with the Constitution and the moral sense of the Nation.". . .

Further evidence of the incorporation of a constitutional standard into Title VI appears in the repeated refusals of the legislation's supporters precisely to define the term "discrimination." Opponents sharply criticized this failure, but proponents of the bill merely replied that the meaning of "discrimination" would be made clear by reference to the Constitution or other existing law. . . .

In view of the clear legislative intent, Title VI must be held to proscribe only those racial classifications that would violate the Equal Protection Clause or the Fifth Amendment.

III

A

Petitioner does not deny that decisions based on race or ethnic origin by faculties and administrations of state universities are reviewable under the Fourteenth Amendment. . . . For his part, respondent does not argue that all racial or ethnic classifications are *per se* invalid. . . . The parties do disagree as to the level of judicial scrutiny to be applied to the special admissions program. Petitioner argues that the court below erred in applying strict scrutiny, as this inexact term has been applied in our cases. . . .

En route to this crucial battle over the scope of judicial review, the parties fight a sharp preliminary action over the proper characterization of the special admissions program. Petitioner prefers to view it as establishing a "goal" of minority representation in the Medical School. Respondent, echoing the courts below, labels it a racial quota.

This semantic distinction is beside the point: The special admissions program is undeniably a classification based on race and ethnic background. To the extent that there existed a pool of at least minimally qualified minority applicants to fill the 16 special admissions seats, white applicants could compete only for 84 seats in the entering class, rather than the 100 open to minority applicants. Whether this limitation is described as a quota or a goal, it is a line drawn on the basis of race and ethnic status.

The guarantees of the Fourteenth Amendment extend to all persons. Its language is explicit: "No State shall . . . deny to any person within its jurisdiction the equal protection of the laws." It is settled beyond question that the "rights created by the first section of the Fourteenth Amendment are, by its terms, guaranteed to the individual. The rights established are personal rights.". . . The guarantee of equal protection cannot mean one thing when applied to one individual and something else when applied to a person of another color. If both are not accorded the same protection, then it is not equal.

Nevertheless, petitioner argues that the court below erred in applying strict scrutiny to the special admissions program because white males, such as respondent, are not a "discrete and insular minority" requiring extraordinary protection from the majoritarian political process. . . . This rationale, however, has never been invoked in our decisions as a prerequisite to subjecting racial or ethnic distinctions to strict scrutiny. Nor has this Court held that discreteness and insularity constitute necessary preconditions to a holding that a particular classification is invidious. . . . These characteristics may be relevant in deciding whether or not to add new types of classifications to the list of "suspect" categories or whether a particular classification survives close examination. . . . Racial and ethnic classifications, however, are subject to stringent examination without regard to these additional characteristics. We declared as much in the first cases explicitly to recognize racial distinctions as suspect:

> Distinctions between citizens solely because of their ancestry are by their very nature odious to a free people whose institutions are founded upon the doctrine of equality. *Hirabayashi* [v. *United States* (1943)].

> [A]ll legal restrictions which curtail the civil rights of a single racial group are immediately suspect. That is not to say that all such restrictions are unconstitutional. It is to say that courts must subject them to the most rigid scrutiny. *Korematsu* [v. *United States* (1944)].

The Court has never questioned the validity of those pronouncements. Racial and ethnic distinctions of any sort are inherently suspect and thus call for the most exacting judicial examination. . . .

Although many of the Framers of the Fourteenth Amendment conceived of its primary function as bridging the vast distance between members of the Negro race and the white "majority" . . . the amendment itself was framed in universal terms, without reference to color, ethnic origin, or condition of prior servitude. As this Court recently remarked in interpreting the 1866 Civil Rights Act to extend to claims of racial discrimination against white persons, "the 39th Congress was intent upon establishing in the federal law a broader principle than would have been necessary simply to meet the particular and immediate plight of the newly freed Negro slaves.". . .

Over the past 30 years, this Court has embarked upon the crucial mission of interpreting the Equal Protection Clause with the view of assuring to all persons "the protection of equal laws. . . " in a Nation confronting a legacy of slavery and racial discrimination. . . . Because the landmark decisions in this area arose in response to the continued exclusion of Negroes from the mainstream of American society, they could be characterized as involving discrimination by the "majority" white race against the Negro minority. But they need not be read as depending upon that characterization for their results. It suffices to say that "[o]ver the years, this Court has consistently repudiated '[d]istinctions between citizens solely because of their ancestry' as being 'odious to a free people whose institutions are founded upon the doctrine of equality.'"". . .

Petitioner urges us to adopt for the first time a more restrictive view of the Equal Protection Clause and hold that discrimination against members of the white "majority" cannot be suspect if its purpose can be characterized as "benign." The clock of our liberties, however, cannot be turned back to 1868. . . . It is far too late to argue that the guarantee of equal protection to *all* persons permits the recognition of special wards entitled to a degree of protection greater than that accorded others. "The Fourteenth Amendment is not directed solely against discrimination due to a 'two-class theory'—that is, based upon differences between 'white' and Negro.". . .

Once the artificial line of a "two-class theory" of the Fourteenth Amendment is put aside, the difficulties entailed in varying the level of judicial review according to a perceived "preferred" status of a particular racial or ethnic minority are intractable. The concepts of "majority" and "minority" necessarily reflect temporary arrangements and political judgments. As observed above, the white "majority" itself is composed of various minority groups, most of which can lay claim to a history of prior discrimination at the hands of the State and private individuals. Not all of these groups can receive preferential treatment and corresponding judicial tolerance of distinctions drawn in terms of race and nationality, for then the only "majority" left would be a new minority of white Anglo-Saxon Protestants. There is no principled basis for deciding which groups would merit "heightened judicial solicitude" and which would not. Courts would be asked to evaluate the extent of the prejudice and consequent harm suffered by various minority groups. Those whose societal injury is thought to exceed some arbitrary level of tolerability then would be entitled to preferential classifications at the expense of individuals belonging to other groups. Those classifications would be free from exacting judicial scrutiny. As these preferences began to have their desired effect, and the consequences of past discrimination were undone, new judicial rankings would be necessary. The kind of variable sociological and political analysis necessary to produce such rankings simply does not lie within the judicial competence—even if they otherwise were politically feasible and socially desirable.

Moreover, there are serious problems of justice connected with the idea of preference itself. First, it may not always be clear that a so-called preference is in fact benign. . . . Second, preferential programs may only reinforce common stereotypes holding that certain groups are unable to achieve success without special protection based on a factor having no relationship to individual worth. . . . Third, there is a measure of inequity in forcing innocent persons in respondent's position to bear the burdens of redressing grievances not of their making.

By hitching the meaning of the Equal Protection Clause to these transitory considerations, we would be holding, as a constitutional principle, that judicial scrutiny of classifications touching on racial and ethnic background may vary with the ebb and flow of political forces. Disparate constitutional tolerance of such classifications well may serve to exacerbate racial and ethnic antagonisms rather than alleviate them. . . . Also, the mutability of a constitutional principle, based upon shifting political and social judgments, undermines the chances for consistent application of the Constitution from one generation to the next, a critical feature of its coherent interpretation. . . . In expounding the Constitution, the Court's role is to discern "principles sufficiently absolute to give them roots throughout the community and continuity over significant periods of time, and to lift them above the level of the pragmatic political judgments of a particular time and place.". . .

IV

We have held that in "order to justify the use of a suspect classification, a State must show that its purpose or interest is both constitutionally permissible and substantial, and that its use of the classification is 'necessary . . . to the accomplishment' of its purpose or the safeguarding of its interest.". . . The special admissions program purports to serve the purposes of: (i) "reducing the historic deficit of traditionally disfavored minorities in medical schools and in the medical profession"; (ii) countering the effects of societal discrimination; (iii) increasing the number of physicians who will practice in communities currently underserved; and (iv) obtaining the educational benefits that flow from an ethnically diverse student body. It is necessary to decide which, if any, of these purposes is substantial enough to support the use of a suspect classification.

A

If petitioner's purpose is to assure within its student body some specified percentage of a particular group merely because of its race or ethnic origin, such a preferential purpose must be rejected not as insubstantial but as facially invalid. Preferring members of any one group for no reason other than race or ethnic origin is discrimination for its own sake. This the Constitution forbids. . . .

B

. . . [T]he purpose of helping certain groups whom the faculty of the Davis Medical School perceived as victims of "societal discrimination" does not justify a classification that imposes disadvantages upon persons like respondent, who bear no responsibility for whatever harm the beneficiaries of the special admissions program are thought to have suffered. To hold otherwise would be to convert a remedy heretofore reserved for violations of legal rights into a privilege that all institutions throughout the Nation could grant at their pleasure to whatever groups are perceived as victims of societal discrimination. That is a step we have never approved. . . .

C

Petitioner identifies, as another purpose of its program, improving the delivery of health-care services to communities currently underserved. It may be assumed that in some situations a State's interest in facilitating the health care of its citizens is sufficiently compelling to support the use of a suspect classification. But there is virtually no evidence in the record indicating that petitioner's special admissions program is either needed or geared to promote that goal. . . .

D

The fourth goal asserted by petitioner is the attainment of a diverse student body. This clearly is a constitutionally permissible goal for an institution of higher education. Academic freedom, though not a specifically enumerated constitutional right, long has been viewed as a special concern of the First Amendment. . . .

. . . As the interest of diversity is compelling in the context of a university's admissions program, the question remains whether the program's racial classification is necessary to promote this interest. . . .

V

A

It may be assumed that the reservation of a specified number of seats in each class for individuals from the preferred ethnic groups would contribute to the attainment of considerable ethnic diversity in the student body. But petitioner's argument that this is the only effective means of serving the interest of diversity is seriously flawed. . . . Petitioner's special admissions program, focused *solely* on ethnic diversity, would hinder rather than further attainment of genuine diversity. . . .

The experience of other university admissions programs, which take race into account in achieving the educational diversity valued by the First Amendment, demonstrates that the assignment of a fixed number of places to a minority group is not a necessary means toward that end. . . .

B

In summary, it is evident that the Davis special admissions program involves the use of an explicit racial classification never before countenanced by this Court. It tells applicants who are not Negro, Asian, or Chicano that they are totally excluded from a specific percentage of the seats in an entering class. No matter how strong their qualifications, quantitative and extracurricular, including their own potential for contribution to educational diversity, they are never afforded the chance to compete with applicants from the preferred groups for the special admissions seats. At the same time, the preferred applicants have the opportunity to compete for every seat in the class.

The fatal flaw in petitioner's preferential program is its disregard of individual rights as guaranteed by the Fourteenth Amendment. . . . Such rights are not absolute. But when a State's distribution of benefits or imposition of burdens hinges on ancestry or the color of a person's skin or ancestry, that individual is entitled to a demonstration that the challenged classification is necessary to promote a substantial state interest. Petitioner has failed to carry this burden. For this reason, that portion of the California court's judgment holding petitioner's special admissions program invalid under the Fourteenth Amendment must be affirmed.

C

In enjoining petitioner from ever considering the race of any applicant, however, the courts below failed to recognize that the State has a substantial interest that legitimately may be served by a properly devised admissions program involving the competitive consideration of race and ethnic origin. For this reason, so much of the California court's judgment as enjoins petitioner from any consideration of the race of any applicant must be reversed.

Opinion of Mr. Justice Brennan, Mr. Justice White, Mr. Justice Marshall, and Mr. Justice Blackmun, concurring in the judgment in part and dissenting in part:

The Court today, in reversing in part the judgment of the Supreme Court of California, affirms the constitutional power of Federal and State Governments to act affirmatively to achieve equal opportunity for all. The difficulty of the issue presented—whether government may use race-conscious programs to redress the continuing effects of past discrimination—and the mature consideration which each of our Brethren has brought to it have resulted in many opinions, no single one speaking for the Court. But this should not and must not mask the central meaning of today's opinions: Government may take race into account when it acts not to demean or insult any racial group, but to remedy disadvantages cast on minorities by past racial prejudice, at least when appropriate findings have been made by judicial, legislative, or administrative bodies with competence to act in this area.

The Chief Justice and our Brothers Stewart, Rehnquist, and Stevens, have concluded that Title VI of the Civil Rights Act of 1964, . . . as amended, . . . prohibits programs such as that at the Davis Medical School. On this statutory theory alone, they would hold that respondent Allan Bakke's rights have been violated and he must, therefore, be admitted to the Medical School. Our Brother Powell, reaching the Constitution, concludes that, although race may be taken into account in university admissions, the particular special admissions program used by petitioner, which resulted in the exclusion of respondent Bakke, was not shown to be necessary to achieve petitioner's stated goals. Accordingly, these Members of the

Court from a majority of five affirming the judgment of the Supreme Court of California insofar as it holds that respondent Bakke "is entitled to an order that he be admitted to the University.". . .

We agree with Mr. Justice Powell that, as applied to the case before us, Title VI goes no further in prohibiting the use of race than the Equal Protection Clause of the Fourteenth Amendment itself. We also agree that the effect of the California Supreme Court's affirmance of the judgment of the Supreme Court of California would be to prohibit the University from establishing in the future affirmative action programs that take race into account. . . . Since we conclude that the affirmative admissions program at the Davis Medical School is constitutional, we would reverse the judgment below in all respects. Mr. Justice Powell agrees that some uses of race in university admissions are permissible and, therefore, he joins with us to make five votes reversing the judgment below insofar as it prohibits the University from establishing race-conscious programs in the future. . . .

II

. . . In our view, Title VI prohibits only those uses of racial criteria that would violate the Fourteenth Amendment if employed by a State or its agencies; it does not bar the preferential treatment of racial minorities as a means of remedying past societal discrimination to the extent that such action is consistent with the Fourteenth Amendment. The legislative history of Title VI, administrative regulations interpreting the statute, subsequent congressional and executive action, and the prior decisions of this Court compel this conclusion. None of these sources lends support to the proposition that Congress intended to bar all race-conscious efforts to extend the benefits of federally financed programs to minorities who have been historically excluded from the full benefits of American life. . . .

III

A

The assertion of human equality is closely associated with the proposition that differences in color or creed, birth or status, are neither significant nor relevant to the way in which persons should be treated. Nonetheless, the position that such factors must be "constitutionally an irrelevance" . . . summed up by the shorthand phrase "[o]ur Constitution is color-blind." *Plessy* v. *Ferguson* [1896] . . . has never been adopted by this Court as the proper meaning of the Equal Protection Clause. Indeed, we have expressly rejected this proposition on a number of occasions.

Our cases have always implied that an "overriding statutory purpose" . . . could be found that would justify racial classifications. . . .

We conclude, therefore, that racial classifications are not *per se* invalid under the Fourteenth Amendment. Accordingly, we turn to the problem of articulating what our role should be in reviewing state action that expressly classifies by race.

B

Respondent argues that racial classifications are always suspect and, consequently, that this Court should weigh the importance of the objectives served by Davis' special admissions program to see if they are compelling. . . .

Unquestionably we have held that a government practice or statute which restricts "fundamental rights" or which contains "suspect classifications" is to be subjected to "strict scrutiny" and can be justified only if it furthers a compelling government purpose and, even then, only if no less restrictive alternative is available. . . . But no fundamental right is involved here. . . . Nor do whites as a class have any of the "traditional indicia of suspectness: the class is not saddled with such disabilities, or subjected to such a history of purposeful unequal treatment, or relegated to such a position of political powerlessness as to command extraordinary protection from the majoritarian political process.". . .

On the other hand, the fact that this case does not fit neatly into our prior analytic framework for race cases does not mean that it should be analyzed by applying the very loose rational-basis standard of review that is the very least that is always applied in equal protection cases. " '[T]he mere recitation of a benign, compensatory purpose is not an automatic shield which protects against any inquiry into the actual purposes underlying a statutory scheme.' ". . . Instead, a number of considerations—developed in gender-discrimination cases but which carry even more force when applied to racial classifications—lead us to conclude that racial classifications designed to further remedial purposes "'must serve important governmental objectives and must be substantially related to achievement of those objectives.'". . .

First, race, like "gender-based classifications too often [has] been inexcusably utilized to stereotype and stigmatize politically powerless segments of society." . . . State programs designed ostensibly to ameliorate the effects of past racial discrimination obviously create the same hazard of stigma, since they may promote racial separatism and reinforce the views of those who believe that members of racial minorities are inherently incapable of succeeding on their own. . . .

Second, race, like gender and illegitimacy . . . is an immutable characteristic which its possessors are powerless to escape or set aside. While a classification is not *per se* invalid because it divides classes on the basis of an immutable characteristic . . . it is nevertheless true that such divisions are contrary to our deep belief that "legal burdens should bear some relationship to individual responsibility or wrongdoing" . . . and that advancement sanctioned, sponsored, or approved by the State should ideally be based on individual merit or achievement, or at the least on factors within the control of an individual. . . .

In sum, because of the significant risk that racial classification established for ostensibly benign purposes can be misused, causing effects not unlike those created by invidious classifications, it is inappropriate to inquire only whether there is any conceivable basis that might sustain such a classification. Instead, to justify such a classification an important and articulated purpose for its use must be shown. In addition, any statute must be stricken that stigmatizes any group or that singles out those least well represented in the political process to bear the brunt of a benign program. Thus, our review under the Fourteenth Amendment should be strict—not "'strict' in theory and fatal in fact," because it is stigma that causes fatality—but strict and searching nonetheless.

IV

Davis' articulated purpose of remedying the effects of past societal discrimination is, under our cases, sufficiently important to justify the use of race-conscious admissions programs where there is a sound basis for concluding that minority underrepresentation is substantial and chronic, and that the handicap of past discrimination is impeding access of minorities to the Medical School. . . .

A

. . . If it was reasonable to conclude—as we hold that it was—that the failure of minorities to qualify for admission at Davis under regular procedures was due principally to the effects of past discrimination, then there is a reasonable likelihood that, but for pervasive racial discrimination, respondent would have failed to qualify for admission even in the absence of Davis' special admissions program.

Thus, our cases under Title VII of the Civil Rights Act have held that, in order to achieve minority participation in previously segregated areas of public life, Congress may require or authorize preferential treatment for those likely disadvantaged by societal racial discrimination. Such legislation has been sustained even without a requirement of findings of intentional racial discrimination by those required or authorized to accord preferential treatment, or a case-by-case determination that those to be benefited suffered from racial discrimination. These decisions compel the conclusion that States also may adopt race-conscious programs designed to overcome substantial, chronic minority underrepresentation where there is reason to believe that the evil addressed is a product of past racial discrimination. . . .

[Section B reviews the facts supporting the existence of discrimination and the underrepresentation of minorities in the Davis and other medical schools.]

C

The second prong of our test—whether the Davis program stigmatizes any discrete group or individual and whether race is reasonably used in light of the program's objectives—is clearly satisfied by the Davis program.

It is not even claimed that Davis' program in any way operates to stigmatize or single out any discrete and insular, or even any identifiable, nonminority group. Nor will harm comparable to that imposed upon racial minorities by exclusion or separation on grounds of race be the likely result of the program. It does not, for example, establish an exclusive preserve for minority students apart from and exclusive of whites. Rather, its purpose is to overcome the effects of segregation by bringing the races together. True, whites are excluded from participation in the special admissions program, but this fact only operates to reduce the number of whites to be admitted in the regular admissions program in order to permit admission of a reasonable percentage—less than their proportion of the California population—of otherwise underrepresented qualified minority applicants.

Nor was Bakke in any sense stamped as inferior by the Medical School's rejection of him. Indeed, it is conceded by all that he satisfied those criteria regarded by the school as generally relevant to academic performance better than most of the minority members who were admitted. Moreover, there is absolutely no basis for concluding that Bakke's rejection as a result of Davis' use of racial preference will affect him throughout his life in the same way as the segregation of the Negro school children in *Brown I* would have affected them. Unlike discrimination against racial minorities, the use of racial preferences for remedial purposes does not inflict a pervasive injury upon individual whites in the sense that wherever they go or whatever they do there is a significant likelihood that they will be treated as second-class citizens because of their color. This distinction does not mean that the exclusion of a white resulting from the preferential use of race is not sufficiently serious to require justification; but it does mean that the injury inflicted by such a policy is not distinguishable from disadvantages caused by a wide range of government actions, none of which has ever been thought impermissible for that reason alone.

In addition, there is simply no evidence that the Davis program discriminates intentionally or unintentionally against any minority group which it purports to benefit. The program does not establish a quota in the invidious sense of a ceiling on the number of minority applicants to be admitted. Nor can the program reasonably be regarded as stigmatizing the program's beneficiaries or their race as inferior. The Davis program does not simply advance less qualified applicants; rather, it compensates applicants, who it is uncontested are fully qualified to study medicine, for educational disadvantages which it was reasonable to conclude were a product of state-fostered discrimination. Once admitted, these students must satisfy the same degree requirements as regularly admitted students; they are taught by the same faculty in the same classes; and their performance is evaluated by the same standards by which regularly admitted students are judged. Under these circumstances, their performance and degrees must be regarded equally with the regularly admitted students with whom they compete for standing. Since minority graduates cannot justifiably be regarded as less well qualified than nonminority graduates by virtue of the special admissions program, there is no reasonable basis to conclude that minority graduates at schools using such programs would be stigmatized as inferior by the existence of such programs.

D

We disagree with the lower courts' conclusion that the Davis program's use of race was unreasonable in light of its objectives. First, as petitioner argues, there are no practical means by which it could achieve its ends in the foreseeable future without the use of race-conscious measures. With respect to any factor (such as poverty or family educational background) that may be used as a substitute for race as an indicator of past discrimination, whites greatly outnumber racial minorities simply because whites make up a far larger percentage of the total population and therefore far outnumber minorities in absolute terms at every socioeconomic level. . . .

Second, the Davis admissions program does not simply equate minority status with disadvantage. Rather, Davis considers on an individual basis each applicant's personal history to determine whether he or she has likely been disadvantaged by racial discrimination. The record makes clear that only minority applicants likely to have been isolated from the mainstream of American life are considered in the special program; other minority applicants are eligible only through the regular admissions program. . . .

V

Accordingly, we would reverse the judgment of the Supreme Court of California holding the Medical School's special admissions program unconstitutional and directing respondent's admission, as well as that portion of the judgment enjoining the Medical School from according any consideration to race in the admissions process.

Mr. Justice Marshall wrote a separate opinion.

Mr. Justice Blackmun wrote a separate opinion.

Mr. Justice Stevens, with whom the Chief Justice, Mr. Justice Stewart, and Mr. Justice Rehnquist join, concurring in the judgment in part and dissenting in part:

Both petitioner and respondent have asked us to determine the legality of the University's admissions program by reference to the Constitution. Our settled practice, however, is to avoid the decision of a constitutional issue if a case can be fairly decided on a statutory ground. "If there is one doctrine more deeply rooted than any other in the process of constitutional adjudication, it is that we ought not to pass on questions of constitutionality . . . unless such adjudication is unavoidable.". . . The more important the issue, the more force there is to this doctrine. In this case, we are presented with a constitutional question of undoubted and unusual importance. Since, however, a dispositive statutory claim was raised at the very inception of this case, and squarely decided in the portion of the trial court judgment affirmed by the California Supreme Court, it is our plain duty to confront it. Only if petitioner should prevail on the statutory issue would it be necessary to decide whether the University's admissions program violated the Equal Protection Clause of the Fourteenth Amendment.

Section 601 of the Civil Rights Act of 1964 . . . provides:

No person in the United States shall, on the ground of race, color, or national origin, be excluded from participation in, be denied the benefits of, or be subjected to discrimination under any program or activity receiving Federal financial assistance.

The University, through its special admissions policy, excluded Bakke from participation in its program of medical education because of his race. The University also acknowledges that it was, and still is, receiving federal financial assistance. The plain language of the statute therefore requires affirmance of the judgment below. A different result cannot be justified unless that language misstates the actual intent of the Congress that enacted the statute or the statute is not enforceable in a private action. Neither conclusion is warranted. . . .

. . . [I]t seems clear that the proponents of Title VI assumed that the Constitution itself required a colorblind standard on the part of government, but that does not mean that the legislation only codifies an existing constitutional prohibition. The statutory prohibition against discrimination in federally funded projects contained in § 601 is more than a simple paraphrasing of what the Fifth or Fourteenth Amendment would require. . . .

In short, nothing in the legislative history justifies the conclusion that the broad language of § 601 should not be given its natural meaning. We are dealing with a distinct statutory prohibition, enacted at a particular time with particular concerns in mind; neither its language nor any prior interpretation suggests that its place in the Civil Rights Act, won after long debate, is simply that of a constitutional appendage. In unmistakable terms the Act prohibits the exclusion of individuals from federally funded programs because of their race. As succinctly phrased during the Senate debate, under Title VI it is not "permissible to say 'yes' to one person; but to say 'no' to another person, only because of the color of his skin.". . .

The University's special admissions program violated Title VI of the Civil Rights Act of 1964 by excluding Bakke from the Medical School because of his race. It is therefore our duty to affirm the judgment ordering Bakke admitted to the University.

Accordingly, I concur in the Court's judgment insofar as it affirms the judgment of the Supreme Court of California. To the extent that it purports to do anything else, I respectfully dissent.

❖❖ How do the standards of judicial scrutiny differ in the Powell and Brennan opinions? Justice Powell wrote, "Racial and ethnic distinctions of any sort are inherently suspect and thus call for the most exacting judicial examination." Applying strict judicial scrutiny, Powell found no compelling justification for the use of racial quotas by the Davis Medical School. Powell reasoned that "the purpose of helping certain groups whom the faculty of the Davis Medical School perceived as victims of 'societal discrimination' does not justify a classification that imposes disadvantages upon persons like respondent [Bakke], who bear no responsibility for whatever harm the beneficiaries of the special admissions program are thought to have suffered." While Powell held that racial quotas are banned, he ruled that race may be taken into account in admissions programs because "the state has a substantial [i.e., compelling] interest that legitimately may be served by a properly devised admissions program involving the competitive consideration of race and ethnic origin."

The dissenting opinion of Justice Brennan supported the use of racial quotas in the Davis admissions program. Underlying Brennan's dissenting opinion was the finding that the classification under review was not "suspect," nor did it affect fundamental rights; therefore, strict judicial scrutiny, under which a compelling state interest has to be demonstrated to uphold the classification, was not required. Justice Brennan and his fellow dissenters used an intermediate standard of judicial scrutiny, which required more than the mere demonstration of a rational relationship between the classification and the goals sought but less than the demonstration of a compelling state interest to uphold the classification. The intermediate standard announced by Justice Brennan was that the classification "must serve important governmental objectives and be substantially related to achievement of those objectives." To uphold a racial classification, stated Brennan, "an important and articulated purpose for its use must be shown. In addition, any statute must be stricken that stigmatizes any group or that singles out those least well represented in the political process to bear the brunt of a benign program." Brennan concluded that the court's review should be "strict," but not at the level of strict judicial scrutiny, which, because it requires the demonstration of compelling state interests, is always fatal to the program under review.

Affirmative action continued to be a major political issue after the Bakke decision. While the use of quotas was banned, race and gender considerations could still be taken into account in school admissions and employment programs. The push for affirmative action that began with President Lyndon B. Johnson, who issued an executive order requiring it for all government contractors and institutions receiving federal aid, continued unabated for over a decade, even during the Republican administrations of Nixon and Ford. However, President Ronald Reagan viewed affirmative action with suspicion, more as an undesirable government interference in private affairs than as a necessary policy to remedy the effects of past discrimination. Under Reagan affirmative action was muted, and the Justice Department even intervened in some cases on the side of plaintiffs challenging affirmative action programs. Opposition to affirmative action was not simply a conservative position, as many liberals also came to feel that the enforcement of affirmative action, which benefited groups, denied individuals the right to be judged on their merits. However, the Supreme Court rejected blanket attacks on affirmative action, holding in several key cases in 1986 that race-conscious practices and even quotas could be used in employment and promotion to remedy the effects of past discrimination.[1] However, the Court in *City of Richmond* v. *Croson* in 1989 overturned an affirmative action program that set aside 30 percent of city construction projects for minority enterprises. Justice Sandra Day O'Connor, who wrote the majority opinion, applied strict judicial scrutiny, finding that absent a finding of past discrimination the Fourteenth Amendment equal protection clause bans state or city government enforcement of racial quotas.

---

[1]*Firefighters* v. *Cleveland* and *Sheet Metal Workers* v. *Equal Employment Opportunity Commission*, decided July 2, 1986.

Equal Protection, Voting Rights, and Racial Gerrymandering

One of the most controversial issues the Supreme Court confronts in the mid-1990s is whether or not states can gerrymander their Congressional or state legislative districts along racial lines to ensure minority representation. Such apportionment schemes constitute racial classifications subject to "strict judicial scrutiny," which requires the demonstration of a compelling state interest to uphold the classification. State racial classifications bring the fourteenth amendment's equal protection clause into play, which requires states to grant all persons within their jurisdictions the equal protection of the laws.

In the following case the Supreme Court confronted first the question of whether a state apportionment plan constituted racial gerrymandering, and secondly whether such gerrymandering can be challenged under the equal protection clause of the Fourteenth Amendment. Plaintiffs in order to sustain an equal protection challenge must show a legislative *intent* to discriminate along racial lines, usually *against* a racial minority. But it can be argued that racial apportionment, giving minorities a majority in designated districts, helps to ensure the election of minority representatives to Congress and state legislatures.

In the case presented below, North Carolina had created a mostly black congressional district that stretched 160 miles along Interstate 85, often no wider than the highway corridor itself, winding, in the words of the court, "in snake-like fashion through tobacco country, financial centers, and manufacturing areas 'until it gobbles in enough enclaves of black neighborhoods.'" Clearly the district was racially gerrymandered, somewhat ironically in response to a Justice Department request under the Voting Rights Act of 1965 that North Carolina create two majority-black districts.[1] In the following opinion the Supreme Court, by a 5–4 majority, ruled that if, on remand, the Federal District Court sustained the allegations of racial gerrymandering that the plaintiffs had made, the apportionment could only be upheld if it was narrowly tailored to advance a compelling governmental interest.

22
Shaw v. Reno
113 S. Ct. 2816 (1993)

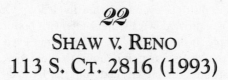

Justice O'Connor delivered the opinion of the Court.

---

[1]Under section 5 of the Voting Rights Act of 1965 Southern states with a history of past voting discrimination had to gain Justice Department approval for reapportionment plans.

This case involves two of the most complex and sensitive issues this Court has faced in recent years: the meaning of the constitutional "right" to vote, and the propriety of race-based state legislation designed to benefit members of historically disadvantaged racial minority groups. As a result of the 1990 census, North Carolina became entitled to a twelfth seat in the United States House of Representatives. The General Assembly enacted a reapportionment plan that included one majority-black congressional district. After the Attorney General of the United States objected to the plan pursuant to § 5 of the Voting Rights Act of 1965, the General Assembly passed new legislation creating a second majority-black district. Appellants allege that the revised plan, which contains district boundary lines of dramatically irregular shape, constitutes an unconstitutional racial gerrymander. The question before us is whether appellants have stated a cognizable claim.

I

The voting age population of North Carolina is approximately 78% white, 20% black, and 1% Native American; the remaining 1% is predominantly Asian. . . . The black population is relatively dispersed; blacks constitute a majority of the general population in only 5 of the State's 100 counties. . . .

The first of the two majority-black districts contained in the revised plan, District 1, is somewhat hook shaped. Centered in the northeast portion of the State, it moves southward until it tapers to a narrow band; then, with finger-like extensions, it reaches far into the southern-most part of the State near the South Carolina border. District 1 has been compared to a "Rorschach ink-blot test.". . .

The second majority-black district, District 12, is even more unusually shaped. It is approximately 160 miles long and, for much of its length, no wider than the I–85 corridor. It winds in snake-like fashion through tobacco country, financial centers, and manufacturing areas "until it gobbles in enough enclaves of black neighborhoods." . . . Northbound and southbound drivers on I–85 sometimes find themselves in separate districts in one county, only to "trade" districts when they enter the next county. Of the 10 counties through which District 12 passes, five are cut into three different districts; even towns are divided. . . . One state legislator has remarked that "'[i]f you drove down the interstate with both car doors open, you'd kill most of the people in the district.'". . . The district even has inspired poetry: "Ask not for whom the line is drawn; it is drawn to avoid thee.". . .

[A]ppellants instituted the present action in the United States District Court for the Eastern District of North Carolina. Appellants alleged not that the revised plan constituted a political gerrymander, nor that it violated the "one person, one vote" principle, see *Reynolds v. Sims,* 377 U. S. 533, 558 (1964), but that the State had created an unconstitutional *racial* gerrymander. Appellants are five residents of Durham County, North Carolina, all registered to vote in that county. Under the General Assembly's plan, two will vote for congressional representatives in District 12 and three will vote in neighboring District 2. . . .

Appellants contended that the General Assembly's revised reapportionment plan violated several provisions of the United States Constitution, including the

Fourteenth Amendment. They alleged that the General Assembly deliberately "create[d] two Congressional Districts in which a majority of black voters was concentrated arbitrarily—without regard to any other considerations, such as compactness, contiguousness, geographical boundaries, or political subdivisions" with the purpose "to create Congressional Districts along racial lines" and to assure the election of two black representatives to Congress. . . .

II

A

"The right to vote freely for the candidate of one's choice is of the essence of a democratic society. . . ." *Reynolds* v. *Sims*, 377 U. S., at 555. For much of our Nation's history, that right sadly has been denied to many because of race. The Fifteenth Amendment, ratified in 1870 after a bloody Civil War, promised unequivocally that "[t]he right of citizens of the United States to vote" no longer would be "denied or abridged . . . by any State on account of race, color, or previous condition of servitude.". . .

But "[a] number of states . . . refused to take no for an answer and continued to circumvent the fifteenth amendment's prohibition through the use of both subtle and blunt instruments, perpetuating ugly patterns of pervasive racial discrimination.". . . Ostensibly race-neutral devices such as literacy tests with "grandfather" clauses and "good character" provisos were devised to deprive black voters of the franchise. Another of the weapons in the States' arsenal was the racial gerrymander—"the deliberate and arbitrary distortion of district boundaries . . . for [racial] purposes.". . . In the 1870's, for example, opponents of Reconstruction in Mississippi "concentrated the bulk of the black population in a 'shoestring' Congressional district running the length of the Mississippi River, leaving five others with white majorities.". . . Some 90 years later, Alabama redefined the boundaries of the city of Tuskegee "from a square to an uncouth twenty-eight-sided figure" in a manner that was alleged to exclude black voters, and only black voters, from the city limits. *Gomillion* v. *Lightfoot*, 364 U. S. 339, 340 (1960).

Alabama's exercise in geometry was but one example of the racial discrimination in voting that persisted in parts of this country nearly a century after ratification of the Fifteenth Amendment. In some States, registration of eligible black voters ran 50% behind that of whites. Congress enacted the Voting Rights Act of 1965 as a dramatic and severe response to the situation. The Act proved immediately successful in ensuring racial minorities access to the voting booth; by the early 1970's, the spread between black and white registration in several of the targeted Southern States had fallen to well below 10%.

But it soon became apparent that guaranteeing equal access to the polls would not suffice to root out other racially discriminatory voting practices. Drawing on the "one person, one vote" principle, this Court recognized that "[t]he right to vote can be affected by a *dilution* of voting power as well as by an absolute prohibition on casting a ballot." *Allen* v. *State Board of Elections*, 393 U. S. 544, 569 (1969) (emphasis added). Where members of a racial minority group vote as a cohesive unit, practices such as multimember or at-large electoral systems can reduce or nullify minority voters' ability, as a group, "to elect the candidate of their choice." *Ibid*. Accordingly, the Court held that such schemes violate the Fourteenth Amendment when they are adopted with a discriminatory purpose and have the effect of diluting minority voting strength. . . .

B

It is against this background that we confront the questions presented here. . . . Our focus is on appellants' claim that the State engaged in unconstitutional racial gerrymandering. That argument strikes a powerful historical chord: It is unsettling how closely the North Carolina plan resembles the most egregious racial gerrymanders of the past.

An understanding of the nature of appellants' claim is critical to our resolution of the case. In their complaint, appellants did not claim that the General Assembly's reapportionment plan unconstitutionally "diluted" white voting strength. They did not even claim to be white. Rather, appellants' complaint alleged that the deliberate segregation of voters into separate districts on the basis of race violated their constitutional right to participate in a "color-blind" electoral process. . . .

Despite their invocation of the ideal of a "color-blind" Constitution, see *Plessy v. Ferguson*, 163 U. S. 537, 559 (1896) (Harlan, J., dissenting), appellants appear to concede that race-conscious redistricting is not always unconstitutional. . . . That concession is wise: This Court never has held that race-conscious state decision-making is impermissible in *all* circumstances. What appellants object to is redistricting legislation that is so extremely irregular on its face that it rationally can be viewed only as an effort to segregate the races for purposes of voting, without regard for traditional districting principles and without sufficiently compelling justification. For the reasons that follow, we conclude that appellants have stated a claim upon which relief can be granted under the Equal Protection Clause. . . .

III

A

The Equal Protection Clause provides that "[n]o State shall . . . deny to any person within its jurisdiction the equal protection of the laws.". . .

Classifications of citizens solely on the basis of race "are by their very nature odious to a free people whose institutions are founded upon the doctrine of equality.". . .

These principles apply not only to legislation that contains explicit racial distinctions, but also to those "rare" statutes that, although race-neutral, are, on their face, "unexplainable on grounds other than race.". . .

B

Appellants contend that redistricting legislation that is so bizarre on its face that it is "unexplainable on grounds other than race,". . . demands the same close scrutiny that we give other state laws that classify citizens by race. Our voting rights precedents support that conclusion.

. . . A reapportionment plan that includes in one district individuals who belong to the same race, but who are otherwise widely separated by geographical and political boundaries, and who may have little in common with one another but the color of their skin, bears an uncomfortable resemblance to political apartheid. It reinforces the perception that members of the same racial group—regardless of their age, education, economic status, or the community in which the live—think alike, share the same political interests, and will prefer the same candidates at the polls. . . .

The message that such districting sends to elected representatives is equally pernicious. When a district obviously is created solely to effectuate the perceived common interests of one racial group, elected officials are more likely to believe that their primary obligation is to represent only the members of that group, rather than their constituency as a whole. This is altogether antithetical to our system of representative democracy. . . .

For these reasons, we conclude that a plaintiff challenging a reapportionment statute under the Equal Protection Clause may state a claim by alleging that the legislation, though race-neutral on its face, rationally cannot be understood as anything other than an effort to separate voters into different districts on the basis of race, and that the separation lacks sufficient justification. It is unnecessary for us to decide whether or how a reapportionment plan that, on its face, can be explained in nonracial terms successfully could be challenged. Thus, we express no view as to whether "the intentional creation of majority-minority districts, without more" always gives rise to an equal protection claim. *Post*, at 11 (White, J., dissenting). We hold only that, on the facts of this case, plaintiffs have stated a claim sufficient to defeat the state appellees' motion to dismiss.

POSTSCRIPT TO *SHAW* V. *RENO*

Upon remand of *Shaw* v. *Reno,* the Federal District Court in North Carolina held that voting districts could be gerrymandered along racial lines to remedy the effects of past discrimination. At the same time, however, another three-judge Federal District Court found in Louisiana against the practice of drawing voting districts along racial lines. The difference between the District Court decisions in North Carolina and Louisiana may be explained by the fact that North Carolina had no black Congressional representatives, while Louisiana had a majority-black Congressional district encompassing New Orleans that had returned a black representative to Congress since 1990. Whatever the reason for the different District Court opinions the Supreme Court will probably have to step in and resolve the racial gerrymandering issue once and for all.

❖❖❖

Part Two

POLITICAL PARTIES, ELECTORAL BEHAVIOR, AND INTEREST GROUPS

Chapter 4

❖❖❖

POLITICAL PARTIES AND THE ELECTORATE

The political process involves the sources, distribution, and use of power in the state. All the institutions and processes of government relate to this area. The role of political parties and the electoral system in determining and controlling political power is examined in this chapter.

Constitutional Background

Political parties and interest groups have developed outside of the original constitutional framework to channel political power in the community, and for this reason they deserve special consideration from students of American government. The Constitution was designed to structure power relationships in such a way that the arbitrary exercise of political power by any one group or individual would be prevented. One important concept held by the framers of the Constitution was that faction, that is, parties and interest groups, is inherently dangerous to political freedom and stable government. This is evident from *Federalist 10*.

23

James Madison

FEDERALIST 10

❖❖❖❖❖❖❖

Among the numerous advantages promised by a well constructed Union, none deserves to be more accurately developed than its tendency to break and control the
violence of faction. The friend of popular governments never finds himself so much
alarmed for their character and fate as when he contemplates their propensity to
this dangerous vice. He will not fail, therefore, to set a due value on any plan
which, without violating the principles to which he is attached, provides a proper
cure for it. The instability, injustice, and confusion, introduced into the public
councils, have, in truth been the mortal diseases under which popular governments
have everywhere perished; as they continue to be the favorite and fruitful topics
from which the adversaries to liberty derive their most specious declamations. The
valuable improvements made by the American constitutions on the popular models, both ancient and modern, cannot certainly be too much admired; but it would
be an unwarrantable partiality, to contend that they have as effectually obviated
the danger on this side, as was wished and expected. Complaints are everywhere
heard from our most considerate and virtuous citizens, equally the friends of public
and private faith, and of public and personal liberty, that our governments are too
unstable; that the public good is disregarded in the conflicts of rival parties; and
that measures are too often decided, not according to the rules of justice, and the
rights of the minor party, but by the superior force of an interested and overbearing
majority. However anxiously we may wish that these complaints had no foundation, the evidence of known facts will not permit us to deny that they are in some
degree true. It will be found, indeed, on a candid review of our situation, that some
of the distresses under which we labor, have been erroneously charged on the operation of our governments; but it will be found, at the same time, that other causes
will not alone account for many of our heaviest misfortunes; and, particularly, for
the prevailing and increasing distrust of public engagements, and alarm for private
rights, which are echoed from one end of the continent to the other. These must be
chiefly, if not wholly, effects of the unsteadiness and injustice, with which a factious
spirit has tainted our public administrations.

By a faction, I understand a number of citizens, whether amounting to a majority or minority of the whole, who are united and actuated by some common impulse
of passion, or of interest, adverse to the rights of other citizens, or to the permanent
and aggregate interest of the community.

There are two methods of curing the mischiefs of faction: the one, by removing its causes; the other, by controlling its effects.

There are again two methods of removing the causes of faction: the one, by destroying the liberty which is essential to its existence; the other, by giving to every citizen the same opinions, the same passions, and the same interests.

It could never be more truly said, than of the first remedy, that it was worse than the disease. Liberty is to faction what air is to fire, an ailment, without which it instantly expires. But it could not be a less folly to abolish liberty, which is essential to political life because it nourishes faction, than it would be to wish the annihilation of air, which is essential to animal life, because it imparts to fire its destructive agency.

The second expedient is as impracticable, as the first would be unwise. As long as the reason of man continues fallible, and he is at liberty to exercise it, different opinions will be formed. As long as the connection subsists between his reason and his self-love, his opinions and his passions will have a reciprocal influence on each other; and the former will be objects to which the latter will attach themselves. The diversity in the faculties of men, from which the rights of property originate, is not less an insuperable obstacle to a uniformity of interests. The protection of those faculties is the first object of government. From the protection of different and unequal faculties of acquiring property, the possession of different degrees and kinds of property immediately results; and from the influence of these on the sentiments and views of the respective proprietors, ensues a division of the society into different interests and parties.

The latent causes of faction are thus sown in the nature of man; and we see them everywhere brought into different degrees of activity, according to the different circumstances of civil society. A zeal for different opinions concerning religion, concerning government, and many other points, as well of speculation as of practice; an attachment to different leaders, ambitiously contending for preeminence and power; or to persons of other descriptions, whose fortunes have been interesting to the human passions, have, in turn, divided mankind into parties, inflamed them with mutual animosity, and rendered them much more disposed to vex and oppress each other, than to cooperate for their common good. So strong is this propensity of mankind, to fall into mutual animosities, that where no substantial occasion presents itself, the most frivolous and fanciful distinctions have been sufficient to kindle their unfriendly passions, and excite their most violent conflicts. But the most common and durable source of factions has been the various and unequal distribution of property. Those who hold, and those who are without property, have even formed distinct interests in society. Those who are creditors, and those who are debtors, fall under a like discrimination. A landed interest, a manufacturing interest, a mercantile interest, a moneyed interest, with many lesser interests, grow up of necessity in civilized nations, and divide them into different classes, actuated by different sentiments and views. The regulation of these various and interfering interests forms the principal task of modern legislation, and involves the spirit of party and faction in the necessary and ordinary operations of government.

No man is allowed to be a judge in his own cause; because his interest will certainly bias his judgment, and, not improbably, corrupt his integrity. With equal, nay, with greater reason, a body of men are unfit to be both judges and parties at the same time; yet what are many of the most important acts of legislation, but so many judicial determinations, not indeed concerning the rights of single persons, but concerning the rights of large bodies of citizens? And what are the different classes of legislators, but advocates and parties to the cause which they determine? Is a law proposed concerning private debts? It is a question to which the creditors are parties on one side, and the debtors on the other. Justice ought to hold the balance between them. Yet the parties are, and must be, themselves the judges; and the most numerous party, or, in other words, the most powerful faction, must be expected to prevail. Shall domestic manufactures be encouraged, and in what degree, by restrictions on foreign manufactures are questions which would be differently decided by the landed and the manufacturing classes; and probably by neither with a sole regard to justice and the public good. . . .

It is vain to say, that enlightened statesmen will be able to adjust these clashing interests, and render them all subservient to the public good. Enlightened statesmen will not always be at the helm; nor, in many cases, can such an adjustment be made at all, without taking into view indirect and remote considerations, which will rarely prevail over the immediate interest which one party may find in disregarding the rights of another, or the good of the whole.

The inference to which we are brought is, that the *causes* of faction cannot be removed; and that relief is only to be sought in the means of controlling its *effects*.

If a faction consists of less than a majority, relief is supplied by the republican principle, which enables the majority to defeat its sinister views, by regular vote. It may clog the administration, it may convulse the society; but it will be unable to execute and mask its violence under the forms of the constitution. When a majority is included in a faction, the form of popular government, on the other hand, enables it to sacrifice to its ruling passion or interest, both the public good and the rights of other citizens. To secure the public good, and private rights, against the danger of such a faction, and at the same time to preserve the spirit and the form of popular government, is then the great object to which our inquiries are directed. Let me add, that it is the great desideratum, by which alone this form of government can be rescued from the opprobrium under which it has so long labored, and be recommended to the esteem and adoption of mankind.

By what means is this object attainable? Evidently by one of two only. Either the existence of the same passion or interest in a majority, at the same time must be prevented; or the majority, having such coexistent passion or interest, must be rendered, by their number and local situation, unable to concert and carry into effect schemes of oppression. If the impulse and the opportunity be suffered to coincide, we well know, that neither moral nor religious motives can be relied on as an adequate control. They are not found to be such on the injustice and violence of individuals, and lose their efficacy in proportion to the number combined together; that is, in proportion as their efficacy becomes needful.

From this view of the subject, it may be concluded, that a pure democracy, by which I mean a society consisting of a small number of citizens, who assemble and administer the government in person, can admit of no cure from the mischiefs of faction. A common passion or interest will, in almost every case, be felt by a majority of the whole; a communication and concert, results from the form of government itself; and there is nothing to check the inducements to sacrifice the weaker party, or an obnoxious individual. Hence it is, that such democracies have ever been spectacles of turbulence and contention; have ever been found incompatible with personal security, or the rights of property; and have, in general, been as short in their lives, as they have been violent in their deaths. Theoretic politicians, who have patronized this species of government, have erroneously supposed that by reducing mankind to a perfect equality in their political rights, they would, at the same time, be perfectly equalized and assimilated in their possessions, their opinions, and their passions.

A republic, by which I mean a government in which the scheme of representation takes place, opens a different prospect, and promises the cure for which we are seeking. Let us examine the points in which it varies from pure democracy, and we shall comprehend both the nature of the cure and the efficacy which it must derive from the union.

The two great points of difference, between a democracy and a republic, are, first, the delegation of the government, in the latter, to a small number of citizens elected by the rest; secondly, the greater number of citizens, and greater sphere of country, over which the latter may be extended.

The effect of the first difference is on the one hand, to refine and enlarge the public views, by passing them through the medium of a chosen body of citizens, whose wisdom may best discern the true interest in their country, and whose patriotism and love of justice, will be least likely to sacrifice it to temporary or partial considerations. Under such a regulation, it may well happen, that the public voice, pronounced by the representatives of the people, will be more consonant to the public good, than if pronounced by the people themselves, convened for the purpose. On the other hand, the effect may be inverted. Men of factious tempers, of local prejudices, or of sinister designs, may by intrigue, by corruption, or by other means, first obtain the suffrages, and then betray the interest of the people. The question resulting is, whether small or extensive republics are most favorable to the election of proper guardians of the public weal; and it is clearly decided in favor of the latter by two obvious considerations.

In the first place, it is to be remarked, that however small the republic may be, the representatives must be raised to a certain number, in order to guard against the cabals of a few; and that however large it may be, they must be limited to a certain number, in order to guard against the confusion of a multitude. Hence, the number of representatives in the two cases not being in proportion to that of the constituents, and being proportionally greatest in the small republic, it follows that if the proportion of fit characters be not less in the large than in the small republic, the former will present a greater option, and consequently a greater probability of a fit choice.

In the next place, as each representative will be chosen by a greater number of citizens in the large than in the small republic, it will be more difficult for unworthy candidates to practice with success the vicious arts, by which elections are too often carried; and the suffrages of the people being more free, will be more likely to center in men who possess the most attractive merit, and the most diffusive and established characters. . . .

The other point of difference is, the greater number of citizens, and extent of territory, which may be brought within the compass of republican, than of democratic government; and it is this circumstance principally which renders factious combinations less to be dreaded in the former, than in the latter. The smaller the society, the fewer probably will be the distinct parties and interests composing it; the fewer the distinct parties and interests, the more frequently will a majority be found of the same party; and the smaller the number of individuals composing a majority, and the smaller the compass within which they are placed, the more easily they will concert and execute their plans of oppression. Extend the sphere, and you take in a greater variety of parties and interests; you make it less probable that a majority of the whole will have a common motive to invade the rights of other citizens; or if such a common motive exists, it will be more difficult for all who feel it to discover their own strength, and to act in unison with each other. . . .

Hence, it clearly appears, that the same advantage, which a republic has over a democracy, in controlling the effects of faction, is enjoyed by a large over a small republic—is enjoyed by the union over the states composing it. Does this advantage consist in the substitution of representatives, whose enlightened views and virtuous sentiments render them superior to local prejudices, and to schemes of injustice? It will not be denied, that the representation of the union will be most likely to possess these requisite endowments. Does it consist in the greater security afforded by a greater variety of parties, against the event of any one party being able to outnumber and oppress the rest? In an equal degree does the increased variety of parties, comprised within the union, increase this security? Does it, in fine, consist in the greater obstacles opposed to the concert and accomplishment of the secret wishes of an unjust and interested majority? Here, again, the extent of the union gives it the most palpable advantage.

The influence of factious leaders may kindle a flame within their particular states, but will be unable to spread a general conflagration through the other states; a religious sect may degenerate into a political faction in a part of the confederacy; but the variety of sects dispersed over the entire face of it, must secure the national councils against any danger from the source; a rage for paper money, for an abolition of debts, for an equal division of property, or for any other improper or wicked project, will be less apt to pervade the whole body of the union, than a particular member of it; in the same proportion as such a malady is more likely to taint a particular county or district, than an entire state.

In the extent and proper structure of the union, therefore, we behold a republican remedy for the diseases most incident to republican government. And according to the degree of pleasure and pride we feel in being republicans, ought to be our zeal in cherishing the spirit, and supporting the character of Federalists.

❖❖ The following selection is taken from E. E. Schattschneider's classic treatise, *Party Government*. In this material he examines both the implications of *Federalist 10* and counterarguments to the propositions stated by Madison with regard to political parties and interest groups.

24

E. E. Schattschneider

PARTY GOVERNMENT

❖❖❖❖❖❖❖

The Convention at Philadelphia provided a constitution with a dual attitude: it was proparty in one sense and antiparty in another. The authors of the Constitution refused to suppress the parties by destroying the fundamental liberties in which parties originate. They or their immediate successors accepted amendments that guaranteed civil rights and thus established a system of party tolerance, i.e., the right to agitate and to organize. This is the proparty aspect of the system. On the other hand, the authors of the Constitution set up an elaborate division and balance of powers within an intricate governmental structure designed to make parties ineffective. It was hoped that the parties would lose and exhaust themselves in futile attempts to fight their way through the labyrinthine framework of the government, much as an attacking army is expected to spend itself against the defensive works of a fortress. This is the antiparty part of the Constitution scheme. To quote Madison, the "great object" of the Constitution was "to preserve the public good and private right against the danger of such a faction [party] and at the same time to preserve the spirit and form of popular government."

In Madison's mind the difference between an autocracy and a free republic seems to have been largely a matter of the precise point at which parties are stopped by the government. In an autocracy parties are controlled (suppressed) at the source; in a republic parties are tolerated but are invited to strangle themselves in the machinery of government. The result in either case is much the same, sooner or later the government checks the parties but *never do the parties control the government*. Madison was perfectly definite and unmistakable in his disapproval of party government as distinguished from party tolerance. In the opinion of Madison, parties were intrinsically bad, and the sole issue for discussion was the means by which bad parties might be prevented from becoming dangerous. What never seems to have occurred to the authors of the Constitution, however, is that parties might be *used* as beneficent instruments of popular government. It is at this point that the distinction between the modern and the antique attitude is made.

The offspring of this combination of ideas was a constitutional system having conflicting tendencies. The Constitution made the rise of parties inevitable yet was incompatible with party government. This scheme, in spite of its subtlety, involved a miscalculation. Political parties refused to be content with the role assigned to them. The vigor and enterprise of the parties have therefore made American political history the story of the unhappy marriage of the parties and the Constitution, a remarkable variation of the case of the irresistible force and the immovable object, which in this instance have been compelled to live together in a permanent partnership. . . .

The Raw Materials of Politics

People who write about interests sometimes seem to assume that all interests are special and exclusive, setting up as a result of this assumption a dichotomy in which the interests on the one side are perpetually opposed to the public welfare on the other side. But there are common interests as well as special interests, and common interests resemble special interests in that they are apt to influence political behavior. The raw materials of politics are not all antisocial. Alongside of Madison's statement that differences in wealth are the most durable causes of faction there should be placed a corollary that the common possessions of the people are the most durable cause of unity. To assume that people have merely conflicting interests and nothing else is to invent a political nightmare that has only a superficial relation to reality. The body of agreement underlying the conflicts of a modern society ought to be sufficient to sustain the social order provided only that the common interests supporting this unity are mobilized. Moreover, not all differences of interest are durable causes of conflict. Nothing is apt to be more perishable than a political issue. In the democratic process, the nation moves from controversy to agreement to forgetfulness; politics is not a futile exercise like football, forever played back and forth over the same ground. The government creates and destroys interests at every turn.

There are, in addition, powerful factors inhibiting the unlimited pursuit of special aims by an organized minority. To assume that minorities will stop at nothing to get what they want is to postulate a degree of unanimity and concentration within these groups that does not often exist in real life. If every individual were capable of having only one interest to the exclusion of all others, it might be possible to form dangerous unions of monomaniacs who would go to great extremes to attain their objectives. In fact, however, people have many interests leading to a dispersion of drives certain to destroy some of the unanimity and concentration of any group. How many interests can an individual have? Enough to make it extremely unlikely that any two individuals will have the same combination of interests. Anyone who has ever tried to promote an association of people having some special interest in common will realize, first, that there are marked differences of enthusiasm within the group and, second, that interests compete with interests for the attention and enthusiasm of every individual. Every organized special interest consists of a group of busy, distracted individuals held together by the efforts of a handful of specialists and enthusiasts who sacrifice other matters in order to concentrate on one. The notion of resolute and unanimous minorities on the point of violence is largely the invention of paid lobbyists and press agents.

The result of the fact that every individual is torn by the diversity of his own interests, the fact that he is a member of many groups, is *the law of the imperfect political mobilization of interests*. That is, it has never been possible to mobilize any interest 100 percent. . . .

It is only another way of saying the same thing to state that conflicts of interests are not cumulative. If it were true that the dividing line in every conflict (or in all major conflicts) split the community identically in each case so that individuals who are opposed on one issue would be opposed to each other on all other issues also, while individuals who joined hands on one occasion would find themselves on the same side on all issues, always opposed to the same combination of antagonists, the cleavage created by the cumulative effect of these divisions would be fatal. But actually conflicts are not cumulative in this way. In real life the divisions are not so clearly marked, and the alignment of people according to interests requires an enormous shuffling back and forth from one side to the other, tending to dissipate the tensions created.

In view of the fact, therefore, (1) that there are many interests, including a great body of common interests, (2) that the government pursues a multiplicity of policies and creates and destroys interests in the process, (3) that each individual is capable of having many interests, (4) that interests cannot be mobilized perfectly, and (5) that conflicts among interests are not cumulative, it seems reasonable to suppose that the government is not the captive of blind forces from which there is no escape. There is nothing wrong about the raw materials of politics.

POLITICAL PARTIES IN DIVIDED GOVERNMENT

A recurring and important theme of commentators on the American political system is that the separation of powers between the President and Congress produces a deadlock of democracy. Major constitutional change to unify the President and Congress by creating a parliamentary system is unrealistic and completely out of the question. Critics of divided government have proposed more disciplined political parties to unify the President and Congress, thereby helping to overcome the effects of the separation of powers. Putting aside the fact that the separation of powers itself makes party government difficult if not impossible, in theory would disciplined political parties that unified the executive and legislative branches make an important difference? In the following selection political scientist David Mayhew presents the provocative and important thesis that the divided government the separation of powers produces works as well as the unified government that party discipline would create.

25

David R. Mayhew

DIVIDED WE GOVERN

❖❖❖❖❖❖❖

Introduction

Since World War II, divided party control of the American national government
has come to seem normal. Between the 1946 and 1990 elections, one of the two
parties held the presidency, the Senate, and the House simultaneously for eighteen
of those years. But control was divided for twenty-six years, it is divided right now,
and we may see more such splits. Some opinion studies suggest that today's voters
prefer divided control on principle: Parties jointly in power are seen to perform a
service by checking each other.

Of course, divided control is not a new phenomenon. During a twenty-two-
year stretch between 1874 and 1896, to take the extreme case, the two parties
shared control of the government for sixteen years. But after that, the country settled into a half-century habit of unified control broken only by two-year transitions
from one party's monopoly to the other's that closed out the Taft, Wilson, and
Hoover administrations. It is against this immediate background that the
post–World War II experience stands out.

Should we care whether party control is unified or divided? That depends on
whether having one state of affairs rather than the other makes any important difference. Does it? Much received thinking says yes. The political party, according to
one of political science's best-known axioms about the American system, is "the indispensable instrument that [brings] cohesion and unity, and hence effectiveness, to
the government as a whole by linking the executive and legislative branches in a
bond of common interest." In the words of Woodrow Wilson, "You cannot compound a successful government out of antagonisms."

At a concrete level, this means at least that significant lawmaking can be expected to fall off when party control is divided. "Deadlock" or "stalemate" will set
in. Variants of this familiar claim could be cited endlessly. Randall B. Ripley argued
in a 1969 study, for example: "To have a productive majority in the American system of government the President and a majority of both houses must be from the
same party. Such a condition does not guarantee legislative success but is necessary

From David R. Mayhew, *Divided We Govern* (New Haven, CT: Yale University Press,
1991).

for it." V. O. Key, Jr., wrote: "Common partisan control of executive and legislature does not assure energetic government, but division of party control precludes it.". . . These authors do not argue that unified party control always generates large collections of notable legislation. But they can be read to predict that it should generate, over a long period of time when contrasted with divided control, considerably more such legislation.

Another familiar claim has to do with congressional oversight. It is that Congress acting as an investigative body will give more trouble to the executive branch when a president of the opposite party holds power. That propensity can be viewed as bad or good. Woodrow Wilson might say that accelerated probing of the executive provides just another kind of unfortunate "antagonism." From another perspective, it can be expected to keep presidents and bureaucrats in line better. Either way, what causes the effect is a predicted difference between unified and divided control. Morris S. Ogul has written, "A congressman of the president's party is less likely to be concerned with oversight than a member of the opposition party.". . .

I . . . argue . . . that the above claims are wrong, or at least mostly or probably wrong. . . . But are there not . . . ways in which unified as opposed to divided party control might make a significant difference?

There are. In closing, five such ways will be introduced here by posing questions and speculating briefly about what their answers might be. In all instances the speculation ends in skepticism: Unified versus divided control has probably *not* made a notable difference during the postwar era. . . .

The first question is: Even if important laws win enactment just as often under conditions of divided party control, might they not be *worse* laws? Isn't "seriously defective legislation" a likelier result? That is sometimes alleged, and if true it would obviously count heavily. The subject is murky, even if kept free of ideological tests of "worseness," but the case seems to have a two-pronged logic. First, enacting coalitions under divided control, being composed of elements not "naturally" united on policy goals, might be less apt to write either clear ends or efficient means into their statutes. Second, such coalitions, absolved from unambiguous "party government" checks by the electorate down the line, might worry less about the actual effects of laws.

These are reasonable enough logics and instances, but the overall case is dubious. . . .

The second question is: Even if important individual statutes can win enactment regardless of conditions of party control, how about programmatic "coherence" across statutes? Isn't that a likelier outcome under unified party control? The argument is sometimes made. Confronted by this claim, one's first response is to note that "coherence" exists in the eyes of beholders, that beholders differ in what they see, and in any event, why is "coherence" necessary or desirable? Democracy, according to some leading models, can function well enough as an assortment of decentralized, unconnected incursions into public affairs. . . .

Still, widespread agreement does exist about the features and importance of at least two patterns of coherence across statutes, and those should be considered. One is *ideological coherence*, for which an argument might go as follows. To permit broadranging change of the sort recommended by ideologies that arise now and then, and to provide a graspable politics to sectors of the public who might be interested in such change, a system needs to allow ideological packaging. That is, it needs to allow, at least sometimes, the enactment of rather large collections of laws thrusting in the same ideological direction. But such packaging has already been discussed. The postwar American system has accommodated it under circumstances of both unified and divided party control—notably in the successfully enacted presidential programs of Johnson (UNI) and Reagan (DIV), and in the liberal legislative surge of 1963 through 1975–76 (UNI then DIV). Presidential programs, given their properties as drama, can probably reach the general public more effectively, but ideological surges arising from "moods" can unquestionably engage appreciable sectors of the public.

Then there is *budgetary coherence*—that is, a match between revenue and expenditure across all government programs. Whether such a match occurs is of course ultimately a matter of statutes, including appropriations bills. It goes without saying that the federal government's immense deficits have daunted and preoccupied the country's political elite as much as anything during the last decade. For some observers, the deficits have also posed a clear test of divided party control, which it has flunked. A single ruling party would have done better, the argument goes, for reasons either of ideological uniformity or electoral accountability. Lloyd N. Cutler made the latter argument in 1988: "If one party was responsible for all three power centers [House, Senate, and presidency] and produced deficits of the magnitude in which they have been produced in recent years, there would be no question of the accountability and the responsibility of that party and its elected public officials for what had happened."

Is this a valid case, finally, against divided party control? That has to remain an open question, since not much scholarship has yet appeared about the history of budgeting as it may have been affected by conditions of party control; also, highly relevant events will no doubt continue to take place. But the case is considerably less compelling than it may first look. For one thing, there is evidently no statistical relation between divided party control and deficit financing over the two centuries of American national history, or more specifically since World War II. That recent period includes the 1950s, it is useful to remember, when Eisenhower, who faced Democratic Congresses for six years, fought major political battles and drew much criticism from liberal intellectuals because he would *not* accept unbalanced budgets. Taking into account size of deficit or surplus, what the postwar pattern does show is a "sudden break" under Reagan. Deficits "blossomed suddenly in 1981." A time series of federal debt as a percentage of gross national product falls almost monotonically from 1946 through 1974, holds more or less steady until 1981, and then surges. The 1980s are the problem.

An explanation that seems to fit this pre-1980 versus post-1980 experience involves not conditions of party control but rather individual presidents' policies. At least since World War II, according to Paul E. Peterson, Congress "has generally followed the presidential lead on broad fiscal policies." Overall congressional appropriations—that is, for each year the total across all programs—have ordinarily come quite close to overall presidential spending requests. Changes in total revenue generated by congressional tax enactments have ordinarily approximated those proposed by presidents. . . .

The third question is: Doesn't government administration suffer as a result of divided party control? Doesn't exaggerated pulling and hauling between president and Congress undermine the implementation of laws and, in general, the functioning of agencies and the administration of programs? High-publicity Capitol Hill investigations, which have been discussed, are relevant to an answer, but the subject is broader than that. It is also vaguer and quite difficult to address. The strategy here will be to present a plausible case *for* an instance of such undermining of administration and then draw a historical comparison. This will scarcely exhaust the topic, but the instances to be compared are important in their own right as well as suggestive about conditions of party control in general.

The plausible instance is Congress's thrust toward "micro-managing" the executive branch in recent decades. That is, Congress has greatly increased its staff who monitor administration, multiplied its days of oversight hearings, greatly expanded its use of the legislative veto (until a federal court ruled that device unconstitutional in 1983), taken to writing exceptionally detailed statutes that limit bureaucratic discretion (notably in environmental law), and tried to trim presidential power through such measures as the War Powers Act of 1973 and the Budget and Impoundment Act of 1974. Whether these moves have helped or harmed the system can be argued either way, but let us stipulate for the moment that they have undermined administration.

Has "micro-management" resulted, at least partly, from divided party control of the government? That too can be argued either way. An abundant list of alternative causes includes public and congressional reaction to the Vietnam war (as conducted by both Johnson and Nixon) and the public's rising distrust of bureaucracy. But let us hypothesize that divided party control is at least partly the cause. Here is the argument. Rather than appearing gradually, "micro-management" came into its own rather quickly under Nixon and Ford in the 1970s—especially during the Nixon-Ford term of 1973–76. To cite some quantitative evidence, days spent per year on congressional oversight hearings, and average number of pages per enacted law (an indicator of statutory detail), achieved *most* of the considerable increase they showed from 1961 through 1984 during just the four years of 1973–76.

That was during a period of divided party control. Obviously, micro-management has not flashed on whenever party control became divided (as under Eisenhower) or flashed off whenever it became unified (as under Carter). Much of it, at least, came in under Nixon-Ford and stayed. One might say that those years saw the initiation of a "regime" of micro-management—that is, a durable set of views and institutionally located practices could survive the transition to Carter and then to Reagan. Their origin is what counts. To implicate divided party control plausibly, one has to argue that two conditions were necessary for this "micro-management regime" to come into existence. First, party control had to be divided: Congress would not have inaugurated such a regime otherwise. Second, there had to occur some unusual shock to the system such as Watergate, Nixon's conduct of the war, or simply Nixon's aggressive presidency: Divided control would not have engendered such a regime otherwise. Divided control, that is, was a necessary *part* of the causal structure that triggered the regime.

That is a plausible, particular argument. Can it be generalized? The broader case would be that members of a relevant class of congressional regimes that includes the micro-management one—that is, regimes that can reasonably be alleged to undermine administration—can be expected to arise under the same circumstances. That is, they require some similar shock to the system plus a background of divided party control.

Has any other such regime ever existed? As it happens, what looks like a particularly good instance of one originated in 1938 and led a vibrant life through 1954. It was that era's "loyalty regime"—the brilliant innovation of Democratic Congressman Martin Dies of Texas, founder of the House Un-American Activities Committee. Dies pioneered a formula that carried through the Hiss, McCarran, Army-McCarthy and other investigations after the war. It was a low-cost, high-publicity, committee-centered way of waging a congressional opposition against the New Deal, the Truman administration, and then Eisenhower. Its chief technique was the hearing where someone could accuse members of the executive branch of being disloyal to the United States. No one should be surprised that that evidently had a pronounced effect on administration. Beyond its effects on the targeted personnel, it could demoralize agencies, preoccupy the White House, put a chill on unorthodox policy options, and even exile whole schools of thought from the government (as with China specialists after 1949).

It seems a good bet that this loyalty regime made as much of a mark on administration—to be sure, its own kind of mark—as has Congress's more recent micromanagement regime. . . .

The fourth question is: Does the conduct of foreign policy suffer under divided party control? That might be a special concern, since "coordination" is often held to be central to effective foreign policy-making. Perhaps an excess of "deadlock" or "non-coordination" occurs under conditions of divided control. But of course such disorderliness, looked at from the other side as by opponents of Truman's China policy or Reagan's Central America policy, figures as a healthy exercise of checks and balances. Foreign policy is often a fighting matter at home. There does not seem to be any way around this. "Coordination," however much sense it may seem to make, does not and cannot dominate every other value.

Yet once past that realization, it is not clear what standards to apply. None will be proposed here. But let the reader try the following thought experiment. Choose any plausible set of standards and, using them, scan through the history of American foreign policymaking since World War II. Here is a prediction of what most readers will conclude: In general, the record was no worse when the two parties shared power. Any appraisal has to accommodate or steer around, for example, the Marshall Plan, which owed to bipartisan cooperation during a time of divided control; the Kennedy-Johnson intervention in Indochina, which, whatever else may be said about it, scarcely took its shape because of a lack of coordination; Nixon's openings to China and the Soviet Union, which were maneuvered with little Capitol Hill dissent during a time of divided control; and Bush's liberation of Kuwait in 1990–91. Given just these items, many readers may agree, considerable ingenuity would be needed to concoct a verdict spanning the four and a half decades that favors unified party control. . . .

The fifth question: Are the country's lower-income strata served less well under divided party control? One can assemble a theory that they might be, assuming for a moment that "serve" refers to direct government action rather than, say, encouragement of long-term economic growth. Separation of powers biases the American regime toward the rich, Progressive theorists used to argue at the outset of the twentieth century. The rich profit when the government does nothing, whereas the non-rich require concerted public action that can all too easily be blocked somewhere in the system's ample array of veto-points. An obvious remedy would be a constitution allowing strict majority rule. But lacking that, according to a conventional argument of political science, much depends on political parties. Their distinctive role is to impose on the country's collection of government institutions a kind of order that serves majority interests. In principle, that might be done by one party embodying the views and experiences of the non-rich (a socialist sort of argument) or by two parties bidding for the votes of the non-rich (a Downsian sort of argument). Either way, unified control is needed to deliver the goods. It allows action, rules out buck-passing, fixes responsibility, permits accountability.

That is a plausible line of argument, and the Great Society as well as the New Deal might be said to bear it out. But altogether too much of the record since World War II does not. What were the origins of the "social safety net" that the Reagan administration—during a time of divided control, for what that is worth—succeeded in widening the holes of? In fact, that net owed much of its weaving to the Nixon and Ford years—also a time of divided control. That period was the source of EEA and CETA jobs, expanded unemployment insurance, low-income energy assistance, post–1974 housing allowances, Pell grants for lower-income college students, greatly multiplied food-stamps assistance, a notable progressivizing of tax incidence, Supplementary Security Income for the aged, blind, and disabled, and Social Security increases that cut the proportion of aged below the poverty line from 25 percent in 1970 to 16 percent in 1974. The laws just kept getting passed. The Reaganite assault against both the Great Society and the 1970s pitted era against era and mood against mood. But it did not pit divided party control against unified party control or even all that clearly Republicans against Democrats.

These five questions are not the only additional ones that might be asked about unified as opposed to divided party control. This work skirts, moreover, the separate and obviously important question of whether the American system of government, with its separation-of-powers features, has been functioning adequately in recent times. Some analysts, for example John E. Chubb and Paul E. Peterson, say no: "When governments of quite different political combinations [that is, unified as well as divided control] all fail to perform effectively, it is worth considering whether the problem is the government itself and not the people or parties that run it." Energy and budgetary policies have been creaking. Each of the last two decades has ended with a riveting spectacle of government inefficacy or disorder—Carter's "malaise" crisis in 1979 and Bush's budget wrangle in 1990. Otherwise, the country is faced with declining voter turnout as well as a rise in election technologies and incumbent-serving practices that seem to be delegitimizing elected officials.

There is no end of taking steps to reform American political institutions, or of good reasons for it. But short of jettisoning the separation-of-powers core of the Constitution—an unlikely event—it would probably be a mistake to channel such concern into "party government" schemes. This work has tried to show that, surprisingly, it does not seem to make all that much difference whether party control of the American government happens to be unified or divided. One reason we assume it does is that "party government" plays a role in political science somewhere between a Platonic form and a grail. When we reach for it as a standard, we draw on abstract models, presumed European practice, and well-airbrushed American experience, but we seldom take a cold look at real American experience. We forget about Franklin Roosevelt's troubles with HUAC and the Rules Committee, Truman's and Kennedy's domestic policy defeats, McCarthy's square-off against Eisenhower, Johnson versus Fulbright on Vietnam, and Carter's energy program and "malaise."

Political parties can be powerful instruments, but in the United States they seem to play more of a role as "policy factions" than as, in the British case, governing instruments. A party as policy faction can often get its way even in circumstances of divided control: Witness the Taftite Republicans in 1947, congressional Democrats under Nixon, or the Reaganites in 1981. How, one might ask, were these temporary policy ascendancies greatly different from that of the Great Society Democrats in 1964–66?

To demand more of American parties—to ask that they become governing instruments—is to run them up against components of the American regime as fundamental as the party system itself. There is a strong pluralist component, for example, as evidenced in the way politicians respond to cross-cutting issue cleavages. There is a public-opinion component that political science's modern technologies do not seem to reach very well. The government floats in public opinion; it goes up and down on great long waves of it that often have little to do with parties. There is the obvious structural component—separation of powers—that brings on deadlock and chronic conflict, but also nudges officials toward deliberation, compromise, and super-majority outcomes. And there is a component of deep-seated individualism among American politicians, who build and tend their own electoral bases and maintain their own relations of responsibility with electorates. This seems to be a matter of political culture—perhaps a survival of republicanism—that goes way back. Unlike most politicians elsewhere, American ones at both legislative and executive levels have managed to navigate the last two centuries of history without becoming minions of party leaders. In this complicated, multi-component setting, British-style governing by party majorities does not have much of a chance.

FUNCTIONS AND TYPES OF ELECTIONS

Most people transmit their political desires to government through elections. Elections are a critical part of the democratic process, and the existence of *free* elections is a major difference between democracies and totalitarian or authoritarian forms of government. Because elections reflect popular attitudes toward governmental parties, policies, and personalities, it is useful to attempt to classify different types of elections on the basis of changes and trends that take place within the electorate. Every election is not the same. For example, the election of 1932 with the resulting Democratic landslide was profoundly different from the election of 1960, in which Kennedy won by less than 1 percent of the popular vote.

Members of the Center for Political Studies at the University of Michigan, as well as V. O. Key, Jr., have developed a typology of elections that is useful in analyzing the electoral system. The most prevalent type of election can be classified as a "maintaining election," "one in which the pattern of partisan attachments prevailing in the preceding period persists and is the primary influence on the forces governing the vote,"[1] Most elections fall into the maintaining category, a fact significant for the political system because such elections result in political continuity and reflect a lack of serious upheavals within the electorate and government. Maintaining elections result in the continuation of the majority political party.

At certain times in American history, what V. O. Key, Jr., has called "critical elections" take place. He discusses this type of election, which results in permanent realignment of the electorate and reflects basic changes in political attitudes.

Apart from maintaining and critical elections, a third type, in which only temporary shifts take place within the electorate, occurs, which can be called "deviating elections." For example, the Eisenhower victories of 1952 and 1956 were deviating elections for several reasons, including the personality of Eisenhower and the fact that voters could register their choice for president without changing their basic partisan loyalties at congressional and state levels. Deviating elections, with reference to the office of president, are probable when popular figures are running for the office.

In "reinstating elections," a final category that can be added to typology of elections, there is a return to normal voting patterns. Reinstating elections take place after deviating elections as a result of the demise of the temporary forces that caused the transitory shift in partisan choice. The election of 1960, in which most of the Democratic majority in the electorate returned to the fold and voted for John F. Kennedy,[2] has been classified as a reinstating election.

26

V. O. Key, Jr.

A THEORY OF CRITICAL ELECTIONS

❖❖❖❖❖❖❖❖

Perhaps the basic differentiating characteristic of democratic order consists in the expression of effective choice by the mass of the people in elections. The electorate

---

[1]Angus Campbell, Philip E. Converse, Warren E. Miller, and Donald E. Stokes, *The American Voter* (New York: John Wiley & Sons, 1960), chap. 19.

[2]See Philip E. Converse, Angus Campbell, Warren E. Miller, and Donald E. Stokes, "Stability and Change in 1960: A Reinstating Election," *The American Political Science Review* 55 (June 1961):269–280.

From V. O. Key, Jr., "A Theory of Critical Elections," *The Journal of Politics* 17 (February 1955):1. Reprinted by permission.

occupies, at least in the mystique of such orders, the position of the principal organ of governance; it acts through elections. An election itself is a formal act of collective decision that occurs in a stream of connected antecedent and subsequent behavior. Among democratic orders elections, so broadly defined, differ enormously in their nature, their meaning, and their consequences. Even within a single nation the reality of election differs greatly from time to time. A systematic comparative approach, with a focus on variations in the nature of elections would doubtless be fruitful in advancing the understanding of the democratic governing process. In behavior antecedent to voting, elections differ in the proportions of the electorate psychologically involved, in the intensity of attitudes associated with campaign cleavages, in the nature of expectations about the consequences of the voting, in the impact of objective events relevant to individual political choice, in individual sense of effective connection with community decision, and in other ways. These and other antecedent variations affect the act of voting itself as well as subsequent behavior. An understanding of elections and, in turn, of the democratic process as a whole must rest partially on broad differentiations of the complexes of behavior that we call elections.

While this is not the occasion to develop a comprehensive typology of elections, the foregoing remarks provide an orientation for an attempt to formulate a concept of one type of election—based on American experience—which might be built into a more general theory of elections. Even the most fleeting inspection of American elections suggests the existence of a category of elections in which voters are, at least from impressionistic evidence, unusually deeply concerned, in which the extent of electoral involvement is relatively quite high, and in which the decisive results of the voting reveal a sharp alteration of the preexisting cleavage within the electorate. Moreover, and perhaps this is the truly differentiating characteristic of this sort of election, the realignment made manifest in the voting in such elections seems to persist for several succeeding elections. All these characteristics cumulate to the conception of an election type in which the depth and intensity of electoral involvement are high, in which more or less profound readjustments occur in the relations of power within the community, and in which new and durable electoral groupings are formed. These comments suppose, of course, the existence of other types of complexes of behavior centering about formal elections, the systematic isolation and identification of which, fortunately, are not essential for the present discussion.

I

The presidential election of 1928 in the New England states provides a specific case of the type of critical election that has been described in general terms. In that year Alfred E. Smith, the Democratic presidential candidate, made gains in all the New England states. The rise in Democratic strength was especially notable in Massachusetts and Rhode Island. When one probes below the surface of the gross election figures it becomes apparent that a sharp and durable realignment also occurred within the electorate, a fact reflective of the activation by the Democratic candidate of low-income, Catholic, urban voters of recent immigrant stock. In New England, at least, the Roosevelt revolution of 1932 was in large measure an Al Smith revolution of 1928, a characterization less applicable to the remainder of the country.

The intensity and extent of electoral concern before the voting of 1928 can only be surmised, but the durability of the realignment formed at the election can be determined by simple analyses of election statistics. An illustration of the new division thrust through the electorate by the campaign of 1928 is provided by the graphs in Figure A, which show the Democratic percentages of the presidential vote from 1916 through 1952 for the city of Somerville and the town of Ashfield in Massachusetts. Somerville, adjacent to Boston, had a population in 1930 of 104,000 of which 28 percent was foreign born and 41 percent was of foreign-born or mixed parentage. Roman Catholics constituted a large proportion of its relatively low-income population. Ashfield, a farming community in western Massachusetts with a 1930 population of 860, was predominantly native born (8.6 percent foreign born), chiefly rural-farm (66 percent), and principally Protestant.

The impressiveness of the differential impact of the election of 1928 on Somerville and Ashfield may be read from the graphs in Figure A. From 1920 the Democratic percentage in Somerville ascended steeply while the Democrats in Ashfield, few in 1920, became even less numerous in 1928. Inspection of graphs also suggests that the great reshuffling of voters that occurred in 1928 was perhaps the final and decisive stage in a process that had been under way for some time. That antecedent process involved a relatively heavy support in 1924 for La Follette in those towns in which Smith was subsequently to find special favor. Hence, in Figure A, as in all the other charts, the 1924 figure is the percentage of the total accounted for by the votes of both the Democratic and Progressive candidates rather than the Democratic percentage of the two-party vote. This usage conveys a minimum impression of the size of the 1924–1928 Democratic gain but probably depicts the nature of the 1920–1928 trend.

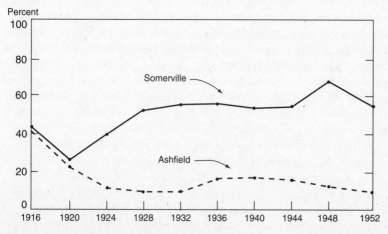

Figure A Democratic Percentages of Major-Party Presidential Vote, Somerville and Ashfield, Massachusetts, 1916–1952

For present purposes, the voting behavior of the two communities shown in Figure A after 1928 is of central relevance. The differences established between them in 1928 persisted even through 1952, although the two series fluctuated slightly in response to the particular influences of individual campaigns. The nature of the process of maintenance of the cleavage is, of course, not manifest from these data. Conceivably the impress of the events of 1928 on individual attitudes and loyalties formed partisan attachments of lasting nature. Yet it is doubtful that the new crystallization of 1928 projected itself through a quarter of a century solely from the momentum given it by such factors. More probably subsequent events operated to reenforce and to maintain the 1928 cleavage. Whatever the mechanism of its maintenance, the durability of the realignment is impressive.

Somerville and Ashfield may be regarded more or less as samples of major population groups within the electorate of Massachusetts. Since no sample survey data are available for 1928, about the only analysis feasible is inspection of election returns for geographic units contrasting in their population composition. Lest it be supposed, however, that the good citizens of Somerville and Ashfield were aberrants simply unlike the remainder of the people of the Commonwealth, examination of a large number of towns and cities is in order. In the interest of both compression and comprehensibility, a mass of data is telescoped into Figure B. The graphs in that figure compare over the period 1916–1952 the voting behavior of the 29 Massachusetts towns and cities having the sharpest Democratic increases, 1920–1928, with that of the 30 towns and cities having the most marked Democratic loss, 1920–1928. In other words, the figure averages out a great many Ashfields and Somervilles. The data of Figure B confirm the expectation that the pattern exhibited by the pair of voting units in Figure A represented only a single case of a much more general phenomenon. Yet by virtue of the coverage of the data in the figure, one gains a stronger impression of the difference in the character of the election of 1928 and the other elections recorded there. The cleavage confirmed by the 1928 returns persisted. At subsequent elections the voters shifted to and fro within the outlines of the broad division fixed in 1928.

Examination of the characteristics of the two groups of cities and towns of Figure B—those with the most marked Democratic gains, 1920–1928, and those with the widest movement in the opposite direction—reveals the expected sorts of differences. Urban, industrial, foreign-born, Catholic areas made up the bulk of the first group of towns, although an occasional rural Catholic community increased its Democratic vote markedly. The towns with a contrary movement tended to be rural, Protestant, native born. The new Democratic vote correlated quite closely with a 1930 vote on state enforcement of the national prohibition law.

Melancholy experience with the eccentricities of data, be they quantitative or otherwise, suggests the prudence of a check on the interpretation of 1928. Would the same method applied to any other election yield a similar result, i.e., the appearance of a more or less durable realignment? Perhaps there can be no doubt that the impact of the events of any election on many individuals forms lasting party loyalties; yet not often is the number so affected so great as to create sharp realignment. On the other hand, some elections are characterized by a large-scale transfer of party affection that is quite short-term, a different sort of phenomenon from that

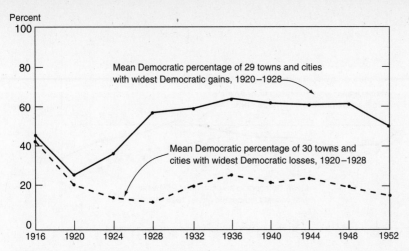

Percent

Figure B Persistence of Electoral Cleavage of 1928 in Massachusetts: Mean Democratic Percentage of Presidential Vote in Towns with Sharpest Democratic Gains, 1920–1928, and in Towns of Widest Democratic Losses, 1920–1928

which occurs in elections marked by broad and durable shifts in party strength. The difference is illustrated by the data on the election of 1932 in New Hampshire in Figure C. The voting records of the twenty-five towns with the widest Democratic gains from 1928 to 1932 are there traced from 1916 to 1952. Observe that Democratic strength in these towns shot up in 1932 but fairly quickly resumed about the same position in relation to other towns that it had occupied in 1928. It is also evident from the graph that this group of towns has on the whole been especially strongly repelled by the Democratic appeal of 1928. Probably the depression drove an appreciable number of hardened Republicans of these towns to vote for a change in 1932, but they gradually found their way back to the party of their fathers. In any case, the figure reflects a type of behavior differing markedly from that of 1928. To the extent that 1932 resembled 1928 in the recrystallization of party lines, the proportions of new Democrats did not differ significantly among the groups of towns examined. In fact, what probably happened to a considerable extent in New England was that the 1928 election broke the electorate into two new groups that would have been formed in 1932 had there been no realignment in 1928.

The Massachusetts material has served both to explain the method of analysis and to present the case of a single state. Examinations of the election of 1928 in other New England states indicate that in each a pattern prevailed similar to that of Massachusetts. The total effect of the realignment differed, of course, from state to state. In Massachusetts and Rhode Island the number of people affected by the upheaval of 1928 was sufficient to form a new majority coalition. In Maine, New Hampshire, and Vermont the same sort of reshuffling of electors occurred, but the proportions affected were not sufficient to overturn the Republican combination, although the basis was laid in Maine and New Hampshire for later limited Democratic success. To underpin these remarks the materials on Connecticut, Maine, New

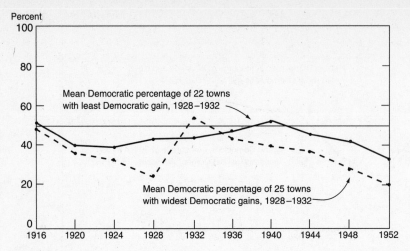

Figure 4.C Impact of Election of 1932 in New Hampshire: Mean Democratic Percentage of Presidential Vote of Towns with Sharpest Democratic Gain, 1928–1932, Compared with Mean Vote of Towns at Opposite Extreme of 1928–1932 Change

Hampshire, and Rhode Island are presented in Figure D. The data on Vermont, excluded for lack of space, form a pattern similar to that emerging from the analysis of the other states.

In the interpretation of all these 1928 analyses certain limitations of the technique need to be kept in mind. The data and the technique most clearly reveal a shift when voters of different areas move in opposite directions. From 1928 to 1936 apparently a good deal of Democratic growth occurred in virtually all geographic units, a shift not shown up sharply by the technique. Hence, the discussion may fail adequately to indicate the place of 1928 as the crucial stage in a process of electoral change that began before and concluded after that year.

II

One of the difficulties with an ideal type is that no single actual case fits exactly its specifications. Moreover, in any system of categorization the greater the number of differentiating criteria for classes, the more nearly one tends to create a separate class for each instance. If taxonomic systems are to be of analytical utility, they must almost inevitably group together instances that are unlike at least in peripheral characteristics irrelevant to the purpose of the system. All of which serves to warn that an election is about to be classified as critical even though in some respects the behavior involved differed from that of the 1928 polling.

Central to our concept of critical elections is a realignment within the electorate both sharp and durable. With respect to these basic criteria the election of 1896 falls within the same category as that of 1928, although it differed in other respects. The persistence of the new division of 1896 was perhaps not so notable as that of 1928; yet the Democratic defeat was so demoralizing and so thorough that

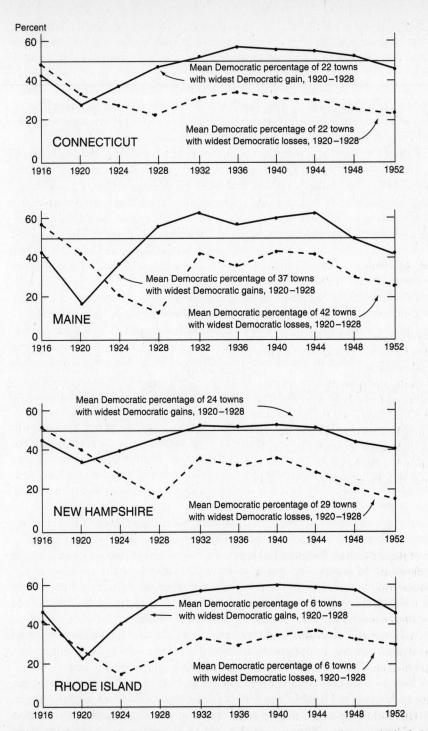

Figure D Realignment of 1928 in Connecticut, Maine, New Hampshire, and Rhode Island

the party could make little headway in regrouping its forces until 1916. Perhaps the significant feature of the 1896 contest was that, at least in New England, it did not form a new division in which partisan lines became more nearly congruent with lines separating classes, religions, or other such social groups. Instead, the Republicans succeeded in drawing new support, in about the same degree, from all sorts of economic and social classes. The result was an electoral coalition formidable in mass but which required both good fortune and skill in political management for its maintenance, given its latent internal contradictions.

If the 1896 election is described in our terms as a complex of behavior preceding and following the formal voting, an account of the action must include the panic of 1893. Bank failures, railroad receiverships, unemployment, strikes, Democratic championship of deflation and of the gold standard, and related matters created the setting for a Democratic setback in 1894. Only one of the eight New England Democratic Representatives survived the elections of 1894. The two 1892 Democratic governors fell by the wayside and in all the states the Democratic share of the gubernatorial vote fell sharply in 1894. The luckless William Jennings Bryan and the free-silver heresy perhaps did not contribute as much as is generally supposed to the 1892–1896 decline in New England Democratic strength; New England Democrats moved in large numbers over to the Republican ranks in 1894.

The character of the 1892–1896 electoral shift is suggested by the data of Figure E, which presents an analysis of Connecticut and New Hampshire made by the technique used earlier in examining the election of 1928. The graphs make plain that in these states (and the other New England states show the same pattern) the rout of 1896 produced a basic realignment that persisted at least until 1916. The graphs in Figure E also make equally plain that the 1892–1896 re-alignment differed radically from that of 1928 in certain respects. In 1896 the net movement in all sorts of geographic units was toward the Republicans; towns differed not in the direction of their movement but only in the extent. Moreover, the persistence of the realignment of 1896 was about the same in those towns with the least Democratic loss from 1892 to 1896 as it was in those with the most marked decline in Democratic strength. Hence, the graphs differ from those on 1928 which took the form of opening scissors. Instead, the 1896 realignment appears as a parallel movement of both groups to a lower plateau of Democratic strength.

If the election of 1896 had had a notable differential impact on geographically segregated social groups, the graphs in Figure E of towns at the extremes of the greatest and least 1892–1896 change would have taken the form of opening scissors as they did in 1928. While the election of 1896 is often pictured as a last-ditch fight between the haves and the have-nots, that understanding of the contest was, at least in New England, evidently restricted to planes of leadership and oratory. It did not extend to the voting actions of the electorate. These observations merit some buttressing, although the inference emerges clearly enough from Figure E.

Unfortunately the census authorities have ignored the opportunity to advance demographic inquiry by publishing data of consequence about New England towns. Not much information is available on the characteristics of the populations of these small geographic areas. Nevertheless, size of total population alone is a fair separator of towns according to politically significant characteristics. Classification of towns according to that criterion groups them roughly according to industrializa-

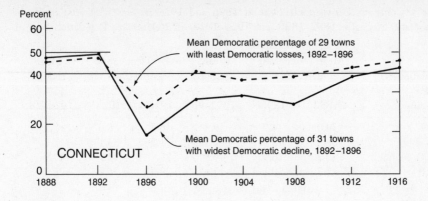

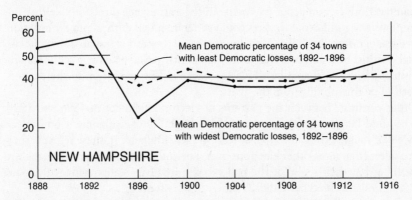

Figure E Realignment of 1896 in Connecticut and New Hampshire

tion and probably generally also according to religion and national origin. Hence, with size of population of towns and cities as a basis, Table 1 contrasts the elections of 1896 and 1928 for different types of towns. Observe from the table that the mean shift between 1892 and 1896 was about the same for varying size groups of towns. Contrast this lack of association between size and political movement with the radically different 1920–1928 pattern which also appears in the table.

Table 1 makes clear that in 1896 the industrial cities, in their aggregate vote at least, moved toward the Republicans in about the same degree as did the rural farming communities. Some of the misinterpretations of the election of 1896 flow from a focus on that election in isolation rather than in comparison with the preceding election. In 1896, even in New England cities, the Democrats tended to be strongest in the poor, working-class, immigrant sections. Yet the same relation had existed, in a sharper form, in 1892. In 1896 the Republicans gained in the working-class wards, just as they did in the silk-stocking wards, over their 1892 vote. They were able to place the blame for unemployment upon the Democrats and to propagate successfully the doctrine that the Republican Party was the party of prosperity and the "full dinner pail." On the whole, the effect apparently was to reduce the degree of coincidence of class affiliation and partisan inclination. Nor was the election of 1896, in New England at least, a matter of heightened tension between city

Table 1 Contrasts Between Elections of 1896 and 1928 in Massachusetts: Shifts in Democratic Strength, 1892–1896 and 1920–1928, in Relation to Population Size of Towns

Population size group	Mean Democratic percentage		Mean change	Mean Democratic percentage		Mean change
	1892	1896	1892–96	1920	1928	1920–28
1–999	34.0	14.7	−19.3	16.5	18.6	+2.1
2000–2999	38.8	18.3	−20.5	21.0	33.1	+12.1
10,000–14,999	46.7	26.9	−19.8	25.8	43.7	+17.9
50,000+	47.7	30.1	−17.6	29.5	55.7	+26.2

and country. Both city and country voters shifted in the same direction. Neither urban employers nor industrial workers could generate much enthusiasm for inflation and free trade; rather they joined in common cause. Instead of a sharpening of class cleavages within New England the voting apparently reflected more a sectional antagonism and anxiety, shared by all classes, expressed in opposition to the dangers supposed to be threatening from the West.

Other contrasts between the patterns of electoral behavior of 1896 and 1928 could be cited but in terms of sharpness and durability of realignment both elections were of roughly the same type, at least in New England. In these respects they seem to differ from most other elections over a period of a half century, although it may well be that each round at the ballot boxes involves realignment within the electorate similar in kind but radically different in extent.

III

The discussion points toward the analytical utility of a system for the differentiation of elections. A concept of critical elections has been developed to cover a type of election in which there occurs a sharp and durable electoral realignment between parties, although the techniques employed do not yield any information of consequence about the mechanisms for the maintenance of a new alignment, once it is formed. Obviously any sort of system for the gross characterization of elections presents difficulties in application. The actual election rarely presents in pure form a case fitting completely any particular concept. Especially in a large and diverse electorate a single polling may encompass radically varying types of behavior among different categories of voters; yet a dominant characteristic often makes itself apparent. Despite such difficulties, the attempt to move toward a better understanding of elections in the terms here employed could provide a means for better integrating the study of electoral behavior with the analysis of political systems. In truth, a considerable proportion of the study of electoral behavior has only a tenuous relation to politics.

The sorts of questions here raised, when applied sufficiently broadly on a comparative basis and carried far enough, could lead to a consideration of basic problems of the nature of democratic orders. A question occurs, for example, about the character of the consequences for the political system of the temporal frequency of critical elections. What are the consequences for public administration, for the legislative process, for the operation of the economy of frequent serious upheavals within the electorate? What are the correlates of that pattern of behavior? And, for those disposed to raise such questions, what underlying changes might alter the situation? Or, when viewed from the contrary position, what consequences flow from an electorate which is disposed, in effect, to remain largely quiescent over considerable periods? Does a state of moving equilibrium reflect a pervasive satisfaction with the course of public policy? An indifference about matters political? In any case, what are the consequences for the public order? Further, what are the consequences when an electorate builds up habits and attachments, or faces situations, that make it impossible for it to render a decisive and clear-cut popular verdict that promises not to be upset by caprice at the next round of polling? What are the consequences of a situation that creates recurring, evenly balanced conflict over long periods? On the other hand, what characteristics of an electorate or what conditions permit sharp and decisive changes in the power structure from time to time? Such directions of speculation are suggested by a single criterion for the differentiation of elections. Further development of an electoral topology would probably point to useful speculation in a variety of directions.

Party Decline and Electoral Decay

Political parties and elections play a central role in democratic theory. Parties aggregate political and economic interests, and party competition, particularly in a two-party system, gives the electorate a choice in determining the course of government. But the American political system is not based solely on democratic theory or party government. On the contrary, the Constitution discourages political parties through the separation of powers, and dampens direct democracy through a number of devices, including the separation of powers, bicameralism, and provisions requiring extraordinary majorities to make treaties, amend the Constitution, and impeach the president. Political parties have nevertheless played a central role in the political process since the adoption of the Constitution. The authors of the following selection suggest that not only may political parties be declining in importance but politics is increasingly carried out by other means.

27

Benjamin Ginsberg and Martin Shefter

POLITICS BY OTHER MEANS

❖❖❖❖❖❖❖

Electoral Decay and Institutional Conflict

For much of America's history, elections have been central arenas of popular choice and political combat. In recent years, however, elections have become less decisive as mechanisms for resolving conflicts and constituting governments in the United States. As a result of party decline and deadlock in the electoral arena, political struggles have come more frequently to be waged elsewhere and crucial choices more often made outside the electoral realm. Rather than engage voters directly, contending political forces have come to rely upon such weapons of institutional combat as congressional investigations, media revelations, judicial proceedings, and alliances with foreign governments. In contemporary America, electoral success often fails to confer the capacity to govern; and political forces have been able to exercise considerable power even if they lose at the polls or, indeed, do not compete in the electoral arena. As the twentieth century draws to a close, America is entering what might be called a *postelectoral era.*

The use of institutional weapons of political combat is not without precedent in American history; but over the past two decades, the importance of these weapons has increased while the significance and decisiveness of elections has diminished. This development has profound consequences for the nation's domestic affairs and international economic and political standing. Because contemporary elections fail to establish conclusively who will—or will not—exercise power, conflict over this question continues to rage throughout the political system. This exacerbates the historic fragmentation of government in the United States, further weakening the American state and making it difficult to achieve collective national purposes. Contending political groups are increasingly able to seize portions of the state apparatus and pursue divergent and often contradictory goals even in the face of serious domestic problems and international challenges. In short, a good deal of the difficulty America has recently faced in maintaining its position in the world is attributable to its politics.

From Electoral to Institutional Combat

Several trends in contemporary American political life bring into focus the declining significance of the electoral arena and the growing importance of other forms of political conflict. American elections in recent decades have been characterized by strikingly low levels of voter turnout and the disappearance of meaningful competition in an increasing number of races. . . .

The extent to which genuine competition takes place in the electoral arena has also declined sharply in recent decades—especially in congressional races, which have come to be dominated by incumbents who are able to use the resources of their office to overwhelm any opponents who might present themselves. . . .

As competition in the electoral arena has declined, the significance of other forms of political combat has increased. One indication of this displacement of conflict from the electoral arena is the growing use of a powerful nonelectoral weapon—the criminal justice system. Between the early 1970s and the late 1980s, there has been more than a tenfold increase in the number of indictments brought by federal prosecutors against national, state, and local officials. . . . Many of those indicted are lower-level civil servants, but large numbers have been prominent political figures—among them more than a dozen members of Congress, several federal judges, and numerous state and local officials. Many of these indictments have been initiated by Republican administrations, and their targets have been primarily Democrats. But a substantial number of high-ranking Republicans in the executive branch—including presidential aides Michael Deaver and Lyn Nofziger, and National Security official Oliver North—have also been the targets of criminal prosecutions stemming from allegations or investigations initiated by Democrats. . . .

There is no reason to believe that the level of political corruption in the United States has actually increased tenfold over the past decade and a half; but it could be argued that this sharp rise in the number of criminal indictments of government officials reflects a heightened level of public concern with governmental misconduct. However, both the issue of government ethics and the growing use of criminal sanctions against public officials have been closely linked to struggles for political power in the United States. In the aftermath of Watergate, institutions were established and processes created to investigate allegations of unethical conduct on the part of public figures. Increasingly, political forces have sought to make use of these mechanisms to discredit their opponents. When scores of investigators, accountants, and lawyers are deployed to scrutinize the conduct of a John Tower of Jim Wright, it is all but certain that something questionable will be found. The creation of these processes, more than changes in the public's moral standards, explains why public officials are increasingly being charged with ethical and criminal violations.

The number of major issues that are fought in the courts has also sharply increased in recent decades, further revealing the importance of nonelectoral conflict in America's current political system. The federal judiciary has become the central institution for resolving struggles over such issues as race relations and abortion and has also come to play a more significant part in deciding questions of social welfare and economic policy. The suits brought by civil rights, environmental, feminist, and other liberal groups seeking to advance their policy goals increased dramatically during the seventies and eighties—reflecting the willingness and ability of these groups to fight their battles in the judicial arena. . . . After the emergence of a conservative majority on the Supreme Court in 1989, forces on the political right formulated plans to use litigation to implement their own policy agenda.

Finally, the national security apparatus has been used as a political weapon in recent decades. One of the best-documented examples of this phenomenon is the substantial expansion that took place during the 1960s and early 1970s in the number of domestic counterintelligence operations directed against groups opposed to the policies of the executive branch. Such activities included wiretaps, surveillance, and efforts to disrupt the activities of these groups. During the 1970s, congressional opposition brought a halt to this particular set of counterintelligence efforts; however, recent revelations have indicated that in the 1980s the FBI placed under surveillance groups opposing the Reagan administration's policies in Central America. The administration also came to rely upon the national security apparatus to circumvent and undercut congressional resistance to its policies.

Party Decline and Electoral Deadlock

Most analyses of American politics assume the primacy of elections. But elections are political institutions, and their significance cannot be taken for granted. The role played by elections has varied over time, and these shifts must be understood in the same terms as changes in the role and power of other institutions. Over the course of American history, political actors have undertaken to transfer decision making on a number of major issues from the electoral to other arenas, such as administrative agencies, the courts, and, in the Civil War, the battlefield. Indeed, forces defeated at the polls have not been averse to using other institutions they control to nullify electoral results. For example, during the late nineteenth and early twentieth centuries, middle- and upper-class "reformers" in American cities were at times able to use state legislative investigations, newspaper exposés, and judicial proceedings to drive from office the machine politicians whom they were unable to defeat through the ballot box.

The declining significance of elections in contemporary America is a product of the electoral deadlock that has developed in the United States over the past quarter century. The duration and scope of this deadlock are without precedent in American history. For eighteen of the twenty-two years between 1968 and 1990, neither the Republican nor the Democratic party was able simultaneously to control the presidency and both houses of Congress. Moreover, for twelve of the eighteen years that the Republicans controlled the White House during this period, the Democrats held majorities in both the House and the Senate.

This deadlock is linked to the decay of America's traditional partisan and electoral institutions. That decay began in the Progressive era, accelerated with the events surrounding the presidencies of Franklin D. Roosevelt and Lyndon Johnson, and has resulted in the virtual destruction of local party organizations and a sharp decline in voting turnout rates. Of course, the Democratic and Republican parties still exist. But they have essentially become coalitions of public officials, office seekers, and political activists; they lack the direct organizational ties to rank-and-file voters that had formerly permitted parties to shape all aspects of politics and government in the United States.

The decay of party organization is a major theme in analyses of contemporary American politics. Political scientists have attributed to it declines in voter turnout, increased electoral volatility, and a diminution in the accountability of public officials to voters. But in focusing on the effects of the decline of party *within* the electoral arena, analysts have paid insufficient heed to its implications for the relationship *between* elections and other political institutions.

Generally speaking, strong party organizations enhance the significance of elections, while declines in party strength reduce the importance of electoral processes. Inasmuch as their influence derives from the electoral arena, political parties are the institutions with the largest stake in upholding the principle that power should be allocated through elections. Thus, a diminution of party influence and an increase in the power of other political agencies is likely not only to reduce the relevance of elections for governmental programs and policies but also to allow electoral results themselves to be circumvented, resisted, or even reversed by forces that control powerful institutions outside the electoral realm.

In contemporary American politics, party decline has fostered a stalemate in the national electoral arena and encouraged contenders for power to look elsewhere for weapons to use against their political foes. . . .

. . . In effect, the decay of America's traditional electoral structures has permitted each of the major contenders for power to establish an institutional stronghold from which it cannot easily be dislodged through electoral means.

Institutional Combat

Party decline and electoral stalemate have had critically important consequences for the locus of political combat in the United States. Of course, the Democrats and Republicans continue to contest elections. But rather than pin all its hopes on defeating its foes in the electoral arena, each party has begun to strengthen the institutions it commands and to use them to weaken its foe's governmental and political base.

President and Congress

The Republicans continue to enter candidates in most congressional races but have reacted to their inability to win control of Congress by seeking to enhance the powers of the White House relative to the legislative branch. Thus, President Nixon impounded billions of dollars appropriated by Congress and sought, through various reorganization schemes, to bring executive agencies under closer White House control while severing their ties to the House and Senate. Presidents Reagan and Bush tolerated budget deficits of unprecedented magnitude in part because these precluded new congressional spending; they also sought to increase presidential authority over executive agencies and diminish that of Congress by centralizing control over administrative rule making in the Office of Management and Budget. In addition, Reagan undertook to circumvent the legislative restrictions on presidential conduct embodied in the War Powers Act.

The Democrats, for their part, compete vigorously in presidential elections but have responded to the Republican presidential advantage by seeking to strengthen the Congress while reducing the powers and prerogatives of the presidency—a sharp contrast to Democratic behavior from the 1930s to the 1960s, when that party enjoyed an advantage in presidential elections. In the 1970s, Congress greatly expanded the size of its committee and subcommittee staffs, thus enabling the House and Senate to monitor and supervise closely the activities of executive agencies. Through the 1974 Budget and Impoundment Act, Congress has sought to increase its control over fiscal policy. Congress has also enacted a number of statutory restrictions on presidential authority in the realm of foreign policy, including the Foreign Commitments Resolution and the Arms Export Control Act.

Finally, congressional investigations, often conducted in conjunction with media exposés and judicial proceedings, have been effective in constraining executive power. Ironically, the techniques that have contributed to the Republican dominance of presidential elections have left them vulnerable to these tactics. The GOP's effective use of television has helped it win presidential elections without engaging in the long and arduous task of building up grass-roots electoral organizations. If it possessed strong organizational ties to its supporters, the GOP would not be so vulnerable to investigations and allegations aired through the media.

Institutional combat of the sort that has characterized American politics in recent years is most likely to occur when the major branches of government are controlled by hostile political forces. . . .

Deadlock in the electoral arena has encouraged contending political forces to attempt to use not only Congress and the presidency but also the federal judiciary, the national security apparatus, and the mass media as instruments of political combat. These institutions, in turn, have been able to ally with such forces and to bolster their own autonomy and power. Through this process, institutions that are not directly subject to the control of the electorate have become major players in contemporary American politics. . . .

Postelectoral Politics and Governmental Disarray

America has now entered an era in which institutional combat has increased in importance relative to electoral competition. This is not to say that electoral outcomes can make no difference. If the Republicans were able to break the Democratic stranglehold on Congress or the Democrats were able more than occasionally to overcome the GOP's advantage in the presidential arena, the stalemate that has characterized American electoral politics for the past quarter century would be broken and the patterns of institutional combat we describe would become less prominent. . . .

Governmental Disarray

The postelectoral political order that has emerged in the United States has three consequences that, taken together, contribute to the disarray of American government and pose problems for the nation's place in the world. First, as each party has strengthened the institutions it commands, the constitutional separation of powers has been transformed into a system of dual sovereignty. The Democrats have undertaken to endow Congress and allied institutions with administrative and coercive capacities that give them the power to govern without controlling the executive branch. In a parallel fashion, the Republicans have worked to make the presidency an institution capable of governing on its own. As a result, the United States often pursues two divergent and contradictory policy agendas. . . .

Second, the American governmental system is increasingly characterized by the absence of political closure. Electoral stalemate and the enhanced political power of non-electoral institutions means that the question of who will govern—and, equally important, who will *not* govern—is less likely to be resolved in the electoral arena. Because the "winners" in the electoral process do not acquire firm control of the government and the "losers" are not deprived of power, governments are characteristically too weak to implement policies that impose costs upon powerful political interests. . . .

Third, the political patterns emerging in the United States are undermining the administrative capabilities of the American state. As Congress and the president struggle to gain control of segments of the state apparatus, administrative agencies become battlegrounds and can be rendered incapable of carrying out their governmental tasks. . . .

Struggles between Congress and the president also provide subordinate officials in the executive branch with the opportunity to increase their autonomy. Officials seeking to pursue an independent course can use the media to generate support in Congress, thereby preventing their superiors from reining them in. . . .

Underlying America's current governmental disarray is the decay of electoral democracy in the United States. The electoral deadlock which helped to produce contemporary patterns of political struggle, as we have noted, emerged from the destruction of the nation's traditional electoral institutions, in particular from the collapse of political party organizations and the concomitant erosion of voter turnout to the point where, at most, 50 percent of the eligible electorate goes to the polls. Today, rather than focus on outmobilizing their opponents in the electoral arena, political leaders increasingly employ institutional weapons of political struggle that neither require nor encourage popular mobilization. Through such techniques as RIP, political actors with a narrow base of popular support (e.g., journalists, federal prosecutors, and public-interest groups) can end the careers of politicians such as presidents and big-city mayors, who enjoy a broader popular base. And when political struggle takes this form, voters are given little reason to participate. Thus the contemporary system of institutional combat emerged from and helps to perpetuate a political order characterized by remarkably limited popular mobilization.

This postelectoral pattern has become increasingly entrenched in recent years because it serves the interests of major political actors. Political forces lacking a broad popular base obviously benefit from forms of competition that do not allocate power in proportion to mass support. Elected officials and party politicians also have reason to be satisfied with the present state of affairs. The constricted electorate helps to maintain the Republicans' hold on the presidency. The Democrats have established an even firmer grip on Congress and have been able to strengthen it as an instrument of both governance and political combat.

Neither party is prepared to assume the risks that seeking to change the present system would entail. To break the electoral deadlock underlying this system, large numbers of new voters would have to be brought into the electorate—and each party fears that a significant expansion of the electorate would threaten its hold on the institution it currently controls. Postelectoral political patterns and the governmental consequences that flow from them have thus become deeply entrenched features of the contemporary American political order.

Voting Behavior: Rational or Irrational?

Parties are supposed to bridge the gap between the people and their government. Theoretically they are the primary vehicles for translating the wishes of the electorate into public policy, sharing this role with interest groups and other governmental instrumentalities in varying degrees. If parties are to perform this aspect of their job properly, the party system must be conducive to securing meaningful debate and action. Party organization and procedure profoundly affect the ability of parties to act in a democratically responsible manner. It should also be pointed out, however, that the electorate has a responsibility in the political process—the responsibility to act rationally, debate the issues of importance, and record a vote for one party or the other at election time. These, at least, are electoral norms traditionally discussed. But does the electorate act in this manner? Is it desirable to have 100 percent electoral participation considering the characteristics of voting behavior? What are the determinants of electoral behavior? These questions are discussed in the following selection.

28

Bernard R. Berelson, Paul F. Lazarsfeld, and William N. McPhee

DEMOCRATIC PRACTICE AND DEMOCRATIC THEORY

❖❖❖❖❖❖❖

Requirements for the Individual

Perhaps the main impact of realistic research on contemporary politics has been to temper some of the requirements set by our traditional normative theory for the typical citizen. "Out of all this literature of political observation and analysis, which is relatively new," says Max Beloff, "there has come to exist a picture in our minds of the political scene which differs very considerably from that familiar to us from the classical texts of democratic politics."

Experienced observers have long known, of course, that the individual voter was not all that the theory of democracy requires of him. As [British Lord James] Bryce put it [in his 1888 treatise, *The American Commonwealth*]:

> How little solidity and substance there is in the political or social beliefs of nineteen persons out of every twenty. These beliefs, when examined, mostly resolve themselves into two or three prejudices and aversions, two or three prepossessions for a particular party or section of a party, two or three phrases or catch-words suggesting or embodying arguments which the man who repeats them has not analyzed.

While our data do not support such an extreme statement, they do reveal that certain requirements commonly assumed for the successful operation of democracy are not met by the behavior of the "average" citizen. The requirements, and our conclusions concerning them, are quickly reviewed.

Interest, Discussion, Motivation

The democratic citizen is expected to be interested and to participate in political affairs. His interest and participation can take such various forms as reading and listening to campaign materials, working for the candidate or the party, arguing politics, donating money, and voting. . . . Many vote without real involvement in the election, and even the party workers are not typically motivated by ideological concerns or plain civic duty.

If there is one characteristic for a democratic system (besides the ballot itself) that is theoretically required, it is the capacity for and the practice of discussion. "It is as true of the large as of the small society," says [A.D.] Lindsay, "that its health depends on the mutual understanding which discussion makes possible; and that discussion is the only possible instrument of its democratic government." How much participation in political discussion there is in the community, what it is, and among whom—these questions have been given answers . . . earlier. . . . In this instance there was little true discussion between the candidates, little in the newspaper commentary, little between the voters and the official party representatives, some within the electorate. On the grass roots level there was more talk than debate, and, at least inferentially, the talk had important effects upon voting, in reinforcing or activating the partisans if not in converting the opposition.

An assumption underlying the theory of democracy is that the citizenry has a strong motivation for participation in political life. But it is a curious quality of voting behavior that for large numbers of people motivation is weak if not almost absent. It is assumed that this motivation would gain its strength from the citizen's perception of the difference that alternative decisions made to him. Now when a person buys something or makes other decisions of daily life, there are direct and immediate consequences for him. But for the bulk of the American people the voting decision is not followed by any direct, immediate, visible personal consequences. Most voters, organized or unorganized, are not in a position to foresee the distant and indirect consequences for themselves, let alone the society. The ballot is cast, and for most people that is the end of it. If their side is defeated, "it doesn't really matter."

Knowledge

The democratic citizen is expected to be well informed about political affairs. He is supposed to know what the issues are, what their history is, what the relevant facts are, what alternatives are proposed, what the party stands for, what the likely consequences are. By such standards the voter falls short. Even when he has the motivation, he finds it difficult to make decisions on the basis of full information when the subject is relatively simple and proximate; how can he do so when it is complex and remote? The citizen is not highly informed on details of the campaign, nor does he avoid a certain misperception of the political situation when it is to his psychological advantage to do so. The electorate's perception of what goes on in the campaign is colored by emotional feeling toward one or the other issue, candidate, party, or social group.

Principle

The democratic citizen is supposed to cast his vote on the basis of principle—not fortuitously or frivolously or impulsively or habitually, but with reference to standards not only of his own interest but of the common good as well. Here, again, if this requirement is pushed at all strongly, it becomes an impossible demand on the democratic electorate.

Many voters vote not for principle in the usual sense but "for" a group to which they are attached—their group. The Catholic vote or the hereditary vote is explainable less as principle than as a traditional social allegiance. The ordinary voter, bewildered by the complexity of modern political problems, unable to determine clearly what the consequences are of alternative lines of action, remote from the arena, and incapable of bringing information to bear on principle, votes the way trusted people around him are voting. . . .

On the issues of the campaign there is a considerable amount of "don't know"—sometimes reflecting genuine indecision, more often meaning "don't care." Among those with opinions the partisans *agree* on most issues, criteria, expectations, and rules of the game. The supporters of the different sides disagree on only a few issues. Not, for that matter, do the candidates themselves always join the issue sharply and clearly. The partisans do not agree overwhelmingly with their own party's position, or, rather, only the small minority of highly partisan do; the rest take a rather moderate position on the political consideration involved in an election.

Rationality

The democratic citizen is expected to exercise rational judgment in coming to his voting decision. He is expected to have arrived at his principles by reason and to have considered rationally the implications and alleged consequences of the alternative proposals of the contending parties. Political theorists and commentators have always exclaimed over the seeming contrast here between requirement and fulfillment. . . . The upshot of this is that the usual analogy between the voting "decision" and the more or less carefully calculated decisions of consumers or businessmen or courts, incidentally, may be quite incorrect. For many voters political preferences may better be considered analogous to cultural tastes—in music, literature, recreational activities, dress, ethics, speech, social behavior. Consider the parallels between political preferences and general cultural tastes. Both have their origin in ethnic, sectional, class, and family traditions. Both exhibit stability and resistance to change for individuals but flexibility and adjustment over generations for the society as a whole. Both seem to be matters of sentiment and disposition rather than "reasoned preferences." While both are responsive to changed conditions and unusual stimuli, they are relatively invulnerable to direct argumentation and vulnerable to indirect social influences. Both are characterized more by faith than by conviction and by wishful expectation rather than careful prediction or consequences. The preference for one party rather than another must be highly similar to the preference for one kind of literature or music rather than another, and the choice of the same political party every four years may be parallel to the choice of the same old standards of conduct in new social situations. In short, it appears that a sense of fitness is a more striking feature of political preference than reason and calculation.

Requirements for the System

If the democratic system depended solely on the qualifications of the individual voter, then it seems remarkable that democracies have survived through the centuries. After examining the detailed data on how individuals misperceive political reality or respond to irrelevant social influences, one wonders how a democracy ever solves its political problems. But when one considers the data in a broader perspective—how huge segments of the society adapt to political conditions affecting them or how the political system adjusts itself to changing conditions over long periods of time—he cannot fail to be impressed with the total result. Where the rational citizen seems to abdicate, nevertheless angels seem to tread. . . .

That is the paradox. *Individual voters* today seem unable to satisfy the requirements for a democratic system of government outlined by political theorists. But the *system of democracy* does meet certain requirements for a going political organization. The individual members may not meet all the standards, but the whole nevertheless survives and grows. This suggests that where the classic theory is defective is in its concentration on the *individual citizen*. What are undervalued are certain collective properties that reside in the electorate as a whole and in the political and social system in which it functions.

The political philosophy we have inherited, then, has given more consideration to the virtues of the typical citizen of the democracy than to the working of the *system* as a whole. Moreover, when it dealt with the system, it mainly considered the single constitutive institutions of the system, not those general features necessary if the institutions are to work as required. For example, the rule of law, representative government, periodic elections, the party system, and the several freedoms of discussion, press, association, and assembly have all been examined by political philosophers seeking to clarify and to justify the idea of political democracy. But liberal democracy is more than a political system in which individual voters and political institutions operate. For political democracy to survive, other features are required: the intensity of conflict must be limited, the rate of change must be restrained, stability in the social and economic structure must be maintained, a pluralistic social organization must exist, and a basic consensus must bind together the contending parties.

Such features of the system of political democracy belong neither to the constitutive institutions nor to the individual voter. It might be said that they form the atmosphere or the environment in which both operate. In any case, such features have not been carefully considered by political philosophers, and it is on these broader properties of the democratic political system that more reflection and study by political theory is called for. In the most tentative fashion let us explore the values of the political system, as they involve the electorate, in the light of the foregoing considerations.

Underlying the paradox is an assumption that the population is homogeneous socially and should be homogeneous politically: that everybody is about the same in relevant social characteristics; that, if something is a political virtue (like interest in the election), then everyone should have it; that there is such as thing as "the" typical citizen on whom uniform requirements can be imposed.

The tendency of classic democratic literature to work with an image of "the" voter was never justified. For, as we will attempt to illustrate here, some of the most important requirements that democratic values impose on a system require a voting population that is not homogeneous but heterogeneous in its political qualities.

The need for heterogeneity arises from the contradictory functions we expect our voting system to serve. We expect the political system to adjust itself and our affairs to changing conditions; yet we demand too that it display a high degree of stability. We expect the contending interests and parties to pursue their ends vigorously and the voters to care; yet, after the election is over, we expect reconciliation. We expect the voting outcome to serve what is best for the community; yet we do not want disinterested voting unattached to the purposes and interests of different segments of that community. We want voters to express their own free and self-determined choices; yet, for the good of the community, we would like voters to avail themselves of the best information and guidance available from the groups and leaders around them. We expect a high degree of rationality to prevail in the decision; but were all irrationality and mythology absent, and all ends pursued by the most coldly rational selection of political means, it is doubtful if the system would hold together.

In short, our electoral system calls for apparently incompatible properties—which, although they cannot all reside in each individual voter, can (and do) reside in a heterogeneous electorate. What seems to be required of the electorate as a whole is a *distribution* of qualities along important dimensions. We need some people who are active in a certain respect, others in the middle, and still others passive. The contradictory things we want from the total require that the parts be different. This can be illustrated by taking up a number of important dimensions by which an electorate might be characterized.

Involvement and Indifference

How could a mass democracy work if all the people were deeply involved in politics? Lack of interest by some people is not without its benefits, too. True, the highly interested voters vote more, and know more about the campaign, and read and listen more, and participate more; however, they are also less open to persuasion and less likely to change. Extreme interest goes with extreme partisanship and might culminate in rigid fanaticism that could destroy democratic processes if generalized throughout the community. Low affect toward the election—not caring much—underlies the resolution of many political problems; votes can be resolved into a two-party split instead of fragmented into many parties (the splinter parties of the left, for example, splinter because their advocates are *too* interested in politics). Low interest provides maneuvering room for political shifts necessary for a complex society in a period of rapid change. Compromise might be based upon sophisticated awareness of costs and returns—perhaps impossible to demand of a mass society—but it is more often induced by indifference. Some people are and should be highly interested in politics, but not everyone is or needs to be. Only the doctrinaire would deprecate the moderate indifference that facilitates compromise.

Hence, an important balance between action motivated by strong sentiments and action with little passion behind it is obtained by heterogeneity within the electorate. Balance of this sort is, in practice, met by a distribution of voters rather than by a homogeneous collection of "ideal" citizens.

Stability and Flexibility

A similar dimension along which an electorate might be characterized is stability-flexibility. The need for change and adaptation is clear, and the need for stability ought equally to be (especially from observation of current democratic practice in, say, certain Latin American countries). . . . [I]t may be that the very people who are most sensitive to changing social conditions are those most susceptible to political change. For, in either case, the people exposed to membership in overlapping strata, those whose former life-patterns are being broken up, those who are moving about socially or physically, those who are forming new families and new friendships—it is they who are open to adjustments of attitudes and tastes. They may be the least partisan and the least interested voters, but they perform a valuable function for the entire system. Here again is an instance in which an individual "inadequacy" provides a positive service for society: The campaign can be a reaffirming force for the settled majority and a creative force for the unsettled minority. There is stability on both sides and flexibility in the middle.

Progress and Conservation

Closely related to the question of stability is the question of past versus future orientation of the system. In America a progressive outlook is highly valued, but, at the same time, so is a conservative one. Here a balance between the two is easily found in the party system and in the distribution of voters themselves from extreme conservatives to extreme liberals. But a balance between the two is also achieved by a distribution of political dispositions through time. There are periods of great political agitation (i.e., campaigns) alternating with periods of political dormancy. Paradoxically, the former—the campaign period—is likely to be an instrument of conservatism, often even of historical regression. . . .

Again, then, a balance (between preservation of the past and receptivity to the future) seems to be required of a democratic electorate. The heterogeneous electorate in itself provides a balance between liberalism and conservatism; and so does the sequence of political events from periods of drifting change to abrupt rallies back to the loyalties of earlier years.

Consensus and Cleavage . . .

[T]here are required *social* consensus and cleavage—in effect pluralism—in politics. Such pluralism makes for enough consensus to hold the system together and enough cleavage to make it move. Too much consensus would be deadening and restrictive of liberty; too much cleavage would be destructive of the society as a whole. . . . Thus again a requirement we might place on an electoral system—balance between total political war between segments of the society and total political indifference to group interests of that society—translates into varied requirements for different individuals. With respect to group or bloc voting, as with other aspects of political behavior, it is perhaps not unfortunate that "some do and some do not."

Individualism and Collectivism

Lord Bryce pointed out the difficulties in a theory of democracy that assumes that each citizen must himself be capable of voting intelligently:

> Orthodox democratic theory assumes that every citizen has, or ought to have, thought out for himself certain opinions, i.e., ought to have a definite view, defensible by argument, of what the country needs, of what principles ought to be applied in governing it, of the man to whose hands the government ought to be entrusted. There are persons who talk, though certainly very few who act, as if they believed this theory, which may be compared to the theory of some ultra-Protestants that every good Christian has or ought to have . . . worked out for himself from the Bible a system of theology.

In the first place, however, the information available to the individual voter is not limited to that directly possessed by him. True, the individual casts his own personal ballot. But, as we have tried to indicate . . . that is perhaps the most individualized action he takes in an election. His vote is formed in the midst of his fellows in a sort of group decision—if, indeed, it may be called a decision at all—and the total information and knowledge possessed in the group's present and past generations can be made available for the group's choice. Here is where opinion-leading relationships, for example, play an active role.

Second, and probably more important, the individual voter may not have a great deal of detailed information, but he usually has picked up the crucial *general* information as part of his social learning itself. He may not know the parties' position on the tariff, or who is for reciprocal trade treaties, or what are the differences on Asiatic policy, or how the parties split on civil rights, or how many security risks were exposed by whom. But he cannot live in an American community without knowing broadly where the parties stand. He has learned that the Republicans are more conservative and the Democrats more liberal—and he can locate his own sentiments and case his vote accordingly. After all, he must vote for one or the other party, and, if he knows the big thing about the parties, he does not need to know all the little things. The basic role a party plays as an institution in American life is more important to his voting than a particular stand on a particular issue.

It would be unthinkable to try to maintain our present economic style of life without a complex system of delegating to others what we are not competent to do ourselves, without accepting and giving training to each other about what each is expected to do, without accepting our dependence on others in many spheres and taking responsibility for their dependence on us in some spheres. And, like it or not, to maintain our present political style of life, we may have to accept much the same interdependence with others in collective behavior. We have learned slowly in economic life that it is useful not to have everyone a butcher or a baker, any more than it is useful to have no one skilled in such activities. The same kind of division of labor—as repugnant as it may be in some respects to our individualistic tradition—is serving us well today in mass politics. There is an implicit division of political labor within the electorate.

Political Campaigns and the Electorate

The voice of the people is always heard in the electoral process, but it is not always clear exactly what the people have chosen. The candidates and their political consultants concentrate upon the projection of images rather than on the serious discussion of public issues. The media, interested in gaining as wide an audience as possible, encourage candidates to be brief in the presentation of their programs and to act with an eye to what is newsworthy in the view of television producers and newspaper editors. A maze confronts the electorate, which must be able to peer through the smoke screen of electoral politics in order to be able to vote intelligently. The following selection, from Key's oft-quoted book, *The Responsible Electorate,* argues that voters are not the fools that many politicians and their advisers often take them to be. The electorate, concludes the author, "behaves about as rationally and responsibly as we should expect, given the clarity of the alternatives presented to it and the character of the information available to it."

29

V. O. Key, Jr.

THE RESPONSIBLE ELECTORATE

In his reflective moments even the most experienced politician senses a nagging curiosity about why people vote as they do. His power and his position depend upon the outcome of the mysterious rites we perform as opposing candidates harangue the multitudes who finally march to the polls to prolong the rule of their champion, to thrust him, ungratefully, back into the void of private life, or to raise to eminence a new tribune of the people. What kinds of appeals enable a candidate to win the favor of the great god, The People? What circumstances move voters to shift their preferences in this direction or that? What clever propaganda tactic or slogan led to

Reprinted by permission of the publishers from *The Responsible Electorate: Rationality in Presidential Voting, 1936–1960* by V. O. Key, Jr., Cambridge, Mass.: The Belknap Press of Harvard University Press, Copyright © 1966 by the President and Fellows of Harvard College.

this result? What mannerism of oratory or style of rhetoric produced another outcome? What band of electors rallied to this candidate to save the day for him? What policy of state attracted the devotion of another bloc of voters? What action repelled a third sector of the electorate?

The victorious candidate may claim with assurance that he has the answers to all such questions. He may regard his success as vindication of his beliefs about why voters vote as they do. And he may regard the swing of the vote to him as indubitably a response to the campaign positions he took, as an indication of the acuteness of his intuitive estimates of the mood of the people, and as a ringing manifestation of the esteem in which he is held by a discriminating public. This narcissism assumes its most repulsive form among election winners who have championed intolerance, who have stirred the passions and hatreds of people, or who have advocated causes known by decent men to be outrageous or dangerous in their long-run consequences. No functionary is more repugnant or more arrogant than the unjust man who asserts, with a color of truth, that he speaks from a pedestal of popular approbation.

It thus can be a mischievous error to assume, because a candidate wins, that a majority of the electorate shares his views on public questions, approves his past actions, or has specific expectations about his future conduct. Nor does victory establish that the candidate's campaign strategy, his image, his television style, or his fearless stand against cancer and polio turned the trick. The election returns establish only that a winner attracted a majority of votes—assuming the existence of a modicum of rectitude in election administration. They tell us precious little about why the plurality was his.

For a glaringly obvious reason, electoral victory cannot be regarded as necessarily a popular ratification of a candidate's outlook. The voice of the people is but an echo. The output of an echo chamber bears an inevitable and invariable relation to the input. As candidates and parties clamor for attention and vie for popular support, the people's verdict can be no more than a selective reflection from among the alternatives and outlooks presented to them. Even the most discriminating popular judgment can reflect only ambiguity, uncertainty, or even foolishness if those are the qualities of the input into the echo chamber. A candidate may win despite his tactics and appeals rather than because of them. If the people can choose only from among rascals, they are certain to choose a rascal.

Scholars, though they have less at stake than do politicians, also have an abiding curiosity about why voters act as they do. In the past quarter of a century they have vastly enlarged their capacity to check the hunches born of their curiosities. The invention of the sample survey—the most widely known example of which is the Gallup poll—enabled them to make fairly trustworthy estimates of the characteristics and behaviors of large human populations. This method of mass observation revolutionized the study of politics—as well as the management of political campaigns. The new technique permitted large-scale tests to check the validity of old psychological and sociological theories of human behavior. These tests led to new hunches and new theories about voting behavior, which could in turn, be checked and which thereby contributed to the extraordinary ferment in the social sciences during recent decades.

The studies of electoral behavior by survey methods cumulate into an imposing body of knowledge which conveys a vivid impression of the variety and subtlety of factors that enter into individual voting decisions. In their first stages in the 1930s the new electoral studies chiefly lent precision and verification to the working maxims of practicing politicians and to some of the crude theories of political speculators. Thus, sample surveys established that people did, indeed, appear to vote their pocketbooks. Yet the demonstration created its embarrassments because it also established that exceptions to the rule were numerous. Not all factory workers, for example, voted alike. How was the behavior of the deviants from "group interest" to be explained? Refinement after refinement of theory and analysis added complexity to the original simple explanation. By introducing a bit of psychological theory it could be demonstrated that factory workers with optimistic expectations tended less to be governed by pocketbook considerations than did those whose outlook was gloomy. When a little social psychology was stirred into the analysis, it could be established that identifications formed early in life, such as attachments to political parties, also reinforced or resisted the pull of the interest of the moment. A sociologist, bringing to play the conceptual tools of his trade, then could show that those factory workers who associate intimately with like-minded persons on the average vote with greater solidarity than do social isolates. Inquiries conducted with great ingenuity along many such lines have enormously broadened our knowledge of the factors associated with the responses of people to the stimuli presented to them by political campaigns.

Yet, by and large, the picture of the voter that emerges from a combination of the folklore of practical politics and the findings of the new electoral studies is not a pretty one. It is not a portrait of citizens moving to considered decision as they play their solemn role of making and unmaking governments. The older tradition from practical politics may regard the voter as an erratic and irrational fellow susceptible to manipulation by skilled humbugs. One need not live through many campaigns to observe politicians, even successful politicians, who act as though they regarded the people as manageable fools. Nor does a heroic conception of the voter emerge from the new analyses of electoral behavior. They can be added up to a conception of voting not as a civic decision but as an almost purely deterministic act. Given knowledge of certain characteristics of a voter—his occupation, his residence, his religion, his national origin, and perhaps certain of his attributes—one can predict with a high probability the direction of his vote. The actions of persons are made to appear to be only predictable and automatic responses to campaign stimuli.

Most findings of the analysts of voting never travel beyond the circle of the technicians; the popularizers, though, give wide currency to the most bizarre—and most dubious—theories of electoral behavior. Public-relations experts share in the process of dissemination as they sell their services to politicians (and succeed in establishing that politicians are sometimes as gullible as businessmen). Reporters pick up the latest psychological secret from campaign managers and spread it through a larger public. Thus, at one time a goodly proportion of the literate population must have placed some store in the theory that the electorate was a pushover for a candidate who projected an appropriate "father image." At another stage, the "sincere" candidate supposedly had an overwhelming advantage. And even so kindly a gentleman as General Eisenhower was said to have an especial attractiveness to those of authoritarian personality within the electorate.

Conceptions and theories of the way voters behave do not raise solely arcane problems to be disputed among the democratic and antidemocratic theorists or questions to be settled by the elegant techniques of the analysts of electoral behavior. Rather, they touch upon profound issues at the heart of the problem of the nature and workability of systems of popular government. Obviously the perceptions of the behavior of the electorate held by political leaders, agitators, and activists condition if they do not fix, the types of appeals politicians employ as they seek popular support. These perceptions—or theories—affect the nature of the input to the echo chamber, if we may revert to our earlier figure, and thereby control its output. They may govern, too, the kinds of actions that governments take as they look forward to the next election. If politicians perceive the electorate as responsive to father images, they will give it father images. If they see voters as most certainly responsive to nonsense, they will give them nonsense. If they see voters as susceptible to delusion, they will delude them. If they see an electorate receptive to the cold, hard realities, they will give it the cold, hard realities.

In short, theories of how voters behave acquire importance not because of their effects on voters, who may proceed blithely unaware of them. They gain significance because of their effects, both potentially and in reality, on candidates and other political leaders. If leaders believe the route to victory is by projection of images and cultivation of styles rather than by advocacy of policies to cope with the problems of the country, they will project images and cultivate styles to the neglect of the substance of politics. They will abdicate their prime function in a democratic system, which amounts, in essence, to the assumption of the risk of trying to persuade us to lift ourselves by our bootstraps.

Among the literary experts on politics there are those who contend that, because of the development of tricks of the manipulation of the masses, practices of political leadership in the management of voters have moved far toward the conversion of election campaigns into obscene parodies of the models set up by democratic idealists. They point to the good old days when politicians were deep thinkers, eloquent orators, and farsighted statesmen. Such estimates of the course of change in social institutions must be regarded with reserve. They may be only manifestations of the inverted optimism of aged and melancholy men who, estopped from hope for the future, see in the past a satisfaction of their yearning for greatness in our political life.

Whatever the trends may have been, the perceptions that leadership elements of democracies hold of the modes of response of the electorate must always be a matter of fundamental significance. Those perceptions determine the nature of the voice of the people, for they determine the character of the input into the echo chamber. While the output may be governed by the nature of the input, over the longer run the properties of the echo chamber may themselves be altered. Fed a steady diet of buncombe, the people may come to expect and to respond with highest predictability to buncombe. And those leaders most skilled in the propagation of buncombe may gain lasting advantage in the recurring struggles for popular favor.

[My] perverse and unorthodox argument . . . is that voters are not fools. To be sure, many individual voters act in odd ways indeed; yet in the large the electorate behaves about as rationally and responsibly as we should expect, given the clarity of the alternatives presented to it and the character of the information available to it. In American presidential campaigns of recent decades the portrait of the American electorate that develops from the data is not one of an electorate straitjacketed by social determinants or moved by subconscious urges triggered by devilishly skillful propagandists. It is rather one of an electorate moved by concern about central and relevant questions of public policy, of governmental performance, and of executive personality. Propositions so uncompromisingly stated inevitably represent overstatements. Yet to the extent that they can be shown to resemble the reality, they are propositions of basic importance for both the theory and the practice of democracy. . . .

Chapter 5

❖❖❖

INTEREST GROUPS

Interest groups are vital cogs in the wheels of the democratic process. Although *Federalist 10* suggests that one major purpose of the separation-of-powers system is to break and control the "evil effects" of faction, modern political theorists take a much more sanguine view of the role that political interest groups as well as parties play in government. No longer are interest groups defined as being opposed to the "public interest." They are vital channels through which particular publics participate in the governmental process. This chapter examines the nature of interest groups and shows how they function.

The Nature and Functions of Interest Groups

Group theory is an important component of democratic political theory. The essence of group theory is that in the democratic process interest groups interact naturally and properly to produce public policy. In American political thought, the origins of this theory can be found in the theory of concurrent majority in John C. Calhoun's *Disquisition on Government*.

It is very useful to discuss the operation of interest groups within the framework of what can best be described as a concurrent majority system. In contemporary usage the phrase *concurrent majority* means a system in which major government policy decisions must be approved by the dominant interest groups directly affected. The word *concurrent* suggests that each group involved must give its consent before policy can be enacted. Thus a concurrent majority is a majority of each group considered separately. If we take as an example an area such as agricultural policy, in which three or four major private interest groups can be identified, we can say that the concurrent majority is reached when each group affected gives its approval before agricultural policy is passed. The extent to which such a system of concurrent majority is actually functioning is a matter that has not been fully clarified by empirical research. Nevertheless, it does seem tenable to conclude that in many major areas of public policy, it is necessary at least to achieve a concurrent majority of the *major* or *dominant* interests affected.

The *theory* of concurrent majority originated with John C. Calhoun. Calhoun, born in 1781, had a distinguished career in public service at both the national and state levels. The idea of concurrent majority evolved from the concept of state nullification of federal law. Under this states' rights doctrine, states would be able to veto any national action. The purpose of this procedure, theoretically, was to protect states in a minority from encroachment by a national majority that could act through Congress, the president, and even the Supreme Court. Those who favored this procedure had little faith in the separation-of-powers doctrine as an effective device to prevent the arbitrary exercise of national power. At the end of his career Calhoun decided to incorporate his earlier views on state nullification into a more substantial theoretical treatise in political science; thus he wrote his famous *Disquisition on Government* (New York: D. Appleton & Co., 1853) in the decade between 1840 and 1850. He attempted to develop a general theory of constitutional (limited) government, the primary mechanism of which would be the ability of the major interest groups (states in Calhoun's time) to veto legislation adverse to their interests. Students should overlook some of the theoretical inconsistencies in Calhoun and concentrate upon the basic justification he advances for substituting his system of concurrent majority for the separation-of-powers device. Under the latter, group interests are not necessarily taken into account, for national laws can be passed on the basis of a numerical majority. And even though this majority may reflect the interests of some groups, it will not necessarily reflect the interests of all groups affected. Calhoun argued that a system in which the major interest groups can dominate the policy process is really more in accord with constitutional democracy than the system established in our Constitution and supported in *Federalist 10.*

The group theory of John C. Calhoun has been updated and carried over into modern political science by several writers, one of the most important being David B. Truman. David Truman's selection, taken from *The Governmental Process* (1951), contains (1) a definition of the term *interest group* and (2) a brief outline of the frame of reference within which the operations of interest groups should be considered. A fairly articulate interest group theory of the governmental process is sketched by Truman. It will become evident to the student of American government that interest groups, like political parties, form an integral part of our political system. Further, interest group theory suggests an entirely new way of looking at government.

30

David B. Truman

THE GOVERNMENTAL
PROCESS

❖❖❖❖❖❖❖

Interest Groups

Interest group refers to any group that, on the basis of one or more shared attitudes, makes certain claims upon other groups in the society for the establishment, maintenance, or enhancement of forms of behavior that are implied by the shared attitudes. . . . [F]rom interaction in groups arise certain common habits of response, which may be called norms, or shared attitudes. These afford the participants frames of reference for interpreting and evaluating events and behaviors. In this respect all groups are interest groups because they are shared-attitude groups. In some groups at various points in time, however, a second kind of common response emerges, in addition to the frame of reference. These are shared attitudes toward what is needed or wanted in a given situation, as demands or claims upon other groups in the society. The term "interest group" will be reserved here for those groups that exhibit both aspects of the shared attitudes. . . .

Definition of the interest group in this fashion . . . permits the identification of various potential as well as existing interest groups. That is, it invites examination of an interest whether or not it is found at the moment as one of the characteristics of a particular organized group. Although no group that makes claims upon other groups in society will be found without an interest or interests, it is possible to examine interests that are not at a particular point in time the basis of interactions among individuals, but that may become such. . . .

Groups and Government: Difficulties in a Group Interpretation of Politics

Since we are engaged in an effort to develop a conception of the political process in the United States that will account adequately for the role of groups, particularly interest groups, it will be appropriate to take account of some of the factors that

From David Truman, *The Governmental Process* (New York: Alfred A. Knopf, 1951). Reprinted by permission of the author.

have been regarded as obstacles to such a conception and that have caused such groups to be neglected in many explanations of the dynamics of government. Perhaps the most important practical reason for this neglect is that the significance of groups has only fairly recently been forced to the attention of political scientists by the tremendous growth in the number of formally organized groups in the United States within the last few decades. It is difficult and unnecessary to attempt to date the beginning of such attention, but Herring in 1929, in his groundbreaking book, *Group Representation Before Congress*, testified to the novelty of the observations he reported when he stated: "There has developed in this government an extra-legal machinery of as integral and of as influential a nature as the system of party government that has long been an essential part of the government. . . ." Some implications of this development are not wholly compatible with some of the proverbial notions about representative government held by specialists as well as laymen. . . . This apparent incompatibility has obstructed the inclusion of group behaviors in an objective description of the governmental process.

More specifically, it is usually argued that any attempt at the interpretation of politics in terms of group patterns inevitably "leaves something out" or "destroys something essential" about the processes of "our" government. On closer examination, we find this argument suggesting that two "things" are certain to be ignored: the individual, and a sort of totally inclusive unity designated by such terms as "society" and "the state."

The argument that the individual is ignored in any interpretation of politics as based upon groups seems to assume a differentiation or conflict between "the individual" and some such collectivity as the group. . . .

Such assumptions need not present any difficulties in the development of a group interpretation of politics, because they are essentially unwarranted. They simply do not square with . . . evidence concerning group affiliations and individual behavior. . . . We do not, in fact, find individuals otherwise than in groups; complete isolation in space and time is so rare as to be an almost hypothetical situation. It is equally demonstrable that the characteristics of any interest group, including the activities by which we identify it, are governed by the attitudes and the circumstances that gave rise to the interactions of which it consists. There are variable factors, and, although the role played by a particular individual may be quite different in a lynch mob from that of the same individual in a meeting of the church deacons, the attitudes and behaviors involved in both are as much a part of his personality as is his treatment of his family. "The individual" and "the group" are at most merely convenient ways of classifying behavior, two ways of approaching the same phenomena, not different things.

The persistence among nonspecialists of the notion of an inherent conflict between "the individual" and "the group" or "society" is understandable in view of the doctrines of individualism that have underlain various political and economic conflicts over the past three centuries. The notion persists also because it harmonizes with a view of the isolated and independent individual as the "cause" of complicated human events. The personification of events, quite apart from any ethical considerations, is a kind of shorthand convenient in everyday speech and, like supernatural explanations of natural phenomena, has a comforting simplicity. Explanations that take into account multiple causes, including group affiliations, are difficult. The "explanation" of a national complex like the Soviet Union wholly in terms of a Stalin or the "description" of the intricacies of the American government entirely in terms of a Roosevelt is quick and easy. . . .

The second major difficulty allegedly inherent in any attempt at a group interpretation of the political process is that such an explanation inevitably must ignore some greater unity designated as society or the state. . . .

Many of those who place particular emphasis upon this difficulty assume explicitly or implicitly that there is an interest of the nation as a whole, universally and invariably held and standing apart from and superior to those of the various groups included within it. This assumption is close to the popular dogmas of democratic government based on the familiar notion that if only people are free and have access to "the facts," they will all want the same thing in any political situation. It is no derogation of democratic preferences to state that such an assertion flies in the face of all that we know of the behavior of men in a complex society. Were it in fact true, not only the interest group but even the political party should properly be viewed as an abnormality. The differing experiences and perceptions of men not only encourage individuality but also . . . inevitably result in differing attitudes and conflicting group affiliations. "There are," says Bentley in his discussion of this error of the social whole, "always some parts of the nation to be found arrayed against other parts." [From *The Process of Government* (1908).] Even in war, when a totally inclusive interest should be apparent if it is ever going to be, we always find pacifists, conscientious objectors, spies, and subversives, who reflect interests opposed to those of "the nation as a whole."

There is a political significance in assertions of a totally inclusive interest within a nation. Particularly in times of crisis, such as an international war, such claims are a tremendously useful promotional device by means of which a particularly extensive group or league of groups tries to reduce or eliminate opposing interests. Such is the pain attendant upon not "belonging" to one's "own" group that if a normal person can be convinced that he is the lone dissenter to an otherwise universally accepted agreement, he usually will conform. This pressure accounts at least in part for the number of prewar pacifists who, when the United States entered World War II, accepted the draft or volunteered. Assertion of an inclusive "national" or "public interest" is an effective device in many less critical situations as well. In themselves, these claims are part of the data of politics. However, they do not describe any actual or possible political situation within a complex modern nation. In developing a group interpretation of politics, therefore, we do not need to account for a totally inclusive interest, because one does not exist.

Denying the existence of an interest of the nation as a whole does not completely dispose of the difficulty raised by those who insist that a group interpretation must omit "the state." We cannot deny the obvious fact that we are examining a going political system that is supported or at least accepted by a large proportion of the society. We cannot account for such a system by adding up in some fashion the National Association of Manufacturers, the Congress of Industrial Organizations, the American Farm Bureau Federation, The American Legion, and other groups that come to mind when "lobbies" and "pressure groups" are mentioned. Even if the political parties are added to the list, the result could properly be designated as "a view which seems hardly compatible with the relative stability of the political system. . . ." Were such the exclusive ingredients of the political process in the United States, the entire system would have torn itself apart long since.

If these various organized interest groups more or less consistently reconcile their differences, adjust, and accept compromises, we must acknowledge that we are dealing with a system that is not accounted for by the "sum" of the organized interest groups in the society. We must go further to explain the operation of such ideals or traditions as constitutionalism, civil liberties, representative responsibility, and the like. These are not, however, a sort of disembodied metaphysical influence, like Mr. Justice Holmes's "brooding omnipresence." We know of the existence of such factors only from the behavior and the habitual interactions of men. If they exist in this fashion, they are interests. We can account for their operation and for the system by recognizing such interests as representing what . . . we called potential interest groups in the "becoming" stage of activity. "It is certainly true," as Bentley has made clear, "that we must accept a . . . group of this kind as an interest group itself." It makes no difference that we cannot find the home office and the executive secretary of such a group. Organization in this formal sense, as we have seen, represents merely a stage or degree of interaction that may or may not be significant at any particular point in time. Its absence does not mean that these interests do not exist, that the familiar "pressure groups" do not operate as if such potential groups were organized and active, or that these interests may not move from the potential to the organized stage of activity.

It thus appears that the two major difficulties supposedly obstacles to a group interpretation of the political process are not insuperable. We can employ the fact of individuality and we can account for the existence of the state without doing violence to the evidence available from the observed behaviors of men and groups. . . .

Interest Groups and the Nature of the State

Men, wherever they are observed, are creatures participating in those established patterns of interaction that we call groups. Excepting perhaps the most casual and transitory, these continuing interactions, like all such interpersonal relationships, involve power. This power is exhibited in two closely interdependent ways. In the first place, the group exerts power over its members; an individual's group affiliations largely determine his attitudes, values, and the frames of reference in terms of which he interprets his experiences. For a measure of conformity to the norms of the group is the price of acceptance within it. . . . In the second place, the group, if it is or becomes an interest group, which any group in society may be, exerts power over other groups in the society when it successfully imposes claims upon them.

Many interest groups, probably an increasing proportion in the United States, are politicized. That is, either from the outset or from time to time in the course of their development they make their claims through or upon the institutions of government. Both the forms and functions of government in turn are a reflection of the activities and claims of such groups. . . .

The institutions of government are centers of interest-based power; their connections with interest groups may be latent or overt and their activities range in political character from the routinized and widely accepted to the unstable and highly controversial. In order to make claims, political interest groups will seek access to the key points of decision within these institutions. Such points are scattered throughout the structure, including not only the formally established branches of government but also the political parties in their various forms and the relationships between governmental units and other interest groups.

The extent to which a group achieves effective access to the institutions of government is the resultant of a complex of interdependent factors. For the sake of simplicity these may be classified in three somewhat overlapping categories: (1) factors relating to a group's strategic position in the society; (2) factors associated with the internal characteristics of the group; and (3) factors peculiar to the governmental institutions themselves. In the first category are: the group's status or prestige in the society, affecting the ease with which it commands deference from those outside its bounds; the standing it and its activities have when measured against the widely held but largely unorganized interests or "rules of the game"; the extent to which government officials are formally or informally "members" of the group; and the usefulness of the group as a source of technical and political knowledge. The second category includes: the degree of appropriateness of the group's organization; the degree of cohesion it can achieve in a given situation, especially in the light of competing group demands upon its membership; the skills of the leadership; and the group's resources in numbers and money. In the third category are: the operating structure of the government institutions, since such established features involve relatively fixed advantages and handicaps; and the effects of the group life of particular units or branches of the government. . . .

A characteristic feature of the governmental system in the United States is that it contains a multiplicity of points of access. The federal system establishes decentralized and more or less independent centers of power, vantage points from which to secure privileged access to the national government. Both a sign and a cause of the strength of the constituent units in the federal scheme is the peculiar character of our party system, which has strengthened parochial relationships, especially those of national legislators. National parties, and to a lesser degree those in the states, tend to be poorly cohesive leagues of locally based organizations rather than unified and inclusive structures. Staggered terms for executive officials and various types of legislators accentuate differences in the effective electorates that participate in choosing these officers. Each of these different, often opposite, localized patterns (constituencies) is a channel of independent access to the larger party aggregation and to the formal government. Thus, especially at the national level, the party is an electing-device and only in limited measure an integrated means of policy determination. Within the Congress, furthermore, controls are diffused among committee chairmen and other leaders in both chambers. The variety of these points of access is further supported by relationships stemming from the constitutional doctrine of separation of powers, from related checks and balances, and at the state and local level from the common practice of choosing an array of executive officials by popular election. At the federal level the formal simplicity of the executive branch has been complicated by a Supreme Court decision that has placed a number of administrative agencies beyond the removal power of the President. The position of these units, however, differs only in degree from that of many that are constitutionally within the Executive Branch. In consequence of alternative lines of access available through the legislature and the Executive and of divided channels for the control of administrative policy, many nominally executive agencies are at various times virtually independent of the Chief Executive.

. . . Within limits, therefore, organized interest groups, gravitating toward responsive points of decision, may play one segment of the structure against another as circumstances and strategic considerations permit. The total pattern of government over a period of time thus presents a protean complex of crisscrossing relationships that change in strength and direction with alterations in the power and standing of interests, organized and unorganized.

❖❖ From Truman's definition *any* group, organized or unorganized, that has a shared attitude toward goals and methods for achieving them should be classified as an interest group. Truman is essentially saying that, since people generally function as members of groups, it is more useful and accurate for the political observer to view the governmental process as the interaction of political interest groups. If one accepts the sociologist's assumption that people act and interact only as members of groups, then it is imperative that the governmental process be viewed as one of interest group interaction.

Within the framework of Truman's definition it is possible to identify both *public* and *private* interest groups. In the political process, governmental groups sometimes act as interest groups in the same sense as private organizations. In many public policies, governmental groups may have more at stake than private organizations. Thus administrative agencies, for example, may lobby as vigorously as their private counterparts to advance their own interests.

Theodore Lowi refers to group theory as "interest-group liberalism." The following selection is taken from his well-known book *The End of Liberalism* (1969), in which he severely criticizes group theory and its pervasive influence upon governmental decision makers. In reading the following selection, remember that the author does not use the term *liberal* in its ordinary sense. The political "liberal" in Lowi's terminology is much like the "economic Liberal" of the early nineteenth century. Just as economic liberalism preached that the public good emerged automatically from the free clash of private interests, the political liberal (in Lowi's terms) supports group theory which holds that the public interest in government is automatically achieved through the interaction of pressure groups.

31

Theodore J. Lowi

THE END OF LIBERALISM:
THE INDICTMENT

❖❖❖❖❖❖❖

The corruption of modern democratic government began with the emergence of interest-group liberalism as the public philosophy. Its corrupting influence takes at least four important forms, four counts, therefore, of an indictment. . . . Also to be indicted, on at least three counts, is the philosophic component of the ideology, pluralism.

Summation 1: Four Counts
Against the Ideology

1. Interest-group liberalism as public philosophy corrupts democratic government because it deranges and confuses expectations about democratic institutions. Liberalism promotes popular decision-making but derogates from the decisions so made by misapplying the notion to the implementation as well as the formulation of policy. It derogates from the processes by treating all values in the process as equivalent interests. It derogates from democratic rights by allowing their exercise in foreign policy, and by assuming they are being exercised when access is provided. Liberal practices reveal a basic disrespect for democracy. Liberal leaders do not wield the authority of democratic government with the resoluteness of men certain of the legitimacy of their positions, the integrity of their institutions, or the justness of the programs they serve.

2. Interest-group liberalism renders government impotent. Liberal governments cannot plan. Liberals are copious in plans but irresolute in planning. Nineteenth-century liberalism was standard without plans. This was an anachronism in the modern state. But twentieth-century liberalism turned out to be plans without standards. As an anachronism it, too, ought to pass. But doctrines are not organisms. They die only in combat over the minds of men, and no doctrine yet exists capable of doing the job. All the popular alternatives are so very irrelevant, helping to

Reprinted from *The End of Liberalism: Ideology, Policy and the Crisis of Public Authority* by Theodore J. Lowi, with permission of W.W. Norton & Company, Inc. Copyright © 1969 by W.W. Norton & Company, Inc.

explain the longevity of interest-group liberalism. Barry Goldwater most recently proved the irrelevance of one. The *embourgeoisement* of American unions suggests the irrelevance of others.

The Departments of Agriculture, Commerce, and Labor provide illustrations, but hardly exhaust illustrations, of such impotence. Here clearly one sees how liberalism has become a doctrine whose means are its ends, whose combatants are its clientele, whose standards are not even those of the mob but worse, are those the bargainers can fashion to fit the bargain. Delegation of power has become alienation of public domain—the gift of sovereignty to private satrapies. The political barriers to withdrawal of delegation are high enough. But liberalism reinforces these through the rhetoric of justification and often even permanent legal reinforcement: Public corporations—justified, oddly, as efficient planning instruments—permanently alienate rights of central coordination to the directors and to those who own the corporation bonds. Or, as Walter Adams finds, the "most pervasive method . . . for alienating public domain is the certificate of convenience and necessity, or some variation thereof in the form of an exclusive franchise, license or permit. . . . Government has become increasingly careless and subservient in issuing them. The net result is a general legalization of private monopoly. . . ." While the best examples still are probably the 10 self-governing systems of agriculture policy, these are obviously only a small proportion of all the barriers the interest-group liberal ideology has erected to democratic use of government.

3. Interest-group liberalism demoralizes government, because liberal governments cannot achieve justice. The question of justice has engaged the best minds for almost as long as there have been notions of state and politics, certainly ever since Plato defined the ideal as one in which republic and justice were synonymous. And since that time philosophers have been unable to agree on what justice is. But outside the ideal, in the realms of actual government and citizenship, the problem is much simpler. We do not have to define justice at all in order to weight and assess justice in government, because in the case of liberal policies we are prevented by what the law would call a "jurisdictional fact." In the famous jurisdictional case of *Marbury v. Madison* Chief Justice Marshall held that even if all the Justices hated President Jefferson for refusing to accept Marbury and the other "midnight judges" appointed by Adams, there was nothing they could do. They had no authority to judge President Jefferson's action one way or another because the Supreme Court did not possess such jurisdiction over the President. In much the same way, there is something about liberalism that prevents us from raising the question of justice at all, no matter what definition of justice is used.

Liberal governments cannot achieve justice because their policies lack the *sine qua non* of justice—that quality without which a consideration of justice cannot even be initiated. Considerations of the justice in or achieved by an action cannot be made unless a deliberate and conscious attempt was made by the actor to derive his action from a general rule or moral principle governing such a class of acts. One can speak personally of good rules and bad rules, but a homily or a sentiment, like liberal legislation, is not a rule at all. The best rule is one which is relevant to the decision or action in question and is general in the sense that those involved with it have no direct control over its operation. A general rule is, hence, *a priori*. Any governing regime that makes a virtue of avoiding such rules puts itself totally outside the context of justice.

Take the homely example of the bull and the china shop. Suppose it was an op art shop and that we consider op worthy only of the junk pile. That being the case, the bull did us a great service, the more so because it was something we always dreamed of doing but were prevented by law from entering and breaking. But however much we may be pleased, we cannot judge the act. We can only like or dislike the consequences. The consequences are haphazard; the bull cannot have intended them. The act was a thoughtless, animal act which bears absolutely no relation to any aesthetic principle. We don't judge the bull. We only celebrate our good fortune. Without the general rule, the bull can reenact his scenes of creative destruction daily and still not be capable of achieving, in this case, aesthetic justice. The whole idea of justice is absurd.

The general rule ought to be a legislative rule because the United States espouses the ideal of representative democracy. However, that is merely an extrinsic feature of the rule. All that counts is the character of the rule itself. Without the rule we can only like or dislike the consequences of the governmental action. In the question of whether justice is achieved, a government without good rules, and without acts carefully derived therefrom, is merely a big bull in an immense china shop.

4. Finally, interest-group liberalism corrupts democratic government in the degree to which it weakens the capacity of governments to live by democratic formalisms. Liberalism weakens democratic institutions by opposing formal procedure with informal bargaining. Liberalism derogates from democracy by derogating from all formality in favor of informality. Formalism is constraining; playing it "by the book" is a role often unpopular in American war films and sports films precisely because it can dramatize personal rigidity and the plight of the individual in collective situations. Because of the impersonality of formal procedures, there is inevitably a separation in the real world between the forms and the realities, and this kind of separation gives rise to cynicism, for informality means that some will escape their collective fate better than others. There has as a consequence always been a certain amount of cynicism toward public objects in the United States, and this may be to the good, since a little cynicism is the father of healthy sophistication. However, when the informal is elevated to a positive virtue, and hard-won access becomes a share of official authority, cynicism becomes distrust. It ends in reluctance to submit one's fate to the governmental process under any condition, as is the case in the United States in the mid-1960s.

Public officials more and more frequently find their fates paradoxical and their treatment at the hands of the public fickle and unjust when in fact they are only reaping the results of their own behavior, including their direct and informal treatment of the public and the institutions through which they serve the public. The more government operates by the spreading of access, the more public order seems to suffer. The more public men pursue their constituencies, the more they seem to find their constituencies alienated. Liberalism has promoted concentration of democratic authority but deconcentration of democratic power. Liberalism has opposed privilege in policy formulation only to foster it, quite systematically, in the implementation of policy. Liberalism has consistently failed to recognize, in short, that in a democracy forms are important. In a medieval monarchy all formalisms were at court. Democracy proves, for better or worse, that the masses like that sort of thing too.

Another homely parable may help. In the good old days, everyone in the big city knew that traffic tickets could be fixed. Not everyone could get his ticket fixed, but nonetheless a man who honestly paid his ticket suffered in some degree a dual loss: his money, and his self-esteem for having so little access. Cynicism was widespread, violations were many, but perhaps it did not matter, for there were so few automobiles. Suppose, however, that as the automobile population increased a certain city faced a traffic crisis and the system of ticket fixing came into ill repute. Suppose a mayor, victorious on the Traffic Ticket, decided that, rather than eliminate fixing by universalizing enforcement, he would instead reform the system by universalizing the privileges of ticket fixing. One can imagine how the system would work. One can imagine that some sense of equality would prevail, because everyone could be made almost equally free to bargain with the ticket administrators. But one would find it difficult to imagine how this would make the total city government more legitimate. Meanwhile, the purpose of the ticket would soon have been destroyed.

Traffic regulation, fortunately, was not so reformed. But many other government activities were. The operative principles of interest-group liberalism possess the mentality of a world of universalized ticket fixing: Destroy privilege by universalizing it. Reduce conflict by yielding to it. Redistribute power by the maxim of each according to his claim. Reserve an official place for every major structure of power. Achieve order by worshipping the processes (as distinguished from the forms and the procedures) by which order is presumed to be established.

If these operative principles will achieve equilibrium—and such is far from proven—that is all they will achieve. Democracy will have disappeared, because all of these maxims are founded upon profound lack of confidence in democracy. Democracy fails when it lacks confidence in its own authority.

Democratic forms were supposed to precede and accompany the formulation of politics so that policies could be implemented authoritatively and firmly. Democracy is indeed a form of absolutism, but ours was fairly well contrived to be an absolutist government under the strong control of consent-building prior to taking authoritative action in law. Interest-group liberalism fights the absolutism of democracy but succeeds only in taking away its authoritativeness. Whether it is called "creative federalism" by President Johnson, "cooperation" by the farmers, "local autonomy" by the Republicans, or "participatory democracy" by the New Left, the interest-group liberal effort does not create democratic power but rather negates it.

❖❖ The following discussion by V. O. Key, Jr., concentrates on private pressure groups and the extent to which they are links between public opinion and government. One interesting conclusion is that the elites of interest groups are not able to influence their members' attitudes to anywhere near the degree commonly thought possible. Pressure group participation in government more often than not reflects highly limited participation by the active elements of the groups. Public policy is often hammered out by very small numbers of individuals both in the government and in the private sphere. Political leaders can never stray too far beyond the boundaries of consent, but these are often very broad.

32

V. O. Key, Jr.

PRESSURE GROUPS

❖❖❖❖❖❖❖

Pressure groups occupy a prominent place in analyses of American politics. In a regime characterized by official deference to public opinion and by adherence to the doctrine of freedom of association, private organizations may be regarded as links that connect the citizen and government. They are differentiated in both composition and function from political parties. Ordinarily they concern themselves with only a narrow range of policies, those related to the peculiar interests of the group membership. Their aim is primarily to influence the content of public policy rather than the results of elections. Those groups with a mass membership, though, may oppose or support particular candidates; in that case they are treated as groups with power to affect election results and, thereby, with capacity to pressure party leaders, legislators, and others in official position to act in accord with their wishes. . . .

Puzzles of Pressure Politics

. . . There is a series of puzzles as we seek to describe the role of pressure groups as links between opinion and government. Clearly the model of the lobbyist who speaks for a united following, determined in its aims and prepared to reward its friends and punish its enemies at the polls, does not often fit reality. Nor is it probable that the unassisted effort of pressure organizations to mold public opinion in support of their position has a large effect upon mass opinion. Yet legislators listen respectfully to representations of the spokesmen of private groups, which in turn spend millions of dollars every year in propagandizing the public. Leaders of private groups articulate the concerns of substantial numbers of persons, even though they

---

may not have succeeded in indoctrinating completely the members of their own groups. All this activity must have some functional significance in the political system. The problem is to identify its functions in a manner that seems to make sense. In this endeavor a distinction of utility is that made . . . between mass-membership organizations and nonmass organizations, which far outnumber the former.

Representation of Mass-Membership Groups

Only the spokesmen for mass-membership organizations can give the appearance of representing voters in sufficient numbers to impress (or intimidate) government. The influence of nonmass groups, which often have only a few hundred or a few thousand members, must rest upon something other than the threat of electoral retribution. As has been seen, the reality of the behavior of members of mass organizations is that in the short run they are not manipulable in large numbers by their leaders. Their party identification anchors many of them to a partisan position, and over the longer run they seem to be moved from party to party in presidential elections by the influences that affect all types and classes of people.

The spokesmen of mass-membership groups also labor under the handicap that they may be made to appear to be unrepresentative of the opinions of their members. When the president of an organization announces to a Congressional committee that he speaks for several million people, the odds are that a substantial proportion of his members can be shown to have no opinion or even to express views contrary to those voiced by their spokesmen. This divergency is often explained as a wicked betrayal of the membership or as a deliberate departure from the mass mandate. Yet it is not unlikely that another type of explanation more often fits the facts. Opinions, as we have seen in many contexts, do not fall into blacks and whites. It may be the nature of mass groups that attachment to the positions voiced by the peak spokesmen varies with attachment to and involvement in the group. At the leadership level the group position is voiced in its purest and most uncompromising form. A substantial layer of group activists subscribes to the official line, but among those with less involvement the faith wins less general acceptance. At the periphery of the group, though, the departure from the official line may be more a matter of indifference than of dissent. Leadership policy is often pictured as the consequence of interaction between leadership and group membership, which may be only partially true. Leaders may be more accurately regarded as dedicated souls who bid for group support of their position. Almost invariably they receive something less than universal acquiescence. This may be especially true in mass organizations in which political endeavor is to a degree a side issue—as, for example, in trade unions and farm organizations. As one traces attitudes and opinions across the strata of group membership, the clarity of position and the extremeness of position become more marked at the level of high involvement and activism.

If it is more or less the nature of mass organizations to encompass a spectrum of opinion rather than a single hue, much of the discussion of the representativeness of group leadership may be beside the point. However that may be, circumstances surrounding the leadership elements of mass organizations place them, in their work of influencing government, in a position not entirely dissimilar to that of leaders of nonmass groups. They must rely in large measure on means not unlike those that must be employed by groups with only the smallest membership. The world of pressure politics becomes more a politics among the activists than a politics that involves many people. Yet politics among the activists occurs in a context of concern about public opinion, a concern that colors the mode of action if not invariably its substance.

Arenas of Decision and Norms of Action

The maneuvers of pressure-group politics thus come ordinarily to occur among those highly involved and immediately concerned about public policy; the connection of these maneuvers with public opinion and even with the opinions of mass-membership organizations tends to be tenuous. Many questions of policy are fought out within vaguely bounded arenas in which the activists concerned are clustered. A major factor in the determination of the balance of forces within each arena is party control of the relevant governmental apparatus. Included among the participants in each issue-cluster of activists are the spokesmen for the pressure groups concerned, the members of the House and Senate committees with jurisdiction, and the officials of the administrative departments and agencies concerned. In the alliances of pressure politics those between administrative agencies and private groups are often extremely significant in the determination of courses of action. The cluster of concerned activists may include highly interested persons, firms, and organizations scattered over the country, though the boundaries delimiting those concerned vary from question to question, from arena to arena. In short, pressure politics among the activists take something of the form that it would take if there were no elections or no concern about the nature of public opinion; that is, those immediately concerned make themselves heard in the process of decision.

In the give and take among the activists, norms and values with foundations in public opinion are conditioning factors. The broad values of the society determine to a degree who will be heard, who can play the game. Those who claim to speak for groups that advocate causes outside the range of consensus may be given short shrift. Some groups advocating perfectly respectable causes may be heard with less deference than others. Subtle standards define what David Truman calls "access" to the decision makers. To some extent this is a party matter: an AFL-CIO delegation does not expect to be heard with much sympathy by a committee dominated by right-wing Republicans. The reality of access, too, may provide an index to the tacit standards in definition of those interests regarded as having a legitimate concern about public policy. The spokesmen of groups both large and small are often heard with respect, not because they wield power, but because they are perceived as the representatives of interests entitled to be heard and to be accorded consideration as a matter of right.

Within the range of the permissible, the process of politics among the activists is governed to some extent by the expectation that all entitled to play the game shall get a fair deal (or at least a fair hearing before their noses are rubbed in the dirt). Doubtless these practices parallel a fairly widespread set of attitudes within the population generally. Probably those attitudes could be characterized as a disposition to let every group—big business and labor unions as well—have its say, but that such groups should not be permitted to dominate the government. In the implementation of these attitudes the legalism of American legislators plays a role. Frequently Congressional committeemen regard themselves as engaged in a judicial role of hearing the evidence and of arriving at decisions based on some sort of standards of equity.

Rituals of the Activists

The maneuvers of group spokesmen, be they spokesmen for mass or nonmass organizations, are often accompanied by rituals in obeisance to the doctrine that public opinion governs. The belief often seems to be that Congressmen will be impressed by a demonstration that public opinion demands the proposed line of action or inaction. Hence, groups organize publicity campaigns and turn up sheaves of editorials in support of their position. They stimulate people to write or to wire their Congressmen; if the labor of stimulation is too arduous, they begin to sign to telegrams names chosen at random from the telephone directory. They solicit the endorsement of other organizations for their position. They lobby the American Legion and the General Federation of Women's Clubs for allies willing to permit their names to be used. On occasion they buy the support of individuals who happen to hold official positions in other organizations. They form fraudulent organizations with impressive letterheads to advance the cause. They attempt to anticipate and to soften the opposition of organizations that might be opposed to their position. Groups of similar ideological orientation tend to "run" together or to form constellations in confederation for mutual advantage.

All these maneuvers we have labeled "rituals"; that is, they are on the order of the dance of the rainmakers. They may be too brutal a characterization, for sometimes these campaigns have their effects—just as rain sometimes follows the rainmakers' dance. Yet the data make it fairly clear that most of these campaigns do not affect the opinion of many people and even clearer that they have small effect by way of punitive or approbative feedback in the vote. Their function in the political process is difficult to divine. The fact that organizations engage in these practices, though, is in itself a tribute to the importance of public opinion. To some extent, too, these opinion campaigns are not so much directed to mass opinion as to other activists who do not speak for many people either but have access to the arena of decision-making and perhaps have a viewpoint entitled to consideration. In another direction widespread publicity, by its creation of the illusion of mass support, may legitimize a position taken by a legislator. If a legislator votes for a measure that seems to arouse diverse support, his vote is not so likely to appear to be a concession to a special interest.

Barnums among the Businessmen

An additional explanation that apparently accounts for a good deal of group activity is simply that businessmen (who finance most of the campaigns of public education by pressure groups) are soft touches for publicity men. The advertising and public-relations men have demonstrated that they can sell goods; they proceed on the assumption that the business of obtaining changes in public policy is analogous to selling soap. They succeed in separating businessmen from large sums of money to propagate causes, often in a manner that sooner or later produces a boomerang effect.

Professional bureaucrats of the continuing and well-established organizations practice restraint in their public-relations campaigns. They need to gain the confidence of Congressmen and other officials with whom they also need to be able to speak the next time they meet. The fly-by-night organization or the business group that falls into the clutches of an unscrupulous public relations firm is more likely to indulge in the fantastic public relations and pressure campaign. Thus the National Tax Equality Association raised some $600,000 to finance a campaign against the tax exemptions of cooperatives, the most important of which are farm coops. Contributions came from concerns as scattered as the Central Power & Light Co., of Corpus Christi, Texas; Fairmont Foods Co., of Omaha, Nebraska; Central Hudson Gas Electric Corporation, of Poughkeepsie, New York; and the Rheem Manufacturing Co., of San Francisco. The late Representative Reed, of New York, who was not one to attack business lightly, declared:

> Mr. Speaker, an unscrupulous racket, known as the National Tax Equality Association, has been in operation for some time, directing its vicious propaganda against the farm co-operatives. To get contributions from businessmen, this racketeering organization has propagandized businessmen with false statements to the effect that if farm co-operatives were taxed and not exempted the revenue to the government would mount annually to over $800,000,000. [The treasury estimate was in the neighborhood of $20,000,000.] This is, of course, absolutely false and nothing more nor less than getting money under false pretenses. . . . This outfit of racketeers known as the Tax Equality Association has led honest businessmen to believe that their contributions were deductible from gross income as ordinary and necessary business expense with reference to their Federal income-tax return.

The Tax Equality Association provided its subscribers with the following form letter to send to their Congressmen:

> Dear Mr. Congressman: You raised my income taxes. Now I hear you are going to do it again. But you still let billions in business and profits escape. How come you raise my taxes, but let co-ops, mutuals, and other profit-making corporations get off scot free, or nearly so? I want a straight answer—and I want these businesses fully taxed before you increase my or anyone else's income taxes again.

Letters so phrased are not well designed to produce favorable Congressional response. The ineptness of this sort of campaign creates no little curiosity about the political judgment of solvent businessmen who put their money or their corporation's money into the support of obviously stupidly managed endeavors.

Autonomous Actors or Links?

This review of the activities of pressure groups may raise doubts about the validity of the conception of these groups as links between public opinion and government. The reality seems to be that the conception applies with greater accuracy to some groups than to others. Certainly group spokesmen may represent a shade of opinion to government even though not all their own members share the views they express. Yet to a considerable degree the work of the spokesmen of private groups, both large and small, proceeds without extensive involvement of either the membership or a wider public. Their operations as they seek to influence legislation and administration, though, occur in a milieu of concern about opinion, either actual or latent. That concern also disposes decision makers to attend to shades of opinion and preference relevant to decision though not necessarily of great electoral strength—a disposition of no mean importance in the promotion of the equitable treatment of people in a democratic order. The changes are that the effects of organized groups on public opinion occur mainly over the long run rather than in short-run maneuvers concerned with particular Congressional votes. Moreover, group success may be governed more by the general balance of partisan strength than by the results of group endeavors to win friends in the mass public. An industry reputed to be led by swindlers may not expect the most cordial reception from legislative committees, especially at times when the balance of strength is not friendly to any kind of business. If the industry can modify its public image, a task that requires time, its position as it maneuvers on particulars (about which few of the public can ever know anything) may be less unhappy. That modification may be better attained by performance than by propaganda.

❖❖ Pressure Group Politics

Both groups theorists, such as David Truman in selection 30, and their critics, such as Theodore Lowi in selection 31, make the apparently reasonable assumption that interest groups represent their constituents. Group theorists argue that such representation defines the public interest, while opponents of "interest group liberalism" charge, as James Madison did in *Federalist 10,* that factions or special interests undermine the national interest. The authors of the following selection shed new light on interest group politics, pointing out that important changes have taken place in special-interest representation since World War II. Their argument fits in nicely with that of V. O. Key, Jr., in selection 32, as both point out that the bureaucratization of interest groups and elite control of group organizations call into question the ability of special interests to link their constituents with government.

33

Walter Isaacson

RUNNING WITH THE PACS

❖❖❖❖❖❖❖

Like electronic images gobbling dots across a video screen, the PAC-men darted among the elegant rooms of the National Republican Club on Capitol Hill. At a

---

fund raiser for Congressman Eldon Rudd of Arizona, they dropped their checks into a basket by the door or pressed them into the candidate's palm, before heading for the shrimp rolls and meatballs. Downstairs, other PAC-men crowded into a reception for Delaware Congressman Tom Evans, which featured piano music and White House luminaries. A few stopped in at the party for Deborah Cochran of Massachusetts. Because she is a long-shot challenger, they mainly left business cards rather than checks. But still she came out ahead; the cost of the event was picked up by the National Rifle Association.

Although Congress has adjourned and most members have headed home for the final stretch of the 1982 campaign, candidates can still be found buzzing back to Capitol Hill. They know that Washington is where the money is these days, or at least where one dips into the honeypot of contributions from political action committees (PACs). In a circular chase that is dominating congressional politics as never before, the candidates are courting the PACs, and the PAC-men are courting the candidates. "Harry Truman said that some people like government so much that they want to buy it," says Democratic Congressman David Obey of Wisconsin. "The 1982 elections will see Truman proved right."

There is nothing inherently evil about PACs: they are merely campaign committees established by organizations of like-minded individuals to raise money for political purposes, a valid aspect of the democratic process. In the wake of Watergate, Congress amended the federal election laws in 1974 to limit the role of wealthy contributors and end secretive payoffs by corporations and unions. The new law formalized the role of PACs, which were supposed to provide a well-regulated channel for individuals to get together and support candidates. But as with many well-intended reforms, there were unintended consequences. Instead of solving the problem of campaign financing, PACs became the problem. They proliferated beyond any expectation, pouring far more money into campaigns than ever before. Today the power of PACs threatens to undermine America's system of representative democracy.

This year there are 3,149 PACs placing their antes into the political pot, up from 2,551 in 1980 and 113 in 1972. The estimated total of funds they will dispense for campaigns this year: a staggering $240 million. There is Back Pac, PeacePac and Cigar-Pac. Beer distributors have a committee named—what else?—SixPAC. Whataburger Inc. has one called Whata-Pac. The Concerned Rumanians for a Stronger America has a PAC, as does the Hawaiian Golfers for Good Government. And so do most major corporations and unions.

By law a PAC can give $5,000 to both a candidate's primary and general election campaigns, while an individual contributor can give only $1,000 to each. Presidential elections are financed by federal funds, so most of the money is channeled into congressional, state and local races. Since PACs tend to run in packs, a popular candidate, particularly a powerful incumbent, may raise more than half his war chest from these special-interest groups. One example: Democratic Congressman Thomas Luken of Ohio, who has sponsored numerous special-interest bills and raised some $100,000 from PACs.

During Campaign '82, PACs will directly donate at least $80 million to House and Senate candidates—a leap of more than 45 percent from 1980. Another $160 million may be spent by PACs on local races, independent political advertising, and administrative activities. Says Democrat James Shannon of Massachusetts: "PACs are visibly corrupting the system."

Critics charge that PACs have distorted the democratic process by making candidates beholden to narrow interests rather than to their constituents. "Dependency on PACs has grown so much that PACs, not constituents, are the focus of a Congressman's attention," says Common Cause President Fred Wertheimer, whose citizens' lobby is fighting to reform the system. Special interests, of course, should be able to fight for their own concerns, but the power of PACs has upset the delicate balance between private interests and the public good. Indeed, PAC victories—continued price supports for dairy farmers, the defeat of a proposed fee on commodity trades, a proposed exemption from antitrust laws for shipping companies—often come at taxpayer expense. "It is not surprising there are no balanced budgets," says Republican Jim Leach of Iowa, who is one of fewer than a dozen members of Congress who refuse to take PAC money.

In addition, the close correlation between special-interest donations and legislative votes sometimes makes it seem that Congress is up for sale. Says Republican Senator Robert Dole of Kansas: "When these PACs give money they expect something in return other than good government." Democratic Congressman Thomas Downey of New York is more blunt: "You can't buy a Congressman for $5,000. But you can buy his vote. It's done on a regular basis." This is one reason why Michigan Democrat William Brodhead decided to quit Congress this year. Says he: "I got sick of feeling indebted to PACs. There is no reason they give money except in the expectation of votes."

Another problem is that PACs have helped raise the cost of campaigning, just as the desire to buy more and more expensive television time increases a candidate's dependency on PACs. Says Democrat Andrew Jacobs of Indiana, a critic of PACs: "It's like getting addicted by a pusher. You become accustomed to lavish campaigns." In 1974 the average cost of campaigning for the House was $50,000; in 1980 the average was $150,000, and this year races costing $500,000 are not uncommon. Says House Republican Leader Robert Michel of Illinois, who has raised more than $220,000 from PACs: "This year I'll pay several hundred thousand dollars for a job that pays $60,000."

Before the sanctioning of PACs in the early 1970s, corporations and unions were generally prohibited from donating to campaigns. Money from large special interests, however, was often funneled secretly in stuffed envelopes; Lyndon Johnson built his power base by serving as a conduit for campaign donations from oil tycoons and construction companies, and one of the key Watergate revelations was the pernicious influence of large corporate payoffs made under the table. But the national parties, and the local political machines, remained the dominant force in the control of campaign funds. By diminishing the role of parties, PACs tend to make elected officials more narrow in their allegiances. This lessens the chance for broad coalitions that balance competing interests. Says Stuart Eizenstat, former domestic affairs adviser to Jimmy Carter: "PACs balkanize the political process."

Labor unions, which organized the first political action committee, will pump some $20 million into the 1982 campaign through 350 separate PACs. Business followed the union lead and soon overtook them: this year 1,497 corporate PACs will give $30 million to the candidates. Trade associations such as the National Association of Realtors and the American Medical Association (A.M.A.) account for 613 PACs, which will chip in another $22 million. An additional 45 PACs are run by cooperatives like the Associated Milk Producers, and will give $2 million this election. By far the greatest, and most worrisome, growth has been among the loose cannons of the PAC arsenal, ideological PACs not connected to any organization. Among them: the National Conservative Political Action Committee (NCPAC) and North Carolina Senator Jesse Helms' Congressional Club. The 644 nonconnected PACs are expected to donate only $6 million directly to candidates. But they will use most of their money for negative propaganda unauthorized by any candidate and for building up direct-mail lists that will help fund future political wars.

PAC money is mainly helping incumbents, since most PACs are guided by the pragmatic desire for access to power. Many corporate PACs that supported successful conservative challengers in 1980 are concentrating this year on solidifying Republican gains. Only 15 percent of the PAC money has gone to challengers so far this election. In the past this bias toward incumbents meant that Democrats fared slightly better with PACs than Republicans, but now the increasing strength of corporate PACs (which give 65 percent of their money to Republicans) relative to labor PACs (which channel 90 percent of their funds to Democrats) could mean that G.O.P. candidates receive slightly more money.

The PACs are playing a dominant role in many races around the country. When Ohio Republican Paul Pfeifer launched his challenge against Senator Howard Metzenbaum last spring, he was given so little chance that the pragmatic PACs shunned him. Metzenbaum's $3 million campaign fund, on the other hand, included $350,000 in PAC money by the end of the summer, mainly from unions. But last month, while Metzenbaum was in Washington conducting a maverick crusade against special-interest bills, Pfeifer began showing strength in the polls. Suddenly PAC money started flowing to the challenger. Says a Pfeifer aide: "More than anything else, a poll will speak to the PAC community. They're like a business trying to invest." One-third of Pfeifer's campaign donations are now from PACs.

Congressmen Ike Skelton and Wendell Bailey of Missouri have been pitted against each other by redistricting. Such a clash of incumbents inevitably triggers heavy PAC spending, and some groups like the A.M.A. have hedged their bets by donating to both. With dairy and labor PACs lining up behind Democrat Skelton, and corporate ones behind Republican Bailey, each side has raised $100,000 from special interests.

Another heated PAC showdown is the California race between Democrat Phillip Burton and Republican Milton Marks. When Marks first flew to Washington to solicit PAC money, he ran into Burton at a restaurant. "I'm here to raise money to run against you," Marks proclaimed jovially. Of his 800 PAC solicitations, Marks hooked 100 donors, raising almost $100,000. Burton piously proclaims he will never take corporate PAC money. But he will take it from labor, progressive groups and conservationist clubs. More than half of his $450,000 reelection fund will come from such PACs.

A far different type of political influence develops when an ideological PAC targets a race. NCPAC, for example, is notorious for mounting negative campaigns against candidates it hopes to see defeated. In these races NCPAC rarely makes direct contributions to a candidate, and thus can spend as much as it wishes. (In 1976 the Supreme Court ruled that parts of the federal election law violated the right of free speech. It said that candidates may personally use as much of their own money as they want, and that unaffiliated groups, like NCPAC, can spend unlimited amounts on their own advocacy campaigns as long as their activity is not authorized by any candidate's official organization.) Moreover, since NCPAC is not affiliated with a candidate, it is less accountable for the tone and content of its campaign. As NCPAC Chairman Terry Dolan has admitted, "A group like ours could lie through its teeth, and the candidate it helps stays clean." NCPAC played a loud but indefinite role in the defeat of four liberal Senators in 1980, but since then it has waned in power if not in dollars.

Liberal groups have responded to NCPAC and other right-wing organizations by forming PACs of their own. Among the new groups is Progressive PAC (ProPAC), which will spend $150,000 in the election, most of it having gone into now abandoned negative campaigns against conservatives. Another is Democrats for the '80s (nicknamed PamPAC for Founder Pamela Harriman), which is spending $500,000. One of the richest ideological PACs is that of the National Organization for Women, which hopes to donate more than $2 million this year to candidates who support its feminist positions and who oppose Reaganomics. Says newly elected NOW President Judy Goldsmith: "We will proceed with work on defeating the right wing."

The growing importance of PAC donations means that the scramble for such money has become an integral part of campaigning. "It used to be that lobbyists lobbied Congressmen," says PAC critic Mike Synar, a Democratic Congressman from Oklahoma. "Now, Congressmen lobby lobbyists—for money." When that inevitable creature of the PAC explosion, the National Association for Association PACs, threw a party, 80 Congressmen showed up. "I've never seen such a group grope," says Democrat Dan Glickman of Kansas. Republican James Coyne of Pennsylvania playfully installed five PacMan video games near the bar of one of his Washington fund raisers in honor of the real PAC-men who have donated $126,000 to his 1982 campaign. Other lawmakers shower the PACs with glossy brochures soliciting money.

Republican Senator Orrin Hatch of Utah has already collected an astounding $750,000 from 531 PACs. Over scrambled eggs at a breakfast last Tuesday in Salt Lake City, he graciously accepted $5,000 more from the Association of Trial Lawyers. Such support, his campaign manager says, "shows a level of commitment to Hatch nationwide by thousands of people." It also shows, critics say, that he is intensely pro-business and chairs the powerful Labor and Human Resources Committee.

Indeed, the pursuit of PAC money has given a national flavor to state campaigns. Two Democratic congressional hopefuls from California, Doug Bosco and Barbara Boxer, ran into each other this year in the Washington waiting room of a PAC they were both courting. Says Bosco: "You get kind of bored with yourself going from PAC to PAC to PAC. You get the feeling you are being processed." San

Diego's Republican mayor Pete Wilson, running for the Senate, made a pilgrimage to Washington a few weeks ago and met with Bernadette Budde of the Business Industry PAC (BIPAC). He also held a $500-per-PAC-man reception at a hotel near the White House. Total take: $75,000.

Houston and Dallas, where the oil money runs thick, have become hubs of PAC activity. "We had a congressional candidate here from North Carolina recently and gave him a few thousand dollars," says Jack Webb, executive director of the Houston PAC. "Then we took him around and introduced him to other oil folks and I'm pretty sure he left with more than $10,000 in pledges." HouPAC plans to give away $200,000 this year, ten times its donations for 1980.

Deciding how to divvy up their bounty can be a complex process for PACs. The 20 trustees of the Realtors PAC held the last of a dozen strategy sessions in Chicago's downtown Marriott Hotel two weeks ago, working late into the night and through the next day to cull the 150 worthy candidates who would receive the last of the $2.5 million allotted for 1982. Each trustee had a folder on supplicants that included voting records and "campaign intelligence reports" prepared with the aid of eight full-time field specialists. Washington staffers gave briefings on where incumbents stand on such issues as the balanced-budget amendment and the mortgage subsidy bill.

Candidates seeking the Realtors' money must submit answers to a six-page questionnaire. In some cases the "correct" answers are all too obvious. "Do you agree or disagree [that] trade associations have a right and a responsibility to hold members of Congress accountable for their votes?" Others are trickier. One asks candidates to rank what contributes most to high interest rates: record deficits, restrictive monetary policy, excessive tax cuts, etc. (A: The Realtors have fought strongly against high deficits.) "Sometimes candidates plead with me to give them the correct answers," says Political Resources Director Randall Moorhead.

Typical of the Realtors' deliberation was their discussion of the Texas Senate race between Democratic Incumbent Lloyd Bentsen and Challenger Jim Collins. Although Republican Collins was very sympathetic to the Realtors' philosophy and had been a supporter in the House, Bentsen is the incumbent and likely victor. He got the $4,250. Challengers are referred to as "risk capital ventures."

The choices for smaller PACs are simpler. At a meeting this month to hand out the last of its $225,000 congressional donations, the PAC of the Grumman Corp., maker of fighter jets, gave another $1,000 to Democrat William Chappell of Florida, who is on the Defense Appropriations Subcommittee. Says Grumman PAC Chairman Dave Walsh: "We have selfish interests. We dole out money to those on committees dealing with defense and to those whose viewpoint is in line with ours."

Small PACs often look to larger ones for guidance. The Chamber of Commerce, BIPAC and the AFL-CIO publish "opportunity lists" to lead like-minded PAC money where it will do the most good. The Chamber recently produced a video version of its list by broadcasting a four-hour, closed-circuit television show called See How They Run to 150 PAC managers in seven cities. It opens with patriotic music and a waving flag as Chamber President Richard Lesher extols "a brighter future for America through political action." Presidential Assistant Kenneth Duberstein joins Chamber analysts in handicapping 50 key races. One of the

Chamber choices, Pennsylvania's Coyne, expresses the sentiment of the rest of the all-Republican lineup: "The key to my race is, Can we marshal the resources?"

An article in *INC.* magazine, which is aimed at independent businessmen, offers advice on "some ways to measure your return" from PAC donations. It explains how to compute the "equity share" and "cost-vote ratio" that can be "bought" for each candidate. "Special interests don't contribute to congressional candidates for the fun of it," the article advises. "They do so to get things done." It dismisses any moral qualms: "If politicians want to sell and the public wants to buy, there is not much you can do to stop the trade."

The question of whether PAC donations actually buy votes or only reward members who tend to vote properly is akin to that of the chicken and the egg. One thing is certain: the combination of chickens and eggs fertilizes the legislative process. The National Automobile Dealers Association, which will contribute more than $850,000 to congressional candidates this election, was able to kill a regulation requiring that buyers be informed of known defects in used cars for sale. The United Auto Workers (U.A.W.) is handing out more than $1 million this year while it lines up support for a "domestic content" bill that requires foreign firms to use a high percentage of American parts and labor in cars they sell in the U.S. Lockheed Corp., like its competitor Boeing, donated heavily to the House and Senate armed services committees as it fought to win a Government contract for its C-5B cargo plane. The National Rifle Association (N.R.A.) will give away $1.3 million this year, some of it to help Senate Judiciary Committee members who approved a law loosening gun-control regulations.

Although lobbyists and Congressmen deny that votes are for sale, the link to donations is often uncomfortably clear. The U.A.W. PAC in New Jersey has long backed Congressman Peter Rodino. But last month Rodino was informed that future support would be contingent on his agreeing to co-sponsor the domestic content bill. When his office said he would, the union publicly announced that its endorsement came "following Rodino's decision to sign on as a co-sponsor" of the bill. The appearance of coercion annoyed Rodino. Said an aide: "He thought it was the most heavyhanded thing he had seen during his career." Rodino withdrew as a co-sponsor, although he is still backing the bill.

An example of how donations and votes go hand in palm is the House passage of a bill that would allow the shipping industry to fix prices, which could raise freight costs by about 20 percent. The Merchant Marine and Fisheries Committee has long been a safe harbor for special interests. "Any bill coming out of the Merchant Marine ought to go straight to the grand jury," jokes one Congressman. Both labor and business groups formed an alliance to pass the price fixing bill, with the Seafarers' Union and Lykes Bros. Steamship Co. leading the lobbying by 13 interested PACs. Their total donations to Merchant Marine Committee members: $47,850. After passing the bill 33 to 0, the committee got the House rules suspended to allow only 40 minutes of debate. Since most Congressmen had little idea of what was in the bill, many voted in response to thumbs-up signs from committee members. The bill passed 350 to 33.

Among other PAC-man specials:

The Professionals Bill. The A.M.A. and American Dental Association have been lobbying for a law that would exempt professionals from Federal Trade Commission regulation and thus permit them to fix prices. The bill is still awaiting House action. Since 1979 the two groups have given $2.3 million to House members, 72 percent of it to 213 co-sponsors of the bill. Each sponsor got an average of $7,598, according to Consumer Advocate Ralph Nader's Congress Watch. Thomas Luken, the prime sponsor, got $14,750. Luken, one of Congress's most notorious PAC-men, also sponsored the bill revoking the used-car regulation.

The Beer Bill. Brewers want to be allowed to designate monopoly territories for their distributors, which could raise the cost of beer 20 percent. The legislation is pending in the House. SixPAC has handed out $35,000 to members of the Judiciary Subcommittee on Monopolies. Democrat Jack Brooks of Texas, the chief sponsor, got a $10,000 contribution, a $1,000 honorarium for a speech and a trip to Las Vegas from SixPAC this year.

The Bankruptcy Bill. The credit industry is pushing for a law that would fundamentally change the legal concept of a "fresh start" for those who go broke. The pending bill would require individual debtors, but not business, to pay back debts after declaring bankruptcy. Six credit PACs, led by the American Bankers Association and Household Finance Corp., have donated $704,297 to 255 Congressmen co-sponsoring the bill.

Commodity Traders' Fee. PACs representing three major groups of commodities brokers have been fighting a Reagan Administration proposal to set a 6¢ to 12¢ fee on each trade to finance the Commodity Futures Trading Commission. They have contributed to most members of the House and Senate agriculture committees, both of which voted to reject the fee. "It isn't buying votes," said Michael McLeod, a lobbyist with the Chicago Board of Trade. "It's just how the political system works."

Clean Air. The House Health and the Environment Subcommittee voted this year to weaken considerably the Clean Air Act. The twelve members who voted for the relaxation got a total of $197,325 from the PACs of the seven major industries affected. Republican Senator Steve Symms of Idaho, who got $97,500 during his 1980 campaign from affected industries, dutifully introduced one industry amendment after another. "It was clear he had no idea what was in those amendments," says one Senator. Members of his committee even privately mocked him, asking, "Which campaign check had that amendment attached to it?"

When a bill emerges from committee, and the debate becomes publicized, it becomes harder for special interests to be effective. Grassroots pressure by those in favor of the Clean Air Act, and perhaps also the growth of environmental PACs, make it likely that the act will pass without being significantly weakened.

Defenders of the PAC system say that contributions are an effect, not a cause; and that they are given to those who are already known to be supportive of a PAC's position. "The idea that there's a *quid pro quo* is balderdash," says Republican Congressman Bill Frenzel of Minnesota. Argues BIPAC's Budde: "Pacs are not buying anyone. They're rewarding." Because a single PAC is limited to $5,000 a race, the power it can command, while large, is not overwhelming. The most you can purchase, proponents claim, is access. Says Grumman PAC Chairman Walsh: "We don't expect contracts because we gave someone $5,000. But the likelihood of us getting in to see the Congressman is much higher."

The backers of PACs point out that, like rivers to the sea, special-interest money will find a way to flow into campaigns, and the PAC channel keeps the process regulated and open to public scrutiny. Small donors, who once felt they had no impact, can now pool their money with like-minded voters. "PACs have redistributed political influence," says Phil Gramm of Texas, "They've taken power away from the smoke-filled room." Agrees Jack Webb of HouPAC: "PACs get people involved who otherwise might not be. They're a damned good thing."

There is no argument about one major PAC fact: within ten years, PACs have become a significant method of financing congressional campaigns, accounting for more than one-fourth of all money raised by candidates, and more than one-third of all money raised by incumbents. The average candidate now gets three times as much money from PACs as from a political party. This year, the national campaign committees of the Republican Party have been revitalized by a surge of donations. Even so, unless the laws are changed, PACs are destined to remain much more important than national parties as a source of funds for candidates. Says Herbert Alexander, a professor at the University of Southern California who has written about campaign finance: "The decline of the parties is, in part, a consequence of election reform gone awry."

PACs have become so important and controversial that they are now an issue of their own on the campaign trail. Their proper role is being debated, for example, in the Senate race in Montana. Democratic Incumbent John Melcher is receiving contributions from a wide array of labor, corporate and association PACs. They have given him more than $350,000, over half his campaign fund. "How can you work for your constituents when you've got $10,000 chits out?" demands Republican Challenger Larry Williams, a self-made millionaire. Melcher is countering by making an issue of the fact that NCPAC has waged an irresponsible $250,000 independent effort to defeat him. One of Melcher's television ads depicts NCPAC operatives flying into the state with money-stuffed briefcases to "defeat Doc Melcher."

Democrat Joseph Kolter is also trying to turn PAC donations into an issue in his bid to unseat Republican Congressman Eugene Atkinson of Pennsylvania. Last year Atkinson made a dramatic switch in party allegiance. As a Democrat, he had piously refused on principle to accept PAC money, but since becoming a Republican he has raised $40,000 from business-oriented PACs. In his campaign speeches, Kolter reels off a list of Atkinson donors, referring to General Public Utilities Corp. as "the people who brought you Three Mile Island" and to a group of major industries as "the filthy five." Kolter has his own PAC sources; he is drawing the maximum donations from the United Steel Workers, the U.A.W. and other unions.

Any attempt to reform the PAC system is vulnerable to the law of unintended consequences. Individuals, groups, corporations and unions will continue to have the desire and resources to support favored candidates. They also have the right, and even the responsibility, to do so. Trying to restrict such efforts too severely could just divert them into other, less worthy approaches, like the one followed by NCPAC. Says Michael Malbin, a political analyst at the American Enterprise Institute: "Unless you repeal the First Amendment, people with private interests in legislation will be active."

Public financing of campaigns would solve many of the problems. The same arguments that were persuasive at the presidential level—the need to lower the role of fat-cat donors and special interests—are at least as compelling when it comes to Congress. (In the primaries, presidential candidates raise money, some of it from PACs, that is matched by federal funds. The general election is fully financed by federal money.) But such a process presents practical difficulties: some districts and states are much more expensive to campaign in than others, and incumbents (who make the laws) are unlikely to vote for a system that removes their own built-in advantage. "It's like sending goats to guard the cabbage patch," says Andrew Jacobs of Indiana, one of the Congressmen who refuse PAC money. Moreover, public financing could be expensive.

Raising the $1,000 limit that an individual can contribute to a campaign would help dilute the power of PACs. The individual limit had stayed the same since 1974 despite inflation. "Individual contributions are far less effective than those from a PAC," says Republican Congresswoman Millicent Fenwick of New Jersey. "The PACs lobbyist will come and twist arms." In her race for a Senate seat, Fenwick has refused PAC money.

Individual donations from corporate leaders, of course, can exert the same type of influence as money from PACs. Indeed, the PAC-stemious Fenwick has raised $13,650 from the top executives of a Wall Street investment firm, far more than the limit imposed on the firm's PAC. But the greatest threat posed by individual contributions in the past was the secrecy surrounding them and their disproportionate amounts. A new $5,000 limit would seem reasonable in light of today's strict reporting requirements.

Another option would be to limit the total amount a House candidate could raise from PACs. A bill setting a $70,000 limit on the amount a House candidate could raise from PACs passed the House in 1979, but died in the Senate. A new measure has been introduced in the House setting the PAC money ceiling at $75,000.

The ideal reform would incorporate elements of each of these proposals. Partial federal financing, either by direct grants or matching funds, could water down the importance of PACs. So could raising the private contribution limit. Increasing the amount people can donate to the national parties, currently $20,000 each year, could strengthen the role of the parties. Finally, setting a reasonable limit on the amount a candidate can get from PACs, certainly no more than $75,000 an election, would rein in the PAC-men.

The difficulty is not so much finding solutions, but persuading Congressmen, who benefit so handsomely, to change the present situation. "It is a lot easier to raise money from PACs than from other sources," observes PAC Critic Barney Frank, a Democratic Congressman from Massachusetts. "You sit there, somebody hands you a check for $3,000, and you say 'Thank you,'" In the end, it is pressure from the voters that may limit the power of the PACs. Some lawmakers, like Missouri Democrat Richard Gephardt, detect rumblings of reform. Says he: "There is a growing sense that the system is getting out of hand."

❖❖ MONEY, PACs, AND ELECTIONS

Political campaigning has become increasingly expensive at all levels of government. Only presidential campaigns are publicly funded, although candidates in presidential primaries have to garner a certain amount of private contributions to qualify for federal matching funds. The rise of political action committees, which the campaign finance laws of the 1970s recognized as legitimate, has enhanced the influence of private money and interest group power in the political process. Money and politics go together in the contemporary political environment, and Political Action Committees are a major source of campaign funds. While PACs are perfectly legitimate organizations, authorized and even encouraged by the campaign finance laws of the 1970s, they are often portrayed as the bad guys of American politics. They are the modern-day "factions" of the James Madison attack in *Federalist 10*. The author of the following selection suggests that PAC-bashing is overdone.

34

Larry J. Sabato

THE MISPLACED OBSESSION WITH PACs

❖❖❖❖❖❖❖

The disturbing statistics and the horror stories about political action committees seem to flow like a swollen river, week after week, year in and year out. Outrage extends across the ideological spectrum: the liberal interest group Common Cause has called the system "scandalous," while conservative former senator Barry Goldwater (R–Ariz.) has bluntly declared, "PAC money is destroying the election process. . . ."

In more and more recent campaigns, political action committees have been portrayed as the central corrupting evil in American politics. In Massachusetts in 1984, for example, all the major contenders for the U.S. Senate in both parties re-

From *Paying for Elections: The Campaign Finance Thicket* (New York, The Twentieth Century Fund, 1989, pp. 9–18), by Larry J. Sabato. Reprinted with permission from the Twentieth Century Fund, New York.

fused to take PAC money, and one candidate even got his Democratic opponent to sign a statement pledging to resign his seat in Congress should he "ever knowingly accept and keep a campaign contribution from a political action committee."

Candidates from Maine to California have scored points by forswearing the acceptance of PAC gifts earlier and more fervently than their opponents. The Democratic party included in its 1984 national platform a call for banning PAC funds from all federal elections, despite its aggressiveness in attracting PAC money to itself and its candidates.

PAC-bashing is undeniably a popular campaign sport, but the "big PAC attack" is an opiate that obscures the more vital concerns and problems in campaign finance. PAC excesses are merely a symptom of other serious maladies in the area of political money, but the near-obsessive focus by public interest groups and the news media on the PAC evils has diverted attention from more fundamental matters. The PAC controversy, including the charges most frequently made against them, can help explain why PACs are best described as agents of pseudo corruption.

The PAC Era

While a good number of PACs of all political persuasions existed prior to the 1970s, it was during that decade of campaign reform that the modern PAC era began. Spawned by the Watergate-inspired revisions of the campaign finance laws, PACs grew in number from 113 in 1972 to 4,196 by 1988, and their contributions to congressional candidates multiplied more than fifteenfold, from $8.5 million in 1971–72 to $130.3 million in 1985–86.

The rapid rise of PACs has engendered much criticism, yet many of the charges made against political action committees are exaggerated and dubious. While the widespread use of the PAC structure is new, special interest money of all types has always found its way into politics. Before the 1970s it simply did so in less traceable and far more disturbing and unsavory ways. And while, in absolute terms, PACs contribute a massive sum to candidates, it is not clear that there is proportionately more interest-group money in the system than before. As political scientist Michael Malbin has argued, we will never know the truth because the earlier record is so incomplete.

The proportion of House and Senate campaign funds provided by PACs has certainly increased since the early 1970s, but individuals, most of whom are unaffiliated with PACs, together with the political parties, still supply about three-fifths of all the money spent by or on behalf of House candidates and three-quarters of the campaign expenditures for Senate contenders. So while the importance of PAC spending has grown, PACs clearly remain secondary as a source of election funding. PACs, then, seem rather less awesome when considered within the entire spectrum of campaign finance.

Apart from the argument over the relative weight of PAC funds, PAC critics claim that political action committees are making it more expensive to run for office. There is some validity to this assertion. Money provided to one candidate funds the purchase of campaign tools that the other candidate must match in order to stay competitive.

In the aggregate, American campaign expenditures seem huge. In 1988, the total amount spent by all U.S. House of Representatives candidates taken together was about $256 million, and the campaign cost of the winning House nominee averaged over $392,000. Will Rogers's 1931 remark has never been more true: "Politics has got so expensive that it takes lots of money to even get beat with."

Yet $256 million is far less than the annual advertising budgets of many individual commercial enterprises. These days it is expensive to communicate, whether the message is political or commercial. Television time, polling costs, consultants' fees, direct-mail investment, and other standard campaign expenditures have been soaring in price, over and above inflation. PACs have been fueling the use of new campaign techniques, but a reasonable case can be made that such expenses are necessary, and that more and better communication is required between candidates and an electorate that often appears woefully uninformed about politics. PACs therefore may be making a positive contribution by providing the means to increase the flow of information during elections.

PACs are also accused of being biased toward the incumbent, and except for the ideological committees, they do display a clear and overwhelming preference for those already in office. But the same bias is apparent in contributions from individuals, who ask the same reasonable, perhaps decisive, economic question: Why waste money on contenders if incumbents almost always win? On the other hand, the best challengers—those perceived as having fair-to-good chances to win—are usually generously funded by PACs. Well-targeted PAC challenger money clearly helped the GOP win a majority in the U.S. Senate in 1980, for instance, and in turn aided the Democrats in their 1986 Senate takeover.

The charge that PACs limit the number of strong challengers is true, because by giving so much money so early in the race to incumbents, they deter potential opponents from declaring their candidacies. On the other hand, the money that PACs channel to competitive challengers late in the election season may actually help increase the turnover of officeholders on election day. PAC money also tends to invigorate competitiveness in open-seat congressional races where there is no incumbent.

One line of attack on PACs that seems fairly justified is the feeling that these important components of our democratic political system are themselves undemocratic in some respects. For example, in some cases their candidate selection process completely severs the connecting link between contributor and candidate. As political scientist David Adamany has noted, this condition is most apparent in many of the politically ideological nonconnected PACs, whose lack of a parent body and whose freestyle organization make them accountable to no one and responsive mainly to their own whims. Leaders of ideological PACs, however, insist that their committees are still democratic, since contributors will simply stop giving if dissatisfied with the PACs' candidate choices.

But ideological PACs raise most of their money by direct mail, which means that the average donor's only source of information about the PAC's activities is their own communication, which, not surprisingly, tends to be upbeat and selective in reporting the committee's work. Moreover, as political scientist Frank Sorauf has stressed, since direct mail can succeed with only a 2 to 5 percent response rate, and since prospecting for new donors is continuous, decisions by even a large number of givers to drop out will have little impact on PAC fundraising.

Ideological PACs are not alone in following undemocratic practices. When the AFL-CIO overwhelmingly endorsed Democrat Walter Mondale for president in 1983, thereby making available to him the invaluable resources of most labor PACs, a CBS News/*New York Times* poll showed that less than a quarter of the union members interviewed had their presidential preferences solicited in any fashion. If a representative sampling had taken place, the AFL-CIO might not have been so pro-Mondale, since the CBS/*Times* poll indicated that Mondale was not favored by a majority of the respondents and was in fact in a statistical dead heat with Senator John Glenn (D–Ohio) for a plurality edge.

Nor can many corporate PACs be considered showcases of democracy. In a few PACs the chief executive officers completely rule the roost, and in many the CEOs have inordinate influence on PAC decisions.

PAC Money and Congressional "Corruption"

The most serious charge leveled at PACs is that they succeed in buying the votes of legislators on issues important to their individual constituencies. It seems hardly worth arguing that many PACs are shopping for congressional votes and that PAC money buys access, or opens doors, to congressmen. But the "vote-buying" allegation is generally not supported by a careful examination of the facts. PAC contributions do make a difference, at least on some occasions, in securing access and influencing the course of events, but those occasions are not nearly as frequent as anti-PAC spokesmen, even congressmen themselves, often suggest.

PACs affect legislative proceedings to a decisive degree only when certain conditions prevail. First, the less visible the issue, the more likely that PAC funds can change or influence congressional votes. A corollary is that PAC money has more effect in the of the legislative process, such as agenda setting and votes in subcommittee meetings, than in later and more public floor deliberations. Press, public, and even "watchdog" groups are not nearly as attentive to initial legislative proceedings.

PAC contributions are also more likely to influence the legislature when the issue is specialized and narrow, or unopposed by other organized interests. PAC gifts are less likely to be decisive on broad national issues such as American policy in Nicaragua or the adoption of a Star Wars missile defense system. But the more technical measures seem tailor-made for the special interests. Additionally, PAC influence in Congress is greater when large PACs or groups of PACs (such as business and labor PACs) are allied. In recent years, despite their natural enmity, business and labor have lobbied together on a number of issues, including defense spending, trade policy, environmental regulation, maritime legislation, trucking legislation, and nuclear power. The combination is a weighty one, checked in many instances only by a tendency for business and labor in one industry (say, the railroads) to combine and oppose their cooperating counterparts in another industry (perhaps the truckers and teamsters).

It is worth stressing, however, that most congressmen are *not* unduly influenced by PAC money on most votes. The special conditions simply do not apply to most legislative issues, and the overriding factors in determining a legislator's votes include party affiliation, ideology, and constituents' needs and desires. Much has been made of the passage of large tax cuts for oil and business interests in the 1981 omnibus tax package. The journalist Elizabeth Drew said there was a "bidding war" to trade campaign contributions for tax breaks benefiting independent oil producers. Ralph Nader's Public Citizen group charged that the $280,000 in corporate PAC money accepted by members of the House Ways and Means Committee helped to produce a bill that "contained everything business ever dared to ask for, and more." Yet as Robert Samuelson has convincingly argued, the "bidding war" between Democrats and Republicans was waged not for PAC money but for control of a House of Representatives sharply divided between Reaganite Republicans and liberal Democrats, with conservative "boll weevil" Democrats from the southern oil states as the crucial swing votes. The Ways and Means Committee actions cited by Nader were also more correctly explained in partisan terms. After all, if these special interests were so influential in writing the 1981 omnibus tax package, how could they fail so completely to derail the much more important (and, for them, threatening) tax reform legislation of 1986?

If party loyalty can have a stronger pull than PAC contributions, then surely the views of a congressman's constituents can also take precedence over those of political action committees. If an incumbent is faced with choice of either voting for a PAC-backed bill that is very unpopular in his district or forgoing the PAC's money, the odds are that any politician who depends on a majority of votes to remain in office is going to side with his constituency and vote against the PAC's interest. PAC gifts are merely a means to an end: reelection. If accepting money will cause a candidate embarrassment, then even a maximum donation will likely be rejected. The flip side of this proposition makes sense as well: if a PAC's parent organization has many members or a major financial stake in the congressman's home district, he is much more likely to vote the PAC's way—not so much because he receives PAC money but because the group accounts for an important part of his electorate. Does a U.S. senator from a dairy state vote for dairy price supports because he received a significant percentage of his PAC contributions from agriculture, or because the farm population of his state is relatively large and politically active? When congressmen vote the National Rifle Association's preferences is it because of the money the NRA's PAC distributes, or because the NRA, unlike gun-control advocates, has repeatedly demonstrated the ability to produce a sizable number of votes in many legislative districts?

If PACs have appeared more influential than they actually are, it is partly because many people believe legislators are looking for opportunities to exclaim (as one did during the Abscam scandal) "I've got larceny in my blood!" It is certainly disturbing that the National Republican Congressional Committee believed it necessary to warn its PAC-soliciting candidates: "Don't *ever* suggest to the PAC that it is 'buying' your vote, should you get elected." Yet knowledgeable Capitol Hill observers agree that there are few truly corrupt congressmen. Simple correlations notwithstanding, when most legislators vote for a PAC-supported bill, it is because of the *merits* of the case, or the entreaties of their party leaders, peers, or constituents, and not because of PAC money.

When the PAC phenomenon is viewed in the broad perspective of issues, party allegiance, and constituent interests, it is clear that *merit* matters most in the votes most congressmen cast. It is naive to contend that PAC money never influences decisions, but it is unjustifiably cynical to believe that PACs always, or even usually, push the voting buttons in Congress.

PACs in Perspective

As the largely unsubstantiated "vote-buying" controversy suggests, PACs are often misrepresented and unfairly maligned as the embodiment of corrupt special interests. Political action committees are a contemporary manifestation of what James Madison called "factions." In his *Federalist, No. 10*, Madison wrote that through the flourishing of these competing interest groups, or factions, liberty would be preserved.

In any democracy, and particularly in one as pluralistic as the United States, it is essential that groups be relatively unrestricted in advocating their interests and positions. Not only is that the mark of a free society, it also provides a safety valve for the competitive pressures that build on all fronts in a capitalistic democracy. And it provides another means to keep representatives responsive to legitimate needs.

This is not to say that all groups pursue legitimate interests, or that vigorously competing interests ensure that the public good prevails. The press, the public, and valuable watchdog groups such as Common Cause must always be alert to instances in which narrow private interests prevail over the commonweal—occurrences that generally happen when no one is looking.

Besides the press and various public interest organizations, there are two major institutional checks on the potential abuses wrought by factions, associations, and now PACs. The most fundamental of these is regular free elections with general suffrage. As Tocqueville commented:

> Perhaps the most powerful of the causes which tend to mitigate the excesses of political association in the United States is Universal Suffrage. In countries in which universal suffrage exists, the majority is never doubtful, because neither party can pretend to represent that portion of the community which has not voted.
>
> The associations which are formed are aware, as well as the nation at large, that they do not represent the majority: this is, indeed, a condition inseparable from their existence; for if they did represent the prepondering power, they would change the law instead of soliciting its reform.

Senator Robert Dole (R–Kan.) has said, "There aren't any poor PACs or Food Stamp PACs or Nutrition PACs or Medicare PACs," and PAC critics frequently make the point that certain segments of the electorate are underrepresented in the PAC community. Yet without much support from PACs, there are food stamps, poverty and nutrition programs, and Medicare. Why? Because the recipients of governmental assistance constitute a hefty slice of the electorate, and *votes matter more than dollars to politicians*. Furthermore, many citizens *outside* the affected groups have also made known their support of aid to the poor and elderly—making yet a stronger electoral case for these PAC-less programs.

The other major institution that checks PAC influence is the two-party system. While PACs represent particular interests, the political parties build coalitions of groups and attempt to represent a national interest. They arbitrate among competing claims, and they seek to reach a consensus on matters of overriding importance to the nation. The parties are one of the few unifying forces in an exceptionally diverse country.

If interest groups and their PACs are useful to a functioning democracy, then political parties are essential. Yet just as PACs began gathering strength in the 1970s, the parties began a steady decline in power. In the past decade the rehabilitation of the party system has begun, but there is a long way to go. A central goal of the campaign financing reform agenda should be to strengthen the political parties, and to grant them a kind of "most favored nation" preferential status in the machinery of elections and campaign finance. Reforms to bolster the parties will also serve to temper the excesses of PACs by reducing their proportional impact on the election of public officials.

However limited and checkmated by political realities PACs may be, they are still regarded by a skeptical public as thoroughly unsavory. PACs have become the embodiment of greedy special interest politics, rising campaign costs, and corruption. It does not seem to matter that most experts in the field of campaign finance take considerable exception to the prevailing characterization of political action committees. PACs have become, in the public's mind, a powerful symbol of much that is wrong with America's campaign process, and candidates for public office naturally manipulate this symbol as well as others for their own ends. It is a circumstance as old as the Republic.

PACs, however, have done little to change their image for the better. Other than the business-oriented Public Affairs Council, few groups or committees have moved to correct one-sided press coverage or educate the public on campaign financing's fundamentals. In fact, many PACs fuel the fires of discontent by refusing to defend themselves while not seeming to care about appearances. Giving to both candidates in the same race, for example—an all-too-common practice—may be justifiable in theory, but it strikes most people as unprincipled, rank influence purchasing. Even worse, perhaps, are PACs that "correct their mistakes" soon after an election by sending a donation to the winning, but not originally PAC-supported, candidate. In the seven 1986 U.S. Senate races where a Democratic challenger defeated a Republican incumbent, there were 150 instances in which a PAC gave to the GOP candidate *before* the election and to the victorious Democrat once the votes were counted. These practices PACs themselves should stop. Every PAC should internally ban double giving, and there should be a moratorium on gifts to previously opposed candidates until at least the halfway point of the officeholder's term.

Whether PACs undertake some necessary rehabilitative steps or not, any fair appraisal of their role in American elections must be balanced. PACs are neither political innocents nor selfless civic boosters. But, neither are they cesspools of corruption and greed, nor modern-day versions of Tammany Hall.

PACs will never be popular with idealistic reformers because they represent the rough, cutting edge of a democracy teeming with different peoples and conflicting interests. Indeed, PACs may never be hailed even by natural allies; it was the business-oriented *Wall Street Journal*, after all, that editorially referred to Washington, D.C., as "a place where politicians, PACs, lawyers, and lobbyists for unions, business or you-name-it shake each other down full time for political money and political support."

Viewed in perspective, the root of the problem in campaign finance is not PACs; it is money. Americans have an enduring mistrust of the mix of money (particularly business money) and politics, as Finley Peter Dunne's Mr. Dooley revealed:

> I niver knew a pollytician to go wrong ontil he'd been contaminated be contact with a business man. . . . It seems to me that th' only thing to do is to keep pollyticians an' business men apart. They seem to have a bad infloonce on each other. Whiniver I see an alderman an' a banker walkin' down th' street together I know th' Recordin' Angel will have to ordher another bottle iv ink.

As a result of the new campaign finance rules of the 1970s, political action committees superceded the "fat cats" of old as the public focus and symbol of the role of money in politics, and PACs inherited the suspicions that go with the territory. Those suspicions are valuable because they keep the spotlight on PACs and guard against undue influence. It may be regrettable that such supervision is required, but human nature—not PACs—demands it.

Part Three

❖❖❖

National Government Institutions

Chapter 6

❖❖❖

THE PRESIDENCY

The American presidency is the only unique political institution that the United States has contributed to the world. It developed first in this country and later was imitated, usually unsuccessfully, in many nations. In no country and at no time has the institution of the presidency achieved the status and power that it possesses in the United States. This chapter will analyze the basis, nature, and implications of the power of this great American institution.

Constitutional Background: Single versus Plural Executive

The change that has taken place in the presidency since the office was established in 1789 is dramatic and significant. The framers of the Constitution were primarily concerned with the control of the arbitrary exercise of power by the legislature; thus they were willing to give the president broad power since he was not to be popularly elected and would be constantly under attack by the coordinate legislative branch. Although the framers were not afraid of establishing a vigorous presidency, there was a great deal of opposition to a potentially strong executive at the time the Constitution was drafted. In *Federalist 70* Alexander Hamilton attempts to persuade the people of the desirability of a strong presidential office, and while persuading, he sets forth the essential constitutional basis of the office.

35

Alexander Hamilton

FEDERALIST 70

❖❖❖❖❖❖❖

There is an idea, which is not without its advocates, that a vigorous executive is inconsistent with the genius of republican government. The enlightened well-wishers to this species of government must at least hope that the supposition is destitute of foundation; since they can never admit its truth, without, at the same time, admitting the condemnation of their own principles. Energy in the executive is a leading character in the definition of good government. It is essential to the protection of the community against foreign attacks; it is not less essential to the steady administration of the laws, to the protection of property against those irregular and high-handed combinations, which sometimes interrupt the ordinary course of justice, to the security of liberty against the enterprises and assaults of ambition, of faction, and of anarchy. Every man, the least conversant in Roman story, knows how often that republic was obliged to take refuge in the absolute power of a single man, under the formidable title of dictator, as well as against the intrigues of ambitious individuals, who aspired to the tyranny, and the seditions of whole classes of the community, whose conduct threatened the existence of all government, as against the invasions of external enemies, who menaced the conquest and destruction of Rome.

There can be no need, however, to multiply arguments or examples on this head. A feeble executive implies a feeble execution of the government. A feeble execution is but another phrase for a bad execution; and government ill executed, whatever it may be in theory, must be, in practice, a bad government.

Taking it for granted, therefore, that all men of sense will agree in the necessity of an energetic executive, it will only remain to inquire, what are the ingredients which constitute this energy? How far can they be combined with those other ingredients, which constitute safety in the republican sense? And how far does this combination characterize the plan which has been reported by the convention?

The ingredients which constitute energy in the executive are: unity; duration; and adequate provision for its support; competent powers.

The ingredients which constitute safety in the republican sense are: a due dependence on the people; a due responsibility.

Those politicians and statesmen, who have been the most celebrated for the soundness of their principles, and for the justness of their views, have declared in favor of a single executive, and a numerous legislature. They have, with great propriety, considered energy as the most necessary qualification of the former, and have regarded this as most applicable to power in a single hand; while they have, with equal propriety, considered the latter as the best adapted to deliberation and wisdom, and best calculated to conciliate the confidence of the people, and to secure their privileges and interests.

That unity is conducive to energy will not be disputed. Decision, activity, secrecy, and dispatch, will generally characterize the proceedings of one man, in a much more eminent degree than the proceedings of any greater number; and in proportion as the number is increased, these qualities will be diminished.

This unity may be destroyed in two ways; either by vesting the power in two or more magistrates, of equal dignity and authority; or by vesting it ostensibly in one man, subject, in whole or in part, to the control and cooperation of others, in the capacity of counsellors to him. . . .

The experience of other nations will afford little instruction on this head. As far, however, as it teaches anything, it teaches us not to be enamored of plurality in the executive. . . .

Wherever two or more persons are engaged in any common enterprise or pursuit, there is always danger of difference of opinion. If it be a public trust of office, in which they are clothed with equal dignity and authority, there is peculiar danger of personal emulation and even animosity. From either, and especially from all these causes, the most bitter dissensions are apt to spring. Whenever these happen, they lessen the respectability, weaken the authority, and distract the plans and operations of those whom they divide. If they should unfortunately assail the supreme executive magistracy of a country, consisting of a plurality of persons, they might impede or frustrate the most important measures of the government, in the most critical emergencies of state. And what is still worse, they might split the community into violent and irreconcilable factions, adhering differently to the different individuals who composed the magistracy. . . .

Upon the principles of a free government, inconveniences from the source just mentioned, must necessarily be submitted to in the formation of the legislature; but it is unnecessary, and therefore unwise, to introduce them into the constitution of the executive. It is here, too, that they may be most pernicious. In the legislature, promptitude of decision is oftener an evil than a benefit. The differences of opinion, and the jarrings of parties in that department of the government, though they may sometimes obstruct salutary plans, yet often promote deliberation and circumspection; and serve to check excesses in the majority. When a resolution, too, is once taken, the opposition must be at an end. That resolution is a law, and resistance to it punishable. But no favorable circumstances palliate, or atone for the disadvantages of dissention in the executive department. Here they are pure and unmixed. There is no point at which they cease to operate. They serve to embarrass and weaken the execution of the plan or measure to which they relate, from the first step to the final conclusion of it. They constantly counteract those qualities in the executive, which are the most necessary ingredients in its composition—vigor and expedition; and this without any counterbalancing good. In the conduct of war, in which the energy of the executive is the bulwark of the national security, everything would be to be apprehended from its plurality.

It must be confessed, that these observations apply with principal weight to the first case supposed, that is, to a plurality of magistrates of equal dignity and authority, a scheme, the advocates for which are not likely to form a numerous sect; but they apply, though not with equal, yet with considerable weight, to the project of a council, whose concurrence is made constitutionally necessary to the operations of the ostensible executive. An artful cabal in that council would be able to distract and to enervate the whole system of administration. If no such cabal should exist, the mere diversity of views and opinions would alone be sufficient to tincture the exercise of the executive authority with the spirit of habitual feebleness and dilatoriness.

But one of the weightiest objections to a plurality in the executive, and which lies as much against the last as the first plan, is, that it tends to conceal faults, and destroy responsibility. . . . It often becomes impossible, amidst mutual accusations, to determine on whom the blame or the punishment of a pernicious measure . . . ought really to fall. It is shifted from one to another with so much dexterity, and under such plausible appearances, that the public opinion is left in suspense about the real author. . . .

A little consideration will satisfy us, that the species of security sought for in the multiplication of the executive, is unattainable. Numbers must be so great as to render combination difficult; or they are rather a source of danger than security. The united credit and influence of several individuals must be more formidable to liberty than the credit and influence of either of them separately. When power, therefore, is placed in the hands of so small a number of men, as to admit of their interests and views being easily combined in a common enterprise, by an artful leader, it becomes more liable to abuse, and more dangerous when abused, than if it be lodged in the hands of one man; who, from the very circumstances of his being alone, will be more narrowly watched and more readily suspected, and who cannot unite so great a mass of influence as when he is associated with others. . . .

I will only add, that prior to the appearance of the constitution, I rarely met with an intelligent man from any of the states, who did not admit as the result of experience, that the unity of the executive of this state was one of the best of the distinguishing features of our constitution.

❖❖ The Nature of the Presidency: Power and Persuasion

What is the position of the presidential office today? There is little doubt that it has expanded far beyond the expectations of the framers of the Constitution. The presidency is the only governmental branch with the necessary unity and energy to meet many of the most crucial problems of twentieth-century government in the United States; people have turned to the president in times of crisis to supply the central direction necessary for survival. In the next selection Clinton Rossiter, one of the leading American scholars of the presidency, gives his view of the role of the office.

36

Clinton Rossiter

THE PRESIDENCY—FOCUS OF LEADERSHIP

❖❖❖❖❖❖❖

No American can contemplate the presidency . . . without a feeling of solemnity and humility—solemnity in the face of a historically unique concentration of power and prestige, humility in the thought that he has had a part in the choice of a man to wield the power and enjoy the prestige.

Perhaps the most rewarding way to grasp the significance of this great office is to consider it as a focus of democratic leadership. Free men, too, have need of leaders. Indeed, it may be argued that one of the decisive forces in the shaping of American democracy has been the extraordinary capacity of the presidency for strong, able, popular leadership. If this has been true of our past, it will certainly be true of our future, and we should therefore do our best to grasp the quality of this leadership. Let us do this by answering the essential question: For what men and groups does the president provide leadership?

First, the president is *leader of the Executive Branch*. To the extent that our federal civil servants have need of common guidance, he alone is in a position to provide it. We cannot savor the fullness of the president's duties unless we recall that he is held primarily accountable for the ethics, loyalty, efficiency, frugality, and responsiveness to the public's wishes of the two and one-third million Americans in the national administration.

Both the Constitution and Congress have recognized his power to guide the day-to-day activities of the Executive Branch, strained and restrained though his leadership may often be in practice. From the Constitution, explicitly or implicitly, he receives the twin powers of appointment and removal, as well as the primary duty, which no law or plan or circumstances can ever take away from him, to "take care that the laws be faithfully executed."

From Congress, through such legislative mandates as the Budget and Accounting Act of 1921 and the succession of Reorganization Acts, the president has received further acknowledgment of his administrative leadership. Although independent agencies such as the Interstate Commerce Commission and the National Labor Relations Board operate by design outside his immediate area of responsibil-

"The Presidency: Focus of Leadership" by Clinton Rossiter, *The New York Times*, November 11, 1956. Copyright © 1956 by The New York Times Company. Reprinted by permission.

ity, most of the government's administrative tasks are still carried on within the
fuzzy-edged pyramid that has the president at its lonely peak; the laws that are executed daily in his name and under his general supervision are numbered in the hundreds.

Many observers, to be sure, have argued strenuously that we should not ask too
much of the president as administrative leader, lest we burden him with impossible
detail, or give too much to him, lest we inject political considerations too forcefully
into the steady business of the civil service. Still, he cannot ignore the blunt mandate of the Constitution, and we should not forget the wisdom that lies behind it.
The president has no more important tasks than to set a high personal example of
integrity and industry for all who serve the nation, and to transmit a clear lead
downward through his chief lieutenants to all who help shape the policies by which
we live.

Next, the president is *leader of the forces of peace and war*. Although authority in
the field of foreign relations is shared constitutionally among three organs—president, Congress, and for two special purposes, the Senate—his position is paramount, if not indeed dominant. Constitution, laws, customs, the practice of other
nations, and the logic of history have combined to place the president in a dominant position. Secrecy, dispatch, unity, continuity, and access to information—the
ingredients of successful diplomacy—are properties of his office, and Congress,
needless to add, possesses none of them. Leadership in foreign affairs flows today
from the president—or it does not flow at all.

The Constitution designates him specifically as "Commander in Chief of the
Army and Navy of the United States." In peace and war he is the supreme commander of the armed forces, the living guarantee of the American belief in "the supremacy of the civil over military authority."

In time of peace he raises, trains, supervises, and deploys the forces that Congress is willing to maintain. With the aid of the Secretary of Defense, the Joint
Chiefs of Staff, and the National Security Council—all of whom are his personal
choices—he looks constantly to the state of the nation's defenses. He is never for
one day allowed to forget that he will be held accountable by the people, Congress,
and history for the nation's readiness to meet an enemy assault.

In time of war his power to command the forces swells out of all proportion to
his other powers. All major decisions of strategy, and many of tactics as well, are his
alone to make or to approve. Lincoln and Franklin Roosevelt, each in his own way
and time, showed how far the power of military command can be driven by a president anxious to have his generals and admirals get on with the war.

But this, the power of command, is only a fraction of the vast responsibility the
modern president draws from the Commander in Chief clause. We need only think
back to three of Franklin D. Roosevelt's actions in World War II—the creation and
staffing of a whole array of emergency boards and offices, the seizure and operation
of more than sixty strike-bound or strike-threatened plants and industries, and the
forced evacuation of 70,000 American citizens of Japanese descent from the West
Coast—to understand how deeply the president's authority can cut into the lives
and liberties of the American people in time of war. We may well tremble in contemplation of the kind of leadership he would be forced to exert in a total war with
the absolute weapon.

The president's duties are not all purely executive in nature. He is also intimately associated, by Constitution and custom, with the legislative process, and we may therefore consider him as *leader of Congress*. Congress has its full share of strong men, but the complexity of the problems it is asked to solve by a people who still assume that all problems are solvable has made external leadership a requisite of effective operation.

The president alone is in a political, constitutional, and practical position to provide such leadership, and he is therefore expected, within the limits of propriety, to guide Congress in much of its lawmaking activity. Indeed, since Congress is no longer minded or organized to guide itself, the refusal or inability of the president to serve as a kind of prime minister results in weak and disorganized government. His tasks as leader of Congress are difficult and delicate, yet he must bend to them steadily or be judged a failure. The president who will not give his best thoughts to leading Congress, more so the president who is temperamentally or politically unfitted to "get along with Congress," is now rightly considered a national liability.

The lives of Jackson, Lincoln, Wilson, and the two Roosevelts should be enough to remind us that the president draws much of his real power from his position as *leader of his party*. By playing the grand politician with unashamed zest, the first of these men gave his epic administration a unique sense of cohesion, the second rallied doubting Republican leaders and their followings to the cause of the Union, and the other three achieved genuine triumphs as catalysts of Congressional action. That gifted amateur, Dwight D. Eisenhower, has also played the role for every drop of drama and power in it. He has demonstrated repeatedly what close observers of the presidency know well: that its incumbent must devote an hour or two of every working day to the profession of Chief Democrat or Chief Republican.

It troubles many good people, not entirely without reason, to watch the president dabbling in politics, distributing loaves and fishes, smiling on party hacks, and endorsing candidates he knows to be unfit for anything but immediate delivery to the county jail. Yet if he is to persuade Congress, if he is to achieve a loyal and cohesive administration, if he is to be elected in the first place (and reelected in the second), he must put his hand firmly to the plow of politics. The president is inevitably the nation's No. 1 political boss.

Yet he is, at the same time, if not in the same breath, *leader of public opinion*. While he acts as political chieftain of some, he serves as moral spokesman for all. It took the line of presidents some time to sense the nation's need for a clear voice, but since the day when Andrew Jackson thundered against the Nullifiers of South Carolina, no effective president has doubted his prerogative to speak the people's mind on the great issues of his time, to serve, in Wilson's words, as "the spokesman for the real sentiment and purpose of the country."

Sometimes, of course, it is no easy thing, even for the most sensitive and large-minded presidents, to know the real sentiment of the people or to be bold enough to state it in defiance of loudly voiced contrary opinion. Yet the president who senses the popular mood and spots new tides even before they start to run, who practices shrewd economy in his appearances as spokesman for the nation, who is conscious of his unique power to compel discussion on his own terms and who talks the language of Christian morality and the American tradition, can shout down any other voice or chorus of voices in the land. The president is the American people's one authentic trumpet, and he has no higher duty than to give a clear and certain sound.

The president is easily the most influential leader of opinion in this country principally because he is, among all his other jobs, our Chief of State. He is, that is to say, the ceremonial head of the government of the United States, the *leader of the rituals of American democracy*. The long catalogue of public duties that the Queen discharges in England and the Governor General in Canada is the President's responsibility in this country, and the catalogue is even longer because he is not a king, or even the agent of one, and is therefore expected to go through of some rather undignified paces by a people who think of him as a combination of scoutmaster, Delphic oracle, hero of the silver screen, and father of the multitudes.

The role of Chief of State may often seem trivial, yet it cannot be neglected by a president who proposes to stay in favor and, more to the point, in touch with the people, the ultimate support of all his claims to leadership. And whether or not he enjoys this role, no president can fail to realize that his many powers are invigorated, indeed are given a new dimension of authority, because he is the symbol of our sovereignty, continuity, and grandeur as a people.

When he asks a senator to lunch in order to enlist his support for a pet project, when he thumps his desk and reminds the antagonists in a labor dispute of the larger interests of the American people, when he orders a general to cease caviling or else be removed from his command, the senator and the disputants and the general are well aware—especially if the scene is laid in the White House—that they are dealing with no ordinary head of government. The framers of the Constitution took a momentous step when they fused the dignity of a king and the power of a prime minister in one elective office—when they made the president a national leader in the mystical as well as the practical sense.

Finally, the president has been endowed—whether we or our friends abroad like it or not—with a global role as *a leader of the free nations*. His leadership in this area is not that of a dominant executive. The power he exercises is in a way comparable to that which he holds as a leader of Congress. Senators and congressmen can, if they choose, ignore the president's leadership with relative impunity. So, too, can our friends abroad; the action of Britain and France in the Middle East is a case in point. But so long as the United States remains the richest and most powerful member of any coalition it may enter, then its president's words and deeds will have a direct bearing on the freedom and stability of a great many other countries.

Having engaged in this piecemeal analysis of the categories of presidential leadership, we must now fit the pieces back together into a seamless unity. For that, after all, is what the presidency is, and I hope this exercise in political taxonomy has not obscured the paramount fact that this focus of democratic leadership is a single office filled by a single man.

The president is not one kind of leader one part of the day, another kind in another part—leader of the bureaucracy in the morning, of the armed forces at lunch, of Congress in the afternoon, of the people in the evening. He exerts every kind of leadership every moment of the day, and every kind feeds upon and into all the others. He is a more exalted leader of ritual because he can guide opinion, a more forceful leader in diplomacy because he commands the armed forces personally, a more effective leader of Congress because he sits at the top of his party. The conflicting demands of these categories of leadership give him trouble at times, but in the end all unite to make him a leader without any equal in the history of democracy.

I think it important to note the qualification: "the history of democracy." For what I have been talking about here is not the Fuehrerprinzip of Hitler or the "cult of personality," but the leadership of free men. The presidency, like every other instrument of power we have created for our use, operates within a grand and durable pattern of private liberty and public morality, which means that the president can lead successfully only when he honors the pattern—by working towards ends to which a "persistent and undoubted" majority of people has given support, and by selecting means that are fair, dignified, and familiar.

The president, that is to say, can lead us only in the direction we are accustomed to travel. He cannot lead the gentlemen of Congress to abdicate their functions; he cannot order our civil servants to be corrupt and slothful; he cannot even command our generals to bring off a coup d'état. And surely he cannot lead public opinion in a direction for which public opinion is not prepared—a truth to which our strongest presidents would make the most convincing witnesses. The leadership of free men must honor their freedom. The power of the presidency can move as a mighty host only with the grain of liberty and morality.

The president, then, must provide a steady focus of leadership—of administrators, ambassadors, generals, congressmen, party chieftains, people, and men of good will everywhere. In a constitutional system compounded of diversity and antagonism, the presidency looms up as the countervailing force of unity and harmony. In a society ridden by centrifugal forces, it is the only point of reference we all have in common. The relentless progress of this continental republic has made the presidency our truly national political institution.

There are those, to be sure, who would reserve this role to Congress, but, as the least aggressive of our presidents, Calvin Coolidge, once testified, "It is because in their hours of timidity the Congress becomes subservient to the importunities of organized minorities that the president comes more and more to stand as the champion of the rights of the whole country." The more Congress becomes, in Burke's phrase, "a confused and scuffling bustle of local agency" the more the presidency must become a clear beacon of national purpose.

It has been such a beacon at most great moments in our history. In this great moment, too, we may be confident it will burn brightly.

❖❖ The constitutional and statutory *authority* of the president is indeed extraordinary. However, it is more important to point out that the actual power of the president depends upon his political abilities. The president must act within the framework of a complex and diversified political constituency. He can use the authority of his office to buttress his strength, but this alone is not sufficient. Somehow he must be able to persuade those with whom he deals to follow him; otherwise, he will be weak and ineffective.

37

Richard E. Neustadt

PRESIDENTIAL POWER

In the United States we like to "rate" a president. We measure him as "weak" or "strong" and call what we are measuring his "leadership." We do not wait until a man is dead; we rate him from the moment he takes office. We are quite right to do so. His office has become the focal point of politics and policy in our political system. Our commentators and our politicians make a specialty of taking the man's measurements. The rest of us join in when we feel "government" impinging on our private lives. In the third quarter of the twentieth century millions of us have that feeling often.

. . . Although we all make judgments about presidential leadership, we often base our judgments upon images of office that are far removed from the reality. We also use those images when we tell one another whom to choose as president. But it is risky to appraise a man in office or to choose a man for office on false premises about the nature of his job. When the job is the presidency of the United States the risk becomes excessive. . . .

We deal here with the president himself and with his influence on governmental action. In institutional terms the presidency now includes 2,000 men and women. The president is only one of them. But *his* performance scarcely can be measured without focusing on *him*. In terms of party, or of country, or the West, so-called, his leadership involves far more than governmental action. But the sharpening of spirit and of values and of purposes is not done in a vacuum. Although governmental action may not be the whole of leadership, all else is nurtured by it and gains meaning from it. Yet if we treat the presidency as the president, we cannot measure him as though he were the government. Not action as an outcome but his impact on the outcome is the measure of the man. His strength or weakness, then, turns on his personal capacity to influence the conduct of the men who make up government. His influence becomes the mark of leadership. To rate a president according to these rules, one looks into the man's own capabilities as seeker and as wielder of effective influence upon the other men involved in governing the country. . . .

"Presidential" . . . means nothing but the president. "Power" means *his* influence. It helps to have these meanings settled at the start.

There are two ways to study "presidential power." One way is to focus on the tactics, so to speak, of influencing certain men in given situations: how to get a bill through Congress, how to settle strikes, how to quiet Cabinet feuds, or how to stop a Suez. The other way is to step back from tactics on those "givens" and to deal with influence in more strategic terms: what is its nature and what are its sources? What can *this* man accomplish to improve the prospect that he will have influence when he wants it? Strategically, the question is not how he masters Congress in a peculiar instance, but what he does to boost his chance for mastery in any instance, looking toward tomorrow from today. The second of these two ways has been chosen for this [selection]. . . .

In form all presidents are leaders, nowadays. In fact this guarantees no more than that they will be clerks. Everybody now expects the man inside the White House to do something about everything. Laws and customs now reflect acceptance of him as the Great Initiator, an acceptance quite as widespread at the Capitol as at his end of Pennsylvania Avenue. But such acceptance does not signify that all the rest of government is at his feet. It merely signifies that other men have found it practically impossible to do *their* jobs without assurance of initiatives from him. Service for themselves, not power for the president, has brought them to accept his leadership in form. They find his actions useful in their business. The transformation of his routine obligations testifies to their dependence on an active White House. A president, these days, is an invaluable clerk. His services are in demand all over Washington. His influence, however, is a very different matter. Laws and customs tell us little about leadership in fact.

Why have our presidents been honored with this clerkship? The answer is that no one else's services suffice. Our Constitution, our traditions, and our politics provide no better source for the initiatives a president can take. Executive officials need decisions, and political protection, and a referee for fights. Where are these to come from but the White House? Congressmen need an agenda from outside, something with high status to respond to or react against. What provides it better than the program of the president? Party politicians need a record to defend in the next national campaign. How can it be made except by "their" Administration? Private persons with a public ax to grind may need a helping hand or they may need a grinding stone. In either case who gives more satisfaction than a president? And outside the United States, in every country where our policies and postures influence home politics, there will be people needing just the "right" thing said and done or just the "wrong" thing stopped in *Washington*. What symbolizes Washington more nearly than the White House?

A modern president is bound to face demands for aid and service from five more or less distinguishable sources: the Executive officialdom, from Congress, from his partisans, from citizens at large, and from abroad. The presidency's clerkship is expressive of these pressures. In effect they are constituency pressures and each president has five sets of constituents. The five are not distinguished by their membership; membership is obviously an overlapping matter. And taken one by one they do not match the man's electorate; one of them, indeed, is outside his electorate. They are distinguished, rather, by their different claims upon him. Initiatives are what they want, for five distinctive reasons. Since government and politics have offered no alternative, our laws and customs turn those wants into his obligations.

Why, then, is the president not guaranteed an influence commensurate with services performed? Constituent relations are relations of dependence. Everyone with any share in governing this country will belong to one (or two, or three) of his "constituencies." Since everyone depends on him why is he not assured of everyone's support? The answer is that no one else sits where he sits, or sees quite as he sees; no one else feels the full weight of his obligations. Those obligations are a tribute to his unique place in our political system. But just because it is unique they fall on him alone. *The same conditions that promote his leadership in form preclude a guarantee of leadership in fact.* No man or group at either end of Pennsylvania Avenue shares his peculiar status in our government and politics. That is why his services are in demand. By the same token, though, the obligations of all other men are different from his own. His Cabinet officers have departmental duties and constituents. His legislative leaders head *Congressional* parties, one in either House. His national party organization stands apart from his official family. His political allies in the states need not face Washington, or one another. The private groups that seek him out are not compelled to govern. And friends abroad are not compelled to run in our elections. Lacking his position and prerogatives, these men cannot regard his obligations as his own. They have their jobs to do; none is the same as his. As they perceive their duty they may find it right to follow him, in fact, or they may not. Whether they will feel obliged *on their responsibility* to do what he wants done remains an open question. . . .

There is reason to suppose that in the years immediately ahead the power problems of a president will remain what they have been in the decades just behind us. If so there will be equal need for presidential expertise of the peculiar sort . . . that has [been] stressed [i.e., political skill]. Indeed, the need is likely to be greater. The president himself and with him the whole government are likely to be more than ever at the mercy of his personal approach.

What may the sixties do to politics and policy and to the place of presidents in our political system? The sixties may destroy them as we know them; that goes without saying. But barring deep depression or unlimited war, a total transformation is the least of likelihoods. Without catastrophes of those dimensions nothing in our past experience suggests that we shall see either consensus of the sort available to F.D.R. in 1933 and 1942, or popular demand for institutional adjustments likely to assist a president. Lacking popular demand, the natural conservatism of established institutions will keep Congress and the party organizations quite resistant to reforms that could give him a clear advantage over them. Four-year terms for congressmen and senators might do it, if the new terms ran with his. What will occasion a demand for that? As for crisis consensus it is probably beyond the reach of the next president. We may have priced ourselves out of the market for "productive" crises on the pattern Roosevelt knew—productive in the sense of strengthening his chances for sustained support *within* the system. Judging from the fifties, neither limited war nor limited depression is productive in those terms. Anything unlimited will probably break the system.

In the absence of productive crises, and assuming that we manage to avoid destructive ones, nothing now foreseeable suggests that our next president will have assured support from any quarter. There is no use expecting it from the bureaucracy unless it is displayed on Capitol Hill. Assured support will not be found in Congress unless contemplation of their own electorates keeps a majority of members constantly aligned with him. In the sixties it is to be doubted . . . that pressure from electors will move the same majority of men in either House toward consistent backing for the president. Instead the chances are that he will gain majorities, when and if he does so, by ad hoc coalition-building, issue after issue. In that respect the sixties will be reminiscent of the fifties; indeed, a closer parallel may well be in the late forties. As for "party discipline" in English terms—the favorite cure-all of political scientists since Woodrow Wilson was a youth—the first preliminary is a party link between the White House and the leadership on both sides of the Capitol. But even this preliminary has been lacking in eight of the fifteen years since the Second World War. If ballot-splitting should continue through the sixties it will soon be "un-American" for president and Congress to belong to the same party.

Even if the trend were now reversed, there is no short-run prospect that behind each party label we would find assembled a sufficiently like-minded bloc of voters, similarly aligned in states and districts all across the country, to negate the massive barriers our institutions and traditions have erected against "discipline" on anything like the British scale. This does not mean that a reversal of the ballot-splitting trend would be without significance. If the White House and the legislative leadership were linked by party ties again, a real advantage would accrue to both. Their opportunities for mutually productive bargaining would be enhanced. The policy results might surprise critics of our system. Bargaining "within the family" has a rather different quality than bargaining with members of the rival clan. But we would still be a long way from "party government." Bargaining, not "discipline," would still remain the key to Congressional action on a president's behalf. The crucial distinctions between presidential party and Congressional party are not likely to be lost in the term of the next president.

❖❖ Presidential Politics

Whether the Founding Fathers intended that the president would be a king or a clerk, they clearly did not foresee the deep involvement of the presidency in *partisan* politics. All presidents after George Washington were party chiefs, a role that grew more important as national parties expanded their electoral bases and began to act in a more disciplined fashion to facilitate their control of government. American parties have never been disciplined in the European sense, but they have managed to achieve sufficient organizational unity at both national and more importantly state and local levels to affect and sometimes determine the course of government.

Presidential parties help to identify and translate the political demands of popular majorities into government action. Theoretically at least, presidents should be able to use their role as party chief to bridge the constitutional gap between the presidency and Congress that the separation of powers created. Before becoming party chief, politicians must capture their party's presidential nomination. Whether or not parties should choose their nominees through "brokered" conventions, in which party power brokers and "bosses" dominate, or through a grass roots process controlled by rank-and-file party members, continues to be hotly debated. Proponents of brokered conventions argue that party leaders tend to choose "better" candidates, those more representative of broad party interests and more likely to appeal to a national electorate, than candidates nominated by a grass roots process that reflects the views of a relatively narrow party electorate.

The author of the following selection argues that the current grass roots arrangement for choosing presidential candidates has neither weakened parties nor undermined the president's role as chief of his party. The reforms in presidential nominating politics were, in the author's view, a proper response to a changing political and social environment that required parties to adapt to new electoral forces.

38

Michael Nelson

THE CASE FOR THE CURRENT PRESIDENTIAL NOMINATING PROCESS

❖❖❖❖❖❖❖

The current process by which Americans nominate their parties' candidates for president is the product of nearly two centuries of historical evolution and two decades of deliberate procedural reform. It can be judged successful because it satisfies reasonably well the three main criteria by which any presidential nominating process may be judged:

- Does the process strengthen or weaken the two major parties, which our political system relies on to provide some measure of coherence to a constitutionally fragmented government?
- Does the process foster or impede the selection of presidents who are suitably skilled for the office?
- Is the process regarded as legitimate by the public? Is it seen to be fair and democratic?

From George Grassmuck, ed. *Before Nomination: Our Primary Problems* (Washington, D.C.: The American Enterprise Institute, 1985). Reprinted by permission.

Political Parties

Have the two major parties been weakened by the reforms of the presidential nomi-nating process that were instituted by the McGovern-Fraser commission and its successors? Much scholarly talent and energy have been devoted to answering this question in the affirmative. Implicit in such analyses are the beliefs that the parties were basically strong before the post-1968 reforms and that they have been consid-erably weaker ever since. In truth, neither of these beliefs is fully accurate. The par-ties were in a state of decline during the 1950s and 1960s, a decline that has been arrested and in most cases reversed during the 1970s and 1980s, as the parties, aided by the reforms, have adapted to the changed social and political environment that underlay their decline. This is true of all three of the components of parties that po-litical scientists, following V. O. Key, have identified as fundamental: the party-in-the-electorate, the party-in-government, and the party organization.

Party-in-the-Electorate

Americans are no longer as loyal to the parties as they were in the early 1950s, when modern survey research on voting behavior first took form. On this there is little room for dispute: as Figure A indicates, voters are far less likely now than in the past to think of themselves as either Democrats or Republicans, to vote a straight-party ticket (even for presidential and House candidates), or to express a favorable evaluation of one or both political parties.

Natural though the tendency may be to explain dramatic changes by equally dramatic causes, one cannot attribute the decline of the party-in-the-electorate to the reform era that began in 1968. The largest falloff in party identification, which had remained steadily high through the 1950s and early 1960s, came between 1964 and 1966. An additional large drop occurred between 1970 and 1972, but since then the decline in party identification seems to have leveled off or even been re-versed. The share of voters who evaluate at least one party favorably, which fell steadily during the 1960s, has stayed very close to 50 percent ever since, rising to 52 percent in 1984. Similarly, split-ticket voting, a more explicitly behavioral indica-tor of weak voter loyalty to the parties, underwent its greatest increases before the reform era and has declined since 1980.

Whether Ronald Reagan's presidency has reversed the "dealignment" of voters that occurred mainly during the 1960s remains to be seen. But well before 1980 most of the indexes of party strength in the electorate at least had stopped falling.

Party-in-Government

Historically, Americans have used the political parties to join what the Constitu-tion put asunder, namely, the executive and legislative branches. The electorate's habit of straight-ticket voting in twentieth-century elections before 1956 meant that the party that controlled the White House also controlled both houses of Con-gress in forty-six of fifty-four years.

The rise of split-ticket voting weakened such interbranch aspects of party-in-government; nowadays control by the same party of the presidency and Congress is

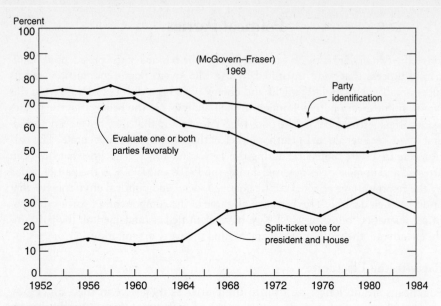

Figure A Indexes of Party Strength
Sources: Stephen J. Wayne, *The Road to the White House,* 2d ed. (New York: St. Martin's Press, 1984), pp. 57, 59; David E. Price, *Bringing Back the Parties* (Washington, D.C.: Congressional Quarterly Press, 1984), p. 18; and Martin P. Wattenberg, "Realignmant without Party Revitalization" (unpublished manuscript).

the exception rather than the rule. As with the party-in-the-electorate, however, the evidence indicates that the party-weakening trend in government began well before the reform era: indeed, it was in 1954 that the new pattern of Republican presidents and divided or Democratic congresses emerged.

Even more significant than the trend in interbranch party strength, perhaps, is the intrabranch trend. During the supposedly halcyon days of parties in the 1950s and 1960s, party unity voting in Congress, as measured by the *Congressional Quarterly,* declined fairly steadily in both parties in both houses, bottoming out in the Ninety-first Congress. During the 1970s and 1980s, in direct contradiction to what the "reform-killed-the-parties" theory would predict, party unity voting has been on the increase. (So has the share of all congressional votes that unite one party against the other.) Nor has this intrabranch development been devoid of interbranch consequences: in 1981 Senate Republicans demonstrated the highest degree of support for a president ever recorded by either party in either house of Congress since the *Congressional Quarterly* began making measurements in 1953.

Party Organization

It is as organizations that the parties were affected most directly by the post-1968 reforms; if party-weakening effects are to be found anywhere, it should be in the realm of party organization. Yet it is here, recent research increasingly is showing, that the opposite is true: the parties in the 1970s and 1980s are institutionally stronger than they were in the 1950s and 1960s.

The regeneration of the parties as organizations has occurred at all levels of the federal system. In the localities and counties there is now far more party activity in the areas of fund raising, campaign headquarters, voter registration, and get-out-the-vote efforts than during the mid-1960s. About twice as many citizens as in the 1950s (some 24 to 32 percent) report that they have been approached personally by party workers in recent presidential campaigns. The share of state party organizations that have permanent headquarters rose from less than half in 1960 to 95 percent in 1982; the size and professionalism of salaried state party staffs have also grown considerably. Judging from his study of party budgets, political scientist Cornelius Cotter concludes that the percentage of state parties whose organization is "marginal" fell from 69 in 1961 to 31 in 1979; the proportion of highly organized state parties rose from 12 percent to 26 percent.

National party organizations, long the stepchild of the party system, have undergone the most striking transformation of all. Since the mid-1970s, when William Brock became chairman, the Republican National Committee has developed a capacity to recruit candidates to run for local office and provide them with funds and professional assistance in such activities as voter registration and television campaigning; to help state parties enhance their own organizational abilities; to do institutional advertising on a "Vote Republican" theme; and so on. As for the opposition, journalist David Broder reports, "Since 1980 the Democrats have been doing what the Republicans did under Brock: raising money and pumping it back to party-building projects at the state and local level."

The Fall and Rise of the Parties

Political parties in the 1980s have arrested or reversed the decline that they were suffering before the reform era that began in 1968 but only because they are different from what they used to be. The recent reforms have helped the parties to adapt relatively successfully to a changing social and political environment.

Organizationally and procedurally, the parties on the eve of the post-1968 reforms were relics of an earlier era. Virtually since the Andrew Jackson years, party strength had continued to rest on the same foundations. Patronage, in the form of government jobs and contracts, had long been one reliable source of workers and funds for party organizations. Party-sponsored charity work—memorably, the Thanksgiving turkey and the winter bucket of coal—helped to cement the loyalties of many voters. Such tangible inducements aside, voters also found the party label the best device for ordering their choices in elections that involved numerous offices, candidates, and issues.

For some years before 1968, developments in government and society had been weakening these foundations. A merit-based civil service and competitive contracting replaced the patronage system of government hiring and purchasing. Income security programs reduced dependence on charity. After World War II education, income, and leisure time rose rapidly throughout the population—voters now had more ability and opportunity to sort out information for themselves about candidates and issues. During the 1950s, television sets became fixtures in the American home, bringing such information to voters in more accessible (if not always more valuable) form.

From these developments, which eroded some of the main props of the traditional political parties, came others that created the basis for new-style parties. First, the issue basis of political participation intensified, both in the movements of the 1960s (civil rights, antiwar, environmental, feminist, and others), which originated mainly outside the party system, and in the parties themselves. In 1962 James Q. Wilson chronicled the rise during the 1950s of the "amateur Democrat," an upper-middle-class reformer whose main concern was for issues and who saw the party as a vehicle for advancing causes, in opposition to professional party people, who viewed elections mainly as a means of achieving the satisfactions and spoils of victory. In 1964 the amateur Democrat's conservative Republican cousin, whom Aaron Wildavsky dubbed the "purist," seized control of the Republican national convention.

Second, the candidate basis of politics intensified, both in presidential politics, where individual aspirants, following John F. Kennedy in 1960, sought to take their own popular paths to the nomination even if that meant detouring around the party professionals, and in congressional politics, where reelection-oriented incumbents, with increasing success, forged personal bonds with their constituents that freed them from much of their dependency on party. Finally, the media basis of politics intensified. As television, radio, and direct mail became available and highly effective routes for reaching voters, media professionals became more valuable politically, as did fundraising specialists who could help to pay for the expensive new forms of campaigning.

Political parties in all their aspects—in the electorate, in government, and as organizations—were weakened during the 1950s and 1960s by these social and political developments. To recover and thrive the parties had to adapt. To adapt they had to accommodate the rise of four main groups: new-style voters, who by virtue of greater education and leisure no longer needed to depend on parties to order their choices in elections; amateur political activists who regarded the parties mainly as vehicles for political change; entrepreneurial candidates who had ceased to regard party fealty as the necessary or even the most desirable strategy for electoral success; and modern political tacticians who practiced the now essential crafts of polling, advertising, press relations, and fund raising. In sum, the reinvigoration of the parties would have to come on terms that accepted the "new politics" in both that label's common uses: policy as the basis for political participation, and modern campaign professionalism as the incentive to channel such participation through the parties.

What made the transformation and reinvigoration of the parties possible was the organizational and procedural fluidity that was hastened by the post-1968 reforms. Once the lingering hold of party professionals of the *ancien régime* on the nominating process was broken, the new groups of voters, activists, candidates, and campaign professionals were able to establish a new equilibrium of power within the parties that reflected the changed social and political realities. Republicans realized this first and strengthened their party by committing it to conservative political ideology and professional campaign services, which in turn tied the party-in-the-electorate, the party-in-government, and the party organization together. Democrats, preoccupied with the reform process more than with the fruits of reform, were slower to adapt. But, responding to the Republican party's success, they now seem to be following a parallel path: new policies and a new professionalism to rebuild the party.

Perhaps the best evidence of the parties' successful adaptation to change is that the old amateurs have become the new professionals: committed to policy but also to party. Summarizing several studies of delegates to recent Republican and Democratic national conventions, William Crotty and John Jackson conclude that "the new professionals are likely to be college graduates working in a service profession . . . familiar with all the paraphernalia of modern campaigning . . . [and] likely to care deeply about at least some issues. . . . They also care, sometimes passionately, about their party . . . and they see the parties as the best vehicles for advancing both their concept of the public interest and their own political careers."

Presidents

Many political analysts have argued vigorously that the influence of the presidential nominating process on the selection of suitably skilled presidents, like its influence on the parties, was benign before the post-1968 reforms were instituted but has been malignant ever since. "In the old way," according to Broder, "whoever wanted to run for president of the United States took a couple of months off from public service in the year of the presidential election and presented his credentials to the leaders of his party, who were elected officials, party officials, leaders of allied interest groups, and bosses in some cases. These people had known the candidate over a period of time and had carefully examined his work." As it happened, the qualities those political peers were looking for, argues political scientist Jeane Kirkpatrick, were the very qualities that make for good presidents: "the ability to deal with diverse groups, ability to work out compromises, and the ability to impress people who have watched a candidate over many years." In contrast, under the post-1968 rules, "the skills required to be successful in the nominating process are almost entirely irrelevant to, perhaps even negatively correlated with, the skills required to be successful at governing."

In a real sense, the old nominating process did work reasonably well to increase the chances of selecting skillful presidents. But then so does the new process. The difference underlying this similarity is the contrast between the political and social environment in which contemporary presidents must try to govern and the environment in which their predecessors as recently as the 1950s and 1960s had to operate.

The contrast is most obvious and significant in the nation's capital. As Samuel Kernell notes, the "old" Washington that was described so accurately by Richard Neustadt in his 1960 success manual for presidents, *Presidential Power,* was "a city filled with hierarchies. To these hierarchies were attached leaders or at least authoritative representatives"—committee chairmen and party leaders in Congress, press barons, umbrella-style interest groups that represented broad sectors such as labor, business, and agriculture, and so on. In this setting to lead was to bargain—the same political "whales," to use Harry MacPhersons's term, who could thwart a president's desires could also satisfy them, and in the same way: by directing the activities of their associates and followers. Clearly a presidential nominating process that placed some emphasis on a candidate's ability to pass muster with Washington power brokers was functional for the governing system.

As the 1960s drew to a close, however, the same social and political changes—and some others as well—that were undermining the foundations of the old party system also were undermining the old ways of conducting the nation's business in Washington. The capital came under the intense and—to many elected politicians—alluring spotlight of television news; a more educated and active citizenry took its heightened policy concerns directly to government officials; interest group activity both flourished and fragmented; and careerism among members of Congress prompted a steady devolution of legislative power to individual representatives and senators and to proliferating committees and subcommittees. From the president's perspective this wave of decentralization meant that Washington had become "a city of free agents" in which "the number of exchanges necessary to secure others' support ha[d] increased dramatically."

What skills do contemporary presidents need if they are to lead in this changed environment, or, to phrase the question more pertinently, what skills should the presidential nominating process foster? Two presidential leadership requirements are familiar and longstanding; first, a strategic sense of the public's disposition to be led during the particular term of office—an ability to sense, shape, and fulfill the historical possibilities of the time; second, some talent for the management of authority, both of lieutenants in the administration who can help the president form policy proposals and of the large organizations in the bureaucracy that are charged with implementing existing programs. Other skills required by presidents are more recent in origin, at least in the form they must take and their importance. Presidents must be able to present themselves and their policies to the public through rhetoric and symbolic action, especially on television. Because reelection-oriented members of Congress "are hypersensitive to anticipated constituent reaction," it is not surprising that the best predictor of a president's success with Congress is his standing in the public opinion polls. Finally, presidents need tactical skills of bargaining, persuasion, and other forms of political gamesmanship to maximize their support among other officials whose help they need to secure their purposes. But in the new Washington these tactical skills must be employed not merely or even mainly on the sort of old-style power brokers who used to be able to help presidents sustain reliable coalitions but on the many elements of a fragmented power system in which tactics must be improvised for new coalitions on each issue.

In several nonobvious and even inadvertent ways, the current nominating process rewards, perhaps requires, most of these skills. The process is, for would-be presidents, self-starting and complex. To a greater extent than ever before, candidates must raise money, develop appealing issues, devise shrewd campaign strategies, impress national political reporters, attract competent staff, and build active organizations largely on their own. They then must dance through a minefield of staggered and varied state primaries and caucuses, deciding and reevaluating weekly or even daily where to spend their time, money, and other resources. What better test of a president's ability to manage lieutenants and lead in a tactically skillful way in the equally complex, fragmented, and uncertain environment of modern Washington or, for that matter, the modern world?

The fluidity of the current nominating process also has opened it to Washington "outsiders." This development, although much lamented by critics of the post-1968 reforms, has done nothing more than restore the traditional place of those who have served as state governors in the ranks of plausible candidates for the presidency, thus broadening the talent pool to include more than senators and vice-presidents. (From 1960 to 1972 every major party nominee for president was a senator or a vice-president who previously had been a senator.) As chief executives of their states, governors may be presumed to have certain skills in the management of large public bureaucracies that senators do not.

Self-presentational skills also are vital for candidates in the current nominating process—not just "looking good on television" but being able to persuade skeptical journalists and others to accept one's interpretation of the complex reality of the campaign. If it does nothing else, the endless contest, which carries candidates from place to place for months and months in settings that range from living rooms to stadiums, probably sensitizes candidates to citizens in ways that uniquely facilitate the choice of a president who has a strong strategic sense of his time.

No earthly good is unalloyed, of course. The length and complexity of the current nominating process, to which so much good can be ascribed, are nonetheless sources of real distraction to incumbent presidents who face renomination challenges and to other contenders who hold public office. To be sure, the post-1968 rules cannot be blamed for all of this. Unpopular presidents have always had to battle, to some extent, for renomination; popular presidents still do not. (In 1984 Reagan not only was unopposed for his party's nomination—the first such president since 1956—but received millions of dollars in federal matching funds for his renomination "campaign.") Most challengers seem to be able to arrange time to campaign, either while holding office (Gary Hart, Alan Cranston, Ernest Hollings, and others in 1984) or by abandoning office for the sake of pursuing the presidency (Walter Mondale in 1984, Howard Baker in 1988). Still, by any standard, the same nominating process that tests a would-be president's leadership skills so well must be said to carry at least a moderate price tag.

Public

Ironically, democratic legitimacy, the paramount value sought by the post-1968 reformers, must be judged as the least achieved of the three main criteria for judging the presidential nominating process: strengthened political parties, skilled presidents, and a satisfied public. Everyone, including journalists, decries the responsibility that the hybrid nature of the process places on the media to interpret who is winning and even which candidates will be taken seriously. Few think it proper that voters in the late primary states have their choices circumscribed by the decisions of voters in Iowa, New Hampshire, and other states with early contests.

The characteristic of the current nominating process that is most corrosive of legitimacy is its sheer complexity. As Henry Mayo notes in his *Introduction to Democratic Theory*:

> If the purpose of the election is to be carried out—to enable the voter to share in political power—the voter's job must not be made more difficult and confusing for him. It ought, on the contrary, to be made as simple as the electoral machinery can be devised to make it.

Yet nothing could be less descriptive of the way we choose presidential candidates. "No school, no textbook, no course of instruction," writes Theodore H. White, "could tell young Americans how their system worked." Or, as Richard Stearns, chief delegate hunter for Senator George McGovern in 1972 and Senator Edward Kennedy in 1980, put it: "I am fully confident that there aren't more than 100 people in the country who fully understand the rules."

What would the public prefer? Nothing that will prove consoling to those who dislike the current process for its excesses of democracy and absence of "peer review." Overwhelmingly, citizens want to select the parties' nominees for president through national primaries: in the most recent Gallup survey on this issue, which was completed in June 1984, 67 percent were in favor, 21 percent were opposed, and 12 percent were undecided. And there are ample reasons to believe that citizens mean what they are saying. For one, the national primary idea has received consistently high support by margins ranging from two-to-one to six-to-one—in Gallup surveys that date back to 1952. More important, the direct primary is the method by which voters are accustomed to nominating almost all party candidates for almost all other offices in the federal system.

A vigorous case can be made for a national primary, and not solely because of the heightened legitimacy it would bring to the nomination process. Still, there are good reasons to stay with the current arrangement. First, the very constancy of rules rewriting is in itself subversive of legitimacy. Second, it also is distracting to the parties, diverting them from the more important task of deciding what they have to offer voters. Finally, to bring the argument of this essay full circle, to the extent that the current process helps the political parties to grow stronger and the presidency to work more effectively, voters ultimately will grow not just used to it but pleased with it, and the legitimacy problem will take care of itself.

❖❖ Presidential Character and Style

The preceding selections in this chapter have focused upon the institutional aspects of the presidency and the constitutional and political responsibilities of the office. Richard Neustadt does focus upon certain personal dimensions of the power equation, the ability to persuade, but he does not deal with presidential character outside the power context. The following selection is taken from one of the most important and innovative of the recent books dealing with the presidency, in which the author, James David Barber, presents the thesis that it is the *total character* of the person who occupies the White House that is the determinant of presidential performance. As he states, "The presidency is much more than an institution." It is not only the focus of the emotional involvement of most people in politics, but also occupied by an emotional person. How that person is able to come to grips with his feelings and emotions often shapes his orientation toward issues and the way in which he makes decisions. From the very beginning the office was thought of in highly personal terms, for the framers of the Constitution, in part at least, built the office around the character of George Washington, who virtually everyone at the time thought would be the first occupant of the office. And evolution of the office since 1787 has added to its personal quotient. James David Barber provides a framework for the analysis of presidential character and its effect upon performance in the White House.

39

James David Barber

THE PRESIDENTIAL CHARACTER

❖❖❖❖❖❖❖

When a citizen votes for a presidential candidate he makes, in effect, a prediction. He chooses from among the contenders the one he thinks (or feels, or guesses) would be the best president. He operates in a situation of immense uncertainty. If he has a long voting history, he can recall time and time again when he guessed wrong. He listens to the commentators, the politicians, and his friends, then adds it all up in some rough way to produce his prediction and his vote. Earlier in the game, his anticipations have been taken into account, either directly in the polls and primaries or indirectly in the minds of politicians who want to nominate someone he will like. But he must choose in the midst of a cloud of confusion, a rain of phony advertising, a storm of sermons, a hail of complex issues, a fog of charisma and boredom, and a thunder of accusation and defense. In the face of this chaos, a great many citizens fall back on the past, vote their old allegiances, and let it go at that. Nevertheless, the citizen's vote says that on balance he expects Mr. X would outshine Mr. Y in the presidency.

This [book] is meant to help citizens and those who advise them cut through the confusion and get at some clear criteria for choosing presidents. To understand what actual presidents do and what potential presidents might do, the first need is

Excerpted from James David Barber, *The Presidential Character,* 2d and 3d editions (Prentice-Hall, Inc.). © 1972, 1977, 1985 by James David Barber. Reprinted by permission of the author.

to see the man whole—not as some abstract embodiment of civic virtue, some scorecard of issue stands, or some reflection of a faction, but as a human being like the rest of us, a person trying to cope with a difficult environment. To that task he brings his own character, his own view of the world, his own political style. None of that is new for him. If we can see the pattern he has set for his political life we can, I contend, estimate much better his pattern as he confronts the stresses and chances of the presidency.

The presidency is a peculiar office. The founding fathers left it extraordinarily loose in definition, partly because they trusted George Washington to invest a tradition as he went along. It is an institution made a piece at a time by successive men in the White House. Jefferson reached out to Congress to put together the beginnings of political parties; Jackson's dramatic force extended electoral partisanship to its mass base; Lincoln vastly expanded the administrative reach of the office, Wilson and the Roosevelts showed its rhetorical possibilities—in fact every President's mind and demeanor has left its mark on a heritage still in lively development.

But the presidency is much more than an institution. It is a focus of feelings. In general, popular feelings about politics are low-key, shallow, casual. For example, the vast majority of Americans knows virtually nothing of what Congress is doing and cares less. The presidency is different. The presidency is the focus for the most intense and persistent emotions in the American polity. The president is a symbolic leader, the one figure who draws together the people's hopes and fears for the political future. On top of all his routine duties, he has to carry that off—or fail.

Our emotional attachment to presidents shows up when one dies in office. People were not just disappointed or worried when President Kennedy was killed; people wept at the loss of a man most had never even met. Kennedy was young and charismatic—but history shows that whenever a president dies in office, heroic Lincoln or debased Harding, McKinley or Garfield, the same wave of deep emotion sweeps across the country. On the other hand, the death of an ex-president brings forth no such intense emotional reaction.

The president is the first political figure children are aware of (later they add Congress, the Court, and others, as "helpers" of the president). With some exceptions among children in deprived circumstances, the president is seen as a "benevolent leader," one who nurtures, sustains, and inspires the citizenry. Presidents regularly show up among "most admired" contemporaries and forebears, and the president is the "best known" (in the sense of sheer name recognition) person in the country. At inauguration time, even presidents elected by close margins are supported by much larger majorities than the election returns show, for people rally round as he actually assumes office. There is a similar reaction when the people see their president threatened by crisis: if he takes action, there is a favorable spurt in the Gallup poll whether he succeeds or fails.

Obviously the president gets more attention in schoolbooks, press, and television than any other politician. He is one of very few who can make news by doing good things. *His* emotional state is a matter of continual public commentary, as is the manner in which his personal and official families conduct themselves. The media bring across the president not as some neutral administrator or corporate executive to be assessed by his production, but as a special being with mysterious dimensions.

We have no king. The sentiments English children—and adults—direct to the Queen have no place to go in our system but to the president. Whatever his talents—Coolidge-type or Roosevelt-type—the president is the only available object for such national-religious-monarchical sentiments as Americans possess.

The president helps people make sense of politics. Congress is a tangle of committees, the bureaucracy is a maze of agencies. The president is one man trying to do a job—a picture much more understandable to the mass of people who find themselves in the same boat. Furthermore, he is the top man. He ought to know what is going on and set it right. So when the economy goes sour, or war drags on, or domestic violence erupts, the president is available to take the blame. Then when things go right, it seems the president must have had a hand in it. Indeed, the flow of political life is marked off by presidents: the "Eisenhower Era," the "Kennedy Years."

What all this means is that the president's *main* responsibilities reach far beyond administering the Executive Branch or commanding the armed forces. The White House is first and foremost a place of public leadership. That inevitably brings to bear on the president intense moral, sentimental, and quasi-religious pressures which can, if he lets them, distort his own thinking and feeling. If there is such a thing as extraordinary sanity, it is needed nowhere so much as in the White House.

Who the president is at a given time can make a profound difference in the whole thrust and direction of national politics. Since we have only one president at a time, we can never prove this by comparison, but even the most superficial speculation confirms the commonsense view that the man himself weighs heavily among other historical factors. A Wilson reelected in 1920, a Hoover in 1932, a John F. Kennedy in 1964 would, it seems very likely, have guided the body politic along rather different paths from those their actual successors chose. Or try to imagine a Theodore Roosevelt ensconced behind today's "bully pulpit" of a presidency, or Lyndon Johnson as president in the age of McKinley. Only someone mesmerized by the lures of historical inevitability can suppose that it would have made little or no difference to government policy had Alf Landon replaced FDR in 1936, had Dewey beaten Truman in 1948, or Adlai Stevenson reigned through the 1950s. Not only would these alternative presidents have advocated different policies—they would have approached the office from very different psychological angles. It stretches credibility to think that Eugene McCarthy would have run the institution the way Lyndon Johnson did.

The burden of this [argument] is that the crucial differences can be anticipated by an understanding of a potential president's character, his world view, and his style. This kind of prediction is not easy; well-informed observers often have guessed wrong as they watched a man step toward the White House. One thinks of Woodrow Wilson, the scholar who would bring reason to politics; of Herbert Hoover, the Great Engineer who would organize chaos into progress; of Franklin D. Roosevelt, that champion of the balanced budget; of Harry Truman, whom the office would surely overwhelm; of Dwight D. Eisenhower, militant crusader; of John F. Kennedy, who would lead beyond moralisms to achievements; of Lyndon B. Johnson, the Southern conservative; and of Richard M. Nixon, conciliator. Spotting the errors is easy. Predicting with even approximate accuracy is going to require some sharp tools and close attention in their use. But the experiment is worth it because the question is critical and because it lends itself to correction by evidence.

My argument comes in layers.

First, a president's personality is an important shaper of his presidential behavior on nontrivial matters.

Second, presidential personality is patterned. His character, world view, and style fit together in a dynamic package understandable in psychological terms.

Third, a president's personality interacts with the power situation he faces and the national "climate of expectations" dominant at the time he serves. The tuning, the resonance—or lack of it—between these external factors and his personality sets in motion the dynamics of his presidency.

Fourth, the best way to predict a president's character, world view, and style is to see how they were put together in the first place. That happened in his early life, culminating in his first independent political success.

But the core of the argument . . . is that presidential character—the basic stance a man takes toward his presidential experience—comes in four varieties. The most important thing to know about a president or candidate is where he fits among these types, defined according to (a) how active he is and (b)whether or not he gives the impression he enjoys his political life.

Let me spell out these concepts briefly before getting down to cases.

Personality Shapes Performance

I am not about to argue that once you know a president's personality you know everything. But as the cases will demonstrate, the degree and quality of a president's emotional involvement in an issue are powerful influences on how he defines the issue itself, how much attention he pays to it, which facts and persons he sees as relevant to its resolution, and finally, what principles and purposes he associates with the issue. Every story of presidential decision-making is really two stories: an outer one in which a rational man calculates and an inner one in which an emotional man feels. The two are forever connected. Any real president is one whole man and his deeds reflect his wholeness.

As for personality, it is a matter of tendencies. It is not that one president "has" some basic characteristic that another president does not "have." That old way of treating a trait as a possession, like a rock in a basket, ignores the universality of aggressiveness, compliancy, detachment, and other human drives. We all have all of them, but in different amounts and in different combinations.

The Pattern of Character, World View, and Style

The most visible part of the pattern is style. *Style is the president's habitual way of performing his three political roles: rhetoric, personal relations, and homework.* Not to be confused with "stylishness," charisma, or appearance, style is how the president goes about doing what the office requires him to do—to speak, directly or through media, to large audiences; to deal face to face with other politicians, individually and in small, relatively private groups; and to read, write, and calculate by himself in order to manage the endless flow of details that stream onto his desk. No president can escape doing at least some of each. But there are marked differences in stylistic emphasis from president to president. The *balance* among the three style elements varies; one president may put most of himself into rhetoric, another may stress close, informal dealing, while still another may devote his energies mainly to study and cogitation. Beyond the balance, we want to see each president's peculiar habits of style, his mode of coping with and adapting to these presidential demands. For example, I think both Calvin Coolidge and John F. Kennedy were primarily rhetoricians, but they went about it in contrasting ways.

A president's *world view consists of his primary, politically relevant beliefs, particularly his conceptions of social causality, human nature, and the central moral conflicts of the time.* This is how he sees the world and his lasting opinions about what he sees. Style is his way of acting; world view is his way of seeing. Like the rest of us, a president develops over a lifetime certain conceptions of reality—how things work in politics, what people are like, what the main purposes are. These assumptions or conceptions help him make sense of his world, give some semblance of order to the chaos of existence. Perhaps most important: a man's world view affects what he pays attention to, and a great deal of politics is about paying attention. The name of the game for many politicians is not so much "Do this, do that" as it is "Look here!"

"Character" comes from the Greek word for engraving; in one sense it is what life has marked into a man's being. As used here, *character is the way the president orients himself toward life*—not for the moment, but enduringly. Character is the person's stance as he confronts experience. And at the core of character, a man confronts himself. The president's fundamental self-esteem is his prime personal resource; to defend and advance that, he will sacrifice much else he values. Down there in the privacy of his heart, does he find himself superb, or ordinary, or debased, or in some intermediate range? No president has been utterly paralyzed by self-doubt and none has been utterly free of midnight self-mockery. In between, the real presidents move out on life from positions of relative strength or weakness. Equally important are the criteria by which they judge themselves. A president who rates himself by the standard of achievement, for instance, may be little affected by losses of affection.

Character, world view, and style are abstractions from the reality of the whole individual. In every case they form an integrated pattern: the man develops a combination which makes psychological sense for him, a dynamic arrangement of motives, beliefs, and habits in the service of his need for self-esteem.

The Power Situation and "Climate of Expectations"

Presidential character resonates with the political situation the president faces. It adapts him as he tries to adapt it. The support he has from the public and interest groups, the party balance in Congress, the thrust of Supreme Court opinion together set the basic power situation he must deal with. An activist president may run smack into a brick wall of resistance, then pull back and wait for a better moment. On the other hand, a president who sees himself as a quiet care-taker may not try to exploit even the most favorable power situation. So it is the relationship between President and the political configuration that makes the system tick.

Even before public opinion polls, the president's real or supposed popularity was a large factor in his performance. Besides the power mix in Washington, the president has to deal with a national climate of expectations, the predominant needs thrust up to him by the people. There are at least three recurrent themes around which these needs are focused.

People look to the president for *reassurance*, a feeling that things will be all right, that the president will take care of his people. The psychological request is for a surcease of anxiety. Obviously, modern life in America involves considerable doses of fear, tension, anxiety, worry; from time to time, the public mood calls for a rest, a time of peace, a breathing space, a "return to normalcy."

Another theme is the demand for a sense *of progress and action*. The president ought to do something to direct the nation's course—or at least be in there pitching for the people. The president is looked to as a take-charge man, a doer, a turner of the wheels, a producer of progress—even if that means some sacrifice of serenity.

A third type of climate of expectations is the public need for a sense of *legitimacy* from, and in, the presidency. The president should be a master politician who is above politics. He should have a right to his place and a rightful way of acting in it. The respectability—even religiosity—of the office has to be protected by a man who presents himself as defender of the faith. There is more to this than dignity, more than propriety. The president is expected to personify our betterness in an in-spiring way, to express in what he does and is (not just in what he says) a moral ide-alism which, in much of the public mind, is the very opposite of "politics."

Over time the climate of expectations shifts and changes. Wars, depressions, and other national events contribute to that change, but there also is a rough cycle, from an emphasis on action (which begins to look too "political") to an emphasis on legitimacy (the moral uplift of which creates its own strains) to an emphasis on reassurance and rest (which comes to seem like drift) and back to action again. One need not be astrological about it. The point is that the climate of expectations at any given time is the political air the President has to breathe. Relating to this cli-mate is a large part of his task.

Predicting Presidents

The best way to predict a president's character, world view, and style is to see how he constructed them in the first place. Especially in the early stages, life is experi-mental; consciously or not, a person tries out various ways of defining and main-taining and raising self-esteem. He looks to his environment for clues as to who he is and how well he is doing. These lessons of life slowly sink in: certain self-images and evaluations, certain ways of looking at the world, certain styles of action get confirmed by his experience and he gradually adopts them as his own. If we can see that process of development, we can understand the product. The features to note are those bearing on presidential performance.

Experimental development continues all the way to death; we will not blind ourselves to midlife changes, particularly in the full-scale prediction case, that of Richard Nixon. But it is often much easier to see the basic patterns in early life histories. Later on a whole host of distractions—especially the image-making all politicians learn to practice—clouds the picture.

In general, character has its *main* development in childhood, world view in adolescence, style in early adulthood. The stance toward life I call character grows out of the child's experiments in relating to parents, brothers and sisters, and peers at play and in school, as well as to his own body and the objects around it. Slowly the child defines an orientation toward experience; once established, that tends to last despite much subsequent contradiction. By adolescence, the child has been hearing and seeing how people make their worlds meaningful, and now he is moved to relate himself—his own meanings—to those around him. His focus of attention shifts toward the future; he senses that decisions about his fate are coming and he looks into the premises for those decisions. Thoughts about the way the world works and how one might work in it, about what people are like and how one might be like them or not, and about the values people share and how one might share in them too—these are typical concerns for the post-child, pre-adult mind of the adolescent.

These themes come together strongly in early adulthood, when the person moves from contemplation to responsible action and adopts a style. In most biographical accounts this period stands out in stark clarity—the time of emergence, the time the young man found himself. I call it his first independent political success. It was then he moved beyond the detailed guidance of his family; then his self-esteem was dramatically boosted; then he came forth as a person to be reckoned with by other people. The *way* he did that is profoundly important to him. Typically he grasps that style and hangs onto it. Much later, coming into the presidency, something in him remembers this earlier victory and reemphasizes the style that made it happen.

Character provides the main thrust and broad direction—but it does not *determine*, in any fixed sense, world view and style. The story of development does not end with the end of childhood. Thereafter, the culture one grows in and the ways that culture is translated by parents and peers shape the meanings one makes of his character. The going world view gets learned and that learning helps channel character forces. Thus it will not necessarily be true that compulsive characters have reactionary beliefs, or that compliant characters believe in compromise. Similarly for style: historical accidents play a large part in furnishing special opportunities for action—and in blocking off alternatives. For example, however much anger a young man may feel, that anger will not be expressed in rhetoric unless and until his life situation provides a platform and an audience. Style thus has a stature and independence of its own. Those who would reduce all explanation to character neglect these highly significant later channelings. For beyond the root is the branch, above the foundation the superstructure, and starts do not prescribe finishes.

Four Types of Presidential Character

The five concepts—character, world view, style, power situation, and climate of expectations—run through the accounts of presidents in [later chapters of Barber's book], which cluster the presidents since Theodore Roosevelt into four types. This is the fundamental scheme of the study. It offers a way to move past the complexities to the main contrasts and comparisons.

The first baseline in defining presidential types is *activity-passivity*. How much energy does the man invest in his presidency? Lyndon Johnson went at his day like a human cyclone, coming to rest long after the sun went down. Calvin Coolidge often slept eleven hours a night and still needed a nap in the middle of the day. In between the presidents array themselves on the high or low side of the activity line.

The second baseline is *positive-negative affect* toward one's activity—this is, how he feels about what he does. Relatively speaking, does he seem to experience his political life as happy or sad, enjoyable or discouraging, positive or negative in its main effect? The feeling I am after here is not grim satisfaction in a job well done, not some philosophical conclusion. The idea is this: is he someone who, on the surfaces we can see, gives forth the feeling that he has *fun* in political life? Franklin Roosevelt's Secretary of War, Henry L. Stimson, wrote that the Roosevelts "not only understood the *use* of power, they knew the *enjoyment* of power, too. . . . Whether a man is burdened by power or enjoys power; whether he is trapped by responsibility or made free by it; whether he is moved by other people and outer forces or moves them—that is the essence of leadership."

The positive-negative baseline, then, is a general symptom of the fit between the man and his experience, a kind of register of *felt* satisfaction.

Why might we expect these two simple dimensions to outline the main character types? Because they stand for two central features of anyone's orientation toward life. In nearly every study of personality, some form of the active-passive contrast is critical; the general tendency to act or be acted upon is evident in such concepts as dominance-submission, extraversion-introversion, aggression-timidity, attack-defense, fight-flight, engagement-withdrawal, approach-avoidance. In everyday life we sense quickly the general energy output of the people we deal with. Similarly we catch on fairly quickly to the affect dimension—whether the person seems to be optimistic or pessimistic, hopeful or skeptical, happy or sad. The two baselines are clear and they are also independent of one another: all of us know people who are very active but seem discouraged, others who are quite passive but seem happy, and so forth. The activity baseline refers to what one does, the affect baseline to how one feels about what he does.

Both are crude clues to character. They are leads into four basic character patterns long familiar in psychological research. In summary form, these are the main configurations:

Active-Positive: There is a congruence, a consistency, between much activity and the enjoyment of it, indicating relatively high self-esteem and relative success in relating to the environment. The man shows an orientation toward productiveness as a value and an ability to use his styles flexibly, adaptively, suiting the dance to the music. He sees himself as developing over time toward relatively well defined personal goals—growing toward his image of himself as he might yet be. There is an emphasis on rational mastery, on using the brain to move the feet. This may get him into trouble; he may fail to take account of the irrational in politics. Not everyone he deals with sees things his way and he may find it hard to understand why.

Active-Negative: The contradiction here is between relatively intense effort and relatively low emotional reward for that effort. The activity has a compulsive quality, as if the man were trying to make up for something or to escape from anxiety into hard work. He seems ambitious, striving upward, power-seeking. His stance toward the environment is aggressive and he has a persistent problem in managing his aggressive feelings. His self-image is vague and discontinuous. Life is a hard struggle to achieve and hold power, hampered by the condemnations of a perfectionistic conscience. Active-negative types pour energy into the political system, but it is an energy distorted from within.

Passive-Positive: This is the receptive, compliant, other-directed character whose life is a search for affection as a reward for being agreeable and cooperative rather than personally assertive. The contradiction is between low self-esteem (on grounds of being unlovable, unattractive) and a superficial optimism. A hopeful attitude helps dispel doubt and elicits encouragement from others. Passive-positive types help soften the harsh edges of politics. But their dependence and the fragility of their hopes and enjoyments make disappointment in politics likely.

Passive-Negative: The factors are consistent—but how are we to account for the man's *political* role-taking? Why is someone who does little in politics and enjoys it less there at all? The answer lies in the passive-negative's character-rooted orientation toward doing dutiful service; this compensates for low self-esteem based on a sense of uselessness. Passive-negative types are in politics because they think they ought to be. They may be well adapted to certain nonpolitical roles, but they lack the experience and flexibility to perform effectively as political leaders. Their tendency is to withdraw, to escape from the conflict and uncertainty of politics by emphasizing vague principles (especially prohibitions) and procedural arrangements. They become guardians of the right and proper way, above the sordid politicking of lesser men.

Active-positive presidents want most to achieve results. Active-negatives aim to get and keep power. Passive-positives are after love. Passive-negatives emphasize their civic virtue. The relation of activity to enjoyment in a President thus tends to outline a cluster of characteristics, to set apart the adapted from the compulsive, compliant, and withdrawn types.

The first four presidents of the United States, conveniently, ran through this gamut of character types. (Remember, we are talking about tendencies, broad directions; no individual man exactly fits a category.) George Washington—clearly the most important president in the pantheon—established the fundamental legitimacy of an American government at a time when this was a matter in considerable question. Washington's dignity, judiciousness, his aloof air of reserve and dedication to duty fit the passive-negative or withdrawing type best. Washington did not seek innovation, he sought stability. He longed to retire to Mount Vernon, but fortunately was persuaded to stay on through a second term, in which, by rising above the political conflict between Hamilton and Jefferson and inspiring confidence in his own integrity, he gave the nation time to develop the organized means for peaceful change.

John Adams followed, a dour New England Puritan, much given to work and worry, an impatient and irascible man—an active-negative president, a compulsive type. Adams was far more partisan than Washington; the survival of the system through his presidency demonstrated that the nation could tolerate, for a time, domination by one of its nascent political parties. As president, an angry Adams brought the United States to the brink of war with France, and presided over the new nation's first experiment in political representation: the Alien and Sedition Acts, forbidding, among other things, unlawful combinations "with intent to oppose any measure or measures of the government of the United States," or "any false, scandalous, and malicious writing or writings against the United States, or the president of the United States, with intent to defame . . . or to bring them or either of them, into contempt or disrepute."

Then came Jefferson. He too had his troubles and failures—in the design of national defense, for example. As for his presidential character (only one element in success or failure), Jefferson was clearly active-positive. A child of the Enlightenment, he applied his reason to organizing connections with Congress aimed at strengthening the more popular forces. A man of catholic interests and delightful humor, Jefferson combined a clear and open vision of what the country could be with a profound political sense, expressed in his famous phrase, "Every difference of opinion is not a difference of principle."

The fourth president was James Madison, "Little Jemmy," the constitutional philosopher thrown into the White House at a time of great international turmoil. Madison comes closest to the passive-positive, or compliant, type; he suffered from irresolution, tried to compromise his way out, and gave in too readily to the "warhawks" urging combat with Britain. The nation drifted into war, and Madison wound up ineptly commanding his collection of amateur generals in the streets of Washington. General Jackson's victory at New Orleans saved the Madison administration's historical reputation; but he left the presidency with the United States close to bankruptcy and secession.

These four presidents—like all presidents—were persons trying to cope with the roles they had won by using the equipment they had built over a lifetime. The President is not some shapeless organism in a flood of novelties, but a man with a memory in a system with a history. Like all of us, he draws on his past to shape his future. The pathetic hope that the White House will turn a Caligula into a Marcus Aurelius is as naive as the fear that ultimate power inevitably corrupts. The problem is to understand—and to state understandably—what in the personal past foreshadows the presidential future. . . .

❖❖ The President and the Media

The media spotlight is on the presidency more than on other governmental institutions. Theodore Roosevelt was the first president to undertake a major effort to co-opt the press, giving Washington reporters space in the White House in order to facilitate his use of them as much as to accommodate the growing presidential press corps. Teddy Roosevelt knew that the press could be an important ally of government, that publicity for presidential policies and actions could help to build public support and ease the job of his administration.

Teddy Roosevelt set a precedent for twentieth-century presidents in recognizing the power of the press and the importance of turning the political reporters' craft to the advantage of the White House by managing the news. Teddy Roosevelt's cousin, Franklin D. Roosevelt, held regular informal press conferences with reporters in the Oval Office, knowing that if he kept them informed of his programs and progress the nation would learn about and, he hoped, support the New Deal.

From the vantage point of the White House, the press, while potentially a useful conduit of managed news, is seen more as a critic than an ally. Presidents tend to view the press as the enemy with which they have to deal. Charged with the responsibility of coping with the press is the presidential press secretary, who conducts daily briefings apprising White House reporters of the president's actions and plans.

A former white House insider, George E. Reedy, portrays the world of the White House reporter and the way in which presidents view and treat the press.

40

George E. Reedy

THE PRESS AND THE PRESIDENT

❖❖❖❖❖❖❖❖

To the leisurely observer of the Washington scene, there is a distinct charm in the startled air of discovery with which the press greets each step in the entirely predictable course of its relationship with the president and the White House staff.

Reprinted from the *Columbia Journalism Review*, May/June, 1983. © 1983. By permission.

Actually, the patterns are as well-established and as foreseeable as the movements of a Javanese temple dance. The timing will vary as well the alternating degrees of adoration and bitterness. But the sequence of events, at least in modern times, appears to be inexorable. It is only the determination of the press to treat each new day as unprecedented that makes the specific events seem to be news.

Seen from a little distance, cries of outrage from the press over the discovery that Mr. Reagan seeks to "manage the news" have the flavor of an Ed Sullivan rerun show on after-midnight television. They are reminiscent of similar protests in the administration of Presidents Carter, Nixon, Johnson, Kennedy, Eisenhower, Truman, and Roosevelt. Presidents before that do not offer much material for discussion simply because they served prior to the FDR era, when press–White House relations were put on a daily-contact basis for the first time in history.

The charge of management is a familiar one because it has a strong element of truth. All presidents seek to manage the news and all are successful to a degree. What is not taken into account is that legitimate management of the news from the White House is inescapable and, human nature being what it is, it is hardly surprising that presidents try to bend this necessity for their own ends. Few men will decline an opportunity to recommend themselves highly.

The press would not be happy with a White House that ended all efforts at news management and either threw the mansion wide open for coverage or closed it to outsiders altogether and told journalists to get facts any way they could. Since the early days of the New Deal, reporters have been relying on daily press briefings, prearranged press conferences, and press pools when the president travels. There would be chaos should all this come to an end.

The point is that the White House is covered by journalists through highly developed and formal structures. It is inherent in the nature of such structures that they must be managed by somebody, and the president's office is no exception. Management technique is employed every time the president decides what stories will be released on Monday and what stories will be released on Saturday; every time he decides that some meetings will be open to press coverage and others will not; every time he decides that some visitors will be fed to the press as they walk out of the Oval Office and others will not. Anybody who believes that he will make decisions on the basis of what makes him look bad will believe a hundred impossible things before breakfast.

There are actually times when the press literally does not want news. This became very clear early in the administration of Lyndon Johnson when he inaugurated the custom of unexpected Saturday morning news conferences. This meant disruption of newspaper production schedules all over the United States. Printing pressmen had to be recalled from weekend holidays to work at exorbitant rates; front pages that had been planned in leisurely fashion in the morning had to be scrapped for new layouts; rewrite men who had looked forward to quiet afternoons with their families worked into the evening hours. It was a mess.

After two such conferences, I began getting calls from top bureau chiefs in Washington pleading with me to put an end to them. They made it clear they wanted stories timed so that they would fit conveniently into news slots. It took some doing on my part; Johnson would have enjoyed the discovery that he was putting newspaper publishers to so much expense and trouble. (I think he started these conferences simply because he became lonely on Saturday mornings when there was little to do.) I talked him into dropping the custom by producing figures which showed that the weekend audiences were not large enough to justify the effort.

While it was actually going on, the episode struck me as just another example of the Johnsonian inability to comprehend the press. It was not until later that I realized the deeper significance. The press had not only acquiesced in news management but had actually asked that it be instituted. The fact that nothing was involved except timing was irrelevant. The ability to control the timing of news is the most potent weapon that any would-be news manipulator can have. No absolute line can be drawn between the occasions when he should have it and those when he should not.

This may well account for the indifference of the public to the periodic campaigns against news management. Even to an unsophisticated audience it is apparent that journalists are not objecting to news management per se but only to the kind of news management that makes their professional lives more difficult. However it may look in Washington, at a distance the issue appears as a dispute over control of the news for the convenience of the president or for the convenience of the press. In such a situation, Americans tend to come down on the side of the president.

Of course, if the president is caught in an outright lie—a lie about something in which the public is really concerned—the public will mobilize against him swiftly. But many charges of news management are directed at statements that Americans do not regard as outright lies. Americans have become so accustomed to the kind of exaggeration and misleading facts that are used to sell products on nightly television that a little White House puffery seems quite natural.

There is, of course, another side to the coin. While presidents always try to manipulate the news—and all too often succeed—there is a very real doubt whether the manipulation performs any real service for them, even in the crassest image-building sense. The presidency is a strange institution. The occupant must accept never-ending responsibilities and must act on never-ending problems. It may be well that what a president does speaks so much more loudly than anything he can say that the normal techniques of public relations are completely futile.

In the first place, a president may be able to time his public appearances but he cannot time his acts. He *is* the United States and anything that affects the United States must have a presidential response. He must react to international crises, to domestic disasters, to unemployment, and to inflation; if he chooses to do nothing in any of these instances his inaction will be writ large in the public media.

In the second place, a president may be able to keep his thoughts to himself but he cannot act in any direction without causing waves that sweep through the Washington community. The federal bureaucracy is shot through with holdovers from previous administrations who do not like him; the Congress is loaded with political opponents with whom he must deal; the lobbying offices of the capital are staffed by skilled president-watchers who can interpret his every act and who have sympathetic journalistic listeners. Finally, there is the overwhelming fact that the president has a direct impact on the lives of every citizen and there is a limit to his capacity to mislead. He cannot convince men and women that there is peace when their sons are dying in a war. He cannot hold up images of prosperity (although he will try) when men and women are out of work. He cannot persuade constituents that there is peace and harmony when there is rioting in the streets. There may be instances when he can escape the blame but only when his political opposition is not on its toes.

Against this background, the efficacy of manipulation is dubious at best. It may have a favorable impact on public opinion in the short run. But I know of no persuasive evidence that it helps to build the long-term support a politician needs. Every instance I have studied bears a close parallel to what happened when Lyndon Johnson held his meaningless meeting with the late Soviet premier Alexei Kosygin at Glassboro, New Jersey, in 1967. He was able to maneuver the press into treating it as a major summit conference for a few days, and his poll ratings rose accordingly. But it soon became clear that the meeting had produced nothing of substance and that there had been no reason to expect that it would. The poll ratings went right back down again.

On the other hand, efforts at manipulation invariably challenge the press to dig deeper than journalists ordinarily would. The stories they write about manipulation have little effect. But the stories they write as a result of the digging may have the kind of substance that does make an impact. The whole exercise can well be merely an invitation to trouble on the part of the president.

The bottom line can be simply stated. The president can, within limits, manipulate the press as a whole, and it is probable that his efforts to do so will always backfire.

❖❖ Presidential Power in Foreign and Domestic Affairs

President George Bush's decision in 1991 to go to war against Iraq to free Kuwait illustrated once again the presidential dominance in military and foreign policy making that has existed since World War II. Presidents have always put their stamp upon foreign policy, but during the nineteenth and early twentieth centuries Congress, particularly the Senate, was more often than not an equal partner with the president in foreign affairs as the Constitution intended.

Franklin D. Roosevelt's administration marked the modern presidency and presidential ascendancy in foreign and military policy making. At the end of FDR's first term in 1936 the Supreme Court acknowledged presidential supremacy in foreign affairs in *United States* v. *Curtiss-Wright*.[1] Writing for the Court's majority, conservative Justice Sutherland referred to "the very delicate, plenary and exclusive power of the president as the sole organ of the federal government in the field of international relations—a power which does not require as a basis for its exercise an act of Congress. . . . It is quite apparent that if, in the maintenance of our international relations, embarrassment—perhaps serious embarrassment—is to be avoided and success for our aims achieved,

---

[1]*United States* v. *Curtiss-Wright*, 299 U.S. 304 (1936).

congressional legislation which is to be made effective through negotiation and inquiry within the international field must often accord to the president a degree of discretion and freedom from statutory restriction which would not be admissible were domestic affairs alone involved."

During World War II the president unilaterally conducted foreign and military affairs, and presidents after FDR followed his example although not always with the same success. Truman did not hesitate to proclaim, "I make foreign policy." President Truman alone essentially made the decision to make war in Korea, although he did symbolically consult Congress and involve the UN. Presidential, not congressional, initiatives brought about the Bay of Pigs fiasco during John F. Kennedy's administration, which also saw the president along with a small group of advisers negotiate the Cuban missile crisis. Lyndon B. Johnson and Richard M. Nixon, the latter acting secretly, escalated the Vietnam war.

Congress passed the War Powers Act in 1973, requiring the president to consult with Congress before involving troops in military action abroad beyond 90 days. The act was one of many attempts made by the resurgent Congress of the 1970s to restrict presidential power in foreign affairs. But the Reagan and Bush presidencies illustrated that regardless of what Congress does presidents will continue to make important foreign policy decisions, even deceiving Congress as in the Iran-Contra affair during the Reagan presidency.

The following selection contrasts presidential power in foreign and domestic affairs, concluding that we have not one but two presidencies. Although the author wrote his classic piece in 1966, his thesis remains valid. The complexities of foreign policy and the recognized need for unity and dispatch in decision making support continued presidential control over foreign affairs.

41

Aaron Wildavsky

THE TWO PRESIDENCIES

The United States has one president, but it has two presidencies; one presidency is for domestic affairs, and the other is concerned with defense and foreign policy.

As appeared in *Trans-Action*, December 1966, Volume 4, Number 2: 7–14. Reprinted with permission of Aaron Wildavsky.

Since World War II, presidents have had much greater success in controlling the nation's defense and foreign policies than in dominating its domestic policies. Even Lyndon Johnson has seen his early record of victories in domestic legislation diminish as his concern with foreign affairs grows.

What powers does the president have to control defense and foreign policies and so completely overwhelm those who might wish to thwart him?

The president's normal problem with domestic policy is to get congressional support for the programs he prefers. In foreign affairs, in contrast, he can almost always get support for policies that he believes will protect the nation—but his problem is to find a viable policy.

Whoever they are, whether they begin by caring about foreign policy like Eisenhower and Kennedy or about domestic policies like Truman and Johnson, presidents soon discover they have more policy preferences in domestic matters than in foreign policy. The Republican and Democratic parties possess a traditional roster of policies, which can easily be adopted by a new president—for example, he can be either for or against Medicare and aid to education. Since existing domestic policy usually changes in only small steps, presidents find it relatively simple to make minor adjustments. However, although any president knows he supports foreign aid and NATO, the world outside changes much more rapidly than the nation inside—presidents and their parties have no prior policies on Argentina and the Congo. The world has become a highly intractable place with a whirl of forces we cannot or do not know how to alter.

The Record of Presidential Control

It takes great crises, such as Roosevelt's hundred days in the midst of the depression, or the extraordinary majorities that Barry Goldwater's candidacy willed to Lyndon Johnson, for presidents to succeed in controlling domestic policy. From the end of the 1930s to the present (what may roughly be called the modern era), presidents have often been frustrated in their domestic programs. From 1938, when conservatives regrouped their forces, to the time of his death, Franklin Roosevelt did not get a single piece of significant domestic legislation passed. Truman lost out on most of his intense domestic preferences, except perhaps for housing. Since Eisenhower did not ask for much domestic legislation, he did not meet consistent defeat, yet he failed in his general policy of curtailing governmental commitments. Kennedy, of course, faced great difficulties with domestic legislation.

In the realm of foreign policy there has not been a single major issue on which presidents, when they were serious and determined, have failed. The list of their victories is impressive: entry into the United Nations, the Marshall Plan, NATO, the Truman Doctrine, the decisions to stay out of Indochina in 1954 and to intervene in Vietnam in the 1960s, aid to Poland and Yugoslavia, the test-ban treaty, and many more. Serious setbacks to the president in controlling foreign policy are extraordinary and unusual.

. . . [P]residents have significantly better records in foreign and defense matters than in domestic policies. When refugees and immigration—which Congress considers primarily a domestic concern—are removed from the general foreign policy area, it is clear that presidents prevail about 70 percent of the time in defense and foreign policy, compared with 40 percent in the domestic sphere.

World Events and Presidential Resources

Power in politics is control over governmental decisions. How does the president manage his control of foreign and defense policy? The answer does not reside in the greater constitutional power in foreign affairs that presidents have possessed since the founding of the Republic. The answer lies in the changes that have taken place since 1945.

The number of nations with which the United States has diplomatic relations has increased from 53 in 1939 to 113 in 1966. But sheer numbers do not tell enough; the world has also become a much more dangerous place. However remote it may seem at times, our government must always be aware of the possibility of nuclear war.

Yet the mere existence of great powers with effective thermonuclear weapons would not, in and of itself, vastly increase our rate of interaction with most other nations. We see [all foreign] events as important because they are also part of a larger worldwide contest, called the cold war, in which great powers are rivals for the control or support of other nations. Moreover, the reaction against the blatant isolationism of the 1930s has led to a concern with foreign policy that is worldwide in scope. We are interested in what happens everywhere because we see these events as connected with larger interests involving, at the worst, the possibility of ultimate destruction.

Given the overriding fact that the world is dangerous and that small causes are perceived to have potentially great effects in an unstable world, it follows that presidents must be interested in relatively "small" matters. So they give Azerbaijan or Lebanon or Vietnam huge amounts of their time. Arthur Schlesinger, Jr., wrote of Kennedy that "in the first two months of his administration he probably spent more time on Laos than on anything else." Few failures in domestic policy, presidents soon realize, could have as disastrous consequences as any one of dozens of mistakes in the international arena.

The result is that foreign policy concerns tend to drive out domestic policy. Except for occasional questions of domestic prosperity and for civil rights, foreign affairs have consistently higher priority for presidents. Once, when trying to talk to President Kennedy about natural resources, Secretary of the Interior Stewart Udall remarked, "He's imprisoned by Berlin."

The importance of foreign affairs to presidents is intensified by the increasing speed of events in the international arena. The event and its consequences follow closely on top of one another. The blunder at the Bay of Pigs is swiftly followed by the near catastrophe of the Cuban missile crisis. Presidents can no longer count on passing along their most difficult problems to their successors. They must expect to face the consequences of their actions—or failure to act—while still in office.

Domestic policy making is usually based on experimental adjustments to an existing situation. Only a few decisions, such as those involving large dams, irretrievably commit future generations. Decisions in foreign affairs, however, are often perceived to be irreversible. This is expressed, for example, in the fear of escalation or the various "spiral" or "domino" theories of international conflict.

If decisions are perceived to be both important and irreversible, there is every reason for presidents to devote a great deal of resources to them. Presidents have to be oriented toward the future in the use of their resources. They serve a fixed term in office, and they cannot automatically count on support from the populace, Congress, or the administrative apparatus. They have to be careful, therefore, to husband their resources for pressing future needs. But because the consequences of events in foreign affairs are potentially more grave, faster to manifest themselves, and less easily reversible than in domestic affairs, presidents are more willing to use up their resources.

The Power to Act

Their formal powers to commit resources in foreign affairs and defense are vast. Particularly important is their power as commander-in-chief to move troops. Faced with situations like the invasion of South Korea or the emplacement of missiles in Cuba, fast action is required. Presidents possess both the formal power to act and the knowledge that elites and the general public expect them to act. Once they have committed American forces, it is difficult for Congress or anyone else to alter the course of events. The Dominican venture is a . . . case in point.

Presidential discretion in foreign affairs also makes it difficult (though not impossible) for Congress to restrict their actions. Presidents can use executive agreements instead of treaties, enter into tacit agreements instead of written ones, and otherwise help create *de facto* situations not easily reversed. Presidents also have far greater ability than anyone else to obtain information on developments abroad through the Departments of State and Defense. The need for secrecy in some aspects of foreign and defense policy further restricts the ability of others to compete with presidents. These things are all well known. What is not so generally appreciated is the growing presidential ability to *use* information to achieve goals.

In the past presidents were amateurs in military strategy. They could not even get much useful advice outside of the military. As late as the 1930s the number of people outside the military establishment who were professionally engaged in the study of defense policy could be numbered on the fingers. Today there are hundreds of such men. The rise of the defense intellectuals has given the president of the United States enhanced ability to control defense policy. He is no longer dependent on the military for advice. He can choose among defense intellectuals from the research corporations and the academies for alternative sources of advice. He can install these men in his own office. He can play them off against each other or use them to extend spheres of coordination.

Even with these advisers, however, presidents and secretaries of defense might still be too bewildered by the complexity of nuclear situations to take action—unless they had an understanding of the doctrine and concepts of deterrence. But knowledge of doctrine about deterrence has been widely diffused; it can be picked up by any intelligent person who will read books or listen to enough hours of conversation. Whether or not the doctrine is good is a separate question; the point is that civilians can feel they understand what is going on in defense policy. Perhaps the most extraordinary feature of presidential action during the Cuban missile crisis was the degree to which the Commander-in-Chief of the Armed Forces insisted on controlling even the smallest moves. From the positioning of ships to the methods of boarding, to the precise words and actions to be taken by individual soldiers and sailors, the president and his civilian advisers were in control.

Although presidents have rivals for power in foreign affairs, the rivals do not usually succeed. Presidents prevail not only because they may have superior resources but because their potential opponents are weak, divided, or believe that they should not control foreign policy. Let us consider the potential rivals—the general citizenry, special interest groups, the Congress, the military, the so-called military-industrial complex, and the State Department.

Competitors for Control of Policy

The Public

The general public is much more dependent on presidents in foreign affairs than in domestic matters. While many people know about the impact of social security and Medicare, few know about politics in Malawi. So it is not surprising that people expect the president to act in foreign affairs and reward him with their confidence. . . .

Although Presidents lead opinion in foreign affairs, they know they will be held accountable for the consequences of their actions. . . . We will support your initiatives, the people seem to say, but we will reserve the right to punish you (or your party) if we do not like the results.

Special Interest Groups

Opinions are easier to gauge in domestic affairs because, for one thing, there is a stable structure of interest groups that covers virtually all matters of concern. The farm, labor, business, conservation, veteran, civil rights, and other interest groups provide cues when a proposed policy affects them. Thus people who identify with these groups may adopt their views. But in foreign policy matters the interest group structure is weak, unstable, and thin rather than dense. In many matters affecting Africa and Asia, for example, it is hard to think of well-known interest groups. While ephemeral groups arise from time to time to support or protest particular policies, they usually disappear when the immediate problem is resolved. In contrast, longer lasting elite groups like the Foreign Policy Association and Council on

Foreign Relations are composed of people of diverse views; refusal to take strong positions on controversial matters is a condition of their continued viability.

The strongest interest groups are probably the ethnic associations whose members have strong ties with a homeland, as in Poland or Cuba, so they are rarely activated simultaneously on any specific issue. They are most effective when most narrowly and intensely focused—as in the fierce pressure from Jews to recognize the state of Israel. But their relatively small numbers limits their significance to presidents in the vastly more important general foreign policy picture—as continued aid to the Arab countries shows. . . .

The Congress

Congressmen also exercise power in foreign affairs. Yet they are ordinarily not serious competitors with the president because they follow a self-denying ordinance. They do not think it is their job to determine the nation's defense policies. . . .

The Military

The outstanding feature of the military's participation in making defense policy is their amazing weakness. Whether the policy decisions involve the size of the armed forces, the choice of weapons systems, the total defense budget, or its division into components, the military have not prevailed. Let us take budgetary decisions as representative of the key choices to be made in defense policy. Since the end of World War II the military has not been able to achieve significant (billion dollar) increases in appropriations by their own efforts. . . .

Military Industrial

But what about the fabled military-industrial complex? If the military alone is divided and weak, perhaps the giant industrial firms that are so dependent on defense contracts play a large part in making policy.

First, there is an important distinction between the questions "Who will get a given contract?" and "What will our defense policy be?" It is apparent that different answers may be given to these quite different questions. There are literally tens of thousands of defense contractors. They may compete vigorously for business. In the course of this competition, they may wine and dine military officers, use retired generals, seek intervention by their congressmen, place ads in trade journals, and even contribute to political campaigns. The famous TFX controversy—should General Dynamics or Boeing get the expensive contract?—is a larger than life example of the pressures brought to bear in search of lucrative contracts.

But neither the TFX case nor the usual vigorous competition for contracts is involved with the making of substantive defense policy. Vital questions like the size of the defense budget, the choice of strategic programs, massive retaliation vs. a counter-[insurgency] strategy, and the like were far beyond the policy aims of any company. Industrial firms, then, do not control such decisions, nor is there much evidence that they actually try. No doubt a precipitous and drastic rush to disarmament would meet with opposition from industrial firms among other interests.

However, there has never been a time when any significant element in the government considered a disarmament policy to be feasible.

. . .

The State Department

Modern presidents expect the State Department to carry out their policies. John F.
Kennedy felt that State was "in some particular sense 'his' department." If a secretary of state forgets this, as was apparently the case with James Byrnes under Truman, a president may find another man. But the State Department, especially the
Foreign Service, is also a highly professional organization with a life and momentum of its own. If a president does not push hard, he may find his preferences somehow dissipated in time. Arthur Schlesinger fills his book on Kennedy [A *Thousand
Days*] with laments about the bureaucratic inertia and recalcitrance of the State
Department.

. . .

[But] Schlesinger comes closest to the truth when he writes that "the White
House could always win any battle it chose over the [Foreign] Service; but the prestige and proficiency of the Service limited the number of battles any White House
would find it profitable to fight." When the president knew what he wanted, he got
it. . . .

The growth of a special White House staff to help presidents in foreign affairs
expresses their need for assistance, their refusal to rely completely on the regular executive agencies, and their ability to find competent men. The deployment of this
staff must remain a presidential prerogative, however, if its members are to serve
presidents and not their opponents. . . . But presidents resolutely refuse to become
prisoners of their advisers by using them as other people would like. Presidents remain in control of their staff as well as of major foreign policy decisions.

How Complete Is the Control?

. . .

Are there significant historical examples which might refute the thesis of presidential control of foreign policy? Foreign aid may be a case in point. For many
years, presidents have struggled to get foreign aid appropriations because of hostility
from public and congressional opinion. Yet several billion dollars a year are appropriated regularly despite the evident unpopularity of the program. . . .

The World Influence

The forces impelling presidents to be concerned with the widest range of foreign
and defense policies also affect the ways in which they calculate their power stakes.
As Kennedy used to say, "Domestic policy . . . can only defeat us; foreign policy can
kill us."

It no longer makes sense for presidents to "play politics" with foreign and defense policies. In the past, presidents might have thought that they could gain by prolonged delay or by not acting at all. The problem might disappear or be passed on to their successors. Presidents must now expect to pay the high costs themselves if the world situation deteriorates. The advantages of pursuing a policy that is viable in the world, that will not blow up on presidents or their fellow citizens, far outweigh any temporary political disadvantages accrued in supporting an initially unpopular policy. Compared with domestic affairs, presidents engaged in world politics are immensely more concerned with meeting problems on their own terms. Who supports and opposes a policy, though a matter of considerable interest, does not assume the crucial importance that it does in domestic affairs. The best policy presidents can find is also the best politics.

The fact that there are numerous foreign and defense policy situations competing for a president's attention means that it is worthwhile to organize political activity in order to affect his agenda. For if a president pays more attention to certain problems he may develop different preferences; he may seek and receive different advice; his new calculations may lead him to devote greater resources to seeking a solution. Interested congressmen may exert influence not by directly determining a presidential decision, but indirectly by making it costly for a president to avoid reconsidering the basis for his action. For example, citizen groups, such as those concerned with a change in China policy, may have an impact simply by keeping their proposals on the public agenda. A president may be compelled to reconsider a problem even though he could not overtly be forced to alter the prevailing policy.

In foreign affairs we may be approaching the stage where knowledge is power. There is a tremendous receptivity to good ideas in Washington. Most anyone who can present a convincing rationale for dealing with a hard world finds a ready audience. The best way to convince presidents to follow a desired policy is to show that it might work. . . . It is, to be sure, extremely difficult to devise good policies or to predict their consequences accurately. Nor is it easy to convince others that a given policy is superior to other alternatives. But it is the way to influence with presidents. For if they are convinced that the current policy is best, the likelihood of gaining sufficient force to compel a change is quite small. The man who can build better foreign policies will find presidents beating a path to his door.

❖❖ Presidential Leadership and Political Parties

Our 18th century constitutional system of divided government weakens political parties. The Founding Fathers did not intend for either the President or Congress to govern through parties. As the following selection reveals, modern presidents have taken a leaf from the founders' notebook by relying more on administrative than party government.

42

Sidney M. Milkis

THE PRESIDENCY AND POLITICAL PARTIES

❖❖❖❖❖❖❖

The relationship between the presidency and the American party system has always been difficult. The architects of the Constitution established a nonpartisan president who, with the support of the judiciary, was intended to play the leading institutional role in checking and controlling the "violence of faction" that the framers feared would rend the fabric of representative democracy. Even after the presidency became a more partisan office during the early part of the nineteenth century, its authority continued to depend on an ability to transcend party politics. The president is nominated by a party but, unlike the British prime minister, is not elected by it.

The inherent tension between the presidency and the party system reached a critical point during the 1930s. The institutionalization of the modern presidency, arguably the most significant constitutional legacy of Franklin D. Roosevelt's New Deal, ruptured severely the limited, albeit significant, bond that linked presidents to their parties. In fact, the modern presidency was crafted with the intention of reducing the influence of the party system on American politics. In this sense Roosevelt's extraordinary party leadership contributed to the decline of the American party system. This decline continued—even accelerated—under the administrations of subsequent presidents, notably Lyndon B. Johnson and Richard M. Nixon. Under Ronald Reagan, however, the party system showed at least some signs of transformation and renewal. Reagan and his successor, George Bush, supported efforts by Republicans in the national committee and congressional campaign organizations to restore some of the importance of political parties by refashioning them into highly untraditional but politically potent national organizations. Yet the 1992 election and its aftermath raised serious doubts about the capacity of these emergent national parties to build popular support for political principles and programs.

New Deal Party Politics, Presidential Reform, and the Decline of the American Party System

The New Deal seriously questioned the adequacy of the traditional natural rights liberalism of John Locke and the framers, which emphasized the need to limit constitutionally the scope of government's responsibilities. The modern liberalism that

313

became the public philosophy of the New Deal entailed a fundamental reappraisal of the concept of rights. As Roosevelt first indicated in his 1932 campaign speech at the Commonwealth Club in San Francisco, effective political reform would require, at a minimum, the development of "an economic declaration of rights, an economic constitutional order," grounded in a commitment to guarantee a decent level of economic well-being for the American people. Although equality of opportunity had traditionally been promoted by limited government interference in society, recent economic and social changes, such as the closing of the frontiers and the growth of industrial combinations, demanded that America now recognize "the new terms of the old social contract."

The establishment of a new constitutional order would require a reordering of the political process. The traditional patterns of American politics, characterized by constitutional mechanisms that impeded collective action, would have to give way to a more centralized and administrative government. As Roosevelt put it, "The day of enlightened administration has come."

The concerns Roosevelt expressed in the Commonwealth Club speech are an important guide to understanding the New Deal and its effects on the party system. The pursuit of an economic constitutional order presupposed a fundamental change in the relationship between the presidency and the party system. In Roosevelt's view, the party system, which was essentially based on state and local organizations and interests and was thus suited to congressional primacy, would have to be transformed into a national, executive-oriented system organized on the basis of public issues.

In this understanding, Roosevelt was no doubt influenced by the thought of Woodrow Wilson. The reform of parties, Wilson believed, depended on extending the influence of the presidency. The limits on partisanship inherent in American constitutional government notwithstanding, the president represented his party's "vital link of connection" with the nation: "He can dominate his party by being spokesman for the real sentiment and purpose of the country, by giving the country at once the information and statements of policy which will enable it to form its judgments alike of parties and men."

. . .

In the final analysis, the "benign dictatorship" that Roosevelt sought to impose on the Democratic party was more conducive to corroding the American party system than to reforming it. His prescription for party reform—extraordinary presidential leadership—posed a serious, if not intractable, dilemma: on the one hand, the decentralized character of politics in the United States can be modified only by strong presidential leadership; on the other, a president determined to alter fundamentally the connection between the executive and the party eventually will shatter party unity.

. . .

The most significant institutional reforms of the New Deal did not promote party government but fostered instead a program that would help the president to govern in the absence of party government. This program, as embodied in the 1937 executive reorganization bill, would have greatly extended presidential authority over the executive branch, including the independent regulatory commissions. The president and the executive agencies would also be delegated extensive authority to govern, making unnecessary the constant cooperation of party members in Congress. As the *Report of the President's Committee on Administrative Management* put it, with administrative reform the "brief exultant commitment" to progressive government that was expressed in the elections of 1932 and, especially, 1936 would now be more firmly established in "persistent, determined, competent, day by day administration of what the Nation has decided to do."

. . .

Roosevelt's leadership transformed the Democratic party into a way station on the road to administrative government. As the presidency developed into an elaborate and ubiquitous institution, it preempted party leaders in many of their limited, but significant, duties: providing a link from government to interest groups, staffing the executive department, contributing to policy development, and organizing election campaigns. Moreover, New Deal administrative reform was directed not just to creating presidential government but to embedding progressive principles (considered tantamount to political rights) in a bureaucratic structure that would insulate reform and reformers from electoral change.

. . .

Lyndon Johnson's Great Society and the Transcendence of Partisan Politics

Presidential leadership during the New Deal prepared the executive branch to be a government unto itself and established the presidency rather than the party as the locus of political responsibility. But the modern presidency was created to chart the course for, and direct the voyage to, a more liberal America. Roosevelt's pronouncement of a "second bill of rights" proclaimed and began this task, but it fell to Johnson, as one journalist noted, to "codify the New Deal vision of a good society."

Johnson's attempt to create the Great Society marked a significant extension of programmatic liberalism and accelerated the effort to transcend partisan politics. Roosevelt's ill-fated efforts to guide the affairs of his party were well remembered by Johnson, who came to Congress in 1937 in a special House election as an enthusiastic supporter of the New Deal. He took Roosevelt's experience to be the best example of the generally ephemeral nature of party government in the United States, and he fully expected the cohesive Democratic support he received from Congress after the 1964 election to be temporary. Thus Johnson, like Roosevelt, looked beyond the party system toward the politics of "enlightened administration."

. . .

Richard Nixon, Nonpartisanship, and the Demise of the Modern Presidency

Considering that the New Deal and Great Society were established by replacing traditional party politics with administration, it is not surprising that when a conservative challenge to liberal reform emerged, it entailed the creation of a conservative "administrative presidency." This development further contributed to the decline of partisan politics.

Until the 1960s, opponents of the welfare state were generally opposed to the modern presidency, which had served as the fulcrum of liberal reform. Nevertheless, by the end of the Johnson administration, it became clear that a strong conservative movement would require an activist program of retrenchment in order to counteract the enduring effects of the New Deal and Great Society. Once the opponents of liberal public policy, primarily housed in the Republican party, recognized this, they looked to the possibility that, ideologically, the modern presidency could be a two-edged sword.

The administrative actions of the Nixon presidency were a logical extension of the practices of Roosevelt and Johnson. The centralization of authority in the White House and the reduction of the regular Republican organization to perfunctory status during the Nixon years was hardly new. The complete autonomy of the Committee for the Re-Election of the President (CREEP) from the regular Republican organization in the 1972 campaign was but the final stage of a long process of White House preemption of the national committee's political responsibilities. And the administrative reform program that was pursued after Nixon's reelection, in which executive authority was concentrated in the hands of White House operatives and four cabinet "supersecretaries," was the culmination of a long-standing tendency in the modern presidency to reconstitute the executive branch as a formidable and independent instrument of government.

Thus, just as Roosevelt's presidency anticipated the Great Society, Johnson's presidency anticipated the administrative presidency of Richard Nixon. Indeed, the strategy of pursuing policy goals through administrative capacities that had been created for the most part by Democratic presidents was considered especially suitable by a minority Republican president who faced a hostile Congress and bureaucracy intent on preserving those presidents' programs. Nixon actually surpassed previous modern presidents in viewing the party system as an obstacle to effective governance.

Yet, mainly because of the Watergate scandal, Nixon's presidency had the effect of strengthening opposition to the unilateral use of presidential power, even as it further attenuated the bonds that linked presidents to the party system. The evolution of the modern presidency now left the office in complete institutional isolation. This isolation continued during the Ford and Carter years, so much so that by the end of the 1970s scholars were lamenting the demise of the presidency as well as of the party system.

The Reagan Presidency and the Revitalization of Party Politics

The development of the modern presidency fostered a serious decline in the traditional local and patronage-based parties. Yet some developments during the Reagan presidency suggested that a phoenix had emerged from the ashes. The erosion of old-style partisan politics had allowed a more national and issue-oriented party system to develop, forging new links between presidents and their parties.

The Republican party in particular developed a formidable organizational apparatus, which displayed unprecedented strength at the national level. . . .

The revival of the Republican party as a force against government by administration seemed to complete the development of a new American party system. The nomination and election of Ronald Reagan, a far more ideological conservative than Nixon, galvanized the Republican commitment to programs, such as "regulatory relief" and "new federalism," that severely challenged the institutional legacy of the New Deal. Had such a trend continued, the circumvention of the regular political process by administrative action may well have been displaced by the sort of full-scale debate about political questions usually associated with critical realignments.

Significantly, it was Reagan who broke with the tradition of the modern presidency and identified closely with his party. The president worked hard to strengthen the Republicans' organizational and popular base, surprising his own political director with his "total readiness" to shoulder such partisan responsibilities as making numerous fund-raising appearances for the party and its candidates. Apparently, after having spent the first fifty years of his life as a Democrat, Reagan brought the enthusiasm of a convert to Republican activities.

The experience of the Reagan administration suggests how the relationship between the president and the party can be mutually beneficial. Republican party strength provided Reagan with the support of a formidable institution, solidifying his personal popularity and facilitating the support of his program in Congress. As a result, the Reagan presidency was able to suspend the paralysis that seemed to afflict American government in the 1970s, even though the Republicans never attained control of the House of Representatives. In turn, Reagan's popularity served the party by strengthening its fund-raising efforts and promoting a shift in voters' party loyalties, placing the Republicans by 1985 in a position of virtual parity with the Democrats for the first time since the 1940s. It may be, then, that the 1980s marked the watershed both for a new political era and for a renewed link between presidents and the party system.

Nevertheless, the separation of political institutions in the United States provides a precarious setting for comprehensive party programs. It is unlikely that the emergence of strong national party organizations will fundamentally alter the limited possibilities for party government under the American Constitution, a fact that will continue to encourage modern presidents, particularly those intent on ambitious policy reform, to emphasize popular appeal and administrative action rather than "collective responsibility." It is not surprising, therefore, that the Reagan presidency frequently pursued its program with acts of administrative discretion that short-circuited the legislative process and weakened efforts to carry out broad-based party policies. The Iran-contra scandal, for example, was not simply a matter of the president's being asleep on his watch. Rather, it revealed the Reagan administration's determination to assume a more forceful anti-communist posture in Central America in the face of a recalcitrant Congress and bureaucracy.

. . .

As such, Reagan did not transform Washington completely. Rather, he strengthened the Republican beachhead in the nation's capital, solidifying his party's recent dominance of the presidency and providing better opportunities for conservatives in the Washington community. Reagan's landslide reelection in 1984 did not prevent the Democrats from maintaining control of the House of Representatives; nor did his plea to the voters during the 1986 congressional campaign to elect Republican majorities prevent the Democrats from recapturing control of the Senate.

Concomitantly, Reagan's two terms witnessed a revitalization of the struggle between the executive and legislative branches; indeed, his conservative program became the foundation for more fundamental philosophical and policy differences between them than in the past. The Iran-contra affair and the battles to control regulatory policy were marked not just by differences between the president and Congress about policy, but by each branch's efforts to weaken the other. The efforts of Republicans to compensate for their inability to control Congress by seeking to circumvent legislative restrictions on presidential conduct were matched by Democratic initiatives to burden the executive with smothering legislative oversight. The opposition to liberal reform, then, did not end in a challenge to national administrative power but in a raw and disruptive battle to control its services.

Reagan's Legacy and the Accession of George Bush

The 1988 election seemed to indicate that divided government had become an enduring characteristic of American politics. The Bush campaign took its shape from the Reagan legacy: in the final analysis, Bush's nomination by the Republican party and his victory by a substantial margin against his Democratic opponent, Gov. Michael Dukakis of Massachusetts, were expressions of the voters' approval of the Reagan administration. Yet the 1988 election also revealed the limits of the Reagan revolution, reflecting in its outcome the underlying pattern that had characterized American politics since 1968: Republican dominance in the White House, Democratic ascendancy almost everywhere else. In fact, the 1988 election represented an extreme manifestation of this pattern. Never before had a president been elected while the other party gained ground in the House, Senate, the state legislatures, and the state governorships. Never before had voters given a newly elected president fewer fellow partisans in Congress than they gave Bush.

. . .

In sum, the closer ties that Reagan and Bush tried to forge between the modern presidency and the Republican party did not alter the unprecedented partisan and electoral divisions that characterized the era of divided government. Indeed, the persistence of divided government itself retarded the restoration of partisanship to the presidency. During the early days of his presidency, Bush attempted to reach out to Democrats in Congress in order to restore the badly frayed consensus in American politics. But he gave no reasonable defense of his pragmatism. Thus, once he abandoned his antitax pledge and lost his top political strategist to illness, Bush's presidency floated adrift. His search for agreement with Congress in the absence of any clear principles threatened the modern presidency with the same sort of isolation and weakness that had characterized the Ford and Carter years.

The 1992 Election and Beyond

The Bush presidency was a painful reminder of the modern executive's "extraordinary isolation." Since FDR, the president had been freed from the constraints of party, only to be enslaved by a volatile political environment that often would rapidly undercut popular support. In 1991, Bush basked in the triumphs of the Gulf and cold wars, his popularity rating at a historic high of about 90 percent; in 1992, he was soundly defeated in his bid for reelection by the governor of Arkansas, William "Bill" Clinton. The Democrats not only captured the presidency but also preserved their majorities in the House and the Senate. For twelve years, the voters' striking ambiguity about the parties had left the government in a cross-fire between a Republican president and Democratic Congress. In 1992, however, an exit poll revealed that a plurality of voters now preferred to have the presidency and Congress controlled by the Democratic party, in the hope that ideological polarization and institutional conflict would be brought to an end. This hope was urged on by Clinton's promise to govern as a "new Democrat," an "agent of change" who would restore political consensus in American politics.

In truth, the 1992 election contained both optimistic and pessimistic portents for the modern presidency. Although the Democrats ran an effective campaign and Clinton skillfully, if not always boldly, addressed his party's liabilities, the election results showed that fundamental conflicts continued to divide Americans, even as they seemed united in their dissatisfaction with the way government worked. Clinton won only 43 percent of the popular vote, roughly the same percentage that losing Democratic candidates had received in the previous three elections. The strong support for the independent candidate H. Ross Perot reflected the continuing erosion of partisan loyalties in the electorate.

. . .

. . . [L]ong after being elected to the presidency, Clinton still faced the profound challenge of establishing the boundaries in which his party and domestic policy could be reformed.

Yet it might be unreasonable, indeed, dangerous, to rely so heavily on presidents to determine the contours of political action. The modern presidency operates in a political arena that is seldom congenial to meaningful political debate and that all too often is guilty of deflecting attention from the painful struggles about the appropriate meaning of liberalism or the relative merits of contemporary liberalism and conservatism. With the liberation of the executive from many of the constraints of party leadership and the rise of the mass media, presidents have resorted to rhetoric and administration, tools with which they have sought to forge new, more personal ties with the public. But this form of politics has perhaps promised the people more security for economic welfare than a free society can tolerate, and it has exposed them to the kind of public figures who will exploit citizens' impatience with the difficult tasks involved in sustaining a healthy constitutional democracy.

Presidents who enjoy prominent places in history have taken the American people to school, educating them about new policy proposals and persuading them to make difficult choices. But they have done so as great party leaders, in the midst of critical partisan realignments. Public education of this sort is rarely encountered on talk shows or in electronic town meetings. Instead, in such forums candidates and presidents are tempted to seek the devotion of the American people in order to manipulate them.

Critical partisan elections have enabled each generation to claim its right to redefine the Constitution's principles and reorganize its institutions. The New Deal continued this unending task to ensure that each generation could affirm its attachment to constitutional government. The burden of this generation is to hold the modern presidency to account, to recapture the understanding of democracy that has made such momentous deliberation and choice so central to the pursuit of America's political destiny. In the nation's present hour of discontent, this effort requires above all the will to acknowledge the limits and appropriate tasks of national administrative power.

❖❖ The Presidency in Divided Government

The preceding selections in this chapter have taken different approaches to an understanding of the presidency. Clinton Rossiter (selection 36) defines the institution in Hamiltonian (selection 35) imperial, terms. Richard Neustadt (selection 37) argues that the President is more a clerk than a king. James David Barber (selection 39) believes that presidential character determines performance. The author of the following selection concludes that the Madisonian system of divided government, set forth in the *Federalist Papers 47, 48,* and *51* (selection 4), has overshadowed all other constitutional and political influences on the presidency.

43

Charles O. Jones

THE PRESIDENCY IN A SEPARATED SYSTEM

❖❖❖❖❖❖❖

Perspectives on the Presidency

The president is not the presidency. The presidency is not the government. Ours is not a presidential system.

Excerpts from *The Presidency in a Separated System* by Charles O. Jones (Washington, DC: The Brookings Institution, 1994, pp. 1–3; 281–285; 297–298). Copyright © 1994 by The Brookings Institution. Reprinted by permission of The Brookings Institution.

I begin with these starkly negative themes as partial correctives to the more popular interpretations of the United States government as presidency-centered. Presidents themselves learn these refrains on the job, if they do not know them before. President Lyndon B. Johnson, who had impressive political advantages during the early years of his administration, reflected later on what was required to realize the potentialities of the office:

> Every President has to establish with the various sectors of the country what I call "the right to govern." Just being elected to the office does not guarantee him that right. Every President has to inspire the confidence of the people. Every President has to become a leader, and to be a leader he must attract people who are willing to follow him. Every President has to develop a moral underpinning to his power, or he soon discovers that he has no power at all.

To exercise influence, presidents must learn the setting within which it has bearing. President-elect Bill Clinton recognized the complexities of translating campaign promises into a legislative program during a news conference shortly after his election in 1992:

> It's all very well to say you want an investment tax credit, and quite another thing to make the 15 decisions that have to be made to shape the exact bill you want.
> It's all very well to say . . . that the working poor in this country . . . should be lifted out of poverty by increasing the refundable income tax credit for the working poor, and another thing to answer the five or six questions that define how you get that done.

For presidents, new or experienced, to recognize the limitations of office is commendable. Convincing others to do so is a challenge. Presidents become convenient labels for marking historical time: the Johnson years, the Nixon years, the Reagan years. Media coverage naturally focuses more on the president: there is just one at a time, executive organization is oriented in pyramidal fashion toward the Oval Office, Congress is too diffuse an institution to report on as such, and the Supreme Court leads primarily by indirection. Public interest, too, is directed toward the White House as a symbol of the government. As a result, expectations of a president often far exceed the individual's personal, political, institutional, or constitutional capacities for achievement. Performance seldom matches promise. Presidents who understand how it all works resist the inflated image of power born of high-stakes elections and seek to lower expectations. Politically savvy presidents know instinctively that it is precisely at the moment of great achievement that they must prepare themselves for the setback that will surely follow.

Focusing exclusively on the presidency can lead to a seriously distorted picture of how the national government does its work. The plain fact is that the United States does not have a presidential system. It has a *separated* system. It is odd that it is so commonly thought of as otherwise since schoolchildren learn about the separation of powers and checks and balances. As the author of *Federalist* 51 wrote, "Ambition must be made to counteract ambition." No one, least of all presidents, the Founders reasoned, can be entrusted with excessive authority. Human nature, being what it is, requires "auxiliary precautions" in the form of competing legitimacies.

The acceptance that this is a separated, not a presidential, system, prepares one to appraise how politics works, not to be simply reproachful and reformist. Thus, for example, divided (or split-party) government is accepted as a potential or even likely outcome of a separated system, rooted as it is in the separation of elections. Failure to acknowledge the authenticity of the split-party condition leaves one with little to study and much to reform in the post–World War II period, when the government has been divided more than 60 percent of the time.

Simply put, the role of the president in this separated system of governing varies substantially, depending on his resources, advantages, and strategic position. My strong interest is in how presidents place themselves in an ongoing government and are fitted in by other participants, notably those on Capitol Hill. The central purpose of this selection is to explore these "fittings." In pursuing this interest, I have found little value in the presidency-centered, party government perspective, as I will explain below. As a substitute, I propose a separationist, diffused-responsibility perspective that I find more suited to the constitutional, institutional, political, and policy conditions associated with the American system of governing. First, however, I offer dramatic cases of how a president's role can change during his term in office, two stories of the highs and lows of serving in the White House.

Landslides and Presidential Power

Surely if any president is to command the government, it will be one who wins so overwhelmingly that no one in Washington can deny his legitimacy for setting and clearing the agenda. Two postwar presidents illustrate that electoral achievement of the highest order is no protection against changing conditions. Lyndon B. Johnson and Richard M. Nixon triumphed at the polls. Both then suffered a dramatic loss in their capacity to lead. Johnson decided not to seek reelection; Nixon resigned in disgrace.

Election does not guarantee power in the American political system. Rather it legitimizes the effort of a president to lead, "to establish . . . the right to govern," in President Johnson's words. Leadership itself depends on opportunity, capability, and resources. By intent, the U.S. government works within a set of limits designed to prevent it from working too well. There is substantial evidence that Americans continue to support the principles of mixed representation, separation of institutions, and distribution of power, with all the checks and balances that follow. These are difficult principles to export or even to explain abroad. It is not certain that Americans understand exactly how a government-in-check works; it is certain that they are consistently critical of government performance. Yet basic constitutional reforms have been few even though institutional adaptation has been substantial.

Lyndon B. Johnson won by a landslide in 1964. His sweeping victory left his conservative opponent, Barry M. Goldwater, with the Dixiecrat states won by Strom Thurmond in 1948 plus a narrow win in his home state of Arizona. On the day following this triumph, a *New York Times* editorial expressed the optimism of most analysts about the victory. Trust had been conveyed, disaster had been averted, and a mandate was declared. It was a "good election" by the criteria of the preferred model of party government.

The American people have given emphatic notice that they want to move forward constructively along the road of international understanding and domestic progress. . . .

Rejected is the thesis that the challenges of an era of dynamic, relentless change in domestic and foreign affairs can be met by dismantling the Federal Government or by shaking a nuclear fist at the rest of the world.

. . .

Thinking about Change

The president is authorized to shape the presidency. The presidency is in a continuous search for its role in the government. Ours is a separated system.

The American presidency carries a burden of lofty expectations that are simply not warranted by the political or constitutional basis of the office. Presidents are important actors in national and world politics, but governments here and abroad must adjust to their inevitable comings and goings. Effective presidents are those who know and understand their potential and variable role in the permanent and continuing government. The natural inclination is to make the president responsible for policies and political events that no one can claim a legitimate right to control. Presidents are well advised to resist this invitation to assume a position of power as though it conveyed authority. Rather they need to identify and define their political capital, and must do so repeatedly in a search for the limits of their influence.

Why are the status and power of the president exaggerated? Why are the constraints of the separation ignored or the president commonly expected to overcome them? Why are the abundant variations of separation not acknowledged as the system's strengths rather than presidential weaknesses? I have puzzled about these questions throughout this volume. My experience in trying to understand just the president's relationships to Congress may offer partial answers. The complexity of a separated system at work is truly imposing, if not always inspiring. It is like an Escher drawing: what rises from one perspective sinks from another. Political analysts, particularly those with deadlines, understandably try to simplify what they observe, and then they criticize when the system does not work as simply as has been described.

For scholars, a presidency-centered, party responsibility perspective may be the consequence of the historical trends in the frequency of split-party government. It was a rarity during the first half of the twentieth century after having occurred often in the latter half of the nineteenth century. Perhaps observers believed that a single-party, presidency-centered government was evolving in the new century as the common solution to the problems identified with the separated system. This hypothesis may have been encouraged by the common interpretation that the Franklin D. Roosevelt administration was the beginning of the modern presidency. With Roosevelt as the model for an evolutionary system of strong presidential leadership, one can then imagine the disillusionment of many scholars with presidents in the post–World War

II era. Most presidents, and surely those governing with opposite-party majorities in Congress, were bound to fail the FDR test, yet it continued to be applied. Finally, one can imagine the frustration for those who believed that presidentialism had arrived, only to discover that the Roosevelt years were the exception, not the rule.

Sidney M. Milkis offers little comfort for the evolutionary perspective, and, indeed, he identifies in the Roosevelt years an emergent separation between presidential government and party government. "Roosevelt's party leadership and the New Deal mark the culmination of efforts, which begin in the Progressive era, to loosen the grip of partisan politics on the councils of power, with a view to strengthening national administrative capacities and extending the programmatic commitments of the federal government." For Milkis, "this shift from party to administrative politics" did not secure single-party government, nor did it usher in an "imperial" presidency. Presidents of either party found "themselves navigating a treacherous and lonely path, subject to a volatile political process that makes popular and enduring achievement unlikely."[1] Thus the big government of the post-New Deal era continues to pose a challenge for presidents that is not met by reconstituted "responsible" political parties.

Principal Observations

I . . . will now summarize my principal observations.

—There are substantial differences in the personal and political background of presidents and how they come to serve in the White House (for example, as elected, reelected, nonelected, and heir apparent presidents and elected vice presidents). These differences can lead to strategies (assertive, compensatory, custodial, guardian, and restorative) that aid in explaining performance in office.

—Organizing a presidency is an adaptive process associated with the circumstances of how a president enters the White House and the set of problems he then encounters in doing the job. Several observations are relevant:

Many postwar presidencies involve same-party transitions: Roosevelt to Truman, Kennedy to Johnson, Nixon to Ford, and Reagan to Bush. These transitions have important organizational implications: the new president in each of the four cases faced the task of adapting to or replacing an existing structure.

Commonly used models of White House organization (the circle or pyramid) fail to account for the substantial variations experienced by postwar presidencies or the changes that are made through a term in office. The variables that should be accounted for in characterizing the organization of the presidency include the nature of access, the president's organizational concepts (if he has any), the degree of interaction between the president and the staff, the nature of staff relations, and, for takeover presidents, the nature of the transition.

Cabinet secretaries represent a public manifestation of a president's effort to connect his White House to the permanent government. But turnover is high among these secretaries, and measuring a president's effectiveness on the basis of a

---

[1]See selection 42.

series of one-on-one interactions with the secretaries is difficult. Most presidents do not meet the challenge of effectively managing the separated system.

—Public standing of presidents, as measured by public approval ratings, is inexactly related to job performance and effectiveness in working with Congress, as would be expected in a separated system of diffused responsibility and a continuing agenda. Still, tests of public approval have increased substantially in recent years, with evaluations typically equating a president's relative standing with his influence in the separated system.

—However inapt the concept of a mandate in American national politics, it will continue to be used in interpreting election results. Three renditions—the mandate for change, the status quo mandate, and the mixed or nonmandate—are commonly employed at election time and then become tests for performance. A fourth concept, that of the "unmandate," may accompany midterm losses by the president's party or other negative events later in a presidency.

—Presidents perform important agenda-setting functions in setting priorities, certifying issues, proposing policy solutions, and reacting to others' policy initiatives. For the most part, the agenda of government itself is continuous from one year to the next. Presidents are judged by their effectiveness as designators within the ongoing policy process.

—Law in the separated system is made by a process, primarily centered in Congress, that is continuous, iterative, representative, informational, sequential, orderly (in setting priorities), and declarative. Most important legislation is worked on over time and is connected with precursory laws that are familiar to those in the permanent government. To be effective, presidents must take these characteristics of the lawmaking process into account so as to judge how, when, and where to participate.

—An analysis of twenty-eight major pieces of legislation in the postwar period reveals the rich variety of presidential-congressional interaction in lawmaking. It demonstrates that presidents are important actors in lawmaking, but there is substantial variation in which branch is preponderant and there are many instances of balanced participation. The engrossing variations in the degree and place of iteration, the sequence of legislative action, and, above all, the mix of partisan strategies at different stages reveal how little is learned from restricting analysis to roll call votes (particularly studies based on presidential support scores).

Taken as a whole, these observations advise presidency watchers against isolating one branch from the other or concentrating on only one president or Congress. Understanding the workings of a separated system of diffused responsibility and mixed representation logically requires attention to the institutional context within which any one part of the system does its work. A presidency-centered perspective is insufficiently attentive to the challenge facing the president in finding his place in the permanent government. Often this perspective invites questioning the legitimacy of other participants, who may be identified as obstructionists. This then leads to the proposal of reforms to orient Congress and the bureaucracy more toward presidential policy preferences, or those preferences it is assumed that presidents should have.

Much of this presidency-centered analysis concludes that the system is not working well, when in fact only a part of the system has been studied—and the most temporary part, at that. One measure of whether the system is working is the production of important legislation. David R. Mayhew challenges those who doubt the capacity of the government to produce important laws under conditions that might be expected to result in stalemate (as in 1973–74).[2] My detailed examination of 28 of Mayhew's list of 267 laws shows an astonishing array of sequences, patterns of iteration, and partisan connections. There is a saying that one does not want to look closely at how either sausage or laws are made. I agree when it comes to sausage. I strongly disagree when it comes to laws. Careful study of how important laws are made impresses one with the creativity and flexibility of the system of separated institutions competing for shared powers. It is an extraordinarily mature process, with a seemingly infinite number of mutations that are bound to challenge the analyst and the reformer.

Reform and Change

Should the separated system be reformed? First, one should understand that it is ever changing. One of the special features of separated institutions is that they are constantly undergoing modification as they compete for shares of power in dealing with policy issues. Further, since there is no one formula by which president and Congress do their work, the object of reform is not easy to stipulate, nor are the effects of reorganization highly predictable. The system changes without reforms, and reforms do not necessarily lead to desired change.

. . .

The Presidency in a Separated System

I come away from this study quite in awe of the American national government. That is not to say I believe it is faultless; angels are not available to govern, as James Madison explained long ago. It does mean that I am impressed with the capacity of a complex set of political institutions to adjust to a remarkable variation in political and policy circumstances. E. E. Schattschneider explained that "democracy is a political system for people who are not too sure that they are right." His formulation draws attention to decisionmaking rather than to the decisions themselves. It is no simple matter to create, maintain, or reform a government forged to represent uncertainty and to approximate, but not necessarily achieve, policy solutions.

The capacity of the separated system to adjust is reflected in the classifications developed throughout this book. Regardless of the topic—how presidents came to be there, how they organized their presidency, their public standing and role in agenda setting, and the patterns of partisan and institutional interactions—I found the differences among and within presidencies to be striking. It simply was not possible to generalize across all postwar presidencies. The manifold determinants of the

[2]See selection 55.

president's strategic position assist in specifying his advantages for certifying and managing items on a continuous agenda, which may be oriented in strikingly different ways, and for participating in a lawmaking process that mostly takes place in another, independent branch of government.

I conclude that it is more important to make the separated system work well than to change systems. The preferred institutional interaction is that of balanced participation, with both branches actively involved in the policy process. The United States has the most intricate lawmaking system in the world. It will not be made better through simplification. Preponderance of one branch over the other should be a cause for concern, not celebration. Presidents are well advised to appreciate the advantages of the separated system and to define their role in it. Most do not have to be counseled on the legitimacy of Congress, but some do. Most know instinctively that their advantages are in certifying the agenda and persuading others to accept their proposals as a basis for compromise, but some have grander conceptions of presidential power. Most understand that they are temporary leaders of a convention of policy choice already in session, but some lack the skills to define the limits or realize the advantages of that status. Most realize that patience, persistence, and sharing are required for effective work in the separated system, but some are overly anxious to take immediate credit for change. And most grasp the purposes of a diffused-responsibility system of mixed representation and shared powers, but some believe that the president is the presidency, the presidency is the government, and ours is a presidential system. Those who believe these things may even have convinced themselves that they are right. They will be proven to be wrong.

❖❖ That divided government has a profound impact upon the presidency and its ability to meet popular expectations is made clear in the following selection. The presidency continues to be the focus of leadership, popular aspirations and expectations. The presidency is the only leadership beacon that shines in our constitutionally divided and pluralistic political system. More realist popular expectations and a better understanding of the presidency will come when people appreciate how the Constitution and political pluralism can strain presidential power just as they limit other political institutions.

44

Thomas Cronin

HOW MUCH IS HIS FAULT?

❖❖❖❖❖❖❖

"Americans pick a President every four years," said Adlai Stevenson, "and for the next four years we pick him apart." It didn't take long for us to begin picking Bill Clinton apart, and we are showing no signs of letting up. Why are we being so tough on him? And, for that matter, why have we been so tough on most all of our recent Presidents?

Midterm elections are rarely America's finest hour. The guns of the out-of-office party pound away at the President. Then he fires back. This is, of course, part of the tribal ritual in which the "outs" trash the "ins" and the "ins" retaliate by castigating the obstructionist opposition, the mean-spirited media and the selfish special interests who are depicted, of course, as all thwarting "progress"—progress, at least, as defined by those in the White House.

But this President-bashing of ours is, I think, about something more than "ins" and "outs." We beat up our Presidents because they invariably disappoint us. And they disappoint us precisely because we still hold exaggerated expectations of what Presidents might be able to achieve. While it is true that the mistakes and misdeeds of Vietnam, Watergate, Iran-contra and Whitewater have made us more skeptical about Presidents, we nevertheless continue to believe that the vitality of our constitutional democracy depends in large measure on creative Presidential leadership. The unwritten Presidential job description, the one we carry around in our heads, calls for a President to be a visionary problem-solver, a unifying force for the nation, a healer and sage. Thus, every four years we search anew for a fresh superstar who is blessed with the judgment of Washington, the brilliance of Jefferson, the genius of Lincoln, the political savvy of F.D.R. and the youthful grace of J.F.K. Expectations always rise. Yet an exaggerated sense of the possibilities of the perfect—or what I have called our notion of "the textbook President"—inevitably blind us to the limits of what a President can accomplish.

The novelist John Steinbeck put it as well as anyone when he wrote in the mid-1960's that "we give the President more work than a man can do, more responsibility than a man should take, more pressure than a man can bear. We abuse him often and rarely praise him. We wear him out, use him up, eat him up. . . . He is ours and we exercise the right to destroy him."

Clinton has most assuredly contributed to his own problems. He lacks discipline and focus. He vacillates and procrastinates. He tries to please everyone and he is a relentless spinmaster. His advisers don't inspire much confidence. He shoots himself in the foot. He plainly doesn't cultivate allies; he doesn't delegate enough; he doesn't laugh enough.

Yet Clinton has achieved more, both with regard to legislation and to foreign policy, than might have been expected of a President elected by 43 percent of the voters in a contest in which the electorate was voting Bush out, not embracing a Democratic platform. Clinton had virtually no mandate. Moreover, he came to office with more baggage—his draft board controversy, Gennifer Flowers and so on— than almost any President in modern times. He tries, justifiably, to claim credit for reducing the deficit, creating more jobs and overseeing the general recovery. Americans, however, are unwilling to give him much credit because they continue to fear the worst—inflation, reduced purchasing power, job loss. Then there is the challenge of charting an appealing and coherent foreign policy in the post-cold-war era. Clinton has had successes in the Middle East; he has been steady with regard to Russia; he won passage of Nafta. But to get to the White House, Clinton concluded he had to talk tougher than his opponents about Bosnia, Haiti and China. What served Clinton well in winning the White House, however, is often making it hard for him to exercise effective leadership as the President. This campaign tough talk haunts him—he has had to commit or waiver, and either way he's been hurt. With the cold war over, Americans are anxious and unsure about where and how they want their country to intervene.

Clinton gets a lot of unfavorable press. The media don't especially like or respect him. Reporters don't feel he levels with them, and members of the national press corps often felt Clinton did end runs around them in the 1992 campaign by going the talk-show route. But it is what Clinton hasn't done about his press relations that has probably hurt him most. He has not, despite his having tried several different press secretaries, chiefs of staff and P.R. handlers (like David Gergen), found anyone who speaks with authority for his Administration. (He gets precious little help from his Cabinet officers.) Moreover, there seems to be no one in the White House creatively capitalizing on good news, as there was in the Reagan and the Bush Administrations. For all the worrying about Clinton's image, there seems little effective effort to associate the President with achievement.

Clinton himself is an effective speaker and he would serve himself better if he had more J.F.K.-style news conferences. He has to counter the negative slant of most media stories by more effective use of the bully pulpit.

Although Clinton has doubtless created some of his own political problems, the larger ones are not of his making but of ours. In fact, all the heated midterm charges and countercharges mostly serve to distract us from appreciating certain enduring realities and fundamental characteristics of our relationship to political leadership.

Today, as ever, we tend to distrust Presidents because Presidents are a prime agent of the Federal Government. We don't like government much, and nowadays we dislike the Federal Government most of all. In times of popular war or dire economic crises, we can be aggressively led by a President, but generally we want a President to preside over and unify us. Further, we subject Presidents to many paradoxical and contradictory expectations—making it hard for a President to remain popular for sustained periods.

Let's face it: Americans are lousy followers. We admire power, yet fear it. We like to unload responsibilities on our leaders, yet we dislike being bossed around. We celebrate the individual and the idea that one person can make a difference, yet we inherently suspect those who have made it to the top—especially those at the top of large institutions.

Every President has to understand the fine line between providing strong, decisive leadership and infringing on the individual rights and liberties of the people. This ambivalence toward executive power is hardly new. The founders of the American Republic knew the new nation needed an office that could exercise leadership, yet they feared the development of a national leader who might incite the people and yield factious or demagogic government. So they wrote a Constitution that makes it possible but difficult for Presidents to exercise decisive leadership.

Alexis de Tocqueville said it well when he wrote that Americans sometimes yearn for leadership but that they also want to be free and left alone. Americans love their country and are highly patriotic. Yet we cherish individualism over collectivism and individual liberty over the rights of the state. We are a difficult people to lead in any predictable manner or direction.

One of the persisting paradoxes of the Presidency is that, on the one hand, it is always too powerful and, on the other, it is always too weak. It is too strong because in many ways it is contrary to our ideals of government by the people and decentralization of power. It is too weak because Presidents seldom are able to keep the promises they make (as on health care). And the Presidency is always too constrained when we believe a President is striving to serve the public interest—as we define it.

We want dynamic, charismatic leadership. "We need leaders of inspired idealism," Teddy Roosevelt wrote. "Leaders to whom are granted great visions, who dream greatly, and strive to make their dreams come true, who can kindle the people with the fire from their own burning souls." However, we also want Presidents to heed our view.

We expect our Presidents to provide bold innovative, programmatic leadership, but expect them, too, to respond pragmatically to public opinion majorities.

We may want a certain amount of visionary innovation, yet Americans routinely resist being led too far in any one direction. Lead us, we say, but also listen to us.

While we want a President who can unify us, the job of being President requires taking firm stands on issues that frequently divide us.

Every now and then, we want change, yet we also fear it. Charlie Brown in the Peanuts cartoon once said, "I have my strong opinions—but they don't last long." So American public opinion shifts—sometimes quickly.

The presidency will surely remain one of our nation's best sources for creative leadership. Indeed, a strong, effective President is a necessity if we are to make our system work. Hamiltonian energy in the Presidency is needed to make our Madisonian system of checks and balances work in such a way as to allow us to achieve those cherished Jeffersonian ends of liberty, freedom and social justice. The paradoxes of the Presidency do not lie in the White House so much as in our own feelings and exalted hopes. There continues to exist some element in the minds of Americans that it is possible to find a savior-hero who will deliver us to some promised land. And then when this pseudo-messiah fails us, we inflict upon him the wrath of our vengeance. It is almost a ritual purifying or savaging—we venerate the Presidency and the White House though we punish the President. Perhaps this is to be expected when we elevate flawed and very human politicians who lust after fame and glory to an office we fill with our hopes and our fears and about which we remain of so many minds.

Chapter 7

❖❖❖

THE BUREAUCRACY

American bureaucracy today is an important fourth branch of the government. Too frequently the administrative branch is lumped under the heading of the "Executive" and is considered to be subordinate to the president. But the following selections will reveal that the bureaucracy is often autonomous, acting outside of the control of Congress, the president, and even the judiciary. This fact raises an important problem for our constitutional democracy: How can the bureaucracy be kept responsible if it does not fit into the constitutional framework that was designed to guarantee limited and responsible government?

Constitutional Background

While the Constitution carefully outlined the responsibilities and powers of the president, Congress, and to a lesser extent the Supreme Court, it did not mention the bureaucracy. The position of the bureaucracy in the separation-of-powers scheme developed by custom and statutory law rather than by explicit constitutional provisions. The following selection makes it clear that, although the Constitution did not provide for an administrative branch, it did have a bearing upon the development of the bureaucracy. Perhaps the most important result of constitutional democracy is that the administrative agencies have become pawns in the constant power struggle between the president and Congress.

45

Peter Woll

CONSTITUTIONAL DEMOCRACY AND BUREAUCRATIC POWER

❖❖❖❖❖❖❖

The administrative branch today stands at the very center of our governmental process; it is the keystone of the structure. And administrative agencies exercise legislative and judicial as well as executive functions—a fact that is often overlooked. . . .

How should we view American bureaucracy? Ultimately, the power of government comes to rest in the administrative branch. Agencies are given the responsibility of making concrete decisions carrying out vague policy initiated in Congress or by the president. The agencies can offer expert advice, closely attuned to the most interested pressure groups, and they often not only determine the policies that the legislature and executive recommend in the first place, but also decisively affect the policy-making process. Usually it is felt that the bureaucracy is politically "neutral," completely under the domination of the president, Congress, or the courts. We will see that this is not entirely the case, and that the president and Congress have only sporadic control over the administrative process.

The bureaucracy is a semi-autonomous branch of the government, often dominating Congress, exercising strong influence on the president, and only infrequently subject to review by the courts. If our constitutional democracy is to be fully analyzed, we must focus attention upon the administrative branch. What is the nature of public administration? How are administration and politics intertwined? How are administrative constituencies determined? What is the relationship between agencies and their constituencies? What role should the president assume in relation to the administrative branch? How far should Congress go in controlling agencies which in fact tend to dominate the legislative process? Should judicial review be expanded? What are the conditions of judicial review? How do administrative agencies perform judicial functions, and how do these activities affect the ability of courts to oversee their actions? These questions confront us with what is called the problem of administrative responsibility: that is, how can we control the activities of the administrative branch? In order to approach an understanding of this difficult problem, it is necessary to appreciate the nature of the administrative process and how it interacts with other branches of the government and with the general public. It is also important to understand the nature of our constitutional system, and the political context within which agencies function.

We operate within the framework of a constitutional democracy. This means, first, that the government is to be limited by the separation of powers and Bill of Rights. Another component of the system, federalism, is designed in theory to provide states with a certain amount of authority when it is not implied at the national level. Our separation of powers, the system of checks and balances, and the federal system help to explain some of the differences between administrative organization here and in other countries. But the Constitution does not explicitly provide for the administrative branch, which has become a new fourth branch of government. This raises the question of how to control the bureaucracy when there are no clear constitutional limits upon it. The second aspect of our system, democracy, is of course implied in the Constitution itself, but has expanded greatly since it was adopted. We are confronted, very broadly speaking, first with the problem of constitutional limitation, and secondly with the problem of democratic participation in the activities of the bureaucracy. The bureaucracy must be accommodated within the framework of our system of constitutional democracy. This is the crux of the problem of administrative responsibility.

Even though the Constitution does not explicitly provide for the bureaucracy, it has had a profound impact upon the structure, functions, and general place that the bureaucracy occupies in government. The administrative process was incorporated into the constitutional system under the heading of "The Executive Branch." But the concept of "administration" at the time of the adoption of the Constitution was a very simple one, involving the "mere execution" of "executive details," to use the phrases of Hamilton in *The Federalist*. The idea, at that time, was simply that the president as Chief Executive would be able to control the Executive Branch in carrying out the mandates of Congress. In *Federalist 72*, after defining administration in this very narrow way, Hamilton stated:

> . . . The persons, therefore, to whose immediate management the different administrative matters are committed ought to be considered as Assistants or Deputies of the Chief Magistrate, and on this account, they ought to derive their offices from his appointment, at least from his nomination, and ought to be subject to his superintendence.

It was clear that Hamilton felt the president would be responsible for administrative action as long as he was in office. This fact later turned up in what can be called the "presidential supremacy" school of thought, which held and still holds that the president is *constitutionally* responsible for the administrative branch, and that Congress should delegate to him all necessary authority for this purpose. Nevertheless, whatever the framers of the Constitution might have planned if they could have foreseen the nature of bureaucratic development, the fact is that the system they constructed in many ways supported bureaucratic organization and functions independent of the president. The role they assigned to Congress in relation to administration assured this result, as did the general position of Congress in the governmental system as a check or balance to the power of the president. Congress has a great deal of authority over the administrative process.

If we compare the power of Congress and the president over the bureaucracy it becomes clear that they both have important constitutional responsibility. Congress retains primary control over the organization of the bureaucracy. It alone creates and destroys agencies, and determines whether they are to be located within the executive branch or outside it. This has enabled Congress to create a large number of *independent* agencies beyond presidential control. Congress has the authority to control appropriations and may thus exercise a great deal of power over the administrative arm, although increasingly the Bureau of the Budget and the president have the initial, and more often than not the final say over the budget. Congress also has the authority to define the jurisdiction of agencies. Finally, the Constitution gives to the legislature the power to interfere in high level presidential appointments, which must be "by and with the advice and consent of the Senate."

Congress may extend the sharing of the appointive power when it sets up new agencies. It may delegate to the president pervasive authority to control the bureaucracy. But one of the most important elements of the separation of power is the electoral system, which gives to Congress a constituency which is different from and even conflicting with that of the president. This means that Congress often decides to set up agencies beyond presidential purview. Only rarely will it grant the president any kind of final authority to structure the bureaucracy. During World War II, on the basis of the War Powers Act, the president had the authority to reorganize the administrative branch. Today he has the same authority, provided that Congress does not veto presidential proposals within a certain time limit. In refusing to give the president permanent reorganization authority, Congress is jealously guarding one of its important prerogatives.

Turning to the constitutional authority of the president over the bureaucracy, it is somewhat puzzling to see that it gives him a relatively small role. He appoints certain officials by and with the advice and consent of the Senate. He has directive power over agencies that are placed within his jurisdiction by Congress. His control over patronage, once so important, has diminished sharply under the merit system. The president is Commander-in-Chief of all military forces, which puts him in a controlling position over the Defense Department and agencies involved in military matters. In the area of international relations, the president is by constitutional authority the "Chief Diplomat," to use [presidential scholar Clinton] Rossiter's phrase. This means that he appoints Ambassadors (by and with the advice and consent of the Senate), and generally directs national activities in the international arena—a crucially important executive function. But regardless of the apparent intentions of some of the framers of the Constitution as expressed by Hamilton in *The Federalist*, and in spite of the predominance of the presidency in military and foreign affairs, the fact remains that we seek in vain for explicit constitutional authorization for the president to be "Chief Administrator."

This is not to say that the president does not have an important responsibility to act as chief of the bureaucracy, merely that there is no constitutional mandate for this. As our system evolved, the president was given more and more responsibility until he became, in practice, Chief Administrator. At the same time the constitutional system has often impeded progress in this direction. The president's Committee on Administrative Management in 1937, and later the Hoover Commissions of 1949 and 1955, called upon Congress to initiate a series of reforms increasing presidential authority over the administrative branch. It was felt that this was necessary to make democracy work. The president is the only official elected nationally, and if the administration is to be held democratically accountable, he alone can stand as its representative. But meaningful control from the White House requires that the president have a comprehensive program which encompasses the activities of the bureaucracy. He must be informed as to what they are doing, and be able to control them. He must understand the complex responsibilities of the bureaucracy. Moreover, he must be able to call on sufficient political support to balance the support which the agencies draw from private clientele groups and congressional committees. This has frequently proven a difficult and often impossible task for the president. He may have the *authority* to control the bureaucracy in many areas, but not enough power.

On the basis of the Constitution, Congress feels it quite proper that when it delegates legislative authority to administrative agencies it can relatively often place these groups outside the control of the president. For example, in the case of the Interstate Commerce Commission . . . Congress has delegated final authority to that agency to control railroad mergers and other aspects of transportation activity, without giving the president the right to veto. The president may feel that a particular merger is undesirable because it is in violation of the antitrust laws, but the Interstate Commerce Commission is likely to feel differently. In such a situation, the president can do nothing because he does not have the *legal authority* to take any action. If he could muster enough political support to exercise influence over the ICC, he would be able to control it, but the absence of legal authority is an important factor in such cases and diminishes presidential power. Moreover, the ICC draws strong support from the railroad industry, which has been able to counterbalance the political support possessed by the president and other groups that have wished to control it. Analogous situations exist with respect to other regulatory agencies.

Besides the problem of congressional and presidential control over the bureaucracy, there is the question of judicial review of administrative decisions. The rule of law is a central element in our Constitution. The rule of law means that decisions judicial in nature should be handled by common law courts, because of their expertise in rendering due process of law. When administrative agencies engage in adjudication their decisions should be subject to judicial review—at least, they should if one supports the idea of the supremacy of law. Judicial decisions are supposed to be rendered on an independent and impartial basis, through the use of tested procedures, in order to arrive at the accurate determination of the truth. Administrative adjudication should not be subject to presidential or congressional control, which would mean political determination of decisions that should be rendered in an objective manner. The idea of the rule of law, derived from the common law and adopted within the framework of our constitutional system, in theory limits legislative and executive control over the bureaucracy.

The nature of our constitutional system poses very serious difficulties to the development of a system of administrative responsibility. The Constitution postulates that the functions of government must be separated into different branches with differing constituencies and separate authority. The idea is that the departments should oppose each other, thereby preventing the arbitrary exercise of political power. Any combination of functions was considered to lead inevitably to arbitrary government. This is a debatable point, but the result of the Constitution is quite clear. The administrative process, on the other hand, often combines various functions of government in the same hands. Attempts are made, of course, to separate those who exercise the judicial functions from those in the prosecuting arms of the agencies. But the fact remains that there is a far greater combination of functions in the administrative process than can be accommodated by strict adherence to the Constitution.

It has often been proposed, as a means of alleviating what may be considered the bad effects of combined powers in administrative agencies, to draw a line of control from the original branches of the government to those parts of the bureaucracy exercising similar functions. Congress would control the legislative activities of the agencies, the president the executive aspects, and the courts the judicial functions. This would maintain the symmetry of the constitutional system. But this solution is not feasible, because other parts of the Constitution, giving different authority to these three branches, make symmetrical control of this kind almost impossible. The three branches of the government are not willing to give up whatever powers they may have over administrative agencies. For example, Congress is not willing to give the president complete control over all executive functions, nor to give the courts the authority to review all the decisions of the agencies. At present, judicial review takes place only if Congress authorizes it, except in those rare instances where constitutional issues are involved.

Another aspect of the problem of control is reflected in the apparent paradox that the three branches do not always use to the fullest extent their authority to regulate the bureaucracy, even though they wish to retain their power to do so. The courts, for example, have exercised considerable self-restraint in their review of administrative decisions. They are not willing to use all their power over the bureaucracy. Similarly, both Congress and the president will often limit their dealings with the administrative branch for political and practical reasons.

In the final analysis, we are left with a bureaucratic system that has been fragmented by the Constitution, and in which administrative discretion is inevitable. The bureaucracy reflects the general fragmentation of our political system. It is often the battleground for the three branches of government, and for outside pressure groups which seek to control it for their own purposes.

❖❖ The Political Roots and Consequences of Bureaucracy

With the exception of those executive departments that all governments need, such as State, Treasury, and Defense, *private*-sector political demands have led to the creation of American bureaucracy. In response to those demands, Congress has over the years created more and more executive departments and agencies to solve economic, political, and social problems. It is important to realize that the bureaucracy is not, as many of its critics have suggested, a conspiracy by government officials to increase their power. The following selection traces the rise of the administrative state and particularly notes how political pluralism has affected the character of the bureaucracy by dividing it into clientele sectors.

46

James Q. Wilson

THE RISE OF THE BUREAUCRATIC STATE

During its first 150 years, the American republic was not thought to have "bureaucracy," and thus it would have been meaningless to refer to the "problems" of a "bureaucratic state." There were, of course, appointed civilian officials: Though only about 3,000 at the end of the Federalist period, there were about 95,000 by the time Grover Cleveland assumed office in 1881, and nearly half a million by 1925. Some aspects of these numerous officials were regarded as problems—notably, the standard by which they were appointed and the political loyalties to which they were held—but these were thought to be matters of proper character and good management. The great political and constitutional struggles were not over the power of the administrative apparatus, but over the power of the President, of Congress, and of the states.

The Founding Fathers had little to say about the nature or function of the executive branch of the new government. The Constitution is virtually silent on the subject and the debates in the Constitutional Convention are almost devoid of reference to an administrative apparatus. This reflected no lack of concern about the matter, however. Indeed, it was in part because of the Founders' depressing experience with chaotic and inefficient management under the Continental Congress and the Articles of Confederation that they had assembled in Philadelphia. Management by committees composed of part-time amateurs had cost the colonies

Reprinted with permission of the author from *The Public Interest*, No. 41 (Fall 1975).

dearly in the War of Independence and few, if any, of the Founders wished to return to that system. The argument was only over how the heads of the necessary departments of government were to be selected, and whether these heads should be wholly subordinate to the President or whether instead they should form some sort of council that would advise the President and perhaps share in his authority. In the end, the Founders left it up to Congress to decide the matter.

There was no dispute in Congress that there should be executive departments, headed by single appointed officials, and, of course, the Constitution specified that these would be appointed by the President with the advice and consent of the Senate. The only issue was how such officials might be removed. After prolonged debate and by the narrowest of majorities, Congress agreed that the President should have the sole right of removal, thus confirming that the infant administrative system would be wholly subordinate—in law at least—to the President. Had not Vice-President John Adams, presiding over a Senate equally divided on the issue, cast the deciding vote in favor of presidential removal, the administrative departments might conceivably have become legal dependencies of the legislature, with incalculable consequences for the development of the embryonic government.

The "Bureaucracy Problem"

The original departments were small and had limited duties. The State Department, the first to be created, had but nine employees in addition to the Secretary. The War Department did not reach 80 civilian employees until 1801; it commanded only a few thousand soldiers. Only the Treasury Department had substantial powers—it collected taxes, managed the public debt, ran the national bank, conducted land surveys, and purchased military supplies. Because of this, Congress gave the closest scrutiny to its structure and its activities.

The number of administrative agencies and employees grew slowly but steadily during the 19th and early 20th centuries and then increased explosively on the occasion of World War I, the Depression, and World War II. It is difficult to say at what point in this process the administrative system became a distinct locus of power or an independent source of political initiatives and problems. What is clear is that the emphasis on the sheer *size* of the administrative establishment—conventional in many treatments of the subject—is misleading.

The government can spend vast sums of money—wisely or unwisely—without creating that set of conditions we ordinarily associate with the bureaucratic state. For example, there could be massive transfer payments made under government auspices from person to person or from state to state, all managed by a comparatively small staff of officials and a few large computers. In 1971, the federal government paid out $54 billion under various social insurance programs, yet the Social Security Administration employs only 73,000 persons, many of whom perform purely routine jobs.

And though it may be harder to believe, the government could in principle employ an army of civilian personnel without giving rise to those organizational patterns that we call bureaucratic. Suppose, for instance, that we as a nation should decide to have in the public schools at least one teacher for every two students. This would require a vast increase in the number of teachers and schoolrooms, but almost all of the persons added would be performing more or less identical tasks, and they could be organized into very small units (e.g., neighborhood schools). Though there would be significant overhead costs, most citizens would not be aware of any increase in the "bureaucratic" aspects of education—indeed, owing to the much greater time each teacher would have to devote to each pupil and his or her parents, the citizenry might well conclude that there actually had been a substantial reduction in the amount of "bureaucracy."

To the reader predisposed to believe that we have a "bureaucracy problem," these hypothetical cases may seem farfetched. Max Weber, after all, warned us that in capitalist and socialist societies alike, bureaucracy was likely to acquire an "overtowering" power position. Conservatives have always feared bureaucracy, save perhaps the police. Humane socialists have frequently been embarrassed by their inability to reconcile a desire for public control of the economy with the suspicion that a public bureaucracy may be as immune to democratic control as a private one. Liberals have equivocated, either dismissing any concern for bureaucracy as reactionary quibbling about social progress or embracing that concern when obviously nonreactionary persons (welfare recipients, for example) express a view toward the Department of health and Human Services indistinguishable from the view businessmen take of the Internal Revenue Service.

Political Authority

There are at least three ways in which political power may be gathered undesirably into bureaucratic hands: by the growth of an administrative apparatus so large as to be immune from popular control, by placing power over a governmental bureaucracy of any size in private rather than public hands, or by vesting discretionary authority in the hands of a public agency so that the exercise of that power is not responsive to the public good. These are not the only problems that arise because of bureaucratic organization. From the point of view of their members, bureaucracies are sometimes uncaring, ponderous, or unfair; from the point of view of their political superiors, they are sometimes unimaginative or inefficient; from the point of view of their clients, they are sometimes slow or unjust. No single account can possibly treat of all that is problematic in bureaucracy; even the part I discuss here—the extent to which political authority has been transferred undesirably to an unaccountable administrative realm—is itself too large for a single essay. But it is, if not the most important problem, then surely the one that would most have troubled our Revolutionary leaders, especially those that went on to produce the Constitution. It was, after all, the question of power that chiefly concerned them, both in redefining our relationship with England and in finding a new basis for political authority in the Colonies.

To some, following in the tradition of [Max] Weber, bureaucracy is the inevitable consequence and perhaps necessary concomitant of modernity. A money economy, the division of labor, and the evolution of legal-rational norms to justify organizational authority require the efficient adaptation of means to ends and a high degree of predictability in the behavior of rulers. To this, Georg Simmel added the view that organizations tend to acquire the characteristics of those institutions with which they are in conflict, so that as government becomes more bureaucratic, private organizations—political parties, trade unions, voluntary associations—will have an additional reason to become bureaucratic as well.

By viewing bureaucracy as an inevitable (or, as some would put it, "functional") aspect of society, we find ourselves attracted to theories that explain the growth of bureaucracy in terms of some inner dynamic to which all agencies respond and which makes all barely governable and scarcely tolerable. Bureaucracies grow, we are told, because of Parkinson's Law: Work and personnel expand to consume the available resources. Bureaucracies behave, we believe, in accord with various other maxims, such as the Peter Principle: In hierarchical organizations, personnel are promoted up to that point at which their incompetence becomes manifest—hence, all important positions are held by incompetents. More elegant, if not essentially different, theories have been propounded by scholars. The tendency of all bureaus to expand is explained by William A. Niskanen by the assumption, derived from the theory of the firm, that "bureaucrats maximize the total budget of their bureau during their tenure"—hence, "all bureaus are too large." What keeps them from being not merely too large but all-consuming is that fact that a bureau must deliver to some degree on its promised output, and if it consistently underdelivers, its budget will be cut by unhappy legislators. But since measuring the output of a bureau is often difficult—indeed, even *conceptualizing* the output of the State Department is mind-boggling—the bureau has a great deal of freedom within which to seek the largest possible budget.

Such theories, both the popular and the scholarly, assign little importance to the nature of the tasks an agency performs, the constitutional framework in which it is embedded, or the preferences and attitudes of citizens and legislators. Our approach will be quite different: Different agencies will be examined in historical perspective to discover the kinds of problems—if any, to which their operations give rise, and how those problems were affected—perhaps determined—by the tasks which they were assigned, the political system in which they operated, and the preferences they were required to consult. What follows will be far from a systematic treatment of such matters, and even farther from a rigorous testing of any theory of bureaucratization. Our knowledge of agency history and behavior is too sketchy to permit that.

Bureaucracy and Size

During the first half of the 19th century, the growth in the size of the federal bureaucracy can be explained, not by the assumption of new tasks by the government or by the imperialistic designs of the managers of existing tasks, but by the addition to existing bureaus of personnel performing essentially routine, repetitive tasks for which the public demand was great and unavoidable. The principal problem facing a bureaucracy thus enlarged was how best to coordinate its activities toward given and noncontroversial ends.

The increase in the size of the executive branch of the federal government at this time was almost entirely the result of the increase in the size of the Post Office.

From 1816 to 1861, federal civilian employment in the executive branch increased nearly eightfold (from 4,837 to 36,672), but 86 percent of this growth was the result of additions to the postal service. The Post Office Department was expanding as population and commerce expanded. By 1869 there were 27,000 post offices scattered around the nation; by 1901, nearly 77,000. In New York alone, by 1894 there were nearly 3,000 postal employees, the same number required to run the entire federal government at the beginning of that century. . . .

The Military Establishment

Not all large bureaucracies grow in response to demands for service. The Department of Defense, since 1941 the largest employer of federal civilian officials, has become, as the governmental keystone of the "military-industrial complex," the very archetype of an administrative entity that is thought to be so vast and so well-entrenched that it can virtually ignore the political branches of government, growing and even acting on the basis of its own inner imperatives. . . .

A "Military-Industrial Complex"?

The argument for the existence of an autonomous, bureaucratically led military-industrial complex is supported primarily by events since 1950. Not only has the United States assumed during this period worldwide commitments that necessitate a larger military establishment, but the advent of new, high-technology weapons has created a vast industrial machine with an interest in sustaining a high level of military expenditures, especially on weapons research, development, and acquisition. This machine, so the argument goes, is allied with the Pentagon in ways that dominate the political officials nominally in charge of the armed forces. There is some truth in all this. We have become a world military force, though that decision was made by elected officials in 1949–1950 and not dictated by a (then nonexistent) military-industrial complex. High-cost, high-technology weapons have become important and a number of industrial concerns will prosper or perish depending on how contracts for those weapons are let. The development and purchase of weapons is sometimes made in a wasteful, even irrational, manner. And the allocation of funds among the several armed services is often dictated as much by inter-service rivalry as by strategic or political decisions. . . .

Bureaucracy and Clientelism

After 1861, the growth in the federal administrative system could no longer be explained primarily by an expansion of the postal service and other traditional bureaus. Though these continued to expand, new departments were added that reflected a new (or at least greater) emphasis on the enlargement of the scope of government. Between 1861 and 1901, over 200,000 civilian employees were added to the federal service, only 52 percent of whom were postal workers. Some of these, of course, staffed a larger military and naval establishment stimulated by the Civil War and the Spanish-American War. By 1901 there were over 44,000 civilian defense employees, mostly workers in government-owned arsenals and shipyards. But even those could account for less than one fourth of the increase in employment during the preceding 40 years.

What was striking about the period after 1861 was that the government began to give formal, bureaucratic recognition to the emergence of distinctive interest in a diversifying economy. As Richard L. Schott has written, "whereas earlier federal departments had been formed around specialized governmental functions (foreign affairs, war, finance, and the like), the new departments of this period—Agriculture, Labor, and Commerce—were devoted to the interests and aspirations of particular economic groups."

The original purpose behind these clientele-oriented departments was neither to subsidize nor to regulate, but to promote, chiefly by gathering and publishing statistics and (especially in the case of agriculture) by research. . . .

Public Power and Private Interests

. . . The New Deal was perhaps the high water mark of at least the theory of bureaucratic clientelism. Not only did various sectors of society, notably agriculture, begin receiving massive subsidies, but the government proposed, through the National Industry Recovery Act (NRA), to cloak with public power a vast number of industrial groupings and trade associations so that they might control production and prices in ways that would end the depression. The NRA's Blue Eagle fell before the Supreme Court—the wholesale delegation of public power to private interests was declared unconstitutional. But the piecemeal delegation was not, as the continued growth of specialized promotional agencies attests. The Civil Aeronautics Board, for example, erroneously thought to be exclusively a regulatory agency, was formed in 1938 "to promote" as well as regulate civil aviation and it has done so by restricting entry and maintaining above-market rate fares.

Agriculture, of course, provides the leading case of clientelism. Theodore J. Lowi finds "at least 10 separate, autonomous, local self-governing systems" located in or closely associated with the Department of Agriculture that control to some significant degree the flow of billions of dollars in expenditures and loans. Local committees of farmers, private farm organizations, agency heads, and committee chairmen in Congress dominate policymaking in this area—not, perhaps, to the exclusion of the concerns of other publics, but certainly in ways not powerfully constrained by them.

"Cooperative Federalism"

The growing edge of client-oriented bureaucracy can be found, however, not in government relations with private groups, but in the relations among governmental units. In dollar volume, the chief clients of federal domestic expenditures are state and local government agencies. . . .

The degree to which such grants, and the federal agencies that administer them, constrain or even direct state and local bureaucracies is a matter of dispute. No general answer can be given—federal support of welfare programs has left considerable discretion in the hands of the states over the size of benefits and some discretion over eligibility rules, whereas federal support of highway construction carries with it specific requirements as to design, safety, and (since 1968) environmental and social impact.

A few generalizations are possible, however. The first is that the states and not the cities have been from the first, and remain today, the principal client group for grants-in-aid. It was not until the Housing Act of 1937 that money was given in any substantial amount directly to local governments and though many additional programs of this kind were later added, as late as 1970 less than 12 percent of all federal aid went directly to cities and towns. The second general observation is that the 1960s mark a major watershed in the way in which the purposes of federal aid are determined. Before that time, most grants were for purposes initially defined by states—to build highways and airports, to fund unemployment insurance programs, and the like. Beginning in the 1960s, the federal government, at the initiative of the President and his advisors, increasingly came to define the purposes of these grants—not necessarily over the objection of the states, but often without any initiative from them. Federal money was to be spent on poverty, ecology, planning, and other "national" goals for which, until the laws were passed, there were few, if any, well-organized and influential constituencies. Whereas federal money was once spent in response to the claims of distinct and organized clients, public or private, in the contemporary period federal money has increasingly been spent in ways that have *created* such clients.

And once rewarded or created, they are rarely penalized or abolished. . . .

Self-Perpetuating Agencies

If the Founding Fathers were to return to examine bureaucratic clientelism, they would, I suspect, be deeply discouraged. James Madison clearly foresaw that American society would be "broken into many parts, interests and classes of citizens" and that this "multiplicity of interest" would help ensure against "the tyranny of the majority," especially in a federal regime with separate branches of government. Positive action would require a "coalition of a majority"; in the process of forming this coalition, the rights of all would be protected, not merely by self-interested bargains, but because in a free society such a coalition "could seldom take place on any other principles than those of justice and the general good." To those who wrongly believed that Madison thought of men as acting only out of base motives, the phrase is instructive: Persuading men who disagree to compromise their differences can rarely be achieved solely by the parceling out of relative advantage; the belief is also required that what is being agreed to is right, proper, and defensible before public opinion.

Most of the major new social programs of the United States, whether for the good of the few or the many, were initially adopted by broad coalitions appealing to general standards of justice or to conceptions of the public weal. This is certainly the case with most of the New Deal legislation—notably such programs as Social

Security—and with most Great Society legislation—notably Medicare and aid to education; it was also conspicuously the case with respect to post–Great Society legislation pertaining to consumer and environmental concerns. State occupational licensing laws were supported by majorities instead in, among other things, the contribution of these statutes to public safety and health.

But when a program supplies particular benefits to an existing or newly created interest, public or private, it creates a set of political relationships that make exceptionally difficult further alteration of that program by coalitions of the majority. What was created in the name of the common good is sustained in the name of the particular interest. Bureaucratic clientelism becomes self-perpetuating, in the absence of some crisis or scandal, because a single interest group to which the program matters greatly is highly motivated and well-situated to ward off the criticisms of other groups that have a broad but weak interest in the policy.

In short, a regime of separated powers makes it difficult to overcome objections and contrary interests sufficiently to permit the enactment of a new program or the creation of a new agency. Unless the legislation can be made to pass either with little notice or at a time of crisis or extraordinary majorities—and sometimes even then—the initiation of new programs requires public interest arguments. But the same regime works to protect agencies, once created, from unwelcome change because a major change is, in effect, new legislation that must overcome the same hurdles as the original law, but this time with one of the hurdles—the wishes of the agency and its client—raised much higher. As a result, the Madisonian system makes it relatively easy for the delegation of public power to private groups to go unchallenged and, therefore, for factional interests that have acquired a supportive public bureaucracy to rule without submitting their interests to the effective scrutiny and modification of other interests. . . .

❖❖ THE COURTS AND ADMINISTRATIVE AGENCIES

Congress makes the courts important, and potentially dominant, actors in the administrative process by providing for judicial review of agency decisions. Judicial review is not automatic, nor does it extend to vast decision-making areas of the bureaucracy that both Congress and the courts define as discretionary. Judicial review primarily operates in the regulatory sphere, where agencies through rule-making and adjudication determine individual rights and obligations under regulatory statutes.

Congress provides for judicial review both in the enabling statutes of regulatory and other agencies, and in the Administrative Procedure Act of 1946 (APA), which pertains to all agencies. Under the APA, private parties injured or aggrieved by agency action may seek judicial review. The courts grant review to cases that meet the appropriate constitutional "case and controversy" requirements, provided the challenged agency action is not exempt from judicial review. On acceptance of a case, the reviewing court decides such questions as whether the agency has acted within its statutory authority and followed required procedures that protect individual rights and interests.

The following selection assesses the impact judicial review has had on agency decision making.

47

R. Shep Melnick

ADMINISTRATIVE LAW AND BUREAUCRATIC REALITY

❖❖❖❖❖❖❖

From the perspective of a political scientist, what is both puzzling and exasperating about the literature on administrative law is how little it has to say about administrators and administration. Administrative law in the United States is almost entirely about *courts*. Articles abound on judicial doctrines relating to scope of review and rulemaking procedures. But no one pays much attention to the tasks performed by administrators, the agency's sense of mission, the conflicting pressures placed on it, or even what happens after judges hand down their decisions.

Others have noticed this lacuna. In a review contribution to this Review, Peter Schuck and Donald Elliott wrote,

> Although the study of administrative law started in earnest more than fifty years ago, we still know little about what is perhaps the central question in that field: how does judicial review *actually* affect agency decisionmaking? This question goes to the fundamental nature and quality of the modern administrative state, yet academic specialists have largely neglected it; the subject remains a matter for uniformed speculation. Despite (or perhaps because of) the lack of data, strong opinions on this question are common.

One such strongly held (but unsubstantiated) opinion is that without "searching and thorough" judicial review, bureaucrats would be running wild, issuing arbitrary and capricious orders with utter abandon. Another view is that without such judicial review agencies would be in the hip pocket of "special interests," captured, we are always told, "by the very interests they are supposed to control." It is bad enough that these two views are incompatible. What is worse is that usually they are both wrong.

Judges' images of the administrative process are of the utmost importance because the central issue in administrative law is the extent to which judges should defer to administrative judgment and expertise. Judges are unlikely to defer to administrators they do not trust—regardless of what the Supreme Court said in *Chevron* v. *NRDC*. It is time administrative law spent less time dissecting the words of judges and more time observing the activities of bureaucrats.

"Administrative Law and Bureaucratic Reality," by R. Shep Melnick, *Administrative Law Review*, Vol. 44, No. 2, 1992, pp. 245–259. Reprinted by permission of the American Bar Association and the author.

In recent years a small group of scholars have taken a closer look at how court decisions have reshaped administrative agencies and their policies. The purpose of this article is to acquaint students of administrative law with some of these findings. As will soon become clear, most of these studies show that judicial intervention has had an unfortunate effect on policymaking. Judicial review has subjected agencies to debilitating delay and uncertainty. Courts have heaped new tasks on agencies while decreasing their ability to perform any of them. They have forced agencies to substitute trivial pursuits for important ones. And they have discouraged administrators from taking responsibility for their actions and for educating the public.

To those who suspect that these findings reflect either the biases of the author or the peculiarities of the cases chosen for close analysis, I offer the following challenge: provide us with detailed studies of cases in which the courts have improved policymaking. There surely must be some. Unsupported assertions about the malevolence of bureaucrats and the good will of judges do not constitute a convincing reply to these empirical studies.

Rulemaking

Let me start with the most obvious problem, rulemaking delay. In the late 1970s William H. Rodgers, Jr. summed up the conventional wisdom about aggressive judicial review of agency rulemaking by saying, "The hard look doctrine plays no favorites; it is advanced as enthusiastically by industry as it is by environmentalists. Its acceptance is deep." Ten years later many people are having second thoughts.

In retrospect, what happened is quite clear. The courts said, consider all the "relevant" evidence, respond to all "significant" comments, and weigh all "reasonable" alternatives. Who could object to that? The problem was that judges failed to explain what they meant by "relevant," "significant," and "reasonable." Like pornography, they knew it only after they saw it. Since agencies do not like losing big court cases, they reacted defensively, accumulating more and more information, responding to all comments, and covering all their bets. The rulemaking record grew enormously, far beyond any judge's ability to review it. As a result, it took longer and longer to complete the rulemaking process. Richard Pierce reports that "the time required to make policy through rulemaking has been stretched to nearly a decade." In some instances the final rules appeared just as the underlying problem had disappeared or changed fundamentally.

Thus began a vicious cycle: the more effort agencies put into rulemaking, the more they feared losing, and the more defensive rulemaking became. Even then, they lost a significant number of cases—it was just too hard to predict what a randomly selected panel of judges would do. Draw two Reagan appointees on a three-judge panel and you might well lose because you regulated too much; draw two Carter appointees, you might lose because you regulated too little. Little wonder that many agencies looked for ways to avoid the rulemaking quagmire. Some agencies decided it would be easier to use adjudication to establish agency policy. Others set policy through interpretive rulings or internal enforcement policies. So instead of more rules, we have more discretion; instead of uniformity, we have particularism. Just as water runs downhill, agencies run away from uncertainty, which is what the judicial review often represented.

Jerry Mashaw and David Harfst's recent book presents a particularly graphic example of how a federal agency has responded to "hard look" judicial review by virtually abandoning rulemaking. After the courts rejected its first set of safety rules, the National Highway Traffic Safety Administration replaced rulemaking with a recall strategy. Decisions of other federal courts made this strategy easy to pursue. The only problem was that recalls do little to improve auto safety. In a similar vein, Richard Pierce has shown that the courts made it impossible for the Federal Energy Regulatory Agency to use rulemaking to revise seriously deficient policies on regulation of natural gas.

This does not mean that agencies never engage in rulemaking or win in court. What do we know about the effects of judicial review for the substance of the rules that are issued? In the area of health and safety standards both my research and the work of John Mendeloff indicate that judicial review has decreased the *number* of standards but increased their *stringency*. Why? Because at the same time that industry is challenging an agency's evidence, public interest groups are charging that the agency has not sufficiently protected the public health.

Judges on key courts have often insisted that EPA and some other agencies take a "health only" approach to standard-setting, especially when a carcinogen is involved. In *Lead Industries Ass'n. v. EPA*, for example, Judge Skelly Wright announced that the legislative history of the Clean Air Act "shows [that] the Administrator may not consider economic or technological feasibility in setting air quality standards." In another decision involving standards for airborne lead, Judge Wright hearkened back to Judge Bazelon's famous claim about the "special judicial interest in favor of protection of the health and welfare of people."

The courts have hardly been consistent on this. The Supreme Court's rulings on OSHA's statutory mandate are far from doctrinaire—in fact they are incoherent. For many years the Supreme Court's inability to speak clearly on such matters left the lower courts—especially the D.C. Circuit—in control. The D.C. Circuit now appears to be pulling back from its previous absolutist position, but in the 1970s and 1980s the message EPA and other agencies often got was this: If you want a standard to survive, collect lots of information, make the rule very stringent, and then use enforcement discretion to avoid the politically dangerous consequences of this stringency. With so few standards being set, environmentalists insisted that the ones that survived were really tough. Seeing these stringent regulations coming down the pike, business fought them tooth and nail, adding to delay.

Mendeloff convincingly argues that this peculiar combination of underregulation and overregulation leads us to get far less safety bang for the buck than European nations, which set more standards, but make them individually more lenient. The courts do not bear sole responsibility for this costly adversarial system, but they surely add to the problem. How is it possible to arrange a grand compromise—more standards for less stringency—if any trade association or environmental group can challenge it in court and have a shot at winning? How is it possible to encourage open horse-trading when the courts are insisting upon "rational" decisionmaking based on the accumulation of enormous amounts of technical information?

Action-Forcing Litigation

Many of the statutes passed by Congress in the 1970s and 1980s were filled with so-called nondiscretionary duties: deadlines, "hammers," and the like. A 1985 study co-authored by the Environmental Law Institute and the Environmental and Energy Study Institute reports that EPA alone was subject to 328 statutory deadlines. Among the other findings of this study were the following:

1. "Very few statutory deadlines (14 percent) have been met."
2. "Congress imposes more deadlines on EPA than it can possibly meet."
3. "Court-ordered deadlines almost always command top management attention at EPA. Top management takes the threat of contempt quite seriously and personally, even though the threat is not real."
4. "The multiplicity of deadlines reduces EPA's ability to assign priority to anything not subject to a deadline."

What this means is that scores of deadlines and other statutory requirements are lying around, usually unused, but still potential weapons in lawsuits—or threatened lawsuits. Do nondiscretionary duties and court enforcement produce "the rule of law"? Of course not; they produce the rule of those who decide which lawsuits to bring. Or, to put it another way, it transfers responsibility for setting agency priority from top administrators to interest groups, some of which use attorneys' fees won in these relatively easy cases to cross-subsidize other activities. It is hard to imagine a worse way to apportion agency resources.

The study cited above asked former EPA administrators what they thought of deadlines and judicial enforcement of them. One said, "From a real world point of view, they are necessary." But another was much more negative, saying, "Deadlines reinforce the sense that we [EPA] are not getting anywhere, to the detriment of public sense of confidence in government." Surprisingly enough, the negative view came from William Ruckelshaus, one of the most outstanding public administrators we have seen in some time, and the positive view came from Anne Gorsuch Burford, who is probably among the worst.

One example will help explain why Ruckelshaus found the deadline-litigation syndrome so detrimental to environmental protection. The Clean Air Act gives the EPA one year to publish regulations setting standards for pollutants it determines are "hazardous." During the Carter administration, EPA determined that radionuclides are carcinogenic, and therefore listed them as hazardous air pollutants. It failed to take any further action. About one year into the Reagan Administration, the Sierra Club sued in the northern district of California. Several years later the matter finally came to a head when Judge Orrick commanded Administrator Ruckelshaus to issue a standard for radionuclides.

At first Ruckelshaus surprised everyone by refusing to obey the court. Not only was the scientific evidence unclear—it always is—but EPA estimated that the health risks were tiny and the potential cost large. Estimated risk from some facilities was one cancer death every fifty years, from other facilities, one cancer death every thirteen to seventeen years. Ruckelshaus was in the middle of a major effort to educate the American public about the nature of environmental risks—to let them know that there is no such thing as a completely safe environment, and to force the government and the public to be honest about the level of safety they are willing to pay for. He told the court, "Given the inevitable burdens that regulation imposes just by its existence, and the shortage of resources to deal with real health risk both in EPA and the society at large, these risks did not appear to me to be large enough to warrant regulation." The judge responded by calling Ruckelshaus a "scofflaw," describing his actions as "outrageous," and expressing shock that such a "responsible person" (and a lawyer to boot) would so cavalierly disregard an order of the U.S. District Court. After being found in contempt of court, Ruckelshaus published regulations that would have virtually no effect on radionuclide levels. EPA estimated that it spent $7.6 million in contract funds and 150 staff-work years on this regulation.

One might conclude from this story that the bureaucracy is filled with scofflaws like William Ruckelshaus who need to be reined in by federal judges. Let me suggest instead that the problem is that too *many* administrators are more than willing to hide behind the argument "don't blame me for stupid policy, the courts made me do it." The law reviews are filled with theoretical discussions of a dialogue between courts and agencies, about using judicial review to stimulate "deliberation." In the real world what happens is that judicial review short-circuits real deliberation about what constitutes good policy. Agencies say, "The courts made me do it"; courts say, "Congress made me do it"; and Congress says, "Protect public health, but don't put anyone out of work, and don't question our right to condemn the agency no matter what it does." The political science literature calls this "blame-avoidance." Most people call it passing the buck. Only a law professor could call it "dialogue."

Separation of Powers

The legal literature is reticent to admit what everyone knows: that a large number of administrative law cases are the outgrowth of divided government. For the first 180 years of the Republic, divided government—control of the presidency by one party and control of Congress by the other—was a rare event. In 1969, however, it became virtually a permanent condition of the American polity. The Democratic Party has had a majority in at least one house of Congress in each of the twenty-two years since 1969, and in both houses for sixteen of those twenty-two years. Barring some electoral miracle, by 1996 Republicans will have held the presidency for twenty-four of twenty-eight years, and Democrats will have controlled the House for forty-two consecutive years.

Those who read the newspaper have noticed that Democrats and Republicans do not always agree on domestic policy or even on foreign affairs. Agencies often find themselves caught between congressional subcommittees (and their persistent staff) that demand more spending or more regulatory activity and the White House (or, more likely, the Office of Management and Budget) that demands less. With relaxed rules on standing, including, at times, even standing for members of Congress, many of these disputes end in court.

It is no coincidence that what Richard Stewart has aptly described as the "reformation of administrative law" began to take shape just as Richard Nixon was assuming the presidency. Nixon had a way of giving a bad odor to everything he touched—including the entire executive branch. Certainly Watergate contributed to judges' insistence that administrators be kept on a short leash. But competition between the presidency and Congress for the control of administrative agencies persisted long after the helicopter lifted Tricky Dick off the White House lawn.

In this decades-old battle between the branches, court intervention has generally given the advantage to the legislative branch. In the process it has added to the already considerable power of congressional subcommittees. The duty of the judiciary, Judge Wright announced in an important administrative law case, is "to see that important legislative purposes, heralded in the halls of Congress, are not lost or misdirected in the vast hallways of the federal bureaucracy." More recently Judge Patricia Wald has described the federal judges as a "trustee for the ghosts of Congresses past." Of course, given unprecedented reelection rates, the ghosts of Congresses past are still in Congress today and are likely to still be there in the year 2000, quite ready to defend their own interest. At least judges have been frank about their "tilt" toward the legislative branch. Congress has paid tribute to its alliance with the courts by relaxing standing and jurisdictional requirements, authorizing attorneys' fees, and recognizing private rights of action.

When courts come to the aid of Congress they usually end up strengthening its subcommittees. Judges intent upon determining the meaning of statutory phrases ambiguous on their face almost always turn to documents produced by congressional committees or other program advocates. Justice Scalia may have exaggerated somewhat when he claimed that "routine deference to the detail of committee reports . . . [is] converting a system of judicial construction into a system of committee-staff prescription," but he was not far from the mark. There are plenty of examples, ranging from the post-hoc legislative "history" produced by subcommittee staff to force HEW to write regulations under section 504, to the stray sentences inserted in a Senate report used to justify the enormous Prevention of Significant Deterioration program.

Many years ago, Justice Jackson warned that heavy reliance on legislative history may lead the courts to impose policies the president would never have accepted. More recently, Solicitor General Starr has pointed out that the use of legislative history "minimizes or ignores the role of the Executive." Moreover, by putting so much emphasis on *technical* justifications for agency policy, the courts have made *political* decisions seem somehow illegitimate. This view of policymaking weakens the position of the Executive Office of the President and of political executives within the agencies whose job it is to insist that whenever possible, agency policy be "in accord with the program of the president."

Given the importance of the presidency in our constitutional system, it is remarkable how seldom the president is mentioned in the legal literature on administrative law. It is hard to know whether this is the result of cynical partisanship (if we ignore Republican presidents, maybe they will go away) or prudish distaste for electoral politics. In many cases, federal judges (not to mention the authors of law review articles) assume the pose of Louis in the movie Casablanca: they are shocked,

shocked!, to find politics going on here. (It is appropriate that "Casablanca" means "White House" in Spanish.) This was particularly evident in the famous air bag case. Given the vagueness of the underlying statute and the inability of previous administrations to decide whether to mandate airbags, one must ask what was wrong with allowing the outcome of a presidential election—a landslide, at that—to determine the outcome of the controversy? If Congress wants to require airbags, it can do so by writing a law to that effect. The courts' solicitude for Congress and its committees would be more justifiable if legislators had few other ways to influence agency activities. The fact is, however, that those members of Congress with a particular interest in a program usually have enormous influence. They have the appropriations process, investigative powers, reauthorization powers, confirmation hearings, and extensive links to the media—not to mention the power of constant harassment.

In his study of six federal bureau chiefs, Herbert Kaufman of the Brookings Institution reports that "[t]he chiefs were constantly looking over their shoulders . . . at the elements of the legislative establishment relevant to their agencies. . . ." He adds, "Not that cues and signals from Capitol Hill had to be ferreted out; the denizens of the Hill were not shy about issuing suggestions, requests, demands, directives, and pronouncements." Members of Congress, he concludes, have an "awesome arsenal" to employ against administrators who ignore their wishes. Anyone who doubts this can read the huge political science literature on the power of Congress and its committees, or one can save a lot of time and simply ask the FSLIC officials who tried to shut down the Lincoln Savings and Loan.

At the very least, it is time for administrative law to be more honest about the role of the Executive Office of the President and political appointees. We should remember that the Constitution makes the president part of the legislative process and gives the president—not judges—the responsibility to "faithfully execute the laws." The Supreme Court's decision in *Chevron* v. *NRDC*, coupled with its recent tendency to avoid reliance on legislative history, may end this tilt toward Congress. As Judge Wald has noted, compared with previous practices these judicial doctrines are "inherently executive enhancing." The Supreme Court, though, has hardly been consistent on these points. And we are only beginning to learn about the lower courts' application of Supreme Court doctrines.

National Uniformity

In some policy areas judicial review has substantially reduced the uniformity of federal law. There is no little irony in this. Ever since the days of John Marshall, federal courts have tried (and often succeeded) to strengthen the Union by reining in the states. Now that we have created a large number of federal agencies charged with carrying out nationally uniform programs, extensive court intervention all too often creates different rules for different circuits. As Peter Strauss has pointed out, "[T]he infrequency of Supreme Court review combines with the formal independence of each circuit's law from that of the other circuits to permit a gradual balkanization of federal law." He notes that the legal profession has "yet to come to grips with the problem."

Although the problem has arisen in a variety of areas—tax law, labor law, education of the handicapped, and welfare, to name a few—it became most apparent in the heated confrontation between the courts and the executive branch over disability benefits. The agency charged with carrying out disability reviews, the Social Security Administration (SSA), is the very embodiment of the New Deal's commitment to national uniformity. The SSA's willingness to engage in "non-acquiescence" in order to preserve this uniformity predated the Reagan Administration's attempt to purge the disability rolls in the early 1980s. The heavy-handedness of the Reagan Administration's policies should not blind us to the larger issue. In her recent book on the SSA, Martha Derthick has this to say about the agency's much-maligned nonacquiescence policy:

> The underlying premise—that policy must be nationally uniform—was not in the least contrived for the occasion. It was contained in law, Congress having stipulated in 1980 that administration of the disability insurance program be "uniform . . . throughout the United States." Just as important, it had long been at the core of the agency's operating code. . . . [T]his code had been reinforced in the SSA's case by the particular historical circumstance that its programs and administrative style were a reaction against the features of American federalism. For the SSA's programs to develop regional differences would be more than an monumental inconvenience to the agency; it would constitute a humiliating retrogression to the time when state governments dominated domestic functions and citizens were treated differently depending on where they happened to live. The SSA's very existence rested on the belief that such differences were unfair.

Compared with agencies like the SSA, the IRS, or even EPA, the federal judiciary is a highly decentralized institution. Constant intervention by the decentralized judiciary can lead to confusion and unfairness. It can also have a corrosive effect on the sense of mission of an agency like the Social Security Administration—a commitment to national uniformity and to prompt determinations, which has served us well since 1935.

Power within the Agency

Aggressive judicial review creates winners and losers within administrative agencies. Clearly the biggest losers are political executives, who are less able to set priorities or to resist demands from congressional committees and interest groups. The biggest winners are lawyers with the agency's Office of General Counsel. Many studies of courts and agencies have come to this conclusion. OGC attorneys are the ones who explain what the courts are likely to accept and reject. Frequently—especially on remand—they end up writing substantial portions of the regulations. At the risk of offending my readers, let me suggest two difficulties with this transfer of power to their "brother" and "sister" attorneys.

First, many of these lawyers work in the agency for a relatively short period of time; they are bright, aggressive young men and women who yearn to "cast a shadow" before moving on to a more lucrative career elsewhere. In that sense they are no different from congressional staffers, law clerks, or many lower-echelon people in the White House. More cocky neophytes with short time horizons is hardly what Washington needs.

Second, few of these lawyers have ever run anything. They seldom have a sense of how hard it is to manage a program at the regional or state level. As Martin Shapiro has put it, the judicial demand for rationality

> tends to shift power within the agencies from those who are really concerned about making policies that work to those concerned with defending them in court . . . from real administrators responsible for the actual operations of programs to lawyers. And it will often lead to a choice of the alternative that can most easily be made to appear synoptic rather than the one that seems best.

This power shift has contributed to some memorable policy disaster. For example, in the early 1970s the D.C. Circuit ordered EPA to promulgate transportation control plans adequate to meet ambient air quality standards, even in cities like Los Angeles. Top administrators considered this politically suicidal. Regional and technical personnel warned that it would be hard to formulate reasonable plans and virtually impossible to implement them. Hard chargers in the Office of General Counsel, though, saw this as their chance to remake the American system of transportation, to fight highways and automobiles, and promote mass transit. The plans, of course, were a political, technical, and management nightmare. The hardest charger in the Office of General Counsel then left the agency—to teach administrative law. As the old saying goes, if you can't do it, teach it.

Get Real, Administrative Law

This article has suggested both that courts often make a mess of policy because they have a poor understanding of administrative agencies and that administrative law has done little to correct judicial misperceptions. What understanding of bureaucracy might be more accurate? Let me propose the following generalization about public bureaucracies in the United States: They are almost always given huge, even utopian, goals and are then saddled with a large number of constraints that prevent them from achieving these goals efficiently—or even at all. We tell EPA, for example, to protect the public health with an adequate margin of safety, but advise it not to spend too much money or put anyone out of work. We tell them to use the best scientific evidence, but refuse to let them pay enough to recruit top-flight scientists, and then we tell them, "By the way, do it within 90 days." We expect bureaucrats to account for every penny of public money, to record every conversation with a member of an interest group, to show that they have treated everyone equally, and to consider all the relevant information and alternatives—but to stop producing all that red tape and being so damn slow.

Courts are particularly likely to make these conflicting demands because they are so decentralized, their exposure to policymaking is so episodic, and the opportunities for forum-shopping are so apparent to interest groups. Courts are good at responding to complaints, and people have lots of complaints about bureaucracy. The problem is that these complaints often require incompatible responses. Today the D.C. Circuit hears a case brought by environmental groups complaining about unconscionable delay. In two years the Sixth Circuit will hear industry complain about shoddy evidence and exorbitant costs. And two years after that a district court judge in Cleveland will be asked to balance the "equities" in order to keep a particular local factory in operation. Who considers the connection among all these decisions? The Supreme Court? Simply to ask this question is to answer it—no one does.

What is to be done? Most obviously, judges should remember a key part of the Hippocratic oath: First, do no harm. In administrative law that translates into the command, defer! defer! Just as importantly, administrative law needs to become less self-absorbed and more concerned about how public bureaucracies work. The best place to start is with James Q. Wilson's recent book, *Bureaucracy: What Government Agencies Do and Why They Do It*, which offers an unequalled discussion of the nature and the varieties of public bureaucracies. In addition to the works previously mentioned, there are a number of other case studies which will acquaint students of the law with the perspective of public administrators.

It is especially important that law students become familiar with some of this nonlegal literature. Like most Americans, law students are contemptuous of bureaucrats. Moreover, in class after class they are asked to adopt the perspective of the judge. If law students fail to learn about public administration in administrative law courses, they never will. Adding studies of agencies to the curriculum will have the further advantage of forcing law professors to descend the Olympian heights of appellate review to wallow in the details of the day-to-day life of government bureaucrats.

My hunch is that this second suggestion will buttress the first. The more that students, law professors, and judges learn about the travails and dilemmas of public administration, the less likely they will be to second-guess agencies or to impose rigid rules and procedures. To purloin Schuck and Elliott's wonderful pun, a better understanding of bureaucratic reality will lead administrative law "To the *Chevron* Station."

Chapter 8

CONGRESS

The United States Congress, exercising supreme legislative power, was at the beginning of the nineteenth century the most powerful political institution in the national government. It was feared by the framers of the Constitution, who felt that unless it was closely guarded and limited it would easily dominate both the presidency and the Supreme Court. Its powers were carefully enumerated, and it was made a bicameral body. This latter provision not only secured representation of different interests but also limited the power of the legislature which, when hobbled by two houses often working against each other, could not act as swiftly and forcefully as a single body could. Although still important, the power and prestige of Congress have declined while the powers of the president and the Supreme Court, not to mention those of the vast governmental bureaucracy, have increased. Congressional power, its basis, and the factors influencing the current position of Congress vis-à-vis coordinate governmental departments are discussed in this chapter.

Constitutional Background: Representation of Popular, Group, and National Interests

Article 1, Section 1 of the Constitution states that "all legislative powers herein granted shall be vested in a Congress of the United States, which shall consist of a Senate and House of Representatives." Section 8 specifically enumerates congressional powers, and provides that Congress shall have power "to make all laws which shall be necessary and proper for carrying into execution the foregoing powers, and all other powers vested by this Constitution in the government of the United States, or in any department or officer thereof."

357

Apart from delineating the powers of Congress, Article 1 provides that the House shall represent the people, and the Senate the states through appointment of members by the state legislatures. The representative function of Congress is written into the Constitution, and at the time of the framing of the Constitution much discussion centered on the nature of representation and what constituted adequate representation in a national legislative body. Further, relating in part to the question of representation, the framers of the Constitution had to determine what the appropriate tasks for each branch of the legislature were, and to what extent certain legislative activities should be within the exclusive or initial jurisdiction of the House or the Senate. All these questions depended to some extent upon the conceptualization the framers had of the House as representative of popular interests on a short-term basis and the Senate as a reflection of conservative interests on a long-term basis. These selections from *The Federalist* indicate the thinking of the framers about the House of Representatives and the Senate.

48

James Madison

FEDERALIST 53

❖❖❖❖❖❖❖

. . . No man can be a competent legislator who does not add to an upright intention and a sound judgment a certain degree of knowledge of the subjects on which he is to legislate. A part of this knowledge may be acquired by means of information, which lie within the compass of men in private, as well as public stations. Another part can only be attained, or at least thoroughly attained, by actual experience in the station which requires the use of it. The period of service ought, therefore, in all such cases, to bear some proportion to the extent of practical knowledge requisite to the due performance of the service. . . .

In a single state the requisite knowledge relates to the existing laws, which are uniform throughout the state, and with which all the citizens are more or less conversant. . . . The great theater of the United States presents a very different scene. The laws are so far from being uniform that they vary in every state; whilst the public affairs of the union are spread throughout a very extensive region, and are extremely diversified by the local affairs connected with them, and can with difficulty be correctly learnt in any other place than in the central councils, to which a knowledge of them will be brought by representatives of every part of the empire. Yet some knowledge of the affairs, and even of the laws of all the states, ought to be possessed by the members from each of the states. . . .

A branch of knowledge which belongs to the acquirements of a federal representative, and which has not been mentioned, is that of foreign affairs. In regulating our own commerce he ought to be not only acquainted with the treaties between the United States and other nations, but also with the commercial policy and laws of other nations. He ought not to be altogether ignorant of the law of nations; for that, as far as it is a proper object of municipal legislation, is submitted to the federal government. And although the House of Representatives is not immediately to participate in foreign negotiations and arrangements, yet from the necessary connection between the several branches of public affairs, those particular subjects will frequently deserve attention in the ordinary course of legislation, and will sometimes demand particular legislative sanction and cooperation. Some portion of this knowledge may, no doubt, be acquired in a man's closet; but some of it also can only be acquired to best effect, by a practical attention to the subject, during the period of actual service in the legislature. . . .

FEDERALIST 56

❖❖❖❖❖❖❖

The . . . charge against the House of Representatives is, that it will be too small to possess a due knowledge of the interests of its constituents.

As this objection evidently proceeds from a comparison of the proposed number of representatives, with the great extent of the United States, the number of their inhabitants, and the diversity of their interests, without taking into view, at the same time, the circumstances which will distinguish the Congress from other legislative bodies, the best answer that can be given to it, will be a brief explanation of these peculiarities.

It is a sound and important principle that the representative ought to be acquainted with the interests and circumstances of his constituents. But this principle can extend no farther than to those circumstances and interests to which the authority and care of the representative relate. An ignorance of a variety of minute and particular objects, which do not lie within the compass of legislation, is consistent with every attribute necessary to a due performance of the legislative trust. In determining the extent of information required in the exercise of a particular authority, recourse then must be had to the objects within the purview of that authority.

What are to be the objects of federal legislation? Those which are of most importance, and which seem most to require knowledge, are commerce, taxation, and the militia.

A proper regulation of commerce requires much information, as has been elsewhere remarked; but as far as this information relates to the laws, and local situation of each individual state, a very few representatives would be sufficient vehicles of it to the federal councils.

Taxation will consist, in great measure, of duties which will be involved in the regulation of commerce. So far the preceding remark is applicable to this object. As far as it may consist of internal collections, a more diffusive knowledge of the circumstances of the state may be necessary. But will not this also be possessed in sufficient degree by a very few intelligent men, diffusively elected within the state?. . . .

With regard to the regulation of the militia there are scarcely any circumstances in reference to which local knowledge can be said to be necessary. . . . The art of war teaches general principles of organization, movement, and discipline, which apply universally.

The attentive reader will discern that the reasoning here used, to prove the sufficiency of a moderate number of representatives, does not, in any respect, contradict what was urged on another occasion, with regard to the extensive information which the representatives ought to possess, and the time that might be necessary for acquiring it. . . .

FEDERALIST 57

❖❖❖❖❖❖❖

. . . The House of Representatives is so constituted as to support in the members an habitual recollection of their dependence on the people. Before the sentiments impressed on their minds by the mode of their elevation, can be effaced by the exercise of power, they will be compelled to anticipate the moment when their power is to cease, when their exercise of it is to be reviewed, and when they must descend to the level from which they were raised; there for ever to remain unless a faithful discharge of their trust shall have established their title to a renewal of it.

I will add, as a . . . circumstance in the situation of the House of Representatives, restraining them from oppressive measures, that they can make no law which will not have its full operation on themselves and their friends, as well as on the great mass of the society. This has always been deemed one of the strongest bonds by which human policy can connect the rulers and the people together. It creates between them that communion of interest, and sympathy of sentiments, of which few governments have furnished examples; but without which every government degenerates into tyranny. If it be asked, what is to restrain the House of Representatives from making legal discriminations in favor of themselves, and a particular class of the society? I answer, the genius of the whole system; the nature of just and constitutional laws; and, above all, the vigilant and manly spirit which actuates the people of America; a spirit which nourishes freedom, and in return is nourished by it.

If this spirit shall ever be so far debased as to tolerate a law not obligatory on the legislature, as well as on the people, the people will be prepared to tolerate anything but liberty.

Such will be the relation between the House of Representatives and their constituents. Duty, gratitude, interest, ambition itself, are the cords by which they will be bound to fidelity and sympathy with the great mass of the people. It is possible that these may all be insufficient to control the caprice and wickedness of men. But are they not all that government will admit, and that human prudence can devise? Are they not the genuine, and the characteristic means, by which republican government provides for the liberty and happiness of the people?. . .

FEDERALIST 58

. . . In this review of the constitution of the House of Representatives . . . one observation . . . I must be permitted to add . . . as claiming, in my judgment, a very serious attention. It is, that in all legislative assemblies, the greater the number composing them may be, the fewer will be the men who will in fact direct their proceedings. In the first place, the more numerous any assembly may be, of whatever characters composed, the greater is known to be the ascendancy of passion over reason. In the next place, the larger the number, the greater will be the proportion of members of limited information and of weak capacities. Now it is precisely on characters of this description that the eloquence and address of the few are known to act with all their force. In the ancient republics, where the whole body of the people assembled in person, a single orator, or an artful statesman, was generally seen to rule with as complete a sway as if a sceptre had been placed in his single hands. On the same principle, the more multitudinous a representative assembly may be rendered, the more it will partake of the infirmities incident to collective meetings of the people. Ignorance will be the dupe of cunning; and passion the slave of sophistry and declamation. The people can never err more than in supposing, that by multiplying their representatives beyond a certain list, they strengthen the barrier against the government of a few. Experience will for ever admonish them, that, on the contrary, after securing a sufficient number for the purposes of safety, of local information, and of diffusive sympathy with the whole society, they will counteract their own views by every addition to their representatives. The countenance of the government may become more democratic; but the soul that animates it will be more oligarchic. The machine will be enlarged, but the fewer, and often the more secret, will be the springs by which its motions are directed. . . .

FEDERALIST 62

Having examined the constitution of the House of Representatives . . . I enter next on the examination of the Senate.

The heads under which this member of the government may be considered are—I. The qualifications of senators; II. The appointment of them by the state legislatures; III. The equality of representation in the Senate; IV. The number of senators, and the term for which they are to be elected; V. The powers vested in the Senate.

I

The qualifications proposed for senators, as distinguished from those of representatives, consist in a more advanced age and a longer period of citizenship. A senator must be thirty years of age at least; as a representative must be twenty-five. And the former must have been a citizen nine years; as seven years are required for the latter. The propriety of these distinctions is explained by the nature of the senatorial trust; which, requiring greater extent of information and stability of character, requires at the same time, that the senator should have reached a period of life most likely to supply these advantages. . . .

II

It is equally unnecessary to dilate on the appointment of senators by the state legislators. Among the various modes which might have been devised for constituting this branch of the government, that which has been proposed by the convention is probably the most congenial with the public opinion. It is recommended by the double advantage of favoring a select appointment, and of giving to the state governments such an agency in the formation of the federal government, as must secure the authority of the former, and may form a convenient link between the two systems.

III

The equality of representation in the Senate is another point, which, being evidently the result of compromise between the opposite pretensions of the large and the small states, does not call for much discussion. If indeed it be right, that among a people thoroughly incorporated into one nation, every district ought to have a *proportional* share in the government: and that among independent and sovereign states bound together by a simple league, the parties, however unequal in size, ought to have an *equal* share in the common councils, it does not appear to be without some reason, that in a compound republic, partaking both of the national and federal character, the government ought to be founded on a mixture of the principles of proportional [as found in the House of Representatives] and equal representation [in the Senate].. . .

. . . The equal vote allowed to each state, is at once a constitutional recognition of the portion of sovereignty remaining in the individual states, and an instrument for preserving that residuary sovereignty. So far the equality ought to be no less acceptable to the large than to the small states; since they are not less solicitous to guard by every possible expedient against an improper consolidation of the states into one simple republic.

Another advantage accruing from this ingredient in the constitution of the senate is, the additional impediment it must prove against improper acts of legislation. No law or resolution can now be passed without the concurrence, first, of a majority of the people, and then, of a majority of the states. It must be acknowledged that this complicated check on legislation may, in some instances, be injurious as well as beneficial; and that the peculiar defense which it involves in favor of the smaller states, would be more rational, if any interests common to them, and distinct from those of the other states, would otherwise be exposed to peculiar danger. But as the larger states will always be able, by their power over the supplies, to defeat unreasonable exertions of this prerogative of the lesser states; and as the facility and excess of law-making seem to be the diseases to which our governments are most liable, it is not impossible, that this part of the constitution may be more convenient in practice than it appears to many in contemplation.

IV

The number of senators, and the duration of their appointment, come next to be considered. In order to form an accurate judgment on both these points, it will be proper to inquire into the purposes which are to be answered by the Senate; and, in order to ascertain these, it will be necessary to review the inconveniences which a republic must suffer from the want of such an institution.

First

It is a misfortune incident to republican government, though in a lesser degree than to other governments, that those who administer it may forget their obligations to their constituents, and prove unfaithful to their important trust. In this point of view, a senate, as a second branch of the legislative assembly, distinct from, and dividing the power with, a first, must be in all cases a salutary check on the government. It doubles the security to the people by requiring the concurrence of two distinct bodies in schemes of usurpation or perfidy, where the ambition or corruption of one would otherwise be sufficient. . . . [A]s the improbability of sinister combinations will be in proportion to the dissimilarity in the genius of the two bodies, it must be politic to distinguish them from each other by every circumstance which will consist with a due harmony in all proper measures, and with the genuine principles of republican government.

Second

The necessity of a senate is not less indicated by the propensity of all single and numerous assemblies, to yield to the impulse of sudden and violent passions, and to be seduced by factious leaders into intemperate and pernicious resolutions. Examples on this subject might be cited without number; and from proceedings within the United States, as well as from the history of other nations. But a position that will not be contradicted need not be proved. All that need be remarked is, that a body which is to correct this infirmity ought itself to be free from it, and consequently ought to be less numerous. It ought, moreover, to possess great firmness, and consequently ought to hold its authority by a tenure of considerable duration.

Third

Another defect to be supplied by a senate lies in a want of due acquaintance with objects and principles of legislation. It is not possible that an assembly of men, called, for the most part, from pursuits of a private nature, continued in appointments for a short time, and led by no permanent motive to devote the intervals of public occupation to a study of the laws, the affairs, and the comprehensive interests of their country, should, if left wholly to themselves, escape a variety of important errors in the exercise of their legislative trust. . . .

Fourth

The mutability in the public councils, arising from a rapid succession of new members, however qualified they may be, points out, in the strongest manner, the necessity of some stable institution in the government. Every new election in the states is found to change one-half of the representatives. From this change of men must proceed a change of opinions; and from a change of opinions, a change of measures. But a continued change even of good measures is inconsistent with every rule of prudence, and every prospect of success. . . .

FEDERALIST 63

A *fifth* desideratum, illustrating the utility of a senate, is the want of a due sense of national character. Without a select and stable member of the government, the esteem of foreign powers will not only be forfeited by an unenlightened and variable policy. . . ; but the national councils will not possess that sensibility to the opinion of the world, which is perhaps not less necessary in order to merit, than it is to obtain, its respect and confidence. . . .

I add, as a *sixth* defect, the want in some important cases of a due responsibility in the government to the people, arising from that frequency of elections, which in other cases produces this responsibility. . . .

Responsibility, in order to be reasonable, must be limited to objects within the power of the responsible party, and in order to be effectual, must relate to operations of that power, of which a ready and proper judgment can be formed by the constituents. The objects of government may be divided into two general classes;

the one depending on measures, which have singly an immediate and sensible operation; the other depending on a succession of well chosen and well connected measures, which have a gradual and perhaps unobserved operation. The importance of the latter description to the collective and permanent welfare of every country, needs no explanation. And yet it is evident that an assembly elected for so short a term as to be unable to provide more than one or two links in a chain of measures, on which the general welfare may essentially depend, ought not to be answerable for the final result, any more than a steward or tenant, engaged for one year, could be justly made to answer for plans or improvements, which could not be accomplished in less than half a dozen years. Nor is it possible for the people to estimate the *share* of influence, which their annual assemblies may respectively have on events resulting from the mixed transactions of several years. It is sufficiently difficult, at any rate, to preserve a personal responsibility in the members of a *numerous* body, for such acts of the body as have an immediate, detached, and palpable operation on its constituents.

The proper remedy for this defect must be an additional body in the legislative department, which, having sufficient permanency to provide for such objects as require a continued attention, and a train of measures, may be justly and effectually answerable for the attainment of those objects.

Thus far I have considered the circumstances, which point out the necessity of a well constructed senate, only as they relate to the representatives of the people. To a people as little blinded by prejudice, or corrupted by flattery, as those whom I address, I shall not scruple to add, that such an institution may be sometimes necessary, as a defense to the people against their own temporary errors and delusions. As the cool and deliberate sense of the community ought, in all governments, and actually will, in all free governments, ultimately prevail over the views of its rulers; so there are particular moments in public affairs, when the people, stimulated by some irregular passion, or some illicit advantage, or misled by the artful misrepresentations of interested men, may call for measures which they themselves will afterwards be the most ready to lament and condemn. In these critical moments, how salutary will be the interference of some temperate and respectable body of citizens, in order to check the misguided career, and to suspend the blow meditated by the people against themselves, until reason, justice and truth can regain their authority over the public mind? What bitter anguish would not the people of Athens have often avoided, if their government had contained so provident a safeguard against the tyranny of their own passions? Popular liberty might then have escaped the indelible reproach of decreeing to the same citizens the hemlock on one day, and statues on the next.

It may be suggested that a people spread over an extensive region cannot, like the crowded inhabitants of a small district, be subject to the infection of violent passions; or to the danger of combining in the pursuit of unjust measures. I am far from denying that this is a distinction of peculiar importance. I have, on the contrary, endeavored in a former paper to show that it is one of the principal recommendations of a confederated republic. At the same time this advantage ought not to be considered as superseding the use of auxiliary precautions. It may even be remarked that the same extended situation, which will exempt the people of America from some of the dangers incident to lesser republics, will expose them to the inconveniency of remaining for a longer time under the influence of those misrepresentations which the combined industry of interested men may succeed in distributing among them. . . .

❖❖ Congress and the Washington Political Establishment

The author of the following selection agrees with David Mayhew (see selection 55) that the principal goal of members of Congress is reelection. That incentive, the author suggests, has led Congress to create a vast federal bureaucracy to implement programs that ostensibly benefit constituents. Congress has delegated substantial authority to administrative departments and agencies to carry out programs, inevitably resulting in administrative decisions that frequently step on constituents' toes. Congress, which has gained credit for establishing the programs in the first place, steps in once again to receive credit for handling constituent complaints against the bureaucracy. The author's provocative thesis is that both the establishment and maintenance of a vast federal bureaucracy is explained by the congressional reelection incentive.

49

Morris P. Fiorina

THE RISE OF THE WASHINGTON ESTABLISHMENT

Dramatis Personae

In this [selection] I will set out a theory of the Washington establishment(s). The theory is quite plausible from a common-sense standpoint, and it is consistent with the specialized literature of academic political science. Nevertheless, it is still a theory, not proven fact. Before plunging in let me bring out in the open the basic axiom on which the theory rests: the self-interest axiom.

I assume that most people most of the time act in their own self-interest. This is not to say that human beings seek only to amass tangible wealth but rather to say that human beings seek to achieve their own ends—tangible and intangible—rather than the ends of their fellow men. I do not condemn such behavior nor do I condone it (although I rather sympathize with Thoreau's comment that "if I knew for a certainty that a man was coming to my house with the conscious design of doing me good, I should run for my life."). I only claim that political and economic theories which presume self-interested behavior will prove to be more widely applicable than those which build on more altruistic assumptions.

What does the axiom imply when used in the specific context of this [selection], a context peopled by congressmen, bureaucrats, and voters? I assume that the primary goal of the typical congressman is reelection. Over and above the [six-figure] salary plus "perks" and outside money, the office of congressman carries with it prestige, excitement, and power. It is a seat in the cockpit of government. But in order to retain the status, excitement, and power (not to mention more tangible things) of office, the congressman must win reelection every two years. Even those congressmen genuinely concerned with good public policy must achieve reelection in order to continue their work. Whether narrowly self-serving or more publicly oriented, the individual congressman finds reelection to be at least a necessary condition for the achievement of his goals.

Moreover, there is a kind of natural selection process at work in the electoral arena. On average, those congressmen who are not primarily interested in reelection will not achieve reelection as often as those who are interested. We, the people, help to weed out congressmen whose primary motivation is not reelection. We admire politicians who courageously adopt the aloof role of the disinterested statesman, but we vote for those politicians who follow our wishes and do us favors.

What about the bureaucrats? A specification of their goals is somewhat more controversial—those who speak of appointed officials as public servants obviously take a more benign view than those who speak of them as bureaucrats. The literature provides ample justification for asserting that most bureaucrats wish to protect and nurture their agencies. The typical bureaucrat can be expected to seek to expand his agency in terms of personnel, budget, and mission. One's status in Washington (again, not to mention more tangible things) is roughly proportional to the importance of the operation one oversees. And the sheer size of the operation is taken to be a measure of importance. As with congressmen, the specified goals apply even to those bureaucrats who genuinely believe in their agency's mission. If they believe in the efficacy of their programs, they naturally wish to expand them and add new ones. All of this requires more money and more people. The genuinely committed bureaucrat is just as likely to seek to expand his agency as the proverbial empire-builder.

And what of the third element in the equation, us? What do we, the voters who support the Washington system, strive for? Each of us wishes to receive a maximum of benefits from government for the minimum cost. This goal suggests maximum government efficiency, on the one hand, but it also suggests mutual exploitation on the other. Each of us favors an arrangement in which our fellow citizens pay for our benefits.

With these brief descriptions of the cast of characters in hand, let us proceed.

Tammany Hall Goes to Washington

What should we expect from a legislative body composed of individuals whose first priority is their continued tenure in office? We should expect, first, that the normal activities of its members are those calculated to enhance their chances of reelection. And we should expect, second, that the members would devise and maintain institutional arrangements which facilitate their electoral activities. . . .

For most of the twentieth century, congressmen have engaged in a mix of three kinds of activities: lawmaking, pork barreling, and casework. Congress is first and foremost a lawmaking body, at least according to constitutional theory. In every postwar session Congress "considers" thousands of bills and resolutions, many hundreds of which are brought to a record vote. . . . Naturally the critical consideration in taking a position for the record is the maximization of approval in the home district. If the district is unaffected by and unconcerned with the matter at hand, the congressman may then take into account the general welfare of the country. (This sounds cynical, but remember that "profiles in courage" are sufficiently rare that their occurrence inspires books and articles.) Abetted by political scientists of the pluralist school, politicians have propounded an ideology which maintains that the good of the country on any given issue is simply what is best for a majority of congressional districts. This ideology provides a philosophical justification for what congressmen do while acting in their own self-interest.

A second activity favored by congressmen consists of efforts to bring home the bacon to their districts. Many popular articles have been written about the pork barrel, a term originally applied to rivers and harbors legislation but now generalized to cover all manner of federal largesse. Congressmen consider new dams, federal buildings, sewage treatment plants, urban renewal projects, etc. as sweet plums to be plucked. Federal projects are highly visible, their economic impact is easily detected by constituents, and sometimes they even produce something of value to the district. The average constituent may have some trouble translating his congressman's vote on some civil rights issue into a change in his personal welfare. But the workers hired and supplies purchased in connection with a big federal project provide benefits that are widely appreciated. The historical importance congressmen attach to the pork barrel is reflected in the rules of the House. That body accords certain classes of legislation "privileged" status: they may come directly to the floor without passing through the Rules Committee, a traditional graveyard for legislation. What kinds of legislation are privileged? Taxing and spending bills, for one: the government's power to raise and spend money must be kept relatively unfettered. But in addition, the omnibus rivers and harbors bills of the Public Works Committee and public lands bills from the Interior Committee share privileged status. The House will allow a civil rights or defense procurement or environmental bill to languish in the Rules Committee, but it takes special precautions to insure that nothing slows down the approval of dams and irrigation projects.

A third major activity takes up perhaps as much time as the other two combined. Traditionally, constituents appeal to their congressman for myriad favors and services. Sometimes only information is needed, but often constituents request that their congressman intervene in the internal workings of federal agencies to affect a decision in a favorable way, to reverse an adverse decision, or simply to speed up the glacial bureaucratic process. On the basis of extensive personal interviews with congressmen, Charles Clapp writes:

> Denied a favorable ruling by the bureaucracy on a matter of direct concern to him, puzzled or irked by delays in obtaining a decision, confused by the administrative maze through which he is directed to proceed, or ignorant of whom to write, a constituent may turn to his congressman for help. These letters offer great potential for political benefit to the congressman since they affect the constituent personally. If the legislator can be of assistance, he may gain a firm ally; if he is indifferent, he may even lose votes.

Actually congressmen are in an almost unique position in our system, a position shared only with high-level members of the executive branch. Congressmen possess the power to expedite and influence bureaucratic decisions. This capability flows directly from congressional control over what bureaucrats value most: higher budgets and new program authorizations. In a very real sense each congressman is a monopoly supplier of bureaucratic unsticking services for his district.

Every year the federal budget passes through the appropriations committees of Congress. Generally these committees make perfunctory cuts. But on occasion they vent displeasure on an agency and leave it bleeding all over the Capitol. The most extreme case of which I am aware came when the House committee took away the entire budget of the Division of Labor Standards in 1947 (some of the budget was restored elsewhere in the appropriations process). Deep and serious cuts are made occasionally, and the threat of such cuts keeps most agencies attentive to congressional wishes. Professors Richard Fenno and Aaron Wildavsky have provided extensive documentary and interview evidence of the great respect (and even terror) federal bureaucrats show for the House Appropriations Committee. Moreover, the bureaucracy must keep coming back to Congress to have its old programs reauthorized and new ones added. Again, most such decisions are perfunctory, but exceptions are sufficiently frequent that bureaucrats do not forget the basis of their agencies' existence. . . . The bureaucracy needs congressional approval in order to survive, let alone expand. Thus, when a congressman calls about some minor bureaucratic decision or regulation, the bureaucracy considers his accommodation a small price to pay for the goodwill its cooperation will produce, particularly if he has any connection to the substantive committee or the appropriations subcommittee to which it reports.

From the standpoint of capturing voters, the congressman's lawmaking activities differ in two important respects from his pork-barrel and casework activities. First, programmatic actions are inherently controversial. Unless his district is homogeneous, a congressman will find his district divided on many major issues. Thus when he casts a vote, introduces a piece of nontrivial legislation, or makes a speech with policy content he will displease some elements of his district. Some constituents may applaud the congressman's civil rights record, but others believe integration is going too fast. Some support foreign aid, while others believe it's money poured down a rathole. Some advocate economic quality, others stew over welfare cheaters. On such policy matters the congressman can expect to make friends as well as enemies. Presumably he will behave so as to maximize the excess of the former over the latter, but nevertheless a policy stand will generally make some enemies.

In contrast, the pork barrel and casework are relatively less controversial. New federal projects bring jobs, shiny new facilities, and general economic prosperity, or so people believe. Snipping ribbons at the dedication of a new post office or dam is a much more pleasant pursuit than disposing of a constitutional amendment on abortion. Republicans and Democrats, conservatives and liberals, all generally prefer a richer district to a poorer one. Of course, in recent years the river damming and stream-bed straightening activities of the Army Corps of Engineers have aroused some opposition among environmentalists. Congressmen happily reacted by absorbing the opposition and adding environmentalism to the pork barrel: water treatment plants are currently a hot congressional item.

Casework is even less controversial. Some poor, aggrieved constituent becomes enmeshed in the tentacles of an evil bureaucracy and calls upon Congressman St. George to do battle with the dragon. Again Clapp writes:

> A person who has a reasonable complaint or query is regarded as providing an opportunity rather than as adding an extra burden to an already busy office. The party affiliation of the individual even when known to be different from that of the congressman does not normally act as a deterrent to action. Some legislators have built their reputations and their majorities on a program of service to all constituents irrespective of party. Regularly, voters affiliated with the opposition in other contests lend strong support to the lawmaker whose intervention has helped them in their struggle with the bureaucracy.

Even following the revelation of sexual improprieties, Wayne Hays won his Ohio Democratic primary by a two-to-one margin. According to a *Los Angeles Times* feature story, Hay's constituency base was built on a foundation of personal service to constituents:

> They receive help in speeding up bureaucratic action on various kinds of federal assistance—black lung benefits to disabled miners and their families, Social Security payments, veterans' benefits and passports.
>
> Some constituents still tell with pleasure of how Hays stormed clear to the seventh floor of the State Department and into Secretary of State Dean Rusk's office to demand, successfully, the quick issuance of a passport to an Ohioan.

Practicing politicians will tell you that word of mouth is still the most effective mode of communication. News of favors to constituents gets around and no doubt is embellished in the process.

In sum, when considering the benefits of his programmatic activities, the congressman must tote up gains and losses to arrive at a net profit. Pork barreling and casework, however, are basically pure profit.

A second way in which programmatic activities differ from casework and the pork barrel is the difficulty of assigning responsibility to the former as compared with the latter. No congressman can seriously claim that he is responsible for the 1964 Civil Rights Act, the ABM, or the 1972 Revenue Sharing Act. Most constituents do have some vague notion that their congressman is only one of hundreds and their senator one of an even hundred. Even committee chairmen may have a difficult time claiming credit for a piece of major legislation, let alone a rank-and-file congressman. Ah, but casework, and the pork barrel. In dealing with the bureaucracy, the congressman is not merely one vote of 435. Rather, he is a nonpartisan power, someone whose phone calls snap an office to attention. He is not kept on hold. The constituent who receives aid believes that his congressman and his congressman alone got results. Similarly, congressmen find it easy to claim credit for federal projects awarded their districts. The congressman may have instigated the proposal for the project in the first place, issued regular progress reports, and ultimately announced the award through his office. Maybe he can't claim credit for the 1965 Voting Rights Act, but he can take credit for Littletown's spanking new sewage treatment plant.

Overall then, programmatic activities are dangerous (controversial), on the one hand, and programmatic accomplishments are difficult to claim credit for, on the other. While less exciting, casework and pork barreling are both safe and profitable. For a reelection-oriented congressman the choice is obvious.

The key to the rise of the Washington establishment (and the vanishing marginals) is the following observation: *the growth of an activist federal government has stimulated a change in the mix of congressional activities*. Specifically, a lesser proportion of congressional effort is now going into programmatic activities and a greater proportion into pork-barrel and casework activities. As a result, today's congressmen make relatively fewer enemies and relatively more friends among the people of their districts.

To elaborate, a basic fact of life in twentieth-century America is the growth of the federal role and its attendant bureaucracy. Bureaucracy is the characteristic mode of delivering public goods and services. Ceteris paribus, the more government attempts to do for people, the more extensive a bureaucracy it creates. As the scope of government expands, more and more citizens find themselves in direct contact with the federal government. Consider the rise in such contacts upon passage of the Social Security Act, work relief projects and other New Deal programs. Consider the millions of additional citizens touched by the veterans' programs of the postwar period. Consider the untold numbers whom the Great Society and its aftermath brought face to face with the federal government. In 1930 the federal bureaucracy was small and rather distant from the everyday concerns of Americans. By 1975 it was neither small nor distant.

As the years have passed, more and more citizens and groups have found themselves dealing with the federal bureaucracy. They may be seeking positive actions—eligibility for various benefits and awards of government grants. Or they may be seeking relief from the costs imposed by bureaucratic regulations—on working conditions, racial and sexual quotas, market restrictions, and numerous other subjects. While not malevolent, bureaucracies make mistakes, both of commission and omission, and normal attempts at redress often meet with unresponsiveness and inflexibility and sometimes seeming incorrigibility. Whatever the problem, the citizen's congressman is a source of succor. The greater the scope of government activity, the greater the demand for his services.

Private monopolists can regulate the demand for their product by raising or lowering the price. Congressmen have no such (legal) option. When the demand

NEED HELP WITH A FEDERAL PROBLEM?

Please feel free to communicate with me in person by phone or by mail Daily from 9 a.m. until 5 p.m. my Congressional District office in Fullerton is open to serve you and your family The staff will be able to help you with information or assistance on proposed Federal legislation and procedures of Federal agencies If you are experiencing a problem with Social Security educational assistance Veterans Administration Immigration Internal Revenue Service Postal Service Environmental Protection Agency, Federal Energy Office or any other Federal agency please contact me through this office If you decide to write to me please provide a telephone number as many times I can call you with information within a day or two

CONGRESSMAN CHARLES E. WIGGINS
Brashears Center, Suite 103
1400 N. Harbor Boulevard
Fullerton, Ca 92635 (714) 870-7266

My Washington address is
Room 2445 Rayburn Building, Washington, D.C.
20515. Telephone (202) 225-4111.

U S House of Representatives
WASHINGTON D C 20515
PUBLIC DOCUMENT
OFFICIAL BUSINESS

Charles E. Wiggins
M C

POSTAL CUSTOMER-LOCAL
39th District
CALIFORNIA

Figure A How the Congressman-as-Ombudsman Drums up Business

for their services rises, they have no real choice except to meet that demand—to supply more bureaucratic unsticking services—so long as they would rather be elected than unelected. This vulnerability to escalating constituency demands is largely academic, though. I seriously doubt that congressmen resist their gradual transformation from national legislators to errand boy-ombudsmen. As we have noted, casework is all profit. Congressmen have buried proposals to relieve the casework burden by establishing a national ombudsman or Congressman Reuss's proposed Administrative Counsel of the Congress. One of the congressmen interviewed by Clapp stated:

> Before I came to Washington I used to think that it might be nice if the individual states had administrative arms here that would take care of necessary liaison between citizens and the national government. But a congressman running for reelection is interested in building fences by providing personal services. The system is set to reelect incumbents regardless of party, and incumbents wouldn't dream of giving any of this service function away to any subagency. As an elected member I feel the same way.

In fact, it is probable that at least some congressmen deliberately stimulate the demand for their bureaucratic fixit services. (See [Figure A].) Recall that the new Republican in district A travels about his district saying:

> I'm you man in Washington. What are your problems? How can I help you?

And in district B, did the demand for the congressman's services rise so much between 1962 and 1964 that a "regiment" of constituency staff became necessary? Or, having access to the regiment, did the new Democrat stimulate the demand to which he would apply his regiment?

In addition to greatly increased casework, let us not forget that the growth of the federal role has also greatly expanded the federal pork barrel. The creative pork barreler need not limit himself to dams and post offices—rather old-fashioned interests. Today, creative congressmen can cadge LEAA money for the local police, urban renewal and housing money for local politicians, educational program grants for the local education bureaucracy. And there are sewage treatment plants, worker training and retraining programs, health services, and programs for the elderly. The pork barrel is full to overflowing. The conscientious congressman can stimulate applications for federal assistance (the sheer number of programs makes it difficult for local officials to stay current with the possibilities), put in a good word during consideration, and announce favorable decisions amid great fanfare.

In sum, everyday decisions by a large and growing federal bureaucracy bestow significant tangible benefits and impose significant tangible costs. Congressmen can affect these decisions. Ergo, the more decisions the bureaucracy has the opportunity to make, the more opportunities there are for the congressman to build up credits.

The nature of the Washington system is . . . quite clear. Congressmen (typically the majority Democrats) earn electoral credits by establishing various federal programs (the minority Republicans typically earn credits by fighting the good fight). The legislation is drafted in very general terms, so some agency, existing or newly established, must translate a vague policy mandate into a functioning program, a process that necessitates the promulgation of numerous rules and regulations and, incidentally, the trampling of numerous toes. At the next stage, aggrieved and/or hopeful constituents petition their congressman to intervene in the complex (or at least obscure) decision processes of the bureaucracy. The cycle closes when the congressman lends a sympathetic ear, piously denounces the evils of bureaucracy, intervenes in the latter's decisions, and rides a grateful electorate to ever more impressive electoral showings. Congressmen take credit coming and going. They are the alpha and the omega.

The popular frustration with the permanent government in Washington is partly justified, but to a considerable degree it is misplaced resentment. *Congress is the linchpin of the Washington establishment.* The bureaucracy serves as a convenient lightning rod for public frustration and a convenient whipping boy for congressmen. But so long as the bureaucracy accommodates congressmen, the latter will oblige with ever larger budgets and grants of authority. Congress does not just react to big government—it creates it. All of Washington prospers. More and more bureaucrats promulgate more and more regulations and dispense more and more money. Fewer and fewer congressmen suffer electoral defeat. Elements of the electorate benefit from government programs, and all of the electorate is eligible for ombudsman services. But the general, long-term welfare of the United States is no more than an incidental by-product of the system.

❖❖ Committee Chairmen as Part of the Washington Establishment

The preceding selection pointed out how the personal power incentive on Capitol Hill supports and expands committee government. Congressional committees became a dominant force in the legislative process towards the end of the nineteenth century. In 1885 Woodrow Wilson was able to state categorically in his famous work, *Congressional Government:*

> The leaders of the House are the chairmen of the principal Standing Committees. Indeed, to be exactly accurate, the House has as many leaders as there are subjects of legislation; for there are as many Standing Committees as there are leading classes of legislation, and in the consideration of every topic of business the House is guided by a special leader in the person of the chairman of the Standing Committee, charged with the superintendence of measures of the particular class to which that topic belongs. It is this multiplicity of leaders, this many-headed leadership, which makes the organization of the House too complex to afford uninformed people and unskilled observers any easy clue to its methods of rule. For the chairmen of the Standing Committees do not constitute a cooperative body like a ministry. They do not consult and concur in the adoption of homogeneous and mutually helpful measures; there is no thought of acting in concert. Each Committee goes its own way at its own pace. It is impossible to discover any unity or method in the disconnected and therefore unsystematic, confused, and desultory action of the House, or any common purpose in the measures which its Committees from time to time recommend.

With regard to the Senate he noted:

> It has those same radical defects of organization which weaken the House. Its functions also, like those of the House, are segregated in the prerogatives of numerous Standing Committees. In this regard Congress is all of a piece. There is in the Senate no more opportunity than exists in the House for gaining such recognized party leadership as would be likely to enlarge a man by giving him a sense of power, and to steady and sober him by filling him with a grave sense of responsibility. So far as its organization controls it, the Senate . . . proceedings bear most of the characteristic features of committee rule.

The Legislative Reorganization Act of 1946 was designed to streamline congressional committee structure and provide committees and individual members of Congress with increased expert staff; however, although the number of standing committees was reduced, subcommittees have increased so that the net numerical reduction is not as great as was originally intended. Further, because Congress still conducts its business through committees, (1) the senior members of the party with the majority in Congress dominate the formulation of public policy through the seniority rule; (2) policy formulation is fragmented, with each committee maintaining relative dominance over policy areas within its jurisdiction; (3) stemming from this fragmentation, party control is weakened, especially when the president attempts to assume legislative dominance.

Although Congress is often pictured as powerless in confrontation with the executive branch, the fact is that the chairmen of powerful congressional committees often dominate administrative agencies over which they have jurisdiction. They are an important part of the broad Washington establishment. This is particularly true of the chairmen of appropriations committees and subcommittees; because of their control of the purse-strings, they are able to wield far more influence over the bureaucracy than are the chairs of other committees. The appropriations committees have a direct weapon—money—that they can wield against administrative adversaries. And, the chairmen of all committees have seniority that often exceeds that of the bureaucrats with whom they are dealing. The secretaries and assistant secretaries of executive departments are political appointments who rarely stay in government more than two years, whereas powerful members of Congress have been around for one or more decades. This gives the latter expertise that the political levels of the bureaucracy often lack. Political appointees in the bureaucracy must rely upon their professional staff in order to match the expertise of senior members of Congress. The power of the chairmen of the appropriations committees often leads them to interfere directly in administrative operations. They become, in effect, part of the bureaucracy, often dominating it and determining what programs it will implement. The constant interaction between committee chairs and agencies results in "government without passing laws," to use the phrase of Michael W. Kirst. (See Michael W. Kirst, *Government Without Passing Laws,* Chapel Hill: University of North Carolina Press, 1969.)

While committees remain an important part of the Washington power establishment, their chairmen often becoming informal "prime ministers" dominating the policy arenas their committees control, the chairmen are no longer the feudal barons Woodrow Wilson portrayed. But committees, more than Congressional parties, continue to define the legislative process. The dispersion of committee power adds new dimensions to divided government. As the President confronts Congress he must deal with multiple power centers, making presidential leadership more complex and difficult.

50

Lawrence C. Dodd

CONGRESS AND THE QUEST FOR POWER

The postwar years have taught students of Congress a very fundamental lesson: Congress is a dynamic institution. The recent congressional changes picture an institution that is much like a kaleidoscope. At first glance the visual images and

From Lawrence C. Dodd and Bruce Oppenheimer, eds., *Congress Reconsidered* (New York: Praeger Publishers, 1977), pp. 269–283. Reprinted by permission.

Author's Note: For critical assistance at various stages in the writing of this essay, I would like to thank Arnold Fleischmann, Michael N. Green, Bruce I. Oppenheimer, Diana Phillips, Russ Renka, Terry Sullivan, and numerous graduate and undergraduate students who shared with me their questions and insights.

structural patterns appear frozen in a simple and comprehensive mosaic. Upon closer and longer inspection the realization dawns that the picture is subject to constant transformations. These transformations seem to flow naturally from the prior observations, yet the resulting mosaic is quite different and is not ordered by the same static principles used to interpret and understand the earlier one. The appreciation and understanding of the moving image requires not only comprehending the role of each colorful geometric object in a specific picture, not developing a satisfactory interpretation of the principles underlying a specific picture or change in specific aspects of the picture, but grasping the dynamics underlying the structural transformations themselves. So it is with Congress. To understand and appreciate it as an institution we must focus not only on particular aspects of internal congressional structure and process, nor on changes in particular patterns. We must seek to understand the more fundamental dynamics that produce the transformations in the congressional mosaic. This essay represents an attempt to explain the dynamics of congressional structure. . . .

I

As with politicians generally, members of Congress enter politics in a quest for personal power. This quest may derive from any number of deeper motives: a desire for ego gratification or for prestige, a search for personal salvation through good works, a hope to construct a better world or to dominate the present one, or a preoccupation with status and self-love. Whatever the source, most members of Congress seek to attain the power to control policy decisions that impose the authority of the state on the citizenry at large.

The most basic lesson that any member of Congress learns on entering the institution is that the quest for power by service within Congress requires reelection. First, reelection is necessary in order to remain in the struggle within Congress for "power positions." Staying in the struggle is important not only in that it provides the formal status as an elected representative without which an individual's influence on national legislative policy lacks legal authority; the quest for power through election and reelection also signals one's acceptance of the myth of democratic rule and thus one's acceptability as a power seeker who honors the society's traditional values. Second, reelection, particularly by large margins, helps create an aura of personal legitimacy. It indicates that one has a special mandate from the people, that one's position is fairly secure, that one will have to be "reckoned with." Third, long-term electoral success bestows on a member of Congress the opportunity to gain the experience and expertise, and to demonstrate the legislative skill and political prescience, that can serve to justify the exercise of power.

Because reelection is so important, and because it may be so difficult to ensure, its pursuit can become all-consuming. The constitutional system, electoral laws, and social system together have created political parties that are weak coalitions. A candidate for Congress normally must create a personal organization rather than rely on her or his political party. The "electoral connection" that intervenes between the desire for power and the realization of power may lead members to emphasize form over substance, position taking, advertising, and credit claiming rather than problem solving. In an effort to sustain electoral success, members of Congress may fail to take controversial and clear positions, fail to make hard choices, fail to exercise power itself. Yet members of Congress generally are not solely preoccupied with reelection. Most members have relatively secure electoral margins. This security stems partially from the fact that members of Congress *are* independent of political parties and are independent from responsibility for selecting the executive, and thus can be judged more on personal qualities than on partisan or executive affiliations. Electoral security is further reinforced because members of Congress personally control financial and casework resources that can help them build a loyalty from their constituents independent of policy or ideological considerations. The existence of secure electoral margins thus allows members to devote considerable effort toward capturing a "power position" within Congress and generating a mystique of special authority that is necessary to legitimize a select decision-making role for them in the eyes of their nominal peers.

The concern of members of Congress with gaining congressional power, rather than just securing reelection, has had a considerable influence on the structure and life of Congress. Were members solely preoccupied with reelection, we would expect them to spend little time in Washington and devote their personal efforts to constituent speeches and district casework. One would expect Congress to be run by a centralized, efficient staff who, in league with policy-oriented interest groups, would draft legislation, investigate the issues, frame palatable solutions, and present the members with the least controversial bills possible. Members of Congress would give little attention to committee work, and then only to committees that clearly served reelection interests. The primary activity of congress-people in Congress, rather, would be extended, televised floor debates and symbolic roll call votes, all for show. Such a system would allow the appearance of work while providing ample opportunity for the mending of home fences. Alternatively, were only a few members of Congress concerned about power, with others concerned with reelection, personal finances, or private lives, one might expect a centralized system with a few leaders exercising power and all others spending their time on personal or electoral matters.

Virtually all members of the U.S. Congress are preoccupied with power considerations. They are unwilling—unless forced by external events—to leave the major decisions in either a centralized, autonomous staff system or a central leadership. Each member wants to exercise power—to make the key policy decisions. This motive places every member in a personal conflict with every other member: to the extent that one member realizes her or his goal personally to control all key decisions, all others must lose. Given this widespread power motive, an obvious way to resolve the conflict is to disperse power—or at least power positions—as widely as possible. One logical solution, in other words, is to place basic policy-making responsibility in a series of discrete and relatively autonomous committees and subcommittees, each having control over the decisions in a specified jurisdictional area. Each member can belong to a small number of committees and, within them, have a significant and perhaps dominant influence on policy. Although such a system denies every member the opportunity to control all policy decisions, it ensures that most members, particularly if they stay in Congress long enough to obtain a subcommittee or committee chair, and if they generate the mystique of special authority necessary to allow them to activate the power potential of their select position, can satisfy a portion of their power drive.

Within Congress, as one would expect in light of the power motive, the fundamental structure of organization is a committee system. Most members spend most of their time not in their district but in Washington, and most of their Washington time not on the floor in symbolic televised debate but rather in the committee or subcommittee rooms, in caucus meetings, or in office work devoted to legislation. While the staff, particularly the personal staff, may be relegated to casework for constituents, the members of Congress sit through hearing after hearing, debate after debate, vote after vote seeking to shape in subcommittee, committee, and floor votes the contours of legislation. This is not to suggest, of course, that members of Congress do not engage in symbolic action or personal casework and do not spend much time in the home district; they do, in their effort at reelection. Likewise, staff do draft legislation, play a strong role in committee investigations, and influence the direction of public policy; they do this, however, largely because members of Congress just do not have enough time in the day to fulfill their numerous obligations. Seen in this perspective, Congress is not solely, simply, or primarily a stage on which individuals intentionally and exclusively engage in meaningless charades. Whatever the end product of their effort may be, members of Congress have actively sought to design a congressional structure and process that would maximize their ability to exercise personal power within Congress and, through Congress, within the nation at large.

The congressional committee structure reflects rather naturally the various dimensions that characterize the making of public policy. There are *authorization* committees that create policies and programs, specify their duties and powers, and establish absolute funding levels. There are *appropriations* committees that specify the actual funding level for a particular fiscal year. There are *revenue* committees that raise the funds to pay for the appropriations necessary to sustain the authorized programs. In addition, since Congress itself is an elaborate institution that must be serviced, there are *housekeeping* committees—those that provide for the day-to-day operation of Congress. In the House of Representatives there is also an *internal regulation* committee, the House Rules Committee, that schedules debate and specifies the rules for deliberation on specific bills.

These committees vary greatly in the nature and comprehensiveness of their impact on national policy making. The housekeeping committees tend to be *service* committees and carry little national weight except through indirect influence obtained from manipulating office and staff resources that other members may want so desperately as to modify their policy stances on other committees. A second set of committees, authorization committees such as Interior or Post Office, have jurisdictions that limit them to the concerns of fairly narrow constituencies; these are "reelection committees that allow members to serve their constituencies' parochial interests but offer only limited potential to effect broad-scale public policy. A third group of committees are *policy* committees, such as Education and Labor or International Relations, that consider fairly broad policy questions, though questions that have fairly clear and circumscribed jurisdictional limits. A fourth set of committees are the *"power"* committees, which make decisions on issues such as the scheduling of rules (the House Rules Committee), appropriations (House and Senate Appropriations committees), or revenues (House Ways and Means or Senate Finance) that allow them to affect most or all policy areas. Within a pure system of committee government, power committees are limited in the comprehensiveness of their control over the general policy-making process. No overarching control committee exists to coordinate the authorization, appropriations, or revenue process.

Because an essential type of legislative authority is associated with each congressional committee, members find that service on any committee can offer some satisfaction of their power drive. There are, nevertheless, inherent differences in the power potential associated with committees, differences that are tied to the variation in legislative function and in the comprehensiveness of a committee's decisional jurisdiction. This variation between committees is sufficient to make some committees more attractive as a place to gain power. Because members are in a quest for power, not simply reelection, they generally will seek to serve on committees whose function and policy focus allow the broadest personal impact on policy.

Maneuvering for membership on the more attractive committees is constrained by two fundamental factors. First, there are a limited number of attractive committee slots, and much competition will exist for these vacancies. Most members cannot realize their goal to serve on and gain control of these committees. For this reason, much pressure exists to establish norms by which members "prove" themselves deserving of membership on an attractive committee. Such norms include courtesy to fellow members, specialization in limited areas of public policy, a willingness to work hard on legislation, a commitment to the institution, adherence to the general policy parameters seen as desirable by senior members of Congress who will dominate the committee nominations process, and a willingness to reciprocate favors and abide by the division of policy domains into the set of relatively independent policy-making entities. Members who observe these norms faithfully will advance to the more desirable committees because they will have shown themselves worthy of special privilege, particularly if they also possess sufficient congressional seniority.

Seniority is particularly important because of the second constraint on the process—the fact that service on the more powerful committees may limit one's ability to mend electoral fences. On the more comprehensive committees, issues often can be more complex and difficult to understand, necessitating much time and concentration on committee work; members may not be able to get home as often or as easily. Issues will be more controversial and will face members with difficult and often unpopular policy choices; members will be less able to engage in the politics of form over substance. The national visibility of the members will be greater, transforming them into public figures whose personal lives may receive considerable attention. Indiscretions that normally might go unreported will become open game for the press and can destroy careers. Thus, although it is undoubtedly true that service on the more comprehensive committees may bring with it certain attributes that can help reelection (campaign contributions from interest groups, name identification and status, a reputation for power that may convince constituents that "our member can deliver"), service on the more attractive committees does thrust members into a more unpredictable world. Although members generally will want to serve on the most powerful committees, it will normally be best for them to put off such service until they have a secure electoral base and to approach their quest for power in sequential steps.

Because of the constraints operating within a system of committee government, congressional careers reflect a set of stages. The first stage entails an emphasis on shoring up the electoral base through casework, service on constituent-oriented reelection committees, and gaining favor within Congress by serving on the housekeeping committees. Of course, the first stage is never fully "completed": there is never a time at which a member of Congress is "guaranteed" long-term reelection or total acceptance within Congress, so both constituent and congressional service are a recurring necessity. But a point is normally reached—a point defined by the circumstances of the member's constituency, the opportunities present in Congress, and the personality and competence of the member—when he or she will feel secure enough, or perhaps unhappy enough, to attempt a move to a second stage. In the second stage members broaden their horizons and seek service on key policy committees that draft important legislation regulating such national policy dimensions as interstate commerce, education, or labor. In this stage, representatives begin to be "legislators," to preoccupy themselves with national policy matters. Because of the limited number of positions on power committees, many members will spend most, perhaps the rest, of their career in this stage, moving up by committee seniority to subcommittee and committee chairs on the policy committees. As they gain expertise in the specific policy area, and create a myth of special personal authority, they will gain power in some important but circumscribed area of national policy. For members who persist, however, and/or possess the right attributes of electoral security and personal attributes, a third stage exists: service on a power committee—Rules, Ways and Means, or Finance, Appropriations, and, in the Senate, Foreign Relations. Service on these committees is superseded, if at all, only by involvement in a fourth stage: service in the party leadership as a floor leader or Speaker. Few individuals ever have the opportunity to realize this fourth and climactic step; in a system of committee government, in fact, this step will be less sought and the battles less bitter than one might expect, considering the status associated with them, because power will rest primarily in committees rather than in the party. Although party leadership positions in a system of committee government do carry with them a degree of responsibility, particularly the obligation to mediate conflicts between committees and to influence the success of marginal legislation on the house floor, members will generally be content to stay on a power committee and advance to subcommittee and committee chair positions rather than engage in an all-out effort to attain party leadership positions.

This career path, presented here in an idealized and simplified fashion, is a general "power ladder" that members attempt to climb in their quest for power within Congress. Some members leave the path voluntarily to run for the Senate (if in the House), to run for governor, to serve as a judge, or to serve as president. Some for special reasons bypass one or another stage, choose to stay at a lower rung, are defeated, or retire. Despite exceptions, the set of stages is a very real guide to the long-term career path that members seek to follow. Implicit within this pattern is the very real dilemma discussed earlier: progress up the career ladder brings with it a greater opportunity for significant personal power, but also greater responsibility. As members move up the power ladder, they move away from a secure world in which reelection interest can be their dominant concern and into a world in which concerns with power and public policy predominate. They take their chance and leave the security of the reelection stage because of their personal quest for power, without which reelection is a largely meaningless victory.

The attempt to prove oneself and move up the career ladder requires enormous effort. Even after one succeeds and gains a power position, this attainment is not in itself sufficient to guarantee the personal exercise of power. To utilize fully the power prerogatives that are implicit in specific power positions, a member must maintain the respect, awe, trust, and confidence of committee and house colleagues; he or she must sustain the aura of personal authority that is necessary to legitimize the exercise of power. Although the norm of seniority under a system of pure committee government will protect a member's possession of a power position, seniority is not sufficient to guard personal authority. In order to pass legislation and dominate policy decisions in a committee's jurisdictional area, a committee chair must radiate an appearance of special authority. The member must abide by the norms of the house and the committee, demonstrate legislative competence, and generate policy decisions that appear to stay within the general policy parameters recognized as acceptable by the member's colleagues. Among reelection efforts, efforts to advance in Congress to power positions, efforts to sustain and nurture personal authority, and efforts to exercise power, the members of Congress confront an incredible array of crosscutting pressures and internal dilemmas—decisions about how to balance external reelection interests with the internal institutional career, how to maximize the possibility of power within Congress by service on particular committees, how to gain and nurture authority within committees by specific legislative actions. The world of the congressman or congresswoman is complicated further, however, by a very special irony.

II

As a form of institutional organization, committee government possesses certain attributes that recommend it. By dividing policy concerns among a variety of committees it allows members to specialize in particular policy areas; this division provides a congressional structure through which the members can be their own expert advisers and maintain a degree of independence from lobbyists or outside specialists. Specialization also provides a procedure whereby members can become acquainted with particular programs and agencies and follow their behavior over a period of years, thus allowing informed oversight of the implementation of public policy. The dispersion of power implicit in committee government is important, furthermore, because it brings a greater number of individuals into the policy-making process and thus allows a greater range of policy innovation. In addition, as stressed above, committee government also serves the immediate power motive of congresspeople by creating so many power positions that all members can seek to gain power in particular policy domains.

Despite its assets, committee government does have severe liabilities, flaws that undermine the ability of Congress to fulfill its constitutional responsibilities to make legislative policy and oversee the implementation of that policy. First, committee government by its very nature lacks strong, centralized *leadership*, thereby undermining its internal decision-making capacity and external authority. Internally, Congress needs central leadership because most major questions of public policy (such as economic or energy policy) cut across individual committee jurisdictions. Since each committee and subcommittee may differ in its policy orientation from all others, and since the support of all relevant committees will be essential to an overall program, it is difficult, if not impossible, to enact a coherent general approach to broad policy questions. A central party leader or central congressional steering committee with extensive control over the standing committees could provide the leadership necessary to assist the development and passage of a coherent policy across the various committees, but committee government rejects the existence of strong centralized power. The resulting dispersion of power within Congress, and the refusal to allow strong centralized leadership, ensures that congressional decisions on major policy matters (unless aided and pushed by an outside leader) will be incremental at best, immobilized and incoherent as a norm. And to the extent that a Congress governed by committees can generate public policy, it faces the external problem of leadership, the inability of outside political actors, the press, or the public to identify a legitimate spokesperson for Congress on any general policy question. The wide dispersion of power positions allows numerous members to gain a degree of dominance over specific dimensions of a policy domain; all of these members can speak with some authority on a policy question, presenting conflicting and confusing approaches and interpretations. In cases where Congress does attempt to act, Congress lacks a viable mechanism through which to publicize and justify its position in an authoritative manner. Should Congress be in a conflict with the president, who can more easily present a straightforward and publicized position, Congress almost certainly will lose out in the eyes of public opinion. Lacking a clearly identifiable legislative leader in its midst, Congress is unable to provide the nation with unified, comprehensible, or persuasive policy leadership.

Closely related to the lack of leadership is a lack of *fiscal coordination*. Nowhere within a system of committee government is there a mechanism to ensure that the decisions of authorization, appropriations, and revenue committees have some reasonable relationship to one another. The authorization committees make their decisions about the programs to authorize largely independent of appropriations committee decisions about how much money the government will spend. The appropriations committees decide on spending levels largely independent of revenue committee decisions on taxation. Since it is always easier to promise (or authorize) than to deliver (or spend), program goals invariably exceed the actual financial outlays and thus the actual delivery of service. And since it is easier to spend money than to make or tax money, particularly for politicians, expenditures will exceed the revenues to pay the bills. Moves to coordinate the authorization, appropriations, and revenue processes are inconsistent with committee government, since such an effort would necessarily create a central mechanism with considerable say over all public policy and thus centralize power in a relatively small number of individuals. Committee government thus by its very nature is consigned to frustration: the policies that it does produce will invariably produce higher expectations than they can deliver; its budgets, particularly in periods of liberal, activist Congresses, will produce sizable and unplanned deficits in which expenditures far exceed revenues. The inability of committee government to provide realistic program goals and fiscal discipline will invite the executive to intervene in the budget process in order to provide fiscal responsibility and coordination. The result, of course, will be a concomitant loss of the congressional control over the nation's purse strings.

A third detriment associated with committee government, and one that is exacerbated by the absence of leadership and committee coordination, is the lack of *accountability* and *responsibility*. A fundamental justification of congressional government is that it allows political decision making to be responsive to the will of a national majority. Committee government distributes this decision-making authority among a largely autonomous set of committees. Since seniority protects each committee's membership from removal and determines who will chair each committee, a committee's members can feel free to follow their personal policy predilections and stop any legislation they wish that falls within their committee's jurisdiction, or propose any that they wish. Within a system of committee government, resting as it does on the norm of seniority, no serious way exists to hold a specific committee or committee chair accountable to the majority views of Congress or the American people, should those views differ from the views held within a particular committee. Because of the process whereby members are selected to serve on major committees—a process that emphasizes not their compatibility with the majority's policy sentiment but rather their adherence to congressional norms, general agreement with the policy views of senior congresspeople, and possession of seniority—the top committees (especially at the senior ranks) are quite likely to be out of step with a congressional or national majority. This lack of representativeness is particularly likely if patterns of electoral security nationwide provide safe seats (and thus seniority) to regions or localities that are unrepresentative of the dominant policy perspectives of the country. Responsiveness is further undermined because the absence of strong central leaders, and a widespread desire among members for procedural protection of their personal prerogatives, require reliance on rigid rules and regulations to govern the flow of legislation and debate, rules such as the Senate's cloture rule that allows the existence of filibusters. Under a system of party government, where limiting rules may exist on the books, strong party leaders can mitigate their effects. In a system of committee government, rules become serious hurdles that can block the easy flow of legislation, particularly major, controversial legislation, thereby decreasing the ability of Congress to respond rapidly to national problems. Committee government thus undermines the justification of Congress as an institution that provides responsive, representative government. Since institutions derive their power not solely from constitutional legalisms but from their own mystique of special authority that comes from their legitimizing myths, committee government undercuts not only Congress's ability to exercise power but also the popular support that is necessary to maintain its power potential.

The lack of accountability and the damage to Congress's popular support are augmented by a fourth characteristic of committee government—a tendency toward *insulation* of congressional decision making. This insulation derives from three factors. First, members of committees naturally try to close committee sessions from public purview, limiting thereby the intrusion of external actors such as interest groups or executive agencies and thus protecting committee members' independent exercise of power within committees. Second, the creation of a multiplicity of committees makes it difficult for the public or the press to follow policy deliberations even if they are open. Third, it is difficult if not impossible to create clear jurisdictional boundaries between committees. The consequent ambiguity that exists between jurisdictional boundaries will often involve committees themselves in extensive disputes over the control of particular policy domains, further confusing observers who are concerned with policy deliberations. By closing its committee doors, creating a multiplicity of committees, and allowing jurisdictional ambiguities, a system of committee government isolates Congress from the nation at large. Out of sight and out of mind, Congress loses the attention, respect, and understanding of the nation and becomes an object of scorn and derision, thus further undermining the authority or legitimacy of its pronouncements and itself as an institution.

Finally, committee government undermines the ability of Congress to perform that one function for which committee government would seem most suited—aggressive oversight of administration. According to the classic argument, the saving grace of committee government is that the dispersion of power and the creation of numerous policy experts ensure congressional surveillance of the bureaucracy. Unfortunately, this argument ignores the fact that the individuals on the committees that pass legislation will be the very people least likely to investigate policy implementation. They will be committed to the program, as its authors or most visible supporters, and will not want to take actions that might lead to a destruction of the program. The impact of publicity and a disclosure of agency or program shortcomings, after all, is very unpredictable and difficult to control and may create a public furor against the program. The better part of discretion is to leave the agency largely to its own devices and rely on informal contacts and special personal arrangements, lest the glare of publicity and the discovery of shortcomings force Congress to deauthorize a pet program, casting aspersions on those who originally drafted the legislation. Members of Congress are unwilling to resolve this problem by creating permanent and powerful oversight committees because such committees, by their ability to focus attention on problems of specific agencies and programs, would threaten the authority of legislative committees to control and direct policy in their allotted policy area. Committee government thus allows a *failure of executive oversight*.

In the light of these five problems, the irony of committee government is that it attempts to satisfy members' individual desires for personal power by dispersing internal congressional authority so widely that the resulting institutional impotence cripples the ability of Congress to perform its constitutional roles, thereby dissipating the value of internal congressional power. Members of Congress thus are not only faced with the daily dilemma of balancing reelection interests with their efforts at upward power mobility within Congress; their lives are also complicated by a cruel paradox, the ultimate incompatibility of widely dispersed power within Congress, on the one hand, and a strong role for Congress in national decision making, on the other. This inherent tension generates an explosive dynamic within Congress as an organization and between Congress and the executive.

In the short run, as members of Congress follow the immediate dictates of the personal power motive, they are unaware of, or at least unconcerned with, the long-term consequences of decentralized power; they support the creation of committee government. The longer committee government operates, the more unhappy political analysts and the people generally become with the inability of Congress to make national policy or ensure policy implementation. With Congress deadlocked by immobilism, political activists within Congress and the nation at large turn to the president (as the one alternative political figure who is popularly elected and thus should be responsive to popular sentiments) and encourage him (or her, if we ever break the sex barrier) to provide policy leadership and fiscal coordination, to open up congressional decision making to national political forces and ensure congressional responsiveness, and to oversee the bureaucracy. Presidents, particularly those committed to activist legislation, welcome the calls for intervention and will see their forthright role as an absolute necessity to the well-being of the Republic. Slowly at first, presidents take over the roles of chief legislator, chief budgetary officer, overseer of the bureaucracy, chief tribune, and protector of the people. Eventually the president's role in these regards becomes so central that he feels free to ignore the wishes of members of Congress, even those who chair very important committees, and impose presidential policy on Congress and the nation at large.

The coming of a strong, domineering, imperial president who ignores Congress mobilizes its members into action. They see that their individual positions of power within Congress are meaningless unless the institution can impose its legislative will on the nation. They search for ways to regain legislative preeminence and constrain the executive. Not being fools, members identify part of the problem as an internal institutional one and seek to reform Congress. Such reform efforts come during or immediately following crises in which presidents clearly and visibly threaten fundamental power prerogatives of Congress. The reforms will include attempts to provide for more centralized congressional leadership, fiscal coordination, congressional openness, better oversight mechanisms, clarification of committee jurisdictions, procedures for policy coordination, and procedures to encourage committee accountability. Because the quest for personal power continues as the underlying motivation of individual members, the reforms are basically attempts to strengthen the value of internal congressional power by increasing the power of Congress vis-à-vis the executive. The reform efforts, however, are constrained by consideration of personal power prerogatives of members of Congress. The attempt to protect personal prerogatives while centralizing power builds structural flaws into the centralization mechanisms, flaws that would not be present were the significance of congressional structure for the national power of Congress itself the only motive. The existence of these flaws provides the openings through which centralization procedures are destroyed when institutional crises pass and members again feel free to emphasize personal power and personal careers. In addition, because policy inaction within Congress often will be identified as the immediate cause of presidential power aggrandizement, and because policy immobilism may become identified with key individuals or committees that have obstructed particular legislation, reform efforts also may be directed toward breaking up the authority of these individuals or committees and dispersing it among individuals and committees who seem more amenable to activist policies. This short-term dispersal of power, designed to break a legislative logjam (and, simultaneously, to give power to additional individuals), will serve to exacerbate immobilism in the long run when the new mechanisms of centralization are destroyed.

Viewed in a broad historical perspective, organizational dynamics within Congress, and external relations of Congress to the president, have a "cyclical" pattern. At the outset, when politicians in a quest for national power first enter Congress, they decentralize power and create committee government. Decentralization is followed by severe problems of congressional decision making, presidential assumption of legislative prerogatives, and an eventual presidential assault on Congress itself. Congress reacts by reforming its internal structure: some reform efforts will involve legislation that attempts to circumscribe presidential action; other reforms will attempt to break specific points of deadlock by further decentralization and dispersal of congressional authority; eventually, however, problems of internal congressional leadership and coordination will become so severe that Congress will be forced to undertake centralizing reforms. As Congress moves to resolve internal structural problems and circumscribe presidential power, presidents begin to cooperate so as to defuse the congressional counterattack; to do otherwise would open a president to serious personal attack as anticongressional and thus anti-democratic, destroying the presidency's legitimizing myth as a democratic institution and identifying presidential motivations as power aggrandizement rather than protection of the Republic. As the immediate threat to congressional prerogatives recedes, members of Congress (many of whom will not have served in Congress during the era of institutional crisis) become preoccupied with their immediate careers and press once again for greater power dispersal within Congress and removal of centralizing mechanisms that inhibit committee and subcommittee autonomy. Decentralization reasserts itself and Congress becomes increasingly leaderless, uncoordinated, insulated, unresponsive, unable to control executive agencies. Tempted by congressional weakness and hounded by cries to "get the country moving," the executive again reasserts itself and a new institutional crisis eventually arises. A review of American history demonstrates the existence of this cycle rather clearly, particularly during the twentieth century. . . .

Congress and the Media

Television has transformed politics in many ways. Perhaps most importantly, because of television, images have become as important as and in some cases more important than issues in political campaigns. On Capitol Hill members of Congress, as the following selection illustrates, spend as much time on the media as they do on their legislative work. The press has always followed members of Congress, but television has changed the rules of the game. Legislators have found that more than in the past media exposure is essential not only to reelection but to a successful Capitol Hill career.

51

Timothy E. Cook

MEDIA POWER AND CONGRESSIONAL POWER

❖❖❖❖❖❖❖❖

The House of Representatives has long witnessed the chaotic comings and goings of its 435 members—from offices to committee rooms to the floor and back again while lobbyists and constituents try to get in a word or two on the run. But increasingly relations with the news media seem to take up legislators' time and effort. Dressed in telegenic blue shirts and red neckties, they stand before television cameras in the swamp, the section of the Capitol lawn set aside for interviews. Inside the Capitol, too, floor debates are often aimed at the discreetly placed cameras that broadcast the proceedings to members' offices, the press galleries, and homes across the country. Staffers and interns dash from one gallery to the next with stacks of press releases to be distributed. Reporters crowd outside hearing rooms to receive a committee report or corner a witness. In short, much of the hubbub of Capitol Hill today is contributed by the press and their would-be subjects. Making laws is far from the only business of the House. It has been supplemented by making news.

Making news was not always so important. Reporters have been present on Capitol Hill for nearly two centuries, but rarely before has seeking publicity been such a significant part of every House member's job. For most of the twentieth century the way to get things done and to advance a career in Washington was to play an inside game, building relationships with colleagues, deferring to senior members, and bargaining, while slowly building up the legislative longevity necessary to achieve a position of power. Legislators paid little attention to reporters except those from the press back home, and they severely restricted the access of radio and television to the House. The House was governed by party leaders and committee chairs who preferred to stay out of the spotlight whenever possible.

Now all that has changed. The media are useful to members for publicity to help them get reelected, of course, but increasingly also in policymaking, wielding influence in Congress and in Washington, and pursuing their personal ambitions. Making news has frequently become integral to the legislative process. Reporters for all kinds of news outlets can now be present at any stage of the legislative process and can be instrumental in shaping the results. Sophisticated House press operations try to create national constituencies for issues on which members can serve as authoritative sources and build reputations. At the very least, legislators who wish to be considered influential experts have to ensure that their media image fits their chosen self-portrait, so few of them, inside or outside leadership circles, can pass up opportunities to be newsworthy. Making news, in short, has become a crucial component of making laws.

This reliance shows few signs of abating, even after the departure of Ronald Reagan, whose presidency has thus far been the high-water mark of going public. His successor, George Bush, has carefully crafted a media strategy, but it has shown him off as more a manager than a great communicator. However, Bush's recent choice of the Iwo Jima Memorial as the backdrop for introducing a constitutional amendment to ban flag burning shows that the adept use of sound bites and visual imagery that marked his presidential campaign could easily turn into a strategy of governing by campaigning. On Capitol Hill the Senate in 1986 finally followed the House's lead in broadcasting floor proceedings, further cementing the conjuncture of making laws and making news. And Tip O'Neill, the self-confessed backroom politician who brought the House into the television age, was succeeded first in 1987 by Jim Wright, whose aggressive, policy-oriented loner style was well-suited for the press, and in 1989 by Thomas Foley, perhaps "the first House Speaker whom most colleagues feel comfortable putting in front of television cameras" and whose tenure as majority leader had been marked by unprecedented attention to publicity.

The conditions that made it not only possible but necessary to use the media to get legislative business accomplished also show few signs of abating. The expansion of congressional staffs in the 1970s will not be reversed; and each new Congress will see members naming more full-time press secretaries. Likewise, the number of Washington reporters should continue to grow steadily. News organizations may be tightening their belts, but the rise of newspaper chains, the abundance of stringers, and the creation of groups such as Conus that contract out television news services mean that virtually any news outlet can have a relatively inexpensive link to Washington. Such easy hookups allow members to add their comments to stories that are bouncing among various newsbeats in the capital. Above all, the news media help House members set the legislative agenda, define the alternatives, influence public moods, and affect outcomes at a time when the political process is confused and unpredictable.

Yet if legislators need reporters, reporters also need legislators to create the events or provide the observations that can become the basis of a story. Even though the needs of the two are rarely identical, they can work in a symbiosis. House members, even at high levels of power, cannot automatically make news. Instead, they must ensure that their information and stories meet journalistic standards of timeliness, pertinence, and interest. Reporters' dependence on authoritative sources to suggest news means that journalism tends to reflect the perspectives of the more powerful. But such power is not absolute, because while politicians control definitions of importance, journalists still decide what is interesting. So House members and reporters negotiate and renegotiate newsworthiness. The question should not then be what the news media have done *to* the House, or what the House has done *to* the news media, but what these two institutions have done *with* one another. What is the effect of this negotiation on policymaking and on representative democracy? The answers must be speculative, but they are well worth contemplating.

Policymaking Processes and the Media

The power of the press often buttresses established power and procedures in the House. Hill traditions of pursuing expertise and influence dovetail with reporters' search for sources who are in a position to know. Reporters accord a reassuring coherence to the legislative process by focusing on "particularly and peculiarly congressional actions," stressing the gradual, orderly nature of the way bills are passed rather than the chaos or stasis that characterizes much of congressional life.

But the priorities of journalists and politicians are now always so synchronized. Reporters have less leeway in whom to report about or when to report it than in the issues that will receive coverage. Some of the coverage of Congress is a by-product of the coverage of issues. Issues most likely to make news are easily described, have clearly characterized sides, affect a large part of the audience, and come with straightforward reform remedies. Journalists tend to pass up matters that are complex, unfamiliar, specialized, or not apparently easily addressed.

If members want news coverage, they must choose clear-cut issues or try to present the complex as simple. But such choices invite distortion or omission of complicating factors. . . .

Setting the agenda is only the first step in the journey of legislation; press attention affects later stages, too. Bargaining among members, once the hallmark of a legislative institution, becomes more difficult when reporters are watching—not so much because members act differently in public than in private but because reporters' dislike for noncommittal stances tends to discourage the fluidity and maneuverability necessary to resolve differences on the fine points and to enact legislation.

Legislators who wish to get something done must be both outside and inside players. Press coverage can enhance their reputations and direct colleagues' attention toward them as people to listen to. Inside strategies can lead to the influential post that can be used to gain the media's attention. Using them together can be synergistic, accomplishing more than using either one on its own. . . .

To the extent that the press spotlights problems and helps set the legislative agenda, an additional complication arises: the clock of Congress will resemble that of the news. The media have a limited attention span. They discover problems suddenly, but their interest rapidly wanes, whether or not the problems have been solved. As entrepreneurial politicians take advantage of the brief window of opportunity to get something done, agenda items can rise and fall in importance with dizzying rapidity. . . .

Yet for all these drawbacks, the conjunction of media strategies and legislative strategies can aid policymaking, particularly in surmounting entrenched interests and facilitating large-scale legislative initiatives. The news suggests problems or alternatives that Congress has bypassed. It helps inform and mobilize public opinion. At the very least it forces legislators to look beyond the interests of organized groups with the most immediate stakes and perhaps toward the larger public interest. When members would prefer to do nothing, publicity can increase the risks of inaction. In short, members in the spotlight are pressured to deal with problems in a way that corresponds to their readings of public opinion.

Congress and Mass-Mediated Democracy

To evaluate more fully the implications of the media's role in the House, though, one must set forth standards for the roles of legislators and legislatures in representative democracy. After all, the Constitution assigned the House in particular to represent the people. At its most basic, political representation means that officials are elected to act on behalf of their constituents' interests. . . .

At the local level the relationship of House member and constituency would initially seem to be working wonderfully. If, as in 1988, nearly 99 percent of the House incumbents standing for reelection are returned for another term, what could possibly be wrong? But as Hanna Pitkin has pointed out, a legislator's reelection "is not absolute proof that he is a good representative; it proves at most that the voters think so." And when reasons for that approval are examined, optimism about the idealness of the relationship must be tempered. Incumbents win reelection more or less by default against invisible opposition. To be sure, even under these circumstances members are constrained by the realization that they might have to account for their actions. To compile a record that can be easily explained back home, when they present themselves in person to as many constituents as possible, they end up anticipating their constituents' will and responding to it. Their accessibility can result in dialogue. But when legislators rely on explaining through the media rather than explaining in person, dialogue is replaced by one-way rhetoric.

The ascendancy of rhetoric might not be a problem if it were informative and balanced, but it is not. Even local news outlets rarely report House elections with the same effort and initiative they devote to statewide or presidential elections. This neglect works to the incumbents' advantage, because in effect they can shape the timing, content, and tone of their own coverage. All of this means that the voters lack enough information and tilt toward incumbents because they have no reason to be against them. Far from being watchdogs, the local media usually reinforce an incumbent's advantage by benign neglect.

What can be done? Cutting back on the incumbent's franking privilege or other perquisites of office is no answer: it can be valuable in a democracy to have legislators communicate with their constituents or travel home. And regulating perks does little to right the balance. Banning mass mailings within sixty days of an election simply moved them from November to September. Regulating the content of postal patron newsletters has created a Franking Commission that diligently counts the number of times a personal pronoun is used but that has little say over substance.

To ensure dialogue and choice, more information must be available. For all the criticism of television advertisements, their content is sometimes more substantive than that allowed by the horse-race mentality of election coverage, and voters may actually learn as much from them. But though campaign managers have considered television the most crucial medium, they rarely buy television time. Airing ads, even those lasting no more than thirty seconds, is so prohibitively expensive that by themselves they are responsible for spiraling campaign expenditures. Reforms must control the expense at its root, or else such proposals as publicly financing congressional elections or placing limits on fundraising (as by restricting the contributions of political action committees) would not improve the quality of information and the quality of voters' decisionmaking.

One answer: since television and radio are regulated by the government, they could be required to broadcast a certain number of messages from the major candidates of each district in the media market, much as stations are already obliged to carry a certain number of public service announcements. Naturally, incumbents are not keen on this idea; in a 1986 survey, 61 percent of the challengers endorsed the idea but only 30 percent of the incumbents. Similar provisions could allow an equal number of campaign mailings sent at government expense by challengers opposing representatives who have sent out newsletters. Members may think twice about blanketing the district with self-serving propaganda if they know their challengers will receive equal treatment. Without some such reforms, elections will remain trials that are all defense and no prosecution.

Of course, providing candidates with free air time does not preclude them from using it to obscure or distort—witness the number of liberal Democrats who used television ads to portray themselves as fiscal conservatives in the Reaganite year of 1984. And reforms aimed at television or at newsletters only indirectly affect newspapers. To answer these concerns, news about House members and House campaigns must be made easier to report. A barrier to providing enough information to the voters is the nature of district boundaries. The few districts that receive complete coverage of House elections correspond closely to television media markets or newspaper circulation areas. The less overlap, the less coverage and the less information about the candidates, especially the challenger. House districts, assembled to meet court standards of population equality, are gerrymandered to protect partisans or incumbents. Their boundaries do not match those of existing political communities or, more importantly, media markets. In 1986 the Supreme Court ruled that political gerrymandering is a justiciable issue, so plans may now be tossed out for favoring particular political outcomes, including protection of incumbents. If state legislatures considered media market boundaries in carving up districts, or if, perhaps more likely, courts took them into account when reviewing redistricting plans, there would be fewer election contests for each news organization to try to cover and probably more information about both incumbent and challenger.

Redrawing district lines would make House races easier to cover, but for re-election to be less routine, journalistic definitions of newsworthiness, balance, and completeness must change. If news organizations are not to give incumbents a boost for reelection, there must be stories other than those instigated by the members themselves. Instead of waiting for legislators to provide a peg for news, local outlets could easily come up with stories out of the public record such as analyses of what the members did in committee or on the floor and how they voted. During the campaign itself, editors and publishers should take care to identify both the incumbent and the challenger as serious candidates, perhaps even assigning different reporters to each one to ensure treatment that is as even-handed as possible. Until this is done, local news organizations, if only by overlooking the House campaigns, will end up being on the incumbent's side, and accountability will be poorly overseen.

At the national level, too, the increasing presence of the media may have some unfavorable effects for representative democracy. Outside strategies tend to converge on only some issues—those that fit the media's preferences. How closely are these issues connected to the people's concerns and preferences? Do media strategies help to open the legislative process to public scrutiny and encourage informed democracy or do they reinforce inequities of access and of power?

To answer these questions, perhaps it would be wise to ask to whom the media themselves are responsive. Though national journalists operate outside of Congress, they are inside the Washington beltway, routinely involved with elected officials, congressional staff, interest-group representatives, bureaucrats, and think-tank scholars. By facilitating communication within Washington, news organizations tend to represent the views of organized groups or otherwise already prominent actors, not only to each other but to the rest of the nation. The debates that Washington reporters discuss are those among organized political and economic groups, and if there is no debate, they do not rush in to fill the void.

Often, the media's role in the political process is akin to recirculating air in a building with no windows. The unexpected becomes so routinized that news itself is almost predictable. Freshness is only occasionally brought in by unanticipated dramatic events: the death of a basketball star from cocaine poisoning, an accident at a Soviet nuclear power plant, hospital waste washing up on New Jersey beaches, a massacre of schoolchildren by a gunman carrying an AK-47. Such disruptions of routine provide an opportunity for sources outside governmental and corporate hierarchies to be heard. But the sources are usually insufficiently organized, and by the time they are ready the spotlight is back to the existing agenda and the usual authoritative sources.

"Washington news gathering, in other words, is an interaction among elites," Stephen Hess has written. "One elite reports on another elite." An advertisement in the New York Times business section even encouraged this interaction.

If the news were about you, you'd read it, wouldn't you?
So Washington reads Washington Talk in the New York Times.
It's where corporate messages will be seen and read by government leaders.

Elites partly adopt and incorporate the concerns of other elites, an interaction only somewhat mitigated by the connections that each has with the people. But if representatives can become detached from constituents, journalists have even fewer direct connections with their readers or viewers, except for fellow reporters, superiors, and sources. Far from giving the public just what it wants, they prefer to avoid information about their mass audiences. Anticipating the latter's needs and reactions adds a potentially paralyzing complication, not to mention a threat to journalists' control of choosing and presenting news. They may ask people outside positions of power for opinions in person-in-the-street interviews or polls, but they choose the subject, which usually reflects issues that are hot in Washington. The result may be top-down policymaking: instead of bringing public opinion to official Washington, the news disseminates the views of Washington across the country.

None of this is the fault of reporters in general or of politicians in general. The Hill reporters I have met are exceedingly conscientious about standards of objectivity and excellence. And even though House press secretaries may present one-sided accounts, their reports are seldom fabrications or distortions of their bosses' records. But these people work within news organizations or political institutions that define what is worth attending to and what may be neglected, and reward workers accordingly. As Warren Breed noted, "Newsmen define their job as producing a certain quantity of what is called 'news' every 24 hours. . . . They are not rewarded for analyzing the social structure, but for getting news." Or in the words of Todd Gitlin, "Political news is like crime news; it's about what went wrong today, not what goes wrong every day."

As House members and their staffs decide what course to pursue and increasingly incorporate a definition of news as something that happened since yesterday, they become directed toward problems that are quickly fixed and away from chronic conditions that find a news peg only with difficulty. Political debate under the spotlight is directed to more technical, less politicized questions of governance instead of essential social concerns that the news rarely directly addresses and that thus remain rarely discussed.

Turning to the news media to help the process of governance is a reasonable option that House members and their staffs may profitably adopt. But merely linking media and legislative strategies, although it could well be a precondition for democratic decisionmaking, is insufficient. Legislating in the spotlight can move politicians away from the influence of organized groups, encourage them to take account of the public interest, and allow them to build coalitions on complex issues. The paradox of the 1980s, however, has been that such results have often occurred without the full-scale public mobilization that marked Reagan's 1981 campaign to cut taxes and spending. Just as theater critics can shut down a play even if the public likes it, so the involvement of the media can turn legislators toward or away from particular issues and particular options whether or not public opinion is on one side or the other.

If representative democracy is to work well, there must be more participation not merely by news organizations on behalf of the people but by the people themselves in shaping the options and decisions of government. Bringing the republic back into politics, of course, entails many possible steps not connected with either Congress or the media. Reforms in House election campaigns to cut down the inherent advantage of the incumbent could help, as would more general reforms, such as easing voter registration requirements. But the democratization of political news to include perspectives besides those provided by Washington is also necessary. It has been suggested that "multiperspectival" news is needed—news that would include opinions of the public as well as those of officials, news about programs as they actually operate rather than as they are intended to work, and news that reflects a much greater variety of sources. None of this need necessarily change how Washington reporters go about their work; but it does require that officials' views be supplemented by others so that news organizations do not become unwitting adjuncts to the already powerful.

Of course, this very willingness on the part of the media to negotiate a relationship favorable to politicians enables House members to use publicity and to craft media strategies in pursuit of legislative goals. By taking advantage of news routines that emphasize a scripted process with authoritative sources, by working to manage journalists' access both formally and informally, by building a professionalized press operation with a full-time press secretary, House members today are adroitly pursuing and using the opportunities presented to them. Media strategies in the House have become valuable, not merely to take positions or gratify egos; they are now crucial ways to attain, maintain, and exert power in Washington.

❖❖ Congress and the Electoral Connection

Throughout the 1970s public opinion polls consistently revealed that Congress was held in low esteem by the American people. The book *Who Runs Congress?*, published by the Ralph Nader Congress Project, reflected and at the same time helped to crystallize public disenchantment with Capitol Hill.[1] The book emphasized the need for citizens to take on Congress to prevent a further flagging of the institution. In his introduction, Ralph Nader summarized the contents of the book by stating that "the people have indeed abdicated their power, their money, and their democratic birthright to Congress. As a result, without the participation of the people, Congress has surrendered its enormous authority and resources to special interest groups, waste, insensitivity, ignorance, and bureaucracy."[2] The 1972 theme of the Nader project that Congress was in crisis continues to be accepted by the vast majority of people.

While Ralph Nader and his colleagues feel that the major cause of the demise of Congress is its detachment from the people, Richard Fenno in the

---

[1]Mark J. Green et al., eds., *Who Runs Congress?* (New York: Bantam/Grossman, 1972).

[2]Ibid., p. 1.

following selection adopts a different viewpoint. He feels that people fault the *institution* of Congress, not their individual representatives on Capitol Hill. In fact, he points out that there is a close connection between legislators and constituents, and often, a feeling of affection by voters for their representatives. Fenno feels that we apply different standards in judging individual members of Congress than we do in assessing the institution, being far more lenient in the former than the latter case. The individual is judged for his or her personality, style, and representativeness, while the institution is judged by its ability to recognize and solve the nation's problems. But the institution cannot be thought of apart from the members that compose it. It is they who have given it its unique character. It is the individual member who, more often than not, has supported a decentralized and fragmented legislature because of the members' incentive to achieve personal power and status on Capitol Hill.

52

Richard F. Fenno, Jr.

IF, AS RALPH NADER SAYS, CONGRESS IS "THE BROKEN BRANCH," HOW COME WE LOVE OUR CONGRESSMEN SO MUCH?

❖❖❖❖❖❖❖

Off and on during the past two years, I accompanied ten members of the House of Representatives as they traveled around in their home districts. In every one of those districts I heard a common theme, one that I had not expected. Invariably, the representative I was with—young or old, liberal or conservative, Northerner, Southerner, Easterner, or Westerner, Democrat or Republican—was described as "the best congressman in the United States." Having heard it so often, I now accept the description as fact. I am even prepared to believe the same thing (though I cannot claim to have heard it with my own ears) of the members of the Senate. Each of our 435 representatives and 100 senators is, indeed, "the best congressman in the

From Richard F. Fenno, Jr., "If, As Ralph Nader Says, Congress Is 'The Broken Branch,' How Come We Love Our Congressmen So Much?" Originally written as part of an editorial project entitled "The Role of Congress: A Study of the Legislative Branch," © 1972 by Time, Inc., and Richard F. Fenno, Jr. Reprinted by permission.

United States." Which is to say that each enjoys a great deal of support and approbation among his or her constituents. Judging by the election returns, this isn't much of an exaggeration. In [recent elections], 96 percent of all House incumbents who ran were reelected; and 85 percent of all Senate incumbents who ran were reelected. These convincing figures are close to the average reelection rates of incumbents for the past ten elections. We do, it appears, love our congressmen.

On the other hand, it seems equally clear that we do not love our Congress. Louis Harris reported in 1970 that only one-quarter of the electorate gave Congress a positive rating on its job performance—while nearly two-thirds expressed themselves negatively on the subject. . . . There [is] considerable concern—dramatized recently by the critical Nader project—for the performance of Congress as an institution. On the evidence, we seem to approve of our legislators a good deal more than we do our legislature. And therein hangs something of a puzzle. If our congressmen are so good, how can our Congress be so bad? If it is the individuals that make up the institution, why should there be such a disparity in our judgments? What follows are a few reflections on this puzzle.

A first answer is that we apply different standards of judgment, those that we apply to the individual being less demanding than those we apply to the institution. For the individual, our standard is one of representativeness—of personal style and policy views. Stylistically, we ask that our legislator display a sense of identity with us so that we, in turn, can identify with him or her—via personal visits to the district, concern for local projects and individual "cases," and media contact of all sorts, for example. On the policy side, we ask only that his general policy stance does not get too frequently out of line with ours. And, if he should become a national leader in some policy area of interest to us, so much the better. These standards are admittedly vague. But because they are locally defined and locally applied, they are consistent and manageable enough so that legislators can devise rules of thumb to meet them. What is more, by their performance they help shape the standards, thereby making them easier to meet. Thus they win constituent recognition as "the best in the United States." And thus they establish the core relationship for a representative democracy.

For the institution, however, our standards emphasize efforts to solve national problems—a far less tractable task than the one we (and he) set for the individual. Given the inevitable existence of unsolved problems, we are destined to be unhappy with congressional performance. The individual legislator knows when he has met our standards of representativeness; he is reelected. But no such definitive measure of legislative success exists. And, precisely because Congress is the most familiar and most human of our national institutions, lacking the distant majesty of the Presidency and the Court, it is the easy and natural target of our criticism. We have met our problem solvers, and they are us.

Furthermore, such standards as we do use for judging the institutional performance of Congress are applied inconsistently. In 1963, when public dissatisfaction was as great as in 1970, Congress was criticized for being obstructionist, dilatory and insufficiently cooperative with regard to the Kennedy programs. Two years later, Congress got its highest performance rating of the decade when it cooperated completely with the executive in rushing the Great Society program into law. But by the late 1960s and early 1970s the standard of judgment had changed radically—from cooperation to counterbalance in Congressional relations with the Executive. Whereas, in 1963, Harris had found "little in the way of public response to the time-honored claim that the Legislative Branch is . . . the guardian against excessive Executive power," by 1968 he found that three-quarters of the electorate wanted Congress to act as the watchdog of the Executive and not to cooperate so readily with it. The easy passage of the Tonkin Resolution reflects the cooperative standards set in the earlier period; its repeal reflects the counterbalancing standards of the recent period. Today we are concerned about Ralph Nader's "broken branch" which, we hear, has lost—and must reclaim from the Executive—its prerogatives in areas such as war-making and spending control. To some degree, then, our judgments on Congress are negative because we change our minds frequently concerning the kind of Congress we want. A Congress whose main job is to cooperate with the Executive would look quite different from one whose main job is to counterbalance the Executive.

Beneath the differences in our standards of judgment, however, lies a deeper dynamic of the political system. Senators and representatives, for their own reasons, spend a good deal more of their time and energy polishing and worrying about their individual performance than they do working at the institution's performance. Though it is, of course, true that their individual activity is related to institutional activity, their first-order concerns are individual, not institutional. Foremost is their desire for reelection. Most members of Congress like their job, want to keep it, and know that there are people back home who want to take it away from them. So they work long and hard at winning reelection. Even those who are safest want election margins large enough to discourage opposition back home and/or to help them float further political ambitions. No matter what other personal goals representatives and senators wish to accomplish—increased influence in Washington and helping to make good public policy are the most common—reelection is a necessary means to those ends.

We cannot criticize these priorities—not in a representative system. If we believe the representative should mirror constituency opinion, we must acknowledge that it requires considerable effort for him to find out what should be mirrored. If we believe a representative should be free to vote his judgment, he will have to cultivate his constituents assiduously before they will trust him with such freedom. Either way we will look favorably on his efforts. We come to love our legislators, in the *second* place, because they so ardently sue for our affections.

As a courtship technique, moreover, they re-enforce our unfavorable judgments about the institution. Every representative with whom I traveled criticized the Congress and portrayed himself, by contrast, as a fighter against its manifest evils. Members run *for* Congress by running *against* Congress. They refurbish their individual reputations as "the best congressman in the United States" by attacking the collective reputation of the Congress of the United States. Small wonder the voters feel so much more warmly disposed and so much less fickle toward the individuals than toward the institution.

One case in point: the House decision to grant President Nixon a spending ceiling plus authority to cut previously appropriated funds to maintain that ceiling.

One-half the representatives I was with blasted the House for being so spineless that it gave away its power of the purse to the President. The other half blasted the House for being so spineless in exercising its power of the purse that the President had been forced to act. Both groups spoke to supportive audiences; and each man enhanced his individual reputation by attacking the institution. Only by raising both questions, however, could one see the whole picture. Once the President forced the issue, how come the House didn't stand up to him and protect its crucial institutional power over the purse strings? On the other hand, if economic experts agreed that a spending ceiling was called for, how come the House didn't enact it and make the necessary budget cuts in the first place? The answer to the first question lies in the proximity of their reelection battles, which re-enforced the tendency of all representatives to think in individualistic rather than institutional terms. The answer to the second question lies in the total absence of institutional machinery whereby the House (or, indeed, Congress) can make overall spending decisions.

Mention of the institutional mechanisms of Congress leads us to a *third* explanation for our prevailing pattern of judgments. When members of Congress think institutionally—as, of course they must—they think in terms of a structure that will be most congenial to the pursuit of their individual concerns—for reelection, for influence, or for policy. Since each individual has been independently designated "the best in the United States," each has an equal status and an equal claim to influence within the structure. For these reasons, the members naturally think in terms of a very fragmented, decentralized institution, providing a maximum of opportunity for individual performance, individual influence, and individual credit.

The 100-member Senate more completely fits this description than the 435-member House. The smaller body permits a more freewheeling and creative individualism. But both chambers tend strongly in this direction, and representatives as well as senators chafe against centralizing mechanisms. Neither body is organized in hierarchical—or even in well-coordinated—patterns of decision-making. Agreements are reached by some fairly subtle forms of mutual adjustment—by negotiation, bargaining, and compromise. And interpersonal relations—of respect, confidence, trust—are crucial building blocks. The members of Congress, in pursuit of their individual desires, have thus created an institution that is internally quite complex. Its structure and processes are, therefore, very difficult to grasp from the outside.

In order to play out some aspects of the original puzzle, however, we must make the effort. And the committee system, the epitome of fragmentation and decentralization, is a good place to start. The performance of Congress as an institution is very largely the performance of its committees. The Nader project's "broken branch" description is mostly a committee-centered description because that is where the countervailing combination of congressional expertise and political skill resides. To strengthen Congress means to strengthen its committees. To love Congress means to love its committees. Certainly when we have not loved our Congress, we have heaped our displeasure upon its committees. The major legislative reorganizations, of 1946 and 1970, were committee-centered reforms—centering on committee jurisdictions, committee democracy, and committee staff support. Other continuing criticisms—of the seniority rule for selecting committee chairmen, for example—have centered on the committees.

Like Congress as a whole, committees must be understood first in terms of what they do for the individual member. To begin with, committees are relatively more important to the individual House member than to the individual senator. The representative's career inside Congress is very closely tied to his committee. For the only way such a large body can function is to divide into highly specialized and independent committees. Policy-making activity funnels through these committees; so does the legislative activity and influence of the individual legislator. While the Senate has a set of committees paralleling those of the House, a committee assignment is nowhere near as constraining for the career of the individual senator. The Senate is more loosely organized, senators sit on many more committees and subcommittees than representatives, and they have easy access to the work of committees of which they are not members. Senators, too, can command and utilize national publicity to gain influence beyond the confines of their committee. Whereas House committees act as funnels for individual activity, Senate committees act as facilitators of individual activity. The difference in functions is considerable— which is why committee chairmen are a good deal more important in the House than in the Senate and why the first modifications of the seniority rule should have come in the House rather than the Senate. My examples will come from the House.

Given the great importance of his committee to the career of the House member, it follows that we will want to know how each committee can affect such careers. . . .

Where a committee's members are especially interested in pyramiding their individual influence, they will act so as to maintain the influence of their committee (and, hence, their personal influence) within the House. They will adopt procedures that enhance the operating independence of the committee. They will work hard to remain relatively independent of the Executive Branch. And they will try to underpin that independence with such resources as specialized expertise, internal cohesion, and the respect of their House colleagues. Ways and Means and Appropriations are committees of this sort. By contrast, where a committee's members are especially interested in getting in on nationally controversial policy action, they will not be much concerned about the independent influence of their committee. They will want to ally themselves closely with any and all groups outside the committee who share their policy views. They want to help enact what they individually regard as good public policy; and if that means ratifying policies shaped elsewhere—in the Executive Branch particularly—so be it. And, since their institutional independence is not a value for them, they make no special effort to acquire such underpinnings as expertise, cohesion, or chamber respect. Education and Labor and Foreign Affairs are committees of this sort.

These two types of committees display quite different strengths in their performance. Those of the first type are especially influential. Ways and Means probably makes a greater independent contribution to policy making than any other House committee. Appropriations probably exerts a more influential overview of executive branch activities than any other House committee. The price they pay, however, is a certain decrease in their responsiveness to noncommittee forces—as complaints about the closed rule on tax bills and executive hearings on appropriations bills will attest. Committees of the second type are especially responsive to non-committee forces and provide easy conduits for outside influence in policy making. Education and Labor was probably more receptive to President Johnson's Great Society policies than any other House committee; it successfully passed the largest part of the program. Foreign Affairs has probably remained as thoroughly responsive to Executive Branch policies, in foreign aid for instance, as any House committee. The price they pay, however, is a certain decrease in their influence—as complaints about the rubber-stamp Education and Labor Committee and about the impotent Foreign Affairs Committee will attest. In terms of the earlier discussions of institutional performance standards, our hopes for a cooperative Congress lie more with the latter type of committee; our hopes for a counterbalancing Congress lie more with the former.

So, committees differ. And they differ to an important degree according to the desires of their members. This ought to make us wary of blanket descriptions. Within the House, Foreign Affairs may look like a broken branch, but Ways and Means does not. And, across chambers, Senate Foreign Relations (where member incentives are stronger) is a good deal more potent than House Foreign Affairs. With the two Appropriations committees, the reverse is the case. It is not just that "the broken branch" is an undiscriminating, hence inaccurate, description. It is also that blanket descriptions lead to blanket prescriptions. And it just might be that the wisest course of congressional reform would be to identify existing nodes of committee strength and nourish them rather than to prescribe, as we usually do, reforms in equal dosages for all committees.

One lesson of the analysis should be that member incentives must exist to support any kind of committee activity. Where incentives vary, it may be silly to prescribe the same functions and resources for all committees. The Reorganization Act of 1946 mandated all committees to exercise "continuous watchfulness" over the executive branch—in the absence of any supporting incentive system. We have gotten overview activity only where random individuals have found an incentive for doing so—not by most committees and certainly not continuously. Similarly, I suspect that our current interest in exhorting all committees to acquire more information with which to combat the executive may be misplaced. Information is relatively easy to come by—and some committees have a lot of it. What is hard to come by is the incentive to use it, not to mention the time and the trust necessary to make it useful. I am not suggesting a set of reforms but rather a somewhat different strategy of committee reforms—less wholesale, more retail.

Since, the best-known target of wholesale committee reform is the seniority rule, it deserves special comment. If our attacks on the rule have any substance to them, if they are anything other than symbolic, the complaint must be that some or all committee chairmen are not doing a good job. But we can only find out whether this is so by conducting a committee-by-committee examination. Paradoxically, our discussions of the seniority rule tend to steer us away from such a retail examination by mounting very broad, across-the-board kinds of arguments against chairmen as a class—arguments about their old age, their conservatism, their national unrepresentativeness. Such arguments produce great cartoon copy, easy editorial broadsides, and sitting-duck targets for our congressmen on the stump. But we ought not to let the arguments themselves, nor the Pavlovian public reactions induced by our cartoonists, editorial writers, and representatives, pass for good institutional analysis. Rather, they have diverted us from that task.

More crucial to a committee's performance than the selection of its chairman is his working relationship with the other committee members. Does he agree with his members on the functions of the committee? Does he act to facilitate the achievement of their individual concerns? Do they approve of his performance as chairman? Where there is real disagreement between chairman and members, close analysis may lead us to fault the members and not the chairman. If so, we should be focusing our criticisms on the members. If the fault lies with the chairman, a majority of the members have the power to bring him to heel. They need not kill the king; they can constitutionalize the monarchy. While outsiders have been crying "off with his head," the members of several committees have been quietly and effectively constitutionalizing the monarchy. Education and Labor, Post Office, and Interior are recent examples where dissatisfied committee majorities have subjected their chairmen to majority control. Where this has not been done, it is probably due to member satisfaction, member timidity, member disinterest, or member incompetence. And the time we spend railing against the seniority rule might be better spent finding out, for each congressional committee, just which of these is the case. If, as a final possibility, a chairman and his members are united in opposition to the majority part or to the rest of us, the seniority rule is not the problem. More to the point, as I suspect is usually the case, the reasons and the ways individual members get sorted onto the various committees is the critical factor. In sum, I am not saying that the seniority rule is a good thing, I am saying that, for committee performance, it is not a very important thing.

What has all this got to do with the original puzzle—that we love our congressmen so much more than our Congress? We began with a few explanatory guesses. Our standards of judgment for individual performance are more easily met: the individual member works harder winning approval for himself than for his institution; and Congress is a complex institution, difficult for us to understand. The more we try to understand Congress—as we did briefly with the committee system—the more we are forced to peel back the institutional layers until we reach the individual member. At that point, it becomes hard to separate, as we normally do, our judgments about congressmen and Congress. The more we come to see institutional performance as influenced by the desires of the individual member, the more the original puzzle ought to resolve itself. For as the independence of our judgments decreases, the disparity between them ought to grow smaller. But if we are to hold this perspective on Congress, we shall need to understand the close individual-institution relationship—chamber by chamber, party by party, committee by committee, legislator by legislator.

This is not a counsel of despair. It is a counsel of sharper focus and a more discriminating eye. It counsels the mass media, for example, to forego "broken branch" type generalizations about Congress in favor of examining a committee in depth, or to forego broad criticism of the seniority rule for a close look at a committee chairman. It counsels the rest of us to focus more on the individual member and to fix the terms of our dialogue with him more aggressively. It counsels us to fix terms that will force him to think more institutionally and which will hold him more accountable for the performance of the institution. "Who Runs Congress," asks the title of the Nader report, "the President, Big Business or You?" From the perspective of this paper, it is none of these. It is the members who run Congress. And we get pretty much the kind of Congress they want. We shall get a different kind of Congress when we elect different kinds of congressmen or when we start applying different standards of judgment to old congressmen. Whether or not we ought to have a different kind of Congress is still another, much larger, puzzle.

❖❖ Richard F. Fenno, Jr., explains in selection 54 that the public holds Congress and its members to different standards. *Congress-bashing,* to use the author's colorful term in the following selection, is popular not only with the public, but more importantly with those who shape public opinion, including political journalists and pundits, network news anchors and television commentators, self-proclaimed public interest representatives, and, perhaps most importantly of all, members of Congress themselves who have found that running against Congress is a successful campaign tactic.

The author of the following selection, a prominent congressional scholar, describes the popular support of Congress-bashing and concludes that criticism of Congress has gone too far.

53

Nelson W. Polsby

CONGRESS-BASHING FOR BEGINNERS

❖❖❖❖❖❖❖❖

On a shelf not far from where I am writing these words sit a half a dozen or so books disparaging Congress and complaining about the congressional role in the constitutional separation of powers. These books date mostly from the late 1940s and the early 1960s, and typically their authors are liberal Democrats. In those years, Congress was unresponsive to liberal Democrats and, naturally enough, aggrieved members of that articulate tribe sought solutions in structural reform.

From *The Public Interest,* No. 100 (Summer 1990):15–23. Copyright 1990 National Affairs, Inc. Reprinted by permission of the author.

In fact, instead of reforms weakening Congress what they—and we—got was a considerably strengthened presidency. This was mostly a product of World War II and not the result of liberal complaints. Before World War II Congress would not enact even the modest recommendations of the Brownlow Commission to give the president a handful of assistants with "a passion for anonymity," and it killed the National Resources Planning Board outright. After World War II everything changed: Congress gave the president responsibility for smoothing the effects of the business cycle, created a Defense Department and two presidential agencies—the NSC and the CIA—that enhanced the potential for presidential dominance of national security affairs, and laid the groundwork for the growth of a presidential branch, politically responsive to both Democratic and Republican presidents.

Congress and the Goring of Oxen

Though it took time for the presidential branch to grow into its potential, the growth of this branch, separate and at arm's length from the executive branch that it runs in the president's behalf, is the big news of the postwar era—indeed, of the last half-century in American government. It is customary today to acknowledge that Harry Truman's primary agenda, in the field of foreign affairs, was quite successfully enacted even though Congress was dominated by a conservative coalition, and what Truman wanted in the way of peacetime international involvement was for the United States quite unprecedented. Dwight Eisenhower's agenda was also largely international in its impact. Looking back, it seems that almost all Eisenhower really cared about was protecting the international position of the United States from diminution by Republican isolationists. Everything else was expendable.

Congress responded sluggishly and in its customary piecemeal fashion. It was right around John Kennedy's first year in office that liberals rediscovered that old roadblock in Congress, a "deadlock of democracy," as one of them put it. It was Congress that had thwarted the second New Deal after 1937, the packing of the Supreme Court, and Harry Truman's domestic program; it was Congress that had stalled civil rights and buried Medicare; it was Congress that had sponsored the Bricker Amendment to limit the president's power to make treaties. Are memories so short that we do not recall these dear, departed days when Congress was the graveyard of the forward-looking proposals of liberal presidents? Then, Congress was a creaky eighteenth-century machine unsuited to the modern age, and Congress-bashers were liberal Democrats.

To be sure, Congress had a few defenders, mostly Republicans and Dixiecrats, who found in its musty cloakrooms and windy debates a citadel (as one of them said) of old-time legislative virtues, where the historic functions of oversight and scrutiny were performed, where the run-away proposals of the presidency could be subjected to the sober second thoughts of the people's own elected representatives, and so on.

Why rehash all this? In part, it is to try to make the perfectly obvious point that Congress-bashing then was what people did when they controlled the presidency but didn't control Congress. And that, in part, is what Congress-bashing is about now. Today, Republicans and conservatives are doing most (although not all) of the complaining. It is worth a small bet that a fair number of editorial pages claimed that the separation of powers made a lot of sense during the Kennedy-Johnson years—but no longer say the same today. On the other side, backers of FDR's scheme to pack the Court have turned into vigorous defenders of the judicial status quo since Earl Warren's time.

There is nothing wrong with letting the goring of oxen determine what side we take in a political argument. In a civilized country, however, it makes sense to keep political arguments civil, and not to let push come to shove too often. There is something uncivil, in my view, about insisting upon constitutional reforms to cure political ailments. What liberal critics of Congress needed was not constitutional reform. What they needed was the 89th Congress, which, in due course, enacted much of the agenda that the Democratic party had built up over the previous two decades. History didn't stop with the rise of the presidential branch and the enactment of the second New Deal/New Frontier/Great Society. President Johnson overreached. He concealed from Congress the costs of the Vietnam War. He created a credibility gap.

This, among other things, began to change Congress. The legislative branch no longer was altogether comfortable relying on the massaged numbers and other unreliable information coming over from the presidential branch. They began to create a legislative bureaucracy to cope with this challenge. They beefed up the General Accounting Office and the Congressional Research Service. They created an Office of Technology Assessment and a Congressional Budget Office. They doubled and redoubled their personal staffs and committee staffs.

Sentiments supporting this expansion began, oddly enough, after a landslide election in which the Democratic party swept the presidency and both houses of Congress. So mistrust between the branches in recent history has by no means been entirely a partisan matter. Nevertheless, Richard Nixon's presidency, conducted entirely in unhappy harness with a Democratic Congress, did not improve relations between the two branches of government. Johnson may have been deceitful, but Nixon, especially after his reelection in 1972, was positively confrontational.

It was Nixon's policy to disregard comity between the branches. This, and not merely his commission of impeachable offenses, fueled the impeachment effort in Congress. That effort was never wholly partisan. Republicans as well as Democrats voted articles of impeachment that included complaints specifically related to obstruction of the discharge of congressional responsibilities.

It is necessary to understand this recent history of the relations between Congress and the president in order to understand the provenance of the War Powers Act, the Boland Amendment, numerous other instances of congressional micromanagement, the unprecedented involvement of the NSC in the Iran-contra affair, and like manifestations of tension and mistrust between Congress and the president. These tensions are, to a certain degree, now embedded in law and in the routines of responsible public officials; they cannot be made to disappear with a wave of a magic wand. They are, for the most part, regrettable in the consequences they have had for congressional-presidential relations, but they reflect real responses to real problems in these relations. Congressional responses, so far as I can see, have been completely legal, constitutional, and—in the light of historical circumstances—understandable. The best way to turn the relations between the legislative and the presidential branches around would be for the presidential side to take vigorous initiatives to restore comity. As head of the branch far more capable of taking initiatives, and the branch far more responsible for the underlying problem, this effort at restoration is in the first instance up to the President.

President Bush and the Item Veto

In this respect, President Bush is doing a decent job, giving evidence of reaching out constructively. It is not my impression that the Bush administration has done a lot of Congress-bashing. After all, what Bush needs isn't a weakened Congress so much as a Republican Congress. Over the long run (though probably not in time to do Bush much good) Republicans are bound to regret despairing of the latter and therefore seeking the former. We have seen enough turns of the wheel over the last half-century to be reasonably confident that sooner or later Republicans will start to do better in congressional elections. The presidential item veto, the Administration's main Congress-bashing proposal, won't help Republicans in Congress deal with a Democratic president when the time comes, as sooner or later it will, for a Democrat to be elected president.

The item veto would effectively take congressional politics out of the legislative process, and would weaken Congress a lot. It would encourage members of Congress, majority and minority alike, to be irresponsible and to stick the president with embarrassing public choices. It would reduce the incentives for members to acquire knowledge about public policy or indeed to serve.

By allocating legislative responsibilities to Congress, the Constitution as originally (and currently) designed forces representatives of diverse interest to cooperate. Because what Congress does as a collectivity matters, legislative work elicits the committed participation of members. The item veto would greatly trivialize the work product of Congress by requiring the president's acquiescence on each detail of legislation. Members would lose their independent capacity to craft legislation. Their individual views and knowledge would dwindle in importance; only the marshalling of a herd capable of overturning a veto would matter in Congress.

The item veto is, in short, a truly radical idea. It is also almost certainly unconstitutional. To espouse it requires a readiness to give up entirely on the separation of powers and on the constitutional design of the American government. There are plenty of people, some of them well-meaning, who are ready to do that. I am not, nor should people who identify themselves as conservatives or liberals or anywhere in the political mainstream.

The separation of powers is actually a good idea. It gives a necessary weight to the great heterogeneity of our nation—by far the largest and most heterogeneous nation unequivocally to have succeeded at democratic self-government in world history. It would take a medium-sized book to make all the qualifications and all the connections that would do justice to this argument. The conclusion is worth restating anyway: the item veto is a root-and-branch attack on the separation of powers; it is a very radical and a very bad idea.

Term Limitations

Less serious in its impact, but still destructive, is the proposal to limit the terms of members of Congress. This proposal relies heavily for its appeal upon ignorance in the population at large about what members of Congress actually do. For in order to take seriously the idea of limiting congressional terms, one must believe that the job of a representative in Congress is relatively simple, and quickly and easily mastered. It is not.

The job of a member of Congress is varied and complex. It includes: (1) Managing a small group of offices that attempt on request to assist distressed constituents, state and local governments, and enterprises in the home district that may have business with the federal government. This ombudsman function gives members an opportunity to monitor the performance of the government in its dealings with citizens and can serve to identify areas of general need. (2) Serving on committees that oversee executive-branch activity on a broad spectrum of subjects (such as immigration, copyright protection, telecommunications, or health policy) and that undertake to frame issues of national scope for legislative action. This entails mastering complicated subject matter; working with staff members, expert outsiders, and colleagues to build coalitions; understanding justifications; and answering objections. (3) Participating in general legislative work. Members have to vote on everything, not merely on the work of their own committees. They have to inform themselves of the merits of bills, and stand ready to cooperate with colleagues whose support they will need to advance their own proposals. (4) Keeping track of their own political business. This means watching over and occasionally participating in the politics of their own states and localities, and mending fences with interest groups, friends and neighbors, backers, political rivals, and allies. (5) Educating all the varied people with whom they come in contact about issues that are high on the agenda and about reasonable expectations of performance. This includes the performance of the government, the Congress, and the member.

Plenty of members never try to master the job, or try and fail, and these members would be expendable. The objection might still be raised that constituents, not an excess of constitutional limitations, ought to decide who represents whom in Congress. But that aside, what about the rather substantial minority of members who learn their jobs, do their homework, strive to make an impact on public policy, and—through long experience and application to work—actually make a difference? Can we, or should we, dispense with them as well?

It is a delusion to think that good public servants are a dime a dozen in each congressional district, and that only the good ones would queue up to take their twelve-year fling at congressional office. But suppose they did. In case they acquired expertise, what would they do next? Make money, I suppose. Just about the time that their constituents and the American people at large could begin to expect a payoff because of the knowledge and experience that these able members had acquired at our expense, off they would go to some Washington law firm.

And what about their usefulness in the meantime? It would be limited, I'm afraid, by the greater expertise and better command of the territory by lobbyists, congressional staff, and downtown bureaucrats—career people one and all. So this is, once again, a proposal merely to weaken the fabric of Congress in the political system at large, and thereby to limit the effectiveness of the one set of actors most accessible to ordinary citizens.

The standard objection to this last statement is that members of Congress aren't all that accessible. Well, neither is Ralph Nader, who has long overstayed the dozen years that contemporary Congress-bashers wish to allocate to members. Neither is the author of *Wall Street Journal* editorials in praise of limitations. And it must be said that a very large number of members take their representational and ombudsman duties very seriously indeed. This includes holders of safe seats, some of whom fear primary-election opposition, some of whom are simply conscientious. A great many of them do pay attention—close attention—to their constituents. That is one of the reasons—maybe the most important reason—that so many of them are reelected. Much Congress-bashing these days actually complains about high reelection rates, as though a large population of ill-served constituents would be preferable.

Congressional Salaries

While we have Ralph Nader on our minds, it is certainly appropriate to pay our disrespects to his completely off-the-wall effort, temporarily successful, at the head of a crazed phalanx of self-righteous disk jockeys and radio talk-show hosts, to deprive members of Congress of a salary increase. The issue of congressional salaries is a straightforward one. Many members, being well-to-do, don't need one. But some do. The expenses of maintaining two places of residence—in Washington and at home—make membership in Congress nearly unique and singularly expensive among upper-middle-class American jobs. Here is the point once more: it is a job, requiring skill and dedication to be done properly. Moreover, membership in Congress brings responsibilities. National policy of the scope and scale now encompassed by acts of the federal government requires responsible, dedicated legislators. People with far less serious responsibilities in the private sector are ordinarily paid considerably better than members of Congress. Think, for example, how far down the organizational chart at General Motors or at CBS or at some other large corporation one would have to go before reaching executives making what members of Congress do, and compare their responsibilities with those of Congress and its members. Actually, most corporations won't say what their compensation packages are like. But at a major auto company, people who make around $100,000 a year are no higher than upper middle management, and certainly don't have responsibilities remotely comparable to those of members of Congress.

There is a case for decent congressional salaries to be made on at least two grounds: one is the rough equity or opportunity-cost ground that we ought not financially to penalize people who serve, and the second is the ground of need for those members who have the expense of families or college educations to think of, and who have no extraordinary private means. The long-run national disadvantage of failing to recognize the justice of these claims is of course a Congress deprived of people for whom these claims are exigent, normal middle-class people with family responsibilities and without money of their own. These are not the sorts of people a sane electorate should wish to prevent from serving.

Members of Congress, knowing very well of the irrational hostilities that the proposal of a congressional pay raise can stir up, have taken the unfortunate precaution of holding hostage the salaries of federal judges, who are now ludicrously underpaid by the admittedly opulent standards of the legal profession, and senior civil servants. An unhealthy impasse has been created owing, at bottom, to Congress-bashing of the most unattractive kind, which exploits the ignorance of ordinary citizens of the dimensions of the members' working lives, and incites citizens to a mindless social envy, in which it is assumed that paying a decent professional salary to professional officeholders is automatically some sort of rip-off.

Members of Congress now make about $98,000. The bottom salary for major-league baseball players is $100,000. Some law firms in New York start new graduates of good law schools at $90,000 or more. How can we argue that members of Congress and others at the top of the federal government should not be paid at least a modest premium above these beginners' wages? There is, evidently, no talking sense to the American people on this subject.

I believe we can dismiss out of hand the charge that large numbers of members individually, or Congress collectively, live in a world all their own, divorced from realities of everyday life. The sophomores who have written attacks of this sort in recent years in the *Atlantic, Newsweek,* and elsewhere simply don't know what they are talking about. They abuse their access to large audiences by neglecting to explain the real conditions that govern the lives of members, conditions that provide ample doses of everyday life.

No doubt scandals involving various members have in recent times made Congress as an institution vulnerable to criticism. But much of this criticism is irresponsible and irrelevant. Suppose we were to discover instances of cupidity, unusual sexual activity, and abuses of power among the rather sizable staff of an important daily newspaper? Or a symphony orchestra? Or, God forbid, a university? I suppose that would shake our confidence in at least part of the collective output, but one would hope for relevant discriminations. One might distrust the ticket office, perhaps, but not the symphony's performance of Mozart; the stock tips, perhaps, but not the Washington page; the basketball program, but not the classics department. I do not think that the existence of scandal excuses us from attempting to draw sensible conclusions about institutions and their performance.

This sort of balanced and discriminating analysis isn't what proposals for item vetoes, limitations on terms of service, or depressed rates of pay are all about. They are about the ancient but now slightly shopworn American custom of Congress-bashing.

❖❖ Congress-bashing continues in the mid-1990s, as voters remain wary of inside-the-beltway politics. But while the public almost rhetorically attacks

Congress as an institution, it continues to reelect incumbents in large numbers. The mid-term 1994 congressional elections, while producing a dramatic changing of the guard, nevertheless reelected incumbents of both parties in great numbers. Ironically, public disillusionment with Congress may increase under Republican rule. The major reason voters give for their persistent Congress-bashing is the failure of the two parties to work together. The party split between the President and Congress can only increase political gridlock. In the following selection two of the *Washington Post's* closest Congressional observers discuss the realities and paradoxes of the continuing public criticism of Congress.

54

Richard Morin and David S. Broder

WHY AMERICANS HATE CONGRESS

❖·❖·❖·❖·❖·❖

Four months before its members face the voters, the 103rd Congress is seen as a do-nothing assemblage of quarrelsome partisans more attuned to the special interests than to its constituents, according to a Washington Post-ABC News Poll. Six out of 10 of those polled disapprove of the way Congress is doing its job, but an equal proportion give thumbs up to the work of their own representatives.

Any comfort incumbents may draw from that has to be balanced by the fact that only 35 percent say they are inclined to reelect their representative, and 54 percent want to look for someone else. Those figures are nearly identical to the 1992 numbers that presaged the biggest turnover in the makeup of the House in almost five decades.

In 19 surveys over the last five years, spanning three congresses and two presidents, the average scores for Congress have been 33 percent approval and 62 percent disapproval. The latest poll—34 percent approval and 61 percent disapproval—is right in line with that.

The disapproval number is down 5 percentage points from the level when the 103rd Congress began in January 1993, but it is 26 points higher than it was 20 years ago, when Congress was confronting President Richard M. Nixon in the impeachment proceedings that led to his resignation.

Unlike many other political attitudes, this one does not split on partisan lines. Six out of 10 Democrats and an equal percentage of Republicans say they disapprove of the job Congress is doing.

In an effort to dig behind the persistent low regard for Capitol Hill, the survey asked about the public's impression of the productivity of Congress and of its members' motivations.

It found large gaps in the public knowledge of what this Congress has done, but discovered that those who know more actually think less of the legislators' performance.

According to the survey, 67 percent of those who are most aware of Congress's accomplishments during the past 17 months said they disapprove, compared with 51 percent of those with little or no knowledge.

Only 31 percent of the knowledgeable approve, compared with 40 percent of the least informed. This relationship between high information and low approval held up even when the results were broken down by party, with the most informed Democrats and Republicans being the most critical of the Democratic-controlled Congress.

Among the best-informed Democrats in the survey, about a third—35 percent—approve of the job that Congress is doing, while 62 percent disapprove. Even informed Democrats in districts with a Democrat in the House gave Congress a negative rating.

The principal reason, as the poll results and interviews make clear, is that the public sees Congress through a lens of deep suspicion. On a series of questions relating to what makes members of Congress tick, the public is notably more negative than it was a decade ago.

Overwhelming majorities say they think that members of Congress care more about special interests than about "people like you" and care more about keeping power than about the best interests of the nation. Few think most members have a high personal moral code. Large numbers say most candidates for Congress make campaign promises they have no intention of fulfilling and quickly lose touch with the people after coming to Washington.

Not surprisingly, the public favors term limits for members of Congress by 3 to 1.

More than a third of those interviewed—37 percent—consistently offered the most negative evaluation when asked their perceptions of the work habits, honesty and integrity of Congress. Less than one-fifth expressed few reservations.

Among the cynical third of the public, only one in four plans to vote to reelect the incumbent, even though 46 percent said they approved of the job he or she is doing. In contrast, three out of four of those with the least cynical views of Congress approve of the job their representative is doing and half say they plan to vote for the incumbent.

Asked to judge how much Congress has accomplished since January 1993, only 4 percent said a great deal, and 20 percent a good amount. An overwhelming 65 percent said not too much and 9 percent said it has done nothing at all.

The blame for this perceived inaction rests largely on partisanship. More than half of those who believe Congress has done little or nothing said the biggest reason for gridlock is the inability of Republicans and Democrats to work together.

One out of five lays the problem on President Clinton's failure to provide adequate leadership. One out of nine says it is the inability of Democrats to work together and an equal portion blame Republicans for blocking programs Democrats want to pass.

The best-known legislation of this Congress is the Brady bill. Seven out of 10 know that its requirement of a five-day delay and background check on anyone trying to buy a handgun is now law. Nearly as many know about the family leave law requiring employers to give workers unpaid time off when there is an illness or new baby in the family.

Half the people know that Congress approved the North American Free Trade Agreement (NAFTA) eliminating trade barriers with Mexico and Canada. But major economic legislation that was the center of an epic struggle in 1993 has vanished from public consciousness.

Only one voter in three credits Congress with raising taxes on the very rich and reducing taxes for millions of working poor. Even fewer acknowledge that Congress cut the annual budget deficit by billions.

As many believe Congress passed a purely mythical bill to control immigration as the real deficit reduction measure. Yet another oddity: Although the House and Senate are deadlocked on going to conference on their separate and conflicting versions of campaign finance reform, nearly four out of 10 of those polled think Congress already has passed changes in the law to restrict special-interest contributions.

House majority leader Richard A. Gephardt of Missouri, says of the poll numbers that he is "surprised they weren't worse," given what he says is the negative tone of congressional news coverage and much of the commentary on talk shows. "People are constantly barraged with negative stories and remarks" about the national legislature, he says. Even serious publications, he says, tend to lose people in the day-to-day process stories inevitable during the lengthy congressional consideration of major bills.

Retired Republican Senate majority leader Howard H. Baker Jr. of Tennessee, whose father and mother served on Capitol Hill, says, "I really grieve for the Congress," but blames its low reputation on the increase in the number of "career politicians" in the House and Senate, perceived as living in a different world from their constituents and driven by different needs.

Two political scientists who have written on Congress, Charles O. Jones of the Brookings Institution and James A. Thurber of American University, say that the public perception of increased partisanship is realistic, backed up by an increase in the important roll-call votes on which the majority of Republicans take the opposite stand from the majority of Democrats.

Jones says the tendency of House Democrats to "freeze Republicans out of the action" has provoked a counterreaction from GOP leaders to "bash the institution," heightening the perception of constant quarreling.

Thurber says that "hyperpluralism," the proliferation of organized interest groups, is a greater barrier to action than partisan divisions, but also notes that the public hears a drumbeat of criticism of Congress, not just from outsiders, but from lawmakers themselves. "Running against the institution is increasingly popular," he says.

The discrepancy between broad disapproval of Congress and equally broad support for its individual members is not a new one—and it may not be as great as the numbers first suggest or as positive for the incumbents' reelection chances.

Figure 54A What The Public Thinks of Congress
Results of a Washington Post–ABC News Poll

Q: Do you approve or disapprove of the way Congress is doing it's job ?

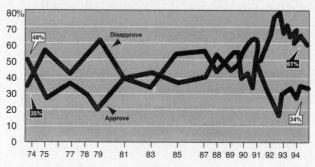

Gallop Poll for results from 1974 through 1988

Q: Do you approve or disapprove of the way your own representative to the U.S.
House of Representatives in Congress is handling his or her job?

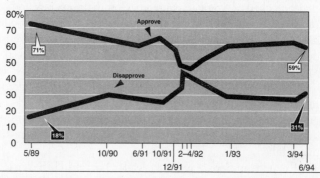

Q: I'm going to read a few statements. For each, can you please tell me if
you tend to agree or disagree with it, or if, perhaps, you have no opinion
about this statement:

	June 26	
	Agree	Disagree
Most members of Congress care more about keeping power than they do about the best interests of the nation	83%	14%
Most members of Congress care more about special interests than they care about people like you	83	12
Generally speaking, those we elect to Congress in Washington lose touch with the people pretty quickly	78	17
To win elections, most candidates for Congress make campaign promises they have no intentions of fulfilling	76	20
Most members of Congress are doing their best in a difficult job	48	48
The Congress is not so bad as it's made out to be	43	51
Most members of Congress have a high personal moral code	30	60
Most members of Congress care deeply about the problems of ordinary citizens	26	69

Q: Overall, how much do you think Congress has accomplished in the past 18 months:

June 26

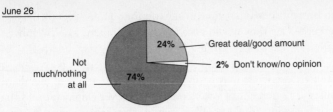

24% — Great deal/good amount

2% Don't know/no opinion

Not much/nothing at all 74%

Q: Of those that I've mentioned, which is the biggest reason that Congress has not done more? (Asked of those who think that Congress has not done much or done nothing at all)

	June 26
The inability of Republicans and Democrats to work together	56%
The failure of Clinton to provide adequate leadership	19
Efforts of Republicans to block programs that the Democrats want to pass	11
The inability of Democrats in Congress to work together	11

Q: Now I'd like you to tell me whether or not Congress has done any of the following things in the past 18 months (Items in **bold** are things Congress has done):

	June 26	
	Has done	Has not done
Required a five-day delay and a background check on anyone trying to buy a handgun	71%	13%
Passed a bill requiring employers to give workers unpaid leave time when there's a new baby or an illness in the workers family	**64**	**14**
Approved an agreement that will end almost all trade barriers between the United States and Mexico	51	17
Changed the finance laws to restrict special interest contributions	37	26
Raised taxes on the very rich and reduced taxes for millions of the working poor	33	49
Passed a bill that makes voter registration almost automatic when you renew your driver's license	32	31
Passed a budget bill that cut the expected federal budget deficit by billions of dollars	24	48
Passed a bill to control immigration into the United States	23	47
Given federal workers the same rights to get involved in politics that private employees have	21	25
Reformed the welfare laws so almost no one can continue receiving assistance for more than two years	19	56
Made it easier for everyone to buy health insurance	11	77

NOTE: Figures may not add up to 100% when "no opinion" is not included. June figures are from a Washington Post–ABC News telephone poll of 1,531 randomly selected adults interviewed June 23–26. Other results are from Washington Post–ABC News polls with samples of similar size. Margin of sampling error for all of the polls is plus or minus 3 percentage points overall. Sampling error is, however, only one of many potential sources of error in these or any polls. Interviewing was conducted by Chilton Research of Radnor, PA.

Even among those who approve of the job their House member is doing, barely half—55 percent—say they would vote for the incumbent in November, while the remainder are inclined to look around for someone else [Fig. 54A].

Although the news is not good for incumbents of either party, the survey suggests that House Democrats may be more vulnerable than GOP members. According to the survey, 37 percent of voters represented by a Democrat said they plan to reelect him or her, compared with 42 percent of those represented by a Republican.

❖❖A commonly held assumption about members of Congress is that their primary incentive is to engage in activities that strengthen their prospects for reelection. David Mayhew, one proponent of this theory, argues in his book *Congress: The Electoral Connection* that both the formal and informal organizations of Congress are oriented principally toward the reelection of its members. For example, the dispersion of committees, which numbered close to three hundred in the 102nd Congress (1991–1992) maximizes the opportunities of committee chairmen to use their power to distribute benefits directly to their districts and states and to take positions on issues that will be appealing to their constituents. Moreover, the weak party structure of Capitol Hill allows individual members to go their own ways in dealing with their diverse constituencies. Unified congressional parties, argues Mayhew, would not allow Congress the necessary flexibility to advertise, claim credit, and take position to gain electoral support. In the following selection Mayhew illustrates the kinds of activities Senate and House members engage in to maximize their electoral support.

55

David Mayhew

CONGRESS: THE ELECTORAL CONNECTION

❖❖❖❖❖❖❖

Whether they are safe or marginal, cautious or audacious, congressmen must constantly engage in activities related to reelection. There will be differences in em-

---

From David R. Mayhew, *Congress: The Electoral Connection* (New Haven, Conn.: Yale University Press, 1974), pp. 49–72. Copyright © 1974 by Yale University. Reprinted by permission of Yale University Press.

phasis, but all members share the root need to do things—indeed, to do things day in and day out during their terms. The next step here is to present a typology, a short list of the *kinds* of activities congressmen find it electorally useful to engage in. The case will be that there are three basic kinds of activities. It will be important to lay them out with some care. . . .

One activity is *advertising,* defined here as any effort to disseminate one's name among constituents in such a fashion as to create a favorable image but in messages having little or no issue content. A successful congressman builds what amounts to a brand name, which may have a generalized electoral value for other politicians in the same family. The personal qualities to emphasize are experience, knowledge, responsiveness, concern, sincerity, independence, and the like. Just getting one's name across is difficult enough; only about half the electorate, if asked, can supply their House members' names. It helps a congressman to be known. "In the main, recognition carries a positive valence; to be perceived at all is to be perceived favorably." A vital advantage enjoyed by House incumbents is that they are much better known among voters than their November challengers. They are better known because they spend a great deal of time, energy, and money trying to make themselves better known. There are standard routines—frequent visits to the constituency, nonpolitical speeches to home audiences, the sending out of infant care booklets and letters of condolence and congratulations. Of 158 House members questioned . . . 121 said that they regularly sent newsletters to their constituents; 48 wrote separate news or opinion columns for newspapers; 82 regularly reported to their constituencies by radio or television; 89 regularly sent out mail questionnaires. Some routines are less standard. Congressman George E. Shipley (D., Ill.) claims to have met personally about half his constituents (i.e. some 200,000 people). For over twenty years Congressman Charles C. Diggs, Jr. (D., Mich.) has run a radio program featuring himself as a "combination disc jockey–commentator and minister." Congressman Daniel J. Flood (D., Pa.) is "famous for appearing unannounced and often uninvited at wedding anniversaries and other events." Anniversaries and other events aside, congressional advertising is done largely at public expense. Use of the franking privilege has mushroomed in recent years; in early 1973 one estimate predicted that House and Senate members would send out about 476 million pieces of mail in the year 1974, at a public cost of $38.1 million—or about 900,000 pieces per member with a subsidy of $70,000 per member. By far the heaviest mailroom traffic comes in Octobers of even-numbered years. There are some differences between House and Senate members in the ways they go about getting their names across. House members are free to blanket their constituencies with mailings for all boxholders; senators are not. But senators find it easier to appear on national television—for example, in short reaction statements on the nightly news shows. Advertising is a staple congressional activity, and there is no end to it. For each member there are always new voters to be apprised of his worthiness and old voters to be reminded of it.

A second activity may be called *credit claiming,* defined here as acting so as to generate a belief in a relevant political actor (or actors) that one is personally responsible for causing the government, or some unit thereof, to do something that the actor (or actors) considers desirable. The political logic of this, from the congressman's point of view, is that an actor who believes that a member can make pleasing things happen will no doubt wish to keep him in office so that he can make pleasing things happen in the future. The emphasis here is on individual accomplishment (rather than, say, party or governmental accomplishment) and on the congressman as doer (rather than as, say, expounder of constituency views). Credit claiming is highly important to congressmen, with the consequence that much of congressional life is a relentless search for opportunities to engage in it.

Where can credit be found? If there were only one congressman rather than 535, the answer would in principle be simple enough. Credit (or blame) would attach in Downsian fashion to the doing of the government as a whole. But there are 535. Hence it becomes necessary for each congressman to try to peel off pieces of governmental accomplishment for which he can believably generate a sense of responsibility. For the average congressman the staple way of doing this is to traffic in what may be called "particularized benefits." Particularized governmental benefits, as the term will be used here, have two properties: (1) Each benefit is given out to a specific individual, group, or geographical constituency, the recipient unit being of a scale that allows a single congressman to be recognized (by relevant political actors and other congressmen) as the claimant for the benefit (other congressmen being perceived as indifferent or hostile). (2) Each benefit is given out in apparently ad hoc fashion (unlike, say, social security checks) with a congressman apparently having a hand in the allocation. A particularized benefit can normally be regarded as a member of a class. That is, a benefit given out to an individual, group, or constituency can normally be looked upon by congressmen as one of a class of similar benefits given out to sizable numbers of individuals, groups, or constituencies. Hence the impression can arise that a congressman is getting "his share" of whatever it is the government is offering. (The classes may be vaguely defined. Some state legislatures deal in what their members call "local legislation.")

In sheer volume the bulk of particularized benefits come under the heading of "casework"—the thousands of favors congressional offices perform for supplicants in ways that normally do not require legislative action. High school students ask for essay materials, soldiers for emergency leaves, pensioners for location of missing checks, local governments for grant information, and on and on. Each office has skilled professionals who can play the bureaucracy like an organ—pushing the right pedals to produce the desired effects. But many benefits require new legislation, or at least they require important allocative decisions on matters covered by existent legislation. Here the congressman fills the traditional role of supplier of goods to the home district. It is a believable role; when a member claims credit for a benefit on the order of a dam, he may well receive it. Shiny construction projects seem especially useful. . . .

The third activity congressmen engage in may be called *position taking*, defined here as the public enunciation of a judgmental statement on anything likely to be of interest to political actors. The statement may take the form of a roll call vote. The most important classes of judgmental statements are those prescribing American governmental ends (a vote cast against the war; a statement that "the war should be ended immediately") or governmental means (a statement that "the way to end the war is to take it to the United Nations"). The judgments may be implicit rather than explicit, as in: "I will support the president on this matter." But judgments may range far beyond these classes to take in implicit or explicit statements on what almost anybody should do or how he should do it: "The great Polish scientist Copernicus has been unjustly neglected" "The way for Israel to achieve peace is to give up the Sinai." The congressman as position taker is a speaker rather than a doer. The electoral requirement is not that he make pleasing things happen but that he make pleasing judgmental statements. The position itself is the political commodity. Especially on matters where governmental responsibility is widely diffused it is not surprising that political actors should fall back on positions as tests of incumbent virtue. For voters ignorant of congressional processes the recourse is an easy one. The following comment [by a Congressman] is highly revealing: "Recently, I went home and began to talk about the————act. I was pleased to have sponsored that bill, but it soon dawned on me that the point wasn't getting through at all. What was getting through was that the act might be a help to people. I changed the emphasis: I didn't mention my role particularly, but stressed my support of the legislation."

The ways in which positions can be registered are numerous and often imaginative. There are floor addresses ranging from weighty orations to mass-produced "nationality day statements." There are speeches before home groups, television appearances, letters, newsletters, press releases, ghostwritten books, *Playboy* articles, even interviews with political scientists. On occasion congressmen generate what amount to petitions; whether or not to sign the 1956 Southern Manifesto defying school desegregation rulings was an important decision for southern members. Outside the roll call process the congressman is usually able to tailor his positions to suit his audiences. A solid consensus in the constituency calls for ringing declarations. . . .

Probably the best position-taking strategy for most congressmen at most times is to be conservative—to cling to their own positions of the past where possible and to reach for new ones with great caution where necessary. Yet in an earlier discussion of strategy the suggestion was made that it might be rational for members in electoral danger to resort to innovation. The form of innovation available is entrepreneurial position taking, its logic being that for a member facing defeat with his old array of positions it makes good sense to gamble on some new ones. It may be that congressional marginals fulfill an important function here as issue pioneers—experimenters who test out new issues and thereby show other politicians which ones are usable. An example of such a pioneer is Senator Warren Magnuson (D., Wash.), who responded to a surprisingly narrow victory in 1962 by reaching for a reputation in the area of consumer affairs. Another example is Senator Ernest Hollings (D., S.C.), a servant of a shaky and racially heterogeneous southern constituency who launched "hunger" as an issue in 1969—at once pointing to a problem and giving it a useful nonracial definition. One of the most successful issue entrepreneurs of recent decades was the late Senator Joseph McCarthy (R., Wis.); it was all there—the close primary in 1946, the fear of defeat in 1952, the desperate casting about for an issue, the famous 1950 dinner at the Colony Restaurant where suggestions were tendered, the decision that "Communism" might just do the trick.

The effect of position taking on electoral behavior is about as hard to measure as the effect of credit claiming. Once again there is a variance problem; congressmen do not differ very much among themselves in the methods they use or the skills they display in attuning themselves to their diverse constituencies. All of them, after all, are professional politicians. . . .

There can be no doubt that congressmen believe positions make a difference. An important consequence of this belief is their custom of watching each other's elections to try to figure out what positions are salable. Nothing is more important in Capitol Hill politics than the shared conviction that election returns have proven a point. . . .

These, then, are the three kinds of electorally oriented activities congressmen engage in—advertising, credit claiming, and position taking. . . .

❖❖ David Mayhew's thesis, part of which is presented in the preceding selection, is that the Washington activities of members of Congress are, with few exceptions, geared toward reelection. In contrast, Richard Fenno argues that the Washington careers of members of Congress may or may not be related to reelection. In his early work on Congress, Fenno pointed out that the *incentives* of members of Congress fall generally into three categories: (1) reelection, (2) internal power and influence on Capitol Hill, and (3) good public policy. While the incentives of House and Senate members cannot always be placed neatly into one of these categories, Fenno's research suggested that the behavior of members *in Congress* tends to be dominated by one of these incentives.[1]

Committee selection, in particular, is made to advance reelection, increase power and status on Capitol Hill, or make a good public policy. For example, such committees as Interior and Insular Affairs in the House serve the reelection incentives of their members by channeling specific benefits, such as water and conservation projects, into their districts. Members seeking influence in the House prefer such committees as Ways and Means and Appropriations, both of which reflect the role of the House in the constitutional system and represent it in the outside world. Representatives on the Ways and Means and the Appropriations committees, particularly the chairmen and ranking minority members, can use their positions effectively to bolster their reputations for power in the House. "Good public policy" committees are those that are used to reflect ideological viewpoints, such as the House Education and Labor Committee, rather than to give particular benefits to constituents or to augment internal influence.

While members of Congress have varying degrees of success in their pursuit of internal power and good public policy, they are overwhelmingly successful in achieving reelection. The power of incumbency is truly formidable.

---

[1]Richard F. Fenno, Jr., *Congressmen in Committees* (Boston: Little, Brown and Co., 1973).

Over 95 percent of House incumbents are regularly reelected, usually by margins in excess of 55 percent and frequently without opposition. Senators are somewhat more vulnerable than representatives, for Senate seats are attractive targets of opportunity for political parties, interest groups, and ambitious politicians. Nevertheless Senate incumbents, too, have great advantages over challengers and normally well over 80 percent of them are easily reelected. Certainly, as David Mayhew points out in selection 55, members of Congress have shaped the legislative environment to enhance their reelection prospects.

Generally, as members of Congress gain seniority, their Washington careers become separated from their constituency activities. The incumbency effect, buttressed by an effective organization within their constituency, leaves them free to pursue goals on Capitol Hill that are not specifically for the purpose of gaining votes. In the following selection Richard Fenno discusses the linkage between the constituency and Washington activities of House and Senate members.

56

Richard F. Fenno, Jr.

HOME STYLE AND WASHINGTON CAREER

❖❖❖❖❖❖❖

. . . When we speak of constituency careers, we speak primarily of the pursuit of the goal of reelection. When we speak of Washington careers, we speak primarily of the pursuit of the goals of influence in the House and the making of good public policy. Thus the intertwining of careers is, at bottom, an intertwining of member goals.

So long as they are in the expansionist stage of their constituency careers, House members will be especially attentive to their home base. They will pursue the goal of reelection with single-minded intensity and will allocate their resources disproportionately to that end. . . . [F]irst-term members go home more frequently, place a larger proportion of their staff in the district, and more often leave their families at home than do their senior colleagues. Building a reelection constituency at home and providing continuous access to as much of that constituency as possible requires time and energy. Inevitably, these are resources that might otherwise be

From Richard F. Fenno, Jr. *Home Style: House Members in Their Districts* (Boston: Little, Brown and Company, 1978). Copyright © 1978 by Little, Brown and Company, Inc. Reprinted by permission.

allocated to efforts in Washington. "The trouble is," said one member near the end of his second term,

> I haven't been a congressman yet. The first two years, I spent all of my time getting myself reelected. The last two years, I spent getting myself a district so that I could get reelected. So I won't be a congressman until next year.

By being "a congressman" he means pursuing goals above and beyond that of reelection (i.e., power in the House and good public policy).

In a House member's first years, the opportunities for gaining inside power and policy influence are limited. Time and energy and staff can be allocated to home without an acute sense of conflict. At rates that vary from congressman to congressman, however, the chances to have some institutional or legislative effect improve. As members stretch to avail themselves of the opportunity, they may begin to experience some allocative strain. It requires time and energy to develop a successful career in Washington just as it does to develop a successful career in the district. Because it may not be possible to allocate these resources to House and home, each to an optimal degree, members may have to make allocative and goal choices.

A four-term congressman with a person-to-person home style described the dilemma of choice:

> I'm beginning to be a little concerned about my political future. I can feel myself getting into what I guess is a natural and inevitable condition—the gradual erosion of my local orientation. I'm not as enthused about tending my constituency relations as I used to be and I'm not paying them the attention I should be. There's a natural tension between being a good representative and taking an interest in government. I'm getting into some heady things in Washington, and I want to make an input into the government. It's making me a poorer representative than I was. I find myself avoiding the personal collisions that arise in the constituency—turning away from that one last handshake, not bothering to go to that one last meeting. I find myself forgetting people's names. And I find myself caring less about it than I used to. Right now, it's just a feeling I have. In eight years I have still to come home less than forty weekends a year. This is my thirty-sixty trip this year. What was it Arthur Rubinstein said? "If I miss one practice, I notice it. If I miss two practices, my teacher notices it. If I miss a week of practice, my audience notices it." I'm at stage one right now—or maybe stage one and stage two. But I'm beginning to feel that I could be defeated before long. And I'm not going to change. I don't want the status. I want to contribute to government.

The onset of a Washington career is altering his personal goals and his established home style. He is worried about the costs of the change; but he is willing to accept some loss of reelection support in exchange for his increased influence in Congress.

The dilemma faces every member of Congress. It is built into the twin requirements that Congress be a representative and a legislative institution. Some members believe they can achieve reelection at home together with influence or policy in Washington without sacrificing either. During Congressman O's first year as a subcommittee chairman, I asked him whether his new position would make it more difficult to tend to district matters. He replied,

> If you mean, am I getting Potomac fever, the answer is, no. If you mean, has the change in my official duties here made me a better congressman, the answer is, yes.

If you mean has it taken away from my activity in the constituency, the answer is no.

Congressman O, we recall, has been going home less; but he has been increasing the number and the activity of his district staff. Although he speaks confidently of his allocative solution, he is not unaware of potential problems. "My staff operation runs by itself. They don't need me. Maybe I should worry about that. You aren't going back and say I'm ripe for the plucking are you? I don't think I am."

A three-term member responded very positively when I paraphrased the worries of the congressman friend of his who had quoted Arthur Rubinstein:

> You can do your job in Washington and in your district if you know how. My quarrel with [the people like him] of this world is that they don't learn to be good politicians before they get to Congress. They get there because some people are sitting around the table one day and ask them to do it. They're smart, but they don't learn to organize a district. Once you learn to do that, it's much easier to do your job in Washington.

This member, however, has not yet tasted the inside influence of his friend. Moreover, he does not always talk with such assurance. His district is not so well organized that he has reduced his personal attentiveness to it.

> Ralph Krug [the congressman in the adjacent district] tells me I spoil my constituents. He says, "You've been elected twice, you know your district; once a month is enough to come home." But that's not my philosophy. Maybe it will be someday. . . . My lack of confidence is still a pressure which brings me home. This is my political base. Washington is not my political base. I feel I have to come home to get nourished, to see for myself what's going on. It's my security blanket—coming home.

For now, he feels no competing pulls; but he is not unaware of his friend's dilemma.

Members pose the dilemma with varying degrees of immediacy. No matter how confident members may be of their ability to pursue their Washington and their constituency careers simultaneously, however, they all recognize the potentiality of conflict and worry about coping with it. It is our guess that the conflict between the reelection goal on the one hand and the power or policy goals on the other hand becomes most acute for members as they near the peak of influence internally. For, at this stage of their Washington career, the resource requirements of the Washington job make it nearly impossible to meet established expectations of attentiveness at home. Individuals who want nothing from their Washington careers except the status of being a member of Congress will never pursue any other goal except reelection. For these people, the dilemma of which we speak is minimal. Our concern is with those individuals who find, sooner or later, that they wish to pursue a mix of goals in which reelection must be weighed along with power or policy.

One formula for managing a mix of goals that gives heavy weight to a Washington career is to make one's influence in Washington the centerpiece of home style. The member says, in effect, "I can't come home to present myself in person as much as I once did, because I'm so busy tending to the nation's business; but my seniority, my influence, my effectiveness in Washington is of great benefit to you." He asks his supportive constituents to adopt a new set of expectations, one that would put less of a premium on access. Furthermore, he asks these constituents to remain sufficiently intense in their support to discourage challengers—especially those who will promise access. All members do some of this when they explain their Washington activity—especially in connection with "explaining power." And, where possible, they quote from favorable national commentary in their campaign literature. But [very few Congressmen] have made Washington influence the central element of [their] home style.

One difficulty of completely adopting such a home style is that the powerful Washington legislator can actually get pretty far out of touch with his supportive constituents back home. One of the more senior members of [Congress], and a leader of his committee, recounted the case when his preoccupation with an internal legislative impasse affecting Israel caused him to neglect the crucial Jewish element of his primary constituency—a group "who contribute two-thirds of my money." A member of the committee staff had devised an amendment to break the deadlock.

> Peter Tompkins looked at it and said to me, "Why don't we sponsor it?" So we put it forward, and it became known as the Crowder-Tompkins Amendment. I did it because I respected the staff man who suggested it and because I wanted to get something through that was reasonable. Well, a member of the committee called people back home and said, "Crowder is selling out." All hell broke loose. I started getting calls at two and three in the morning from my friends asking me what I was doing. So I went back home and discussed the issue with them. When I walked into the room, it made me feel sad and shocked to feel their hostility. They wanted me to know that they would clobber me if they thought I was selling out. Two hours later, we walked out friends again. I dropped the Crowder-Tompkins Amendment. That's the only little flare up I've ever had with the Jewish community. But it reminded me of their sensitivity to anything that smacks of discrimination.

The congressman survived. But he would not have needed so forceful a reminder of his strongest supporters' concerns were he nearer the beginning of his constituency career. But, of course, neither would he have been a committee leader, and neither would the imperatives of a House career bulked so large in his mix of goals.

Another way to manage conflicting reelection and Washington career goals might be to use one's Washington influence to alter support patterns at home. That is, instead of acting—as is the normal case—to reenforce home support, to keep what he had "last time," the congressman might act to displace that old support with compensating new support. He might even accomplish this inadvertently, should his pursuit of power or policy attract, willy-nilly, constituents who welcome his new mix of goals. The very Washington activity that left him out of touch with previously supportive constituents might put him in touch with newly supportive ones. A newly acquired position of influence in a particular policy area or a new reputation as an effective legislator might produce such a feedback effect....

... [There is] a tendency for successful home styles to harden over time and to place stylistic constraints on the congressman's subsequent behavior. The pursuit of a Washington career helps us explain this constituency phenomenon. That is, to the degree that a congressman pursues power or policy goals in the House, he will have that much less time or energy to devote to the consideration of alternative home styles. His predisposition to "do what we did last time" at home will be further strengthened by his growing preoccupation with Washington matters. Indeed, the speed with which a congressman begins to develop a Washington career will affect the speed with which his home style solidifies. . . .

In all of this speculation about career linkages, we have assumed that most members of Congress develop, over time, a mix of personal goals. We particularly assume that most members will trade off some of their personal commitment to reelection in order to satisfy a personal desire for institutional or policy influence. It is our observation . . . that House members do, in fact, exhibit varying degrees of commitment to reelection. All want reelection in the abstract, but not all will pay any price to achieve it; nor will all pay the same price. . . .

One senior member contemplated retirement in the face of an adverse redistricting but, because he had the prospect of a committee chairmanship, he decided to run and hope for the best. He wanted reelection because he wanted continued influence; but he was unwilling to put his present influence in jeopardy by pursuing reelection with the same intensity that marked his earlier constituency career. As he put it,

> Ten years ago, I whipped another redistricting. And I did it by neglecting my congressional duties. . . . Today I don't have the time, and I'm not going to neglect my duties. . . . If I do what is necessary to get reelected and thus become chairman of the committee, I will lose the respect and confidence of my fellow committee members because of being absent from the hearings and, occasionally, the votes.

He did not work hard at reelection, and he won by his narrowest margin ever. But he succeeded in sustaining a mix of personal goals very different from an earlier one. . . .

The congressman's home activities are more difficult and taxing than we have previously recognized. Under the best of circumstances, the tension involved in maintaining constituency contact and achieving legislative competence is considerable. Members cannot be in two places at once, and the growth of a Washington career exacerbates the problem. But, more than that, the demands in both places have grown recently. The legislative workload and the demand for legislative expertise are steadily increasing. So is the problem of maintaining meaningful contact with their several constituencies. Years ago, House members returned home for months at a time to live among their supportive constituencies, soak up the home atmosphere, absorb local problems at first hand. Today, they race home for a day, a weekend, a week at a time. [Few] maintain a family home in their district. [Many] stay with relatives or friends or in barely furnished rooms when they are at home. The citizen demand for access, for communication, and for the establishment of trust is as great as ever. So members go home. But the quality of their contact has suffered. "It's like a one-night stand in a singles bar." It is harder to sustain a genuine two-way communication then it once was. House member worries about the home relationship—great under any circumstances, but greater now—contribute to the strain and frustration of the job. Some cope; but others retire. It may be those members who cannot stand the heat of the home relationship who are getting out of the House kitchen. If so, people prepared to be more attentive to home . . . are likely to replace them.

The interplay between home careers and Washington careers continues even as House members leave Congress. For, in retirement or in defeat, they still face a choice—to return home or to remain in Washington. The subject of postcongressional careers is too vast to be treated here. But students of home politics can find, in these choices, indications of the depth and durability of home attachments in the face of influential Washington careers. It is conventional wisdom in the nation's capital that senators and representatives "get Potomac fever" and that "they don't go back to Pocatello" when their legislative careers end. Having pursued the goals of power and policy in Washington with increasing success, they prefer, it is said, to continue their Washington career in some nonlegislative job rather than to go back home. In such a choice, perhaps, we might find the ultimate displacement of the constituency career with the Washington career.

An examination of the place of residence of 370 individuals who left the House between 1954 and 1974, and who were alive in 1974, sheds considerable doubt on this Washington wisdom. It appears that most House members do, indeed, "go back to Pocatello." Of the 370 former members studied, 253 (68 percent) resided in their home states in 1974; 91 lived in the Washington, D.C., area; and 26 resided someplace else. Of those 344 who chose either Washington or home, therefore, nearly three-quarters chose home. This simple fact underscores the very great strength of the home attachments we have described in this [selection].

No cross section of living former members will tell us for sure how many members lingered in Washington for a while before eventually returning home. Only a careful tracing of all individual cases, therefore, will give us a full and accurate description of the Washington-home choice. Even so, among the former members most likely to be attracted to Washington—those who left Congress from 1970 to 1974—only 37 percent have chosen to remain there. A cursory glance at all those who have chosen to prolong their Washington careers, however, tell us what we might expect—that they have already had longer congressional careers than those who returned home. Our data also tell us that these members are younger than those who choose to return home. Thus, we speculate, the success of a member's previous career in Congress and the prospect that he or she still has time to capitalize on that success in the Washington community are positive inducements to stay. And these inducements seem unaffected by the manner of his or her leaving Congress—whether by electoral defeat (for renomination or reelection) or retirement. Those who were defeated, however, had shorter congressional careers and were younger than those who had voluntarily retired.

Whether or not the 1994 elections changed fundamentally the landscape of Congressional politics is the subject of the following selections.

57

Norman Ornstein

THE NEW REPUBLICAN CONGRESS

❖❖❖❖❖❖❖

When the 104th Congress convened on January 4, 1995, it was surrounded by a level of hoopla and media attention virtually unprecedented in modern American politics. All three major network news anchors came to Washington to report on the events of the day, which included blanket live coverage of the opening speech of newly-elected Speaker of the House Newt Gingrich (R–GA). Speaker Gingrich's face was on the cover of every major newsmagazine. The events of the remarkable first day, which ended well after 2:00 AM, underscored the scope of political change that the November 1994 elections had brought. Congress enacted rules changes that combined into the most sweeping changes in nearly fifty years of congressional procedures.

The reasons for the excitement were obvious. The 104th Congress became the first Republican-controlled Congress in 40 years. It was the first Republican Congress to face a Democratic president in 46 years. Not a single Republican member of the House had *ever* been in the majority in the House before (one, Bill Emerson of Missouri, had been in the House during the last GOP majority—as a young page!). Not a single Democrat in the House had ever been in the minority there (although the Democrats had their own page from minority days, their senior member, John Dingell of Michigan). The new Speaker, Newt Gingrich, had only recently been a minority backbencher known more for his fiery statements and all-out assaults on congressional Democrats and Congress itself—and suddenly, he was in charge of the institution he had so fiercely criticized.

The difference in politics was accompanied by a sharp difference in policy, both in substance and process. Especially for the House, the 1994 election had been fought in major part on the battlefield of the Republicans' proposed "Contract with America," a document signed in September 1994 with fanfare on the steps of the Capitol by nearly all GOP candidates for the House. The Contract was printed verbatim in an insert in *TV Guide* during the campaign.

The Contract promised up or down votes in the House, under open rules, on ten major measures during the first hundred days of the 104th Congress. The ten items included a series of Constitutional Amendments on a balanced budget, a line-item veto, term limits for Congress (and possibly to ban unfunded mandates to state and local governments), and sweeping action through a series of tax cuts, money for the elderly, tort reform, and welfare and defense reform, among other things. It also pledged, on Congress's first day, to enact—not just vote on—sweeping congressional reforms. The first day accomplished that goal, providing some impetus for the remainder of the Contract, and elevating Congress' approval in the eyes of the American public.

But there were some sobering realities that contrasted with the first day's euphoria. In a CNN/USA Today poll taken just after that first day, public approval of Congress went up nearly forty percent—but that meant rising from 23% to 31%. Even after the drama, 50% of Americans disapproved of Congress's performance, underscoring the deep resentment voters had developed about the legislative branch, deep enough not to be erased by one good day.

Early controversies surrounded the new Speaker, including his abortive decision to accept a $4.5 million advance from a publishing house, and his highly controversial appointment of a House historian which was hastily withdrawn after criticism of her background and views. These reversed decisions suggested that the early momentum, built in part around the remarkable personal drive of the new Speaker, could be dampened if the initial minor problems escalated.

The U.S. Senate's first day underscored another reality. Late in the first day, in debate lasting just over one hour, the House passed its first piece of substantive legislation—the Congressional Accountability Act, creating an Office of Compliance to ensure that Congress applied to itself all laws it applied to the private sector. The Senate had hoped to do the same thing.

But the Senate spent its first day tied up in lengthy debate over the future of the filibuster, the Senate's Rule XXII that allowed extended debate and delay on bills and nominations. When the Senate finally got to its own version of the Congressional Accountability Act, extended debate and a succession of amendments offered by the minority Democrats drew out the discussion over several days. The Act finally passed on January 11, one week after the House had dispatched with it in one hour.

The House nonetheless intrepidly moved forward. After just one week, the House Judiciary Committee reported out a Constitutional Amendment to balance the budget, moving it rapidly toward the House floor and ignoring, for the moment, the brewing controversy across party lines about a provision in the draft amendment requiring a three-fifths vote of both houses of Congress for any tax increase. The House and the Senate moved almost as rapidly to pass through bills blocking or limiting unfunded mandates, i.e., requirements which federal legislation impose on state and local governments without any funding to pay for them. Committees began to mobilize to put together other pieces of legislation reflecting the priorities of the Contract with America.

If revolution had come to the House, the Senate showed that all that had changed was the party majority. Its balky, slow, decentralized and individualized traditions and procedures remained in place. The new majority Republicans had used these same techniques as a minority to slow down and kill multiple initiatives of the Clinton Administration, but were now bedeviled by them as they tried to match their colleagues in the House.

Whatever the actual outcomes in policy in the 104th Congress, the fact remained that even early in January of its first year it was historic and important. However, there were key questions to ask to determine *how* historic and *how* important.

How Enduring Would Republican Rule of Congress Be?

The forty-year Democratic majority in the House of Representatives that preceded the 104th Congress lasted more than twice as long as any partisan majority at any time in American history. There were many reasons for this unprecedented achievement, including the underlying party identification of voters; the sharp increase in perquisites and powers of Democratic incumbents; the sharply increased cost of campaigns and the resultant barriers for challengers.

There was one other ironic reason: Republicans were dominant in the White House. The longer a party holds the White House, in fact, the more its position in Congress erodes. Midterm elections inexorably cost the president's party seats in Congress. Presidential year contests rarely provide enough cushion in presidential party gains in Congress to offset the midterm losses.

From the GOP perspective, at least one historical parallel was sobering. The 1946 midterm election had much in common with the one held in 1994. In it, the Democratic president Harry Truman suffered sharp losses in his first midterm, including 56 seats dropped in the House and 13 in the Senate, costing the Democrats their longstanding majorities in both houses of Congress. But two years later in 1948, Truman's come-from-behind presidential victory was accompanied by a whopping 75 seat Democratic *gain* in the House, along with a gain of nine in the Senate, and the recapture of control of Congress.

To be sure, enough has changed in America and in American politics in the past 48 years that it would be foolish to suggest that 1996 would in any way parallel 1948. But one aspect of this historical record also resonated with Newt Gingrich. In his first address to the newly-elected Republican members of the House, he noted that if 1994 brought with it the first Republican majority in Congress in forty years, we would have to go back nearly *seventy* years, to 1928, for the last time a Republican Congress was *re*-elected to a second consecutive term.

What Would Make Americans Continue Republicans in the Majority in Congress?

Focus this question another way: will voters be happier with Republicans if the system *works*, passing lots of policy changes, or if the system doesn't work? Can Republicans make the case that it would work if they only had the missing piece of the puzzle, the presidency?

Consider, in that context, the 1946–1948 parallel. In 1948, the Democrats held the White House and recaptured Congress when Harry Truman ran by condemning the "Do Nothing 80th Congress," a charge that stuck. Could such an approach work in 1996?

The more hardline conservative Republicans in the 104th House considered a 180 degree variation on this strategy—to pass a series of tough, uncompromising bills, and send them to President Clinton to force him into a Hobson's choice—or to sign the bills, infuriating his liberal Democratic base, or veto them and allow the Republicans to run against a "Do-Nothing President." But can both the House and

Senate agree on and pass tough and uncompromising legislation on welfare, balanced budgets, tort reform, regulatory reform, tax cuts, budget cuts, and so on? With the Senate divided 53 Republicans to 47 Democrats, and with at least eight of the Republicans considered to be moderates or even liberals, that strategy could be shaky at best.

Indeed, any strategy of blaming the other party might be shaky. Voters *did* collectively reject continuing Democratic control of Congress in 1994, a reality underscored by the unprecedented perfect success of Republican incumbents in both the House and Senate. However, polls also suggested that one reason for this collective decision was a collective desire to return to divided government, with one party in charge of Congress, the other in charge of running the presidency.

Thus, the answer to this question might give us the answer to another key question.

How Would the Republican 104th Congress Get Along with a Democratic President?

Although Speaker-designate Gingrich said soon after the election that Republicans would cooperate—but not compromise—with the president, the dynamics of politics in 1995 added considerable pressure for major compromises as well. The case could be made that it was in everyone's political interest to have Republicans running Congress and Democrats in the White House, to show government working while passing legislation that allowed all sides to declare victory.

Mixed in with that kind of political pressure was the more partisan and ideological pressure each party felt from its base. Any set of issues resulting in compromises in the middle would be matched by another set of issues with the parties drawing lines in the dust and facing off with confrontational postures, leading to vetoes and votes on veto overrides.

One other major question floated over the political calculus early in 1995.

How Would the Republican House Get Along with the Republican Senate?

If a majority was wholly new to Republicans in the House, it was more familiar territory to Republicans in the Senate. They had held the majority from 1981 through 1986 through the first six years of the Reagan presidency. Nearly half the Republican members of the 104th Senate had been in the majority during the earlier period; their approach to governing was more restrained than their House counterparts—almost an attitude of "been there; done that."

The likelihood of frequent clashes between the hard-charging House and the deliberate, sloth-like Senate was very high as the 104th Congress began. The slow, individualized and decentralized nature of the Senate as an institution combined with the difficulty the majority party in the Senate would have generating the near-perfect party unity necessary to build a reliable majority. The possibility of fili-busters was high, requiring sixty votes, not just 51, to achieve success.

The likelihood of House–Senate tension was in turn exacerbated by personal-ity conflicts built in to the political dynamic. Speaker Newt Gingrich (R–GA), the recipient of almost unprecedented attention as the singular focal point of Congress, had to interact with Senate Majority Leader Bob Dole (R–KS), a strong potential presidential candidate in 1996, along with another presidential hopeful like Sena-tor Phil Gramm (R–TX). Watching the interplay between the Republican House, the Republican Senate, and the Democratic president, who might be able at times to play one house of Congress against the other for his own ends, was one of the most fascinating prospects for Congress-watchers in 1995–96.

There was one final question to ask as the 104th Congress began.:

What Did the 1994 Election and the Likely Actions of the 104th Congress Suggest About the Future of Political Parties in America?

Public opinion data in 1994 and beyond underscored another large political reality: even as partisanship increased in Washington, it was declining among voters throughout the country. Compared to earlier decades, fewer people identified with one or the other of the two major parties. The intensity of identification among the remaining partisans had waned as well. The opportunity for third-party or indepen-dent candidates to emerge was thus heightened, although structural barriers sharply limited their prospects for electoral success. But the ability of the parties to interact successfully in the 104th Congress, balancing and juggling their disparate political ambitions, ideological bases, and partisan histories, would go a long way toward de-termining whether a third or independent force, as a party or an individual candi-date for president, would take hold as America approached the millennium.

Congress and Campaign Finance Reform

Congressional incumbents have always benefited from free-wheeling cam-paign finance, which gives them a special advantage over challengers. Special interests have followed the axiom that a bird in the hand is worth two in the bush. Money flows freely to congressional incumbents of both parties. Al-though legislators reap the benefits of free enterprise campaigning, public pressure has forced Congress to put campaign finance reform on its legislative agenda. The public demands reform because of its conviction that politics is intrinsically dishonest. The following selection discusses the unique ways in which public images define campaign finance politics.

58

Frank J. Sorauf

THE SPECIAL POLITICS OF CAMPAIGN FINANCE

❖❖❖❖❖❖❖

The images of campaign finance in the public mind are hopelessly intertwined with the public's impressions about politics generally, about the integrity or knavery of politicians, about the nature of campaigning and campaign tactics, even about the pay and perquisites of public officials. The politics of campaign finance, therefore, features the same double standard—higher standards for the public than the private sector—that American public brings to all of the politics of representation. Just as it easily accepts salaries of more than a million dollars in corporate management while denying one of $100,000 to members of Congress, it is shocked at costs of campaigns that are easily dwarfed by everyday commercial transactions. It abhors skillful avoidance of FECA limits while at the same time employing millions of lawyers, accountants, financial planners, and tax preparers to help avoid paying personal taxes. Popular distrust of politics and politicians is an unavoidable cost of holding public office.

Much of this attitude springs from the Progressive and populist traditions. Many of the relationships of representation involve money, campaign finance most purely, and they easily validate the central proposition of the Progressive worldview: that interests, money, and influence are integrally linked and that they form the driving force behind the major decisions of the political system. Above all, Progressive images and predispositions create their own reality, and it is that reality that is the chief justification for the attack on the post-1974 status quo. It drives reform by defining what is wrong, by defining the acceptable reforms, and by defining the political rewards and punishments for action or inaction on them.

Considered more broadly, the politics of campaign finance has a number of special characteristics. It is, as I have just noted, a politics centered in a broader politics of representation and, therefore, a politics of politics. Naturally, it is a politics to which the members of Congress are enormously sensitive, for it is the politics of their reelection and political careers. It is also a politics that is almost pure populism, driven by mass fears, mass opinion, and mass voting, a politics easily inflamed whether by somber editorialists or by the demagogues of the radio talk shows. It is a politics that looks not at a member of Congress's legislative record but at personal qualities and political styles. And it is a politics complicated and heightened by the fact that the members of Congress legislate about themselves, by the fact that self-interest is central to the policies they choose.

More specifically, the intense mass concern about campaign finance can best be seen by looking at recent history. Certainly the intermittent episodes of PAC-bashing cater to popular fears, as does the rhetoric that nourishes myths of the growth of campaign money. The failure of maintenance and repair of the regulatory structures reflects the same fears, for repairs are scorned for merely propping up a discredited system, a self-serving preservation of the status quo. Ironically, even the reformers may have set in motion perceptions that come back to haunt them. Their charges about the effect of campaign money on the Congress have undoubtedly given support to opinion that rejects the use of public funds to pay for campaigns.

Even though some of the popularly held images may be in error, the issues behind them are not trivial. The politics of representation—the politics of politics, that is—is in a real sense the politics of democracy. It is the politics of who will be listened to in the American political system. One sees, for example, the "enfranchisement" of a new political constituency, a campaign funding constituency. People may disagree over the extent of its influence in the final accounting of political influence, but it would be a foolhardy soul who would assert that it had no substantial influence. The alliance of a part of the funding constituency with well-established group lobbying only gives the question greater force. Moreover, the new constituency is national and organized, and its interests are to some extent at variance with the interests of the local, grass-roots constituencies that vote and whose opinions make up mass public opinion. The rejection of PACs and their works is, therefore, an attempt to repulse foreign or hostile interests and to protect local voter hegemony.

These politics of campaign finance add a dense and complicated layer to the stratified politics that have led for more than 10 years to legislative deadlock over reforming the regime of 1974. The fact that the politics of politics are at stake pits strong and irreconcilable party interests against each other; it sets the House against the Senate, and at a time of divided control of the elected branches, it positions a president of one party against the majority party in the Congress. Deadlock, too, reflects and springs from the difficulties of making policy, even of framing policy proposals, when not only interests and opinion but even images of reality, are fragmented. Placating mass opinion becomes the first priority in a politics of representation. But there are limits to placating, for the politics of representation is often marked by an inherently destructive dynamic that leads it either to inaction or to ineffective or inept public policy that in turn creates further mass cynicism and displeasure.

Campaign finance regimes change or evolve either by legislated design or by their own internal dynamic and processes. The attempts at legislated reform go on, but political deadlock appears to doom them. Even if limited change comes, it seems unlikely that it will abandon the outlines of the regime that has evolved since 1974. Increasingly, indeed, it seems that short-term changes in the regime may come instead through changes in its political environment. That is the fascination of the 1992 campaigns. Fundamental change in the environment, however, seems as distant as a party realignment or a constitutional amendment limiting the terms of members of Congress. Perhaps, indeed, the end of the post-1974 regime will come only in the same way it was born—in the aftermath of great and disillusioning events.

❖❖ The Courts and the Congress: Interpreting Legislative Intent

A major issue in the relationship between the courts and Congress is "legislative intent." In the broader picture the Supreme Court rarely has held congressional statutes to be unconstitutional. Over its entire history the court has declared only approximately 195 provisions of congressional statutes to be unconstitutional. On the other hand both the Supreme Court and lower federal courts have shaped public policy through their interpretations of *statutory* law.

The courts exercise statutory review when groups and individuals who are injured by executive or administrative enforcement of statutory law challenge the action in court. In such cases injured parties often claim that administrators have exceeded their authority by misinterpreting the statutes they are enforcing. Confronted with such claims the courts must interpret the relevant statutes to determine exactly what Congress meant or intended when it passed the law and delegated enforcement authority to the executive branch. In such cases courts look first at the *text* of the statute, but more often than not, especially in regulatory areas, the text is far from clear. Under such circumstances judges must next turn to the "legislative history" of the law to determine what is commonly referred to as congressional intent. Administrative and on review judicial discretion is broad when statutory texts are ambiguous. Administrative agencies first fill in the details of the law, using their own judgments and policy preferences. Agencies act as quasi-legislative bodies in this way. Judicial review of the "legislative" actions of administrative agencies also gives the courts an important role in defining public policies by choosing among competing statutory interpretations.

In the following selection Supreme Court Justice Stephen Breyer discusses the dilemma courts often face in interpreting unclear statutory language, when judges are forced to turn to legislative history to define congressional intent.

59

Stephen R. Breyer

ON THE USES OF LEGISLATIVE HISTORY IN INTERPRETING STATUTES

Until recently an appellate court trying to interpret unclear statutory language would have thought it natural, and often helpful, to refer to the statute's "legislative history." The judges might have examined congressional floor debates, committee reports, hearing testimony, and presidential messages in an effort to determine what Congress really "meant" by particular statutory language. Should courts refer to legislative history as they try to apply statutes correctly? Is this practice wise, helpful, or proper? Lawyers and judges, teachers and legislators, have begun to reexamine this venerable practice, often with a highly critical eye. Some have urged drastically curtailing, or even totally abandoning, its use. Some argue that courts use legislative history almost arbitrarily. Using legislative history, Judge Leventhal once said, is like "looking over a crowd and picking out your friends." Others maintain that it is constitutionally improper to look beyond a statute's language, or that searching for "congressional intent" is a semi-mystical exercise like hunting the snark.

. . .

The Problem of Congressional "Intent"

Critics sometimes argue that the use of legislative history depends upon a mistaken belief that behind every statute lies a congressional "intent." Congressional intent, they say, is a myth; some say that the concept itself lacks intellectual coherence. How can a document written by a committee staffer indicate the inner workings of the mind of even one legislator, let alone the several hundred who voted for the law, perhaps each for different individual reasons? Moreover, a branch of political science, called "public choice" theory, argues that legislation simply reflects the conflicting interactions of interest groups; the resulting law sometimes reflects their private, selfish interests, and sometimes serves no purpose at all. Does it make any

From Stephen Breyer, "On the Uses of Legislative History in Interpreting Statutes," *Southern California Law Review,* 65, 1992, pp. 845–874. Reprinted with the permission of the Southern California Law Review.

sense in such circumstances to ascribe a responsible-sounding purpose to the statute's words?

Conceptually, however, one can ascribe an "intent" to Congress in enacting the words of a statute if one means "intent" in its, here relevant, sense of "purpose," rather than its sense of "motive." One often ascribes "group" purposes to group actions. A law school raises tuition to obtain money for a new library. A basketball team stalls to run out the clock. A tank corps feints to draw the enemy's troops away from the main front. Obviously, one of the best ways to find out the purpose of an action taken by a group is to ask some of the group's members about it. But, this does not necessarily mean that the group's purposes and the members' motives or purposes must be identical. The members of the group participating in the group activity—indeed, whose actions are necessary conditions for its action—may have different, private *motives* for their own actions; but that fact does not necessarily change the proper characterization of the group's purpose. Perhaps several key members of the faculty voted for the tuition increase, not because they cared about the library, but simply in order to please the Dean. Is a better library any the less the object of the *law school's* action? Indeed, must it always matter if many, or even most, of the group do not fully understand the group objective of the specific action? Perhaps the basketball team is simply reacting instinctively with long-practiced, set plays, the basic function of which the individual members do not have time to consider, or perhaps have forgotten. Is the purpose of those plays any the less the running of the clock? Perhaps the members of the tank corps do not understand why they head in the direction they take; indeed, perhaps even the commanding general does not understand fully the function of each specific action, the exact purposes of which are spelled out only in a memorandum written by a lowly intelligence officer at brigade headquarters (which officer himself was killed sometime before the attack began). Does this story make any difference at all in respect to the purpose of the individual troop movements?

All this is to say that ascribing purposes to groups and institutions is a complex business, and one that is often difficult to describe abstractly. But that fact does not make such ascriptions improper. In practice, we ascribe purposes to group activities all the time without many practical difficulties.

Of course, the relationship between individual group members' purposes and the group's purpose itself may (depending on the type of group) be particularly complex. It may depend upon the group's internal rules and practices, upon background understandings of the group's role in its social context, and upon the kind of individual purposes or motives at issue, along with the individual statements and actions that reveal those individual purposes. But again, those who understand the group do not ordinarily have trouble properly ascribing purposes to its activities, at least in ordinary cases. A legislator, for example, may vote for language that the legislator believes will extend a statute of limitations solely to obtain campaign contributions, to gain political support, or to defeat the bill on the floor. Those personal motives, however, do not change the purpose of the bill's language, namely, to extend the limitations period. A legislator may vote for technical language that the legislator does not understand, knowing that committee members believe (perhaps because of their faith in the drafting process) that it has a proper function. That fact does not necessarily *change* its function or its purpose. . . . If I am correct in believing that ascribing a purpose to a human institution is an activity related to, but different from, ascribing a purpose to an individual, then I do not see how one can criticize courts that use legislative history on *conceptual* grounds. To refuse to ascribe a "purpose" to Congress in enacting statutory language simply because one cannot find three or four hundred legislators who have claimed it as a personal purpose, is rather like refusing to believe in the existence of Oxford University because one can find only colleges.

The public choice theory arguments against the use of legislative history are more substantial, for they seek to dissolve our belief that ascribing purpose serves any useful descriptive function. Public choice theory describes legislative outcomes in terms of interest-group interaction. The description resembles a psychoanalytic explanation of an individual's actions. Normally such an explanation can coexist with, but not replace, a person's own ordinary purposive account of his behavior. But if an individual's behavior is quite bizarre, if his own long, ordinary-purpose-related accounts of what he is doing do not seem to make much sense, and if the psychoanalytic account is good enough, observers will begin to disregard the individual's own purposive accounts as mere window-dressing, and they will begin to consider the psychoanalytic account as the only (or the most) accurate description and explanation of what is going on. Such is the hope of public choice theorists in respect to their explanation of congressional behavior.

Public choice theory, however, does not yet seem able to explain legislation well enough to warrant abandoning the use of legislative history. Public choice proponents sometimes seem to say that a legislature cannot enact laws in the "public interest" if those laws lack strong private interest group support and face strong private interest group opposition. Empirically, however, this seems wrong. The deregulation movement, for example, began in the airline and trucking industries with virtually no interest-group support. The relevant industries were, in fact, strongly opposed to deregulation and the positions of key labor unions ranged from the unenthusiastic to the adamantly opposed. At other times, the theory's proponents seem to deduce from the fact that legislation was enacted that strong private interest groups supported the legislation. As so used, however, the theory becomes tautological.

Moreover, the experience of those who have worked in legislatures does not confirm many public choice theorists' descriptions of the legislative process. Chief Judge Mikva of the District of Columbia Circuit, a congressman for many years, writes:

> The politicians and other people I have known in public life just do not fit the "rent-seeking" egoist model that the public choice theorists offer. . . . Not even my five terms in the Illinois state legislature—that last vestige of democracy in the "raw"—nor my five terms in the United States Congress, prepared me for the villains of the public choice literature.

My experience running the staff of the Senate Judiciary Committee led me to conclude that elected officials seriously consider public interest arguments and act upon them far more often than the press, the public choice theorists, or the cynics would lead one to believe.

Finally, one should recall that legislative history is a *judicial* tool, one judges use to resolve difficult problems of judicial interpretation. It can be justified, at least in part, by its ability to help judges interpret statutes, in a manner that makes sense and that will produce a workable set of laws. If judicial use of legislative history achieves this kind of result, courts might use it as part of their overarching interpretive task of producing a coherent and relatively consistent body of statutory law, even were the "rational member of Congress" a pure fiction, made up out of whole cloth. . . .

When legislators enact statutes against the backdrop of current judicial practice, they know that they need not spend scarce time entering thorny, technical, legal debates about language when all concerned agree about substance. They can often more easily achieve their substantive objectives by explaining clearly, in a report or on the floor, their agreed-upon purposes in enacting a particular form of words. Senator Williams, for example, in the midst of floor debate about the Urban Mass Transportation Act's labor protection, noted a misstatement and said, "[The] *legislative history* has to be corrected . . . because if the bill shall be enacted, we must have a record that shows that the bill does not preempt State law. . . ."

If suddenly courts applied a new interpretation system to the Act's language, the court would frustrate Senator William's understanding of what he was accomplishing. To change interpretive horses in midstream would defeat the expectations of the legislators who enacted a statute, and, if the change were sufficiently sudden and radical, it could defeat the expectations of the voters as well.

The complex legislative process I have described relies heavily upon interactions of legislators, staff, and interest groups to create, review, criticize, and amend legislative language, reports, and floor statements. The process is reasonably open and fair so long as those whom the legislation will likely affect have roughly equal access to the legislative process. However, critics of the congressional process challenge this assumption strongly and often. Most critics concede that trade associations, labor unions, executive departments, and certain public interest groups, all under the watchful eye of the press, participate fully in the process on behalf of those they represent. But they ask several familiar questions. For example, are there not many disadvantaged groups who are excluded from the legislative process? Indeed, is the ordinary citizen adequately represented as a "typical citizen" rather than as a member of some organized interest group? Moreover, does ideology drive congressional staff more than the desire to reflect the will of the voter? Perhaps because we are all familiar with such criticism, my description of the legislative process did not fully dispel doubts about the legitimacy of the use of legislative history.

If these questions disturb you, then you might ask yourself whether judicial abandonment of the use of legislative history would make matters better or worse. Certainly abandonment would eliminate one factor that favors public hearings, public reports vetted by staff, and fairly detailed floor debates. It would also make it easier for legislators to justify amending legislation after it leaves committee, while it is on the floor of the House or Senate, or even while both Houses of Congress confer upon the bill after it passed each in different versions. To the extent that a change weakens the publicly accessible committee system and diminishes the need for public justification, it increases the power of the "special interests" (and here I use that term pejoratively) to secure legislation that is not in the "public interest." Thus, if judges abandon the use of legislative history, Congress will not necessarily produce better laws.

To the contrary, insofar as courts discourage Congress from using the regular committee, floor debate, and conference process, the technical quality of statutory law is likely to deteriorate significantly. The statutory language inserted by amendment on the floor of Congress produces absurd, anomalous, or unfair results. Recently, for example, the First Circuit had to interpret a section of the Anti-Drug Amendments Act of 1986 that changed one part of a "cocaine possession" penalty from "special parole" to "supervised release." Although the section said that the change would take effect at once, the words "supervised release" (in the section taking effect at once) referred to procedures that a different law, the Sentencing Reform Act, said would not take effect until one year later. What law applied to the offenders convicted during this one-year interval? The old law abolished parole; the new procedure did not yet exist. The courts produced conflicting solutions at the circuit level and eventually the Supreme Court simply picked one of those solutions as the best. The very point of congressional committee hearings is to scrutinize legislative language carefully to prevent this kind of drafting error.

Consider a worse example. A recently enacted statutory provision, apparently a House floor amendment, imposes high mandatory prison terms upon those convicted two or three times of possessing crack cocaine. The language of the provision triggers these high "subsequent possession" penalties only when the prior convictions were convictions *under this subsection.* The "subsection," however, involves simple *possession* of crack, not the much more serious crime of possessing crack with intent to sell it to others. The result is that the less serious recidivist (the crack possessor) is punished more severely than the more serious recidivist (the crack distributor). Had this provision gone through committee, Congress would likely have heard the Sentencing Commission and other experts explain how punishments for related crimes should relate to one another, and this anomaly would not have escaped notice.

I did not dwell upon the problems of the legislative process, however, because my focus was the judiciary. I have simply argued that, viewed in light of the judiciary's important objective of helping to maintain coherent, workable statutory law, the case for abandoning the use of legislative history has not yet been made. Present practice has proved useful; the alternatives are not promising; radical change is too problematic. The "problem" of legislative history is its "abuse," not its "use." Care, not drastic change, is all that is warranted.

Chapter 9

THE JUDICIARY

An independent judicial system is an important part of constitutional government. The United States Supreme Court was created with this view, and its members were given life tenure and guaranteed compensation to maintain their independence. However, Congress was given power to structure the entire subordinate judicial system, including control over the appellate jurisdiction of the Supreme Court. Regardless of any initial lack of power and various attempts made by and through Congress to curb its power, the Supreme Court today occupies a predominant position in the governmental system. The evolution of the Court, its present powers, and their implications are analyzed in this chapter.

Constitutional Background: Judicial Independence and Judicial Review

The Supreme Court and the judicial system play important roles in the intricate separation-of-powers scheme. Through judicial review, both legislative and executive decisions may be overruled by the courts for a number of reasons. To some extent, then, the judiciary acts as a check upon arbitrary action by governmental departments and agencies. The intent of the framers of the Constitution regarding the role of the judiciary, particularly the Supreme Court, in our governmental system is examined in *Federalist 78*.

60

Alexander Hamilton

FEDERALIST 78

❖❖❖❖❖❖❖

We proceed now to an examination of the judiciary department of the proposed government.

In unfolding the defects of the existing confederation, the utility and necessity of a federal judicature have been clearly pointed out. It is the less necessary to recapitulate the considerations there urged; as the propriety of the institution in the abstract is not disputed; the only questions which have been raised being relative to the manner of constituting it, and to its extent. To these points, therefore, our observations shall be confined.

The manner of constituting it seems to embrace these several objects: 1st. The mode of appointing the judges; 2nd. The tenure by which they are to hold their places; 3rd. The partition of the judiciary authority between different courts, and their relations to each other.

First

As to the mode of appointing the judges: This is the same with that of appointing the officers of the union in general, and has been so fully discussed . . . that nothing can be said here which would not be useless repetition.

Second

As to the tenure by which the judges are to hold their places: This chiefly concerns their duration in office; the provisions for their support; the precautions for their responsibility.

According to the plan of the convention, all the judges who may be appointed by the United States are to hold their offices *during good behavior;* which is conformable to the most approved of the state constitutions. . . . The standard of good behavior for the continuance in office of the judicial magistracy is certainly one of the most valuable of the modern improvements in the practice of government. In a monarchy, it is an excellent barrier to the despotism of the prince; in a republic, it is a no less excellent barrier to the encroachments and oppressions of the representative body. And it is the best expedient which can be devised in any government, to secure a steady, upright, and impartial administration of the laws.

Whoever attentively considers the different departments of power must perceive, that, in a government in which they are separated from each other, the judiciary, from the nature of its functions, will always be the least dangerous to the political rights of the constitution; because it will be least in a capacity to annoy or injure them. The executive not only dispenses the honors, but holds the sword of the community. The legislature not only commands the purse, but prescribes the rules by which the duties and rights of every citizen are to be regulated. The judiciary, on the contrary, has no influence over either the sword or the purse; no direction either of the strength or of the wealth of the society; and can take no active resolution whatever. It may truly be said to have neither FORCE NOR WILL, but merely judgment; and must ultimately depend upon the aid of the executive arm for the efficacious exercise even of this faculty.

This simple view of the matter suggests several important consequences: It proves incontestably, that the judiciary is beyond comparison, the weakest of the three departments of power, that it can never attack with success either of the other two; and that all possible care is requisite to enable it to defend itself against their attacks. It equally proves, that, though individual oppression may now and then proceed from the courts of justice, the general liberty of the people can never be endangered from that quarter; I mean so long as the judiciary remains truly distinct from both the legislature and executive. For I agree, that "there is no liberty, if the power of judging be not separated from the legislative and executive powers." It proves, in the last place, that as liberty can have nothing to fear from the judiciary alone, but would have everything to fear from its union with either of the other departments; that, as all the effects of such a union must ensue from a dependence of the former on the latter, notwithstanding a nominal and apparent separation; that as, from the natural feebleness of the judiciary, it is in continual jeopardy of being overpowered, awed or influenced by its coordinate branches; that, as nothing can contribute so much to its firmness and independence as PERMANENCY IN OFFICE, this quality may therefore be justly regarded as an indispensable ingredient in its constitution; and, in a great measure, as the CITADEL of the public justice and the public security.

The complete independence of the courts of justice is peculiarly essential in a limited constitution. By a limited constitution, I understand one which contains certain specified exceptions to the legislative no ex post facto laws, and the like. Limitations of this kind can be preserved in practice no other way than through the medium of the courts of justice, whose duty it must be to declare all acts contrary to the manifest tenor of the constitution void. Without this, all the reservations of particular rights or privileges would amount to nothing.

Some perplexity respecting the right of the courts to pronounce legislative acts void, because contrary to the constitution, has arisen from an imagination that the doctrine would imply a superiority of the judiciary to the legislative power. It is urged that the authority which can declare the acts of another void, must necessarily be superior to the one whose acts may be declared void. As this doctrine is of great important in all the American constitutions, a brief discussion of the grounds on which it rests cannot be unacceptable.

There is no position which depends on clearer principles than that every act of a delegated authority, contrary to the tenor of the commission under which it is exercised, is void. No legislative act, therefore, contrary to the constitution, can be valid. To deny this would be to affirm, that the deputy is greater than his principal; that the servant is above his master; that the representatives of the people are superior to the people themselves; that men, acting by virtue of powers, may do not only what their powers do not authorize, but what they forbid.

If it be said that the legislative body are themselves the constitutional judges of their powers, and that the construction they put upon them is conclusive upon the other departments, it may be answered, that this cannot be the natural presumption, where it is not to be collected from any particular provisions in the constitution. It is not otherwise to be supposed that the constitution could intend to enable the representatives of the people to substitute their *will* to that of their constituents. It is far more rational to suppose that the courts were designed to be an intermediate body between the people and the legislature, in order, among other things, to keep the latter within the limits assigned to their authority. The interpretation of the laws is the proper and peculiar province of the courts. A constitution is, in fact, and must be, regarded by the judges as a fundamental law. It must therefore belong to them to ascertain its meaning, as well as the meaning of any particular act proceeding from the legislative body. If there should happen to be an irreconcilable variance between the two, that which has the superior obligation and validity ought, of course, to be preferred; in other words, the constitution ought to be preferred to the statute, the intention of the people to the intention of their agents.

Nor does this conclusion by any means suppose a superiority of the judicial to the legislative power. It only supposes that the power of the people is superior to both; and that where the will of the legislature declared in its statutes, stands in opposition to that of the people declared in the constitution, the judges ought to be governed by the latter, rather than the former. They ought to regulate their decisions by the fundamental laws, rather than by those which are not fundamental. . . .

It can be no weight to say, that the courts, on the pretense of a repugnancy, may substitute their own pleasure to the constitutional intentions of the legislature. This might as well happen in the case of two contradictory statutes; or it might as well happen in every adjudication upon any single statute. The courts must declare the sense of the law; and if they should be disposed to exercise WILL instead of JUDGMENT, the consequence would equally be the substitution of their pleasure to that of the legislative body. The observation, if it proved anything, would prove that there ought to be no judges distinct from the body.

If then the courts of justice are to be considered as the bulwarks of a limited constitution, against legislative encroachments, this consideration will afford a strong argument for the permanent tenure of judicial officers, since nothing will contribute so much as this to that independent spirit in the judges, which must be essential to the faithful performance of so arduous a duty.

This independence of the judges is equally requisite to guard the constitution and the rights of individuals, from the effects of those ill-humors which the arts of designing men, or the influence of particular conjunctures, sometimes disseminate among the people themselves, and which, though they speedily give place to better information, and more deliberate reflection, have a tendency, in the meantime, to occasion dangerous innovations in the government, and serious oppression of the minor party in the community. . . . Until the people have, by some solemn and authoritative act, annulled or changed the established form, it is binding upon themselves collectively, as well as individually; and no presumption, or even knowledge of their sentiments, can warrant their representatives in a departure from it, prior to such an act. But it is easy to see, that it would require an uncommon portion of fortitude in the judges to do their duty as faithful guardians of the constitution, where legislative invasions of it had been instigated by the major voice of the community.

But it is not with a view to infractions of the constitution only, that the independence of the judges may be an essential safeguard against the effects of occasional ill-humors in the society. These sometimes extend no farther than to the injury of the private rights of particular classes of citizens, by unjust and partial laws. Here also the firmness of the judicial magistracy is of vast importance in mitigating the severity, and confining the operation of such laws. It not only serves to moderate the immediate mischiefs of those which may have been passed, but it operates as a check upon the legislative body in passing them; who, perceiving that obstacles to the success of an iniquitous intention are to be expected from the scruples of the courts, are in a manner compelled by the very motives of the injustice they mediate, to quality their attempts. . . .

That inflexible and uniform adherence to the rights of the constitution, and of individuals, which we perceive to be indispensable in the courts of justice, can certainly not be expected from judges who hold their offices by a temporary commission. Periodical appointments, however regulated, or by whomsoever made, would, in some way or other, be fatal to their necessary independence. If the power of making them was committed either to the executive or legislature, there would be danger of an improper compliance to the branch which possessed it; if to both, there would be an unwillingness to hazard the displeasure of either; if to the people, or to persons chosen by them for the special purpose, there would be too great a disposition to consult popularity to justify a reliance that nothing would be consulted but the constitution and the laws.

There is yet a further and a weighty reason for the permanency of judicial offices, which is deducible from the nature of the qualifications they require. It has been frequently remarked, with great propriety, that a voluminous code of laws is one of the inconveniences necessarily connected with the advantages of a free government. To avoid an arbitrary discretion in the courts, it is indispensable that they should be bound down by strict rules and precedents, which serve to define and point out their duty in every particular case that comes before them; and it will readily be conceived, from the variety of controversies which grow out of the folly and wickedness of mankind, that the records of those precedents must unavoidably swell to a very considerable bulk, and must demand long and laborious study to acquire a competent knowledge of them. Hence it is, that there can be but few men in the society, who will have sufficient skill in the laws to qualify them for the stations of judges. And making the proper deductions for the ordinary depravity of human nature, the number must be still smaller, of those who unite the requisite integrity with the requisite knowledge. . . .

❖❖ From *Federalist 78* students can observe that the intent of the framers of the Constitution, at least as expressed and represented by Hamilton, was to give to the courts the power of judicial review over legislative acts. Students should note that this concept was not explicitly written into the Constitution. Although the cause of this omission is not known, it is reasonable to assume that the framers felt that judicial power implied judicial review. Further, it is possible that the framers did not expressly mention judicial review because they had to rely on the states for adoption of the Constitution; judicial power would extend to the states as well as to the coordinate departments of the national government.

The power of the Supreme Court to invalidate an act of Congress was stated by John Marshall in *Marbury* v. *Madison,* 1 Cranch 137 (1803). At issue was a provision in the Judiciary Act of 1789 which extended the *original jurisdiction* of the Supreme Court by authorizing it to issue writs of mandamus in cases involving public officers of the United States and private persons, a power not conferred upon the Court in the Constitution. Marbury had been appointed a justice of the peace by President John Adams under the Judiciary Act of 1801, passed by the Federalists after Jefferson and the Republican party won the elections in the fall of 1800 so that President Adams could fill various newly created judicial posts with Federalists before he left office in March 1801. Marbury was scheduled to receive one of these commissions, but when Jefferson took office on March 4, with Madison as his secretary of state, it had not been delivered. Marbury filed a suit with the Supreme Court requesting it to exercise its original jurisdiction and issue a writ of mandamus (a writ to compel an official to perform his or her duty) to force Madison to deliver the commission, an act which both Jefferson and Madison were opposed to doing. In his decision, Marshall, a prominent Federalist, stated that although Marbury had a legal right to his commission, and although mandamus was the proper remedy, the Supreme Court could not extend its original jurisdiction beyond the limits specified in the Constitution; therefore, that section of the Judiciary Act of 1789 permitting the court to issue such writs to public officers was unconstitutional. Incidentally, the Republicans were so outraged at the last-minute appointments of Adams that there were threats that Marshall would be impeached if he issued a writ of mandamus directing Madison to deliver the commission. This is not to suggest that Marshall let such considerations influence him; however, politically his decision was thought to be a masterpiece of reconciling his position as a Federalist with the political tenor of the times.

61
MARBURY V. MADISON
1 CRANCH 137 (1803)

❖❖❖❖❖❖❖❖

Mr. Chief Justice Marshall delivered the opinion of the Court, saying in part:

. . . The authority, therefore, given to the Supreme Court, by the [Judiciary Act of 1789] . . . establishing the judicial courts of the United States, to issue writs of mandamus to public officers, appears not to be warranted by the Constitution [because it adds to the original jurisdiction of the Court delineated by the framers of the Constitution in Article III; had they wished this power to be conferred upon the Court it would be so stated, in the same manner that the other parts of the Court's original jurisdiction are stated]; . . . it becomes necessary to inquire whether a jurisdiction so conferred can be exercised.

The question whether an act repugnant to the Constitution can become the law of the land, is a question deeply interesting to the United States; but, happily, not of an intricacy proportioned to its interests. It seems only necessary to recognize certain principles supposed to have been long and well established, to decide it.

That the people have an original right to establish, for their future government, such principles as, in their opinion, shall most conduce to their own happiness, is the basis on which the whole American fabric has been erected. The exercise of this original right is a very great exertion; nor can it nor ought it to be frequently repeated. The principles, therefore, so established, are deemed fundamental. And as the authority from which they proceed is supreme, and can seldom act, they are designed to be permanent.

This original and supreme will organizes the government, and assigns to different departments their respective powers. It may either stop here, or establish certain limits not to be transcended by those departments.

The government of the United States is of the latter description. The powers of the legislature are defined and limited; and that those limits may not be mistaken, or forgotten, the Constitution is written. To what purpose are powers limited, and to what purpose is that limitation committed to writing, if these limits may, at any time, be passed by those intended to be restrained? The distinction between a government with limited powers is abolished, if those limits do not confine the persons on whom they are imposed, and if acts prohibited and acts allowed, are of equal obligation. It is a proposition too plain to be contested, that the Constitution controls any legislative act repugnant to it; or, that the legislature may alter the Constitution by an ordinary act.

Between these alternatives there is no middle ground. The Constitution is either a superior paramount law, unchangeable by ordinary means, or it is on a level with ordinary legislative acts, and, like other acts, is alterable when the legislature shall please to alter it.

If the former part of the alternative be true, then a legislative act contrary to the Constitution, is not law; if the latter part be true, then written constitutions are absurd attempts, on the part of the people, to limit a power in its own nature illimitable.

Certainly all those who have framed written constitutions contemplate them as forming the fundamental and paramount law of the nation, and, consequently, the theory of every such government must be, that an act of the legislature, repugnant to the constitution, is void.

This theory is essentially attached to a written constitution, and is consequently to be considered, by this court, as one of the fundamental principles of our society. It is not, therefore, to be lost sight of in the further consideration of this subject.

If an act of the legislature, repugnant to the Constitution, is void, does it, notwithstanding its invalidity, bind the courts, and oblige them to give it effect? Or, in other words, though it be not law, does it constitute a rule as operative as if it was a law? This would be to overthrow in fact what was established in theory; and would seem, at first view, an absurdity too gross to be insisted on. It shall, however, receive a more attentive consideration.

It is emphatically the province and duty of the judicial department to say what the law is. Those who apply the rule to particular cases, must of necessity expound and interpret that rule. If two laws conflict with each other, the courts must decide on the operation of each.

So if the law be in opposition to the Constitution; if both the law and the Constitution apply to a particular case, so that the court must either decide that case conformably to the law, disregarding the Constitution, or conformably to the Constitution, disregarding the law, the court must determine which of these conflicting rules governs the case. This is of the very essence of judicial duty.

If, then, the courts are to regard the Constitution, and the Constitution is superior to any ordinary act of the legislature, the Constitution, and not such ordinary act, must govern the case to which they both apply.

Those, then, who controvert the principle that the Constitution is to be considered, in court, as a paramount law, are reduced to the necessity of maintaining that courts must close their eyes on the Constitution, and see only the law.

This doctrine would subvert the very foundation of all written constitutions. It would declare that an act which, according to the principles and theory of our government, is entirely void, is yet, in practice, completely obligatory. It would declare that if the legislature shall do what is expressly forbidden, such act, notwithstanding the express prohibition, is in reality effectual. It would be giving to the legislature a practical and real omnipotence, with the same breath which professes to restrict their powers within narrow limits. It is prescribing limits, and declaring that those limits may be passed at pleasure.

That it thus reduces to nothing what we have deemed the greatest improvement on political institutions, a written constitution, would of itself be sufficient, in America, where written constitutions have been viewed with so much reverence, for rejecting the construction. But the peculiar expressions of the Constitution of the United States furnish additional arguments in favor of its rejection.

The judicial power of the United States is extended to all cases arising under the Constitution.

Could it be the intention of those who gave this power, to say that in using it the Constitution should not be looked into? That a case arising under the Constitution should be decided without examining the instrument under which it arises?

This is too extravagant to be maintained.

In some cases, then, the Constitution must be looked into by the judges. And if they can open it at all, what part of it are they forbidden to read or obey?

There are many other parts of the Constitution which serve to illustrate this subject.

It is declared that "no tax or duty shall be laid on articles exported from any State." Suppose a duty on the export of cotton, of tobacco, or of flour; and a suit instituted to recover it. Ought judgment to be rendered in such a case? Ought the judges to close their eyes on the Constitution, and only see the law?

The Constitution declares "that no bill of attainder or ex post facto law shall be passed."

If, however, such a bill should be passed, and a person should be prosecuted under it, must the court condemn to death those victims whom the Constitution endeavors to preserve?

"No person," says the Constitution, "shall be convicted of treason unless on the testimony of two witnesses to the same overt act, or on confession in open court."

Here the language of the Constitution is addressed especially to the courts. It prescribes, directly for them, a rule of evidence not to be departed from. If the legislature should change that rule, and declare one witness, or a confession out of court, sufficient for conviction, must the constitutional principle yield to the legislative act?

From these, and many other selections which might be made, it is apparent that the framers of the Constitution contemplated that instrument as a rule for the government of courts, as well as of the legislature.

Why otherwise does it direct the judges to take an oath to support it? This oath certainly applies in an especial manner to this conduct in their official character. How immoral to impose it on them, if they were to be used as the instruments, and the knowing instruments, for violating what they swear to support!

The oath of office, too, imposed by the legislature, is completely demonstrative of the legislative opinion on this subject. It is in these words: "I do solemnly swear that I will administer justice without respect to persons, and do equal right to the poor and to the rich; and that I will faithfully and impartially discharge all the duties incumbent on me as ———, according to the best of my abilities and understanding, agreeably to the Constitution and laws of the United States."

Why does a judge swear to discharge his duties agreeably to the Constitution of the United States, if that Constitution forms no rule for his government—if it is closed upon him, and cannot be inspected by him?

If such be the real state of things, this is worse than solemn mockery. To prescribe, or to take this oath, becomes equally a crime.

It is also not entirely unworthy of observation, that in declaring what shall be the supreme law of the land, the Constitution itself is first mentioned; and not the laws of the United States generally, but those only which shall be made in pursuance of the Constitution, have that rank.

Thus, the particular phraseology of the Constitution of the United States confirms and strengthens the principle, supposed to be essential to all written constitutions, that a law repugnant to the Constitution is void; and that courts, as well as other departments, are bound by that instrument.

The rule must be discharged.

❖❖ Powers and Limitations of the Supreme Court

Paul A. Freund, in his book *On Understanding the Supreme Court* (1949), notes that the Supreme Court has a definite political role. He asks:

Is the law of the Supreme Court a reflection of the notions of "policy" held by its members? The question recalls the controversy over whether judges "make" or "find" the law. A generation or two ago it was thought rather daring to insist that judges make law. Old Jeremiah Smith, who began the teaching of law at Harvard after a career on the New Hampshire Supreme Court, properly deflated the issue. "Do judges make law?" he repeated. "Course they do. Made some myself." Of course Supreme Court Justices decide cases on the basis of their ideas of policy.

To emphasize this point today is to repeat the familiar. The Court makes policy. It would be difficult to conceive how a Court having the power to interpret the Constitution could fail to make policy, that is, could fail to make rulings that have *general* impact upon the community as a whole. The essential distinction between policymaking and adjudication is that the former has a general effect while the latter touches only a specifically designated person or group.

If the Supreme Court has this power of constitutional interpretation, how is it controlled by the other governmental departments and the community? Is it, as some have claimed, completely arbitrary in rendering many of its decisions? Is it potentially a dictatorial body? The Supreme Court and lower courts are limited to the consideration of cases and controversies brought before them by outside parties. Courts cannot initiate law. Moreover, all courts, and the Supreme Court in particular, exercise judicial self-restraint in certain cases to avoid difficult and controversial issues and to avoid outside pressure to limit the powers of the judiciary. John P. Roche, in the next selection, deals with the background, the nature, and the implications of judicial doctrines of self-restraint.

62

John P. Roche

JUDICIAL SELF-RESTRAINT

Every society, sociological research suggests, has its set of myths which incorporate and symbolize its political, economic, and social aspirations. Thus, as medieval society had the Quest for the Holy Grail and the cult of numerology, we, in our enlightened epoch, have as significant manifestations of our collective hopes the dream of impartial decision-making and the cult of "behavioral science." While in my view these latter two are but different facets of the same fundamental drive, namely, the

John P. Roche, "Judicial Self-Restraint," *APSR*, September 1955. Washington, DC: American Political Science Association.

age-old effort to exorcise human variables from human action, our concern here is with the first of them, the pervasive tendency in the American political and constitutional tradition directed toward taking the politics out of politics, and substituting some set of Platonic guardians for fallible politicians.

While this dream of objectivizing political Truth is in no sense a unique American phenomenon, it is surely true to say that in no other democratic nation has the effort been carried so far and with such persistence. Everywhere one turns in the United States, he finds institutionalized attempts to narrow the political sector and to substitute allegedly "independent" and "impartial" bodies for elected decision-makers. The so-called "independent regulatory commissions" are a classic example of this tendency in the area of administration, but unquestionably the greatest hopes for injecting pure Truth-serum into the body politic have been traditionally reserved for the federal judiciary, and particularly for the Supreme Court. The rationale for this viewpoint is simple: "The people must be protected from themselves, and no institution is better fitted for the role of chaperone than the federal judiciary, dedicated as it is to the supremacy of the rule of law."

Patently central to this function of social chaperonage is the right of the judiciary to review legislative and executive actions and nullify those measures which derogate from eternal principles of truth and justice as incarnated in the Constitution. Some authorities, enraged at what the Supreme Court has found the Constitution to mean, have essayed to demonstrate that the framers did not intend the Court to exercise this function, to have, as they put it, "the last word." I find no merit in this contention; indeed, it seems to me undeniable not only that the authors of the Constitution intended to create a federal government, but also that they assumed *sub silentio* that the Supreme Court would have the power to review both national and state legislation.

However, since the intention of the framers is essentially irrelevant except to antiquarians and polemicists, it is unnecessary to examine further the matter of origins. The fact is that the United States Supreme Court, and the inferior federal courts under the oversight of the high Court, have enormous policy-making functions. Unlike their British and French counterparts, federal judges are not merely technicians who live in the shadow of a supreme legislature, but are fully equipped to intervene in the process of political decision making. In theory, they are limited by the Constitution and the jurisdiction it confers, but, in practice, it would be a clumsy judge indeed who could not, by a little skillful exegesis, adapt the Constitution to a necessary end. This statement is in no sense intended as a condemnation; on the contrary, it has been this perpetual reinvigoration by reinterpretation, in which the legislature and the executive as well as the courts play a part, that has given the Constitution its survival power. Applying a Constitution which contains at key points inspired ambiguity, the courts have been able to pour the new wine in the old bottle. Note that the point at issue is not the legitimacy or wisdom of judicial legislation; it is simply the enormous scope that this prerogative gives to judges to substitute their views for those of past generations, or, more controversially, for those of a contemporary Congress and President.

Thus it is naive to assert that the Supreme Court is limited by the Constitution, and we must turn elsewhere for the sources of judicial restraint. The great power exercised by the Court has carried with it great risks, so it is not surprising that American political history has been sprinkled with demands that the judiciary be emasculated. The really startling thing is that, with the notable exception of the McCardle incident in 1869, the Supreme Court has emerged intact from each of these encounters. Despite the plenary power that Congress, under Article III of the Constitution, can exercise over the appellate jurisdiction of the high Court, the national legislature has never taken sustained and effective action against its House of Lords. It is beyond the purview of this analysis to examine the reasons for Congressional inaction; suffice it here to say that the most significant form of judicial limitation has remained self-limitation. This is not to suggest that such a development as statutory codification has not cut down the area of interpretive discretion, for it obviously has. It is rather to maintain that when the justices have held back from assaults on legislative or executive actions, they have done so on the basis of self-established rationalizations. . . .

The remainder of this paper is therefore concerned with two aspects of this auto-limitation: first, the techniques by which it is put into practice; and, second, the conditions under which it is exercised. . . .

Techniques of Judicial
Self-Restraint

The major techniques of judicial self-restraint appear to fall under the two familiar rubrics: procedural and substantive. Under the former fall the various techniques by which the Court can avoid coming to grips with substantive issues, while under the latter would fall those methods by which the Court, in a substantive holding, finds that the matter at issue in the litigation is not properly one for judicial settlement. Let us examine these two categories in some detail.

Procedural Self-Restraint

Since the passage of the Judiciary Act of 1925, the Supreme Court has had almost complete control over its business. United States Supreme Court *Rule 38*, which governs the certiorari policy, states, (§ 5) that discretionary review will be granted only "where there are special and important reasons therefor." Professor Fowler Harper has suggested in a series of detailed and persuasive articles on the application of this discretion [*University of Pennsylvania Law Review*, vols. 99–101; 103] that the Court has used it in such a fashion as to duck certain significant but controversial problems. While one must be extremely careful about generalizing in this area, since the reasons for denying certiorari are many and complex, Harper's evidence does suggest that the Court in the period since 1949 has refused to review cases involving important civil liberties problems which on their merits appeared to warrant adjudication. As he states at one point: "It is disconcerting when the Court will review a controversy over a patent on a pin ball machine while one man is deprived of his citizenship and another of his liberty without Supreme Court review of a plausible challenge to the validity of government action.". . .

Furthermore, the Supreme Court can issue certiorari on its own terms. Thus in *Dennis v. United States*, appealing the Smith Act convictions of the American communist leadership, the Court accepted the evidential findings of the Second Circuit as final and limited its review to two narrow constitutional issues. This, in effect, burked the basic problem: whether the evidence was sufficient to demonstrate that the Communist Party, U.S.A., was *in fact* clear and present danger to the security of the nation, or whether the communists were merely shouting "Fire!" in an empty theater.

Other related procedural techniques are applicable in some situations. Simple delay can be employed, perhaps in the spirit of the Croatian proverb that "delay is the handmaiden of justice." . . . However, the technique of procedural self-restraint is founded on the essentially simple gadget of refusing jurisdiction, or of procrastinating the acceptance of jurisdiction, and need not concern us further here.

Substantive Self-Restraint

Once a case has come before the Court on its merits, the justices are forced to give some explanation for whatever action they may take. Here self-restraint can take many forms, notably, the doctrine of political questions, the operation of judicial parsimony, and—particularly with respect to the actions of administrative officers of agencies—the theory of judicial inexpertise.

The doctrine of political questions is too familiar to require much elaboration here. Suffice it to say that if the Court feels that a question before it, e.g., the legitimacy of a state government, the validity of a legislative apportionment, or the correctness of executive action in the field of foreign relations, is one that is not properly amenable to judicial settlement, it will refer the plaintiff to the "political" organs of government for any possible relief. The extent to which this doctrine is applied seems to be a direct coefficient of judicial egotism, for the definition of a political question can be expanded or contracted in accordian-like fashion to meet the exigencies of the times. A juridical definition of the term is impossible, for at root the logic that supports it is circular: political questions are matters not soluble by the judicial process; matters not soluble by the judicial process are political questions. As an early dictionary explained, violins are small cellos, and cellos are large violins.

Nor do examples help much in definition. While it is certainly true that the Court cannot mandamus a legislature to apportion a state in equitable fashion, it seems equally true that the Court is without the authority to force state legislators to implement unsegregated public education. Yet in the former instance the Court genuflected to the "political" organs and took no action, while in the latter it struck down segregation as violative of the Constitution.

Judicial parsimony is another major technique of substantive self-restraint. In what is essentially a legal application of Occam's razor, the court has held that it will not apply any more principles to the settlement of a case than are absolutely necessary, e.g., it will not discuss the constitutionality of a law if it can settle the instant case by statutory construction. Furthermore, if an action is found to rest on erroneous statutory construction, the review terminates at that point: the Court will not go on to discuss whether the statute, properly construed, would be constitutional. A variant form of this doctrine, and a most important one, employs the "case of controversy" approach, to wit, the Court, admitting the importance of the issue, inquires as to whether the litigant actually has standing to bring the matter up. . . .

A classic use of parsimony to escape from a dangerous situation occurred in connection with the evacuation of the Nisei from the West Coast in 1942. Gordon Hirabayashi, in an attempt to test the validity of the regulations clamped on the American-Japanese by the military, violated the curfew and refused to report to an evacuation center. He was convicted on both counts by the district court and sentenced to three months for each offense, the sentences to run *concurrently*. When the case came before the Supreme Court, the justices sustained his conviction for violating the *curfew*, but refused to examine the validity of the evacuation order on the ground that it would not make any difference to Hirabayashi anyway; he was in for ninety days no matter what the Court did with evacuation.

A third method of utilizing substantive self-restraint is particularly useful in connection with the activities of executive departments or regulatory agencies, both state and federal. I have entitled it the doctrine of judicial *inexpertise*, for it is founded on the unwillingness of the Court to revise the findings of experts. The earmarks of this form of restraint are great deference to the holdings of the expert agency usually coupled with such a statement as "It is not for the federal courts to supplant the [Texas Railroad] Commission's judgment even in the face of convincing proof that a different result would have been better." In this tradition, the Court has refused to question *some* exercises of discretion by the National Labor Relations Board, the Federal Trade Commission, and other federal and state agencies. But the emphasis on *some* gives the point away; in other cases, apparently on all fours with those in which it pleads its technical *inexpertise*, the Court feels free to assess evidence de novo and reach independent judgment on the technical issues involved. . . .

In short, with respect to expert agencies, the Court is equipped with both offensive and defensive gambits. It if chooses to intervene, one set of precedents is brought out, while if it decides to hold back, another set of equal validity is invoked. Perhaps the best summary of this point was made by Justice Harlan in 1910, when he stated bluntly that "the Courts have rarely, if ever, felt themselves so restrained by technical rules that they could not find some remedy, consistent with the law, for acts . . . that violated natural justice or were hostile to the fundamental principles devised for the protection of the essential rights of property."

This does not pretend to be an exhaustive analysis of the techniques of judicial self-restraint; on the contrary, others will probably find many which are not given adequate discussion here. The remainder of this paper, however, is devoted to the second area of concern: the conditions under which the Court refrains from acting.

The Conditions of Judicial Self-Restraint

The conditions which lead the Supreme Court to exercise auto-limitation are many and varied. In the great bulk of cases, this restraint is an outgrowth of sound and quasi-automatic legal maxims which defy teleological interpretation. It would take a master of the conspiracy theory of history to assign meaning, for example, to the great majority of certiorari denials; the simple fact is that these cases do not merit review. However, in a small proportion of cases, purpose does appear to enter the picture, sometimes with a vengeance. It is perhaps unjust to the Court to center our attention on this small proportion, but it should be said in extenuation that these cases often involve extremely significant political and social issues. In the broad picture, the refusal to grant certiorari in 1943 to the Minneapolis Trotskyites convicted under the Smith Act is far more meaningful than the similar refusal to grant five hundred petitions to prison "lawyers" who have suddenly discovered the writ of habeas corpus. Likewise, the holding that the legality of Congressional apportionment is a "political question" vitally affects the operation of the whole democratic process.

What we must therefore seek are the conditions under which the Court holds back *in this designated category of cases*. Furthermore, it is important to realize that there are positive consequences of negative action; as Charles Warren has implied, the post-Civil War Court's emphasis on self-restraint was a judicial concomitant of the resurgence of states' rights. Thus self-restraint may, as in wartime, be an outgrowth of judicial caution, or it may be part of a purposeful pattern of abdicating national power to the states.

Ever since the first political scientist discovered Mr. Dooley, the changes have been run on the aphorism that the Supreme Court "follows the election returns," and I see no particular point in ringing my variation on this theme through again. Therefore, referring those who would like a more detailed explanation to earlier analyses, the discussion here will be confined to the bare bones of my hypothesis.

The power of the Supreme Court to invade the decision-making arena, I submit, is a consequence of that fragmentation of political power which is normal in the United States. No cohesive majority, such as normally exists in Britain, would permit a politically irresponsible judiciary to usurp decision-making functions, but, for complex social and institutional reasons, there are few issues in the United States on which cohesive majorities exist. The guerrilla warfare which usually rages between Congress and the President, as well as the internal civil wars which are endemic in both the legislature and the administration, give the judiciary considerable room for maneuver. If, for example, the Court strikes down a controversial decision of the Federal Power Commission, it will be supported by a substantial bloc of congressmen; if it supports the FPC's decision, it will also receive considerable congressional support. But the important point is that *either* way it decides the case, there is no possibility that Congress will exact any vengeance on the Court for its action. A disciplined majority would be necessary to clip the judicial wings, and such a majority does not exist on this issue.

On the other hand, when monolithic majorities do exist on issues, the Court is likely to resort to judicial self-restraint. A good case here is the current tidal wave of anti-communist legislation and administrative action, the latter particularly with regard to aliens, which the Court has treated most gingerly. About the only issues on which there can be found cohesive majorities are those relating to national defense, and the Court has, as Clinton Rossiter demonstrated in an incisive analysis [*The Supreme Court and the Commander-in-Chief*, Ithaca, 1951], traditionally avoided problems arising in this area irrespective of their constitutional merits. Like the slave who accompanied a Roman consul on his triumph whispering "You too are mortal," the shade of Thad Stevens haunts the Supreme Court chamber to remind the justices what an angry Congress can do.

To state the proposition in this brief compass is to oversimplify it considerably. I have, for instance, ignored the crucial question of how the Court knows when a majority *does* exist, and I recognize that certain aspects of judicial behavior cannot be jammed into my hypothesis without creating essentially spurious epicycles. However, I am not trying to establish a monistic theory of judicial action; group action, like that of individuals, is motivated by many factors, some often contradictory, and my objective is to elucidate what seems to be one tradition of judicial motivation. In short, judicial self-restraint and judicial power seem to be opposite sides of the same coin: it has been by judicious application of the former that the latter has been maintained. A tradition beginning with Marshall's *coup* in *Marbury* v. *Madison* and running through *Mississippi* v. *Johnson* and *Ex Parte Vallandigham* to *Dennis* v. *United States* suggests that the Court's power has been maintained by a wise refusal to employ it in unequal combat.

❖❖ Judicial Decision Making

Judicial decision making is not quasi-scientific, always based clearly upon legal principles and precedent, with the judges set apart from the political process. The interpretation of law, whether constitutional or statutory, involves a large amount of discretion. The majority of the Court can always read its opinion into law if it so chooses.

Justice William J. Brennan, Jr., a former member of the Supreme Court, discusses below the general role of the Court and the procedures it follows in decision making.

63

William J. Brennan, Jr.

HOW THE SUPREME COURT ARRIVES AT DECISIONS

❖❖❖❖❖❖❖

Throughout its history the Supreme Court has been called upon to face many of the dominant social, political, economic and even philosophical issues that confront the nation. But Solicitor General Cox only recently reminded us that this does not

"How the Supreme Court Arrives at Decisions," by William S. Brennan, Jr., *The New York Times,* October 12, 1963. Copyright © 1963 by The New York Times Company. Reprinted by permission.

mean that the Court is charged with making social, political, economic or philosophical decisions.

Quite the contrary, the Court is not a council of Platonic guardians for deciding our most difficult and emotional questions according to the Justices' own notions of what is just or wise or politic. To the extent that this is a government function at all, it is the function of the people's elected representatives.

The Justices are charged with deciding according to law. Because the issues arise in the framework of concrete litigation they must be decided on facts embalmed in a record made by some lower court or administrative agency. And while the Justices may and do consult history and the other disciplines as aids to constitutional decisions, the text of the Constitution and relevant precedents dealing with that text are their primary tools.

It is indeed true, as Judge Learned Hand once said, that the judge's authority

> depends upon the assumption that he speaks with the mouth of others: the momentum of his utterances must be greater than any which his personal reputation and character can command; if it is to do the work assigned to it—if it is to stand against the passionate resentments arising out of the interests he must frustrate—he must preserve his authority by cloaking himself in the majesty of an over-shadowing past, but he must discover some composition with the dominant trends of his times.

Answers Unclear

However, we must keep in mind that, while the words of the Constitution are binding, their application to specific problems is not often easy. The Founding Fathers knew better than to pin down their descendants too closely.

Enduring principles rather than petty details were what they sought.

Thus the Constitution does not take the form of a litany of specifics. There are, therefore, very few cases where the constitutional answers are clear, all one way or all the other, and this is also true of the current cases raising conflicts between the individual and governmental power—an area increasingly requiring the Court's attention.

Ultimately, of course, the Court must resolve the conflicts of competing interests in these cases, but all Americans should keep in mind how intense and troubling these conflicts can be.

Where one man claims a right to speak and the other man claims the right to be protected from abusive or dangerously provocative remarks the conflict is inescapable.

Where the police have ample external evidence of a man's guilt, but to be sure of their case put into evidence a confession obtained through coercion, the conflict arises between his right to a fair prosecution and society's right to protection against his depravity.

Where the orthodox Jew wishes to open his shop and do business on the day which non-Jews have chosen, and the Legislature has sanctioned, as a day of rest, the Court cannot escape a difficult problem of reconciling opposed interests.

Finally, the claims of the Negro citizen, to borrow Solicitor General Cox's words, present a "conflict between the ideal of liberty and equality expressed in the Declaration of Independence, on the one hand, and, on the other hand, a way of life rooted in the customs of many of our people."

Society Is Disturbed

If all segments of our society can be made to appreciate that there are such conflicts, and that cases which involve constitutional rights often require difficult choices, if this alone is accomplished, we will have immeasurably enriched our common understanding of the meaning and significance of our freedoms. And we will have a better appreciation of the Court's function and its difficulties.

How conflicts such as these ought to be resolved constantly troubles our whole society. There should be no surprise, then, that how properly to resolve them often produces sharp division within the Court itself. When problems are so fundamental, the claims of the competing interests are often nicely balanced, and close divisions are almost inevitable.

Supreme Court cases are usually one of three kinds: the "original" action brought directly in the Court by one state against another state or states, or between a state or states and the federal government. Only a handful of such cases arise each year, but they are an important handful.

A recent example was the contest between Arizona and California over the waters of the lower basin of the Colorado River. Another was the contest between the federal government and the newest state of Hawaii over the ownership of lands in Hawaii.

The second kind of case seeks review of the decisions of a federal Court of Appeals—there are eleven such courts—or of a decision of a federal District Court—there is a federal District Court in each of the fifty states.

The third kind of case comes from a state court—the Court may review a state court judgment by the highest court of any of the fifty states, if the judgment rests on the decision of a federal question.

When I came to the Court seven years ago the aggregate of the cases in the three classes was 1,600. In the term just completed there were 2,800, an increase of 75 percent in seven years. Obviously, the volume will have doubled before I complete ten years of service.

How is it possible to manage such a huge volume of cases? The answer is that we have the authority to screen them and select for argument and decision only those which, in our judgment, guided by pertinent criteria, raise the most important and far-reaching questions. By that device we select annually around 6 percent—between 150 and 170 cases—for decision.

Petition and Response

That screening process works like this: when nine Justices sit, it takes five to decide a case on the merits. But it takes only the votes of four of the nine to put a case on the argument calendar for argument and decision. Those four voters are hard to come by—only an exceptional case raising a significant federal question commands them.

Each application for review is usually in the form of a short petition, attached to which are any opinions of the lower courts in the case. The adversary may file a response—also, in practice usually short. Both the petition and response identify the federal questions allegedly involved, argue their substantiality, and whether they were properly raised in the lower courts.

Each Justice receives copies of the petition and response and such parts of the record as the parties may submit. Each Justice then, without any consultation at this stage with the others, reaches his own tentative conclusion whether the application should be granted or denied.

The first consultation about the case comes at the Court conference at which the case is listed on the agenda for discussion. We sit in conference almost every Friday during the term. Conferences begin at ten in the morning and often continue until six, except for a half-hour recess for lunch.

Only the Justices are present. There are no law clerks, no stenographers, no secretaries, no pages—just the nine of us. The junior Justice acts as guardian of the door, receiving and delivering any messages that come in or go from the conference.

Order of Seating

The conference room is a beautifully oak-paneled chamber with one side lined with books from floor to ceiling. Over the mantel of the exquisite marble fireplace at one end hangs the only adornment in the chamber—a portrait of Chief Justice John Marshall. In the middle of the room stands a rectangular table, not too large but large enough for the nine of us comfortably to gather around it.

The Chief Justice sits at the south end and Mr. Justice Black, the senior Associate Justice, at the north end. Along the side to the left of the Chief Justice sit Justices Stewart, Goldberg, White and Harlan. On the right side sit Justice Clark, myself and Justice Douglas in that order.

We are summoned to conference by a buzzer which rings in our several chambers five minutes before the hour. Upon entering the conference room each of us shakes hands with his colleagues. The handshake tradition originated when Chief Justice Fuller presided many decades ago. It is a symbol that harmony of aims if not of views is the Court's guiding principle.

Each of us has his copy of the agenda of the day's cases before him. The agenda lists the cases applying for review. Each of us before coming to the conference has noted on his copy his tentative view whether or not review should be granted in each case.

The Chief Justice begins the discussion of each case. He then yields to the senior Associate Justice and discussion proceeds down the line in order of seniority until each Justice has spoken.

Voting goes the other way. The junior Justice votes first and voting then proceeds up the line to the Chief Justice, who votes last.

Each of us has a docket containing a sheet for each case with appropriate places for recording the votes. When any case receives four votes for review, that case is transferred to the oral argument list. Applications in which none of us sees merits may be passed over without discussion.

Now how do we process the decisions we agree to review?

There are rare occasions when the question is so clearly controlled by an earlier decision of the Court that a reversal of the lower court judgment is inevitable. In these rare instances we may summarily reverse without oral argument.

Each Side Gets Hour

The case must very clearly justify summary disposition, however, because our ordinary practice is not to reverse a decision without oral argument. Indeed, oral argument of cases taken for review, whether from the state or federal courts, is the usual practice. We rarely accept submissions of cases on briefs.

Oral argument ordinarily occurs about four months after the application for review is granted. Each party is usually allowed one hour, but in recent years we have limited oral argument to a half-hour in cases thought to involve issues not requiring longer arguments.

Counsel submit their briefs and record in sufficient time for the distribution of one set to each Justice two or three weeks before the oral argument. Most of the members of the present Court follow the practice of reading the briefs before the argument. Some of us often have a bench memorandum prepared before the argument. This memorandum digests the facts and the arguments of both sides, highlighting the matters about which we may want to question counsel at the argument.

Often I have independent research done in advance of argument and incorporate the results in the bench memorandum.

We follow a schedule of two weeks of argument from Monday through Thursday, followed by two weeks of recess for opinion writing and the study of petitions for review. The argued cases are listed on the conference agenda on the Friday following argument. Conference discussions follow the same procedure I have described for the discussions of certiorari petitions.

Opinion Assigned

Of course, it is much more extended. Not infrequently discussion of particular cases may be spread over two or more conferences.

Not until the discussion is completed and a vote taken is the opinion assigned. The assignment is not made at the conference but formally in writing some few days after the conference.

The Chief Justice assigns the opinions in those cases in which he has voted with the majority. The senior Associate Justice voting with the majority assigns the opinion in the other cases. The dissenters agree among themselves who shall write the dissenting opinion. Of course, each Justice is free to write his own opinion, concurring or dissenting.

The writing of an opinion always takes weeks and sometimes months. The most painstaking research and care are involved.

Research, of course, concentrates on relevant legal materials—precedents particularly. But Supreme Court cases often require some familiarity with history, economics, the social and other sciences, and authorities in these areas, too, are consulted when necessary.

When the author of an opinion feels he has an unanswerable document he sends it to a print shop, which we maintain in our building. The printed draft may be revised several times before his proposed opinion is circulated among the other Justices. Copies are sent to each member of the Court, those in the dissent as well as those in the majority.

Some Change Minds

Now the author often discovers that his work has only begun. He receives a return, ordinarily in writing, from each Justice who voted with him and sometimes also from the Justices who voted the other way. He learns who will write the dissent if one is to be written. But his particular concern is whether those who voted with him are still of his view and what they have to say about his proposed opinion.

Often some who voted with him at conference will advise that they reserve final judgment pending the circulation of the dissent. It is a common experience that dissents change votes, even enough votes to become the majority.

I have had to convert more than one of my proposed majority opinions into a dissent before the final decision was announced. I have also, however, had the more satisfying experience of rewriting a dissent as a majority opinion for the Court.

Before everyone has finally made up his mind a constant interchange by memoranda, by telephone, at the lunch table continues while we hammer out the final form of the opinion. I had one case during the past term in which I circulated ten printed drafts before one was approved as the Court opinion.

Uniform Rule

The point of this procedure is that each Justice, unless he disqualifies himself in a particular case, passes on every piece of business coming to the Court. The Court does not function by means of committees or panels. Each Justice passes on each petition, each time, no matter how drawn, in long hand, by typewriter, or on a press. Our Constitution vests the judicial power in only one Supreme Court. This does not permit Supreme Court action by committees, panels, or sections.

The method that the Justices use in meeting an enormous caseload varies. There is one uniform rule: Judging is not delegated. Each Justice studies each case in sufficient detail to resolve the question for himself. In a very real sense, each decision is an individual decision of every Justice.

The process can be a lonely, troubling experience for fallible human beings conscious that their best may not be adequate to the challenge.

"We are not unaware," the late Justice Jackson said, "that we are not final because we are infallible; we know that we are infallible only because we are final."

One does not forget how much may depend on his decision. He knows that usually more than the litigants may be affected, that the course of vital social, economic and political currents may be directed.

This then is the decisional process in the Supreme Court. It is not without its tensions, of course—indeed, quite agonizing tensions at times.

I would particularly emphasize that, unlike the case of a Congressional or White House decision, Americans demand of their Supreme Court judges that they produce a written opinion, the collective expression of the judges subscribing to it, setting forth the reason which led them to the decision.

These opinions are the exposition, not just to lawyers, legal scholars and other judges, but to our whole society, of the bases upon which a particular result rests— why a problem, looked at as disinterestedly and dispassionately as nine human beings trained in a tradition of the disinterested and dispassionate approach can look at it, is answered as it is.

It is inevitable, however, that Supreme Court decisions—and the Justices themselves—should be caught up in public debate and be the subjects of bitter controversy.

An editorial in *The Washington Post* did not miss the mark by much in saying that this was so because

> one of the primary functions of the Supreme Court is to keep the people of the country from doing what they would like to do—at times when what they would like to do runs counter to the Constitution. . . . The function of the Supreme Court is not to count constituents; it is to interpret a fundamental charter which imposes restraints on constituents. Independence and integrity, not popularity, must be its standards.

Freund's View

Certainly controversy over its work has attended the Court throughout its history. As Professor Paul A. Freund of Harvard remarked, this has been true almost since the Court's first decision:

> When the Court held, in 1793, that the state of Georgia could be sued on a contract in the federal courts, the outraged Assembly of that state passed a bill declaring that any federal marshal who should try to collect the judgment would be guilty of a felony and would suffer death, without benefit of clergy, by being hanged. When the Court decided that state criminal convictions could be reviewed in the Supreme Court, Chief Justice Roane of Virginia exploded, calling it a "most monstrous and unexampled decision. It can only be accounted for by that love of power which history informs us infects and corrupts all who possess it, and from which even the eminent and upright judges are not exempt."

But public understanding has not always been lacking in the past. Perhaps it exists today. But surely a more informed knowledge of the decisional process should aid a better understanding.

It is not agreement with the court's decisions that I urge. Our law is the richer and the wiser because academic and informed lay criticism is part of the stream of development.

Consensus Needed

It is only a greater awareness of the nature and limits of the Supreme Court's function that I seek.

The ultimate resolution of questions fundamental to the whole community must be based on a common consensus of understanding of the unique responsibility assigned to the Supreme Court in our society.

The lack of that understanding led Mr. Justice Holmes to say fifty years ago:

> We are very quiet there, but it is the quiet of a storm center, as we all know. Science has taught the world skepticism and has made it legitimate to put everything to the test of proof. Many beautiful and noble reverences are impaired, but in these days no one can complain if any institution, system, or belief is called on to justify its continuance in life. Of course we are not excepted and have not escaped.

Painful Accusation

Doubts are expressed that go to our very being. Not only are we told that when Marshall pronounced an Act of Congress unconstitutional he usurped a power that the Constitution did not give, but we are told that we are the representatives of a class—a tool of the money power.

I get letters, not always anonymous, intimating that we are corrupt. Well, gentlemen, I admit that it makes my heart ache. It is very painful, when one spends all the energies of one's soul in trying to do good work, with no thought but that of solving a problem according to the rules by which one is bound, to know that many see sinister motives and would be glad of evidence that one was consciously bad.

But we must take such things philosophically and try to see what we can learn from hatred and distrust and whether behind them there may not be a germ of inarticulate truth.

The attacks upon the Court are merely an expression of the unrest that seems to wonder vaguely whether law and order pay. When the ignorant are taught to doubt they do not know what they safely may believe. And it seems to me that at this time we need education in the obvious more than investigation of the obscure.

❖❖ Interpreting the Constitution

Justice William J. Brennan, Jr., in his discussion of how the Supreme Court arrives at decisions in the preceding selection, points out that inevitably Supreme Court decisions and the justices are the subjects of public debate and often bitter controversy. It is not surprising that when Supreme Court justices and lower-court judges as well follow the early dictum of Chief Justice John Marshall, which he stated in *Marbury* v. *Madison* in 1803, that "It is emphatically the province and duty of the judicial department to say what the law is," they will become the center of political storms stirred up by those who feel the Court has overstepped its bounds.

While the Supreme Court may not enter unequal political combat, as John Roche contends in selection 63, it has made many highly controversial decisions since Roche wrote his article in 1955. (For example, see selections 18–22.) One conservative law scholar has gone so far as to state, "In the years since *Brown* v. *Board of Education* (1954) nearly every fundamental change in domestic social policy has been brought about not by the decentralized democratic (or, more accurately, republican) process contemplated by the Constitution, but simply by the Court's decree."[1]

Conservatives, clearly unhappy with the trend in Supreme Court decision making not only during the Warren era (1953–1969) but under the chief justiceship of Warren Burger (1969–1986), charged that the Court's "loose" constitutional interpretations have been contrary to the wishes of the majority of the people and have made a mockery of the Constitution itself. Responding to their conservative constituencies, Republican presidential candidates Richard M. Nixon in 1968 and Ronald Reagan in 1980 promised to take action to reverse the Supreme Court's alleged liberalism by appointing conservative justices.

Ironically, one of Nixon's appointees, Harry Blackmun, authored the Court's controversial abortion decision in 1973 (see selection 19). Another Nixon appointee, Lewis Powell, joined the more liberal justices in the *Bakke* case (see selection 21) to allow universities and the colleges to take race into account in their admissions processes, a tacit although far from direct support for the affirmative action programs conservatives so strongly opposed. Nixon found, as had Dwight D. Eisenhower who appointed Earl Warren to be chief justice in 1953, that presidents have no control over their appointees once they are on the Court.

For his part in the conservative cause, President Ronald Reagan, while choosing Sandra Day O'Connor as the first woman Supreme Court justice, tried to make certain beforehand that she would support conservative positions on such issues as abortion. Reagan added three conservative Supreme Court justices and had an even greater impact upon the lower federal judiciary, which he "stacked" with conservative judges.

Debate over the role of the Supreme Court intensified during Reagan's second term. His attorney general, Edwin Meese, in a speech given before the American Bar Association, attacked the Supreme Court for interpreting the Constitution according to its own values rather than the intent of the Founding Fathers. In response, Associate Justice William J. Brennan, speaking to a Georgetown University audience, called the attorney general "arrogant" and "doctrinaire," stating that it is impossible to "gauge accurately the intent of the framers on the application of principle to specific, contemporary questions." Another Supreme Court justice, John Paul Stevens, joined the attack on Meese.

---

[1]Lino A. Graglia, "How the Constitution Disappeared," *Commentary*, February 1986, p. 19.

The arguments in the 1980s over the proper role of the Supreme Court recalled the debate in the early days of the Republic between proponents of "strict" construction of the Constitution on the one hand and "loose" construction on the other. No less an intellectual and political giant than Thomas Jefferson favored the former approach, arguing that judges should not interpret the Constitution to reflect their own political values. He particularly opposed Chief Justice John Marshall's "loose" construction of congressional authority under Article I and the implied powers clause, which supported an expansion of national power over the states. Prior to Marshall's historic decisions in *McCulloch v. Maryland* (1819) and *Gibbons v. Ogden* that flexibly interpreted the Constitution to support broad congressional powers over the states (see selection 9), Alexander Hamilton had provided the rationale for loose construction in *The Federalist*. He suggested that Congress should be able to carry out its enumerated powers by whatever means it considered to be necessary and proper.

An old adage states that where one stands on political issues depends upon whose ox is being gored. Liberal supporters of Franklin D. Roosevelt attacked the conservative Supreme Court during the early New Deal when it was systematically declaring the core of FDR's program to be unconstitutional. After his overwhelming 1936 electoral victory Roosevelt attempted to "pack" the Court by seeking congressional approval of legislation that would give him the authority to appoint one new justice for each justice over 70 years of age. The legislation would have given him at the time the authority to appoint a Supreme Court majority because there were seven septuagenarian justices on the Court. Conservatives attacked Roosevelt's plan, charging that it was an unconstitutional and even un-American attempt to undermine the Supreme Court's independence. They wanted the Court to continue acting as a superlegislature as long as it advocated conservative views. However, when the tables were turned, and the Court became the advocate of "liberal" views during the Warren era, conservatives were quick to attack it for acting as a superlegislature against the will of the majority, which was the same argument liberals had used against the Court in the 1930s.

THE CONTEMPORARY DEBATE OVER CONSTITUTIONAL INTERPRETATION

Robert H. Bork, to most Americans an obscure figure before his Senate confirmation hearings in 1987 after President Ronald Reagan nominated him to fill a Supreme Court vacancy, became a cause célèbre both for the conservatives who supported him and the liberals who opposed him.

Before his nomination Bork had a distinguished career. He served in the U.S. Marine Corps, became a partner in a major law firm, taught constitutional law at the Yale Law School, served as solicitor general and acting attorney general of the United States under Richard M. Nixon, and finally as a circuit court judge in the U.S. Court of Appeals for the District of Columbia circuit.

At the time of Bork's nomination most political observers expected that he would be confirmed, although not without a fight. He had written many articles during his tenure at Yale expressing what liberals considered to be unacceptable conservative and unorthodox opinions on important issues of constitutional law. As professors are wont to be he was often purposely provocative. Most importantly, although he had not written on the subject, he had publicly denied that a constitutional right to privacy existed, an opinion that his liberal opponents felt would put him on the side of Supreme Court justices who favored overturning *Roe* v. *Wade* (1973), which had affirmed the right to privacy as the basis of the right to abortion.

Bork's confirmation became a bitter struggle between liberals and conservatives, the former emerging victorious when the Senate failed to confirm him. In answer to his critics Bork wrote *The Tempting of America* (New York: The Free Press, 1990) from which the following selection is taken. He presents a viewpoint that contrasts sharply with that of a former justice, William J. Brennan, Jr., in selection 63.

64

Robert H. Bork

THE TEMPTING OF AMERICA

❖❖❖❖❖❖❖

The Supreme Court and the
Temptations of Politics

A popular style in complaining about the courts is to contrast modern judges with those of a golden or, at least, a less tarnished age. Many people have a fuzzy impression that the judges of old were different. They did things like "follow precedent" and "apply the law, not make it up." There is a good deal to be said for that view. The practice of judicial lawmaking has certainly accelerated spectacularly in this century, particularly in the past four or five decades. Nevertheless, the whole truth is rather more complicated.

From the establishment of the federal judiciary at the end of the eighteenth century, some judges at least claimed the power to strike down statutes on the basis

---

Excerpts (pp. 15–18 and pp. 351–355) from *The Tempting of America: The Political Seduction of the Law* by Robert H. Bork. Copyright © 1990 by Robert H. Bork. Reprinted with the permission of The Free Press, a Division of Simon & Schuster, Inc.

of principles not to be found in the Constitution. Judges who claimed this power made little or no attempt to justify it, to describe its source with any specificity, or to state what principles, if any, limited their own power. No more have the activist judges of our time. Justifications for such judicial behavior had, for the most part, to await the ingenuity of modern law faculties. But the actions of the federal judiciary, and in particular those of the Supreme Court, have often provoked angry reaction, though rarely a systematic statement of the appropriate judicial role. The appropriate limits of judicial power, if such there be, are thus the center of an ancient, if not always fruitful, controversy. Its confused and unfocused condition constitutes a venerable tradition, which is one tradition, at least, modern scholarship leaves intact. . . .

. . . [I]t is important to keep in mind that any court seen engaging in overt revisionism will, in all probability, have engaged in many more instances of disguised departures from the Constitution. A court that desires a result the law does not allow would rather, whenever possible, through misuse of materials or illogic, publish an opinion claiming to be guided or even compelled to its result by the Constitution than state openly that the result rests on other grounds. That is because popular support for judicial supremacy rests upon the belief that the court is applying fundamental principles laid down at the American founding. We would hardly revere a document that we knew to be no more than an open warrant for judges to do with us as they please.

Disguised or not, the habit of legislating policy from the bench, once acquired, is addictive and hence by no means confined to constitutional cases. The activist or revisionist judge, as we shall see, can no more restrain himself from doing "good" in construing a statute than when he purports to speak with the voice of the Constitution.

The values a revisionist judge enforces do not, of course, come from the law. If they did, he would be revising. The question, then, is where such a judge finds the values he implements. Academic theorists try to provide various philosophical apparatuses to give the judge the proper values. We may leave until later the question of whether any of these systems succeed. The important point, for the moment, is that no judge has ever really explained the matter. A judge inserting new principles into the Constitution tells us their origin only in a rhetorical, never an analytical, style. There is, however, strong reason to suspect that the judge absorbs those values he writes into law from the social class or elite with which he identifies.

It is a commonplace that moral views vary both regionally within the United States and between socio-economic classes. It is similarly a commonplace that the morality of certain elites may count for more in the operations of government than that morality which might command the allegiance of a majority of the people. In no part of government is this more true than in the courts. An elite moral or political view may never be able to win an election or command the votes of a majority of a legislature, but it may nonetheless influence judges and gain the force of law in that way. That is the reason judicial activism is extremely popular with certain elites and why they encourage judges to think it the highest aspect of their calling. Legislation is far more likely to reflect majority sentiment while judicial activism is likely to represent an elite minority's sentiment. The judge is free to reflect the "better" opinion because he need not stand for reelection and because he can deflect the majority's anger by claiming merely to have been enforcing the Constitution. Constitutional jurisprudence is mysterious terrain for most people, who have more pressing things to think about. And a very handy fact that is for revisionists.

The opinions of the elites to which judges respond changes as society changes and one elite replaces another in the ability to impress judges. Thus, judicial activism has had no single political trajectory over time. The values enforced change, and sometimes those of one era directly contradict those of a prior era. That can be seen in the sea of changes constitutional doctrine has undergone in our history. There will often be a lag, of course, since judges who have internalized the values of one elite will not necessarily switch allegiances just because a new elite and its values have become dominant. When that happens, when judges are enforcing values regarded by the dominant elite as passé, the interim between the change and the replacement of the judges will be perceived as a time of "constitutional crisis." The fact of judicial mortality redresses the situation eventually, and new judges enforce the new "correct" values. This has happened more than once in our history. The intellectuals of the newly dominant elite are then highly critical of the activist judges of the prior era for enforcing the wrong values while they praise the activist judges of their own time as sensitive to the needs of society. They do not see, or will not allow themselves to see, that the judicial performances, judged as judicial performances, are the same in both eras. The Supreme Court that struck down economic regulation designed to protect workers is, judged as a judicial body, indistinguishable from the Court that struck down abortion laws. Neither Court gave anything resembling an adequate reason derived from the Constitution for frustrating the democratic outcome. So far as one can tell from the opinions written, each Court denied majority morality for no better reason than that elite opinion ran the other way.

. . . [T]he Supreme Court's activism was at various times enlisted in the protection of property, the defense of slave owners, the protection of business enterprise in an industrializing nation, the interests of groups in the New Deal coalition, and, today, the furtherance of the values of the elite or cluster of elites known as the "new class" or the "knowledge class." The point ought not be overstated. We are discussing a strong tendency, not invariable conduct. No Court behaves in this way all of the time, in every case. Few judges are so willful as that. The structure of the law does have force, and, in any event, most cases do not present a conflict between elite morality and the law's structure. Yet such occasions arise in important matters, and it is those occasions that give the Court of each era its distinctive style.

Part of any revisionist Court's style, in addition to the nature of the nonconstitutional values enforced, is the rhetoric employed. The Court of each era is likely to choose different provisions of the Constitution or different formulations of invented rights as the vehicles for its revisory efforts. These are different techniques for claiming that what is being done is "law." The shifts in terminology do not alter the reality of the judicial performance as such. Still, the rhetoric employed will often disclose what values are popular with the elites to which the Court responds. Thus, the Court's shift from the use of the word "liberty" in the due process clause, popular in the closing decades of the last century and the opening decades of this century, to the idea of equality in the equal protection clause signified a shift in dominant values. It also signified a change in the social groups to which the Court responded, a decline in the influence of the business class and a rise in that of the New Deal political coalition and its intellectual spokesmen. Similarly, the change from "liberty of contact," used in striking down economic reform legislation, to the "right of privacy" employed to guarantee various aspects of sexual freedom, signals a change in dominant values from capitalist free enterprise to sexual permissiveness, and, again, a change in dominant elites from the business class to the knowledge class, though now with less concern than previously for the social values of those who made up the New Deal coalition.

Conclusion

The Constitution has been many things to Americans. It has been and remains an object of veneration, a sacred text, the symbol of our nationhood, the foundation of our government's structure and practice, a guarantor of our liberties, and a moral teacher.

But the Constitution is also power. That is why we see political struggle over the selection of the judges who will wield that power. In our domestic affairs and even to some degree in our foreign dealings, the Constitution provides judges with the ultimate coercive power known to our political arrangements. In the hands of judges, words become action: commands are issued by courts, obeyed by legislatures, and enforced by executives. The reading of the words becomes freedoms and restrictions for us; the course of the nation is confirmed or altered; the way we live and the ways we think and feel are affected.

It will not do to overstate the matter. We are an incredibly complex and intricate society and no power is without checks, some obvious and direct in operation, some subtle and intangible. But a major check on judicial power, perhaps the major check, is the judges' and our understanding of the proper limits to that power. Those limits may be pressed back incrementally, case by case, until judges rule areas of life not confided to their authority by any provision of the Constitution or other law. We have, in fact, witnessed just that process. The progression of political judging, judging unrelated to law . . . has greatly accelerated in the past few decades and now we see the theorists of constitutional law urging judges on to still greater incursions into Americans' right of self-government.

This is an anxious problem and one that can be met only by understanding that judges must always be guided by the original understanding of the Constitution's provisions. Once adherence to the original understanding is weakened or abandoned, a judge, perhaps instructed by a revisionist theorist, can reach any result, because the human mind and will, freed of the constraints of history and "the sediment of history which is law," can reach any result. As we have seen, no set of propositions is too preposterous to be espoused by a judge or a law professor who has cast loose from the historical Constitution.

The judge's proper task is not mechanical. "History," Cardinal Newman reminded us, "is not a creed or a catechism, it gives lessons rather than rules." No body of doctrine is born fully developed. That is as true of constitutional law as it is of theology. The provisions of the Constitution state profound but simple and general ideas. The law laid down in those provisions gradually gains body, substance, doctrines, and distinctions as judges, equipped at first with only those ideas, are forced to confront new situations and changing circumstances. It is essential, however, that the new developments always be weighed in the light of the lessons history provides about the principles meant to be enforced. Doctrine must be shaped and reshaped to conform to the original ideas of the Constitution, to ensure that the principles intended are those which guide and limit power, and that no principles not originally meant are invented to deprive us of the right to govern ourselves. The concept of original understanding itself gains in solidity, in articulation and sophistication, as we investigate its meanings, implications, and requirements, and as we are forced to defend its truths from the constitutional heresies with which we are continually tempted.

Among the stakes is the full right of self-government that the Founders bequeathed us and which they limited only as to specified topics. In the long run, however, there may be higher stakes than that. As we move away from the historically rooted Constitution to one created by abstract, universalistic styles of constitutional reasoning, we invite a number of dangers. One is that such styles teach disrespect for the actual institutions of the American nation. A great many academic theorists state explicitly, and some judges seem easily persuaded, that elected legislators and executives are not adequate to decide the moral issues that divide us, and that judges should therefore take their place. But, when Americans are morally divided, it is appropriate that our laws reflect that fact. The often untidy responses of the elected branches possess virtues and benefits that the "principled" reactions of courts do not. Our popular institutions, the legislative and executive branches, were structured to provide safety, to achieve compromise when we are divided, to slow change, to dilute absolutisms. They both embody and produce wholesome inconsistencies. They are designed, in short, to do the very things that abstract generalizations about moral principle and the just society tend to bring into contempt. That is a dangerous civics lesson to teach the citizens of a republic. As Edmund Burke put it:

> All government, indeed every human benefit and enjoyment, every virtue, and every prudent act, is founded on compromise and barter. We balance inconveniences; we give and take; we remit some rights, that we may enjoy others; and we choose rather to be happy citizens, than subtle disputants.

It may be significant that this passage is from Burke's speech on *Moving His Resolutions for Conciliation with the Colonies*, delivered to Parliament in 1775. The English government elected to stand on abstract principles of sovereignty and lost the American colonies.

The attempt to define individual liberties by abstract moral philosophy, though it is said to broaden our liberties, is actually likely to make them more vulnerable. I am not referring here to the freedom to govern ourselves but to the freedoms from government guaranteed by the Bill of Rights and the post–Civil War amendments. Those constitutional liberties were not produced by abstract reasoning. They arose out of historical experience with unaccountable power and out of political thought grounded in the study of history as well as in moral and religious sentiment. Attempts to frame theories that remove from democratic control areas of life our nation's Founders intended to place there can achieve power only if abstractions are regarded as legitimately able to displace the Constitution's text and structure and the history that gives our legal rights life, rootedness, and meaning. It is no small matter to discredit the foundations upon which our constitutional freedoms have always been sustained and substitute as a bulwark only the abstract propositions of moral philosophy. To do that is, in fact, to display a lightmindedness terrifying in its frivolity. Our freedoms do not ultimately depend upon the pronouncements of judges sitting in a row. They depend upon their acceptance by the American people, and a major factor in that acceptance is the belief that these liberties are inseparable from the founding of the nation. The moral systems urged as constitutional law by the theorists are not compatible with the moral beliefs of most Americans. Richard John Neuhaus wrote that law is "a human enterprise in response to human behavior, and human behavior is stubbornly entangled with beliefs about right and wrong." Law will not be recognized as legitimate if it is not organically related to "the larger universe of moral discourse that helps shape human behavior." Constitutional doctrine that rests upon a parochial and class-bound version of morality, one not shared by the general American public, is certain to be resented and is unlikely to prove much of a safeguard when crisis comes.

Robert Bolt's play about Thomas More, *A Man for All Seasons*, makes the point. When More was Lord Chancellor, his daughter, Margaret, and his son-in-law, Roper, urged him to arrest a man they regarded as evil. Margaret said, "Father, that man's bad." More replied, "There is no law against that." And Roper said, "There is! God's law!" More then gave excellent advice to judges: "Then God can arrest him. . . . The law, Roper, the law. I know what's legal not what's right. And I'll stick to what's legal. . . . I'm *not* God. The currents and eddies of right and wrong, which you find such plain sailing, I can't navigate. I'm no voyager. But in the thickets of the law, oh, there I'm a forester."

Roper would not be appeased and he leveled the charge that More would give the Devil the benefit of law.

> MORE Yes. What would you do? Cut a great road through the law to get after the Devil?
>
> ROPER I'd cut down every law in England to do that?
>
> MORE . . . Oh? . . . And when the last law was down, and the Devil turned round on you—where would you hide, Roper, the laws all being flat? . . . This country's planted thick with laws from coast to coast—man's laws, not God's—and if you cut them down— . . . d'you really think you could stand upright in the winds that would blow then? . . . Yes, I'd give the Devil benefit of law, for my own safety's sake.

This is not a romanticized version of the man, for the historic More is reported to have said of his duty as a judge: "[I]f the parties will at my hands call for justice, then, all were it my father stood on the one side, and the Devil on the other, his cause being good, the Devil should have right." It is a hard saying and a hard duty, but it is the duty we must demand of judges.

Judges will always be tempted to apply what they imagine to be "God's law," cutting a great road through man's law. When they have done, when man's law has been thoroughly weakened and discredited, and when powerful forces have a different version of God's law or the higher morality, we may find that the actual rights of the Constitution and the democratic institutions that protect us may have all been flattened.

The difference between our historically grounded constitutional freedoms and those the theorists, whether of the academy or of the bench, would replace them with is akin to the difference between the American and the French revolutions. The outcome for liberty was much less happy under the regime of the abstract "rights of man" than it has been under the American Constitution. What Burke said of the abstract theorists who produced the calamities of the French Revolution might equally be said of those, judges and professors alike, who would remake our constitution out of moral philosophy: "This sort of people are so taken up with their theories about the rights of man that they have totally forgotten his nature." Those who made and endorsed our Constitution knew man's nature, and it is to their ideas, rather than to the temptations of utopia, that we must ask that our judges adhere.

❖❖ Justice William J. Brennan, Jr., argues in the next selection that strict construction is a myth. Many constitutional provisions, by their very nature, are vague and require judicial interpretation. "It is arrogant to pretend," writes Brennan, "that from our vantage we can gauge accurately the intent of the Framers on application of principle to specific, contemporary questions." The Supreme Court must apply the Constitution in a contemporary context, and adapt it to present needs. "Our Constitution was not intended to preserve a preexisting society," concludes Brennan, "but to make a new one, to put in place new principles that the prior political community had not sufficiently recognized."

65

William J. Brennan, Jr.

FOR "LOOSE" CONSTRUCTION

I am deeply grateful for the invitation to participate in the "Text and Teaching" symposium. This rare opportunity to explore classic texts with participants of such

---

Address to the Text and Teaching Symposium, Georgetown University, October 12, 1985, Washington, D.C.

wisdom, acumen and insight as those who have preceded and will follow me to this podium is indeed exhilarating. But it is also humbling. Even to approximate the standards of excellence of these vigorous and graceful intellects is a daunting task. I am honored that you have afforded me this opportunity to try.

It will perhaps not surprise you that the text I have chosen for exploration is the amended Constitution of the United States, which, of course, entrenches the Bill of Rights and the Civil War amendments, and draws sustenance from the bedrock principles of another great text, the Magna Carta. So fashioned, the Constitution embodies the aspiration to social justice, brotherhood, and human dignity that brought this nation into being. The Declaration of Independence, the Constitution and the Bill of Rights solemnly committed the United States to be a country where the dignity and rights of all persons were equal before all authority. In all candor we must concede that part of this egalitarianism in America has been more pretension than realized fact. But we are an aspiring people, a people with faith in progress. Our amended Constitution is the lodestar for our aspirations. Like every text worth reading, it is not crystalline. The phrasing is broad and the limitations of its provisions are not clearly marked. Its majestic generalities and ennobling pronouncements are both luminous and obscure. This ambiguity of course calls forth interpretation, the interaction of reader and text. The encounter with the constitutional text has been, in many senses, my life's work.

My approach to this text may differ from the approach of other participants in this symposium to their texts. Yet such differences may themselves stimulate reflection about what it is we do when we "interpret" a text. Thus I will attempt to elucidate my approach to the text as well as my substantive interpretation.

Perhaps the foremost difference is the fact that my encounters with the constitutional text are not purely or even primarily introspective; the Constitution cannot be for me simply a contemplative haven for private moral reflection. My relation to this great text is inescapably public. That is not to say that my reading of the text is not a personal reading, only that the personal reading perforce occurs in a public context, and is open to critical scrutiny from all quarters.

The Constitution is fundamentally a public text—the monumental charter of a government and a people—and a Justice of the Supreme Court must apply it to resolve public controversies. For, from our beginning, a most important consequence of the constitutionally created separation of powers has been the American habit, extraordinary to other democracies, of casting social, economic, philosophical and political questions in the Form of lawsuits, in an attempt to secure ultimate resolution by the Supreme Court. In this way, important aspects of the most fundamental issues confronting our democracy may finally arrive in the Supreme Court for judicial determination. Not infrequently, these are the issues upon which contemporary society is most deeply divided. They arouse our deepest emotions. The main burden of my twenty-nine terms on the Supreme Court has thus been to wrestle with the Constitution in this heightened public context, to draw meaning from the text in order to resolve public controversies.

Two other aspects of my relation to this text warrant mention. First, constitutional interpretation for a federal judge is, for the most part, obligatory. When litigants approach the bar of court to adjudicate a constitutional dispute, they may justifiably demand an answer. Judges cannot avoid a definitive interpretation because they feel unable to, or would prefer not to, penetrate to the full meaning of the Constitution's provisions. Unlike literary critics, judges cannot merely savor the tensions or revel in the ambiguities inhering in the text—judges must resolve them.

Second, consequences flow from a Justice's interpretation in a direct and immediate way. A judicial decision respecting the incompatibility of Jim Crow with a constitutional guarantee of equality is not simply a contemplative exercise in defining the shape of a just society. It is an order—supported by the full coercive power of the State—that the present society change in a fundamental aspect. Under such circumstances the process of deciding can be a lonely, troubling experience for fallible human beings conscious that their best may not be adequate to the challenge. We Justices are certainly aware that we are not final because we are infallible; we know that we are infallible only because we are final. One does not forget how much may depend on the decision. More than the litigants may be affected. The course of vital social, economic and political currents may be directed.

These three defining characteristics of my relation to the constitutional text— its public nature, obligatory character, and consequentialist aspect—cannot help but influence the way I read that text. When Justices interpret the Constitution they speak for their community, not for themselves alone. The act of interpretation must be undertaken with full consciousness that it is, in a very real sense, the community's interpretation that is sought. Justices are not platonic guardians appointed to wield authority according to their personal moral predilections. Precisely because coercive force must attend any judicial decision to countermand the will of a contemporary majority, the Justices must render constitutional interpretations that are received as legitimate. The source of legitimacy is, of course, a wellspring of controversy in legal and political circles. At the core of the debate is what the late Yale Law School Professor Alexander Bickel labeled "the counter-majoritarian difficulty." Our commitment to self-governance in a representative democracy must be reconciled with vesting in electorally unaccountable Justices the power to invalidate the expressed desires of representative bodies on the ground of inconsistency with higher law. Because judicial power resides in the authority to give meaning to the Constitution, the debate is really a debate about how to read the text, about constraints on what is legitimate interpretation.

There are those who find legitimacy in fidelity to what they call "the intentions of the Framers." In its most doctrinaire incarnation, this view demands that Justices discern exactly what the Framers thought about the question under consideration and simply follow that intention in resolving the case before them. It is a view that feigns self-effacing deference to the specific judgments of those who forged our original social compact. But in truth it is little more than arrogance cloaked as humility. It is arrogant to pretend that from our vantage we can gauge accurately the intent of the Framers on application of principle to specific, contemporary questions. All too often, sources of potential enlightenment such as records of the ratification debates provide sparse or ambiguous evidence of the original intention. Typically, all that can be gleaned is that the Framers themselves did not agree about the application or meaning of particular constitutional provisions, and hid their differences in cloaks of generality. Indeed, it is far from clear whose intention is relevant—that of the drafters, the congressional disputants, or the ratifiers in the state—or even whether the idea of an original intention is a coherent way of thinking about a jointly drafted document drawing its authority from a general assent of the states. And apart from the problematic nature of the sources, our distance of two centuries cannot but work as a prism refracting all we perceive. One cannot help but speculate that the chorus of lamentations calling for interpretation faithful to "original intention"—and proposing nullification of interpretations that fail this quick litmus test—must inevitably come from persons who have no familiarity with the historical record.

Perhaps most importantly, while proponents of this facile historicism justify it as a depoliticization of the judiciary, the political underpinnings of such a choice should not escape notice. A position that upholds constitutional claims only if they were within the specific contemplation of the Framers in effect establishes a presumption of resolving textual ambiguities against the claim of constitutional right. It is far from clear what justifies such a presumption against claims of right. Nothing intrinsic in the nature of interpretation—if there is such a thing as the "nature" of interpretation—commands such a passive approach to ambiguity. This is a choice no less political than any other; it expresses antipathy to claims of the minority rights against the majority. Those who would restrict claims of right to the values of 1789 specifically articulated in the Constitution turn a blind eye to social progress and eschew adaptation of overarching principles to changes of social circumstance.

Another, perhaps more sophisticated, response to the potential power of judicial interpretation stresses democratic theory: because ours is a government of the people's elected representatives, substantive value choices should by and large be left to them. This view emphasizes not the transcendent historical authority of the Framers but the predominant contemporary authority of the elected branches of government. Yet it has similar consequences for the nature of proper judicial interpretation. Faith in the majoritarian process counsels restraint. Even under more expansive formulations of this approach, judicial review is appropriate only to the extent of ensuring that our democratic process functions smoothly. Thus, for example, we would protect freedom of speech merely to ensure that the people are heard by their representatives, rather than as a separate, substantive value. When, by contrast, society tosses up to the Supreme Court a dispute that would require invalidation of a legislature's substantive policy choice, the Court generally would stay its hand because the Constitution was meant as a plan of government and not as an embodiment of fundamental substantive values.

The view that all matters of substantive policy should be resolved through the majoritarian process has appeal under some circumstances, but I think it ultimately will not do. Unabashed enshrinement of majority will would permit the imposition of a social caste system or wholesale confiscation of property so long as a majority of the authorized legislative body, fairly elected, approved. Our Constitution could not abide such a situation. It is the very purpose of a Constitution—and particularly of the Bill of Rights—to declare certain values transcendent, beyond the reach of temporary political majorities. The majoritarian process cannot be expected to rectify claims of minority right that arise as a response to the outcomes of that very majoritarian process. As James Madison put it:

> The prescriptions in favor of liberty ought to be levelled against that quarter where the greatest danger lies, namely, that which possesses the highest prerogative of power. But this is not found in either the Executive or Legislative departments of Government, but in the body of the people, operating by the majority against the minority. (I Annals 437)

Faith in democracy is one thing, blind faith quite another. Those who drafted our Constitution understood the difference. One cannot read the text without admitting that it embodies substantive value choices; it places certain values beyond the power of any legislature. Obvious are the separation of powers; the privilege of the Writ of Habeas Corpus; prohibition of Bills of Attainder and *ex post facto* laws; prohibition of cruel and unusual punishments; the requirement of just compensation for official taking of property; the prohibition of laws tending to establish religion or enjoining the free exercise of religion; and, since the Civil War, the banishment of slavery and official race discrimination. With respect to at least such principles, we simply have not constituted ourselves as strict utilitarians. While the Constitution may be amended, such amendments require an immense effort by the People as a whole.

To remain faithful to the content of the Constitution, therefore, an approach to interpreting the text must account for the existence of these substantive value choices, and must accept the ambiguity inherent in the effort to apply them to modern circumstances. The Framers discerned fundamental principles through struggles against particular malefactions of the Crown; the struggle shapes the particular contours of the articulated principles. But our acceptance of the fundamental principles has not and should not bind us to those precise, at times anachronistic, contours. Successive generations of Americans have continued to respect these fundamental choices and adopt them as their own guide to evaluating quite different historical practices. Each generation has the choice to overrule or add to the fundamental principles enunciated by the Framers; the Constitution can be amended or it can be ignored. Yet with respect to its fundamental principles, the text has suffered neither fate. Thus, if I may borrow the words of an esteemed predecessor, Justice Robert Jackson, the burden of judicial interpretation is to translate "the majestic generalities of the Bill of Rights, conceived as part of the pattern of liberal government in the eighteenth century, into concrete restraints on officials dealing with the problems of the twentieth century." *Board of Education* v. *Barnette*, [319 U.S. 624, 639 (1943),].

We current Justices read the Constitution in the only way that we can: as Twentieth Century Americans. We look to the history of the time of framing and to the intervening history of interpretation. But the ultimate question must be, what do the words of the text mean in our time? For the genius of the Constitution rests not in any static meaning it might have had in a world that is dead and gone, but in the adaptability of its great principles to cope with current problems and current needs. What the constitutional fundamentals meant to the wisdom of other times cannot be their measure to the vision of our time. Similarly, what those fundamentals mean for us, our descendants will learn, cannot be the measure to the vision of their time. This realization is not, I assure you, a novel one of my own creation. Permit me to quote from one of the opinions of our Court, *Weems v. United States*, [217 U.S. 349,] written nearly a century ago:

> Time works changes, brings into existence new conditions and purposes. Therefore, a principle to be vital must be capable of wider application than the mischief which gave it birth. This is peculiarly true of constitutions. They are not ephemeral enactments, designed to meet passing occasions. They are, to use the words of Chief Justice John Marshall, "designed to approach immortality as nearly as human institutions can approach it." The future is their care and provision for events of good and bad tendencies of which no prophesy can be made. In the application of a constitution, therefore, our contemplation cannot be only of what has been, but of what may be.

Interpretation must account for the transformative purpose of the text. Our Constitution was not intended to preserve a preexisting society but to make a new one, to put in place new principles that the prior political community had not sufficiently recognized. Thus, for example, when we interpret the Civil War Amendments to the charter—abolishing slavery, guaranteeing blacks equality under law, and guaranteeing blacks the right to vote—we must remember that those who put them in place had no desire to enshrine the status quo. Their goal was to make over their world, to eliminate all vestige of slave caste.

Having discussed at some length how I, as a Supreme Court Justice, interact with this text, I think it time to turn to the fruits of this discourse. For the Constitution is a sublime oration on the dignity of man, a bold commitment by a people to the ideal of libertarian dignity protected through law. Some reflection is perhaps required before this can be seen.

The Constitution on its face is, in large measure, a structuring text, a blueprint for government. And when the text is not prescribing the form of government it is limiting the powers of that government. The original document, before addition of any of the amendments, does not speak primarily of the rights of man, but of the abilities and disabilities of government. When one reflects upon the text's preoccupation with the scope of government as well as its shape, however, one comes to understand that what this text is about is the relationship of the individual and the state. The text marks the metes and bounds of official authority and individual autonomy. When one studies the boundary that the text marks out, one gets a sense of the vision of the individual embodied in the Constitution.

As augmented by the Bill of Rights and the Civil War amendments, this text is a sparkling vision of the supremacy of the human dignity of every individual. This vision is reflected in the very choice of democratic self-governance: the supreme value of a democracy is the presumed worth of each individual. And this vision manifests itself most dramatically in the specific prohibitions of the Bill of Rights, a term which I henceforth will apply to describe not only the original first eight amendments, but the Civil War amendments as well. It is a vision that has guided us as a people throughout our history, although the precise rules by which we have protected fundamental human dignity have been transformed over time in response to both transformations of social condition and evolution of our concepts of human dignity.

Until the end of the nineteenth century, freedom and dignity in our country found meaningful protection in the institution of real property. In a society still largely agricultural, a piece of land provided men not just with sustenance but with the means of economic independence, a necessary precondition of political independence and expression. Not surprisingly, property relationships formed the heart of litigation and of legal practice, and lawyers and judges tended to think stable property relationships the highest aim of the law.

But the days when common law property relationships dominated litigation and legal practice are past. To a growing extent economic existence now depends on less certain relationships with government—licenses, employment, contracts, subsidies, unemployment benefits, tax exemptions, welfare and the like. Government participation in the economic existence of individuals is pervasive and deep. Administrative matters and other dealings with government are at the epicenter of the exploding law. We turn to government and to the law for controls which would never have been expected or tolerated before this century, when a man's answer to economic oppression or difficulty was to move two hundred miles west. Now hundreds of thousands of Americans live entire lives without any real prospect of the dignity and autonomy that ownership of real property could confer. Protection of the human dignity of such citizens requires a much modified view of the proper relationship of individual and state.

In general, problems of the relationship of the citizen with government have multiplied and thus have engendered some of the most important constitutional issues of the day. As government acts ever more deeply upon those areas of our lives once marked "private," there is an even greater need to see that individual rights are not curtailed or cheapened in the interest of what may temporarily appear to be the "public good." And as government continues in its role of provider for so many of our disadvantaged citizens, there is an even greater need to ensure that government act with integrity and consistency in its dealings with these citizens. To put this another way, the possibilities for collision between government activity and individual rights will increase as the power and authority of government itself expands, and this growth, in turn, heightens the need for constant vigilance at the collision points. If our free society is to endure, those who govern must recognize human dignity and accept the enforcement of constitutional limitations on their power conceived by the Framers to be necessary to preserve that dignity and the air of freedom which is our proudest heritage. Such recognition will not come from a technical understanding of the organs of government, or the new forms of wealth they administer. It requires something different, something deeper—a personal confrontation with the wellsprings of our society. Solutions of constitutional questions from that perspective have become the great challenge of the modern era. All the talk in the last half-decade about shrinking the government does not alter this reality or the challenge it imposes. The modern activist state is a concomitant of the complexity of modern society; it is inevitably with us. We must meet the challenge rather than wish it were not before us.

The challenge is essentially, of course, one to the capacity of our constitutional structure to foster and protect the freedom, the dignity, and the rights of all persons within our borders, which it is the great design of the Constitution to secure. During the time of my public service this challenge has largely taken shape within the confines of the interpretive question whether the specific guarantees of the Bill of Rights operate as restraints on the power of State government. We recognize the Bill of Rights as the primary source of express information as to what is meant by constitutional liberty. The safeguards enshrined in it are deeply etched in the foundation of America's freedoms. Each is a protection with centuries of history behind it, often dearly bought with the blood and lives of people determined to prevent oppression by their rulers. The first eight amendments, however, were added to the Constitution to operate solely against federal power. It was not until the Thirteenth and Fourteenth Amendments were added, in 1865 and 1868, in response to a demand for national protection against abuses of state power, that the Constitution could be interpreted to require application of the first eight amendments to the states.

It was in particular the Fourteenth Amendment's guarantee that no person be deprived of life, liberty or property without process of law that led us to apply many of the specific guarantees of the Bill of Rights to the States. In my judgment, Justice Cardozo best captured the reasoning that brought us to such decisions when he described what the Court has done as a process by which the guarantees "have been taken over from the earlier articles of the federal bill of rights and brought within the Fourteenth Amendment by a process of absorption . . . [that] has had its source in the belief that neither liberty nor justice would exist if [those guarantees] . . . were sacrificed." *Palko* v. *Connecticut*, [302 U.S. 319, 326 (1937),]. But this process of absorption was neither swift nor steady. As late as 1922 only the Fifth Amendment guarantee of just compensation for official taking of property had been given force against the states. Between then and 1956 only the First Amendment guarantees of speech and conscience and the Fourth Amendment ban of unreasonable searches and seizures had been incorporated—the latter, however, without the exclusionary rule to give it force. As late as 1961, I could stand before a distinguished assemblage of the bar at New York University's James Madison Lecture and list the following as guarantees that had not been thought to be sufficiently fundamental to the protection of human dignity so as to be enforced against the states: the prohibition of cruel and unusual punishments, the right against self-incrimination, the right to assistance of counsel in a criminal trial, the right to confront witnesses, the right to compulsory process, the right not to be placed in jeopardy of life or limb more than once upon accusation of a crime, the right not to have illegally obtained evidence introduced at a criminal trial, and the right to a jury of one's peers.

The history of the quarter century following that Madison Lecture need not be told in great detail. Suffice it to say that each of the guarantees listed above has been recognized as a fundamental aspect of ordered liberty. Of course, the above catalogue encompasses only the rights of the criminally accused, those caught, rightly or wrongly, in the maw of the criminal justice system. But it has been well said that there is no better test of a society than how it treats those accused of transgressing against it. Indeed, it is because we recognize that incarceration strips a man of his dignity that we demand strict adherence to fair procedure and proof of guilt beyond a reasonable doubt before taking such a drastic step. These requirements are, as Justice Harlan once said, "bottomed on a fundamental value determination of our society that it is far worse to convict an innocent man than to let a guilty man go free." *In re Winship*, [397 U.S. 358, 372 (1970),] (concurring opinion). There is no worse injustice than wrongly to strip a man of his dignity. And our adherence to the constitutional vision of human dignity is so strict that even after convicting a person according to these stringent standards, we demand that his dignity be infringed only to the extent appropriate to the crime and never by means of wanton infliction of pain or deprivation. I interpret the Constitution plainly to embody these fundamental values.

Of course the constitutional vision of human dignity has, in this past quarter century, infused far more than our decisions about the criminal process. Recognition of the principle of "one person, one vote" as a constitutional one redeems the promise of self-governance by affirming the essential dignity of every citizen in the right to equal participation in the democratic process. Recognition of so-called "new property" rights in those receiving government entitlements affirms the essential dignity of the least fortunate among us by demanding that government treat with decency, integrity and consistency those dependent on its benefits for their very survival. After all, a legislative majority initially decides to create governmental entitlements; the Constitution's Due Process Clause merely provides protection for entitlements thought necessary by society as a whole. Such due process rights prohibit government from imposing the devil's bargain of bartering away human dignity in exchange for human sustenance. Likewise, recognition of full equality for women—equal protection of the laws—ensures that gender has no bearing on claims to human dignity.

Recognition of broad and deep rights of expression and of conscience reaffirm the vision of human dignity in many ways. They too redeem the promise of self-governance by facilitating—indeed demanding—robust, uninhibited and wide-open debate on issues of public importance. Such public debate is of course vital to the development and dissemination of political ideas. As importantly, robust public discussion is the crucible in which personal political convictions are forged. In our democracy, such discussion is a political duty, it is the essence of self government. The constitutional vision of human dignity rejects the possibility of political orthodoxy imposed from above; it respects the right of each individual to form and to express political judgments, however far they may deviate from the mainstream and however unsettling they might be to the powerful or the elite. Recognition of these rights of expression and conscience also frees up the private space for both intellectual and spiritual development free of government dominance, either blatant or subtle. Justice Brandeis put it so well sixty years ago when he wrote: "Those who won our independence believed that the final end of the State was to make men free to develop their faculties; and that in its government the deliberative forces should prevail over the arbitrary. They valued liberty both as an end and as a means." *Whitney v. California* [274 U.S. 357, 375 (1927),] (concurring opinion).

I do not mean to suggest that we have in the last quarter century achieved a comprehensive definition of the constitutional ideal of human dignity. We are still striving toward that goal, and doubtless it will be an external quest. For if the interaction of this Justice and the constitutional text over the years confirms any single proposition, it is that the demands of human dignity will never cease to evolve.

Indeed, I cannot in good conscience refrain from mention of one grave and crucial respect in which we continue, in my judgment, to fall short of the constitutional vision of human dignity. It is in our continued tolerance of State-administered execution as a form of punishment. I make it a practice not to comment on the constitutional issues that come before the Court, but my position on this issue, of course, has been for some time fixed and immutable. I think I can venture some thoughts on this particular subject without transgressing my usual guideline too severely.

As I interpret the Constitution, capital punishment is under all circumstances cruel and unusual punishment prohibited by the Eighth and Fourteenth Amendments. This is a position of which I imagine you are not unaware. Much discussion of the merits of capital punishment has in recent years focused on the potential arbitrariness that attends its administration, and I have no doubt that such arbitrariness is a grave wrong. But for me, the wrong of capital punishment transcends such procedural issues. As I have said in my opinions, I view the Eighth Amendment's prohibition of cruel and unusual punishments as embodying to a unique degree moral principles that substantively restrain the punishments our civilized society may impose on those persons who transgress its laws. Foremost among the moral principles recognized in our cases and inherent in the prohibition is the primary principle that the State, even as it punishes, must treat its citizens in a manner consistent with their intrinsic worth as human beings. A punishment must not be so severe as to be utterly and irreversibly degrading to the very essence of human dignity. Death for whatever crime and under all circumstances is a truly awesome punishment. The calculated killing of a human being by the State involves, by its very nature, an absolute denial of the executed person's humanity. The most vile murder does not, in my view, release the State from constitutional restraints on the destruction of human dignity. Yet an executed person has lost the very right to have rights, now or ever. For me, then, the fatal constitutional infirmity of capital punishment is that it treats members of the human race as nonhumans, as objects to be toyed with and discarded. It is, indeed, "cruel and unusual." It is thus inconsistent with the fundamental premise of the Clause that even the most base criminal remains a human being possessed of some potential, at least, for common human dignity.

This is an interpretation to which a majority of my fellow Justices—not to mention, it would seem, a majority of my fellow countrymen—does not subscribe. Perhaps you find my adherence to it, and my recurrent publication of it, simply contrary, tiresome, or quixotic. Or perhaps you see in it a refusal to abide by the judicial principle of *stare decisis*, obedience to precedent. In my judgment, however, the unique interpretive role of the Supreme Court with respect to the Constitution demands some flexibility with respect to the call of *stare decisis*. Because we are the last word on the meaning of the Constitution, our views must be subject to revision over time, or the Constitution falls captive, again, to the anachronistic views of long-gone generations. I mentioned earlier the judge's role in seeking out the community's interpretation of the Constitutional text. Yet, again in my judgment, when a Justice perceives an interpretation of the text to have departed so far from its essential meaning, that Justice is bound, by a larger constitutional duty to the community, to expose the departure and point toward a different path. On this issue, the death penalty, I hope to embody a community striving for human dignity for all, although perhaps not yet arrived.

You have doubtless observed that this description of my personal encounter with the constitutional text has in large portion been a discussion of public developments in constitutional doctrine over the last century. That, as I suggested at the outset, is inevitable because my interpretive career has demanded a public reading of the text. This public encounter with the text, however, has been a profound source of personal inspiration. The vision of human dignity embodied there is deeply moving. It is timeless. It has inspired Americans for two centuries and it will continue to inspire as it continues to evolve. That evolutionary process is inevitable and, indeed, it is the true interpretive genius of the text.

If we are to be as a shining city upon a hill, it will be because of our ceaseless pursuit of the constitutional ideal of human dignity. For the political and legal ideals that form the foundation of much that is best in American institutions—ideals jealously preserved and guarded throughout our history—still form the vital force in creative political thought and activity within the nation today. As we adapt our institutions to the ever-changing conditions of national and international life, those ideals of human dignity—liberty and justice for all individuals—will continue to inspire and guide us because they are entrenched in our Constitution. The Constitution with its Bill of Rights thus has a bright future, as well as a glorious past, for its spirit is inherent in the aspirations of our people.

Appendix 1

❖❖❖

THE DECLARATION OF INDEPENDENCE[1]

In Congress, July 4, 1776

The unanimous Declaration of the thirteen United States of America

When in the Course of human events it becomes necessary for one people to dissolve the political bands which have connected them with another, and to assume among the Powers of the earth, the separate and equal station to which the Laws of Nature and of Nature's God entitle them, a decent respect to the opinions of mankind requires that they should declare the causes which impel them to the separation.

We hold these truths to be self-evident, that all men are created equal, that they are endowed by their Creator with certain unalienable Rights, that among these are Life, Liberty and the pursuit of Happiness. That to secure these rights, Governments are instituted among Men, deriving their just powers from the consent of the governed. That whenever any Form of Government becomes destructive of these ends, it is the Right of the People to alter or to abolish it, and to institute new Government, laying its foundation on such principles and organizing its powers in such form, as to them shall seem most likely to effect their Safety and Happiness. Prudence, indeed, will dictate that Governments long established should not be changed for light and transient causes; and accordingly all experience hath shown, that mankind are more disposed to suffer, while evils are sufferable, than to right themselves by abolishing the forms to which they are accustomed. But when a long train of abuses and usurpations, pursuing invariably the same Object evinces a design to reduce them under absolute Despotism, it is their right, it is their duty, to

---

[1]This text retains the spelling, capitalization, and punctuation of the original.

throw off such Government, and to provide new Guards for their future security.—
Such has been the patient sufferance of these Colonies; and such is now the necessity which constrains them to alter their former Systems of Government. The
history of the present King of Great Britain is a history of repeated injuries and
usurpations, all having in direct object the establishment of an absolute Tyranny
over these States. To prove this, let Facts be submitted to a candid world.

He has refused his Assent to Laws, the most wholesome and necessary for the
public good.

He has forbidden his Governors to pass Laws of immediate and pressing importance, unless suspended in their operation till his Assent should be obtained; and
when so suspended, he has utterly neglected to attend to them.

He has refused to pass other Laws for the accommodation of large districts of
people, unless those people would relinquish the right of Representation in the Legislature, a right inestimable to them and formidable to tyrants only.

He has called together legislative bodies at places unusual, uncomfortable, and
distant from the depository of their Public Records, for the sole purpose of fatiguing
them into compliance with his measures.

He has dissolved Representative Houses repeatedly, for opposing with manly
firmness his invasions on the rights of the people.

He has refused for a long time, after such dissolutions, to cause others to be
elected; whereby the Legislative Powers, incapable of Annihilation, have returned
to the People at large for their exercise; the State remaining in the mean time
exposed to all the dangers of invasion from without, and convulsions within.

He has endeavored to prevent the population of these States; for that purpose
obstructing the Laws for Naturalization of Foreigners; refusing to pass others to encourage their migration hither, and raising the conditions of new Appropriations of Lands.

He has obstructed the Administration of Justice, by refusing his Assent to Laws
for establishing Judiciary Powers.

He has made Judges dependent on his Will alone, for the tenure of their offices,
and the amount and payment of their salaries.

He has erected a multitude of New Offices, and sent hither swarms of Officers
to harass our People, and eat out their substance.

He has kept among us, in times of peace, Standing Armies without the Consent
of our Legislature.

He has affected to render the Military independent of and superior to the Civil Power.

He has combined with others to subject us to a jurisdiction foreign to our constitution, and unacknowledged by our laws; giving his Assent to their acts of pretended Legislation:

For quartering large bodies of armed troops among us:

For protecting them, by a mock Trial, from Punishment for any Murders which they should commit on the Inhabitants of these States:

For cutting off our Trade with all parts of the world:

For imposing taxes on us without our Consent:

For depriving us in many cases, of the benefits of Trial by Jury:

For transporting us beyond Seas to be tried for pretended offenses:

For abolishing the free System of English Laws in a neighboring Province, establishing therein an Arbitrary government, and enlarging its Boundaries so as to render it at once an example and fit instrument for introducing the same absolute rule into these Colonies:

For taking away our Charters, abolishing our most valuable Laws, and altering fundamentally the Forms of our Government:

For suspending our own Legislature, and declaring themselves invested with Power to legislate for us in all cases whatsoever.

He has abdicated Government here, by declaring us out of his Protection and waging War against us.

He has plundered our seas, ravaged our Coasts, burnt our towns, and destroyed the lives of our people.

He is at this time transporting large armies of foreign mercenaries to compleat the works of death, desolation and tyranny, already begun with circumstances of Cruelty & perfidy scarcely paralleled in the most barbarous ages, and totally unworthy the Head of a civilized nation.

He has constrained our fellow Citizens taken Captive on the high Seas to bear Arms against their Country, to become the executioners of their friends and Brethren, or to fall themselves by their Hands.

He has excited domestic insurrections amongst us, and has endeavored to bring on the inhabitants of our frontiers, the merciless Indian Savages, whose known rule of warfare, is an undistinguished destruction of all ages, sexes and conditions.

In every stage of these Oppressions We have Petitioned for Redress in the most humble terms: Our repeated Petitions have been answered only by repeated injury. A Prince, whose character is thus marked by every act which may define a Tyrant, is unfit to be the ruler of a free People.

Nor have We been wanting in attention to our British brethren. We have warned them from time to time of attempts by their legislature to extend an unwarrantable jurisdiction over us. We have reminded them of the circumstances of our emigration and settlement here. We have appealed to their native justice and magnanimity, and we have conjured them by the ties of our common kindred to disavow these usurpations, which, would inevitably interrupt our connections and correspondence. They too have been deaf to the voice of justice and consanguinity. We must, therefore, acquiesce in the necessity, which denounces our Separation, and hold them, as we hold the rest of mankind, Enemies in War, in Peace Friends.

We, therefore, the Representatives of the united States of America, in General Congress, Assembled, appealing to the Supreme Judge of the world for the rectitude of our intentions, do, in the Name, and by Authority of the good People of these Colonies, solemnly publish and declare, That these United Colonies are, and of Right ought to be Free and Independent States; that they are Absolved from all Allegiance to the British Crown, and that all political connection between them and the State of Great Britain, is and ought to be totally dissolved; and that as Free and Independent States, they have full Power to levy War, conclude Peace, contract Alliances, establish Commerce, and to do all other Acts and Things which Independent States may of right do. And for the support of this Declaration, with a firm reliance on the Protection of Divine Providence, we mutually pledge to each other our Lives, our Fortunes and our sacred Honor.

John Hancock

New Hampshire

Josiah Bartlett,   Matthew Thornton.
WM. Wimple,

Massachusetts Bay

Saml. Adams,   Robt. Treat Paine,
John Adams,   Elridge Gerry.

Rhode Island

Step. Hopkins,   William Ellery.

Connecticut

ROGER SHERMAN,   WM. WILLIAMS,
SAM'EL HUNTINGTON,   OLIVER WOLOOT.

New York

WM. FLOYD,   FRANS. LEWIS,
PHIL. LIVINGSTON,   LEWIS MORRIS.

New Jersey

RICHD. STOCKTON,   JOHN HART,
JNO. WITHERSPOON,   ABRA. CLARK.
FRAS. HOPKINSON,

Pennsylvania

ROBT. MORRIS,   JAS. SMITH,
BENJAMIN RUSH,   GEO. TAYLOR,
BENJA. FRANKLIN,   JAMES WILSON,
JOHN MORTON,   GEO. ROSS.
GEO. CLYMER,

Delaware

CAESAR RODNEY,   THO. M'KEAN.
GEO. READ

Maryland

SAMUEL CHASE,   THOS. STONE,
WM. PACA,   CHARLES CAROLL OF CARROLLTON.

Virginia

GEORGE WYTHE,   THOS. NELSON, JR.,
RICHARD HENRY LEE,   FRANCIS LIGHTFOOT LEE,
TH. JEFFERSON,   CARTER BRAXTON.
BENJA. HARRISON,

North Carolina

WM. HOOPER,   JOHN PENN.
JOSEPH HEWES,

South Carolina

EDWARD RUTLEDGE,   THOMAS LYNCH, JNR.,
THOS. HEYWARD, JUNR.,   ARTHUR MIIDDLETON.

Georgia

BUTTON GWINNETT,   GEO. WALTON.
LYMAN HALL,

Appendix 2

·········

THE CONSTITUTION OF THE UNITED STATES

We the People of the United States, in Order to form a more perfect Union, establish Justice, insure domestic Tranquility, provide for the common defence, promote the general Welfare, and secure the Blessings of Liberty to ourselves and our Posterity do ordain and establish this CONSTITUTION for the United States of America.

Article I

Section 1.
All legislative Powers herein granted shall be vested in a Congress of the United States, which shall consist of a Senate and House of Representatives.

Section 2.
[1] The House of Representatives shall be composed of members chosen every second Year by the People of the several States, and the Electors in each State shall have the Qualifications requisite for Electors of the most numerous Branch of the State Legislature.

[2] No Person shall be a Representative who shall not have attained to the Age of twenty-five Years, and been seven Years a Citizen of the United States, and who shall not, when elected, be an Inhabitant of that State in which he shall be chosen.

[3] [Representatives and direct Taxes[1] shall be apportioned among the several States which may be included within this Union, according to their respective Numbers, which shall be determined by adding to the whole Number of free Persons, including those bound to Service for a Term of Years, and excluding Indians

---

[1]The Sixteenth Amendment replaced this with respect to income taxes.

not taxed, three fifths of all other Persons.]² The actual Enumeration shall be made within three Years after the first Meeting of the Congress of the United States, and within every subsequent Term of ten years, in such Manner as they shall by Law direct. The Number of Representatives shall not exceed one for every thirty Thousand, but each State shall have at Least one Representative; and until such enumeration shall be made, the State of New Hampshire shall be entitled to choose three, Massachusetts eight, Rhode-Island and Providence Plantations one, Connecticut five, New York six, New Jersey four, Pennsylvania eight, Delaware one, Maryland six, Virginia ten, North Carolina five, South Carolina five, and Georgia three.

[4] When vacancies happen in the Representation from any State, the Executive Authority thereof shall issue Writs of Election to fill such Vacancies.

[5] The House of Representatives shall choose their Speaker and other Officers; and shall have the sole Power of Impeachment.

Section 3.

[1] The Senate of the United States shall be composed of two Senators from each State, [chosen by the Legislature]³ thereof, for six Years; and each Senator shall have one Vote.

[2] Immediately after they shall be assembled in Consequence of the first Election, they shall be divided as equally as may be into three Classes. The Seats of the Senators of the first Class shall be vacated at the Expiration of the second Year, of the second Class at the Expiration of the fourth Year, and of the third Class at the Expiration of the sixth Year, so that one-third may be chosen every second Year; [and if Vacancies happen by Resignation, or otherwise, during the Recess of the Legislature of any State, the Executive thereof may make temporary Appointments until the next Meeting of the Legislature, which shall then fill such Vacancies].⁴

[3] No person shall be a Senator who shall not have attained to the Age of thirty Years, and been nine Years a Citizen of the United States, and who shall not, when elected, be an Inhabitant of that State for which he shall be chosen.

[4] The Vice President of the United States shall be President of the Senate, but shall have no Vote, unless they be equally divided.

[5] The Senate shall choose their other Officers, and also a President pro tempore, in the absence of the Vice President, or when he shall exercise the Office of President of the United States.

[6] The Senate shall have the sole Power to try all Impeachments. When sitting for that Purpose, they shall be on Oath or Affirmation. When the President of the United States is tried, the Chief Justice shall preside: And no Person shall be convicted without the Concurrence of two thirds of the Members present.

[7] Judgment in Cases of Impeachment shall not extend further than to removal from Office, and disqualification to hold and enjoy any Office of honor, Trust or Profit under the United States: but the Party convicted shall nevertheless be liable and subject to Indictment, Trial, Judgment and Punishment according to Law.

---

²Repealed by the Fourteenth Amendment.
³Repealed by the Seventeenth Amendment, Section 1.
⁴Changed by the Seventeenth Amendment.

Section 4.

[1] The Times, Places and Manner of holding Elections for Senators and Representatives, shall be prescribed in each State by the Legislature thereof; but the Congress may at any time by Law make or alter such Regulations, except as to the Places of Choosing Senators.

[2] The Congress shall assemble at least once in every Year, and such Meeting shall [be on the first Monday in December,][5] unless they shall by Law appoint a different Day.

Section 5.

[1] Each House shall be the Judge of the Elections, Returns and Qualifications of its own Members, and a Majority of each shall constitute a Quorum to do Business; but a smaller number may adjourn from day to day, and may be authorized to compel the Attendance of absent Members, in such Manner, and under such Penalties as each House may provide.

[2] Each House may determine the Rules of its Proceedings, punish its Members for disorderly Behavior, and, with the Concurrence of two thirds, expel a Member.

[3] Each House shall keep a Journal of its Proceedings, and from time to time publish the same, excepting such Parts as may in their Judgment require Secrecy; and the Yeas and Nays of the Members of either House on any question shall, at the Desire of one fifth of those Present, be entered on the Journal.

[4] Neither House, during the Session of Congress, shall, without the Consent of the other, adjourn for more than three days, nor to any other Place than that in which the two Houses shall be sitting.

Section 6.

[1] The Senators and Representatives shall receive a Compensation for their Services, to be ascertained by Law, and paid out of the Treasury of the United States. They shall in all Cases, except Treason, Felony and Breach of the Peace, be privileged from Arrest during their Attendance at the Session of their respective Houses, and in going to and returning from the same; and for any Speech or Debate in either House, they shall not be questioned in any other Place.

[2] No Senator or Representative shall, during the Time for which he was elected, be appointed to any civil Office under the Authority of the United States, which shall have been created, or the Emoluments whereof have been increased during such time; and no Person holding any Office under the United States, shall be a Member of either House during his Continuance in Office.

Section 7.

[1] All Bills for raising Revenue shall originate in the House of Representatives; but the Senate may propose or concur with Amendments as on other Bills.

[2] Every Bill which shall have passed the House of Representatives and the Senate, shall, before it become a Law, be presented to the President of the United States; If he approve he shall sign it, but if not he shall return it, with his Objections to that House in which it shall have originated, who shall enter the Objections at large on their Journal, and proceed to reconsider it. If after such Reconsideration two thirds of that House shall agree to pass the Bill, it shall be sent, together with

---

[5]Changed by the Twentieth Amendment, Section 2.

the Objections, to the other House, by which it shall likewise be reconsidered, and if approved by two thirds of that House, it shall become a Law. But in all such Cases the Votes of both Houses shall be determined by Yeas and Nays, and the Names of the Persons voting for and against the Bill shall be entered on the Journal of each House respectively. If any Bill shall not be returned by the President within ten Days (Sundays excepted) after it shall have been presented to him, the Same shall be a Law, in like Manner as if he had signed it, unless the Congress by their Adjournment prevent its Return, in which Case it shall not be a Law.

[3] Every Order, Resolution, or Vote to which the Concurrence of the Senate and House of Representatives may be necessary (except on a question of Adjournment) shall be presented to the President of the United States; and before the Same shall take Effect, shall be approved by him, or being disapproved by him, shall be repassed by two thirds of the Senate and House of Representatives, according to the Rules and Limitations prescribed in the Case of a Bill.

Section 8.

[1] The Congress shall have Power To lay and collect Taxes, Duties, Imposts and Excises, to pay the Debts and provide for the common Defence and general Welfare of the United States; but all Duties, Imposts and Excises shall be uniform throughout the United States;

[2] To borrow money on the credit of the United States;

[3] To regulate Commerce with foreign Nations, and among the several States, and with the Indian Tribes;

[4] To establish an uniform Rule of Naturalization, and uniform Laws on the subject of Bankruptcies throughout the United States;

[5] To coin Money, regulate the Value thereof, and of foreign Coin, and fix the Standard of Weights and Measures;

[6] To provide for the Punishment of counterfeiting the Securities and current Coin of the United States;

[7] To establish Post Offices and post Roads;

[8] To promote the Progress of Science and useful Arts, by securing for limited Times to Authors and Inventors the exclusive Right to their respective Writings and Discoveries;

[9] To constitute Tribunals inferior to the supreme Court;

[10] To define and punish Piracies and Felonies committed on the high Seas, and Offences against the Law of Nations;

[11] To declare War, grant Letters of Marque and Reprisal, and make Rules concerning Captures on Land and Water;

[12] To raise and support Armies, but no Appropriation of Money to that Use shall be for a longer Term than two Years;

[13] To provide and maintain a Navy;

[14] To make rules for the Government and Regulation of the land and naval Forces;

[15] To provide for calling forth the Militia to execute the Laws of the Union, suppress Insurrections and repel Invasions;

[16] To provide for organizing, arming, and disciplining the Militia, and for governing such Part of them as may be employed in the Service of the United States,

reserving to the States respectively, the Appointment of the Officers, and the Authority of training the Militia according to the discipline prescribed by Congress;

[17] To exercise exclusive Legislation in all Cases whatsoever, over such District (not exceeding ten Miles square) as may, by Cession of particular States, and the acceptance of Congress, become the Seat of the Government of the United States, and to exercise like Authority over all Places purchased by the Consent of the Legislature of the State in which the Same shall be, for the Erection of Forts, Magazines, Arsenals, dock-Yards, and other needful Buildings;—And

[18] To make all Laws which shall be necessary and proper for carrying into Execution the foregoing Powers, and all other Powers vested by this Constitution in the Government of the United States, or in any Department or Officer thereof.

Section 9.

[1] The Migration or Importation of such Persons as any of the States now existing shall think proper to admit, shall not be prohibited by the Congress prior to the Year one thousand eight hundred and eight, but a tax or duty may be imposed on such Importation, not exceeding ten dollars for each Person.

[2] The privilege of the Writ of Habeas Corpus shall not be suspended, unless when in Cases of Rebellion or Invasion the public Safety may require it.

[3] No Bill of Attainder or ex post facto Law shall be passed.

[4] No capitation, or other direct, Tax shall be laid, unless in Proportion to the Census or Enumeration herein before directed to be taken.[6]

[5] No Tax or Duty shall be laid on Articles exported from any State.

[6] No Preference shall be given by any Regulation of Commerce or Revenue to the Ports of one State over those of another: nor shall Vessels bound to, or from, one State, be obliged to enter, clear, or pay Duties in another.

[7] No Money shall be drawn from the Treasury, but in Consequence of Appropriations made by Law; and a regular Statement and Account of the Receipts and Expenditures of all public Money shall be published from time to time.

[8] No Title of Nobility shall be granted by the United States: And no Person holding any Office of Profit or Trust under them, shall, without the Consent of the Congress, accept of any present, Emolument, Office, or Title, of any kind whatever, from any King, Prince, or foreign State.

Section 10.

[1] No State shall enter into any Treaty, Alliance, or Confederation; grant Letters of Marque and Reprisal; coin Money; emit Bills of Credit; make any Thing but gold and silver Coin a Tender in Payment of Debts; pass any Bill of attainder, ex post facto Law, or Law impairing the Obligation of Contracts, or grant any Title of Nobility.

[2] No State shall, without the Consent of the Congress, lay any Imposts or Duties on Imports or Exports, except what may be absolutely necessary for executing its inspection Laws: and the net Produce of all Duties and Imposts, laid by any State on Imports or Exports, shall be for the Use of the Treasury of the United States; and all such Laws shall be subject to the Revision and Control of the Congress.

---

[6]Changed by the Sixteenth Amendment.

[3] No State shall, without the Consent of Congress, lay any duty of Tonnage, keep Troops, or Ships of War in time of Peace, enter into any Agreement or Compact with another State, or with a foreign Power, or engage in War, unless actually invaded, or in such imminent Danger as will not admit of delay.

Article II

Section 1.

[1] The executive Power shall be vested in a President of the United States of America. He shall hold his Office during the Term of four Years, and, together with the Vice-President, chosen for the same Term, be elected, as follows

[2] Each State shall appoint, in such Manner as the Legislature thereof may direct, a Number of Electors, equal to the whole Number of Senators and Representatives to which the State may be entitled in the Congress; but no Senator or Representative, or Person holding an Office of Trust or Profit under the United States, shall be appointed an Elector.

[The Electors shall meet in their respective States, and vote by Ballot for two persons, of whom one at least shall not be an Inhabitant of the same State with themselves. And they shall make a List of all the Persons voted for, and of the Number of Votes for each; which List they shall sign and certify, and transmit sealed to the Seat of the Government of the United States, directed to the President of the Senate. The President of the Senate shall, in the Presence of the Senate and House of Representatives, open all the Certificates, and the Votes shall then be counted. The Person having the greatest Number of Votes shall be the President, if such Number be a Majority of the whole Number of Electors appointed; and if there be more than one who have such Majority, and have an equal Number of Votes, then the House of Representatives shall immediately choose by Ballot one of them for President; and if no Person have a Majority, then from the five highest on the List the said House shall in like Manner choose the President. But in choosing the President, the Votes shall be taken by States, the Representation from each State having one Vote; A quorum for this Purpose shall consist of a Member or Members from two-thirds of the States, and a Majority of all the States shall be necessary to a Choice. In every Case, after the Choice of the President, the Person having the greatest Number of Votes of the Electors shall be the Vice-President. But if there should remain two or more who have equal Votes, the Senate shall choose from them by Ballot the Vice-President.][7]

[3] The Congress may determine the Time of choosing the electors, and the Day on which they shall give their Votes; which Day shall be the same throughout the United States.

[4] No person except a natural born Citizen, or a Citizen of the United States, at the time of the Adoption of this Constitution, shall be eligible to the Office of President; neither shall any Person be eligible to that Office who shall not have

---

[7]This paragraph was superseded in 1804 by the Twelfth Amendment.

attained to the Age of thirty-five Years, and been fourteen Years a Resident within the United States.

[5] In case of the Removal of the President from Office, or of his Death, Resignation, or Inability to discharge the Powers and Duties of the said Office, the same shall devolve on the Vice-President, and the Congress may by Law provide for the Case of Removal, Death, Resignation or Inability, both of the President and Vice-President, declaring what Officer shall then act as President, and such Officer shall act accordingly, until the Disability be removed, or a President shall be elected.[8]

[6] The President shall, at stated Times, receive for his Services, a Compensation, which shall neither be increased nor diminished during the Period for which he shall have been elected, and he shall not receive within that Period any other Emolument from the United States, or any of them.

[7] Before he enter on the Execution of his Office, he shall take the following Oath or Affirmation:—"I do solemnly swear (or affirm) that I will faithfully execute the Office of President of the United States, and will to the best of my Ability, preserve, protect and defend the Constitution of the United States."

Section 2.

[1] The President shall be Commander in Chief of the Army and Navy of the United States, and of the Militia of the several States, when called into the actual Service of the United States; he may require the Opinion in writing, of the principal Officer in each of the executive Departments, upon any subject relating to the Duties of their respective Offices, and he shall have Power to Grant Reprieves and Pardons for Offenses against the United States, except in Cases of Impeachment.

[2] He shall have Power, by and with the Advice and Consent of the Senate, to make Treaties, provided two-thirds of the Senators present concur; and he shall nominate, and by and with the Advice and Consent of the Senate, shall appoint Ambassadors, other public Ministers and Consuls, Judges of the supreme Court, and all other Officers of the United States, whose Appointments are not herein otherwise provided for, and which shall be established by Law: but the Congress may by Law vest the Appointment of such inferior Officers, as they think proper, in the President alone, in the Court of Law, or in the Heads of Departments.

[3] The President shall have Power to fill up all Vacancies that may happen during the Recess of the Senate, by granting Commissions which shall expire at the End of their next Session.

Section 3.

He shall from time to time give to the Congress Information of the State of the Union, and recommend to their Consideration such Measures as he shall judge necessary and expedient; he may, on extraordinary Occasions, convene both Houses, or either of them, and in Case of Disagreement between them, with Respect to the Time of Adjournment, he may adjourn them to such Time as he shall think proper; he shall receive Ambassadors and other public Ministers; he shall take Care that the Laws be faithfully executed, and shall Commission all the Officers of the United States.

---

[8]Changed by the Twenty-fifth Amendment.

Section 4.

The President, Vice President and all civil Officers of the United States, shall be removed from Office on Impeachment for, and Conviction of, Treason, Bribery, or other high Crimes and Misdemeanors.

Article III

Section 1.

The judicial Power of the United States, shall be vested in one supreme Court, and in such inferior Courts as the Congress may from time to time ordain and establish. The Judges, both of the supreme and inferior Courts, shall hold their Offices during good Behavior, and shall, at stated Times, receive for their Services a Compensation which shall not be diminished during their Continuance in Office.

Section 2.

[1] The judicial Power shall extend to all Cases, in Law and Equity, arising under this Constitution, the Laws of the United States, and Treaties made, or which shall be made, under their Authority;—to all Cases affecting Ambassadors, other public Ministers and Consuls;—to all Cases of admiralty and maritime Jurisdiction;—to Controversies to which the United States shall be a Party;—to Controversies between two or more States;—[between a State and Citizens of another State];[9]—between Citizens of different States;—between Citizens of the same State claiming Lands under Grants of different States, and [between a State, or the Citizens thereof, and foreign States, Citizens or Subjects].[10]

[2] In all Cases affecting Ambassadors, other public Ministers and Consuls, and those in which a State shall be Party, the supreme Court shall have original Jurisdiction. In all the other Cases before mentioned, the supreme Court shall have appellate Jurisdiction, both as to Law and Fact, with such Exceptions, and under such Regulations as the Congress shall make.

[3] The trial of all Crimes, except in Cases of Impeachment, shall be by Jury; and such Trial shall be held in the State where the said Crimes shall have been committed: but when not committed within any state, the Trial shall be at such Place or Places as the Congress may by Law have directed.

Section 3.

[1] Treason against the United States, shall consist only in levying War against them, or in adhering to their Enemies, giving them Aid and Comfort. No Person shall be convicted of Treason unless on the Testimony of two Witnesses to the same overt Act, or on Confession in open Court.

[2] The Congress shall have power to declare the Punishment of Treason, but no Attainder of Treason shall work Corruption of Blood, or Forfeiture except during the Life of the Person attained.

---

[9]Restricted by the Eleventh Amendment.
[10]Restricted by the Eleventh Amendment.

Article IV

Section 1.
Full faith and Credit shall be given in each State to the public Acts, Records, and judicial Proceedings of every other State. And the Congress may by general Laws prescribe the Manner in which such Acts, Records and Proceedings shall be proved, and the Effect thereof.

Section 2.
[1] The Citizens of each State shall be entitled to all Privileges and Immunities of Citizens in the several States.

[2] A Person charged in any State with Treason, Felony, or other Crime, who shall flee from Justice, and be found in another State, shall on demand of the executive Authority of the State from which he fled, be delivered up, to be removed to the State having Jurisdiction of the Crime.

[3] [No Person held to Service or Labor in one State, under the Laws thereof, escaping into another, shall, in Consequence of any Law or Regulation therein, be discharged from such Service or Labor, but shall be delivered up on Claim of the Party to whom such Service or Labor may be due.][11]

Section 3.
[1] New States may be admitted by the Congress into this Union; but no new State shall be formed or erected within the Jurisdiction of any other State; nor any State be formed by the Junction of two or more States, or parts of States, without the Consent of the Legislatures of the States concerned as well as of the Congress.

[2] The Congress shall have Power to dispose of and make all needful rules and Regulations respecting the Territory or other Property belonging to the United States; and nothing in this Constitution shall be so construed as to Prejudice any Claims of the United States, or of any particular State.

Section 4.
The United States shall guarantee to every State in this Union a Republican Form of Government, and shall protect each of them against Invasion; and on Application of the Legislature, or of the Executive (when the Legislature cannot be convened) against domestic Violence.

Article V

The Congress, whenever two-thirds of both Houses shall deem it necessary, shall propose Amendments to this Constitution, or, on the Application of the Legislatures of two-thirds of the several States, shall call a Convention for proposing Amendments, which, in either Case, shall be valid to all Intents and Purposes, as part of this Constitution, when ratified by the Legislature of three-fourths of the several States, or by Conventions in three-fourths thereof, as the one or the other Mode of Ratification may be proposed by the Congress; Provided that no Amendment which may be made prior to Year One thousand

---

[11]This paragraph has been superseded by the Thirteenth Amendment.

eight hundred and eight shall in any Manner affect the first and fourth Clauses in the Ninth Section of the first Article; and that no State, without its Consent, shall be deprived of its equal Suffrage in the Senate.

Article VI

[1] All Debts contracted and Engagements entered into, before the Adoption of this Constitution, shall be as valid against the United States under this Constitution, as under the Confederation.

[2] This Constitution, and the Laws of the United States which shall be made in Pursuance thereof; and all Treaties made, or which shall be made, under the Authority of the United States, shall be the supreme Law of the Land; and the Judges in every State shall be bound thereby, any Thing in the Constitution or Laws of any State to the Contrary notwithstanding.

[3] The Senators and Representatives before mentioned, and the Members of the several State Legislatures, and all executive and judicial Officers, both of the United States and of the several States, shall be bound by Oath or Affirmation, to support this Constitution; but no religious Test shall ever be required as a Qualification to any Office or public Trust under the United States.

Article VII

The Ratification of the conventions of nine States, shall be sufficient for the Establishment of this Constitution between the States so ratifying the Same.

DONE   in Convention by the Unanimous Consent of the States present the Seventeenth Day of September in the Year of our Lord one thousand seven hundred and Eighty seven and the Independence of the United States of America the Twelfth. In Witness whereof We have hereunto subscribed our Names,

Go Washington
President and deputy from Virginia
Articles in Addition to, and Amendment of, the Constitution of the United States of America, Proposed by Congress, and Ratified by the Legislatures of the Several States, Pursuant to the Fifth Article of the Original Constitution.

Article I[12]

Congress shall make no law respecting an establishment of religion, or prohibiting the free exercise thereof; or abridging the freedom of speech, or of the press; or the right of the people peaceably to assemble, and to petition the Government for a redress of grievances.

---

[12]The first ten amendments were adopted in 1791.

Article II

A well regulated Militia, being necessary to the security of a free State, the right of the people to keep and bear Arms, shall not be infringed.

Article III

No Soldier, shall, in time of peace he quartered in any house, without the consent of the Owner, nor in time of war, but in a manner to be prescribed by law.

Article IV

The right of the people to be secure in their persons, houses, papers, and effects, against unreasonable searches and seizures, shall not be violated, and no Warrants shall issue, but upon probable cause, supported by Oath or affirmation, and particularly describing the place to be searched, and the persons or things to be seized.

Article V

No person shall be held to answer for a capital, or otherwise infamous crime, unless on a presentment or indictment of a Grand Jury, except in cases arising in the land or naval forces, or in the Militia, when in actual service in time of War or public danger; nor shall any person be subject for the same offence to be twice put in jeopardy of life or limb; nor shall be compelled in any criminal case to be witness against himself, nor be deprived of life, liberty, or property, without due process of law; nor shall private property be taken for public use, without just compensation.

Article VI

In all criminal prosecutions, the accused shall enjoy the right to a speedy and public trial, by an impartial jury of the State and district wherein the crime shall havebeen committed, which district shall have been previously ascertained by law, and to be informed of the nature and cause of the accusation; to be confronted with the witnesses against him; to have compulsory process for obtaining witnesses in his favor, and to have the Assistance of Counsel for his defence.

Errors on page 11
Error 3 Column 1 ERROR: Column ran short by 4p4.724

Article VII

In suits at common law, where the value in controversy shall exceed twenty dollars, the right of trial by jury shall be preserved, and no fact tried by a jury, shall be otherwise reexamined in any Court of the United States, than according to the rules of the common law.

Article VIII

Excessive bail shall not be required, nor excessive fines imposed, nor cruel and unusual punishments inflicted.

Article IX

The enumeration in the Constitution, of certain rights, shall not be construed to deny or disparage others retained by the people.

Article X

The powers not delegated to the United States by the Constitution, nor prohibited by it to the States, are reserved to the States respectively, or to the people.

Article XI[13]

The Judicial power of the United States shall not be construed to extend to any suit in law or equity, commenced or prosecuted against one of the United States by Citizens of another State, or by Citizens or Subjects of any Foreign State.

Article XII[14]

The Electors shall meet in their respective states and vote by ballot for President and Vice-President, one of whom, at least, shall not be an inhabitant of the same state with themselves; they shall name in their ballots the person voted for as President, and in distinct ballots the person voted for as Vice-President, and they shall make distinct lists of all persons voted for as President, and of all persons voted for as Vice-President, and of the number of votes for each, which lists they shall sign and certify, and transmit sealed to the seat of the government

---

[13]Adopted in 1798.
[14]Adopted in 1804.

of the United States, directed to the President of the Senate;—The President of the Senate shall, in presence of the Senate and House of Representatives, open all the certificates and the votes shall then be counted;—The person having the greatest number of votes for President, shall be the President, if such number be a majority of the whole number of Electors appointed; and if no person have such majority, then from the persons having the highest numbers not exceeding three on the list of those voted for as President, the House of Representatives shall choose immediately, by ballot, the President. But in choosing the President, the votes shall be taken by states, the representation from each state having one vote; a quorum for this purpose shall consist of a member or members from two-thirds of the states, and a majority of all the states shall be necessary to a choice. [And if the House of Representatives shall not choose a President whenever the right of choice shall devolve upon them, before the fourth day of March next following, then the Vice-President shall act as President, as in the case of the death or other constitutional disability of the President.][15]—The person having the greatest number of votes as Vice President, shall be the Vice-President, if such number be a majority of the whole number of Electors appointed, and if no person have a majority, then from the two highest numbers on the list, the Senate shall choose the Vice-President; a quorum for the purpose shall consist of two-thirds of the whole number of Senators, and a majority of the whole number shall be necessary to a choice. But no person constitutionally ineligible to the office of President shall be eligible to that of Vice-President of the United States.

Article XIII[16]

Section 1.
Neither slavery nor involuntary servitude, except as a punishment for crime whereof the party shall have been duly convicted, shall exist within the United States, or any place subject to their jurisdiction.
Section 2.
Congress shall have power to enforce this article by appropriate legislation.

Article XIV[17]

Section 1.
All persons born or naturalized in the United States, and subject to the jurisdiction thereof, are citizens of the United States and of the State wherein they reside. No state shall make or enforce any law which shall abridge the privileges or immunities of citizens of the United States; nor shall any State deprive any person of life, liberty, or property, without due process of law; nor deny to any person within its jurisdiction the equal protection of the laws.

---

[15]Superseded by the Twentieth Amendment, Section 3.
[16]Adopted in 1865.
[17]Adopted in 1868.

Section 2.

Representatives shall be apportioned among the several States according to their respective numbers, counting the whole number of persons in each State, excluding Indians not taxed. But when the right to vote at any election for the choice of electors for President and Vice-President of the United States, Representatives in Congress, the Executive and Judicial officers of a State, or the members of the Legislature thereof, is denied to any of the male inhabitants of such State, being twenty-one years of age, and citizens of the United States, or in any way abridged, except for participation in rebellion, or other crime, the basis of representation therein shall be reduced in the proportion which the number of such male citizens shall bear to the whole number of male citizens twenty-one years of age in such State.

Section 3.

No person shall be a Senator or Representative in Congress, or elector of President and Vice-President, or hold any office, civil or military, under the United States, or under any State, who, having previously taken an oath, as a member of Congress, or as an officer of the United States, or as a member of any State legislature, or as an executive or judicial officer of any State, to support the Constitution of the United States, shall have engaged in insurrection or rebellion against the same, or given aid or comfort to the enemies thereof. But Congress may by a vote of two-thirds of each House, remove such disability.

Section 4.

The validity of the public debt of the United States, authorized by law, including debts incurred for payment of pensions and bounties for services in suppressing insurrection or rebellion, shall not be questioned. But neither the United States nor any State shall assume or pay any debt or obligation incurred in aid of insurrection or rebellion against the United States, or any claim for the loss or emancipation of any slave; but all such debts, obligations and claims shall be held illegal and void.

Section 5.

The Congress shall have power to enforce, by appropriate legislation, the provisions of this article.

Article XV[18]

Section 1

The right of citizens of the United States to vote shall not be denied or abridged by the United States or by any State on account of race, color, or previous condition of servitude—

---

[18]Adopted in 1870.

Errors on page 14

Error 4 Column 1 WARNING: Paragraph 4 depth has changed 1 lines.

Error 5 Column 1 ERROR: Column ran short by p9.871

Section 2
The Congress shall have power to enforce this article by appropriate legislation.

Article XVI[19]

The Congress shall have power to lay and collect taxes on incomes, from whatever source derived, without apportionment among the several States, and without regard to any census or enumeration.

Article XVII[20]

The Senate of the United States shall be composed of two Senators from each State, elected by the people thereof, for six years; and each Senator shall have one vote. The electors in each State shall have the qualifications requisite for electors of the most numerous branch of the State legislatures.

When vacancies happen in the representation of any State in the Senate, the executive authority of such State shall issue writs of election to fill such vacancies: *Provided*, That the legislature of any State may empower the executive thereof to make temporary appointments until the people fill the vacancies by election as the legislature may direct.

This amendment shall not be so construed as to affect the election or term of any Senator chosen before it becomes valid as part of the Constitution.

Article XVIII[21]

Section 1
After one year from the ratification of this article the manufacture, sale, or transportation of intoxicating liquors within, the importation thereof into, or the exportation thereof from the United States and all territory subject to the jurisdiction thereof for beverage purposes is hereby prohibited.

Section 2
The Congress and the several States shall have concurrent power to enforce this article by appropriate legislation.

Section 3
This article shall be inoperative unless it shall have been ratified as an amendment to the Constitution by the legislatures of the several States, as provided in the Constitution, within seven years from the date of the submission hereof to the States by the Congress.

---

[19]Adopted in 1913.
[20]Adopted in 1913.
[21]Adopted in 1919. Repealed by Section 1 of the Twenty-first Amendment.

Article XIX[22]

The right of citizens of the United States to vote shall not be denied or abridged by the United States or by any State on account of sex.

Congress shall have power to enforce this article by appropriate legislation.

Article XX[23]

Section 1.
The terms of the President and Vice-President shall end at noon on the 20th day of January, and the terms of Senators and Representatives at noon on the 3d day of January, of the years in which such terms would have ended if this article had not been ratified; and the terms of their successors shall then begin.

Section 2.
The Congress shall assemble at least once in every year, and such meeting shall begin at noon on the 3d day of January, unless they shall by law appoint a different day.

Section 3.
If, at the time fixed for the beginning of the term of the President, the president elect shall have died, the Vice-President elect shall become President. If a President shall not have been chosen before the time fixed for the beginning of his term, or if the President elect shall have failed to qualify, then the Vice-President elect shall act as President until a President shall have qualified; and the Congress may by law provide for the case wherein neither a President elect nor a Vice-President elect shall have qualified, declaring who shall then act as President, or the manner in which one who is to act shall be selected, and such person shall act accordingly until a President or Vice-President shall have qualified.

Section 4.
The Congress may by law provide for the case of the death of any of the persons from whom the House of Representatives may choose a President whenever the right of choice shall have devolved upon them, and for the case of the death of any of the persons from whom the Senate may choose a Vice-President whenever the right of choice shall have devolved upon them.

Section 5.
Section 1 and 2 shall take effect on the 15th day of October following the ratification of this article.

Section 6.
This article shall be inoperative unless it shall have been ratified as an amendment to the Constitution by the legislatures of three-fourths of the several States within seven years from the date of its submission.

---

[22]Adopted in 1920.
[23]Adopted in 1933.

Article XXI[24]

Section 1.
The eighteenth article of amendment to the Constitution of the United States is hereby repealed.
Section 2.
The transportation or importation into any State, Territory, or possession of the United States for delivery or use therein of intoxicating liquors, in violation of the laws thereof, is hereby prohibited.
Section 3.
This article shall be inoperative unless it shall have been ratified as an amendment to the Constitution by conventions in the several States, as provided in the Constitution, within seven years from the date of the submission hereof to the States by the Congress.

Article XXII[25]

Section 1.
No person shall be elected to the office of the President more than twice, and no person who has held the office of President, or acted as President, for more than two years of a term to which some other person was elected President shall be elected to the office of the President more than once. But this Article shall not apply to any person holding the office of President when this Article was proposed by the Congress, and shall not prevent any person who may be holding the office of President, or acting as President, during the term within which this Article becomes operative from holding the office of President or acting as President during the remainder of such term.
Section 2.
This article shall be inoperative unless it shall have been ratified as an amendment to the Constitution by the legislatures of three-fourths of the several States within seven years from the date of its submission to the States by the Congress.

Article XXIII[26]

Section 1.
The District constituting the seat of Government of the United States shall appoint in such manner as the Congress may direct:

A number of electors of President and Vice-President equal to the whole number of Senators and Representatives in Congress to which the District would be entitled if it were a State, but in no event more than the least populous State; they shall

---

[24]Adopted in 1933.
[25]Adopted in 1951.
[26]Adopted in 1961.

be in addition to those appointed by the States, but they shall be considered, for the purposes of the election of President and Vice-President, to be electors appointed by a State; and they shall meet in the District and perform such duties as provided by the twelfth article of amendment.

Section 2.

The Congress shall have power to enforce this article by appropriate legislation.

Article XXIV[27]

Section 1.

The right of citizens of the United States to vote in any primary or other election for President or Vice-President, for electors for President or Vice-President, or for Senator or Representative in Congress, shall not be denied or abridged by the United States or any state by reasons of failure to pay any poll tax or other tax.

Section 2.

The Congress shall have power to enforce this article by appropriate legislation.

Article XXV[28]

Section 1.

In case of the removal of the President from office or of his death or resignation, the Vice-President shall become President.

Section 2.

Whenever there is a vacancy in the office of the Vice-President, the President shall nominate a Vice-President who shall take office upon confirmation by a majority vote of both Houses of Congress.

Section 3.

Whenever the President transmits to the President pro tempore of the Senate and the Speaker of the House of Representatives his written declaration that he is unable to discharge the powers and duties of his office, and until he transmits to them a written declaration to the contrary, such powers and duties shall be discharged by the Vice-President as Acting President.

Section 4.

Whenever the Vice-President and a majority of either the principal officers of the Executive departments or of such other body as Congress may by law provide transmit to the President pro tempore of the Senate and the Speaker of the House of Representatives their written declaration that the President is unable to discharge the powers and duties of his office, the Vice-President shall immediately assume the powers and duties of the office as Acting President.

---

[27]Adopted in 1964.
[28]Adopted in 1967.

Thereafter, when the President transmits to the President pro tempore of the Senate and the Speaker of the House of Representatives his written declaration that no inability exists, he shall resume the powers and duties of his office unless the Vice-President and a majority of either the principal officers of the Executive departments or of such other body as Congress may by law provide transmit within four days to the President pro tempore of the Senate and the Speaker of the House of Representatives their written declaration that the President is unable to discharge the powers and duties of his office. Thereupon Congress shall decide the issue, assembling within forty-eight hours for that purpose if not in session. If the Congress, within twenty-one days after receipt of the latter written declaration, or, if Congress is not in session, within twenty-one days after Congress is required to assemble, determines by two-thirds vote of both houses that the President is unable to discharge the powers and duties of his office, the Vice-President shall continue to discharge the same as Acting President; otherwise, the President shall resume the powers and duties of his office.

Article XXVI[29]

Section 1.
The right of citizens of the United States, who are 18 years of age or older, to vote shall not be denied or abridged by the United States or any state on account of age.

Section 2.
The Congress shall have power to enforce this article by appropriate legislation.

---

[29]Adopted in 1971.